Economies of the World

EDITED BY

NITA WATTS

THE EAST ASIAN INSTITUTE OF
COLUMBIA UNIVERSITY

The East Asian Institute is Columbia University's centre
for research, education, and publication on modern East
Asia. The Studies of the East Asian Institute were
inaugurated in 1962 to bring to a wider public the results
of significant new research on modern and contemporary
East Asia.

China's Political Economy

The Quest for Development since 1949

CARL RISKIN

OXFORD UNIVERSITY PRESS

Oxford University Press, Walton Street, Oxford OX2 6DP
Oxford New York
Athens Auckland Bangkok Bombay
Calcutta Cape Town Dar es Salaam Delhi
Florence Hong Kong Istanbul Karachi
Kuala Lumpur Madras Madrid Melbourne
Mexico City Nairobi Paris Singapore
Taipei Tokyo Toronto
and associated companies in
Berlin Ibadan

Oxford is a trade mark of Oxford University Press

Published in the United States by
Oxford University Press Inc., New York

First published 1987
Paperback edition reprinted 1988, 1991, 1995, 1996

British Library Cataloguing in Publication Data
Riskin, Carl
China's political economy: the quest for
development since 1949.—(Economies of
the world)
1. China—Economic conditions—1949-
I. Title II. Series
330.951'05 HC427.9
ISBN 0-19-877089-8
ISBN 0-19-877090-1 (Pbk)

Library of Congress Cataloging in Publication Data
Riskin, Carl.
China's political economy.
(Economics of the world)
Bibliography: p.
Includes index.
1. China—Economic policy—1949-
2. Agriculture and state—China. I. Title.
II. Series.
HC427.9.R57 1987 338.951 87-16267
ISBN 0-19-877089-8
ISBN 0-19-877090-1 (Pbk)

Printed in Hong Kong

PREFACE

This book was begun at an inauspicious moment, just as China's economy and recent history began a metamorphosis that has continued to this day. Perhaps it would have been better to let the dust settle before writing, but there was no telling how long that would take. The changes need to be understood in historical context, and because I believed that such a task could be accomplished, even if imperfectly under the circumstances, I decided to accept the risks inherent in aiming at a moving target. The chief penalty was that extensive parts of the book had to be rewritten more than once as new information became available and my own ideas changed. The completion of the project was therefore much delayed.

Under such conditions, the help and encouragement of family, friends, and colleagues were even more than usually needed and appreciated. I am especially indebted to Tom Bernstein, Padma Desai, Charles Hoffmann, Janos Kornai, Dinyar Lalkaka, Roland Lew, Maurice Meisner, Jeanne Oi, the late Suzanne Paine, James Polachek, K. N. Raj, Mark Selden, James Seymour, Marilyn Young, N. T. Wang, Madeleine Zelin, and Andrew Zimbalist, all of whom read and commented on parts of the manuscript. Dorothy Borg has my gratitude not only for her good advice and constant encouragement, but also for prodding me mercilessly toward the finish line. Many others offered aid and support, of whom I should like particularly to thank Michael Edelstein, Hong Junyan, Paul Lin, Amartya Sen, Mark Sidel, and Ajit Singh. Len Rodberg's help with computer matters beginning midway through the project made its completion more enjoyable than its pre-electronic beginnings. Robert Azar provided research assistance and Kimiko Hahn clerical support.

My gratitude to my wife, Mary Murphree, who encouraged and sustained me unfalteringly, cannot be adequately expressed. Jessica Riskin, who kept well ahead of the project as it matured, finally ordered it finished and got her way.

This research was assisted by a grant from the Subcommittee on Reseach on the Chinese Economy of the Joint Committee on Contemporary China of the American Council of Learned Societies and the Social Science Research Council. Additional assistance came in the form of a sabbatical grant from Queens College, which has been a sustaining home institution. The intellectual stimulus provided by my Queens colleagues and the material and logistic aid extended by the college are both much appreciated. The Word Processing office did the laborious typing of the early chapters.

Much of the research and writing was done at Columbia University's East Asian Institute. The Institute faculty and leadership, including its capable administrative assistant, Deborah Bell, have my gratitude for their encouragement and backing over the years.

In 1980 I interviewed scholars at the Chinese Academy of Social Sciences in Beijing, especially its Institute of Industrial Economics. I am indebted to Ma Hong, then director of that Institute and later President of the Academy, and to

Xu Dixin, then director of the Institute for Economic Research, for welcoming me to CASS and arranging a series of fruitful and informative discussions. Among the economists and officials from various parts of CASS who made themselves available were Dong Furen, Du Mengkun, Hong Huiru, Jiang Yiwei, Liu Suinian, Qian Junrui, Wang Gengjin, Wang Zhenzhi, Wu Jiazun, Wu Jinglian, Xu Ming, Yi Hongren, Yuan Wenqi, Zhang Liuzheng, Zhang Peiji, Zhao Renwei. Interviews were also arranged with representatives of Beijing industrial firms, including Hu Quanyi, deputy head of finance, and Han Long, external affairs officer, of the Beijing Construction Machinery Company; Zhao Jingyuan, head of the finance office of the Beijing Automative Company; Xu Changde, financial officer of the Beijing Diesel Engine Plant; and Fu Jingli, general accountant of the Beijing Heavy Construction Machinery Company.

Chen Daisun, eminent chairman of the economics department at Beijing University, was a most gracious host during a memorable visit to the campus. Zhu Peixing and Zhu Yijin added warm friendship to my stay in Beijing. Zou Yimin provided arrangements, news clippings and general help in negotiating Beijing institutions, as well as translation when my Chinese fell short.

This book is a hybrid, striking off on its own at times but also depending heavily on the work of others. The many text citations give a good indication of the extent and direction of my debts to the community of scholars who have laboured to understand the Chinese economy. Without their work this book would have been inconceivable. All the more reason then to exonerate them, along with the other friends and colleagues mentioned here, from any responsibility for the book's errors and shortcomings, and for those interpretations and views to which they take exception. I hope the latter will give rise to fruitful debate; they were an important reason for doing this book.

New York
April 1986

For my father
and
in memory of my mother

CONTENTS

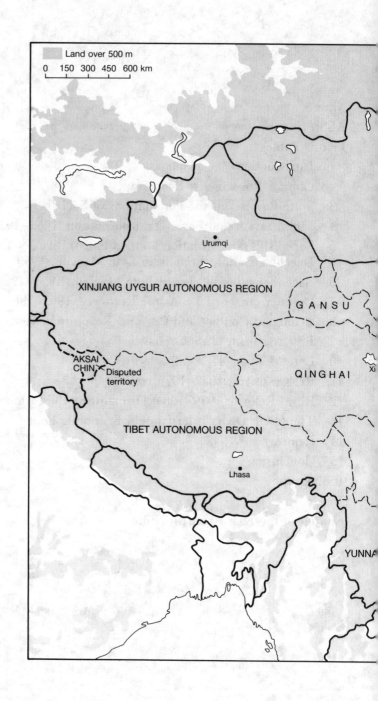

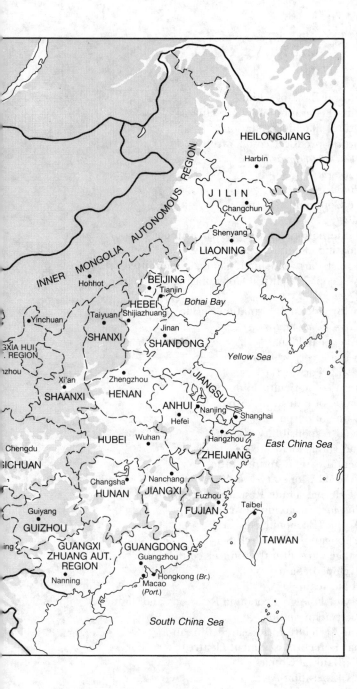

ABBREVIATIONS

ABC	Agricultural Bank of China
ACFTU	All-China Federation of Trade Unions
AMS	agricultural machinery station
APC	agricultural producer co-operative
AWSJ	*Asian Wall Street Journal*
BR	*Beijing Review*
CBR	*China Business Review*
CCP	Chinese Communist Party
CD	*China Daily*
CITIC	China International Trust and Investment Corporation
COCOM	Coordinating Committee
CPCCC	Communist Party of China, Central Committee
CPPCC	Chinese People's Political Consultative Conference
CQ	*China Quarterly*
FBIS	Foreign Broadcast Information Service
FEER	*Far Eastern Economic Review*
FFYP	First Five Year Plan
FTC	foreign trade corporation
GLF	Great Leap Forward
GVAO	gross value of agricultural output
GVIO	gross value of industrial output
GVO	gross value of output
HRS	household responsibility system
HSYA	high and stable yield area
ICOR	incremental capital–output ratio
IMF	International Monetary Fund
JETRO	Japan External Trade Research Organization
JJGL	*Jingji Guanli* (Economic Management)
JJYJ	*Jingji Yanjiu* (Economic Research)
JPRS	Joint Publications Research Service
LAPC	lower-stage agricultural producer co-operative
LDC	less developed country
MAT	mutual aid team
MOFERT	Ministry of Foreign Economic Relations and Trade
MTS	machine tractor station
NARB	National Agricultural Research Bureau
NFAC	National Foreign Assessment Centre
PBC	People's Bank of China
PLA	People's Liberation Army
PPS	'planned purchase and supply'
PR	*Peking Review* (former name of *Beijing Review*)
PRC	People's Republic of China

RMB	*renminbi*
RMRB	*Renmin Ribao* (People's Daily)
SEZ	Special Economic Zone
SPC	State Planning Commission
SPRCM	Survey of People's Republic of China Magazines
SSB	State Statistical Bureau
SYOC	*Statistical Yearbook of China*
TGY	*Ten Great Years*
USCIA	United States Central Intelligence Agency
USCJEC	United States Congress, Joint Economic Committee
WD	*World Development*
ZJN	*Zhongguo Jingji Nianjian* (Economic Yearbook of China)
ZMWTZ	*Zhongguo Maoyi Wujia Tongji Ziliao* (Statistical Material on Chinese Trade and Prices)
ZNJQ	*Zhongguo Nongye Jiben Qingkuang* (Basic Situation of China's Agriculture)
ZNN	*Zhongguo Nongye Nianjian* (Agricultural Yearbook of China)
ZRGGTJ	Zhonghua Renmin Gongheguo Guojia Tongji Ju (State Statistical Bureau of the PRC)
ZTN	*Zhongguo Tongji Nianjian* (Statistical Yearbook of China)
ZTZ	*Zhongguo Tongji Zhaiyao* (Statistical Abstract of China)

TABLES

CHAPTER 1

INTRODUCTION

This book is about the emergence of China as an industrializing nation in the second half of the twentieth century. Occurring suddenly against the rhythms of world history, this is a development with great import for our time and beyond. One of my objectives has been to tell the story in its essential details. Since it is not an easy one to make sense of, however, my second goal has been to offer an analytical guide to the rough roads and switchbacks of recent Chinese history, from the perspective of political economy.

This perspective is one that broadly takes into account the impact of economic events on social and political structures and attitudes, and vice versa. In other words, I am concerned with links between what Marx called the forces and relations of production, rather than with chronicling changes in the former alone. This seems to me the only sensible way to understand economic development in rapidly changing societies. It does not mean that one should expect to find here a political or social history of contemporary China. The starting point is economic development, and its intersections with social and political dynamics are dealt with where it seemed necessary for understanding the development record. As an economist, I fear I may already have trespassed into areas that others are more competent to explore.

Part of the significance of China's development is obvious: whatever the vicissitudes of the past thirty-five years, and even taking into account a major famine in the early 1960s (see Chs. 6 and 7), China is no longer the international paradigm of mass destitution it was in the past. This is not only because of substantial progress in economic development and in provision for the basic needs of the population, but also because China's new strength has eliminated one of the world's oft-trod battlefields. For more than a century after the 1839–42 Opium War, China's weakness had made it a locus of conflict among adventurous foreign powers seeking commercial advantage and domestic factions competing for political power. Ironically, and against all the evidence, the first Chinese government in a century capable of keeping the peace within its own borders was, in the West, long branded an aggressive and expansionist threat to peace.

Beyond these lie other deep ramifications of the Chinese development experience. In 1949 China was not only the most populous country, but among the poorest; yet it was led by a communist party professing a Marxist outlook and committed to establishing a socialist society. These facts singly and collectively raise a number of issues.

Consider the population question, for instance. It is an article of faith that the larger and more rapidly growing populations of today's poor countries, as compared with those of the early industralizers, constitute a new and potent obstacle to their development. With some 22 per cent of the world's population living on 5 per cent of its arable land, China can be said to be on the cutting edge of the conflict between population growth and economic development, facing a problem unlike any confronted by its predecessors.

Over the centuries, the Chinese sought to protect their living standards from the erosive effects of growth in numbers by spreading into potentially productive and unoccupied regions of the south and west, and finally the north-east, and at the same time by gradually intensifying cultivation. By the middle of the present century, however, the potential for squeezing more output from the soil with traditional techniques had been all but used up. In this respect, too, China is not unlike other densely populated areas of the Third World. It is not feasible under such circumstances to neglect agriculture in the quest for industrialization. For one thing, to do so would be to condemn to lasting misery the great bulk of the population that is rural and makes its living from the land. This conclusion gains force from the fact that the industrial technologies inherited from the developed world have been fashioned to fit its circumstances of relatively expensive labour and thus can absorb very few rural inhabitants into urban industrial employment. But even putting aside the moral and political problems a peasant-based revolution would face in turning its back on its first constituents, industrialization itself would be held back by shortages of raw materials and exports, inadequate markets, rising prices of food and other wage goods, and lack of savings, all of which would result from a moribund agriculture.

There are various attitudes towards this problem. One harks back to the experience of Meiji Japan, holding that, if appropriate changes can be made in the organization of credit, markets, extension services, and tenurial institutions, then relatively cheap and labour-intensive means exist for bringing about substantial rises in farm yields. Another view is that agricultural development requires most of all a modern chemical and machine industry and modern biological research—that is, the substitution of an entirely new production function for a traditional one encountering sharply diminishing returns. This must be accompanied by market incentives to make the adoption of the new technology profitable, and by institutional changes, such as land reform and the establishment of supply, credit, and marketing co-operatives, to ensure access to it by the right people—usually better-off farmers. A third view, common among Indian Marxist scholars, sees the transformation of the pre-capitalist rural class structure as the key requirement for agricultural development since, irrespective of the availability of improved techniques, this structure conditions the possibility of their adoption.

Chinese experience incorporates elements from all three approaches— labour-intensive cultivation and irrigation methods, new modern inputs, and radical change in rural socioeconomic institutions. Indeed, as is suggested in Chapter 12, China's recent return to individual household farming, *after* an era of collectivization during which great advances in chemical and biological technology were made and extensive farmland capital construction and rationalization of land use occurred, can be interpreted as an unexpected wedding of the 'new technology' and 'class structure' schools, which has produced rapid advances in output and productivity in its first half-decade.

It is China's allegiance to socialism, however, that raises some of the most interesting questions about its post-1949 development experience. If Lenin's theory of the 'weakest link' explained why victory of the revolution came in relatively backward Russia rather than in the realm of advanced capitalism, as Marx had expected, this explanation can hardly suffice in the case of China. True, capitalism in China was stunted, and the world capitalist system in the aftermath of the Second World War could not rescue the Nationalist regime from the consequences of its own folly and of the superior morale, commitment, and organization of the revolutionaries. But in China there was even less objective basis for the development of a communist movement in the classical Marxist sense than in Russia. Industry was far less developed, its economic and regional weight in the national economy far smaller. The proletariat, although organized and militant in the few enclaves of industrialization, such as Shanghai, was but a tiny fraction of the population and labour force. Given the circumstances, it is possible to understand how the Chinese revolution succeeded—but how could it have been a *socialist* revolution?

We can never be sure what sort of regime Mao Zedong and the Chinese Communist Party might have built in different international circumstances. But with the Cold War at its height and the new government at war with the United States in Korea within months of its establishment, it is not surprising that it opted for policies of maximum control and an approach to political organization and economic planning that would benefit from close alliance with the Soviet bloc, its one source of international support. By the late 1950s, despite early successful attempts to encourage and direct private industry and commerce, almost all private enterprise had been abolished and the state found itself having to plan and manage, without benefit of a market, the whole sprawling, complex network of activities that made up the economy. It is at this point that, looking back, the reformist leadership of the 1980s sees things beginning to go seriously wrong.

When the USSR dismantled its own market and began administering resources by plan, it was natural that questions were raised about the feasibility of abandoning the economic order as it had been known. Maurice Dobb used the introduction to his classic history of the Soviet economy (1966) to argue that it was the *tempo* of development, rather than the prevailing paradigm of efficient equilibrium, that was the appropriate criterion for evaluating economic performance in a growing country. The charting of an economic growth path for a poor country, he suggested, was analogous to the military problem of choice among a limited number of discrete strategies. Similarly, he raised questions about the role of the interest rate in investment planning, and about the relevance of 'consumer sovereignty' for a growing economy where many types of goods are new and unfamiliar.

China's recent history, as well as that of other centrally planned economies, shows that such issues have not become obsolete. It is by now clear that a centrally planned economy can survive, grow rapidly, and provide for the basic material needs of its people. At an early stage of development, with limited resources and options, the choice of investment projects can be made without great computational sophistication. And, despite the current vogue of *laissez-faire* economics in the United States and Britain, state intervention is a fact of life in all advanced economies. Western economic theory leaves very large loopholes through which government may legitimately enter, and the issue of plan *v.* market has come to be posed less in rigidly absolutist terms and more in terms of degree, except perhaps in the White House, which, to be sure, does not act in accordance with its own rhetoric. At the level of system survival, economic growth, and the meeting of basic needs, Dobb's answers turn out to be right.

But the questions have not gone away; they have only changed form. Granted that a centrally planned and administered economy[1] can survive, grow, and industrialize quickly, what determines the direction in which it develops, its investment priorities, its choice of consumer goods to produce? Granted that consumers cannot be familiar with future alternatives, how can they influence allocation decisions when the future has arrived and the alternatives are before them? As the simple, pre-industrial economy becomes more complex, how can intelligent investment decisions be made in the many cases that are not intuitively obvious? What do the enormous information and supervision requirements of central planning imply about the growth of bureaucratism in the state? What does the essentially passive role played by enterprises and their personnel in this system imply for the likelihood of innovation and the search for efficiency? Above all, the political economy of the central planning regime itself is placed on the agenda, for we cannot posit as the socialist counterpart of the myth of perfect competition a fiction of a transparent state peopled by omniscient and selfless planners.

The role of the socialist state has been central to China's economic drama. In capturing power, the Chinese Communist Party found its winning formula in the mobilization of the rural population, among which its leaders and cadres lived for many years. That political alliance, together with the conditions facing the new regime as it began economic construction, made it next to impossible to avoid the question of accountability of Party and State to the population at large. Struggles around this issue, linked first to Mao's crusade against the remnants of centuries of bureaucratic rule, then to his successors' crusade against the remnants of his own rule, have been a recurrent feature of PRC history.

Among the economic causes of this ongoing contest, a chief one is undoubtedly the fact that, given the sheer size of the rural population, the countryside will retain the bulk of the population for a long time. This fact has posed new problems for the socialist mission in China. In contrast to the USSR, which managed within twelve years of the start of its First Five Year Plan to reduce agriculture's share of total employment from 71 per cent to around one-half, China is still largely rural more than three decades after the initiation of development planning, with almost 70 per cent of its labour force still engaged in agriculture.[2] No feasible rate of industrialization, however rapid, can quickly incorporate the bulk of the population into the modern non-agricultural economy.[3] Development policy, therefore, cannot ignore the countryside in the expectation that quick urbanization will progressively reduce its importance. The needs and problems of rural development have been on the agenda from the beginning.

The problem of large rural population, furthermore, is compounded by the capital-intensive nature of the technology that China is adopting from industrialized countries. A unit of income withheld from current consumption and used to make or buy capital goods creates far fewer jobs today than it would have done fifty or seventy-five years ago. Industrial production thus can grow quickly without changing very much the sectoral distribution of the labour force and the geographical disposition of the population. Development proceeds apace, yet most of the population remains poor, equipped with traditional technologies. The gap in productivity between the minority of workers in the modern sectors and the majority in the indigenous economy has grown continuously since the early 1950s (Eckstein, 1973). China has striven mightly to prevent personal incomes from following sectoral labour productivity rates in becoming ever more unequal; yet, as we shall see, the urban–rural gap nevertheless increased, while the attempt to suppress it was part of a policy that kept consumption generally low and broke the promise of socialism to raise living standards steadily.

It has been a temptation to compensate for the technological legacy of modernization—fewer jobs per yuan of investment than in the past—with correspondingly higher aggregate savings and investment rates. The modernization mission, together with various institutional biases of bureaucratic socialism towards ever more capital construction, has driven these rates to great heights in China. If economic development obeyed simple mathematical rules, such sacrifice of current consumption on behalf of growth would have produced the intended structural transformation, and China's population today would be considerably more urbanized, with a larger proportion of it employed in high-productivity modern pursuits, than is actually the case.

In fact, the growth of the investment rate was accompanied by a decline in efficiency. Capital construction projects took longer to complete and produced less output per yuan when finished. Moreover, they were built in the wrong industries and lacked supplies of fuel and raw materials. Forcing the pace of growth led to sectoral imbalances and lagging consumption, which in turn impacted on productivity. By the end of the 1970s China's leaders had concluded that there was a better approach to development: moderate and balanced growth together with rising per capita consumption.

These results are not explicable in terms of mathematics or economic logic alone, nor were the conclusions of the post-Mao leadership drawn from dispassionate analysis or clinical social experiments. On the contrary, the struggle over development policy has been turbulent and, during the Cultural Revolution, violent. Class, sectoral, regional, and élite power interests were at stake; Marxist ideology became intertwined with old cultural traditions. It is a purpose of this book to sort out some of the ingredients that have gone into the irregular evolution of development policy.

First among the problems facing policy-makers has been that of getting farmers to produce the surpluses essential for industrialization. Such a surplus existed in the early 1950s, as it had before (Lippit 1974; Perkins 1969; Riskin 1975a), but it was small by international standards. Soviet foodgrain production per capita in the disastrous year of 1932 was actually some 45 per cent higher than the comparable figure for China in the average year of 1957. Even after subtracting from the former figure grain extracted from the countryside to feed the urban population and for export, the Soviet farmers still had a per capita grain availability some 30 per cent higher than the Chinese.[4] While China's farm situation was better than that of some other poor countries (e.g., India, Pakistan, Ceylon) during the same period, it was certainly not good enough to provide the raw materials, urban food supplies, and exports needed by an ambitious industrialization programme. Development demanded agricultural growth, the agents of which must be the farmers themselves.

A growth strategy that discriminated against the countryside would leave mainly coercive means of getting the required results. Aside from its political implications, coercion would hardly have been the most effective means of eliciting sustained efforts from the farm population. Political and economic considerations thus both militated against the development of an urban-based bureaucracy catering to its immediate constituency in industry, finance, and administration. Yet precisely such a tradition was inherited from the USSR and embodied in the approach of central administrative planning. Almost from the outset, Mao Zedong criticized this approach for its extreme centralization of authority, its technocratic cast, and its neglect of human initiative.

Also from early on, China rebelled against some of the features of the Soviet model. 'One-man management' was rejected in the mid-1950s, and piece rates never figured as prominently in Chinese as in Soviet factories. Mao experimented with new organizational and administrative institutions, from various kinds of 'communes' to revolutionary committees, which in their initial forms often implied considerable decentralization and dispersal of political authority. In a similar vein, he periodically attempted to transfer economic decision-making power to lower levels; advocated relying on the 'mass line', which was meant to subject leaders to frequent contact with the rank-and-file; and promoted the unpopular policy of sending urban secondary school graduates to settle in the countryside.

These institutional responses impacted sharply on the lives of most Chinese. Fed by messianic expectations and often ruled by the momentum of mass movements, they discriminated haphazardly among different groups of the population. Ironically, their attack on China's functional bureaucracy and on the values of system and order finally increased the arbitrary power of the top leadership, which gained the capacity to determine the political orthodoxy of virtually all acts and thoughts. Yet, to an economist, the striking characteristic of the Maoist response to central administrative planning was its failure to put forward an alternative. While Mao objected to hierarchical and bureaucratic prerequisites of a central planning regime, he also rejected reliance on the market as an institution that inevitably encouraged the 'restoration of capitalism'. Full of ideas for the proper structuring of authority and participation at the microeconomic level, Maoism had virtually nothing positive to say about the fashioning of an integrated, cohesive macroeconomy.

In some respects, the period referred to here as 'late Maoism'—roughly, 1958–76—witnessed a sustained attempt to beg this question. Much of the period was dominated by an ethic of 'self-reliance', one of whose implications was the de-emphasis on complex linkages between economic units and regions and therefore of the planning and administrative apparatus needed for such connections. If Mao rejected the 'one-big-workshop' model of the macroeconomy, in which central decision-makers distribute materials and products among its many units, his alternative seems to have been a 'many-workshops' approach, in which each unit and locality, largely independent of others, distributed resources for itself.

This result, in any case, came about if only by default. It was never formally proposed as a model; indeed, one can scour the literature of Maoism without finding a serious discussion of socialist macroeconomic organization. Moreover, the centre continued throughout to allocate and redistribute resources nationally. But, in the face of continuous Maoist assaults on the ideology of central planning and on the corps of specialists that implemented it, the centre progressively lost the capacity to plan effectively. Yet when the disorganization produced by mass campaigns became excessive, Mao, seeing no alternative, would acquiesce in the restoration of central planning, crippled as it was. At the same time, individual administrative organs, localities, and enterprises, unable to rely on the centre for the resources needed to carry out their plans, increasingly sought to ensure their own operations through 'self-reliance', which came to mean the hoarding of materials and the establishment of duplicative productive operations. China got caught on a path between two poles—rigid centralism and chaotic administrative decentralization—each of which seemed a lesser evil only when farthest away.

A watershed was reached in this history with the death of Mao in 1976 and the arrest immediately afterward of his principal followers. Gradually, but with increasing momentum since then, the locus of conflict has shifted from Mao's ideological, populist attack on central planning to the relations between plan and market. Starting first in the countryside with the dismantling of the commune system, and moving then to the urban economy, the post-Mao leadership has sought to roll back aspects of the 'relations of production'—ownership and payment systems and relations of authority in the work-place—to a level commensurate in their view with the still primitive development of the 'forces of production'. They have sought to replace the 'central workshop' model with a more complex system of semi-autonomous enterprises producing commodities for sale on the market under varying degrees of planned constraints; to return to material self-interest as a primary source of motivation for individuals and enterprises; and to make use of foreign capital and technology on an unprecedented scale for China's development.

These reforms, halting and self-contradictory in some respects and by no means yet providing a coherent picture of what China's economy is meant to look like in the end, are still very much in progress as this book goes to press.

Economic growth and industrialization are of course only partial goals. The late Alexander Eckstein (1977) summarized China's main development objectives as follows: 'economic growth . . . combined with a commitment to improve income distribution, assure full employment free of inflation, and promote development with honor through a policy of self-reliance, that is, by minimizing or obviating China's dependence on foreign countries' (p. 4). To these must be added the goal of establishing socialism. What that implies for social policy, however, is precisely what much of the conflict has been about. Starting from conditions of extreme backwardness ('a blank page'), Mao tried to build a society that would progressively part with modes of social organization and thought that he associated with capitalism; the first steps towards communism would be taken even in the present. To his successors, however, the page was not blank; it was corrupted with pre-capitalist, 'feudal' ideas and attitudes that gained strength from the attempt to bypass a progressive stage of quasi-capitalism. They see the socialist transition from pre-capitalist conditions as requiring a wide development of quasi-capitalist institutions, such as commodities and markets, private trade and material incentives, the separation of government and economy, and the establishment of formal legal institutions, all of which Mao himself regarded as 'taking the capitalist road'. The utopianism associated in Maoist thought with communism has been transferred by his heirs to the concept of 'modernization'; how communism figures in modern society is an issue that the post-Mao leadership is willing to relegate to the distant future.

The general organization of the book is chronological. Chapter 2 sets the stage by sketching the broad contours of China's long economic history and discussing economic conditions in the decades immediately preceding the PRC's establishment. The initial steps taken by the new regime to take control of an economy ravaged by occupation, war, and hyperinflation, and to carry out land reform, are the focus of Chapter 3. Chapter 4 covers mobilization for development under the First Five Year Plan and the simultaneous beginning of co-operative formation in agriculture.

The approach taken to long-term development planning combined policies and systems closely modelled on the Soviet example with indigenous Chinese methods, the latter noticeable in the initially gradual, step-by-step, approach to agricultural collectivization. The combination proved problematic in many respects, and new solutions began to be sought to problems of agricultural organization and production, choice of techniques, urban–rural relations, educational policy, wages and incentives, planning and management, etc. By the mid-1950s new policy directions, the seeds of which had already existed in the Yanan period, started to emerge. These were conditioned by the imperatives of China's natural, demographic, and cultural conditions on the one hand, and by the progressive formulation of Maoist principles of social and economic organization on the other. Ironically, while the changes in industry moved China away from the Soviet model, the decision to speed up collectivization moved it closer, albeit by different methods. Chapter 5 deals with this period of transition between the era of high Soviet influence and what is here called 'late Maoism'.

'Late Maoism', encompassing the period from the Great Leap Forward of 1958–60 and the famine years that overlapped it to Mao's death in 1976, is the subject of Chapters 6–10. Of these, the first three present historical analyses, while the last two summarize the record of this period with respect to two of its principal concerns: self-reliance and egalitarian distribution.

The final four substantive chapters concern the post-Mao period. Chapter 11 presents a prosecutor's brief for the reformers, with respect to both central command planning *per se* and the truncated Chinese version as amended and distorted by collision with Maoism. Chapters 12 and 13 deal, respectively, with the decollectivization of agriculture after 1979 and the simultaneous reopening of China to the world market. The issue of reform in industry and in the planning and management system generally is treated in a final chapter, which also attempts to identify the main parameters governing China's current progress towards modernity.

The passage from a war-torn and backward economy to one of the ten biggest industrial powers in the world, with a record of great economic and technological achievement, is the subject of this book. But, as the above outline indicates, its main sub-themes concern the rise and fall of Maoism as an approach to economic development, and the nature and origins of the very different policies of Mao's successors. From this turbulent story emerge possible lessons about the promise and the limits of socialist economic development under conditions of backwardness. But such lessons can only be tentative because, like all histories, this one is sparked by the friction of its own momentum against the random conjunctures of world events. Moreover, the story is unfinished.

Notes

1. There is a semantic problem here. 'Central planning' can refer to any regime in which central planners set and attempt to implement priorities for economic activity. However, it has come to imply a particular form of central intervention: one in which virtually all enterprises are either state-owned or treated as though they were, and in which the central government not only sets priorities, but carries them out *administratively* by distributing materials and finance to, and ordering output from, the various enterprises. It is in this sense that I use the term in this book.
2. According to State Statistical Bureau figures, the proportion of the total labour force engaged in agriculture was 83.5 per cent in 1952 and 68.4 per cent in 1984 (year-end figures). See *ZTZ* (1985:26); *ZTN* (1984:107, 109).
3. This argument can be illustrated by the following example. Imagine that China's modern sectors employed a number of workers equal to the total labour force of the United States. There would still remain some 350 million Chinese workers and their families unaccounted for—i.e., who would still be living largely in rural areas and engaging in agriculture and traditional handicrafts and services—although Chinese

GNP would exceed the current US level (assuming similar labour productivities in the modern sectors of the two countries). At present, in contrast, China's aggregate GNP is less than one-tenth that of the United States by conventional methods of measurement, perhaps one-fifth by methods that better reflect the relative purchasing power of the two currencies.

4. The figures for the USSR in 1932 are: 415 kg (national average per capita availability) and 375 kg (remaining for farm consumption after extractions) (Tang 1968:467). For China, the per capita availability in 1957 was 286 kg (Perkins 1969:302). Tang (1968:467) gives a figure of 256 kg, but this appears to be based on an underestimate of 1957 grain production. 'Availability' refers to domestic production plus exports minus imports.

CHAPTER 2

CHINA'S PRE-SOCIALIST ECONOMY

1 Introduction

The economy inherited by the Chinese Communists in 1949 was an anomaly. Among the most backward in the world in terms of income per capita, it nevertheless had a well-developed commerce, a sophisticated monetary system, a relatively high degree of literacy, long experience with complex organizations, and some highly industrialized regions. Whereas much of the countryside still practised subsistence production, other areas had already come under the commercial pull of the large coastal cities and, ultimately, the world market. In much of North China land reform had been carried out before Liberation (1 October 1949), and years of experience had been accumulated by the leadership in running the economy of the occupied areas. In contrast, Shanghai, the biggest and most industrialized and Westernized city, was the epitome of *laissez-faire* capitalism, with enormous commercial vitality and equally great indifference to human life and welfare. In Shanghai and other former treaty ports, foreign goods of all kinds filled the markets, but a few miles inland they met stiff competition from native goods, and country folk in the interior used them rarely, if at all. The complexity of the economy that greeted the victorious Communists in 1949 helps explain the shifting and innovative character of development policy over the subsequent decades.

2 Centuries of stability and change

Unlike many contemporary Third World nations, China had had a more or less unified economy over many centuries. Emerging from clusters on the North China Plain from the fourth and fifth centuries on, the population gradually spread southward, notably into the Yangtze River valley, where it was to develop and refine techniques of wet rice cultivation. It grew to a size of perhaps 100 million by the end of the Song dynasty in the twelfth century, before the devastation of the Mongol conquest reversed the trend. In the early years of the Ming dynasty (1368–1644), the population is estimated to have numbered between 65 and 80 million, from which it increased to perhaps 200 million by the end of the sixteenth century, and again to some 410 million by 1850.[1]

Economic growth went hand in hand with these trends. 'From the tenth to the fourteenth century China advanced to the threshold of a systematic experimental investigation of nature, and created the world's earliest mechanized industry', forging ahead in mathematics, astronomy, medicine, metallurgy, and manufacture (Elvin 1973:179). The Song economy was characterized by elaborate trade and commerce and the use of sophisticated mechanical devices in textile manufacturing and metallurgy. As Elvin (1973:

Chs. 12–13; 1975) has shown, Song China possessed both the scientific knowledge and the mechanical ability to have experienced a full-fledged industrial revolution some four centuries before it occurred in the West. But, for reasons still not fully understood, the Chinese economy instead entered a period of decline, during which many previously known technologies were lost; when growth commenced again in the sixteenth century, it consisted of change in quantity rather than in kind, and 'invention was almost entirely absent' (Elvin 1973:203).

In agriculture, too, technology changed little during the six centuries beginning with the Ming. Over this long period, farm output rose by more or less enough to keep up with population, which grew by an average rate of less than 0.5 per cent per year. This was sufficient, however, to generate a four- or five-fold increase in both population and food production by the middle of the nineteenth century. Such progress resulted from an expansion in cultivated area and a gradual increase in intensity of cultivation (Perkins 1969:6, 184–5). It is argued by some (notably Dwight H. Perkins) that by the nineteenth century the filling up of potentially arable areas had made it difficult for the traditional methods of farming to produce enough food. This thesis suggests that a long-postponed confrontation between Chinese society and its technological foundations was brewing just at the time when the first shocks from abroad jolted the Chinese Empire.

The West thus intervened in a country that had been changing slowly for many centuries but within the context of general social and technological stability. Culturally as well as economically, it looked backward to its golden ages, but these had not been entirely lost. Nineteenth-century China was a country with a long experience of literacy, artisan production and manufacture, commerce, and banking. Its forced entry into the world economy traded on these virtues, stimulating their further development in some respects while blocking it in others.

3   Imperialism and its impact

The evolving attitude of the People's Republic towards intercourse with the West and Japan can hardly be understood independently of the century-old gauntlet of humiliation, exploitation, and threat to survival that had characterized the relationship. That crucial period of seemingly unending insult provided the formative atmosphere in which the revolutionary leadership matured.

The symbolism of the fact that opium was the *casus belli* for imperialism's first major thrust against China has often been pointed out. China had permitted the development of some foreign trade, treating it as part of the system by which vassal states paid tribute to the Empire in return for imperial largesse. Tightly controlled, this exchange was confined to Canton and was monopolized on the Chinese side by a group of merchants (the 'Cohong'). In the course of the eighteenth century, the growing trade between Britain and China was compromised, from the British point of view, by an inability to sell China enough goods to balance the tea and silk that Britain purchased. These had to be paid for in silver, until English merchants discovered the expedient of selling the Chinese opium shipped from India. Despite a Chinese government ban on both the import and the use of opium, British sales to China increased greatly from the second half of the eighteenth century, until in 1830 they comprised no less than three-fifths of China's imports.[2] By this time the balance of trade had reversed itself, so that specie now flowed out of China at an increasing rate. The Chinese government's attempt to correct this situation by stopping the opium trade triggered the Opium War of 1840–2.

This was but the first of a series of armed conflicts by which Western powers forced a number of 'unequal treaties' on China. These included the cession of territory; the opening of designated 'treaty ports'—forty-eight of them by 1913 (Dernberger 1975:32)—in which foreigners enjoyed rights of extra-territoriality; the restriction of Chinese customs duties; and, ultimately, the provision of the right for foreigners to establish manufacturing facilities in the treaty ports.[3] Despite the proliferation of contact points between China and the imperialist powers, however, Shanghai dominated the treaty port system, accounting for almost two-thirds of China's foreign trade in 1870 and almost half of direct foreign investment in 1931.[4] Shanghai's predominance was an important legacy inherited by the People's Republic, and was to give that city a peculiarly important role into the 1980s.

As in many other Third World areas that became targets for Western economic imperialism, total trade increased sharply in consequence—from an annual average of $209 million for the period 1871–84 to $1,419 million in 1920–9.[5] Annual exports were about $2\frac{1}{2}$ per cent of gross domestic product in the earlier period and over 7 per cent of GDP in the later one. In size, therefore, this trade was small but not unusually so, given China's size, backwardness, and location. Exports were dominated by tea and silk until the beginning of the twentieth century, when tea especially declined (silk to a lesser extent), to be replaced by a variety of goods of agricultural origin, such as beans and beancake, seeds and oils, and hides and skins.[6] Such a pattern had little stimulative effect on either user or supplier industries, and was thus of negligible importance for economic growth (Dernberger 1975:34).

The pattern of Chinese imports, dominated in the nineteenth century by opium, also had little positive impact on growth. Opium, 'a deadweight loss in the Chinese economy' (Dernberger 1975:34), still accounted for about 40 per cent of imports in 1880, declining thereafter to some 15 per cent in 1900 and 7 per cent in 1913 (see note 6). At the turn of the century, opium, cereal, sugar, and paraffin together comprised almost half of China's imports. Consumer goods, they were largely devoid of forward linkage (i.e., stimulative influence on user industries).

It used to be thought that these imports played an extremely destructive role by flooding the market with cheap foreign goods and thus ruining native handicrafts. More recent scholarship has established a somewhat more complex view, which recognizes (1) that some handicrafts (especially cotton spinning, the largest nineteenth century handicraft industry) were indeed severely crippled by foreign competition, while others (e.g., weaving) were not; and (2) that handicrafts as a whole could not have been hurt much, since they still constituted more than 10 per cent of GDP in the 1930s, whereas imports potentially competitive with them made up less than 0.5 per cent of GDP (Perkins 1975b:121).

As for foreign investment, its direct economic impact can be summarized quite briefly. Total foreign investment in China rose to about $1 billion in 1902 and to more than $3 billion in the 1930s, by which time it amounted to $6–$8 per capita. Total investment was not very high in the 1930s (perhaps 5 per cent of GDP), but one-fifth of this was net foreign private investment—a not insubstantial proportion. Before direct foreign investment was 'legalized' by the Treaty of Shimonoseki (1895), the foreign financial commitment consisted chiefly of loans to the Chinese government. But by the 1930s, three-quarters of it was direct equity investment (Gurley 1976:95–6).

The immediate impact of foreign investment is symbolized by the fact that, in 1931, half of the accumulated total directly served the needs of foreign inhabitants (e.g., investment in public utilities, banks, real estate, and inventories). Another quarter was devoted to transport—railroads and steamships; these at least made some infrastructural contribution to the economy and stimulated some commercial crop development (Dernberger 1975:37–8; Myers 1970). However, direct investment in manufacturing accounted for only 17 per cent of total foreign investment in 1931, and in 1933 foreign-owned factories produced only about one-third of the total output of China's modern manufactures.[7]

What, then, was the net impact of the imperialist penetration of China from the mid-nineteenth century onward? This question is still controversial, with some assigning to imperialism the major share of blame for blocking industrialization and growth, and others seeing it as a stimulus blunted by weaknesses in the domestic fabric of Chinese society. An intermediate position regards the foreign encroachment as largely irrelevant, the treaty ports as 'economically . . . extraneous and tiny outposts of a system which remained foreign to China and made little impact on it' (Murphey 1970:59). The relative size of foreign activity in the economy as a whole, however, tells us little about its dynamic role, which depends more upon its impact on the still small potential growth-points in the economy. But what there were of these had been largely created by imperialism itself, for no signs can be detected in the period before foreign penetration of anything that might have led to an indigenous industrial revolution. While introducing modern technology and organizational methods, which some Chinese learned from,[8] imperialism at the same time put blocks in the way of exploiting such opportunities fully, had the determination to do so existed.

Most directly, imperialism siphoned off resources that *could* have (not necessarily would have) been devoted to capital formation and economic growth. In the years between 1895 and 1911—that is, from the end of the Sino–Japanese War to the fall of the Qing (Ch'ing) dynasty—total payments to foreigners by the Chinese government on account of the Boxer and Japanese war indemnities equalled more than twice the initial total value of all manufacturing enterprises established in China between 1895 and 1913 (Feuerwerker 1969:71–2). Such considerations lead Feuerwerker to conclude that after 1895, even had active economic development policies been desired, 'the imperial government . . . was without the facilities to reverse the largely passive economic role it had hitherto assumed' (Feuerwerker 1969:68–9, 71–2).

Similarly, the denial of tariff autonomy prevented China from protecting its nascent industries,[9] while the drain on government revenues occasioned by indemnities, service of foreign loans, and military expenditures severely limited the government's financial capacity to promote their development.[10] The impact that an intelligent import substitution policy might have had is suggested by the spurt in industrial growth during the First World War, when 'foreign competitors diverted their attention, though only temporarily, from Chinese markets' and 'as a result, the domestic industries of China made substantial gains . . .'[11]

Less tangible than, but at least as important as, these considerations is what Feuerwerker (1968:75) calls 'the ideological and political disequilibrium which was the most profound consequence of the impact of the West'. Having weakened, humiliated, and helped to delegitimize the Qing (Ch'ing) government, the foreigners proceeded to help put down the great Taiping revolution of the 1850s and 1860s[12] while simultaneously both shoring up the central government and continuing to make it an object of contempt. However, the imperial government never displayed interest in the kind of modernization promoted by its Meiji Japanese counterparts. Both the government and the social forces it represented feared the potentially erosive impact of industrialization upon their rule, and almost until the end of the regime this fear dominated other considerations. It is equally clear that imperialism was never central to the Empire's survival, and that it therefore cannot be held responsible for blocking earlier development by propping up a conservative regime.[13]

The most persuasive conclusion is that domestic factors were mainly responsible for the perpetuation of China's backwardness into the mid-twentieth century, but that imperialism, while providing a catalyst for economic and social change and stimulating Chinese nationalism, vastly complicated—and bloodied—the process by which these changes were to be accomplished.

4   Economic modernization during the first half of the twentieth century

For a time, at the very end of the dynasty, it seemed that forces were gathering within China that would sweep away the old barriers to fundamental reform. The first decade of the twentieth century was marked by a growing awareness of the foreign threat to China's integrity, and by the development of nationalist consciousness and organized opposition, often led by a reformist local gentry in the provinces, to what was perceived as the imperial government's subservience to the imperialist powers. From the same sources came local support for modern educational reforms and railroad development free of foreign control.[14] With the fall of the Qing dynasty in 1911, however, centrifugal forces prevailed, and the new, would-be emperor, Yuan Shih-k'ai, with foreign financial support, was able to 'by-pass and ultimately overwhelm this province-based gentry nationalism' (Esherick 1972:14).

The warlordism that followed the failure of the 1911 revolution ushered in a period of over three decades of almost continuous warfare, political instability, and widespread misery. Divisive regionalism, dominating China until the Guomindang (Kuomintang) unification drive of 1927, was punctuated by periodic manifestations of growing revolutionary sentiment, notably the May 4th Movement of 1919 and the May 30th Movement of 1925. The Guomindang's Northern Expedition, designed to unify the country, actually inaugurated in earnest the civil war that was to last until 1949. In April 1927, three weeks after capturing Shanghai with the aid of a Communist-led uprising in the city, Chiang K'ai-shek turned on his former allies and executed thousands of Communists and radicals throughout China. Four years later, Japan took over the north-east provinces of Manchuria, and, after incessant pressure against the rest of the country, attacked in force in 1937. For more than a decade thereafter, China was a battleground. Accompanying these political and military events were natural disasters—a northern drought in 1920–1 and the Yangtze River flood in 1931, as well as the deliberate flooding of the Yellow River during the war to slow the Japanese advance—all of which caused enormous devastation and loss of life.

It would be surprising if any economic growth had occurred in such a turbulent period. Abstracting from Japanese heavy industrial development in Manchuria, total national output in 1948 was probably similar to that of the turn of the century.[15] Between these two periods, however, and until the onset of total war, there was some growth. More important, the decades before the Second World War provided China with technical, organizational, and management skills that were to prove of value after 1949.

The first examples of modern industry appeared in the 1860s, in the form of several arsenals and shipyards. The establishment in 1890 of a *guandu shangban*[16] mechanized weaving enterprise in Shanghai marked the beginning of the leading modern industry in early twentieth-century China: cotton textiles. The tempo of industrialization picked up after the Treaty of Shimonoseki (1895) forced China to accept foreign direct investment.

According to rather impressionistic figures subject to wide margins of error, gross domestic product (GDP) grew by about 28 per cent between the First World War and 1933 (Perkins 1975b:117). More is known about the small modern sector than about the rest of the economy. For instance, an index of modern industrial production combining fifteen commodities and, over the period in question, representing perhaps 40 per cent of factory output, registered an average annual growth rate of 9.4 per cent between 1912 and 1936 (Chang 1969). This period encompasses an extraordinary spurt during 1912–20 when, freed temporarily from foreign competition by the First World War, Chinese industrial output advanced at an annual rate of 13.4 per cent. On the

Table 2.1. *Growth and structural change, 1914–1918 to 1933*

Sector	Share of GDP, 1957 prices (%)		Index of growth 1914–18 = 100
	1914–18	1933	1933
Industry[a]	17.6	19.8	144
Agriculture	61.8	59.2	122
Services	20.7	21.0	130
GDP	100.0	100.0	128
Population			116
GDP per capita			109.6

[a] Industry includes handicrafts and transport. See source for exact definitions and coverage.

Source: Perkins (1975b: 117, Table I, Appendix). The growth indexes are computed from absolute figures given by Perkins.

other hand, the index of modern industrial output in 1949 was virtually the same as in 1935[17]

Up to the 1930s, modern industry had made only minor inroads in the economy as a whole. In 1933 factories, mines, and utilities altogether produced no more than 3.4 per cent of net domestic product, less than one-half the output of handicrafts, and they employed fewer than 2 million workers.[18] After 1931 significant industrialization occurred only in Manchuria, which was cut off from the rest of China.

Much less is known about the fate of agriculture, handicrafts, and services during the first half of the twentieth century. Perkins (1975b) argues plausibly that agricultural output grew slowly as a result of both migration into newly opened areas such as Manchuria, and a gradual increase in the intensity of cultivation. Handicrafts present a mixed picture: of those competitive with foreign and domestic manufactures, most were probably not affected seriously. Modern and traditional services can be assumed to have grown at rates similar to those for the material-goods-producing sectors to which they were linked. Perkins's attempt to assign plausible numbers to all this is shown in Table 2.1, which indicates that gross domestic product per capita may have increased by about 10 per cent between the Great War and 1933. But the figures are not very firm; Rawski (1982b; 1983) makes a vigorous argument for higher growth in agriculture and per capita product, putting the latter at some 30 per cent over the same period; but his estimates too leave many questions unanswered.

Less ambiguous is the lack of significant change in the structure of output. Bearing in mind that the *modern* portion of 'industry' contributed only about 39 per cent of industrial output in 1933, its share of total GDP (in 1957 prices) was only about 7½ per cent.[19] Adding the output of modern services would raise this figure to no more than 10 per cent, which therefore represents the order of magnitude of the entire modern share of China's output in 1933. On the other hand, this share was not abnormally small in comparison with that of other Asian less developed countries (LDCs); even in the 1960s, this amounted to only 11 per cent in East Pakistan (now Bangladesh) and to 13 per cent in Burma and Afghanistan.

Moreover, the small modern sector did provide a foundation for the rapid economic growth that was to come later. In the few 'growth poles' where it was concentrated, notably Shanghai and its environs and southern Manchuria, 'the full panoply of changes that accompany the spread of modern economic growth' could be found (Rawski 1983). Its impact outside these centres is a matter of debate, however. Whereas Rawski (1983) states that 'few communities, however primitive and isolated, escaped the influence of economic change', others follow Rhoads Murphey (1970:66–7) in regarding the modernizing coastal nubs as 'tiny and isolated islands in an alien Chinese sea which all along resisted, and then rejected them'.[20]

Because labour productivity was considerably greater in modern than in pre-modern activities, and in non-agriculture than in agriculture, the sectoral division of the labour force was even more backward than that of output. Even if we double the fewer than 2 million workers estimated to be employed in 1933 (Feuerwerker 1968:7), in order to account for workers in other modern activities, the 'modern' labour force would still constitute only about $8\frac{1}{2}$ per cent of the non-agricultural working population and a minute 1.7 per cent of the entire working population.[21] The beginnings of economic modernization had directly involved only a small fraction of the population.

5   China's lagging economy: technology or society?

From the late nineteenth century on, Japan, unlike China, was rapidly building itself into a world economic and military power. China's failure to proceed in the same manner has puzzled many scholars, past and present, who have tried to identify what ailed the 'sick man of Asia'. The impact of imperialism does not seem to offer a sufficient explanation. Alleged defects in Chinese culture and society, such as the absence of primogeniture, the importance of the extended family, or the relative fluidity of class structure that permitted wealthy merchants to purchase entry into the landed gentry and officialdom, were emphasized by some earlier writers, but such explanations are now generally discounted.[22]

One influential school of thought sought the answer in a technological variant of the 'vicious circle of poverty' doctrine. Over the centuries, the potential for generating improvements in the traditional farm technology had been exhausted, so that farm surplus above the subsistence needs of the population tended to decline, discouraging investment and innovation.[23] A simpler version of this view avowed that 'the basic difficulty in rural China during the past century was that too many people were trying to make a living off too little land using a primitive technology.'[24] While stagnation obviously was linked to technological backwardness and low productivity, the underlying causal pattern cannot be technological. From the mid-nineteenth century on, China had access to the advanced technology of the world. That sufficient means and will to exploit it did not exist requires other than a technological explanation. Even in the depressed conditions of the 1930s, China produced a sufficient potential surplus above the average standard of living of the working population to finance a considerably higher rate of investment and growth than in fact occurred.[25] It is primarily to social and political conditions that one must look for explanation. In Feuerwerker's (1968:28–9) words, 'the structure of the agrarian economy and rural society combined with the absence of effective political leadership to dissipate potential output surpluses or to prevent their mobilization for investment in further economic growth'; thus it was 'a social system which guaranteed continued stagnation'.

In late nineteenth-century Japan, per capita agricultural output, and possibly total income per capita, were no higher than in China, yet the radical reforms of the Meiji era led to sharp increases in savings and investment (Eckstein 1968:44; Nakamura 1966). The weakness of similar forces for change within a China dominated by a conservative governing bureaucracy based on a rural élite prevented the available economic surplus from being put to use in growth-inducing ways.[26] This is not to deny the importance of population pressure, land scarcity, low per capita incomes, and pre-modern technologies in keeping China poor. Rather, it is to argue, with Tawney (1939:xii–xiii), that 'the extensive introduction of technical improvements is . . . improbable, until the social fabric within which they must function has been drastically modified.'

Industrial growth during the first third of the twentieth century does not seem to have refuted Tawney's judgement of the late 1930s. Modern economic activity contributed a very small share of total output, absorbed even less of the labour force, and was to a significant degree controlled by foreigners (see Sections 4, 6). Depression and civil war had brought about a deterioration in agrarian conditions, so that by the 1930s land concentration, tenancy, and general rural poverty were probably greater than they had been several decades earlier.[27] The economy inherited by the Chinese Communists—to which we now turn—was in ruinous condition.

6 The economic legacy: industry

Behind the devastation and dislocation created by continuous war and hyperinflation lay more deep-rooted structural problems. One such was the domination of large sectors of modern industry by foreign capital. In all, foreigners owned about 42 per cent of industrial assets just prior to the Second World War (Chao 1957:89; cited in Chen and Galenson 1969:20). More than three-fifths of national coal output came from foreign establishments in 1937, as did 86 per cent of iron ore, 80 per cent of pig iron, 88 per cent of steel, and 76 per cent of electric power. Foreign entrepreneurs owned 54 per cent of spindles and 44 per cent of looms in the textile industry, 68 per cent of power-generating capacity, 73 per cent of shipping tonnage, and the bulk of public utilities. Over half the output of shipbuilding and of a variety of light industries, such as woodworking, tanning, cigarette manufacturing, and soda production, was produced in foreign establishments. Banking, insurance, and external trade were foreign-dominated (SSB 1958:4; Xue *et al.* 1960:1).

The Nationalist government took over Japanese, German, and Italian enterprises after the war, extending state control to 67 per cent of modern industrial capital in 1946. Mao Zedong regarded this as the use of state power by a small number of 'bureaucratic capitalists' to achieve monopoly control of industry, and he dubbed it 'compradore–feudal state-monopoly capitalism' (Xue *et al.* 1960:18). This was to be distinguished from the 'national capitalism' of small and medium enterprises. Bureaucratic capitalism was seen as obstructive of development:

This type of capitalism did not grow mainly through increased production, but through open plunder with the aid of the state machine, through exploiting the laboring people and crowding out and swallowing up the medium-sized and small capitalist enterprises by means of speculation, currency inflation, and various measures of economic control. Like imperialism and feudalism, it seriously impeded the growth of the productive forces. [Xue *et al.* 1960:27][28]

The origin of extensive parts of 'bureaucratic capital' in the expropriated properties, expecially of Japan and Germany can be seen by comparing the above list of industries dominated in the 1930s by foreign capital with one of state-run industries after the Second World War. In 1947 the National Resources Commission controlled 90 per cent of national iron and steel production, 33 per cent of coal, 67 per cent of electric power, 45 per cent of cement, all petroleum and nonferrous metals, and 90 per cent of sugar. The major banks, all railways, highways, and airlines, 44 per cent of shipping tonnage, and several trading corporations were also in the 'state capitalist' sphere (Xue *et al.* 1960:27–8; Cheng 1963:8).

This great concentration of economic power in the hands of the state (and of the Guomindang élite[29]) was a windfall for the new regime; it permitted a rapid takeover of much of China's modern, large-scale industry, the transport and communications network, and most banking and foreign and domestic trade. Of course, this massive take-over left in its wake many problems, centring on the contradiction between the new ownership on the one hand and the old managements, business methods, and motivations on the other. Such problems would probably have been far greater, however, had it been necessary to undertake a more protracted process of nationalizing many thousands of individual enterprises in such a manner as to prevent production from falling.[30]

The most basic structural problem, of course, was the limited development of modern industry. Within the latter, moreover, small-scale enterprises were dominant. In 1936 (the last year of relative peace), handicraft production (both factory and individual) accounted for no less than 65 per cent of the gross value of national industrial output, leaving only 35 per cent for modern industries that used machines for their main processes. According to an investigation of eleven provinces and four cities carried out by the Nationalist Ministry of Industries, the size distribution of factories employing thirty or more workers,[31] by number of workers in the sample area at the end of 1935, was as shown in Table 2.2.

Table 2.2. *Size distribution of factories, 1935*

No. of workers per factory	No. of factories	% of all factories with 30 or more workers
30–50	544	48.7
51–500	517	46.3
More than 500	56	5.0
Total	1117	100.0

N.B. Figures are based upon a survey of factories employing thirty or more workers, in eleven provinces and four cities (Shanghai, Nanjing, Hankou, and Peiping), late 1935.
Source: Chao (1957:14).

Thus, in contrast to the USSR, whose well-known predilection for large-scale industry was fed by the fact that a majority of pre-revolutionary industrial workers were employed in factories with over 500 employees,[32] Chinese workers were widely dispersed in smaller factories. This situation was changed somewhat by the Japanese buildup of heavy industries in Manchuria during the war; when rebuilt with Russian help in the 1950s, these provided the locus for transmission into China of Soviet-type large-scale industry.

In terms of capitalization, as well, industrial enterprises were small, and Chinese-owned firms were generally much smaller than foreign-owned ones.[33] On the other hand, small Chinese enterprises were linked together skilfully in a complex division of labour that, while complicating the tasks of central planners, did realize some gains of specialization. One factory (the Continental Machine Plant) actually contracted with some forty-four small factories to process parts for it (Chao 1957:14–15). There has been a running debate in China over the relative merits of comprehensive and specialized enterprises, and post-Mao reformers decry what they regard as the overcentralizing trend of the late 1950s and 1960s that sacrificed such systems of specialization and division of labour (see Chapter 11).

It was also characteristic of Chinese industry that it was dominated by consumer goods.[34] The most important industries in terms of output value were cotton textiles, flour milling, cigarettes, and oil pressing (Feuerwerker 1968:117). This pattern was in part a legacy of the foreign interest in processing Chinese materials for immediate resale. It was also due to the inability of Chinese entrepreneurs to amass the capital and technological knowledge needed for producer goods industries, the riskiness of such investment under prevailing political conditions, and the lack of demand for capital equipment by a small industrial sector that could satisfy its limited needs through imports.

Finally, because of the foreign origins of modern industry, its location was heavily skewed towards the coastal provinces, and within these towards the treaty ports, especially Shanghai, Tianjin, Qingdao, and Guangzhou. The Treaty of Shimonoseki had limited foreign direct investment to the treaty ports, and this constraint was buttressed economically by the lack of infrastructure and of legal and military security in the interior, where, moreover, cruder but cheaper Chinese handicrafts competed effectively. For the same reasons, Chinese merchants and industrialists were also attracted to the port cities.[35] In 1949 the coastal areas, containing only one-tenth of China's area, produced over three-quarters of gross factory output (Chen and Galenson 1969:21). As Feuerwerker (1968:13) summarizes the situation, 'modern factory industry remained almost totally unknown in the interior provinces of China before the outbreak of the war with Japan.' Such geographical disposition ensured that factories were rarely placed near their sources of raw materials, were often located irrationally with respect to markets, and left most of the population in the interior out of the picture altogether.

7 The legacy: the rural economy

The pre-socialist economy was overwhelmingly rural; about 85 per cent of people lived in the countryside, the great majority of them farmers. John Lossing Buck (1956:165)[36] estimated that in the early 1930s about 362,000 square miles were under cultivation in the eight agricultural areas of China, which would make the cultivated area only about 10 per cent of a gross land area of about 3.7 million square miles. Dominated by arid grasslands in the northwest, high plateaux and massive mountain ranges in the west, and uneven hills in the south and south-west, the topography of China begrudges its people good farmland. What there is of it is limited almost entirely to five specific areas (*Geography of China* 1972:6–9):

1. *the North-east or Heilongjiang Plain*: including parts of the three north-eastern provinces (formerly Manchuria) of Liaoning, Jilin, and Heilongjiang, this region is China's principal producer of *gaoliang* (sorghum) and soybeans and is a spring wheat area;
2. *the North China Plain*: beginning near Beijing in the north and stretching downward through Hebei and eastern Henan, Shandong and northern Anhui, and Jiangsu. The 'cradle of Chinese civilization' and earliest as well as largest cultivated area of the country, this region is dominated by the Yellow River, which deposits there the alluvial soil originating in the loess regions upstream. Winter wheat, *gaoliang*, maize, and cotton are among the principal crops;
3. *the Middle and Lower Changjiang Plain*, following the banks of the Yangtze (Changjiang) from Yichang eastward towards Shanghai: warm and humid, with fertile, easily irrigated soil, it is a major rice area, but also produces wheat, silk and cotton;
4. *the Chengdu Plain*, in western Sichuan: a basin lying 500 metres above sea level amidst the higher mountains formed by the gradual descent from the Qinghai–Tibet Plateau towards the plains of the east; an extremely fertile rice-growing area and very heavily populated;
5. *South China valleys*, especially the Pearl River delta of southern Guangdong: ribbons of lush rice and subtropical cultivation amidst the hills of the region.

This physical geography explains why 90 per cent of China's population lives in only one-sixth of the total land area. In fact, the last four of these regions account for about three-quarters of the population. Within this heavily populated region, density averages around 250 persons per square kilometre, or 500 per square kilometre of cultivated land, but over considerable areas of the Chengdu Plain rural density reaches 660 per square kilometre.

The pattern of land use observed by Buck (1964:268) in the 1930s follows directly from these demographic realities. In order to squeeze as many calories as possible from the land, 90 per cent of the farm area was devoted to crops and only 1.1 per cent to pasture for animals (as compared with US figures of 42 and 47 per cent, respectively, in the same period). Moreover, Chinese farms were very small, with a median crop area of only 0.97 hectares (2.37 acres). Over 70 per cent of all farms were under 1 hectare (2.47 acres). Although the corresponding figures for certain other LDCs (e.g., Japan) were even smaller, China's farm size contrasts sharply with the 157 acres that constituted an average farm in the United States at that time.

One might anticipate that population pressure would cause a particularly high proportion of land to be under crops. Yet Buck found that 7.6 per cent of farm land was not in productive use (10.2 per cent for small farms, 6.7 per cent for larger ones), compared with only 4.6 per cent in the United States. To some extent this difference was due to the higher density of the Chinese rural population and its requirement of more housing, etc., per acre. In addition, private ownership implied the need to demarcate one's land from that of others and have access to it via paths. Partible inheritance and free commerce in land also encouraged fragmentation of the land. The typical farm, though small to begin with, was divided into an average of six parcels, whose average distance from the farmstead was 0.4 miles. Thus, additional land had to be removed from production for use as boundaries and paths between parcels. Not only was land wasted by parcelization; during the busy season, much labour time was spent transporting farmer, equipment, and animals from field to field. Irrigation and drainage were both rendered difficult by fragmentation, which led to endless disputes over ownership and access.

Among the most densely populated poor countries in terms of cultivable area, China furnished a paradigm for development models, fashionable in the 1950s and 1960s, that assumed 'unlimited' supplies of labour. It is thus interesting to find Buck using this term in 1937, in a famous and, on the face of it, paradoxical characterization of labour supply in rural China:

The amount of man labor in China is almost unlimited and one of the great problems is the discovery of enough production work to keep this vast human army profitably employed. Paradoxically, the problem is also one of reducing the amount of human labor required during periods of peak labor requirements for important farm operations, such as planting and harvesting, and for tasks which man labor alone cannot accomplish, such, for instance, as pumping water to great heights or distances. [Buck 1964:289]

Buck found that, while 35 per cent of all able-bodied men of working age were engaged in full-time work and 58 per cent were without work part of the time, this idleness was heavily concentrated in the four winter months of

November–February. During the busy seasons of the farm year, most localities reported labour *shortages*. It is clear, then, that the Chinese farm economy did not have surplus labour in the sense that, *ceteris paribus*, large amounts of labour could be removed *permanently* from agriculture without farm output declining. It is also clear, however, that there was a potential for much more effective use of China's huge rural labour force, if land could be consolidated, labour organized for off-season farmland capital construction projects, and selective technical improvements introduced.

Production relations in the countryside were extremely complex; for instance, the renting in and out of land and the hiring of labour extended over a wide socioeconomic range. Some scholars have argued that 'the amount of land held by landowners who did not themselves farm was clearly too small to serve in and of itself as an adequate basis for a distinct and socially dominated class' (Elvin 1973:255). In the same vein, rural society has been described as highly 'competitive' (Elvin 1973:259; Myers 1980:173; Rawski 1979:67–71), even 'egalitarian', with the fortunes of individual families continually rising and falling (Elvin 1973:259).

Such statements raise a number of issues: (1) Was rural society egalitarian with respect to the distribution of income and wealth and was it characterized by a high degree of both upward and downward social mobility? (2) Did landlords form a distinct and dominant class? (3) Did socioeconomic conditions in the villages tend to hinder investment, innovation, and growth? These issues, about which debate still flourishes, cannot be explored exhaustively here, but each demands a brief comment.

First, regarding mobility: unlike Japan, traditional China did not have rigid barriers of status to prevent social mobility. Anecdotal accounts of steep rises and falls in individual family fortunes over two or three generations have created an impression of great mobility in both directions. Partible inheritance made it difficult for each generation of families to keep its estates intact over the generational change. However, there are hardly any statistical studies of social mobility of the population at large against which to check such impressions, and none at all of national scope. Conclusions must be based upon fragmentary data, demographic logic, and a grasp of the relevant institutions of rural society.

Powerful forces besides partible inheritance did indeed make for *downward* mobility in rural China. One such was recurrent famine. Buck's (1937:19) data on the incidence of famines between 1850 and 1932 imply that, on average, 4.5 per cent of each generation died from famine conditions, with the rate of death reaching 8.8 per cent in North China (Moise 1977:7). These deaths were concentrated among the poorest families, those without assets to tide them over the crisis or make them eligible for credit. Thus, each generation of poorest families, being survivors, had been on average better off than the poorest in the *previous* generation, and had thus declined in relative economic standing (Moise 1977:5–7). Similarly, the higher infant mortality rate for girls, owing to female infanticide and differentially inferior care, gave rise to a marked sex imbalance in the adult population, so that approximately one man in ten was unable to marry. These too tended to be the poorest. Thus, as Moise (1977:4) concludes, 'the simple fact is that the families at the bottom of the economic scale tended to die out.'[37]

Under such circumstances, even if the average per capita income was rising and there was significant social mobility in both directions, the predominant direction of relative change—at least for individual men and for families—was probably downward; that is, 'the average Chinese man was significantly poorer than his father' (Moise 1977:4), and the same was true of his family relative to that of his father. Other factors, such as widespread indebtedness and the extravagance required at ceremonial occasions, contributed to the difficulty peasants experienced in accumulating assets. What Feuerwerker (1968:37) calls 'the pervasiveness and crushing burden of rural indebtedness' was overwhelmingly due to the inability of large numbers of peasants to accumulate enough food and/or income to survive the 'spring famine' and reach the next harvest. Most rural borrowing was for such consumption purposes (or to meet extraordinary ceremonial requirements), and led to a vicious cycle of borrowing to repay past debts and interest ('for the poorer peasants permanent indebtedness was the rule'—Feuerwerker 1968:38). Estimates of the incidence of peasant indebtedness in the 1930s range from 39 to 56 per cent (Feuerwerker 1968:38). More than three-fourths of farm credit was provided by merchants, landlords, wealthy farmers, and village shops; interest rates, while concentrated in the 20–40 per cent range, not uncommonly reached over 100 per cent per annum. Thus, rural usury, while occasionally permitting the temporary survival of indigent peasants, did so 'at the ultimate cost of preserving intact a landlord-dominated rural society' (Feuerwerker 1968:38–9).

Through luck, extraordinary diligence, or shrewdness, peasants could and did occasionally improve their economic positions (see Huang 1975:145–6, for a case in point). Those who had inherited assets and lived in areas near thriving metropolitan regions could invest in commerce or lend out their money, accumulate land, and pass on larger estates than they had inherited. But such opportunities were not often available to poorer peasants: one survey (undertaken by the University of Nanking in 1934–5) of four provinces ascertained that only 1.6 per cent of part-owners and 0.6 per cent of full owners had advanced from being agricultural labourers (Feuerwerker 1968:37). By the second and third decades of this century, poorer peasants, preoccupied chiefly with avoiding disaster, could not realistically look forward to either absolute or relative advance on the socioeconomic scale.

'Egalitarian' also seems a poor characterization of Chinese rural society. As in other Asian LDCs, the overall scale of landholdings was microcosmic in comparison with the extensive agriculture practised in North America. The *largest* farms in China—that is the less than 0.5 per cent of all farms averaging 23.38 acres (Buck 1964:271–3)—would have been uneconomically *small* in the United States even in the early 1930s, when farm size averaged only 157 acres (1964:174). Similarly, although there were concentrations of great wealth in China, the typical village landlord would not have been considered wealthy by Western standards. Therefore, there is a superficial plausibility to the view that poverty must have been shared equally.

A closer look belies this view. We have already seen that the most basic 'good'—the expectation of survival until the next generation—was very unequally distributed, with a substantial section of the poorest men unable to reproduce itself. This fact provides an insight: when average income is very low, it does not require an *absolutely* large degree of inequality to have profound economic, social, and political consequences. Although 'only a few acres' separated landlords from poor peasants (Elvin 1970:165), when the median farm size is only 3.31 acres, these 'few acres' could spell the difference between prestige and authority on the one hand, and destitution and social power-lessness on the other.

Among the factors that bear on the distribution of wealth and income in the rural areas are: (1) the extent of tenancy; (2) the distribution of landownership; (3) the distribution of land cultivated; and (4) the distribution of other assets.

The facts regarding the importance of tenancy in the 1930s are uncertain. J. L. Buck found that a national average of 28.7 per cent of land owned by private individuals was rented out. Adding institutionally owned land yields an estimate of 33.5 per cent of all farmland being farmed by tenants (Lippit 1974:64).[38] However, Buck's estimate is generally felt to be on the low side because his sample of localities under-represented the south, where tenancy was more widespread.

The incidence of tenancy from the perspective of population (rather than of land) is treated in Table 2.3. It can be seen that estimates of pure tenancy (i.e., farm households renting all their cultivated land) range from the Buck Farm Survey's 17 per cent (panel B) to the NARB's 1937 figure of 30 per cent (panel A) to 50 per cent in Hunan Province immediately before land reform. NARB regional estimates range as high as 58 per cent in Sichuan (Feuerwerker 1968:35).

Tenancy rates tended to be highest in the most fertile, productive, and commercialized regions, such as the Chengdu Plain of Sichuan, the lower Yangtze Valley, and the Pearl River delta of Guangdong. Since the impulse for technological change should have been strongest in just such regions, the question arises whether tenancy posed a barrier to improvement. On this issue, too, past scholarship has not been unanimous.

Two of the most important aspects of landlord–tenant relations are the form of rent and security of tenure. Perkins (1969), largely on the basis of these two considerations, concludes that tenancy did not exercise a retarding effect on productivity growth. He argues that fixed rent and long-term tenure, conditions that give tenants an incentive to increase productivity, were both prevalent in areas where tenancy was widespread (1969:106).

Aside from the spotty nature of some of the evidence, there are caveats suggested by additional considerations. First, the level of rents, which generally amounted to 50 per cent of the annual crop, limited tenants' *capacity* to invest, whatever their incentive to do so. Second, other forms of exactions, such as land deposits, collection of rent in advance, labour services, etc. (Lippit 1974:61–2), must have affected both capacity and incentive. Third, where investment involved significant risk, fixed rent, which allots risk to the tenant alone, might

Table 2.3. *Incidence of tenancy, pre-land reform China (percentages)*

(A) National Agricultural Research Bureau				
	1912	1931	1933	1937
Owner	49	46	45	46
Part-owner	23	23	23	24
Tenant	28	31	32	30

Source: Feuerwerker (1968:34).

(B) J. L. Buck, Land Utilization in China, 1929–33		
	Farm survey	Agricultural survey
Owner	54	44
Part-owner	29	23
Tenant	17	33

Source: Buck (1964:196).

(C) National Land Commission, 1934–5	
Landlord	2.05
Landlord–owner	3.15
Landlord–owner–tenant	0.47
Owner	47.61
Owner–tenant	20.81
Tenant	15.78
Tenant–Labourer	0.02
Labourer	1.57
Other	8.43

Source: Feuerwerker (1968:34).

(D) Hunan before land reform, 1950	
Owners	22
Part-owners	28
Tenants	50

Source: Yen *et al.* (1955:278); cited in Huang (1975:137).

(E) Kwangtung Province, 1933

	% of peasant families		
	Owners	Tenants[a]	Agricultural labourers[a]
152 villages, 38 districts	32.6	57.2	10.2
69 villages, Pan-yu District	12.0	77.4	10.6
22 villages, Hwa County	22.2	73.3	4.5

[a]'Tenants' is defined as peasants who lease all or most of land they cultivate; 'Agricultural labourers' is defined as peasants who depend on wages as principal source of livelihood.
Source: Chen (1936:115–22).

have been less advantageous to investment than sharecropping, which splits it between landlord and tenant. Fourth, landlords, who were also local monopolistic suppliers of credit, were in a position to charge high interest rates and to undervalue collateral as additional means of extracting income from tenants. Finally, there is some indication that long-term tenure was declining in the twentieth century.[39]

Regardless of its impact on productivity growth, however, tenancy was not a good indicator of class in rural China. First, as can be seen from panel (C) of Table 2.3, the demarcations between landlord, owner, and tenant were anything but rigid. Many farmers fell simultaneously into two of these categories, and there were even landlords who were also tenants. Moreover, it was not uncommon to find wealthy peasants who owned no land, but rented large holdings which they farmed with the help of hired labourers. Therefore, we must look beyond tenancy to such criteria as land distribution by ownership and by operation.

Information about the distribution of landownership on a national scale is scanty. Two available estimates, presented in panels (A) and (B) of Table 2.4, suggest that, although very large properties were rare, land was nevertheless quite unequally distributed. On a national scale, the great majority of peasants owning 1 hectare (15 *mu*) or less accounted for only 28 per cent of cultivated land, while the slightly more than one-quarter of farmers owning larger properties accounted for 72 per cent of cultivated land (panel B). Because this conclusion masks considerable regional variation, however, some local surveys, including one made by Mao Zedong in 1931 (panel D), are presented in panels (C)–(F). These indicate varying degrees of inequality, with the least concentration of ownership appearing in the backward area of Shanxi Province studied by William Hinton (panel E).

Landownership was an important source of income, security, and access to credit. However, the effect of ownership inequality on *production* was partly ameliorated by the rental market, which somewhat smoothed the distribution of land *holdings* relative to that of landownership. Columns (1), (4), and (5) of Table 2.5 indicate that the 61 per cent of farm households *cultivating* farms of less than 3.88 acres accounted for 32.5 per cent of the cultivated area, whereas the distribution of *ownership* (Table 2.4) shows a higher percentage (73 per cent) of households owning smaller farms (2.47 acres or less) and accounting for a smaller proportion (28 per cent) of total cultivated area. This result was

Table 2.4. *Distribution of land owned, rural China, 1930s to 1950*

	% of households	% of cultivated land
(A) *China as a whole*		
Landless	10.03	0
Owning less than 5 *mu*	17.34	2.46
Owning 5–20 *mu*	40.21	21.58
Owning 21–50 *mu*	21.53	30.51
Owning 51–100 *mu*	7.96	24.59
Owning 101–200 *mu*	2.47	14.65
Owning more than 200 *mu*	0.47	6.21

Source: Liu (1953:19); cited in Zao (1964:35).

Table 2.4. *Cont.*

	% of households	% of cultivated land
(B) *China as a whole*		
Owning 15 *mu* or less	72.77	28.26
Owning more than 15 *mu*	27.23	71.74
Owning 1000 *mu* or more	0.015	1.75

Source: National Land Commission Survey, 1934/35; cited in Feuerwerker (1968: 31–2).

(C) *Panyu District, Guangdong (1933)*		
Landless labourers	9.0	0
Poor peasants	58.5	22.1
Middle peaseants	20.9	28.3
Rich peasants (incl. landlords)	11.6	49.6

Source: Chen (1936:126).

(D) *Xinguo County, Jiangxi (1931)*		
Landless labourers	1.0	0
Poor peasants	60.0	5.0
Middle peasants	20.0	15.0
Rich peasants	5.0	30.0
Landlords	1.0	40.0

Source: Mao Zedong, 'Rural Investigation of Hsinkuo', in Chao (1960:30).

(E) *"Longbow" Village, Shanxi (1944)*		
Landless labourers	6.0	0
Poor peasants	46.8	24.8
Middle peasants	40.0	45.3
Rich peasants	2.7	5.4
Landlords	4.0	12.2
Institutional land	—	12.3

Source: Hinton (1966); cited in Huang (1975:142).

(F) *Hunan (1950)*		
Landless labourers	10.0	0
Poor peasants	39.0	7.0
Middle peasants	30.0	26.0
Rich peasants	5.0	13.0
Landlords	3.0	55.0[a]

[a] Including institutional land.

Source: Huang (1975:142).

Table 2.5. *Distribution of farm holdings by size class, 1929–1933: Buck (acres)*

	(1) Range of area means	(2) Mean	(3) Median	(4) % of farms	(5) % cultiv. area	(6) % farm area rented	(7) Persons per household	(8) Mean farm size per person	(9) % farms w/o draught animals	(10)(a) Fertilizer per acre (lb)	(10)(b) of which, manure (%)
Very small	0.77–1.61	1.43	1.46	1 }	7.9	29.5	4.2 }	0.33	65	9 314	83
Small	0.74–2.00			23 }			4.4 }				
Medium	2.00–3.88	2.84	2.79	37	24.6	29.7	5.5	0.52	38	9 515	76
Med.–large	3.93–6.67	4.92	4.79	20	22.5	29.2	6.9	0.71	18	10 033	67
Large	5.73–9.83	7.17	6.92	11	18.0	28.1	8.3	0.86	12	9 691	58
Very large	8.45–23.70	13.02		7	21.8 }		10.1	1.29 }			
Larger still	16.16–31.09	21.97	11.56 }	1	4.0 }	24.3 }	10.7	2.05 }	7	10 381	55
Largest	16.73–40.20	23.38		negl.	1.1 }		11.6	2.02 }			
All farms	0.74–40.20	4.18	3.16	100	100	28.7	6.2	0.67	35	n.a.	
Wheat region		5.63	4.05	—	—	12.7	6.5	0.87	31	n.a.	
Rice region		3.11	2.52	—	—	40.3	5.9	0.53	38	n.a.	

Source: Buck (1964:Chs. VI, VIII, IX).

Table 2.6. *Distribution of farm households by size of farm: NARB (hectares)*

Farm size (ha)	% of farm households
Less than 0.67	36
0.67–1.33	25
1.33–2.00	14
2.00–3.33	17
More than 3.33	8

Source: National agricultural Research Bureau, 1933–7 Agricultural Survey; cited in Shen (1951:141).

achieved by the widespread practice of renting land. Farms in all size classes rented in one-fourth or more of their land (Table 2.5, col. (6)).[40]

The somewhat greater equality of distribution of landholdings does not signify an 'egalitarian' rural society. Land, after all, is a factor of production, and its availability to tenants was as much of benefit to its owners as it was a means of sustaining its occupants. One would not deduce from an equal distribution of lathes among machine operators that industrial democracy reigned within the factory; similarly, holding size did not by itself determine class status in rural China.

Farm area was more equally distributed per person (col. (8)) than per household because larger farms had larger households (col. (7)). The 7 per cent of households with 'very large' farms still had almost four times as much land per capita as 'small' and 'very small' farms, however.

There is very little information about the distribution of assets other than land in rural China before 1949, but some indication is provided by columns (9) and (10) of Table 2.5. These suggest that the distribution of draught animals and chemical fertilizer were both highly correlated with farm size. An indication of the generally more favourable resource endowment of larger farms is given by Buck's (1964:279) finding that per capita grain production of large farms was three times higher than that of small ones, even though average family size was also larger.

Seeking to understand rural social structure, the Chinese Communists went through a process of trying out various simple criteria, such as those investigated above. Mao's initial approach (in 1926) assumed a simple dichotomy between landlords and tenants, with rent the predominant form of exploitation, and paid little attention to the use of hired labour, subletting of land, or money-lending (Huang 1975:136–7). By the time the Agrarian Reform Law of 1950 was written, however, this concept had been replaced by a far more complex conception, which divided rural society into five main classes. (1) *Landlords* were owners of land who mostly did not engage in labour but depended on labour exploitation for their income, which was principally land rent but might also include interest and profits. Moreover, a class of sub-landlords was recognized, which rented in large areas of land in order to sublet them out again. (2) *Rich peasants* generally owned land, but might rent in all or part of it; they generally owned better means of production and some liquid capital, laboured themselves, but derived most of their livelihood from the exploitation of hired labour. (3) *Middle peasants* owned all, some, or none of their land, some of their tools, and depended wholly or principally on their own labour for their living. They generally did not exploit others, but might do so in a minor way; they might also be exploited on a small scale via land rent and loan interest. (4) *Poor peasants* might own some inadequate tools and part of their land, but generally had to rent land and were exploited through rent, interest, and profit on their labour for others. (5) Finally, *workers*, including farm labourers, generally had neither land nor tools and depended wholly or mainly on wage labour for their living (*Agrarian Reform Law* 1959:18–23).

Despite the hedged nature of these definitions, as promulgated by the 'Decisions Concerning the Differentiation of Class Status in the Countryside', many additional pages were needed for a host of further considerations, such as the definitions of 'supplementary labour', 'well-to-do middle peasant', and 'idlers', dealing with the class status resulting from inter-marriage between classes, etc. The document as a whole suggests a full recognition of the actual complexity and fluidity of Chinese rural class composition, even as its principal skeletal structure was affirmed.

Provisional answers can now be offered for the three questions with which this discussion of rural class structure began. (1) Chinese rural society was hardly egalitarian with respect to the distribution of income and wealth: and although characterized by substantial social mobility, the predominant direction of the latter was downward, at least in relative terms. (2) The incidence and significance of landlordism varied greatly by region. Where it was most prevalent, landlords were absentees, living in towns and cities where they used income siphoned from the countryside for commercial or speculative activities or for consumption. Conversely, in areas where little land was rented and landlords were less differentiated from other rural classes, they tended to remain in their native villages, where, ironically, they were probably able to play a larger social and political role. In any event, the proportion of land rented is by itself an inadequate indicator of landlord economic strength and social dominance. (3) Socioeconomic conditions in the villages broadly understood, did hinder investment, innovation, and growth. High rents and increasingly insecure tenancy discouraged investment by tenants, while fragmentation of holdings discouraged technical improvements. Where commercialization might have stimulated investment, innovation, and specialization, inadequate credit and high interest rates made borrowing for such purposes a major gamble; few peasants were in a position to undertake it, or were willing to trust their fate to an unpredictable market.

The ultimate test of the impact of socioeconomic conditions upon rural economic growth is the relation between the surplus potentially available for generating such growth and the actual rate of investment. My estimate of this surplus for 1933, including output lost owing to underutilized land and labour, comes to more than 24 per cent of net domestic product (Riskin 1975a:70; see also note 25). In contrast, net investment in that year was less than 2 per cent of NDP and did not exceed 3 per cent in any of the years (1931–6) for which estimates are available, and it is unlikely that investment in agriculture accounted for more than half of this total. The clue to this disparity lies neither in the lap of God nor in the size of China's population, but must be sought in the nature of the traditional rural society.

8   The economy on the eve of liberation

In one of his best known passages, Mao characterized the Chinese people as 'both poor and blank' (Mao 1956). These qualities he saw as both an indictment of the past and a source of hope for the future: on a blank sheet of paper 'the newest and most beautiful words can be written'. The inherited economy fits this image well. Decades of war and civil war had destroyed much of the pre-existing industrial capacity, and much of what was left was removed to Hong Kong and Taiwan ahead of the advancing People's Liberation Army. At the same time, rampant corruption and hyperinflation had left the reputation of the old regime in shreds and created a broad receptivity to initiatives by the new authorities. In short, the very severity of the chaos and depth of economic depression in the late 1940s posed a severe test for the incoming government but at the same time created opportunities for it to gain legitimacy.

Industrial production in 1949 was only 56 per cent of its prewar peak level. Producer goods industries, built up in the north-east by the Japanese, were most seriously affected. At the war's end, the Soviet Union occupied Manchuria and carted home over half the surviving capital stock. Rural production was less affected by the disruption of transport and trade; food output in 1949 was estimated at 70–75 per cent of its prewar peak. Light industry, also producing 70 per cent of its previous peak, was hampered by lack of raw materials, particularly in its most developed base, Shanghai, which was cut off from trade by a Nationalist blockade.

The most dramatic characteristic of the economy in the late 1940s was the inflation, which began in 1938 and by the mid-1940s had evolved into a chronic hyperinflation. It started with the Japanese seizure of the most productive areas of the country and the chief sources of national government revenue; continued with the failure of the government to institute effective tax reform or to finance mushrooming military expenditures other than by the printing press; and finally produced a wholesale public flight from money. A brief respite following the Japanese surrender gave way to a renewed upward spiral with the intensification of the civil war. By the beginning of August 1948, Shanghai wholesale prices had reached a level 4.7 million times that of early 1937, and the time path of the inflation had become nearly vertical (Chen and Galenson 1969:19; Gurley 1976:109).

The aggravated economic problems of the late 1940s contributed to, but were not the basic cause of, the Communist victory. The Communists had of course gained considerable national support already from their unambiguous leadership of the anti-Japanese resistance. Moreover, their main political base of support was in the countryside, where the economy as a whole had survived the turbulent 1930s and 1940s better than the cities. It was the long-term, underlying agrarian crisis that had created the possibility for the mobilization of poorer peasants into a powerful movement with revolutionary aspirations. In the urban areas, however, the Communists were a less well-known quantity and the great inflation undoubtedly played an important role in their victory. Its impact on Chinese society was profound. In the words of its chief historian,

Public servants and servicemen were demoralized by a degree of poverty extreme even for China and were antagonized by the growth of a wealthy class which had achieved its position by engaging in activities inimical to the general welfare. By its failure to avoid the economic conditions leading to this outcome and its further failure to correct the situation that emerged, the government earned the disaffection of the army and of the administrative services. These conditions led toward the loss of support which eventually brought the downfall of the Nationalist Government and the triumph of Communism in China. [Chang 1958:68]

By bringing about the economic ruin of much of the urban population, including the intelligentsia, the inflation narrowed the base of the Nationalists' political support almost out of existence and made any alternative seem preferable to many who would not otherwise have favoured the Communists. At the same time, the inflation faced the latter with the first great test of their own capacity for national leadership.

Notes

1. See Ho (1959); Perkins (1959:16, App. A); and Elvin (1973:255, 309–10).
2. Eckstein (1968:47). Eckstein cites the figure of 56 per cent, but points out that this figure is incomplete, omitting 'the quantities smuggled in'. It seems safe to assume that the figure must have reached 60 per cent.
3. The last concession was won by Japan in the Treaty of Shimonoseki (1895) and automatically applied to the other powers via the most favoured nation clauses won by them earlier.
4. Dernberger (1975:33). Most remaining foreign investment in 1931 consisted of Japanese and Russian investment in Manchuria (Dernberger 1975:33).
5. Dernberger (1975:27). Figures are in current prices converted to US dollars at the exchange rates ruling during the years in question.
6. Eckstein (1968:47, Table 2; 56, Table 3; 72–3, Table 8).
7. Dernberger (1975:38). The latter observations have been cited (Hou 1965) in support of the proposition that foreign activity did not inhibit the growth of native Chinese manufactures. This is a *non sequitur*. By themselves, these figures do not imply that native manufactures might not have grown faster (or slower) in the absence of competition from foreign-owned firms (Feuerwerker 1968).
8. Thus, Chinese-owned factories accounted for two-thirds of the total output of modern manufactures in 1933, and, though much smaller and less capitalized than foreign factories, outnumbered the latter by ten to one.
9. China's tariffs were set at 5 per cent ad valorem in 1843. Foreigners (principally

Britain) took over direct administration of Chinese customs between 1856 and 1861. When China finally regained control in 1928, the effective rate rose to 8.5 per cent in 1929, 10 per cent in 1932, and 30 per cent in 1935 (Dernberger 1975:44). The argument that denial of tariff autonomy harmed China has been challenged (e.g., by Dernberger 1975:44, and Lippit 1978:280), on the ground that the government could have resorted to the alternative of subsidizing domestic enterprises. However, it is doubtful that the imperialist powers, having ruled out protectionism in one form, would blithely have accepted it in another. See also note 10.

10. For this argument, as well as evidence of Western opposition to such attempts at domestic favouritism and of general Chinese fear of taking actions that would provoke imperialist retaliation, see Moulder (1977:194–7).

11. Chang (1969:72). See also Esherick (1972). Although, as is often pointed out, foreign control of customs was relatively free of corruption and provided the Chinese government with its one secure and predictable source of revenue, the main effect of this, especially after 1895, was to secure China's ability to pay indemnities and service foreign loans, a task for which it was increasingly inadequate.

12. See Wolfgang Franke, 'The Taiping Rebellion', in Schurmann and Schell (1967), for a brief history of this great social eruption.

13. These arguments are both put forcefully in Lippit (1978).

14. See Wright (1969) for a dramatic account of these developments.

15. Ashbrook (1975) gives GNP in 1952 as 68 per cent greater than in 1949, while Perkins (1975b) gives 1952 GDP as only 36 per cent above that of 1914–18. Together, these comparisons imply that 1949 output was below that of 1914–18. Of course, the figures used are in some cases very crude and contain large margins of error, and they are cited here only to support the general impression suggested in the text.

16. *Guandu shangban* means literally 'official supervision, merchant management', and refers to a common form of industrial organization in late Qing China in which private enterprises were established under official patronage and protection but were also subject to official interference and 'squeeze'. See Feuerwerker (1959).

17. Chang (1969:72). Japanese-sponsored heavy industrial growth in Manchuria continued into the early 1940s, causing the overall index to reach a peak in 1942 above the 1935 and 1949 levels. See Chang (1969:Table 14, 61, 72, and App. A).

18. Feuerwerker (1968:10). See also Chang (1969:109), citing Yeh (1964). 'Factories' refers to manufacturing establishments using mechanical power, and does not include handicrafts, which employed more than 12 million workers.

19. Calculated from Perkins (1975b:117, Table 1). This percentage differs from the one cited earlier and based on Feuerwerker (1968) (see note 18) both in prices used and in coverage. Yeh's (1979) estimate of the modern sector's share of GDP in the 1930s (in 1933 prices) is 7.5 per cent. Excluding Japanese-controlled Manchuria, this share falls to 6.8 per cent. See Rawski (1982b:20).

20. Rawski (1982b:57–60) correctly argues that 'modern-oriented fixed investment, while modest in relation to the national economic aggregates, was a regional and sectoral rather than a national phenomenon.' He makes this point in criticizing, with some validity, this author's (Riskin 1975a) emphasis on the very low proportion of national net investment in total economic surplus in 1933 (see note 25 below). However, it is a double-edged argument, also serving to underscore how little investment occurred in the great bulk of the economy outside Manchuria and Shanghai, and it rather serves to weaken the argument in Rawski (1983) concerning 'the wide sectoral and spatial ramifications of developments in the modern sector'.

21. The estimates are about 212 million for the agricultural working population and 47 million for the non-agricultural working population, making the entire working

population some 259 million (Feuerwerker 1968:6,7). These estimates are taken by Feuerwerker from Liu and Yeh (1965:185, 188, Tables 54, 55).

22. A critical review of some of these sociocultural arguments can be found in Perkins (1975a).

23. This argument is part of the notion of a 'high-level equilibrium trap', associated with Radha Sinha and Mark Elvin and expounded in the latter's *The Pattern of the Chinese Past* (1973). Elvin (1973), however, withdraws somewhat from this argument as a sufficient overall explanation of Chinese backwardness.

24. Potter (1968:180). A similar view is expressed by Myers (1970:293).

25. Lippit (1974). Building on this work, I have attempted to estimate roughly the size of the potential surplus above the actual level of consumption of the working population in all sectors of the economy. The result varies from over one-quarter to over one-third of net domestic product in 1933, depending upon the concept of 'surplus' employed (see Riskin 1975a:64–77). In contrast, net domestic investment was less than 2 per cent of NDP in the same year (p. 79). See also Section 7 of this chapter.

26. For a discussion of the role of China's class structure in impeding economic development, see Lippit (1978).

27. This proposition is denied by Rawski (1983), who argues that rural living standards improved in the decades leading up to the 1930s.

28. In Chinese Communist parlance, 'feudalism' refers to the pre-capitalist socioeconomic structure and culture in China.

29. Especially the 'four big families'—Chiang, Soong, Kung, and Ch'en.

30. The actual number of 'bureaucratic–capitalist' industrial enterprises confiscated by the new state was 2,858, employing a total of over 750,000 industrial workers (Xue *et al*. 1960:29).

31. It is unclear whether 'workers' (*gongren*) refers only to production workers.

32. Chao (1957:14). Chao uses the term 'enterprise' (*qiye*) in the Russian case, as opposed to 'factory' (*gongchang*) in the Chinese. This renders the comparison inexact, since a single enterprise could encompass several factories.

33. Feuerwerker (1968:14), citing an industrial survey published in 1937.

34. Chao (1957:15) reports that in the mid-1930s some 92 per cent of industrial capital was invested in consumer goods industries.

35. Of 468 non-mining Chinese-owned enterprises established between 1895 and 1913, well over half (239) were located in treaty port cities, and their initial capitalization averaged about twice that of those located inland (Feuerwerker 1969:41–2). According to industrial statistics for twenty principal cities collected in 1947 by the Nationalist economics ministry, as many as 63 per cent of factories were located in Shanghai and Tianjin alone, and they employed 62 per cent of the total factory work force (Chao 1957:15–16). Shanghai alone possessed 54 per cent of both factories and labour force. In 1943 Japanese-occupied Manchuria produced more than 90 per cent of all iron and steel, while before the war the coastal provinces possessed 94 per cent of electrical generating capacity, 75 per cent of metal-working factories, 90 per cent of looms and 88 per cent of spindles.

36. The information in this section comes primarily from Buck (1964:Chs. VI, IX and X).

37. The quote continues: 'The poorest men often were unable to have children at all; any children they did have were rather likely to die young. This means that the poorest 15 per cent of the men in one generation could not be the children of the poorest 15 per cent of the preceding generation; very few such children existed. They had to be the children of parents farther up the economic scale.'

38. This national picture conceals great regional variation: in Guangdong and Sichuan Provinces almost half of all land was rented, whereas the corresponding proportion was

about two-fifths in the Yangtze Valley and one-fifth in the North China Plain (Elvin 1973:255).
39. By 1935, according to Feuerwerker (1968:35) 'in seven out of ten leases the duration of tenure was not fixed, which usually meant that they were annual or biennial contracts.'
40. There were pronounced regional variations in this respect, too: the proportion of land rented in was more than three times as high in the rice region as in the wheat (Shen 1951:142).

CHAPTER 3

STATE POWER AND THE FOUNDATIONS OF SOCIALISM

1 Theory of the 'New Democratic State'

With the inauguration of the People's Republic of China on 1 October 1949, and the flight of the Nationalist government to Taiwan two months later. China was unified (except for Taiwan) and at peace for the first time in decades. The attention of the Chinese Communist Party turned from fighting to building. Since it had had to administer liberated territories of fluctuating size over extended periods in the 1930s and 1940s, administration and economic construction were not entirely foreign to it. But taking up the reins of power in a country of China's size was a different matter, particularly since it meant moving back into the cities, from which almost a generation of revolutionaries had largely been excluded:

From 1927 to the present the center of gravity of our work has been in the villages . . . The period for this method of work has now ended . . . The center of gravity of the Party's work has shifted from the village to the city . . . Attention must be given to both city and village and it is necessary to link closely urban and rural work, workers and peasants, industry and agriculture. Under no circumstances should the village be ignored and only the city given attention; such thinking is entirely wrong. Nevertheless, the center of gravity of the work of the Party and the army must be in the cities; we must do our utmost to learn how to administer and build the cities. [Mao 1967:364–5]

The problems facing China's revolutionary government on achieving state power were formidable. First, national administrative control had to be established and consolidated. Second, a prostrate economy had to be revived, the hyperinflation afflicting it ended, economic direction brought under government control, and reconstruction and development begun. Third, the transition to socialist relations of production were to begin, in keeping with the Party's ideological beliefs and the expectations of its political base. These various requirements did not dovetail neatly with one another. In particular, there was an uneasy relation between the objective of socialist transformation, on the one hand, and that of rapid restoration and growth of production, on the other. The urgency of the new government's immediate tasks was matched by the delicacy of their interrelations.

A channel through these shoals was provided by Mao's doctrine of the 'new democracy'. Worked out originally in 1939–40 (Mao 1967, II:305–34, 339–84), this concept was an adaptation of the Marxist category of 'bourgeois democratic revolution' to the situation of a 'semi-feudal, semi-colonial' country ruled by a communist party. The principal tasks of this phase of development—such as the creation of a centralized state and national market, the assertion of national economic interests, the curbing of pre-capitalist rural élites, and industrialization—are pre-socialist, in this view. They are in the interests of not only the proletariat and poor peasantry but virtually all social classes and groups except for a small number of 'bureaucratic monopoly capitalists' and 'feudal landlords'. Moreover, it was also considered essential to win the support of these intermediate classes and groups if the tasks of antifeudal and anti-imperialist reform and of beginning industrialization were to be achieved.

The idea of rule by a coalition of revolutionary classes—workers, peasants, national bourgeoisie, and petty bourgeoisie—under the leadership of the proletariat was in 1949 renamed 'people's democratic dictatorship', a term that Meisner calls 'semantically obscure and socially ambiguous, but . . . convey[ing] the Maoist view that the revolution remained within bourgeois limits' (Meisner 1977:61).

The political strategy of the 'new democracy' period was to gain the support of or to neutralize the intermediate groups that were seen as part of the alliance of 'people,' in order to isolate the landlords and the representatives of 'bureaucratic capital'. Economically, the strategy aimed at fostering production and economic growth through protecting the private property of 'national capitalists' and small producers, including farmers. In 'The Present Situation and Our Tasks' (Mao 1967, IV:157–76), written in December 1947, Mao stated these themes most bluntly: 'Confiscate the land of the feudal class and turn it over to the peasants. Confiscate monopoly capital . . . and turn it over to the new-democratic state. Protect the industry and commerce of the national bourgeoisie. These are the three major economic policies of the new-democratic revolution' (p. 167).

Mao went on to stress that the 'new democratic revolution' was aimed 'not at wiping out capitalism in general, the upper petty bourgeoisie or the middle bourgeoisie'. The reason for this was straightforward: 'In view of China's economic backwardness, even after the country-wide victory of the revolution, it will still be necessary to permit the existence for a long time of a petty bourgeoisie and middle bourgeoisie . . . This capitalist sector will still be an indispensable part of the whole national economy' (p. 168). Mao defined the 'upper petty bourgeoisie referred to here' as 'small industrialists and merchants employing workers or assistants', and he identified the petty bourgeoisie as 'great numbers of small independent craftsmen and traders who employ no workers or assistants and, needless to say, . . . should be firmly protected' (p. 168).

While protecting private businesses, Mao at the same time called for 'well-measured and flexible policies for restricting capitalism from several directions . . . in the scope of its operation and by tax policy, market prices and labor conditions' (Mao 1967, IV:368). The essence of economic strategy under the 'new democratic state', then, was to permit private capitalism some leeway and motivation to encourage its productive potential, but to harness it to the goals and priorities of the new state.

These principles were embodied in the 'Common Program
the Chinese People's Political Consultative Conference in Septe.
CPPCC was composed of delegates from the various classes a

made up the united front of the 'new democracy', and the 'Common Programme' served as a national constitution until 1954. Articles 26–31 of this programme spelled out the economic strategy of the new democracy, as earlier mapped out by Mao, and divided the economy into four sectors according to degree of public ownership:

1. The state-owned sector: 'All enterprises vital to the economic life of the country and to the people's livelihood shall come under unified operation by the State' (Article 28);
2. the co-operative economy, regarded as semi-socialist in nature and to be accorded preferential treatment (Article 29);
3. the private sector, to be 'encouraged and fostered' where beneficial to the national welfare (Article 30);
4. the state–capitalist sector, an amorphous concept embodying various means by which private production was subordinated to state priorities: 'For example, producing for state-owned enterprises and exploiting the state-owned resources through the form of concessions' (Article 31).

It is a commonplace that the Chinese Communists inherited an economy more backward in most respects than that taken over by the Bolsheviks in 1917 (see Chapter 4, Sec. 1). Yet in some respects the Chinese Communists were in a better position than their Soviet predecessors—for instance, in having a thought-out general strategy for organizing the country, dealing with major social forces, and beginning economic construction. Lenin in 1917 had no such strategy. Power came suddenly and 'prematurely', and its survival was thought to depend on immediate socialist revolution in the advanced capitalist countries. It was not until more than three years later that the need for a long-term, nationally self-reliant basis of power and organization had fully registered. The Chinese Communists came to power at the end of a long civil war in which they gained strength and self-confidence; the Bolsheviks took power only to face a civil war that complicated their tasks of consolidating power and beginning economic construction. Mao Zedong was seen as a national saviour who had heroically resisted the Japanese; Lenin was vilified in many circles as one who had capitulated to Germany in order to make peace. The Chinese Communists were based in the countryside and could discipline the weak industrial proletariat in order to gain the support of private business; the Bolsheviks' only political base was among the urban workers, whose demands brought about early nationalization and ruled out such an alliance. Moreover, the Chinese Communists had long been administering territories and governing populations of fluctuating size and so had a corps of relatively experienced cadres and a fund of administrative competence to rely on.

Perhaps the biggest single advantage of the Chinese was the existence of the Soviet Union. However checkered their past and future record of co-operation, there is no question that the presence of a powerful ally afforded the new regime a degree of security beyond what Lenin and the Bolsheviks had had three decades earlier. Mao bluntly recognized this:

Just imagine! If the Soviet Union had not existed, if there had been no victory in the anti-fascist Second World War . . . if the People's Democracies had not come into being, [etc.] . . . if not for all these in combination, the international reactionary forces bearing down upon us would certainly be many times greater than now. In such circumstances, could we have won victory? Obviously not. And even with victory, there could be no consolidation. [Mao 1967, IV:416–17]

2 Establishing control

The formal inauguration of the People's Republic of China took place on 1 October 1949, before the civil war had ended. Organized Guomindang resistance came to an end in remote Xinjiang (Sinkiang) Province only in March 1950, leaving just Taiwan under Nationalist control. Preparations to take this island province, apparently planned for the summer of 1950 (Meisner 1977:75), were foiled by Truman's decision of 27 June 1950 to 'neutralize' the Taiwan Straits.

The fact that consolidation began before fighting ceased affected the political institutions that were established. The supreme executive organ set up by the CPPCC was called the Government Administrative Council (GAC) until 1954, when, under the new constitution, its name was changed to State Council. Zhou Enlai was the first premier, appointed by Mao as head of state. The country was initially divided into six 'greater administrative regions' which were placed under military administrative control. Below these regions, the principal administrative levels consisted of the provinces (including province-level 'autonomous regions', and the municipalities of Beijing, Shanghai, and Tianjin, which were under direct central control); over two thousand counties (*xian*), and, on the same level, municipalities (*shi*); and below that the 'administrative villages' (*xiang*), each comprising several natural villages. In addition, of fluctuating importance over subsequent years were the 'special (or administrative) district' (*zhuan qu*), between the province and the county; and the 'district' (*qu*), between county and *xiang* (Donnithorne 1967:21–2). The Communist Party organization paralleled this administrative subdivision, and often party and government positions were occupied by the same persons. The Party, of course, played the main role in formulating and overseeing the execution of basic national policies.

If 'taking control' had a fairly clear political meaning, its economic significance was far from straightforward. The new regime, while preserving private ownership of enterprise, had to get resources allocated on behalf of its own objectives. This requirement had two dimensions. First, appropriate institutions (e.g., a banking and monetary system, wholesale trading network, etc.) had to be created for the making and implementation of economic decisions. Second, it was necessary to reduce or eliminate the power over economic affairs wielded by opponents of party goals—chiefly, rural landlords and urban commercial and industrial capitalists.

In the countryside, the Communists at least had the benefit of long experience with rural conditions and a close working relationship with much of the peasantry. They were largely an unknown quantity to the urban population, however. In 1949 there were over 60 million urbanites (in cities with populations of more than 100,000). Shanghai alone had more than 6 million inhabitants, as well as a large proportion of surviving industry and trade. In the short run, it was the urban situation that most demanded attention because of what Meisner (1977:86) calls 'the final legacy of the Guomindang era—the utter destitution of the cities'. Starvation and malnutrition were widespread; elementary sanitation was lacking; organized crime preyed on the population; factories were closed for lack of materials; unemployment soared; and the great inflation had reduced much of the population to a simple bartering of goods and services.

The inflation provided the new government's first major test of authority and competence. Given the lack of control over resources, the absence of a developed system of raising revenues, and the continued need for large military outlays, the Communists at the outset had no choice but to print money (Xue 1977, part 1:5). In the ten months after the fall of Shanghai in May 1949, prices rose ten to twenty-fold. Shanghai capitalists gave the Communists 'full marks' for their military successes, '80' for their political skills, and 'no marks at all' in the economic field. The effort to curb inflation provided a popular basis for the achievement of government control of the banking and financial system and the commercial networks. Before the inflation was ended, 'we could not exercise leadership and the capitalists refused to accept our leadership. After the prices were stabilized, they had no way out but to submit' (1977, part 1:5, 8).

The government's first move was administrative: a ban on circulation of gold, silver, and foreign currencies and the arrest of 200-odd speculators. Thereafter, speculation was concentrated in the hoarding of goods, especially grain and cotton piece goods; its administrative suppression was impossible because everyone who could hoarded such goods.

The core of the monetary aspect of policy was to centralize control of the new currency, the *renminbi* (RMB or yuan) in the People's Bank of China (PBC), which had been established as central bank in the winter of 1948. All government offices, military units, and enterprises were required to deposit their holdings of all but petty cash in the PBC, thus depriving private banks of deposits. Y300 million of government bonds were issued and sold with great vigour in order to reduce currency in circulation. These acts destroyed many private banks; the few that remained were merged into joint public–private banks, which brought them entirely under government control. Public savings were encouraged by indexing savings deposits to the value of a bundle of common commodities.

Fiscal policy included strenuous efforts to reduce the government deficit, in part by reorganizing and stepping up tax collection in the urban areas, but principally by enforcing stringent economies in government spending. Public employees were paid largely in subsistence goods with a small money supplement.

As a complement to its demand-side monetary and fiscal attacks, the government moved to increase the supply of goods, especially in the hard-pressed cities. This involved a crash programme to restore the transport system, especially the railroads, as well as a state take-over of wholesale trade. Although less than half the country's rail lines were in operation in October 1949, by the middle of 1951 the entire system was functioning, and at far greater intensity than in the past (Eckstein 1954:244). In the major towns and cities, state trading companies were established that bought up supplies of food, cotton and other raw materials. The state quickly became the principal supplier of the goods that made up the average person's budget. Reserves of such goods could be thrown on the market at vital moments to break speculatively induced price increases, as was done in Shanghai following the Spring Festival of 1950 (Xue 1977, part 1:6). With firm command of cotton and grain supplies, the state gained control over textile and food processing enterprises, the two largest industries remaining in private hands, by agreeing to supply them with raw materials and purchase their products at fixed prices. The profits of state trading companies, meanwhile, further buttressed state revenues and thereby became subject to the fiscal economy measures.

As a result of these various policies, the inflationary spiral was broken by March 1950, and prices even declined immediately thereafter, although the cost of the draconian deflationary measures was a crisis in the private sector marked by widespread bankruptcy and a fall in production. The Korean War brought about a resumption of inflationary pressures, especially after China's entry in October. However, the overall rise in the price level was limited to 20 per cent in 1951, and by the following year inflation in its open manifestation had been brought to a virtual halt.

This was significant beyond the immediate issue of inflation. Between the end of 1949 and the end of 1950, categories of industry directly or indirectly subject to state control grew from 45 to about 63 per cent of total industrial output. In commerce the state did not achieve dominance so quickly, but it did get more than a foot in the door. State-owned commercial enterprises and supply and marketing co-operatives together accounted for about 24 per cent of wholesale trade and 15 per cent of retail trade in 1950 (Xue 1977, part 1:8).[1] State hegemony in foreign trade and banking was almost total.

In industry, under the transition policies of the Common Programme, the chief large-scale industries were confiscated and nationalized outright. This was made easier by the fact that these 'bureaucratic-capitalist' industries had already come under highly concentrated ownership, and a large part of them had been taken over by the Guomindang's National Resources Commission during the war. Some 35 per cent of modern industrial output (i.e., excluding handicrafts) was already produced by state-owned industry in 1949. That figure reached 57.5 per cent in 1953, the first year of the First Five Year Plan (*Ten Great Years* 1960:38).

Nationalized industries were run by industrial ministries established under the State Council (or 'Government Administrative Council', as it was called until 1954). Until 1952, however, when the State Planning Commission was established, there existed no agency for formulating and implementing long-term development plans. The chief problem was a simpler one: how to operate and manage the enterprises successfully and to restore production.

These goals required administrative, managerial, and technical skills that were in short supply in a movement that had been predominantly rural for twenty years. The Communists had three sources of authority and potential leadership within factories:[2] the People's Liberation Army, which sent representatives to assert the authority of the new government in individual factories; the small, highly disciplined Communist Party organization in the urban areas, including some skilled and experienced workers; and 'skilled, literate workers who, with the blessings of the Communist Party, were quickly promoted to positions of leadership in the factories by the trade unions' (Andors 1977:48). These leadership groups by themselves were inadequate to run Chinese industry. Even in 1953, the total of urban communists, promoted workers, factory directors and vice-directors appointed by the Party, party committee secretaries, and trade union officials altogether amounted to only 20 per cent of all managerial and technical personnel in industry (Andors 1977:49). It was thus necessary to make use of the corps of retained technical and managerial personnel, while eliminating the urban criminal influence long endemic in much of Chinese industry and reforming management practices. Inevitably, however, skills and services would be bought at the price of retaining management practices associated with the past.

Despite the highly centralist character of communist policies immediately after 1949, decentralized participative and 'mass line' methods that characterized Chinese Communist Party (CCP) practice during the guerrilla period continued to play a role in many aspects of early PRC policy, including that of industrial management. The Common Programme authorised for State-owned enterprises a system of worker participation in management, in the form of 'factory administrative committees . . . under the leadership of the factory director' (Article 32). These committees took a wide variety of forms, and could include technicians and co-operative former owners as well as military personnel, plant workers and former underground party members (Andors 1977:51). They were chaired by the factory director, who generally had veto power over committee decisions. The scope of their operations was broad, covering enterprise plans, personnel, organization, and welfare (Andors 1977:51).

This system of collective leadership under the factory director, sometimes referred to as the Shanghai or East China system, gave rein to rank-and-file participation while preserving the formal hegemony of the director. Its social impact was relatively egalitarian: until mid-1955 party cadres were paid according to the old pre-Liberation supply system, which provided them with little but their daily needs. Yet held-over technical and managerial personnel retained high salaries. As production developed and the need for inter-regional and inter-enterprise co-ordination grew, so did the potential for conflict between the local and political orientation of the administrative committees, on the one hand, and the interests of the director, who was held responsible for meeting targets assigned from above, on the other. It is a moot point whether the resolution of this conflict would have embodied a continued role for collective participation in factory management, had not the Soviet example, working its way south from the north-eastern provinces of former Manchuria, provided an orthodox rationale for abandoning such an approach in favour of 'one-man management'.

The spread of the Soviet 'one-man management' system stemmed from the influence achieved by the USSR as a result of the Sino-Soviet Treaty of February 1950 and the surrounding series of agreements providing for Soviet economic aid, as well as from its historical role as the pioneer of socialist planned development. The Soviet system of factory management was in essence a combination of 'scientific management' and a hierarchical 'responsibility system' of leadership. The former entailed the formulation of precise work plans for all phases of factory operations, and their translation into minutely specified job tasks. The latter put one person in complete control of each unit and level of a factory, with supreme authority vested in the plant director.[3]

The advantages of this system for central planners needing clear channels of communication and reliable levers of control are obvious. Lines of authority and responsibility were unambiguous; the link between plan and enterprise could be established with the utmost precision; and the chief responsibility of rank-and-file enterprise personnel was to fulfil tasks that were specified in as much detail as possible. The most obvious problem was how to motivate the conscientious performance of such passive roles. The logical solution lay in adopting a 'scientific' system of incentives to reward good performance and punish bad. Accordingly, more than a third of all industrial workers were on piece rates by 1952 (Richman 1969:314), and bonus systems were adopted that paid higher bonuses for senior than for junior staff and up to 90 per cent of basic salaries for managers (Howe 1973:121).[4]

'By the end of 1953 the Soviet concept of industrial management had gained general, though only tentative acceptance' (Andors 1977:53). As will be seen (Chapter 4), problems concerning both the ideological complications and the practical applicability to Chinese conditions of this system arose from the very beginning, and its dominance was both short-lived and partial. But, in retrospect, it is not hard to explain its attractiveness to China's leadership at a time when they were establishing control of the economy, yet worrying about the role of the inherited managerial corps.

The private sector of the urban economy was thrown into disarray by the deflationary policies of early 1950. Private banks and commercial enterprises were forced to suspend operations or close entirely. More than half of Shanghai's banks and a tenth of its commercial establishments shut down. Private output of cotton cloth in May 1950 was 38 per cent below that of January, and other commodities suffered similar declines in production (Xue et al. 1960:46-7).

The government now acted to resuscitate private industry and commerce, chiefly by placing processing and purchase orders with private firms and allowing profitable trading opportunities for commercial enterprises. This policy was strengthened by the outbreak of war in Korea in June 1950 and the entry of China into that war in October, which led to heavy government demand for war-related goods, such as hardware, canned food, and medicine

(Xue 1977, part 2:14). The end of 1950 thus saw a revival of the private urban economy.

But the *long-run* significance of the Korean War for private industry was anything but expansionary. The US entry into Korea provided the rationalization for President Truman's decision to order the Seventh Fleet into the Taiwan Straits (although China was certainly not involved in the origin of the Korean conflict). This war, in which China suffered great losses, represented the combined threat of both external intervention and internal counter-revolution. As Meisner (1977:80) states, 'the essentially external threat to the survival of the revolution turned the initially moderate policies and practices of the new state into increasingly repressive ones . . .' The harsh movement of 1951 to suppress counter-revolutionaries, followed by the 'three-anti' (*sanfan*) and 'five-anti' (*wufan*) campaigns of the following year, were in part responses to an environment that had become threatening and that consequently had increased the premium placed on security and control.

The 'three-anti' campaign, which began at the end of 1951, was a rectification movement for cadres in government offices and state enterprises. Directed against 'corruption, waste, and bureaucracy', it was designed to correct problems inherent in the political–administrative situation of the early 1950s, when the state apparatus was run largely by retained Nationalist officials, 'democratic personages, capitalists, and bourgeois specialists', and by an influx of hastily recruited cadres of varied competence, experience, and integrity. Some older cadres as well, accustomed to rough rural living, were believed by Mao to be susceptible to corruption upon exposure to the luxuries and temptations of the cities, with their 'sugar-coated bullets'. It is this element that links the movement to the private sector, even though it was aimed primarily at the state bureaucracy. The growing ties between the state and the private sector, through which the former restricted and dominated the latter, created fertile ground for corruption, such as the 'five evils' (bribery of government workers, tax evasion, theft of state property, cheating on government contracts, and stealing economic information from the state).

The 'five-anti' movement, aimed at the private sector, used mass accusation, denunciation, and 'struggle meetings' as substitutes for the still-weak formal mechanisms of control. It began in early 1952, resulted in the investigation of more than 450,000 private industrial and commercial enterprises in the nine biggest cities, and found that three-quarters of them had engaged in one or another of the 'five evils' in varying degrees 'to make excessive profits' (Xue *et al.* 1960:51–2). Schurmann (1938:318) calls the 'five-anti' movement 'an onslaught against a class as a whole', but not one intended to obliterate it. In the end, although only a few persons were imprisoned as serious offenders, financial penalties taking the form of fines and collection of back taxes were heavy and resulted in a depletion of resources of the private sector and a great accretion of state revenue.[5]

The 'five-anti' movement caused widespread distress in the private economy. Another rescue operation by the state resulted in further restriction of private sector autonomy, so that 'from this time on, the greater part of the capitalist

Table 3.1. *Socialist transformation of industry and trade, 1949–1952*

	1949	1950	1952
Industry: % of GVIO produced by:			
State-owned enterprises	34.7	45.3	56.0
Joint state-private enterprises and private enterprises receiving orders from the state for processing and manufacturing goods, or selling their products to the state	9.5	17.8	26.9
Private enterprises producing and selling their own products	55.8	36.9	17.1
Trade: Proportion of sales by state-owned stores and supply maketing co-operatives in			
Wholesale trade	—	23.9	63.7
Retail trade	—	14.9	42.6

Source: Xue (1977, part 2:15).

sector was directed into the orbit of the state plan under the leadership of the state sector . . .' Xue *et al*. 1960:53). As Table 3.1 demonstrates, by 1952 more than half of gross industrial output was produced by state-owned factories, and more than one-fourth more came from enterprises within the 'state capitalist' orbit, leaving only 17 per cent to 'purely' private enterprises. A similar degree of dominance is evident in wholesale trade, and a lesser but rapidly growing one in retail trade.

Foreign capital was also a victim of the Korean War. Property of the Axis Powers had already been taken over by the Guomindang government after the war; that of the United States, Britain, France, and other Western countries was initially left intact by the new regime. Political and economic developments conspired to make this period of coexistence very brief, however. The United States embargœd all trade with China at the end of 1950 after China's entry into Korea, and in addition froze bank accounts and other assets in the United States owned by China or its nationals. US-registered ships and planes were prohibited from stopping at Chinese ports and from transporting goods destined for China. 'Thus, in less than three weeks, the Administration had imposed a total embargo on American trade and payment transactions with China' (Garson 1971:7–8). Under US pressure, the Co-ordinating Committee (Cocom), established in November 1949 to organize Western strategic controls on trade with the Soviet bloc, agreed to more stringent prohibitions on that with China (1971:8–9). The embargo crippled activities of foreign enterprises in China, and they began closing. When China froze US assets in retaliation for the US seizure of Chinese property, the continued operation of US enterprises became impossible (Xue *et al*. 1960:33).

The complicated task of keeping alive the private sector while leading it into state-directed channels was on the whole handled successfully, for the number of private industrial establishments actually increased from 133,000 in 1950 to 150,000 in 1953, and their employment grew from 1.8 million to 2.2 million (Richman 1969:899). Yet this enterprise had the advantage of being confined to a few major cities, and even within these the important components of the urban economy were highly concentrated. In contrast, the rural economy was dispersed over several hundred thousand villages, each with distinct characteristics, and containing in all some 100 million families. In the long run, economic development depended upon the ability to reach and mobilize the peasants, to persuade them to make the efforts and investments for which, in a country of China's size and poverty, no amount of foreign assistance could substitute. Despite the Communists' long immersion in rural China, they were far from having established political control of the villages in 1949, and control of the rural economy was still a matter for the future. A fifth, at most, of the villages had already undergone land reform, the convulsive event that provided the necessary conditions for the extension of governmental authority to the countryside.

3 Land reform

Land reform proceeded from the summer of 1950 to the spring of 1953. Its redistributive principles are best conveyed by the stark pronouncements of the *Agrarian Reform Law* (1959:1–4):

Article 1
   The land ownership system of feudal exploitation by the landlord class shall be abolished and the system of peasant land ownership shall be introduced in order to set free the rural productive forces, develop agricultural production, and thus pave the way for New China's industrialization.

Article 2
   The land, draught animals, farm implements and surplus grain of the landlords, and their surplus houses in the countryside shall be confiscated, but their other properties shall not be confiscated.

Article 4
   Industry and commerce shall be protected from infringement.
   Industrial and commercial enterprises operated by landlords and the land and other properties used by landlords directly for the operation of industrial and commercial enterprises shall not be confiscated . . .

Article 6
   Land owned by rich peasants and cultivated by themselves or by hired labour and their other properties shall be protected from infringement . . .

Article 7
   Land and other properties of the middle peasants . . . shall be protected from infringement.

Article 10

All land and other means of production thus confiscated and requisitioned . . . shall be taken over . . . for unified, equitable, and rational distribution to poverty-stricken peasants who have little or no land and who lack other means of production. Landlords shall be given an equal share so that they can make their living by their own labour and thus reform themselves through labour.

Although Article 1 stresses the economic objective of the land reform ('set free the rural productive forces'), it is clear that the very first principle mentioned—abolition of the system of feudal exploitation by the landlord class—entailed an equally important political objective: elimination of the potential counter-revolutionary threat of the landlord–gentry. Moreover, mobilizing the peasants to participate in the confiscation and redistribution of land, and to confront their former rulers, assured that 'the previous patterns of authority and subservience could never again be resurrected' (Lippit 1974:25). Finally, the acquisition of land by more than three-fifths of the peasantry would forge bonds of support and commitment to the new government.

The orientation of the 'new democracy' was expressed by Article 4, which protected the industrial and commercial operations of landlords. In practice it was very difficult to distinguish between the 'feudal exploitative' and 'progressive capitalistic' personae of one and the same landlord, especially since the law provided an incentive for the latter to place as much wealth as possible under the protective shelter of mill or shop.

Article 6 protected the rich peasant economy, including its use of hired labour. More than any other provision, this one indicates the Party's production-oriented and moderate intent in the land reform, following the violence and 'ultra-left excesses' of the 1947–8 land revolution in the liberated areas of North China.[6]

The two overriding objectives of land reform—to eliminate landlordism and prepare for development of production—were quite compatible, since the former, where most prevalent, was of the absentee sort (Ch. 2, Sec. 7). As Meisner (1977:103) remarks, 'the gentry had nothing to offer to society. They were a class dispensable on economic grounds as well as socially and politically undesirable.'

China's involvement in Korea began within a few months of the promulgation of the Agrarian Reform Law, and had the same kind of impact on this movement as it had on urban developments. By subjecting the new regime to the threat of attack and rekindling the hopes of the former ruling groups, it led to a heightened urgency and bitterness in the movement. Moreover, the areas reached last, especially those in the south, were precisely those of most powerful landlord dominance where resistance would normally have been greater, and considerable friction developed between northern cadres sent down to lead the movement, on the one hand, and the localist sentiments and social ties of southern cadres, on the other (Vogel 1969:Ch. 3). In the end, the tenor of the movement was more bitter, and the treatment of landlords harsher, than had originally been signalled by the Reform Law.

Its aims, however, were accomplished. The landlord class was eliminated, the material conditions of the poorer strata of peasants were improved, and an organizationally tempered local peasant cadre oriented towards the Communist Party developed. According to official statements, 'over 300 million peasants . . . received 700 million *mu* [117 million acres] of arable land and other means of production free of charge' (*Ten Great Years* 1960:34). (700 million *mu* constituted over 44 per cent of the official estimates of cultivated land.) Ambiguities surrounding the pre-1949 estimates of land distribution (see Ch. 2, Sec. 7) make it difficult to state precisely how this was changed by land reform, but a general idea is conveyed by Table 3.2, which is based on some broad assumptions. Poor peasants and landlords were most affected. The former (which here include 57 per cent of the farm population) doubled their share of ownership of all cropland from under a quarter to almost half, and their average crop area owned per farm from about 1 acre (6 *mu*) to 2; their average cultivated area per farm grew by almost 50 per cent, from under 9 *mu* to over 12. Landlords lost heavily, their ownership share dropping from almost 30 per cent to only 2 per cent.

The position of the other two classes changed as well, although not as sharply. Middle peasants ended by operating slightly smaller farms than before land reform (the difference may not be statistically significant), but both the proportion and absolute amount they owned increased substantially. Rich peasants lost heavily in terms of ownership of land as well as amount cultivated.

Inequality of land ownership and operation was thus greatly reduced, and with it the inequality of income distribution. Yet in the end, the average rich peasant owned and operated more than twice as much land as did the average poor peasant (col. (7)), and the middle peasant 50 per cent more. Land reform had deliberately stopped short of complete economic equality and was incapable of eradicating rural poverty. Indeed, economic conditions were in some ways worsened by the reform, and the class structure that emerged was inherently unstable (see Ch. 4). The chief significance of the land reform therefore was in creating the political and social conditions for change in the direction planned by Mao and the Party—towards a collectivized and ultimately industrialized agriculture.

The means by which the CCP established and consolidated its control helped to shape the direction of subsequent conflict and change. Concurrently, the Party began mobilizing resources and organizing for economic development. These two objectives were not mutually independent, as witness the preservation of the 'rich peasant economy' in the land reform, and the repeated resuscitation of nearly defunct private enterprise in the cities. Both were examples of temporary compromises in the short-run quest for control that were adopted to stimulate production and thus make possible greater political security in the long run. But in the interest of control and security, the Party was also willing temporarily to sacrifice production, as it did in the harsh struggles that marked the initial stages of social transformation. Tension between the objectives of control and development has marked Chinese development policy ever since.

Table 3.2. *Impact of land reform on distribution of landownership and of cultivated land*

Class status, pre-Reform	(1) Share of households (%)	(2) Share crop area owned (%) 1929–33	(3) Post-Reform	(4) Ave. crop area owned (mu) 1929–33	(5) Post-Reform	(6) Ave. area cultivated (mu) 1929–33	(7) Post-Reform
Poor peasant	57.1	23.5	46.8	6.25	12.14	8.89	12.46
Middle peasant	35.8	30.3	44.8	15.81	18.53	22.18	19.01
Rich peasant	3.6	17.7	6.4	35.75	26.30	47.22	25.09
Landlord	2.6	28.7	2.1	116.10	11.98	0	12.16

Source: Schran (1969:14–27). These figures are based on Buck's distributions by farm size for the 1929–33 period, and on a sample survey carried out by the State Statistical Bureau in 1955, and they depend on the crucial assumption that Buck's farm size classes correspond to the SSB's class statuses. For Schran's argument that these two distributions 'may well be consistent', see Schran (1969:15–16).

Notes

1. 'Supply and marketing co-operatives were the main channel through which the state sector was linked with the individual sector in trade' (Xue *et al*. 1960:55). The total membership of these organizations grew from 10 million at the end of 1949 to 156 million in 1955. Predominantly rural, their main functions were to purchase grain and other produce from the peasants on behalf of the state and to sell consumer goods and farm inputs to the peasants. They also became chief processors of farm products. Initially under collective ownership, their organs at county level and above became state-owned, and their activities were under close state supervision. See Xue *et al*. (1960:54–9) and Donnithorne (1967:277–80).

2. The following paragraphs lean heavily on Andors (1977: Ch. 3).

3. This brief description of the Soviet management system is oversimplified. For a fuller discussion, see Berliner (1957), Granick (1954), or Nove (1961); also Andors (1977:53–62).

4. Wage and incentive systems are discussed more fully in Chapter 4.

5. Mao (1977a, V:80) announced in August 1952 that 'the money that came from the settling of accounts in the movements against the "three evils" and the "five evils" can see us through another eighteen months of war.' (I am grateful to Larry Weiss for bringing this statement to my attention.)

6. While fighting Japan, the CCP had promoted rent and interest reduction rather than land redistribution so as not to compromise the wartime united front. Pressure for land from poor peasants and farm labourers mounted after the war and resulted in a May 1946 directive from the Central Committee ordering redistribution on a very moderate scale. Rich peasants' holdings were exempted from confiscation. This directive was like an *hors d'œuvre* for a poor peasantry expecting a banquet. Pressure for more land increased simultaneously with the Party's need for poor peasant support in the civil war. On 13 September 1947 a new Land Law was passed giving village Peasants' Associations the right to take over the 'surplus' portions of rich peasants' properties as well as all properties of landlords, and to redistribute them with an equal share allotted to landlords. During the winter and spring of 1947–8 poor peasants carried out 'struggle' and 'settle accounts' meetings, often leading to violence against the landlords. There is no reliable estimate of the number of executions that occurred in the course of the long land revolution (as distinct from the civil war itself and other movements), but there is no doubt that tens of thousands were killed. Property and interests of middle peasants were infringed on as well, and great tension and fear were created in the rural areas. The Communist leadership reacted with warnings against 'ultra-leftist excesses' and acted to moderate the land movement to protect middle and rich peasants. See Chao (1960:74–93), on which this note draws extensively.

CHAPTER 4

MOBILIZATION AND SOCIAL TRANSFORMATION, 1952–1955

1 Introduction

'Three years of recovery, then ten years of development' was the goal announced in 1949. The first three years, known as the Rehabilitation period, were to see production in all major sectors and industries restored to past peak levels of performance in preparation for a long term development programme.

This objective had been realized, and in many respects exceeded, by 1952. According to official statistics, the gross value of industrial output (GVIO) had grown to two and a half times that of 1949, and exceeded prewar levels by almost a quarter (Chao 1957:20). Output of almost all important products had reached or exceeded past peak levels, as can be seen from the selection presented in Table 4.1. In agriculture as well, production of most—but not all—major crops equalled or surpassed past levels. Producer goods output grew by almost one-half *each year*, consumer goods by almost a third.[1] GVIO in 1952 prices[2] more than doubled over the Rehabilitation period.

In agriculture, the gross value of output (GVAO) in 1952 prices increased by almost one-half between 1949 and 1952, according to the official statistics, while foodgrain output grew only slightly less rapidly (*Ten Great Years* 1960:118). The more careful Western estimate of foodgrain output (Wiens 1978) still yields an annual growth rate of 7.4 per cent for these years. Thus, it must be concluded that the growth performance of the Rehabilitation period was outstanding.

On the basis of these accomplishments, China began its first essay at long term development planning. Despite Rehabilitation growth rates, the absolute levels of production reached, especially per capita, were extraordinarily low. In comparison with the Soviet Union on the eve of its own First Five Year Plan in 1928, China's per capita grain output in 1952 was less than half as great, its per capita railroad mileage less than 10 per cent, and its per capita production of electric power, coal, steel, and cement all less than half the Soviet level (Chen and Galenson 1969:35). This substantial difference in initial conditions was in part responsible for China's later departures from Soviet development objectives and methods, but in 1953 the slogan was 'let's be modern and Soviet'.

2 The First Five Year Plan

Planning was adopted gradually in China, being first tried experimentally with Soviet advice and assistance in the heavy industrial regions of the North-east (formerly Manchuria). National economic planning had to await the establishment of an elementary infrastructure, including planning and statistical capacities. The State Statistical Bureau was set up only in October

Table 4.1. *Output of selected products, pre-1949 peak, 1949, and 1952*

	Output				
	Pre-'49 peak	1949	1952	1952 as % of 1949	1952 as % of past peak
Industry					
Elec. power (m. kWh)	5 955	4 308	7 261	168.5	121.9
Coal ('000 tons)	61 875	30 984	63 528	205.0	102.7
Crude petroleum ('000 tons)	320	122	436	357.7	136.3
Pig iron ('000 tons)	1 801	246	1 900	773.3	105.5
Crude steel ('000 tons)	923	158	1 349	851.4	146.1
Sulphuric acid ('000 tons)	227	27	181	674.0	80.1
Metal-cutting (no. of machine tool sets)	5 390	1 582	13 734	868.1	254.8
Cement ('000 tons)	2 293	661	2 861	432.9	124.8
Cotton yarn ('000 bales)	2 447	1 803	3 618	200.7	147.8
Cotton cloth (m. bolts)	45 008	30 178	89 273	295.8	198.3
Cigarettes ('000 crates)	2 363	1 600	2 650	165.6	112.1
Agriculture					
Foodgrains (m. metric tons)	138.7	108.1	154.4	142.8	111.3
		(126.8)	(157.3)	(124.0)	(113.4)
Paddy rice	57.4	48.7	68.5	140.7	119.3
		(56.9)	(69.7)	(122.5)	(121.4)
Wheat	23.3	13.8	18.1	131.2	77.8
		(14.1)	(18.4)	(130.5)	(79.0)
Misc. grains	51.7	35.8	51.5	143.9	99.6
		(44.8)	(52.5)	(117.2)	(101.5)
Potatoes	6.4	9.9	16.4	165.9	257.9
		(11.0)	(16.7)	(151.8)	(260.9)
Cotton (m. metric tons)	0.85	0.44	1.30	293.4	153.6
		(0.45)	(1.33)	(295.6)	(156.5)

N.B. Potato output is given in 'grain equivalent' form, equal to one-quarter the actual weight; i.e., potatoes are converted into grain equivalent at the ratio of 4 lbs. to 1 lb. Numbers in parentheses are estimates by Wiens (1978), which correct for probable underestimation in the official statistics of cultivated area and yield during the early post-Liberation years.

Sources: Industry: Chao (1857:20). (For later revisions of some of these figures, see *TGY* (1960:95–100).) Agriculture: *TGY* (1960:119–20); Wiens (1978).

1952, provincial and municipal statistical departments in 1953, and below them administrative and special district offices in 1954. The chief organ of planning, the State Planning Commission (SPC), was established in 1952 and placed under the State Council when the latter was made supreme executive body by the 1954 Constitution. At the same time, a State Construction Commission was organized to oversee capital investment under the Plan; and later, in 1956, a State Economic Commission was established to take over short-term (up to annual) plan responsibilities, leaving the SPC to concentrate on long term and perspective planning. Also born in 1956 were the General Bureau for Supply of Raw Materials, to handle materials allocation, and the State Technological Commission, to plan long term technical development. Thus, the planning organizational infrastructure was only half formed when the First Five Year Plan was inaugurated in 1953.

The method of central planning adopted, based on Soviet experience, was that of 'material balances', according to which tables are prepared indicating how the output of each industry or sector of the economy is distributed—given existing technology—among all producing industries or sectors, plus final demand. With such a table of intersectoral balances, it is then possible to project the pattern of demand for each sector's output that will be generated by a given planned rate and pattern of growth, and to compare it with the supplies likely to be made available by existing capacities and their planned expansions. If balance between anticipated supply and demand is lacking, the plan is adjusted and the possibility of using foreign trade to fill the gaps is explored.[3]

Until November 1957, China's planning system was highly centralized, in the sense that a fairly large number of targets of different kinds were drawn up, and their fulfilment directly supervised, from the centre, for an originally small but rapidly growing number of goods.[4] As both the number of commodities and the number of enterprises for which the centre assumed responsibility grew rapidly in the course of the 1950s, the maintenance of such a high degree of centralization of both planning and management became increasingly cumbersome. In 1957 and 1958 the government adopted a series of decentralization measures (see Chapter 5) in order to unburden some of its responsibilities onto the localities, increase the scope for local initiative, and strengthen central control of the most important plan targets and enterprises.

The First Plan was by no means a purely technocratic document. In fact, of the three most general tasks to which it addressed itself, only the first—to build 694 specific large-scale industrial construction projects, especially 156 Soviet-aid projects (FFYP 1956:21–2)—concerned economic construction *per se*; the other two had to do with 'relations of production': to foster growth of farm and handicraft co-operatives, and to bring the bulk of private industry and commerce into the orbit of state capitalism. Note that, at this most general level, the principal themes of the Plan did not include agricultural production.[5]

Total planned investment by the state for the five-year period 1953–7 came to Y76,640 million ($31,154 million at the then official exchange rate of 2.46 yuan to the dollar). The allocation of this total, and particularly of the capital construction[6] component of it, is detailed in Figure 4.1. Altogether, some three-fifths of state investment was to be devoted to capital construction, and a similar proportion of the latter was earmarked for industry, most of it for the ministries of heavy industry, fuel industry, and machine-building industry.

Agriculture was to be limited to a little more than Y1 billion, or 2.4 per cent of planned capital construction investment, with another 3.3 per cent allotted to

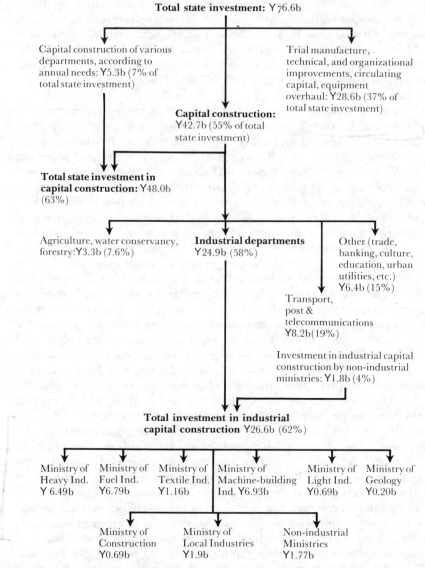

Fig. 4.1. First Five Year Plan: distribution of state investment. (In billions of yuan and percentages of total; percentages of items below 'Capital construction' take investment in capital construction as the base.)

investments in water conservancy. However, these figures are somewhat misleading in three respects: first, they exclude certain miscellaneous expenditures allocated by the state to agriculture; second, the state expected some Y10 billion to be invested by individual farmers and co-operatives; finally, the real issue for the technical modernization of agriculture concerned investment *within* industry in expanding the capacity of the farm input and equipment manufacturing sectors and the development of scientific research. In these respects also, however, the Plan was modest.[7] It is clear, then, that the real goods counterpart of the planned and hoped-for investments in agriculture by both state and farmers would consist largely of *traditional* inputs produced by handicraft enterprises.

The approach of the Plan to the farm question was no doubt affected by the state of flux regarding it within the Party at the time the Plan was being formulated. The leadership was always acutely aware of the need for agricultural surpluses as a condition for rapid industrialization (Walker 1966:3). On the other hand, up to 1954 it also firmly believed that some prior industrialization was a prerequisite for rapid and sustained growth of agriculture, and that only when the means for its technical transformation were at hand would collectivization be possible. This view implied that initial industrialization would depend on squeezing more output from agriculture *before* collectivization and mechanization were begun. Co-operatives evolving gradually, were to be the principal tool for this purpose, permitting more rational use of land, equipment, and animals, greater self-financed investment, and improved incentives while preparing the way for eventual collectivization.

By 1954, however, some aspects of this analysis had changed. In particular, given a much heightened appreciation of the barrier that slow agricultural growth posed for industrialization, and of the problems inherent in the very gradualness of progress towards collectivization (see Section 4 below), it was now argued that the latter would have to occur *before* technical modernization. Only collectives could mobilize the resources for urgently needed improvements that would increase yields and lead to later 'technical revolution'. This view, which was dominant at the time the Plan was formulated, 'made agricultural growth more a function of socialist organization than [of] the amount of industrial assistance available; institutional reform would permit technical advances which were largely *independent of industry*' (Walker 1966:8). Hence the Plan's neglect of agricultural technology.

The First Plan was ambitious not only in the scope of its capital construction projects, but also in its projected growth rates of output, especially that of modern industry. But Table 4.2 indicates that actual results surpassed even these ambitious targets, with industrial production growing by an average annual rate of 18 per cent.[8] GVAO, foodgrain, and cotton growth targets were all slightly overfulfilled, but the targets themselves had been scaled down at least twice before publication in 1955 (Walker 1966:25), and there is reason to suspect an upward bias in the official growth rates because of an underestimation of output in the early years. In any event, the statistically satisfactory performance of agriculture masked increasingly acute difficulties.

Table 4.2. *Major First Five Year Plan targets and results*

	1952 Output[a]	1957 Plan target		1957 results	
		Output[a]	Growth rate (%)	Output[b]	Growth rate (%)
Industry[c] (bn. 1952 yuan)	27.0	53.6	14.7	65.0	18.0
Industry ('Modern')[d] (bn. 1952 yuan)	22.1	45.0	15.3	55.6	20.3
Handicrafts[e] (bn. 1952 yuan)	12.2	20.3	10.7	22.8	13.1
Agriculture (bn. 1952 yuan)	48.4	59.7	4.3	60.4	4.5
Foodgrain (bn. catties)	308.8	363.2	3.3	370.0	3.7
Cotton (bn. catties)	2.61	3.27	4.6	3.28	4.7
'National Income' (bn. 1957 yuan)[f]					8.9
Gross Domestic Product[g] (bn. 1957 yuan)	70.4			104.7	8.3

N.B. All value figures (except those for GDP) are for gross output value.
[a]All '1952 output' (except that for GDP) and '1959 Plan Target' figures are from the First Five Year Plan (1956).
[b]All '1957 output results' are from *Ten Great Years* (1960).
[c]'Industry' here includes mining, manufacturing, and utilities, and also 'factory handicrafts' (operations with four or more hired workers) but not 'individual handicrafts'.
[d]'Modern industry' excludes 'factory handicrafts' from the 'Industry' definition.
[e]'Handicrafts' includes factory, individual, and collective handicrafts.
[f]'National income' is 'the sum of net output value of agriculture, industry, construction, transport, and commerce' and excludes most services (*SYOC* 1983:579). It is thus equivalent to the Western concept of net domestic material product.
[g]The GDP figures are D. H. Perkins's 'I' estimates: see Perkins (1980).

Two measures of aggregate output are shown in Table 4.2: the official estimate of growth of 'national income'—which, in the Soviet definition adopted by China, is roughly equivalent to net domestic material product—and an estimate by D. H. Perkins of the growth rate of gross domestic product. Both indicate a healthy annual growth of more than 8 per cent for aggregate product.

In keeping with the Plan's emphasis on heavy industry, particularly high growth rates were planned for producer goods industries. Official statistics indicate that their output (in 1952 prices) more than trebled over the Plan period, while that of consumer goods grew by 83 per cent, so that the ratio of producer goods output to GVIO was almost one-half by 1957 (*Ten Great Years* 1960:88,90).

The Plan had an ambitious geographic dimension. It sought to shift industry inland from its locus along the eastern coastline by committing 55 per cent of all industrial investment—and about three-quarters of investment in new plant construction—to inland regions. The strategy was one of developing gradually, from north-east to south-west, major new interior industrial bases which would become focal points for the eventual spread of industry thoughout the country. The Plan itself was to complete the major part of the north-eastern base, centred on the integrated iron and steel complex at Anshan (Liaoning Province), and to work towards the establishment of similar bases in north and central China based on similar complexes being established at Baotou (Inner Mongolia) and Wuhan (central China).

Was the First Plan 'Stalinist'? In establishing urban industries, setting up management systems, embarking on long-term planning, and providing for scientific and technical education, the Chinese Communists in the early 1950s had only the USSR to turn to for models, assistance, and advice. Soviet success in building a large heavy industrial base from very backward conditions had much impressed them. Although not overawed by the Russians' Marxist credentials, Mao nevertheless regarded the Soviet Union as heir to Marxism's leadership. And, of course, the USSR was willing to provide assistance in the form of plants, machinery, and systems of organization and management, which inevitably resembled their counterparts at home.

So China 'leaned to one side.' The preponderant stress of the First Plan on very large-scale and capital-intensive producer goods industries was certainly consistent with the Stalinist development approach. So were its complements, a highly centralized mode of command planning, a hierarchical 'one-man management' system, and a highly articulated structure of individual material incentives in industry (see Section 3).

These Soviet imports had both internal consistency and a certain relevance to China's most acute needs. Technology tends to dictate its own preferred conditions, including the systems of command and control that shape its human environment. Thus it is hardly surprising that so many aspects of past Soviet practice were incorporated in China's development approach at this time. Massive, capital-intensive projects called for highly centralized control, an exalted role for scarce experts and technicians, and unambiguous lines of managerial authority. Gathering the reins of decision-making power in the centre implied the need for elaborate functional hierarchies to amass and process information and check on results, as well as for external incentive systems to encourage good performance in implementing central directives. The Chinese were aware of, and quoted, Lenin's technological determinist view of the social impact of large-scale industry:

Any large-scale industry—which is the material source and foundation of production in socialism—unconditionally must have a rigorous, unified will to direct the collective work of hundreds, thousands, and even millions of men. But how can the rigorous unity of wills be assured? Only by the wills of the thousands and millions submitting to the will of a single individual.[9]

Soviet methods seemed to speak to China's pressing *national* needs. After decades of internal chaos and victimization by foreign powers, the establishment of a powerful, centralized authority was a national imperative. The unbalanced location of industry, as well as its unsatisfactory composition, reinforced the urge for centralization.

Fast development of heavy industry also made sense in Chinese conditions of the early 1950s. The inherited industrial structure was highly skewed towards consumer goods production. Yet increasing the living standards of the population as a whole, which required above all the technological trans-formation of agriculture, could not be imagined without construction of the fuel, power, metallurgical, machine-building, and chemical industries. Con-siderations of military security reinforced this demand. Much that China was able to accomplish later, when priorities and strategy had changed, rested on the heavy industrial achievements of the 'Stalinist' period.

Yet Mao's phrase, 'lean to one side', was in retrospect a clue to the impermanence of this phase. 'Leaning' is a temporary posture of necessity. In fact, the Soviet model never had a clear field in China. Within industry, in such matters as management and wage systems, its spread was widely resisted. Successful mainly in the core Soviet-aid enterprises themselves, it did not gain predominance in the thousands of smaller establishments outside that orbit.

There is no doubt that the Soviet approach was imitated excessively in many areas. In retrospect, however, its contributions to Chinese development were considerable (see Section 6), while many of its objectively unsuitable aspects were recognized early and triggered a critique of mounting intensity.

3   Mobilizing workers

In 1949 total non-agricultural employment came to over 26 million workers and staff, including some 8 million in 'modern' sectors. Of these, industry and construction employed 3.3 million, but by 1952 this figure had grown by 94 per cent to reach 6.3 million (Emerson 1967:462). As big an increase as this was in percentage terms, it amounted to only 3 million new jobs, despite the fact that industrial production increased two and a half times. Yet the rate of employment creation was actually to fall thereafter (see Table 4.3).

The problem of mobilizing workers thus did not include finding them, for the regime inherited a sizeable amount of urban unemployment which it had great difficulty in eliminating. There is no reliable estimate of its precise magnitude; *Ten Great Years* (1960:177) put the amount at 4 million; one Western estimate (Hou 1968:369) put it at between 5 and 12.5 million in 1950.[10] The government at first assumed that the unemployment problem would quickly yield to economic growth. By 1952, with the adoption of the 'Decisions on the Problem of Employment', this simple faith had been replaced by recognition that aspects of the transition period itself—for example, the oppression of the private sector by the *wufan* campaign—were contributing to the problem. Not until 1954, however, did the long-term and structural character of unemployment receive public recognition (Howe 1971:Chapters 5–6).

The chief organs for administering labour and employment policy were the Labour Bureaux, established at the provincial and municipal levels in

Table 4.3. *State and private employment in industry and trade, 1939, 1952, and 1955 (Thousands)*

	1949	1952	1955
Total non-agricultural employment	26 267[a]	36 752[a]	38 864[a]
	(34 552)[b]	(44 864)[b]	(45 352)[b]
Workers and Employees[c]	8 004	15 804	19 076
Industry	3 060	5 260	5 981
State and co-op. enterprises	1 311	2 955	3 886
State–private joint enterprises	105	248	785
Private enterprises	1 644	2 057	1 310
Trade and restaurants	1 222	2 724	n.a.
State and co-op. enterprises	n.a.	1 246	2 223
State–private joint enterprises	n.a.	436	n.a.
Private enterprises	n.a.	917	315
Restaurants	n.a.	125	222

Sources and notes
[a]Emerson (1965:133).
[b]Hou (1968:366). These alternative estimates of non-agricultural employment differ from Emerson's because of differences in both coverage and methodology: see Hou (1968:362–4).
[c]All figures for 'workers and employees' and its sub-categories are official figures or estimates, based on official definitions, by Nai-ruenn Chen (*Source*: Chen 1967:474–5). Up to 1958, 'Workers and employees' essentially meant wage- and salary-earners, as opposed to self-employed persons in handicrafts, traditional transport, trade, services, etc., plus co-operative enterprise members who were paid by dividing enterprise net income.

May 1950. In the early years, their principal duties concerned unemployment, welfare, and the mediation of labour disputes in the private sector. The last was especially complicated because of the New Democracy's toleration of capitalist industrialization. The private sector had to be permitted some flexibility in hiring and firing labour if it was to survive and expand, yet the unemployment rate had to be contained. Unemployment was periodically swelled by state pressures on the private sector, such as during the *wufan* campaign, which resulted in the disgorging of labour by bankrupted and depressed businesses (Howe 1971). Over the longer run, such pressures were especially significant in commerce, where private employment fell from a high of 7.4 million in 1951 to virtually zero in 1956, while *total* employment in trade actually declined by over 2 million (Emerson 1967:448). Policies towards the registered unemployed included temporary assignments to public works, formation of small-scale enterprises, provision of assistance in returning to one's native village, and, if all else failed, pure relief (Howe 1971:93; Hoffmann 1974:52).

The weak demand for labour, which contributed to the persistence of unemployment, was due in part to the capital-intensive nature of the First Five Year Plan. But the Plan also influenced labour *supply*, by building expectations of high-paying jobs in industry and thus encouraging rural–urban migration, a principal contributor to open unemployment throughout the 1950s. Continuing social ferment in the countryside following land reform made some peasants migrate, as did the occurrence of poor harvests. But the most important factor behind migration was probably the widening gap between urban wages and rural incomes.

Estimating this gap is not a straightforward problem. Several attempts were made in China in the mid-1950s to compare the income level of peasants with that of urban workers, and the results ranged from near equality to a differential of 2 to 1, depending on the locality studied and the method of comparison (Riskin 1975c:205). One Western study of average per capita consumption in rural and urban areas in the mid-1950s puts the gap at 15–26 per cent (Roll 1974)—probably an underestimate, since average urban consumption was no doubt lower than that of regular state workers.

Urban wages rose much faster than rural incomes. The average wage of workers and staff increased by 70 per cent from 1949 to 1952, and another 43 per cent during the First Plan period, for an overall gain of 143 per cent; while peasant incomes rose by a total of 69 per cent (*Ten Great Years* 1960:211–12). Whatever the absolute size of the gap, therefore, it evidently was increasing, which must have acted as a powerful incentive for enterprising peasants to seek their fortunes in the cities.

Not only the level of money incomes favoured urban workers; so did the job security and social insurance they enjoyed after the Labour Insurance Regulations were promulgated in February 1951.[11] No rural equivalent existed in the 1950s (nor today, although co-operative social insurance schemes have spread in rural areas) between the medical, hospitalization, disability, and retirement coverage available to full-status industrial workers, on the one hand, and the meagre private, co-operative, and state relief resources provided in the countryside, on the other (Riskin 1975c:206–7).

The market is not an ideal means of allocating labour when there is a great surplus. With more than enough unskilled workers to go around, the chief problem was to limit their hiring by individual enterprises so as to contain costs. With respect to highly skilled personnel, their total number was small enough (there were but 31,000 engineers at the beginning of 1956[12]) to permit direct physical allocation (Perkins 1966:146). Elaborate wage systems for allocating labour efficiently were hardly necessary at this point.

Nevertheless, the leadership did have an idea as to the appropriate inter-industry structure of wages, its chief principle being that, in industries making producer goods or requiring arduous or dangerous work, pay should be somewhat higher than average. During the first half of the 1950s the wage structure was adjusted accordingly, and one result was a striking reduction in overall inter-industry differentials (Howe 1973:45).

Such differentials were relied on to some degree to provide incentives for workers to work hard and acquire new skills. The ideal, however, carried over from the ideology and practice of Yanan, was to inspire performance by developing political consciousness and group identity on the part of the individual. In conditions of short supply, this had the advantage—as long as it worked to motivate people—of permitting direct distribution of subsistence goods in lieu of wages, which was the method of paying government cadres until 1955. In older enterprises that remained in operation after 1949, spontaneous reforms by workers led to reductions in pay differentials from the forty- to fifty-fold spreads common before to spans of two- to four-fold (Howe) 1973:35–6).

Lessened reliance on wage differentials to inspire performance was consistent with the 'Shanghai', or 'East China', system of factory management, which was widely adopted in the older industrial centres of the east coast. Stressing collective responsibility for plant management and encouraging worker and staff participation via 'factory administrative committees', this system fostered the identification of workers with plant objectives and encouraged group solidarity. Such sources of motivation tend to be eroded by differentiated pay and to thrive in relatively egalitarian environments with common goals.

Even before 1949, however, the principle of egalitarianism, especially the 'very mistaken advocacy of so-called "equal livelihood" for technical personnel and ordinary workers' (Chen 1948:1), came under attack by the party leadership as antithetical to the development of production in the New Democracy period. Chen Boda (Chen Po-ta), then a Central Committee member, discussing the Party's labour policies from Yanan in April 1948, argued against relying 'exclusively on political stimulus' and called for a wage policy that included use of piece rates and progressive wage grades. He rejected the criticism that such a system would encourage workers to regard themselves as mere 'employees', pointing out that China was committed to 'permitting the development of liberal capitalism, . . . so that wiping out the workers' "employee" concept is impossible . . . Under the system of piece work wages and so forth, the workers' "employee" concept of obtaining increased emoluments because of increased production—or carrying on increased production to acquire increased emoluments—is not detrimental but rather is rational and progressive.'

In practice, because of the wide variety of inherited wage conditions, and the necessarily piecemeal approach taken to reforming them, a unified wage system did not come into existence until the wage reform of 1956. However, the state consistently opposed the levelling tendencies of the early years, so that by the mid-1950s intra-enterprise wage spans appear to have reached the target range of five- to seven-fold (Howe 1973:35–6), and the piece rate system had been widely adopted, covering 42 per cent of industrial workers at its peak in 1956 (Richman 1969:314).[13]

Greater wage differentiation was compatible with the one-man management system that became the national model for industrial management at the start of the Plan in 1953. Schurmann (1968:256) writes: 'The factory, under one-man management, was conceived of as a coldly rational arrangement of individual workers commanded by an authoritarian manager.' The stress this system necessarily put on administrative hierarchy, division of labour, individual responsibility, standardized tasks, and objective controls—the accoutrements of 'scientific management'—made an articulated system of individual incentives mandatory for both administrative staff and workers. In the 1955 shift from supply to salaries, government cadres (down to foremen and clerical personnel in state enterprises) were divided into twenty-six grades with salaries from Y30 to Y560. Technical personnel were also graded (Andors 1977:55).

One-man management lost favour before differentiated incentives did, perhaps because it was identified with the discredited Gao Gang (Kao Kang), the party leader in the North-east and first head of the State Planning Commission,[14] but also because it violated ideological principles favoured by Mao, such as that of the supremacy of Party and politics. In addition, it had encountered practical problems. The great number and variety of firms of different sizes and technologies did not augur well for 'scientific management' and unified systems of control. Such systems require much precise and accurate data about all aspects of plant capacity and performance, but this information was simply not available.[15]

While one-man management was being scrapped, however, wage differentiation proceeded apace, reaching its apex in the major wave reform of late 1956. This reform had two main purposes: first, to raise the overall wage level (which had grown only 6.9 per cent between 1953 and 1955 despite an official increase in labour productivity of 41.8 per cent); second, to replace the old wage structure, which 'had virtually ceased to be an incentive to greater output' (Liu 1956:14–15) with a more differentiated one. Wages rose 14.5 per cent for the average worker, and grades were widened to reflect skill differences, locational factors, and riskiness of work environment. Especially great increases (averaging 36 per cent for university professors and research fellows of the Chinese Academy of Sciences), as well as eligibility for large bonuses, were granted to senior scientists and technicians.

The year 1956 also witnessed the crest of the trend towards differentiating labour incomes in other ways, such as by means of piece rates and labour emulation campaigns. The latter involved honorific awards for model workers and campaigns to emulate them, and were applied not only to production but also to accounting and statistical work, safety, quality control, and technical innovation (Howe 1973:130).[16]

These various systems of individual differentiation advanced against constant criticism and resistance during the first half of the 1950s. Piece rates and emulation campaigns were unpopular with workers, who resented the glorification of individuals, the erosion of group morale, the influence of the 'rate-busting' model performance on standard work norms, and the 'endlessly soaring accident rates' produced by overstrenuous and prolonged competitive pressures (Howe 1973:120, 131–2). Moreover, the technical conditions for efficient and fair implementation of such incentive systems were generally lacking: where technologies differ among plants, where machines break down frequently, where raw material supplies are erratic, and where management and administration are patchy and uneven, there will be large variations in output over which the workers have no control. It then becomes impossible to assess their individual productivities, even if administrative staffs are not overburdened and underskilled; and the inevitably resulting inequities create resentment and erode support for the system.

Among the chief organizers of emulation campaigns were the trade unions, amalgamated in the All-China Federation of Trade Unions (ACFTU).[17] Unions 'transmit the party line to workers, encourage production . . ., engage in political education, and execute a range of welfare chores' (Hoffmann 1974:134). An anomalous instrument for mobilizing workers, they functioned as explained by Lenin in 1920:

In its work, the Party relies directly on the *trade unions* . . . which are *formally non-party*. Actually, all the directing bodies of the vast majority of the unions . . . consist of Communists and carry out all the directives of the Party. Thus, on the whole, we have a formally non-Communist, flexible, and relatively wide and very powerful proletarian apparatus, by means of which the Party is closely linked up with the *class* and with the *masses*, and by means of which, under the leadership of the Party, the *dictatorship of the class* is exercised. [cited in Harper 1969:86]

To be a proper 'transmission belt' between Party and workers requires that unions not only transmit directives downward, but also keep the higher levels informed about the needs and opinions of their members. Moreover, for the unions to gain respect from their constituency, they must, at most, represent its interests when these inevitably conflict with the objectives of Party and state, and, at least, protect the membership against overzealous managements. Failing this, unions will tend to be seen by their members as 'tails of the administration' or the 'workers' control department', as a high union official acknowledged happened on occasion (Harper 1969:108). Yet to grant some independence to the unions risks their building an independent power base around localist and 'economist' demands at variance with the overall social interest as identified by the Party. Twice during the 1950s (in 1951 and 1957), crises arose over this issue, with sections of the union leadership striving for greater independence and the Party in turn accusing them of economism. In both cases, the Party prevailed and its absolute control of the union movement was reinstated.[18]

Thus, the mobilization of workers after Liberation was carried out in a number of partly contradictory ways. It was nevertheless successful in creating an expanding and ever more skilled labour force, which helped generate a high rate of industrial growth. At the same time, however, the stubborn problem of unemployment seemed no closer to solution, and the systems of management and motivation, originally taken from the Soviet example, increasingly appeared alien both to Chinese economic conditions and to the political traditions and principles of the CCP. An evolution to something new was begun, but its ultimate shape was far from clear.

4 Mobilizing peasants

The land reform had a profound impact on the distribution of rural wealth and income and, through this, on both the motivation and the capacity of the farm population to invest, improve techniques, and increase production. It also made available new flows of income to the state for investment in industry.

Table 4.4. *Size of household, labour force, and cultivated area, by rural class, 1954*

	Share of households (%)	Ave. size of household (persons)	Ave. size of labour force (persons)	Ave. cultivated area (acres)	Ave. no. of work-days Hired in	Ave. no. of work-days Hired out
Poor peasant	29.0	4.2	2.0	1.88	7.0	25.7
Middle peasant	62.2	5.0	2.5	2.96	17.2	18.7
Rich peasant	2.1	6.2	3.0	5.20	78.6	11.7
Former landlord	2.5	4.2	2.2	2.14	11.8	20.5
Co-op. member	4.2	5.1	2.6	2.70		
All households	100.0	4.8	2.4	2.64		

Source: *Tongji Gongzuo*, no. 10, 1957:31–2; cited in Schran (1969:25).

The class composition of the countryside after land reform is suggested by Table 4.4. 'Poor peasants' now made up about 29 per cent of the rural population and cultivated about ½ acre per capita. Land reform obviously had not solved the problem of land scarcity for the poor. Indeed, the average per capita amount of land received by *all* beneficiaries, while varying by region, was but a fraction of an acre, as shown in Table 4.5. Robert Ash (1976:529) calculates that the 'poor peasant' farm of average size in south Kiangsu Province—1½ acres—could produce less than 80 per cent of its minimum caloric requirements (estimated at 1,900 calories per capita), and certainly could not realize a surplus for investment.

Table 4.5. *Average per capita area reallocated by land reform to peasants in selected provinces*

Province or region	Ave. per capita land received (acres)
Northern Manchuria[a]	1.17
Southern Manchuria[a]	0.50
Honan[a]	0.33–0.50
Hopei[a]	0.17–0.42
Hunan[a]	0.17–0.42
East China (Shantung, North Kiangsu, South Kiangsu Chekiang, North Anhwei, South Anhwei)	0.33
South Shensi[b]	0.25–0.33
North Shensi[b]	0.67
Shensi: mountains region[b]	1.67

Sources:
[a]Chao (1960:99).
[b]Ash (1976:521).

Those most able to improve their economic positions were the 2.1 per cent of the rural population classified as 'rich peasants', whose average farm size of 5.2 acres was almost three times that of 'poor peasants' and 75 per cent larger than that of 'middle peasants'. This inequality in land ownership surviving the land reform was more than matched by inequality in possession of other assets. 'Poor peasants' in 1954 had one draught animal per two households, one plow per three households, and one water wheel per seventeen households. 'Rich peasants', on the other hand, had two draught animals and one plow per household and a water wheel for every three households (Xue *et al*. 1960:99,101). The poor, although their lot had improved, were still at a disadvantage in competing both for survival and for growth.

This result was not accidental. Land reform had the dual purpose, it will be recalled, of ending 'feudal exploitation' and promoting growth of farm production. The second objective meant preserving the rich peasant economy, which best embodied the potential for private agricultural development. The fruits of this strategy, however, were disappointing: 'as a capitalist type, rich peasant farming in China was still in a low stage of development. Their capitalist activities were mainly directed towards commercial speculation and usury; their management of farming in a capitalist way did not show any marked advance; and their production did not display much superiority over that of the peasants working on their own' (Xue *et al*. 1960:101).

Yet investment did take place. The land reform's income redistribution brought roughly 300 million beneficiaries an initial increment in annual income estimated at about Y9.4 billion, or over 13 per cent of net domestic product (NDP) in 1952. Of this, the government in various ways extracted almost three fifths, leaving some Y3.9 billion as increased disposable income (Lippit 1974:125). This amounts to roughly Y13 per person per year, or almost 20 per cent of estimated per capita peasant consumption in 1952, and a 25 per cent increase in the disposable income of the beneficiaries (Schran 1969:133; Lippit 1974:146). In that year, self-financed (gross) investment in agriculture reached about Y1,620 million (Eckstein 1961:154), or 3.3 per cent of GVAO.

To survive, poorer farmers needed credit, of which there was an acute shortage in the post-reform period. Better-off farmers were often loath to make loans for fear of not being able to collect on them; when given the necessary assurances, they would often charge high interest rates (rates of 5–10 per cent per month were reported)—a reflection of the short supply and the high risk of default. Moreover, a good many of the newly prosperous peasants were rural party cadres. With some farmers going into debt and having to sell their land and hire out as labourers, the class structure threatened to revert to its pre-reform character; but now there was the added danger of rural party members being co-opted into the ranks of the privileged (Cheng 1963:28–9).

Because post-reform distribution of farm assets remained unequal, it was imperative to find a way of allocating them more rationally and equitably. The mechanism chosen was the mutual aid team (MAT), which was built on traditional rural practices of reciprocal aid, as refined in the Communist-held areas before 1949. The earliest form of MAT consisted of three to five households that banded together to help each other during the heavy farming seasons. Only a rough attempt was made to keep track of each member's contribution to the joint effort. The more advanced MAT was larger (up to twenty households) and worked together year-around. These 'practice[d] mutal aid in all matters, including labour power, draught cattle and farm tools, in purely agricultural production as well as in side occupations . . .' (*Agriculture in New China* 1953:14). They were seen as transitional forms, gradually preparing the ground for larger-scale co-operative farming proper, with merged and consolidated fields. By 1952, 40 per cent of farm households were in MATs, half of them in permanent ones.

Simultaneously with the spread of MATs in 1952 came the introduction of elementary or lower-stage agricultural producer co-operatives (LAPCs).[19] By the autumn harvest of 1954, these numbered 114,000 and encompassed about 2 per cent of peasant households (Xue *et al*. 1960:117). The distinctive feature of LAPCs was that their members' land, draught animals, and large tools, while still owned privately, were pooled and used collectively. Members were paid for their work and also a rent for their property investment, the former payment in principle exceeding the latter. LAPCs varied considerably in size: most contained between ten and twenty households, but some reached 200. Their average holding of farmland was around 82 acres (33 ha), although some had as much as 640 acres (260 ha) (*Agriculture in New China* 1953:15). Since the means of production were still owned privately, provided income to their owners, and (in principle) could be withdrawn from the co-operative, the LAPCs were regarded as 'semi-socialist' institutions.

LAPCs had certain advantages compared with MATs or private farming. Since the land was pooled, its use could be planned more rationally. Each plot did not have to feed its owners, regardless of suitability for grain production; a certain amount of crop specialization was now possible. Draught animals and implements, subject to unified management, could be allocated more efficiently. The LAPC organized labour to build irrigation and drainage canals and terrace the fields. It put aside a portion of its net income to acquire tools and equipment of benefit to all members, including those who could not individually have afforded them.

On the other hand, the co-operatives encountered a number of problems, some of them inherent in the contradictory aspects of their 'semi-socialist' nature. The fact that land could still be withdrawn inevitably restricted its integration into land planning and development: what family would consent to *its* land being flooded in a water conservancy project, for instance? The same was true of draught animals, whose feeding and breeding were a source of endless conflict. Perhaps most importantly, management of the co-operatives demanded leadership and planning on a scale new to the countryside, and in their absence a good deal of cadre inefficiency and 'commandism' emerged. The size and use of the reserve fund was a particularly delicate issue, pitting as it did the interests of the collective as a whole against those of its individual members. Finally, public awareness that the LAPCs were transitional to full collectivization dampened incentives to invest and improve land on the part of the great majority of peasants who remained private farmers.

By early 1955, when the first push forward had organized some 14 per cent of rural households into co-operatives, many of these problems had become apparent. Violations of the principle of 'voluntariness and mutual benefit' were widespread; cadres pressured richer peasants to join the co-operatives, whose prospects were brighter with than without the superior land and equipment of the better-off peasants. In some cases, their assets were undervalued or arbitrarily taken over, with the result that property came to be hidden or destroyed and pigs and draught animals were slaughtered or sold off to avoid confiscation. The total stock of pigs declined from 102 million in 1954 to 88 million in 1955 (Walker 1965; Chen 1967:340).

Simultaneous with—and in part because of—the problems being encountered by co-operativization, farm production had begun to lag and thus to threaten the success of the newly launched First Five Year Plan. The growth of foodgrain output had fallen to only 1.6 per cent in 1953 and 2.3 per cent in 1954, well below its Rehabilitation period record (*Ten Great Years* 1960:119). Investment in 1953, the Plan's first year, was 84 per cent greater than in 1952, exports were up 28 per cent, and the urban population had grown by 8.4 per cent (or by 6 million persons). Thus, demand for farm products was exceptionally high, whereas supply was lagging: in 1953 'the state's sales of grain were running several billion catties ahead of its purchases' (Perkins 1966:41). Not only had production growth slowed, but the land reform had sharply reduced the proportion of output marketed by the peasants, since its poor peasant beneficiaries had a higher propensity to consume and a lower marketing ration than the expropriated landlords and rich peasants had had.[20] In the 1920s and 1930s, inequality of wealth and income and the extraction of surplus as rent, interest, and profits had allowed as much as half the crop to be marketed; but in 1953 the marketing ratio was only 28 per cent (Perkins 1966:41).

To have either accepted the reduced rate of commercialization or raised it by increasing purchase prices greatly would have forced curtailment of the Plan's investment programme. The short-run alternative to these unattractive choices was to eliminate the market and procure farm goods administratively. In November 1953 a system of compulsory purchase quotas was introduced for grain, and shortly thereafter for cotton and oil-bearing seeds as well. This system, known as 'planned purchase and supply' (PPS), set sales quotas for each farm household based upon its requirement of food, seed, and fodder, as well as upon demand from grain deficit areas. Any surplus produced above-quota could be kept, sold to the state, or exchanged with other peasants. 'Planned supply' meant that the state undertook to provide to the urban population, at fixed prices, rations of grain, edible oil, and cotton cloth, and to supply cloth and, if necessary, grain to the peasants (Xue *et al*. 1960:60–1). Private trade in these commodities was banned.

For other major farm commodities a system of 'unified purchase and sale' was instituted in 1954. Like PPS, it outlawed private trade in the commodities affected, but it did not initially ration their distribution (Perkins 1966:53–4).

By 1954, then, two general methods of compulsory procurement of agricultural goods existed: a tax in kind, and the 'planned' and 'unified' purchase systems. These methods had different effects on production incentives. The tax was fixed as a proportion of 'normal' yield in 1953, and this base was kept constant for five years.[21] The marginal tax rate on increases in yield achieved by the peasants was thus zero in the short run, and the average proportion of crop paid in tax in fact fell from 13.2 per cent in 1952 to 11.3 per cent in 1957.[22] On the whole, as Perkins (1966:48) points out, 'the agricultural tax had relatively little influence at the margin on either the level of production or selection of crops to be planted in a given area . . . . it even approached the "ideal tax" (from the point of view of economic efficiency) of Western economists, the "lump sum" tax.'

The compulsory purchase programme, on the other hand, was initially implemented in a near-confiscatory manner, causing purchases to grow by twice the (official) increase in grain output between the 1952–3 and 1954–5 grain years (Perkins 1966:51), and leaving the peasants with insufficient food to meet their own needs. This coercive, bureaucratic, and extractive approach hurt incentives. Politically, it threatened the Party's relations with the poor and middle peasants, while economically it epitomized the myopia that Mao later dubbed 'draining the pond to catch the fish'. The Party acted to redress the situation by instituting in mid-1955 the 'three-fix' policy.

The 'three-fix' approach structured compulsory procurement to resemble the agricultural tax, that is, tied it to an estimate of normal production (based on spring 1955 production conditions). The state purchased a fixed amount (generally 80–90 per cent) of the surplus (if any) of 'normal' output above consumption, tax, seed, and fodder needs from agriculture producer co-operatives (APCs) or households. Grain deficit households were guaranteed 'fixed sales' of grain by the state. 'Normal production' quotas were to remain unchanged for three years (i.e., through 1957), and so were purchase quotas.[23]

The 'three-fix' policy did relax pressure on the peasantry: state grain purchases fell in the next two grain years (1955–6 and 1956–7) to stand at the end of the First Five Year Plan (FFYP) period some $7\frac{1}{2}$ per cent below the level of 1954–5 (see Table 4.6). In 1956–7, for the first time, state sales of grain far exceeded purchases and reserve stocks were drawn down by some 17 per cent. Over the Plan period as a whole, therefore, there was 'practically no growth at all in the amount of agricultural products available to the planners (Denny 1970:9, 17).

By 1955 the problem had become clear: the growth rate of raw and processed farm product exports had fallen, as had that of consumer goods production (highly dependent on raw materials from agriculture), and even the high priority producer goods sector had been affected. Although the farm problem was not the sole cause of these troubles, it was the main one (Perkins 1966:55). 'Planned' and 'unified' purchase had merely postponed the crisis for a couple of years; to solve it would require raising farm productivity itself.

The mobilization of the peasantry was a vast process still very much

Table 4.6. *State procurement of grain, 1952–1957 (millions of metric tons)*

Grain year	Total procurement (purchases + tax)[a]
1952–3	35.5 (38.6)
1953–4	41.5 (44.9)
1954–5	45.1 (46.8)
1955–6	43.0 (46.0)
1956–7	41.7 (46.0)

[a]Husked grain, including soybeans.

Source: Perkins (1966:248). Alternative estimates in parentheses by Denny (1970).

unfinished in 1955. Moreover, the rural situation was dynamic and unstable. Landlordism had been abolished, redistribution carried out, and the welfare of the poorer majority of peasants improved, all without sacrificing the rapid recovery of farm production. But continued growth would depend on equipping agriculture with better technologies. In Mao Zedong's view, to attempt this within the context of individual small peasant agriculture would risk the re-polarization of rural society. On the other hand, the co-operative movement itself was advancing very slowly in the face of resistance from better-off peasants. The mere prospect of co-operativization—especially when forced by autocratic cadres and activists—discouraged private investment. Finally, there was no way of coercing from the farm population, even had the Party been so inclined, the increasing surpluses needed for industrialization, without thereby crippling production incentives and eliminating future surpluses. Mao's sudden intervention of July 1955, which led swiftly to total collectivization, thus broke what he saw as an impasse that was becoming untenable.

5 Mobilizing domestic resources: investment

In 1933, gross investment had been barely large enough to keep China's capital stock from diminishing (Liu and Yeh 1965:68). One of the new regime's highest priorities, whose achievement can be seen in Table 4.7, was to raise investment sharply. The rate of gross investment in fact climbed above 20 per cent in 1953 and remained there for the entire FFYP period. This compares with an average investment rate of 15–17 per cent for all low-income countries in 1958 and is a rate of capital formation reached in Japan only in the mid-1930s.[24]

This record was due in part to the government's success in using the national budget to channel resources into investment. State budget revenues rose rapidly during the 1950s, both absolutely and in proportion to GDP, constituting about 22 per cent of GDP in 1952 and 29 per cent in 1957.[25] Of the rising proportion of

Table 4.7. *Gross domestic investment and the investment rate, 1952–1957 (billions of 1957 yuan)*

	Net inventory investment[a]	Gross domestic fixed capital formation[b]	Gross domestic investment (GDI)[c]	GDP[d]	$\dfrac{\text{GDI}}{\text{GDP}}$
1952	6.02	7.70	13.72	77.16	0.178
1953	6.33	11.14	17.47	(81.77)	(0.214)
1954	6.66	12.88	19.54	(86.38)	(0.226)
1955	5.93	13.76	19.69	(94.44)	(0.208)
1956	1.81	20.05	21.86	(101.35)	(0.217)
1957	3.43	19.52	22.95	107.86	0.213

[a]Net inventory investment in 1952 yuan was obtained as follows:

	Yeh (1968:511) estimate of total investment (bn. 1952 yuan) (1)	Yeh (1968:519) estimate of change in inventories (% of (1)) (2)	Change in inventories (bn. 1952 yuan): (1) × (2) ÷ 100 (3)
1952	14.56	47.5	6.92
1953	18.81	38.7	7.28
1954	20.31	37.7	7.66
1955	21.46	31.8	6.82
1956	26.04	8.0	2.08
1957	23.72	16.6	3.94

These figures were then converted to 1957 yuan by using Field's 1957 price index of 86.98 (1952 = 100) for all producer goods, as 'derived from officially reported aggregates for producer and consumer goods' (Field 1980:377, 380).
[b]Field (1980:233).
[c]This column is the sum of the two preceeding columns.
[d]Gross domestic product from Field (1980:390).

N.B. Numbers in parentheses are derived by applying the annual rate of increase of GNP (in 1973 dollars), implied by Ashbrook's (1975:23) GNP series, to the 1952 GDP figure in the table. The ratio of 1957 GNP to 1952 GNP in Ashbrook's table is about 1.4, almost identical to that in the above table.

total product captured by the budget, an increasing share was in turn devoted to investment expenditures.[26]

The sources of expanding state revenue are indicated in Table 4.8, which reveals a pattern of declining importance of agricultural taxes and miscellaneous revenues of various kinds, compensated by the growing weight of state enterprise profits and depreciation allowances. A complex bundle of industrial and commercial taxes, simplified at various times in the 1950s, continued to provide over 30 per cent of state revenues until the end of the decade. But it is clear that increasing reliance was put on profit taxes, including the direct collection of state enterprise profits, rather than on sales-type taxes such as the Soviet turnover tax. As more industry and commerce entered the

Table 4.8. *State budget revenue and its sources, 1950–1959*

	Total govt revenue (bn. current yuan)	Sources of government revenue (%)			
		Agricult. taxes	Industr., commercial taxes	State enterprise profits, deprec. allowances	All other[a]
1950	6.5	29	36	13	22
1951	13.0	17	36	24	23
1952	17.6	15	35	32	17
1953	21.8	12	38	35	15
1954	26.2	13	34	38	16
1955	27.2	11	32	41	16
1956	28.7	10	35	47	8
1957	31.0	10	36	46	8
1958	41.9	8	34	53	6
1959	54.2	6	29	62	3

[a] Includes salt and miscellaneous taxes, customs receipts, receipts from foreign loans and domestic bonds, receipts from insurance operations, and other income.

Source: Ecklund (1966:Table 1, p. 20).

state orbit, the share of state enterprise profits in government revenue rose, until by the end of the 1950s it constituted more than three-fifths of total revenue. Both the policy of keeping industrial goods prices high relative to wages and salaries, and the automatic growth of depreciation allowances as capital stock increased, contributed to this result.

This system of revenue collection had some major virtues: (1) it produced rapidly growing revenue to finance the ambitious investment programme without excessive inflationary pressures; (2) it bore most heavily on consumer goods, especially luxuries, which discouraged their use and expedited the state's policy of shifting resources to investment; and (3) the growing share of revenue coming from state enterprise profits and the resulting simplification of the tax structure made the system progressively less bureaucratic and costly to run (Ecklund 1966: Chapter 3; Gurley 1976:143).

Against these merits must be placed its lack of stimulus to seek greater efficiency. Enterprises did not keep their profits and thus had no incentive to increase them; they merely transferred the costs of inefficiency to the state via reduced profits and profit taxes. However, it was at least a feasible system to administer. Enterprises at that time were of widely divergent size and technology and their numbers were being increased daily by inefficient new units. A system of sales taxes linked to (fixed) prices would have resulted in losses for many firms, and, consequently, would have required an administratively burdensome system of centrally directed subsidies to individual enterprises (Perkins 1966:113–14). Three decades later, the government, having concluded that enterprise incentives needed to be restored, was again wrestling with the trade-off between incentives and administrative costs (see Chapter 14).

6 External resources and Soviet aid

China's foreign trade rose steadily throughout the 1950s (see Table 4.9), growing somewhat faster than GNP, so that the ratio of two-way trade[27] to GNP rose from about 6 per cent in 1952 to about 9 per cent in 1959 (Eckstein 1966:121). During this period, China used trade as a means of increasing its investment rate, importing such producer goods as metal-cutting tools, forging-press equipment, and rolled steel in exchange for exports of raw and processed agricultural goods, textiles, and minerals (Eckstein 1966:126).

Between 1950 and 1961 the Soviet Union provided about 45 per cent of China's imports and was the main source of producer goods from the rest of the world. Soviet exports to China over the period came to about $7.7 billion, of which about one-quarter took the form of complete industrial plants and another 16 per cent, other machinery and equipment. Most of these imports were paid for by means of current exports, but about 27 per cent were financed with Soviet credits (Gurley 1976:163–4). The availability of Soviet loans enabled China to run a trade deficit with the USSR from 1950 to 1955, tapping Soviet savings to supplement Chinese investment at a crucial point in time (see Table 4.10).

Soviet credits[28] financed four types of purchases by China: capital goods, including complete sets of plant and equipment; military equipment, especially in connection with the Korean War; military stockpiles turned over to China when the Soviets vacated Port Arthur and Dairen in 1955; and Soviet shares of four joint-stock companies turned over to sole Chinese control in 1954 (Eckstein 1966:156). While the precise division of credits among these uses is unknown, the First Five Year Plan itself makes clear the strategic economic significance of Soviet aid in the development programme, describing the Soviet-aid projects as 'the core of our industrial construction plans' (FFYP 1956:38).

These projects included seven iron and steel plants, twenty-four electric power stations, and sixty-three machinery plants, and involved aid in all aspects of the construction process, from prospecting to the training of Chinese personnel. In all, Soviet aid projects plus those directly supporting them absorbed over half of all capital construction investment in the FFYP. In addition, some 10,800 Soviet and 1,500 East European technicians and specialists went to China in the 1950s, about 8,000 Chinese engineers and skilled workers trained in the USSR, and more than 7,000 Chinese students received instruction in Soviet schools and research institutes.

All of the aid except blueprints, licences, and technical documents had to be paid for. The degree of 'aid'—as opposed to 'trade'—involved in the transactions thus depends on payment terms, including prices, interest rates, and repayment periods. No convincing evidence of exploitative pricing has been found (Eckstein 1966:171–4); interest rates were in the 1–2 per cent range

Table 4.9. *China's trade balances, 1950–1957 (billions of current yuan)*

	Total trade				Socialist countries				Capitalist countries			
	Total	X	M	Balance	Total	X	M	Balance	Total	X	M	Balance
1950	1.20	0.62	0.59	0.03	0.35	0.21	0.14	0.07	0.86	0.41	0.45	−0.04
1951	1.90	0.78	1.12	−0.34	0.98	0.47	0.52	−0.05	0.92	0.31	0.61	−0.30
1952	1.89	0.88	1.02	−0.14	1.32	0.61	0.71	−0.10	0.58	0.27	0.31	−0.04
1953	2.30	1.04	1.26	−0.22	1.56	0.67	0.89	−0.22	0.74	0.37	0.37	0.00
1954	2.35	1.06	1.29	−0.23	2.25	0.95	1.30	−0.35	0.79	0.43	0.36	0.07
1955	3.04	1.38	1.66	−0.29	2.25	0.95	1.30	−0.35	0.79	0.43	0.36	0.07
1956	3.12	1.64	1.49	0.15	2.06	1.05	1.01	0.04	1.07	0.59	0.48	0.12
1957	3.06	1.62	1.44	0.18	1.97	1.09	0.88	0.21	1.09	0.53	0.56	−0.03

Source: USCIA (1972:9).

Table 4.10. *Sino-Soviet trade, 1950–1965 (millions of US dollars)*

	Exports to USSR	Imports from USSR	Net trade balance
1950	190	135	55
1951	305	445	−140
1952	415	550	−135
1953	475	690	−215
1954	550	720	−170
1955	645	1055	−410
1956	745	715	30
1957	750	545	205
1958	880	635	245
1959	1100	955	145
1960	850	815	35
1961	550	365	185
1962	515	235	280
1963	415	185	230
1964	315	135	180
1965	225	190	35

Source: Chen (1975:648).

(Mah 1968:705), well below the 5–6 per cent on long-term loans charged by the World Bank at that time; but repayment periods appear to have been significantly shorter.[29] This imposed on China after 1955 a heavier annual debt service burden than would a typical World Bank loan. Indeed, after 1955, debt service requirements made China a net capital exporter. Soviet credits ended in 1957 and were not renewed.[30] During the bitter dispute that raged between the two countries in the early 1960s, China rushed to repay its debt early, and did so in 1965.

The exact amount and composition of Soviet aid is still a matter of uncertainty, and its contribution to China's development cannot be quantified with precision.[31] But enough is known to make it apparent that China's tempo of industrialization in the 1950s would have been considerably slower without Soviet help. China could neither have produced itself nor obtained elsewhere the modern industrial technology obtained from the USSR.[32] Despite its relatively short repayment terms, this aid can hardly be deemed ungenerous. It provided goods and services badly needed by the USSR itself so soon after the devastation of the Second World War. Perhaps its chief cost to China was the dependency it created—a cost that became clear only when the Soviet experts were abruptly withdrawn in 1960.

China's trade with the West, on the other hand, was severely limited by the embargo imposed by the United States at the outbreak of the Korean War, and by accompanying controls imposed by other Western countries and Japan.

From 1950 to 1957, restrictions on trade with China were tighter than with other socialist countries, but this 'China differential' was frequently circumvented or even ignored by European countries.

Nevertheless, China's trade with the capitalist world fell to less than half that with Communist countries for most of the 1950s (Table 4.9). It remained important to China as a source of certain materials (e.g., rubber, cotton, and chemicals) and of foreign exchange. Hong Kong was (and still is) the crucial market for earning the latter, as well as a useful entrepôt for hiding banned trade with other countries.

7   Industrialization and living standards

It is widely believed that rapid industrialization during the First Plan period was accomplished by reducing the living standards of the rural population.[33] The issue of urban–rural relations and of the nature of net resource flows between these sectors is a complex one that is examined further in Chapter 10, Section 4. However, the increase in investment in the early to mid 1950s clearly did *not* result in a *decline* in mass living standards.

This is apparent on several counts. First, the investment rate rose most sharply—from 10 to about 21 per cent of GDP—in the early years, 1950–3, after which it remained fairly constant for the rest of the Plan period (Table 4.7). Yet, during those early years GDP grew by at least 13 per cent per year (Ashbrook 1975:23, *Ten Great Years* 1960:20). Simple arithmetic indicates that this was more than enough to account for the increase in investment and still leave room for greater consumption per capita. Second, consumer goods output rose by an average annual rate of 29 per cent during 1950–2, and by 13 per cent during the Plan period (*Ten Great Years* 1960:89), while foodgrain output grew by 7 per cent and between 2.9 and 3.7 per cent, respectively, over the two periods.[34] Thus, consumer goods production and food grain production both grew faster than population.

Finally, there is the issue of distribution. A massive redistribution of industrial and commercial capital and of land did of course occur in the early 1950s. As Perkins (1975c:176) points out, such a redirection of wealth could easily have raised both the investment rate and the consumption level of the poorest half of the population. Lippit's analysis of just this process (see Section 3) concluded that the land reform redistributed some 13 per cent of net domestic product in 1952, of which the peasants retained enough after taxes and compulsory sales at low prices to increase their per capita disposable income by a quarter. Land reform alone may have provided almost one-half the increase in national savings between 1950 and 1952 while still raising consumption for most peasants. To this must be added a substantial increase in public consumption in the form of public health and sanitation measures, and the provision of elementary education to increasing numbers of people.

In sum, Ashbrook's (1975:22) characterizations of the Rehabilitation period ('End of civil war, inflation, gross starvation; hope rekindled') and of the First Five Year Plan period ('Stabilization of living standard at spartan but improved levels') is probably more accurate than the image of a peasantry impoverished by the investment requirements of rapid industrialization.

In this apparent success story, only hints have been seen of the issues that led to abandonment of the First Plan strategy in 1958. The latter half of the Plan period, to which we now turn, bridges the gap between the Soviet-oriented strategy of the Plan, itself, and the era of 'late Maoism' that dominated China from the late 1950s until the Chairman's death.

Notes

1. The annual rates were 48.5 per cent for heavy industry, 29 per cent for light industry (calculated from *Ten Great Years* 1960:88).
2. The use of 1952 prices, however, results in some upward bias in the growth rate of industrial output value.
3. For a general discussion of the evolution of material balances planning in China, see Perkins (1968). See also Ellman (1979).
4. Such targets included: total national capital investment; major development projects; new productive capacity for important commodities; output of important commodities; balancing and inter-provincial transfers of important raw materials, equipment, and consumer goods; foreign trade totals, and volumes of individual important import and export goods; national budget revenues and expenditures; total wages; total employment; labour allocation for centrally directed enterprises; allocation of scientific and technical workers; railway freight volume and freight turnover; planning for individual centrally operated enterprises and institutions; 'overall arrangements' for higher educational enrolment plans and for students being sent abroad; total gross value of industrial output; 'irrigated acreage, arable acreage, total circulation of commodities, total retail sales, turnover of goods, local transport, rate of and total cost reduction, and the volume of building and installation work' (Donnithorne 1967:462).
5. At the time the Plan was being written, most of agriculture was still in private hands, with some co-operatives in existence. This may explain the absence of agricultural production targets from the Plan's general themes, although more recently the government has not hesitated to announce such targets even though most of agriculture has been in the collective—rather than the state—sector.
6. In Chinese accounting terminology, investment in capital construction (*jiben jianshe*—lit., 'basic construction') means investment that results in the increase or replenishment of fixed assets, and also includes ancillary expenditures such as those for geological surveys and exploration, engineering design, scientific testing and research, workers' training, etc. (Chen 1967:20; Ishikawa 1965:128).
7. It envisaged construction of only one tractor factory (for completion in 1959) and four chemical fertilizer plants, plus reconstruction of a number of others. Moreover, agriculture was not among the eleven fields of research to which the plan directed the Academia Sinica to 'pay particular attention' (FFYP:186–7).
8. With regard to the question of accuracy of official statistics, Rawski (1980b), after an exhaustive review, dismisses the possibility of deliberate falsification during the period in question and concludes that official statistics provide generally meaningful measures of Chinese industrial performance.
9. Lenin, *Selected Works* (Moscow, 1952, II:398); cited in Schurmann (1968:255).

Schurmann goes on to point out that the 1953 Chinese article containing this quote quickly added that such highly concentrated management must not be arbitrary and autocratic, but must be based on 'close reliance on the working masses'.

10. Hou's estimate must be read only as indicating a serious problem, since it calculates unemployment as a residual between estimates of labour force and of employment, both subject to wide margins of error.

11. These were amended in January, 1953; see Hoffmann (1974:App. B) for the text.

12. There were another 63,600 technicians doing engineers' work. The total number of engineering and technical personnel of all kinds was 164,000 in 1952 and 344,000 in 1955 (Orleans 1961:130, 165).

13. This figure, however, compares with a corresponding peak of 74 per cent for the Soviet Union (Howe 1973:119).

14. Gao was the principal subject of a drawn-out political struggle from 1953 to the announcement of his suicide in March 1955. As head of his 'independent kingdom' in the North-east and as Commissioner of State Planning, Gao was the 'one man' at the apex of the hierarchical one-man management system, and it was his power and authority that stood to gain from that system's successful implementation. One-man management came under increasingly open criticism from 1954 on (Gao was replaced by Li Fuchun (Li Fu-ch'un) as head of the State Planning Commission in September of that year), and was officially abolished in favour of 'factory manager responsibility under the leadership of the Party committee', at the Eighth Party Congress in summer 1956. See Schurmann's account of this affair (1968, Ch. IV).

15. These and other criticisms of the one-man management system are discussed in Andors (1977:56–8).

16. This fact illustrates the artificiality of the distinction between 'material' and 'non-material' incentives. A more significant distinction is that between 'external' (or 'extrinsic') and 'internal' ('intrinsic') incentives; see Riskin (1975b). Both honorific awards and individual material incentives are examples of external incentives.

17. Industrial membership in the ACFTU rose from 2.8 million in 1948 to over 16 million in 1957, in addition to which there were as many members from 'non-industrial' sectors such as trade and commerce (Richman 1969:269). Neither compulsory nor universal, union membership nevertheless brings important social insurance and welfare benefits that supplement those provided by the state. For the functions, structure, and funding of trade unions, see Hoffmann (1974:Ch. 5), Richman (1969:267–70), Chen and Galenson (1969:191–5); see also Gardner (1969); Harper (1969).

18. This paragraph is based on Harper (1969), which presents an informative history of Party-union relations.

19. LAPCs existed prior to 1952 but on an insignificant scale. In 1950 there were only 219 households in LAPCs in all of China, and in 1951 only 1,618 such households (Ten Great Years 1960:34).

20. A 1955 survey found that, even then, rich peasants marketed 43.9 per cent of their grain, while middle and poor peasants marketed 25.2 and 22.1 per cent, respectively (Perkins 1966:29). Additional reasons for the decline in the marketing ratio may be found on pp. 29–40 of Perkins's work.

21. In 1958 it was raised somewhat and the tax rate lowered, with the net effect of increasing the tax by about 5 per cent.

22. The details of the agricultural tax and procurement policies can be found in Donnithorne (1967: Ch. 13).

23. Unless severe shortages of grain elsewhere necessitated procuring more. In such

cases, the additional amount purchased was not to exceed 40 per cent of the surplus of actual over 'normal' output for any household.

24. Kuznets (1966:406). The countries concerned are those with a per capita GDP of less than $350 in 1958. China's GDP per capita, as conventionally measured, was under $100 (in 1957 dollars) for the period in question (Perkins 1975:134).

25. Estimated by using budget revenue figures from Ecklund (1966:20) and GDP estimates of Field (1980). Since the latter are in 1957 yuan, the 1952 GDP was inflated back to 1952 prices by the use of sectoral price indexes in Field.

26. 'Growing budgetary allocations to economic construction, rising from 26 per cent [of expenditures] in 1950 to 61 per cent in 1959, were the primary source of financing Communist China's industrial growth' (Ecklund 1966:18). Such allocations came out of government saving, which rose even more quickly than did revenue, starting at about 50 per cent of the latter in 1952 and reaching over 80 per cent by 1957.

27. Valued at the 1957 adjusted official exchange rate of Y2.62 = $1: see Eckstein (1966:App. C). The ratio given in the text is very sensitive to the choice of exchange rate.

28. These totalled some Y5,294 million between 1950 and 1957.

29. The only one definitely known is for the 1950 loan, which provided for repayments in ten equal annual instalments beginning in 1954. Typical World Bank loans at the time ran for twenty to twenty-five years.

30. An interest-free payments moratorium was granted China in 1960, however, as was a 1961 interest-free loan of sugar, both at the height of the post-Great Leap Forward famine.

31. There are several reasons for this. First, not enough is known about the actual use of Soviet loans. Second, data on capital goods exports to China (as well as of imports from China) are obtained from trade partners (in this case the USSR) and valued in the partners' currencies; there is no ideal way of converting these figures into yuan to obtain 'true' scarcity values within China. Third, the counter-factual question of what China could have accomplished in the absence of Soviet aid is unanswerable.

32. Alexander Eckstein estimated very roughly that capital goods imports from the USSR contributed somewhere between 15 and 46 per cent of China's growth rate during the First Plan period; see Eckstein (1966:124).

33. See, e.g., Eckstein (1966:30), who refers to 'rapid industrial expansion . . . at the expense . . . of rural standards of living', and Meisner (1977:124), who writes of 'industrialization of the cities . . . based largely on the exploitation of the countryside.'

34. Wiens (1978), 3.7 per cent is the official figure (see Table 4.2) and 2.9 per cent is based on Wiens's upward revision of 1952 output. It is generally accepted that gross value of agricultural output grew faster than foodgrains alone.

CHAPTER 5

SOCIALIST TRANSFORMATION AND ADMINISTRATIVE DECENTRALIZATION: PRELUDE TO LATE MAOISM, 1955–1957

1 Introduction

In retrospect, the two decades to which we now turn were a period of increasingly irreconcilable conflict within the Chinese leadership. The consolidation of political rule and the mobilization for economic development under a regime of material balances planning had concentrated great power at the centre. The government moved rapidly to take over what remained of the private sector in industry and commerce, but then found it increasingly difficult to exercise effective control from the centre over an ever larger and more complex economy. In agriculture, slower growth after the quick recovery of production in the early 1950s, and the unanticipated complexities of gradual co-operativization, threatened to fulfilment of the First Five Year Plan and called into question its strategy of rapid heavy industrialization.

Mao perceived in the situation of the mid-1950s a whole series of contradictions—between industry and agriculture, coast and interior, centre and localities, heavy industry and light industry, to name a few—which demanded resolution. At the core of these contradictions was the problem of monopoly of political power by the Party and by its national leadership. This situation gave rise to the attempt to *administer* the economy by means of a centralized bureaucracy, to stress accumulation and rapid growth over raising living standards, to develop autocratic or manipulative relations with the population—in contrast to the more interdependent links of the revolutionary and civil war periods. In this last respect, China's age-old tradition of bureaucratism was quick to find expression in the fertile new ground of centralized socialism.

At the cost of oversimplification, one can identify two broad options in attacking this range of problems, in so far as they pertain to economic affairs. The first is to attack the base of centralized political power over the economy by expanding the power of individual enterprises at the expense of government administrative organs, either central or local. This would require a large role for the market in co-ordinating the activities of autonomous enterprises. At the beginning of the period in question only Yugoslavia, regarded as a renegade from the socialist camp, was taking such 'market socialism' seriously. The second option was to decentralize many economic matters to local control, keeping them within the political sphere. It may turn out to be one of Mao's chief contributions to history that under his leadership China explored the administrative decentralization route during two turbulent decades. It is the view of the post-Mao leadership that this cure turned out to be worse than the disease.

From a structural point of view, the political decentralization option required local organizations capable of exercising effective leadership to achieve politically acceptable goals. This meant socialist institutions. Impatient with the slow formation of co-operatives in the countryside, and unwilling to accept the consequences for rapid industrialization that it entailed, Mao intervened dramatically in July 1955 to force the pace. In a decisive break with the previous strategy of planned and voluntary gradualism, almost the entire peasantry was organized into collectives in a single year. Two years later, in the course of the Great Leap Forward, these were further amalgamated into rural people's communes, enormous units containing thousands of members.

The Great Leap rejected the model of central administrative planning in two fundamental ways. First, it substituted spontaneously initiated, mass economic activity for the blueprints worked out by professional planners. Second, it gave great economic and political authority to local and regional units—the communes and provinces, respectively. With the communes able to mobilize labour and investment on a large scale, they were then ideologically whipped up to make a maximum effort to raise China's economic and technological level qualitatively in a few brief years.

When the Great Leap collapsed and economic crisis set in at the turn of the 1960s, the combination of administrative decentralization and political mobilization was abandoned. Central planning was resurrected on an annual basis, while opportunities for market-oriented activities were extended, especially for the rural population. Where Mao's collectivist policies had dispersed authority from the top down while concentrating it from the bottom up, the 'new economic policy' of the early 1960s did the opposite on both counts. This policy worked to tide the economy over the immediate crisis and bring about a recovery that gathered momentum into the middle 1960s.

Through these various twists and turns, the three opposing themes can be observed tensely interacting in various combinations. The central, administrative planning approach of the 'command economy', inherited from the Soviet Union, was in the defensive position. During the Cultural Revolution it would come to be identified with Liu Shaoqi (Liu Shao-ch'i), then Chief of State. Its structural defenders were the political and administrative cadres whose careers it legitimized. In one opposing corner there was the 'market socialism' option, propounded most eloquently by the economist, Sun Yefang. Mao opposed both of these paths. The first he saw as unwieldy and ineffective economically, and as giving rise to a class of bureaucratic rulers, divorced from the masses politically. The second played to bourgeois values, opposing the socialist values of co-operation and solidarity in favour of individualism and profit orientation. Mao's goal, instead, was an economy that centralized control only of major macroeconomic variables and of the large-scale modern industries that he regarded as the 'backbone' of the economy. Other activities would be the province of the regions and localities, using technologies appropriate to their sizes and resource bases and adopting the policy of 'self-reliance'. A principal theme of the 1960s and early 1970s, 'self-reliance' functioned to relieve the centre of investment responsibilities outside the modern, large-scale sector; to stimulate the full exploitation of locally available resources; and to provide a clear link between a region's development and its own efforts, as a kind of collective incentive to spur local development (see Chapter 9).

Towards the lagging agricultural sector, Mao urged neither an extractive approach (which he called 'draining the pond to catch the fish') nor one based on coaxing growth from the peasantry by means of market incentives. Instead, local self-reliance was to provide the peasantry with both the incentive and the means to raise yields and output rapidly. Under the auspices of the communes, small rural industries were to spread rapidly over the country, and take on the task of upgrading and modernizing agricultural technology. Initial surpluses for supporting this diversification were to be produced by herculean efforts by the peasantry in intensive cultivation ('deep plowing and close planting') and in the construction of dams, reservoirs, and irrigation and drainage ditches.

All of the outstanding characteristics of the Great Leap are consistent with the logic of Mao's solution to the twin problems of bureaucratism and administrative overcentralization: the establishment of quasi-autonomous localities with the power to allocate resources and distribute income, according to broad criteria enunciated from the centre, but worked out in constant consultation with lower levels (the 'mass line'). The strategy of 'walking on two legs' reserved for the centre control of the major, large-scale modern industries, especially those with substantial forward linkage to other sectors, while ceding other industries to provincial or local control. The rural people's communes were to be institutions of local governance with sufficient size and resource-mobilizing power to make local efforts effective, but also large enough (and few enough) to be effective channels of communication from the centre to the peasantry. The extraordinary labour-intensive efforts of the Leap stemmed from the need to capitalize on the one resource in abundant supply at the local level.

More than anything else, however, what stands out about the Great Leap, as well as about the Cultural Revolution that followed it, is the extreme politicization of economic decision-making (along with virtually all other kinds, as well). This aspect of Chinese life from the late 1950s to the mid-1970s has often been written off as a product of Mao's 'Utopian' ideology, his insistence upon an idealistic view of society that contradicts both the specific requirements of modernization at the moment, and 'human nature' more generally.

By the phrase 'politicization of economic decision-making', I mean three things: first, the extensive use of general criteria of choice (e.g., that industry should support agriculture, that each locality should strive to build up a comprehensive and relatively independent industrial system, that rural incomes should be distributed basically according to work done and secondarily on a per capita 'supply' basis, etc.) that were passed down from the central party and government organs as general directives; second, the fact that these and other guidelines for choice were often expressed in slogan form ('walk on two legs', 'go all out, aim high, strive to build socialism more, faster, better, and more economically', 'both red and expert', 'get going with local methods', etc.);

third, the fact that ideological values came to be substituted for objective engineering or economic standards of choice.

These characteristics of 'politicization' can be seen to follow directly from Mao's response to the problem of bureaucratization. Hostile to both centralized commands and the apolitical market, Mao needed a means of aligning the quasi-autonomous decisions of provinces, municipalities, counties, and communes with the broad directions mapped by the centre. The widespread broadcast of these directions in simple form, capable of being grasped in their essence by everyone and general enough to be adapted to local circumstances, was his solution. The structure of administrative decentralization required such an alternative to market criteria or central commands. At the same time, of course, this alternative did rest upon an anti-élitist and anti-bureaucratic value system, as well as one that had no place for the individualistic values associated with impersonal market forces. And, in seeking to discredit its more conservative opposition, the Maoist response took on a quality of messianic irrationality that led to major disasters and ultimately compromised its own credibility. In retrospect, its weaknesses and failures can be seen to be due in part to problems intrinsic in the 'logic' of the approach itself, and in part to intractability of the social conditions in which the approach was tried—if such a distinction can be made with validity.

The rest of the present chapter deals with the events of the 1955–7 period, during which Mao and the Communist Party groped in a relatively orderly way towards what I have called the administrative decentralization solution to the problems facing China in the mid-1950s.

2 Socialist transformation completed

In the last two chapters we have traced the processes by which private industry and trade were restricted, brought under state control, and partially nationalized and co-operativized; and by which agriculture was gradually reorganized following land reform through the institutions first of mutual aid teams and then of lower-stage co-operatives (LAPCs). We have also seen that, in the case of agriculture, a severe problem of lagging growth and stagnant procurement interacted with—and was in part caused by—the contradictions inherent in the gradual pace of co-operative formation.

Mao Zedong's decisive intervention in July 1955 was meant to resolve these contradictions by pushing co-operativization forward at a much faster rate. In the event, the actual pace far exceeded even his schedule. The ensuing 'socialist high tide' swept industry and commerce into its path as well, in one year virtually eliminating private ownership in the former and vastly reducing it in the latter. In the post-Mao period, many of the problems plaguing China's economy would be traced to the shift in 1955–6 from a policy of gradual collectivization based on progressive development of the productive forces and the principle of persuasion and voluntary agreement, to one of rapid, forward achievement of 'advanced' forms of socialist production relations at a still primitive level of technology and productivity.

2.1   *Collectivization of agriculture*

Midway through the 1950s, the carefully worked out policy of step-by-step progress towards full collectivization of agriculture was abandoned. Until 1954, as Table 5.1 shows, the post-land reform transformation of the villages was limited to the gradual formation of mutual aid teams (MATs). At the end of 1953 about two farm families in five belonged to such teams, less than one-third of which were permanent, year-around teams. The formation of MATs was hardly a radical break with the past, for it built on a long tradition in rural China of banding together for mutual aid during heavy seasons. At the same time, only a few thousand elementary APCs had been formed (see Chapter 4, Sec. 4), with average membership of between twenty and thirty households per co-operative, encompassing only 0.2 per cent of rural households. Even so, the process of organizing MATs and APCs had been marred by widespread violations by local cadres of the principles of stages (e.g., by jumping prematurely to permanent MATs without first going through the stage of seasonal ones, or by jumping directly to co-operative formation); voluntariness (e.g., by accusing peasants refusing to join teams of being counter-revolutionaries, expelling them from peasants' associations, and barring them from obtaining loans or hiring labour); and mutual benefit (e.g., by overvaluing labour relative to draught animals, or using the latter without compensation). These violations, and the resulting decline in peasant incentives, which gave rise to the slaughter of pigs, the sale of draught animals, a decline in subsidiary production, etc., were frankly acknowledged by the government (Walker 1966:11–14).

The first surge of co-operative formation came in 1954, in the course of which some 11 per cent of peasant households were organized into elementary APCs. This campaign occurred simultaneously with the change in party perspective regarding the relative priorities of mechanization and co-operativization, respectively; in the course of 1954, the official position became one of regarding the formation of co-operatives and collectives as the precondition for both agricultural growth in the short run, and mechanization in the long run (Chapter 4, Sec. 2). The need for more rapid agricultural growth, as well as the perceived tendency for 'capitalist' farming practices to arise (often with the explicit encouragement of local cadres), and for social repolarization to occur in the countryside, both seemed to indicate that co-operative formation should be pushed forward. However, the problem lay in achieving this objective without hurting production.

The 1954 campaign to form co-operatives suffered from an even more serious and widespread incidence of the same kinds of errors that occurred in 1952. Walker (1966:19) states that 'perhaps the main single feature of the 1954 campaign was the widespread *discrimination against* the middle peasants in the treatment of their privately owned resources once they had joined cooperatives.' The result was the slaughter, neglect, or sale of large numbers of livestock, a decline in investment and fertilizer collection, especially by middle peasants, and a reduction in winter sown area (Walker 1966:20–1). These

Table 5.1 Steps from private farming to the collectivization of agriculture, 1950–1958 (percentage of all peasant households)

	1950	1951	1952	1953	1954	1955		1956				1958			
						June	Dec.	Jan.	Feb.	June	Dec.	Apr.	Aug.	Sep.	Dec.
Mutual aid teams	11	18	40	39	58	50	n.a.	n.a.	n.a.	n.a.	n.a.	—	—	—	—
of which: Permanent MATs	2	n.a.	10	11	26	28	n.a.	n.a.	n.a.	n.a.	n.a.	—	—	—	—
Elementary APCs	—	—	0.1	0.1	11	14	59	50	36	29	9	—	—	—	—
Advanced APCs	—	—	—	—	—	0.03	4	11	51	63	88	100	70	n.a.	n.a.
Rural people's communes	—	—	—	—	—	—	—	—	—	—	—	—	30	98	99

N.B. Figures are as of the *end* of respective year or month.

Sources: Selden (1981:Table 1); Walker (1965:Table 1, p. 14; 1966).

problems were compounded by unusually severe weather, and gave rise to a suspension of new co-operative formation at the beginning of 1955. Some 20,000 weak and trouble-ridden co-operatives were disbanded, leaving 650,000 in place by June of 1955.

Abuses of the kind mentioned above were so widely discussed in the press that we may get an exaggerated view of their incidence. The fact of their open discussion, and of emphasis on the importance of correcting them, plus the general approach of encouraging flexible local formulas for protecting the interests of both middle and poor peasants, are consistent with the organization of 15 per cent of rural households into co-operatives without disaster, a major accomplishment in itself. Yet, from the viewpoint of Mao Zedong in mid-1955, it was not enough. We have seen (Chapter 4, Sec. 4) that by 1955 it was apparent that the growth rates of agricultural output and of state procurements of agricultural products were falling far short of the requirements of the FFYP. The attempt to meet this problem by putting drastic pressure on the peasants to sell to the state had encountered great resistance and proven counter-productive, and so had been replaced by the 'three-fix' policy, which, while meant to restore peasant incentives, was a step away from solution of the procurement problem in the short run.

In his speech of 31 July 1955, 'On the Cooperative Transformation of Agriculture', which broke the impasse, Mao drew the link between industrialization, agricultural surpluses, and co-operative transformation:

[Some] comrades fail to understand that socialist industrialization cannot be carried out in isolation from the co-operative transformation of agriculture. In the first place, as everyone knows, China's current level of production of commodity grain and raw materials for industry is low, whereas the state's need for them is growing year by year, and this presents a sharp contradiction. If we cannot basically solve the problem of agricultural co-operation within roughly three five-year plans, that is to say, if our agriculture cannot make a leap from small-scale farming with animal-drawn implements to large-scale mechanized farming, along with extensive state-organized land reclamation by settlers using machinery . . ., than we shall fail to resolve the contradiction between the ever-increasing need for commodity grain and industrial raw materials and the present generally low output of staple crops, and we shall run into formidable difficulties in our socialist industrialization and be unable to complete it. [Mao 1977a:196–7]

Until Mao's speech, the majority of the leadership favoured a policy of slowing down co-operative formation to provide time for strengthening rural leadership and solving the difficulties of already existing co-operatives. The process promised to be a very long and drawn-out one, with little prospect of significantly improved output and procurement. As Mao observed, it seemed to dictate rather drastic changes in the heavy industrialization strategy on which the FFYP was based. Yet it was an approach that was perfectly consistent with Mao's own insistence on the principles of voluntariness and mutual benefit.

Mao's speech, delivered to an enlarged work conference of the Central Committee and Party secretaries of provinces and municipalities, considered and rejected the arguments for a slower pace. Dividing the middle peasants into upper and lower-middle strata, Mao argued that the poor and lower-middle peasants, constituting 60–70 per cent of the rural population, were ahead of the party leadership in demanding co-operativization; that the problem of inadequate leadership could be solved only by actual participation of large numbers of people in the struggle to form co-operatives; that the success of most existing APCs in raising output showed that the many problems encountered by the movement could be solved; and that, 'as is clear to everyone', a spontaneous development of capitalism in the countryside was occurring which would lead to increasing class polarization in the absence of more rapid development of co-operatives. Mao continued to insist on careful preparation and adherence to the principles of stages (MAT, elementary APC, advanced APC), of voluntariness, and of mutual benefit. On the other hand, he repeatedly held up the experience of the Soviet collectivization as a model to emulate, a model that conspicuously ignored these principles. While agreeing that China should avoid the 'impetuousness and rashness' that briefly characterized the Soviet experience but was 'quickly corrected', he insisted that 'on no account should we allow these comrades to use the Soviet experience as a cover for their idea of moving at a snail's pace' (Mao 1977a:198): 'Eventually, by a great effort, the Soviet Union successfully accomplished the socialist transformation of the whole of its agriculture and at the same time achieved a massive technical reconstruction of agriculture. This road traversed by the Soviet Union is our model' (1977a:199).

The pace of co-operativization urged by Mao remained a gradual one, even though it was speeded up. By October 1956 the number of APCs would double to 1.3 million and they would embrace 28 per cent of the farm population. By spring of 1958 one-half the farming population would be included; the other half would be organized by 1960. Thus, the entire process of co-operative transformation would take some five years. During that time, advanced APCs (collectives) would gradually begin to form, in unspecified numbers.

This pace contrasts with that published only a few weeks earlier as part of the First Five Year Plan (which, though covering the period 1953–7, was ratified in final form by the National People's Congress only on 30 July 1955—*one day* before Mao's historic speech!). The Plan called for organizing about one-third of farm households into elementary co-operatives by 1957, and 'basically realizing' elementary co-operativization *in the principal agricultural regions* by the end of the *Second* Five Year Plan, i.e. 1962.

The contrast is even greater, however, between Mao's proposed schedule and the actual pace of events immediately following his speech (Table 5.1). By the end of 1955, 59 per cent of peasant households had been organized into elementary co-operatives—thus overachieving Mao's goal for 1958. More stunning still, only one year later the great bulk of rural households—88 per cent—were already in *advanced* co-operatives, or collectives. These facts alone establish that a very large proportion of collectives had been formed without even a single harvest having been experienced in elementary co-operative form. In addition, many households became members of co-operatives, and even of collectives, without passing through the stage of mutual aid teams.

There are a number of reasons why events took on their own logic and left behind the careful formulations of Mao. First, the campaign that started with his 31 July speech quickly made one's attitude towards co-operativization a litmus test of political correctness; in this atmosphere, local cadres won credit not for carefully adhering to voluntariness and mutual benefit, but by organizing co-operatives, one way or another. Second, the poorer peasants appear to have pushed hard for full collectivization as another redistribution of income and wealth benefiting them. In the collectives, the rent portion of co-operative income (i.e., the portion accruing to land shares invested in the APC) was abolished, and all personal income depended on labour alone. Therefore, poorer peasants who had contributed little land stood to gain at the expense of better-off peasants who had contributed relatively large land-holdings.

Third, the process of negotiating formulas for property valuation and income distribution for the co-operatives that would satisfy both the poor peasant interest in a large labour share and the wealthier peasant interest in a large property share (including livestock, fishponds, tools, and fruit trees, in addition to land) was a complicated and difficult task. 'Rather than spend several weeks, even months, trying to solve these difficult problems, it seemed better to leave them behind by forming collectives' (Walker 1966:38). Fourth, the rent share of income was regarded by the government and local cadres as a potential source of additional investment funds. Fifth, the continuing contradictions concerning land use within the co-operatives could be solved at one blow by collec-tivization; as long as private ownership of land was maintained, peasants would be reluctant to allow their own land to be used in ways disadvantageous to them (e.g., flooded for irrigation) while their right to withdraw or sell their land interfered with its full integration into co-operative use.

Sixth, the larger size of collectives would permit the mobilization of more capital and labour for carrying out farmland capital construction, and also would provide better conditions for the introduction of improved machinery and equipment. Seventh, the larger scale, smaller numbers, and lack of property income in collectives were conducive to greater government control of agriculture, an attractive property from the state's viewpoint (Walker 1968:401).

Finally, the current crisis of agricultural production and extraction, which had thrown doubt on the possibility of fulfilling the First Plan, put great pressure on rural cadres to raise agricultural productivity rapidly. In 1956 two events occurred that promised a way out of this impasse: the publication of the draft Twelve Year Programme for Agriculture, and the introduction of the double-wheel double-share plough. Both events were intimately linked with the collectivization movement, and were intended to give the fledgling collectives the vision and the means to bring about substantial output growth.

The draft National Programme for Agricultural Development, 1956–67,[1] was not a plan at all. Its forty articles combine specific targets for yield increases, by broad region of the country, with exhortations about the means of achieving them. What it did not do was provide plans for specific increases in supplies of modern inputs and machinery and equipment for agriculture. Oriented towards social mobilization, it stressed increasing farm labour inputs (to 250 working days per year for men, 120 for women with household responsibilities). The double-wheel double-share plough was a piece of 'intermediate technology' imported from the Soviet Union; it was said to permit a single farmer to plough more land in a given time. The plough had proved useful on dry flatlands, but it turned out to be too bulky and heavy for the wet paddy fields. Before this became clear to the central leadership, however, Mao personally championed the device as the technical secret weapon of the new co-operatives—unlike most individual families, the co-operatives could afford the new ploughs, and would therefore use them to achieve technical superiority over private agriculture. In 1956 and 1957 3.6 million of these ploughs were produced (Chao 1970:102), representing a substantial commitment of steel, before the implement all but disappeared from the scene.[2]

It is easy to fault the 'high tide' of collectivization in retrospect. Yet the choices facing China's leadership in 1955 were hard ones. It seemed to Mao that a failure to stimulate rapid agricultural growth would force the curtailment of the rapid industrialization strategy centred on heavy industrial growth. The inherent contradictions of gradualism in the socialist transformation of agriculture seemed to rule out, for a long time, fast enough growth in farm production. Once an accelerated pace was adopted, it became difficult and risky for better-off peasants to choose to remain outside the co-operatives; whereas—as Bernstein (1967:45) points out—'the regime did not turn collectivization and related policies such as grain purchase into a complete disaster for the middle peasants, as had been the case in the Soviet Union. This circumstance greatly facilitated their compliance.'

Thus the political strength of the Party in the countryside, the enthusiasm of a large fraction of poorer peasants for a further redistribution of land and productive assets, and the widespread—if short-lived—enthusiasm for the potential of collectivization to raise output dramatically brought about full collectivization against surprisingly little resistance. One might speculate about the possible outcomes of an alternative strategy: one of much less emphasis on heavy industry, with substantially more resources within industry devoted to farm inputs (e.g., chemical fertilizer), and with greater investment in agriculture itself; of adherence to the original, gradual programme of voluntary co-operation, with the state differentially allocating increased supplies of machinery, equipment, and current inputs to the co-operatives to encourage their success.[3] But the impact of the Korean War, together with the Soviet example, seemed to make rapid heavy industrialization a *sine qua non*, at least to Mao Zedong. From that constraint followed Mao's case for the forced pace that collectivization actually took. However, Mao and his central supporters alone could not have brought about the 'high tide'. As one student of collectivization concludes, 'The peasant constituency for a swifter transition was clearly in place; the demand for it was voiced by a restless village cadre force. Mao merely advocated that the potential for swift action on behalf of the poorest be utilized . . .' (Shue 1981:332).

During its 'adventurist' phase in late 1955 and early 1956, the drive to collectivize ignored central directives on protecting the right of co-operative and collective members to retain private plots equal to 5 per cent of per capita cultivated land in their village, and peasants were frequently underpaid for their tools and draught animals. The result was a decline in the already inadequate population of draught animals and a sharp fall in the number of pigs and poultry (Walker 1965:54, 59–63).

In addition, collectivization for the first time subjected virtually the entire peasantry to direct control of productive activities by the government. That such control was a prime motive of the leadership in encouraging rapid collectivization is made clear by statements such as the following by Deng Zihui (Teng Tzu-hui), a Central Committee specialist on agriculture, in 1955: 'Individual peasants cannot be directly controlled by the State plan. They formulate their production plans according to their own requirements and particularities; they cannot formulate plans according to the requirements of the State' (Chao 1960:152).

In this respect, the *de jure* independence of collectively owned entities was not respected *de facto*. The forcing of the double-wheel double-share plough on the collectives was only the most dramatic example of this centralization of decision-making in agriculture. County-level cadres, themselves under pressure from higher levels to meet excessively high plan targets, in turn dictated to the collectives concerning double-cropping, close planting, use of new seed types, and other technical measures that were frequently unsuitable to local conditions (Walker 1966:418–25; Shue 1981:312–13). Finally, in the autumn of 1956 the government moved to correct the worst abuses by returning operational autonomy to the collectives, condemning the undervaluation of collectivized animals, reaffirming the importance of private plots, and otherwise restoring material incentives.

The size of the collective was also reduced in 1957 in the attempt to improve management and incentives. The several hundred advanced APCs that had already existed before the 'high tide' had an average membership of 76 households. During 1956 the amalgamation of elementary APCs to form collectives gave rise to very large units, averaging some 344 households per collective. When these were split up in 1957, Chinese agriculture consisted of some 740,000 collectives averaging 164 households in each, but with considerable variation in size by region of the country (Chao 1960:162, 293).

The collective was the basic unit of organization in rural China for about two years. It owned the land, draught animals, and large farm implements previously owned by its individual members, who were supposed to have been compensated at rates worked out in group discussion. 'Household goods . . . and small holdings of trees, poultry, domestic animals, small farm tools, and tools needed for subsidiary cottage occupations' were to be retained as the private property of individual members ('Model Regulations for Advanced APC', in Chao 1960:314). Also, land not exceeding 5 per cent of the average per capita cultivated area was to be allocated to individual households for raising vegetables, poultry, and so forth.

The collective had to pay the agricultural tax, deduct from gross income the production expenses of the coming year, and set aside an accumulation fund (for investment in capital construction and repayment of loans) limited to 8 per cent of net income, and a welfare fund limited to 2 per cent. The remainder was to be distributed to members in accordance with the total number of labour-days credited to each. These could be accumulated for agricultural and subsidiary work, for management work within the co-operative, and as bonuses to both work brigades and individuals.

The production brigade (later called 'small brigade' or 'team' under the communes) was the basic unit of work organization within the collective and was roughly equivalent in size to the former elementary co-operative (where these had existed at all) of twenty or thirty households. This unit had comparative longevity in rural China, taking on even greater importance as the 'basic accounting unit' under the commune system from the early 1960s on. Production brigades existed both for basic field work and for subsidiary occupations. Thus, the level at which income accrued and was distributed (i.e., the collective) differed from that at which labour was organized and work done (the brigade). This was to be regarded as a 'contradiction' that was overcome only with the decentralization of the commune in the early 1960s. The collective had—and often exercised—the ability to redistribute income from more productive to less productive brigades. Done arbitrarily or excessively, this hurt incentives in both kinds of brigades.

Within brigades, income depended upon each individual's accumulation of labour-days or work-points (a standard labour-day generally was equal to ten work-points). There were several methods of calculating labour-days (see Shue 1981:300–8; and Parish and Whyte 1978:62–7 for good discussions). One was to evaluate each member's strength and skill and assign him/her a basic labour-day value accordingly, adding to or subtracting from it daily according to the quantity and quality of the day's work. Another was to evaluate *tasks* and assign work-points to individuals or teams in accordance with their performance of the tasks. A popular version of this system (*sanbao yijiang*, or 'three guarantees and one reward') judged performance by ultimate output: the co-operative guaranteed the capital and equipment needed by the team, which in turn guaranteed the necessary work and resulting output, and received a bonus for overfulfilment. However allotted, the work-point's value was precisely known only when the harvest was in, for it was determined by dividing the total net income of the collective by the total number of work-points awarded.

The work-point system bore a heavy burden. Previously, each peasant household's income depended mainly upon the quantity and quality of its work—given its land, equipment, and weather conditions. The whip of necessity was a goad to careful and diligent labour. In the collectives, however, each household's income was calculated as a portion of the total income of from one to three hundred households. The method of calculation determined the closeness of the linkage between individual effort and reward, but this relation could not be as immediate or as automatic as it had been previously. Moreover, the process of working out and implementing the linkage formula now required care and effort. There were several important issues involved in this process that continued to demand attention until the collectives were dismantled after 1978.

First, there was the issue of size: over what unit should the value of the work-point be calculated? The larger the unit, the more averaging of output from fields of different fertility and from teams and individuals of different productivity; hence the weaker the link between individual effort and individual income. The smaller the unit, the stronger this link, but the smaller also the incentive for individuals and teams to feel responsibility for their neighbours' work and conditions: hence less concern for comprehensive water conservancy projects or for helping to combat natural disasters in surrounding areas. This issue was initially decided in favour of calculating work-point value at the level of the collective itself; but, especially in 1956, when collectives were very large, this decision aroused resentment among more diligent individuals and groups and those with better conditions. Even the smaller collectives of 1957–8 (166 households) required considerably more averaging than later during the 1960s, when the production team of 20–30 households became the basic income-distributing unit.

Second, there was the problem of allocating labour among different tasks. The individual farmer, with survival at stake, could determine more or less accurately what needed to be done and when. At the collective level, however, the number of tasks multiplied, and the allocation had to be determined for tens or even hundreds of individuals. In one county in Hebei Province, 123 farm tasks were identified and divided into five categories according to strength and skill requirements, relative unpleasantness of work, etc. Standards of performance had to be worked out for each task, and then work-point values attached to the standards (Walker 1966:428). Unless such evaluation was done very carefully, peasants would seek to avoid those tasks they considered undervalued and would cluster to the well-rewarded ones; or, if technical standards were badly set, they would finish tasks in quantity to earn the work-points, but would do a poor job. The preoccupation with work-point systems could and did give rise to an attitude of 'work-pointism' on the part of peasants—a substitution of the pursuit of work-points for the high-quality performance of farm tasks themselves.

Third, how often should the work of small groups or individuals be evaluated? Possibilities ranged from checking each day's work in the evening and allocating work-points daily—an exhausting and time-consuming process—to evaluating an individual's overall performance only once or twice a year. Alternatively, as in the 'three guarantees and one reward' system, the final output could be taken as evidence of performance; this system entailed considerable decentralization of authority down to the individual household or small work group. Different tasks were suitable to different systems: those of a long-term nature with a definite output might be handled by long-term contract ('three guarantees and one reward'), whereas short-run and seasonal tasks required a more frequently evaluated piecework system.

Fourth, there was the issue of proper criteria for evaluation of individual performance. While it was generally agreed that quantity and quality of work were primary considerations, other things than brute strength and dextrous hands went into being a good farmer: the ability to take initiative in responding to sudden emergencies and unanticipated difficulties, helpfulness to others, etc. Collectivization both put a premium on such group-oriented qualities and created for them a previously non-existent quasi-market in which they required valuation in work-points. Yet by nature these qualities were intangible and not easily evaluated.

Fifth, how should the productive contribution of women be treated? In theory, government and Party operated by the principle of equal pay for equal work, regardless of sex. In practice, 'women's work' was almost universally undervalued relative to that of men, and women automatically received lower work-point norm ratings. A number of rationales existed for this (Croll 1979: 28–31). In practice, it led to reduced enthusiasm for collective labour on the part of women, who often found that it made more sense to keep to household tasks or work on their private plots.

Sixth, any capital construction work undertaken during the off-season—e.g., building water conservancy works, irrigation canals, etc.—unless it increased farm output immediately, had the effect of diluting the value of the work-point for the year in question. This was widely resented in 1956, when much labour was thrown into construction projects during the winter season. The government reacted by directing that work be concentrated on projects with immediate pay-offs, that work-points for long-range projects be 'banked' until the higher output occurred, and that some work be done voluntarily by collective members. While such measures were in and of themselves sensible, they, too, were capable of being abused, as by requiring too much 'voluntary' labour or undertaking insufficient amounts of long-term construction work. This issue of 'labour accumulation' and the proper way to organize and pay for it was to remain a problem throughout subsequent years.

Seventh, members with special problems required special consideration. Dependants of soldiers, old people without grown children to support them, and the disabled and ill needed help, ranging from the assignment of light tasks carrying work-point values to outright relief payments. The existence of the collective, with its welfare fund, meant a margin of security that did not exist under private farming for the especially needy. On the other hand, some previously available means of handling such problems now disappeared; for example, before collectivization, an elderly or disabled person with a bit of land could rent it out and live on the proceeds. The relative responsibility assigned to family members and to the collective for supporting such people would determine the size of the welfare fund and therefore would affect the value of the work-point.

Finally, there was the problem of paying for administration and management activities. These constituted an entire range of work that had not previously existed, and for which, moreover, the link with output was neither direct nor obvious. The model regulations for collectives laid down certain limits: the number of labour-days assigned for full- and part-time managerial work should not exceed 2 per cent of the total number of labour-days earned by collective

members (Chao 1960:320). Inflation of management costs would reduce the
work-point value for labouring members: but there was also the possibility that
members would reduce wages of managers to levels that would breed
resentment or apathy among the latter (Walker 1966:427-8).

From this list it is evident that the problems of organizing production and
distribution in the new units were formidable—even after the added compli-
cation of deducting a *property share* had been eliminated by collectivization.
The fact that farm output continued to rise throughout this tempestuous
period (Wiens 1980:68) is a tribute to the efforts of cadres and peasants in
handling such problems.

2.2   Socialist transformation of industry and commerce

The 'high tide' of collectivization in agriculture gave rise to a similar movement
in industry and trade: for a few months in 1956, virtually all economic activity
in China was undergoing rapid and clamorous reorganization. In industry, the
target of this activity was the formation not of collectives, but rather of joint
state–private enterprises, referred to as 'state-capitalist' in character. The
former owners/managers in essence became state employees while receiving
interest payments on the value—estimated by the state—of their shares in the
enterprises.

We have seen in Chapter 3 (Table 3.1) that by 1952, the end of the
Rehabilitation period, state-owned enterprises already produced over half of
gross industrial output value, and another 27 per cent was produced by
'state-capitalist' enterprises—a term that designates not only joint state–
private ownership, but also privately owned firms producing on government
order. At that time the former variant, under which state control is direct and
virtually complete, was in the minority, producing only 5 per cent of industrial
output (Table 5.2).

By 1953, after the 'five-anti' movement, there were more than a thousand
joint enterprises, employing 270,000 people and producing about Y2 billion
annually. The first spurt in the formation of joint enterprises came in 1954.
Relatively large private establishments were the target, and by the end of the
year the proportion of industrial output produced in jointly owned firms had
more than doubled (Table 5.2). Additional if somewhat slower progress was
made in 1955, at the end of which private industry accounted for only 16.2
per cent of gross industrial output, and more than three-quarters of this was
produced to state order and thus within the sphere of 'state capitalism'.

The final transformation began in January 1956, in the atmosphere of the
rural 'high tide'. It reflected a realization on the part of remaining private
businesspeople that their end was in sight, that their ability to hold out as
private owners was fast disappearing, and that it was best to avoid acquiring
the reputation of die-hard capitalists. Mao Zedong also intervened strategically
in November 1955 by assuring a group of representative businessmen that,
following their transformation, adequate arrangements would be made for their
work, livelihood, income, and political status (Xue *et al*. 1960:219). From

Table 5.2. Socialist transformation of industry: percentage distribution of gross value of industrial output (excluding handicrafts)

	(1) Socialist Industry	State-capitalist industry			(5) 'Pure capitalist' industry	(6) Private industry (4) + (5)
		(2) Total	(3) Joint state–private enterprises	(4) Private enterprises executing state orders		
1949	34.7	9.5	2.0	7.5	55.8	63.3
1950	45.3	17.8	2.9	14.9	36.7	51.6
1951	45.9	25.4	4.0	21.4	28.7	50.0
1952	56.0	26.9	5.0	21.9	17.1	39.0
1953	57.5	28.5	5.7	22.8	14.0	36.8
1954	62.8	31.9	12.3	19.6	5.3	24.9
1955	67.7	29.3	16.1	13.2	3.0	16.2
1956	67.5	32.5	32.5	—	—	—

Source: Ten Great Years (1960:38).

January 1956 on, the capitalists of Beijing, Shanghai, Tianjin, and other major cities petitioned to change over to joint operation by entire trades, and private enterprise in industry was virtually eliminated. Moreover, whereas before the 'high tide' former owners shared profits of joint enterprises with their new state partners, and continued to exercise some influence on management, this was no longer the case after 1956. Their ownership status was now reduced to coupon-clipping, and their managerial role to carrying out state orders.

The assessment of private assets and liabilities resulted in a grand total of Y2.4 billion (about $1 billion) of private shares in joint enterprises of all kinds in China at the end of 1956. This broke down into Y1.7 billion for industrial enterprises, Y0.6 billion for commercial, catering, and personal service firms, and Y0.1 billion for transport and communications enterprises (Xue *et al.* 1960:220).

For giving up control as well as ownership of their firms, capitalists received in return fixed interest payments, irrespective of profitability. Usually equal to 5 per cent of the assessed value of their shares, these payments began on 1 January 1956 and were to continue for seven years until the end of 1962. The time period was later extended and came to an end finally in September 1966 amidst a new 'high tide'—that of the Cultural Revolution (*BR*, 28 April 1980:19).

A total of 1,140,000 persons received fixed interest from the state, including some 380,000 'small shareholders who were not themselves capitalists' and 760,000 'private industrialists and businessmen' (*BR*, 28 April 1980:20–1).[4] Of the latter number, about one-third were said to be still working in various enterprises in 1980, the rest having died or retired. The total amount of money paid out in fixed interest over the roughly ten years ending September 1966 came to Y1.2 billion (US$0.5 billion at the then rate of exchange), or one-half the estimated value of private shares, amounting to an average annual payment of $44 per recipient. Recent (but undated) statistics on those former capitalists still working in Beijing, Shanghai, Tianjin, and Guangzhou give the following distribution of their monthly salary incomes:

% of former capitalists	Earning category (yuan/month)
21.3	less than 50
58.0	50–100
17.7	100–200
2.3	200–300
0.7	more than 300

As the source points out, this distribution 'places the wages of most former industrialists and businessmen roughly on a par with ordinary skilled workers' (*BR*, 28 April 1980:20–1).

The pace of handicraft transformation basically followed that of industry and agriculture. Handicrafts were (and remain) a very important part of the Chinese economy. In 1954 there were some 20 million people engaged in individual handicraft production, of whom between 8 and 9 million were independent artisans and the rest peasants who engaged part-time in commercial handicraft production. Together, these two groups produced about one-fifth of the gross industrial output.[5] Besides being a principal source of supply of everyday consumer goods, tools, and utensils for most of the population, handicrafts provided employment, a chance to supplement meagre agricultural earnings, and a large number of traditional art and craft products that have remained earners of foreign exchange.

In handicrafts, socialist transformation took the form of co-operativization. As in agriculture, intermediate forms of organization were devised—especially supply and marketing groups, and co-operatives that enabled individual craftspeople to join forces in procuring raw materials and selling output while remaining independent units of production. But, also as in agriculture, this step-by-step process was swept aside in the 'high tide' of 1956. Whereas in 1955 about 27 per cent of artisans were organized in groups of co-operatives of some kind (see Table 5.3, which is inclusive of all such co-operative arrangements), at the beginning of 1956 'the handicraftsmen in entire regions and trades became organized right away into producers' co-operatives based on collective ownership, bypassing the step of the supply and marketing co-operatives' (Xue et al. 1960:154).

Even before the 'high tide', quite a few handicraft occupations had suffered difficulties owing to the increasing competition from state-operated factories which enjoyed superior access to raw materials. Native oil-pressing, cotton spinning, and sugar refining were among occupations that suffered between 1953 and 1956, as a by-product of the drive to modernize and centralize production, with concomitant losses to rural income and employment (Selden 1981:23–5). The 'high tide' of 1956 was later called too hasty, with its premature attempts to centralize production, pool profits and losses over entire trades, and concentrate management. The result was to deprive handicrafts of much of the flexibility, variety, and responsiveness to local demand that were its hallmarks.

There was also a tendency to raid handicrafts for skilled workers for state industry. During the first nine months of 1956, for example, more than 12,000 skilled workers in Tianjin handicraft trades were transferred to state factories and industrial construction projects (Xue et al. 1960:143). The amalgamation of handicraft co-operatives into state factories and the shift of their personnel to factory and construction work is probably responsible for the sharp drop of more than 1.6 million, or around 20 per cent, in total handicraft employment between 1955 and 1956.[6] This problem would become much sharper two years later during the Great Leap Forward.

The state moved quickly to control the bulk of wholesale trade in the early 1950s (Chapter 3, Sec. 2). Retail trade progressed more slowly. The temporal pattern of its transformation appears in Table 5.4 to resemble that of industry (Table 5.2), but there is evidence that in fact it lagged considerably behind, particularly in that much of the trade labelled 'state capitalist and other co-operative' was transformed largely in name only (Solinger 1980:3). This was

Table 5.3. *Formation of handicraft co-operatives*

	No. of handicraft persons ('000)			Percentage distribution	
	Total	In co-ops	In individual handicrafts	In co-ops	In individual handicrafts
1952	7364	228	7136	3.1	96.9
1953	7789	301	7488	3.9	96.1
1954	8910	1213	7697	13.6	86.4
1955	8202	2206	5996	26.9	73.1
1956	6583	6039	544	91.7	8.3

Source: *Ten Great Years* (1960:36).

due to its generally small scale and scattered nature: there were millions of small shopkeepers, stall operators, pushcart and pole pedlars, and itinerant merchants in urban and rural China. Their value lay precisely in their flexibility, mobility, and adaptability; there were few if any technological advantages to be gained from amalgamation and concentration. Although the same kinds of excesses in this direction occurred in trade as in other sectors during the 'high tide', they seem to have been halted more quickly.

By 1957, the first step in a two-step attack on the 'contradictions' facing Chinese society and economy had been completed. With farm production lagging, state procurement of agricultural goods stagnant, centralized control of the economy proving increasingly inefficient, unemployment a persistent problem, and the issues dubbed by Mao the 'ten major relations' calling for attention, the Chairman pushed the leadership towards a strategy more in keeping with his own predilections. Instead of a highly centralized,

Table 5.4. *Transformation of the ownership system in retail trade (percentage distribution of retail sales)*

	State-owned stores and supply and marketing co-ops	State capitalist and other co-operative trade	Private trade
1950	14.9	0.1	85.0
1951	24.4	0.1	75.5
1952	42.6	0.2	57.2
1953	49.7	0.4	49.9
1954	69.0	5.4	25.6
1955	67.6	14.6	17.8
1956	68.3	27.5	4.2
1957	65.7	31.6	2.7

Source: *Ten Great Years* (1960:40); Xue (1977:15).

bureaucratic command system, there was to be administrative decentralization, with greater initiative in the hands of local party and government organs.

Collectivization, especially in agriculture, established the basic-level units on which such a system would rest. It provided a political impetus for the social mobilization strategy inherent in the administrative decentralization approach by once again playing to the interests of the poorer peasants. The new units—collectives, co-operatives, joint state–private enterprises—were now subject to direct control by local party cadres. The close organizational and ideological links of these cadres with the centre would ensure the exercise of their new powers of initiative on behalf of correct policies.

The second step was to make the system of planning and management compatible with the new approach. Less than a year after completion of the 'high tide', this reform was begun.

3   The 1957–8 decentralization

In late 1957 and 1958, a series of State Council directives were announced decentralizing the planning and management system for industry, commerce, and finance. Although further changes occurred subsequently, including another major decentralization in 1970, the reform of the late 1950s was until recently generally taken to have established the principal outlines of the planning and management system that endured until the reforms of the mid-1980s began (see Chapter 14). Indeed, Mao's answer to the problem of rigid overcentralization and heavy-handed bureaucratism inherent in the acquired Soviet system of planning and management is usually seen as achieving its structural foundations in the 1957–8 reforms. More recently, the extent to which these reforms actually decentralized control over resource allocation has been sharply questioned, notably by Nicholas Lardy (1978a). Moreover, the critique of China's system of planning and management launched within China in the late 1970s suggests that the reforms in question marked less a watershed in the economic history of the People's Republic than one phase of a recurrent cycle of tightening and loosening of central control, as the leadership struggled alternately to check extremes of centralization and anarchy. Nevertheless, as the first attempt to restructure the planning and management system to suit Chinese conditions, and as the move which set the stage for the Great Leap Forward, the 1957–8 reforms deserve attention. More than that, the issues surrounding the reform are not only the same ones that would haunt China for the next quarter-century (at least); they are also the same issues that face other centrally planned economies, and whose treatment will ultimately determine the future evolution of these economies.

Under the Soviet-type system, the central government translated its broad economic objectives into a set of specific output targets for individual industries. The process of establishing these targets, or quotas, was to be grounded on certain givens: the current production capacity of industries, the supply of resources, technical coefficients of industries (i.e., required amounts of specific inputs per unit of output), opportunities for utilizing foreign trade. The problem was to expand the economy in the direction desired by the planners while avoiding or minimizing shortages of some products and surpluses of others—in other words, to achieve a consistent plan in which all output was fully used and none was redundant. The objective of matching supply and demand required the establishment of various balances—material balances for production and distribution of goods, labour balances for the allocation of available labour supplies, energy balances for fuel and power production and allocation. Corresponding to the material balances were financial balances, consisting chiefly of arrangements for the money income and expenditures of the population, the state budget, the cash and credit plans of the banking system, and the income and expenditure plans of economic sectors, compiled from those of individual enterprises.[7] The central plan not only encompassed economic sectors *per se*, but extended as well to the development of the health care, educational, and cultural systems.

The most important producer goods and raw materials—steel, coal, power, etc.—were balanced directly by the central government. There were only 28 such centrally allocated goods in the year before the First Plan, 1952, but this number grew steadily, reaching 235 by 1956 (Lardy 1978a:15). Moreover, the activities of the individual enterprises producing such goods in the central state sector were largely determined from above. Thus, output quantity, variety, and quality targets; equipment utilization, maintenance, and repair schedules; sources of supply and consumption rates of raw materials and working capital; distribution of the product; total work-force, working hours, wage rates; and much else as well were specified in the enterprise annual plan, which was negotiated with and approved by the State Economic Commission.

Central plans were vertically organized; the plan for each economic sector was supervised by the relevant central ministry and was national in scope. In addition, provinces and localities also made plans that were 'horizontally' organized on the territorial principle and covered all sectors within the relevant jurisdiction but only those enterprises that were under provincial (or local) control. In the early 1950s the predominance of handicrafts and small privately owned firms among industrial and commercial enterprises caused a large share of non-agricultural output to remain in the horizontal planning system. But the heavy commitment of the First Plan to development of central state-operated enterprises increased the centre's share of total industrial output to almost one-half by the end of the Plan. Moreover, the central government increasingly encroached upon the nominal authority of local governments to plan the activities of their own enterprises (Lardy 1978a:7–19).

Mao in 1956 described the situation quizzically:

At present scores of hands are reaching out to the localities, making things difficult for them . . . Since the various ministries don't think it proper to issue them [orders] to the Party committees and people's councils at the provincial level, they establish direct contact with the relevant departments and bureaus in the provinces and municipalities and give them orders every day. These orders are all supposed to come from the central authorities, even though neither the Central Committee of the Party nor the State Council knows anything about them, and they put a great strain on the local authorities.

There is such a flood of statistical forms that they become a scourge. This state of affairs must be changed. [Mao 1977d:16]

The pronounced centralization that developed in the course of the First Plan had its advantages. Structural change was the order of the day. The rapid shift in the relative proportions of consumer goods and producer goods in total output, and in the geographic disposition of industry from the coastal regions to the hinterland, arguably required highly centralized allocation of resources. There was also the consideration of equity; the Party was committed to reducing the sharp regional inequalities in the level of development and distribution of services; and, as we shall see, central control over resources was effectively used to this end during the First Plan period. A greater degree of regional and local autonomy would very likely have pushed Chinese development along the common international path of widening distributive inequality.

But the costs of centralization were also high, and as the desired structural shifts were brought about, while the size and complexity of the economy rapidly increased, the balance of benefits and costs shifted against the former. Especially was this the case after the sudden elimination of the private sector in 1956, which drastically increased the number of enterprises under the direct jurisdiction of the central planning apparatus, and simultaneously eliminated the role of the market in distributing many goods and services, which now had to be handled exclusively by state distribution channels.

An extensive discussion of the costs of centralization took place after the circulation of Mao's 'Ten Major Relationships' speech in April 1956 (Mao 1977). Mao advocated enlarging the powers of the provinces and localities and also called more vaguely for increasing the authority of the individual enterprise.

In the wake of this speech, many pressing problems of co-ordination, control, and motivation were revealed as consequences of excessive centralization. Central decisions were often based on inadequate or erroneous information, while local governments possessing the correct information were powerless to use it. Local governments were also unable effectively to plan and co-ordinate activities within their jurisdiction, because so many of these activities came under the authority of the vertically organized central planning system. Often, local and central authorities would duplicate each other's efforts within a region, leading to waste, redundancy, and competition for materials. The 'local initiative' problem was particularly severe: under the consolidated state budget system, local expenditures were determined by the centre and bore no relation to local revenues. This of course weakened the incentive of the localities to increase their revenues and to engage in local development efforts.

Not only were the costs of excessively centralized control over resource allocation and financial affairs growing unacceptably high as the economy increased in size and complexity; other policy considerations that came to the fore in the mid-1950s also militated in favour of a less centralized approach. First, it became apparent that agricultural development would require more attention than it had received under the FFYP. But effective stimulation of agriculture was clearly beyond the reach of the central government; paying more attention to agriculture meant necessarily enlarging the role of provincial and local authorities. Second, by the mid-1950s the cost of the long gestation periods associated with the large-scale, heavy industrial FFYP projects had become apparent. The biggest of these projects had been financed with Soviet credits, no more of which had been made available to China after 1955. Accordingly, the government began to plan for more medium- and small-scale projects which would be less dependent on external support, quicker to begin producing, and capable of providing more employment. This, too, lent impetus to the cause of decentralization.[8]

Although, as we have seen, Mao's 1956 speech on 'The Ten Major Relationships' included a vague call for increased enterprise authority, the bulk of its discussion of decentralization concerned giving greater power to local administrative units, which is indeed what happened. Lardy (1978a:25–8) suggests several reasons for this outcome: the less developed state of China's economy relative to those of the Soviet Union and Eastern Europe, where market-oriented reforms began to be discussed seriously in the 1950s; China's continuing labour surplus, in contrast to the increasing tightness of the labour market in the more advanced socialist countries; and the relatively unimportant role of foreign trade in China's quasi-continental economy, as opposed to the dependence of small countries, such as Hungary, on the world market, whose prices and incentives they may need to adopt to be competitive.

Nevertheless, the idea of giving greater autonomy to enterprises and allowing the market a greater role did get some support in the course of the debate. At least two of China's pre-eminent economists—Chen Yun, then Minister of Commerce, and Xue Muqiao, then chief of the State Statistical Bureau—favoured it (Schurmann 1968:196–7). Their suggestions focused on an aspect of central planning usually not highlighted in Western discussions, viz., the distinction between control by economic agencies directly under the State Council, on the one hand, and by the separate ministries, on the other.[9] Ministerial control is associated with professionalism and expertise, whereas State Council jurisdiction means the primacy of political over economic objectives. More authority for the ministries implies more professional direction of economic affairs according to economic criteria, but without the uncertainties associated with the market. An imperfect foreign analogue of ministerial control is the large corporation, efficiently organized and somewhat sheltered from market forces. This approach would in fact be attacked during the Cultural Revolution as equivalent to monopoly control by 'trusts' in capitalist countries.

As Schurmann (1968:197–8) interprets the Chen Yun–Xue Muqiao position of 1956–7, it had the following dimensions: (1) an increased role for the market in co-ordinating production and distribution and providing incentives to the individual producing units; (2) greater attention to light industry, especially consumer goods industries, in order to make market incentives effective; (3) a trimming of the authority of provinces and localities between the enhanced power of the central ministries, on the one hand, and the greater autonomy of market-oriented enterprises, on the other; and hence (4) a reduced role for the powerful regional party apparatus that dominated provincial administrations. In this view, the Chen–Xue strategy implied (1) less emphasis on social mobilization of the 'socialist high tide' sort and greater use of material incentives; and (2) less dependence on Soviet or other external assistance in comparison with what had been required by the heavy industry approach of the FFYP. Most parties to the debate agreed on the need for some kind of decentralization, and on the importance of stepping up agricultural growth as well as the growth of light industry; what they disagreed about was the *kind* of decentralization, the approach to speeding up growth in agriculture, and the desirable target rate of growth.

At stake was the question of *control*—how much direct control the Party should continue to exercise over economic affairs. The market socialist option (which Schurmann calls 'decentralization I', or decentralization to the individual enterprise) involves a loss of direct control by the Party as a whole; the administrative decentralization approach (Schurmann's 'decentralization II') means a redistribution of party control from centre to regions.

In addition to (although linked with) the question of control was one of *distribution*. Both kinds of decentralization were likely to increase the relative access to resources of more advanced provinces and localities, in comparison with the highly centralized system under which resources were routinely transferred from richer to poorer regions. There was also a question of *values* at issue: centralized control could be exercised according to broad, political criteria (control by the State Council) or according to narrower, economic criteria (control by the ministries). Decentralized control would clearly be less political in nature under a market-oriented variant, but even administrative decentralization would give rise to a range of possible objectives, from the 'purely' economic (e.g., maximizing local growth) to the largely ideological, and including the desire to enhance local bureaucratic power. Finally, there was an *incentive* problem to consider: how could workers, managers, and local planners best be motivated towards diligence and efficiency while gearing their work to the central plan?

Mao's chosen strategy—administrative decentralization—contained an answer to these questions: social mobilization and the intense propagation of correct ideological values would ensure appropriate distribution, effective incentives, the right use of local powers, and, *therefore*, adequate central control. The State Council decisions announced on 18 November 1957 embraced the organizational underpinnings of this strategy by endorsing administrative decentralization.[10]

The directive reforming industrial management passed control of the vast majority of light industrial enterprises (with the exception of textiles) from the central government to provincial governments, along with heavy industrial enterprises other than large-scale units in strategically important sectors.[11] It also applied the principle of 'dual leadership' by both central and provincial authorities to all enterprises still under central control. Unlike the case for enterprises that were originally under local control, however, the profits of the newly decentralized enterprises were to be split between centre and province with the former retaining 80 per cent. The same 80–20 division was applied for the profits of enterprises (e.g., textiles) still under central control, except for those in certain large-scale and/or strategically important heavy industries. The result of these provisions was, at least on paper, a substantial increase in the share of total industrial profits going to localities. Provincial governments were also given greater authority over the distribution of materials in their jurisdictions, including materials supplied to centrally managed enterprises; over the distribution of output of provincial factories producing goods subject to unified distribution; and over the allocation of personnel in centrally operated enterprises.

Enterprise managers got some greater measure of authority from the reduction in the number of mandatory targets set by the State Council from twelve to only four: (1) quantities of important products; (2) total employment; (3) the total wage bill; and (4) total profit. Such previously assigned norms as rate of cost reduction, average wage, and labour productivity were now left up to the individual enterprise management. Schurmann (1968:209) argues that if this reform had been fully carried out along with the others, which increased provincial authority, 'a kind of checks-and-balance condition would have been created, marked by the juxtaposed authorities of provincial cadres and enterprise managers. This would have impeded centralization of power at the regional level.' Since such provincial centralization in fact occurred, he argues, the provision enlarging enterprise authority must have remained largely unimplemented.

However, a closer look at the latter would seem to indicate that its implementation was not really a threat to greater provincial authority. Enterprises were allowed somewhat greater flexibility in running their own affairs, instead of being bound by detailed orders that left them absolutely no initiative. For instance, given the (still prescribed) profit target, the enterprise now had some room for manoeuvre in trying to achieve it, whereas previously the profit target had been a more or less redundant supplement to the mandatory targets for output quantity and value, rate and amount of cost reduction, important technical economic quotas, average wage, and total wage bill. However, significant control over resource allocation, such as the right to obtain supplies and sell products on the market, or to keep and use a substantial share of profits, or to decide product quantity and variety, was *not* given to enterprises by the reform; and it was only power of these kinds that would have constituted a contradiction with the administrative decentralization measures. In short, the enhancement of enterprise authority was designed to permit more effective enterprise management by those closest to the problems concerned, but not to enlarge the role of the market in any significant sense.

The *commercial* reforms passed control over the vast majority of commercial enterprises to local management. Provincial authority to set prices was greatly expanded. The number of targets of commercial enterprises set by the centre was reduced to four, as in the case of industry, and a similar profit-sharing arrangement between centre and localities was instituted. Provinces were also given an increased say over the planned purchase and supply of grain, and, after a five-year period during which their quotas for grain deliveries to the centre were fixed, control of future increases in this quota (Donnithorne 1967:287–8; Lardy 1978:32–3). The main features of the *financial* reform are summarized as follows by Lardy:

Provincial tax authority was expanded by setting forth a number of cases in which provinces could adjust tax rates and change the coverage of certain taxes. Decentralization of financial management expanded the scope of revenues and expenditures of local governments and in addition gave provincial governments more control over the composition of their expenditures. Extra budgetary revenues of local governments also were expanded and local governments were given increased authority over the use of budgetary surpluses. [Lardy 1978a:33]

The decentralization of authority from centre to provinces was matched by an analogous handing down of power from the latter to sub-provincial units. Administrative districts and counties now found themselves controlling small enterprises that had previously been under provincial jurisdiction.

The trend marked by the November 1957 reforms towards increasing the scope of horizontal (or territorial) planning at the expense of vertical control was considerably strengthened by additional measures announced in September 1958, which gave the provinces the power to plan for *all* enterprises within their territory, including those operated by the central government. In addition, the provinces were now given very far-reaching control over commodity distribution, the allocation of production materials, and the labour plan for their territories; and the number of targets set for them by the central government was greatly reduced (Donnithorne 1967:461–3). Such crucial targets as the output of the most important products, total capital investment and major construction projects, total wages and employment, and the allocation of scientific and technical labour (nine targets in all, although some of multiple dimensions) remained under central control. However, the actual administration of economic activity in order to meet these targets—as well as the many other targets now set by the provinces themselves—was now largely a provincial responsibility. Although vertical and horizontal planning were to proceed nominally in co-operation with each other, the horizontal element was now predominant.

The Chinese decentralization followed close on the heels of a similar reform that took place in the Soviet Union in 1957, which replaced the vertical, industrial ministerial system with a territorial one based upon regional economic councils (called *sovnarkhozy*). However, unlike the Soviet reform, China's retained the vertical structure (ministries).

From this description of the reforms, one might conclude that they had done away with centralized, vertical planning altogether, and that subsequently the central plan would be a simple aggregation of provincial plans. Such a change would have been dramatic, indeed, with profound consequences for the interregional and intersectoral structure of growth. However, as Lardy has convincingly argued, the centre was careful to retain far-reaching power over the interregional allocation of resources, the level and nature of capital investment, the production quantities of the most important industrial and agricultural goods, the total expenditures (and even their composition) of provinces, and the total wage bill.

Thus, for example, before the reforms each province's annual revenues were provided by the central government in the amount required by the centrally approved expenditure plan for the year in question. After the reforms the provinces had in their expanded tax base and profit-sharing powers a broad, independent, and expanding source of revenues. However, the size of their revenue base was carefully calculated to cover only about three-quarters of their expenditures, so that they continued to depend upon annually adjusted central subsidies, which could be used to control the growth and composition of provincial expenditures. Moreover, the most developed provincial units—Shanghai, Liaoning, Beijing, and Tianjin—were excluded both from the profit-sharing arrangements that obtained elsewhere and from sharing in industrial, commercial, and agricultural taxes collected in their jurisdictions; whereas, on the other hand, the autonomous regions, the poorest areas in China, were allowed to keep all enterprise profits (rather than just 20 per cent) as well as being given additional revenue concessions.

The centre's firm hold on the fiscal levers of resource allocation was further strengthened by an additional reform in 1959 eliminating the potentially most significant feature of the 1957–8 reform, viz., the fixed revenue-sharing rates, which had promised the provinces regular and growing sources of income. Instead, each province was now to have its own share of its total revenues set annually at a level just sufficient to cover its approved expenditures. Furthermore, although provinces that had been excluded from profit-sharing previously (e.g., Shanghai) now had this ban lifted, they were not permitted to spend their new revenues; instead, approved expenditures were kept well below revenues and the large resulting surpluses were remitted to the central budget. Throughout the 1960s and 1970s, this system gave rise to widely differing provincial revenue-sharing rates: advanced regions such as Shanghai and Liaoning turned over the great bulk of their revenues to the centre, while backward provinces such as Xinjiang and Qinghai received central subsidies equal to large fractions of their own revenues (Lardy 1978a:128–236 and *passim*).

The decentralization of the late 1950s enhanced the ability of provinces and localities to arrange material supplies and allocate labour within their territories, and thus to administer and co-ordinate economic activity more effectively than when vertical and horizontal control systems existed side by side and virtually independent of each other. The institution of 'dual leadership' was a novel attempt to unburden the central authorities of the impossible details of administering thousands of individual enterprises on to the shoulders of the provinces, while maintaining central supervision of their activities. These reforms somewhat rationalized the overcentralized planning system of the FFYP period. However, they left unsolved the crucial issues common to all attempts at central command planning.

First, management of the economy was still a highly bureaucratized affair. It must be kept in mind that the provinces, to which some planning and management powers had been handed down, are very large administrative units. The provincial level of decision-making is not materially closer to the actual producers than the national level, and the quality of provincial planning and administrative resources and personnel was probably lower on average. Also, any material incentive for the provinces to use their new authority efficiently was weakened by the centre's retention of control over provincial expenditures; superior performance in raising output, cutting costs, and enlarging profits was rewarded merely by the higher remission of profit to the centre.

Second, the problem of work and management incentives was not solved by the decentralization. As we have seen, its *administrative* form was not intended to provide a material link between an enterprise's performance and the income of its personnel. Administrative decentralization was associated in the debates within the Party with dependence on social mobilization, as Schurmann points out, rather than with material incentives. The motivational accoutrements of social mobilization, in Chinese experience, have been a heavy reliance on ideology (or political incentives); on non-material external incentives (such as the granting of honorific titles or other symbolic awards); and on changes in production relations within enterprises, especially attacks on social and economic stratification and attempts to erect participatory forms of work and management. During the Great Leap Forward, for which the reforms in a sense set the stage, the new institution of the rural people's commune came into being. At the level of the production team, the commune's smallest sub-unit, administrative decentralization may have been compatible with group material incentives, because effective management and hard work would result in greater and more diversified output for the entire team and higher living standards for its members; and this linkage occurred on a scale small enough for it to be perceived and thus to serve as a source of motivation. Even at this level, however, there were major problems with the approach, especially the tendency of social mobilization to give rise to 'commandism', or the issuing of arbitrary orders by local cadres (see Chapter 6). At higher levels, however, as in provincial and central state-operated enterprises, the system of administrative decentralization did not build any link between enterprise performance and reward, and motivation depended entirely upon the non-material forms enumerated above. While these may be effective during periods of great social unity and national fervour, they tend quickly to fail in an atmosphere of political disillusionment, economic retreat, perceived factionalism among the leadership, and the pursuit of inequitable privileges by the élite. Much of the post-Leap history of China has been marked by just such conditions.

Third, the decentralization did not lead to qualitative improvement in resource allocation. Some allocative problems were indeed alleviated by the enhanced power of regions and localities to arrange material and labour use within their territories. One basic allocative problem, however, *worsened* in the wake of the decentralization: the tendency to overemphasize capital investment and ignore consumption and living standards. This is directly evident in the persistent rise in the accumulation rate (roughly, the ratio of fixed capital investment plus increases in working capital to material product) to well over 40 per cent during the Great Leap Forward. It is also indirectly evident in the persistent failure of living standards to grow significantly after 1957 (to be dealt with in later chapters).

The relation between the structure of economic management and the ratio of accumulation to consumption is a complex one. It concerns the means by which popular aspirations for improved living standards are conveyed to the leadership. Administrative decentralization seems to have increased the ability of regional and local officials to mobilize resources for investment, but not to have provided similar incentives for them—or pressures on them—to attend to improving the standard of living of their people; instead, accumulation was pushed irrationally and to counter-productive ends. The effect of this was also felt in the sphere of incentives: ideological, participatory, and other nonmaterial incentives depend upon the state's fulfilment of its part of the 'social contract' by regular delivery of the promised increases in income. While the often violent conflicts that characterized the period of 'late Maoism' could be blamed alternately by each side for failure to deliver, the combination of that failure itself, and the ongoing struggle that rationalized it, must have eroded the basis for a collective incentive system to work effectively.[12]

4   The political reaction, 1956–7

The progression from socialist 'high tide' to decentralization, however logical, was not smooth and uncontested. On the contrary, the many problems created by the pace of the 'high tide' and by the over-ambitious investment programme in 1956 (see below) brought together a coalition within the leadership that succeeded temporarily in shelving Mao's high-speed, social mobilizational approach. At the same time, popular disaffection with the course of events burst forth in unanticipated strength in the Hundred Flowers movement, and many of the views then expressed (as well as their authors) were subsequently attacked in a harsh anti-rightist campaign. In a sense, these were intervening events between 'high tide' and decentralization. Because ideology played such as important role in Mao's approach, it was necessary to deal with the ideological problems left behind by the 'high tide'. Mao's original intention may have been to foster unity by means of full discussion. Because of the fundamental nature of much of the criticism, however, he ended by opting for a large measure of suppression.

In his preface to the book *Socialist Upsurge in China's Countryside* (1956),[13] Mao sharply criticized 'rightist conservative ideas' that underestimated the potential for high-speed development. In fact, taking advantage of the very good harvest of 1955, the momentum of the 'high tide', and the state revenues deriving from transformation of the private sector, the leadership carried out a leap forward in 1956. Total investment in capital construction increased by 60 per cent over 1955 (*Ten Great Years* 1960:55–6); gross value of industrial output increased by 28 per cent (p. 18), the number of industrial workers by 33 per cent (p. 183).

Such a sudden and massive increase in investment and production gave rise to considerable imbalances in the economy: shortages of fuels and raw materials, idle capacity in some sectors, bottlenecks in others, and inflationary pressures. These problems were exacerbated by a poor harvest in 1956.

The Party was therefore forced to cut back the scale of capital construction in 1957, and to moderate policy towards the agricultural collectives, handicraft co-operatives, and newly transformed commercial and industrial enterprises. At the Eighth National Party Congress in September 1956, a moderate set of proposals for the Second Five Year Plan was announced, according to which the pace of development over the period 1958–62 would be slightly faster than obtained in the FFYP period (a 65 per cent increase in gross value of industrial and agricultural output, as compared with 60 per cent during the First Plan). Mao's Twelve Year Plan for Agriculture, launched with much publicity in January, was all but ignored.

The Eighth Congress took the position that, as a result of the basic completion of socialist transformation of ownership in all sectors, the class struggle in China had been 'basically resolved'; accordingly, the main contradiction had become that between the objective of industrialization and the reality of agrarian backwardness ('Resolution' 1956, I:116). This was a view with which Mao strongly disagreed, as he made clear directly after the Congress (Selden 1979:69). Throughout 1956 and early 1957, he repeatedly expressed concern not only about the survival of 'bourgeois' opposition to party leadership and policy, but also about the growing problem of bureaucratism, élitism, and autocratic behaviour on the part of the new officialdom. Such leadership characteristics were incompatible with a development strategy that stressed mobilization of local initiative. With the 1956 events in Poland and Hungary still fresh in mind, Mao declined to take the spotlight off politics and ideology and shift it to technology. In a sense, the Hundred Flowers movement bore him out. Begun as a rectification campaign, in which intellectuals were encouraged to criticize and expose bureaucratic and élitest tendencies in the leadership, it soon exposed as well the depth of intellectual opposition to the Party's monopoly of political power and to the absence of civil liberties.

5   From long-term planning to Great Leap Forward

The First Five Year Plan scored major successes in laying the foundations for industrialization in China. Yet despite the nominal existence of subsequent five year plans, it was the only period in the three decades following the Rehabilitation period in which planning was actually carried out for more than a year at a time. This apparent paradox can be explained by the political predilections of the 'left' leadership group that was dominant for much of the twenty years after 1957. However, this explanation seems inadequate unless the objective difficulties—both political and economic—that arose out of the First Plan strategy to inform the left ideological position are recognized.

Three of these in particular are worth mentioning or recalling in summary. First, there was the inadequate growth of agricultural production and procurement: a stagnation of grain output because of poor incentives had been averted by the 'three-fix' policy in mid-1955, but at the cost of a decline in state procurement of foodgrain (Chapter 4, Sec. 4, and Table 4.6). Some means had to be found around the unhappy choice between too little growth and inadequate procurement.

Second, planning and administration, in their highly centralized form, had become increasingly ineffective as the economy grew in size and complexity, and especially after virtually all industry and commerce came under direct state control in 1956 (see Sec. 3 above). The decentralization measures of 1957–8 were supposed to deal with this problem by giving provincial authorities more scope for planning regional development and managing local enterprises. In line with the emphasis on local initiative, central ministries in 1957–8 worked out designs for small-scale factories to be built and operated locally, and called local cadres to Beijing to learn about them. In sum, China's leaders were looking to a rather different distribution of authority between centre and localities during the Second Five Year Plan.

Third, the industrialization strategy of the First Plan had proved incapable of solving the unemployment problem. Quantitative information about the extent of open urban unemployment at the end of the plan period is scarce and contradictory. On the one hand, a 1957 article put 1956 unemployment at only 1 million (Howe 1971:31), and *Beijing Review* (11 February 1981:14) has claimed that 'we basically eliminated unemployment' by 1957. On the other hand, a variety of information published in China makes it clear that urban unemployment remained a serious problem in 1957. It was fed by a continuing flow of rural migrants escaping poverty, natural disasters, and the turmoil of collectivization, and seeking secure and better-paying jobs in the cities. Howe (1971:73) calculates that such migration may have added 17 per cent to the supply of job-seekers in Shanghai, almost doubling unemployment there. Rawski (1970b:29, 35) roughly estimates urban unemployment in 1957 at 7.8 million, or 8.5 per cent of the urban population and about 20 per cent of the urban labour force. China's basic demographics dictated that more attention be paid to creating employment. The total labour force may have increased by some 40–50 million between 1952 and 1957, whereas total non-agricultural employment grew by less than 5 million, leaving perhaps 90 per cent of the increased labour force to be absorbed in already highly labour-intensive agriculture. Moreover, the pressure that liquidated almost all of the private sector in 1956 thereby also eliminated a potentially flexible and responsive source of employment and left the entire burden of allocating labour to the overworked labour bureaus. Thus, neither the capital-intensive strategy of the First Plan nor the administrative capacity of the government was capable of responding adequately to the problem.

What was needed, therefore, was a strategy that—in comparison with the First Five Year Plan—would give greater attention to agriculture, reduce centralization, give greater initiative to localities (and/or to enterprises), and turn China's redundant labour force into a strength instead of a weakness. Such objectives fitted very nicely Mao's ideological predilection for a mobilizational strategy based on administrative decentralization.

Notes

1. The National Programme for Agricultural Development, 1956–67, drafted by Mao Zedong, appeared in late January 1956 as a 'draft'. It was then caught up in internal party disputes over rural policy and led a checkered history until finally being ratified by the National People's Congress in April 1960 (see Schurmann 1968:200). The text is excerpted in Selden (1979:358–63).

2. Wiens (1978:693–5), in discussing this episode, rebuts the common ascription of the double-wheel double-share plough fiasco to 'blind commandism or technical stupidity'. He argues that there was reason to believe at the time that the plough could be made to operate successfully under paddy conditions; that the reasons for its failure are several, involving overly optimistic generalizations from experimental use, inaccurate assessment of the peasants' willingness and ability to modify the plough and/or the shape of their fields, the high opportunity cost of the additional draught animals needed, the high steel requirements, etc. Nevertheless, he points out that 'the fact that the plow is still produced today attests to its ultimate profitability to at least some north China purchasers.'

3. Selden (1981) restrospectively favours such an alternative strategy. It is also interesting to speculate about the likely results had private farming evolved directly into the 'household responsibility system' of today, without first going through collectivization. In Chapter 12 it is argued that the success of this reform in the 1980s was based in part on the prior contributions of the era of collective agriculture.

4. This is one possible interpretation of the figures given in *BR* (28 April 1980:20–21). Another is that the phrase, 'private industrialists and businessmen numbered 760,000 in 1956', excludes those capitalists already transformed before 1956, whereas the total of 1.14 million recipients of fixed interest is inclusive of these. The latter interpretation leaves indeterminate the number of 'small shareholders who were themselves not capitalists'.

5. These figures exclude two additional groups of craftspeople: those working in 'handicraft factories' (included in the category of industry proper and not in individual handicrafts), and peasants engaged in subsidiary craft production for their own use (Xue *et al*. 1960:139).

6. The actual decline in individual craftspeople was even sharper than appears, since the 1956 figure includes 'more than 1,000,000 handicraftsmen belonging to fishing and salt co-ops' (*Ten Great Years* 1960:36, n. 2), who were presumably excluded from handicraft employment figures in previous years. Note 1 of the source's table explains the decline in individual handicraft employment in 1955 and 1956 as due to the absorption of some craftspeople into agricultural collectives in rural areas, and of others into industrial enterprises in the cities.

7. For a good basic description of Soviet-type central planning, see Ellman (1979: Chapter 2). Lardy (1978b) contains a selection of Chinese articles describing the planning process and system there. The early evolution of China's planning system is chronicled in Donnithorne (1967:Chapter 17).

8. The most thorough discussion of the decentralization of the late 1950s is Lardy (1978a). The above discussion relies heavily upon Chapter 1 of this work.

9. This distinction is clearly regarded as important by Chinese economists, who sometimes use the term 'centrally allocated' to refer only to the first category (i.e., commodities balanced by the State Council agencies). In late 1980, according to the director of the State Bureau of Supplies (an agency under the State Council), Li Kaixin, this agency and the State Planning Commission directly balanced 256 kinds of producer goods (e.g., coal, steel products, non-ferrous metals, various kinds of

machinery and electrical products, etc.); another 581 product types, encompassing 'important means of production with specialized uses, such as power plant equipment', were balanced by individual industrial and transport ministries; 'ordinary means of production' totaling over 10,000 kinds of goods were handled at the provincial and municipal levels; and consumer goods were distributed 'through commercial channels' (*CBR*, November–December 1980: 14–15).

10. The high growth rates favoured by Mao required continued emphasis on heavy industry and therefore on Soviet help. Schurmann (1968:204–5) contends that several events in the autumn of 1957 (including the launching of Sputnik), which enhanced Soviet prestige and appeared to signal Soviet willingness to expand trade and aid with China, helped tip the balance in China's Central Committee towards Mao's position.

11. See the list of such exceptions in the text of the directive, as excerpted in Selden (1979:432–5). The term 'provincial level' or 'provincial' includes autonomous regions and municipalities directly under the central government.

12. This formulation of the problem avoids the issue of whether such an incentive system is possible, under the best of political circumstances, in very low-income conditions. It is the position of the post-Mao leadership of China that economic underdevelopment itself rules out what Marxists would regard as advanced relations of production. This issue will be taken up again in the concluding chapters.

13. This book was a collection of several hundred case studies of successful agricultural co-operatives, and was published in three volumes in January 1956. It was intended to provide a source of inspiration and guidance to the peasantry in forming co-operatives. See Jack Gray's analysis of these examples in Gray (1970).

CHAPTER 6

ASCENDANCY AND CRISIS OF LATE MAOISM, 1958–1962

1 Introduction

The Great Leap Forward (GLF), which gathered momentum in the winter and spring of 1957–8, epitomized Mao Zedong's response to the complex set of problems left by history and, more immediately, by the First Five Year Plan strategy. Observing the GLF in retrospect, it is easy to recognize its structural relevance to these problems. This does not mean, however, that the Leap was a carefully designed bundle of policies that could legitimately be called a 'plan'. Schurmann (1968) captures the essence of the GLF in calling it 'the product of a vision rather than of a plan'. Because this 'vision' dominated Chinese economic activity and thought for several years, Schurmann's explication is worth quoting at some length:

A plan is a carefully worked-out blueprint of action based on a matching of goals with capabilities. A vision is a total insight into the essential interrelationships of a situation ... Late in 1957 [the draft Second Five Year Plan] was abandoned and a program initiated which was based on Mao Tse-tung's vision of Chinese society. Since the core of that vision was the insight that Chinese society was marked by essential economic, political and social contradictions, and that rapid development could take place by resolving those contradictions, we shall call it the dialectical conception of Chinese society. Whereas the plan was essentially economic, Mao's vision encompassed all factors of societal dynamics: political, social as well as economic. [Schurmann 1968:74]

In Mao's ontology, contradiction is the permanent state of things, equilibrium between contradictory forces being always temporary and fleeting, and disequilibrium the normal condition. The principal contradictions facing Chinese society in the late 1950s were, in Mao's view, due partly to the scientific policies followed during the first seven years of the People's Republic. In his talks to the Chengdu Conference in March 1958, Mao applied the label of 'dogmatism' to previous Chinese policies towards heavy industry, planning, banking, and statistics, because, lacking native experience and competence in these areas, China had rigidly copied Soviet practices regardless of their appropriateness to Chinese conditions. Now the situation had changed, he said, and China was better able to summarize its own experiences and apply the lessons to forging its own path of development.

The chief contradictions of an economic nature that concerned Mao were the first five 'relations' set out in his 'Ten Major Relationships' speech of April 1956 (Mao 1977a:284). The first is the relation between heavy industry on the one hand, and light industry and agriculture on the other. Although China had not erred to the same degree as the Soviet Union and some East European countries in overemphasizing heavy industry, Mao held that it was still necessary to increase the proportion of investment allocated to agriculture and light industry. In so doing, China would lay a more solid foundation for heavy industrial development by raising living standards and promoting saving.

The second relation is that between coast and interior. Mao emphasized the *long-run* nature of the goal of alleviating the existing imbalance by developing the interior. To accomplish this, he argued, it was necessary in the short run to take better advantage of the existing industrial base along the coast, in the North-east and East China regions.

The third relation juxtaposes investment in economic development and defense. Mao argued for a substantial cut (from 30 to 20 per cent) in the share of defense and administrative spending in the total budget, on the grounds that faster economic construction would enhance China's military power in the long run.

Relations 4 and 5 have received considerably more attention than the first three. They concern the reconciliation of the interests of state, enterprise, and individual worker, and of central and local authorities, respectively. We have already discussed these sections as they concern the decentralization measures of 1957-8 (Chapter 5, Sec. 3). Mao here reiterates the need to improve wages and working conditions as production increases; to avoid the Soviet example of squeezing the peasantry and ensure that 90 per cent of peasants get more income each year in which production grows; and to enlarge the inde-pendence of enterprises and the powers of local authorities.

Mao was later to characterize this speech as containing his first attempt to formulate an approach to socialist construction based on China's own conditions.[1] Schram (1974:42) writes, 'As for economic policy, most of the main themes of the "Great Leap Forward" which Mao promoted in 1958 are to be found' in the 'Ten Major Relationships'. But this was a judicious speech that proposed relatively marginal changes (e.g., 'the proportion for agriculture and light industry must be somewhat increased'; 'our attention should now be focused on how to enlarge the powers of the local authorities to some extent'; etc.), whereas there was nothing judicious about the Great Leap, which abandoned altogether the principles of central planning. There is no *a priori* conflict between the goals of the 'Ten Major Relationships' speech and the use of central planning techniques to achieve them. Indeed, the decentralization measures of 1957, as well as other policies adopted in the last two years of the First Plan, were precisely attempts to realize those goals through planning. The dynamic, spontaneous, and chaotic nature of the Leap must be traced elsewhere than to the balanced formulations of the 'Ten Major Relationships'.

It might seem idealistic to search for the answer in Mao's thought. Yet Schurmann (1968:74) is undoubtedly right in saying that the Great Leap Forward, based on Mao's conception of Chinese society, 'must be regarded as the most momentous instance of ideology in action in the brief history of Communist China'. It is therefore not surprising that Maoist dialectics, viewed against the background of the objective difficulties inherent in the FFYP strategy (summarized at the end of Chapter 5), should explain a large part of what happened in the Leap. Schurmann's (1968:73–104) complex and insightful analysis of the chief economic, political, and social contradictions preoccupying Mao in the China of the late 1950s, and of the respective biases of the Leap and the FFYP towards opposite poles in this amalgam of dualities, informs much of the discussion below.

Several of these biases do help to explain the wave-like, unplanned, and ultimately chaotic nature of the GLF: for instance, among 'political contradictions', the bias towards initiative 'from the bottom up' rather than 'from the top down', and towards region rather than centre; among social contradictions, the stress on political redness rather than technical expertise, on masses and cadres rather than bureaucrats, on ideology rather than material incentives. In addition to these elements that contributed to the rapid decay of planning and orderly administration, however, we must also take into account Mao's notion of 'uninterrupted revolution'. Point 21 of the 'Sixty Points on Working Methods'[2] drafted by Mao in January 1958, is devoted to this idea. 'Our revolutions come one after another', Mao wrote, sketching the sequence of conquest of state power, land reform, socialist 'high tide', and the anti-rightist campaign of 1957:[3] 'Our revolutions are like battles. After a victory, we must at once put forward a new task. In this way cadres and the masses will forever be filled with revolutionary fervor . . .' Elsewhere in the 'Sixty Points', the politicization of economic goals (see Introduction to Chapter 5 for a definition of this phrase) is made quite clear. Point 13 calls for making 'a basic change in the appearance of most areas in three years' and states: 'Our slogan: Bitter struggle for three years. Our method: Arouse the masses in an entirely uninhibited manner and everything must be tried out first.' It is not that planning was explicitly repudiated; on the contrary, several of the early paragraphs of the 'Sixty Points' emphasize the importance of 'over-all planning, regular inspection, and annual reviews and comparisons'. But the decisive targets that are put forward in this first guiding document of the GLF implicitly rule out planning, since they are chosen without regard to means, or to the balancing of supply with demand. Consider, for example, the target of making the industrial output of localities overtake their agricultural output within five, seven, or ten years (point 11). In setting this goal, no reference is made either to the possibility of accomplishing it in all localities, or to its rationality, given locally varying factor endowments and the desirability of some regional specialization and division of labour. Similarly, one of the key slogans of the Leap—'Overtake Britain in iron and steel and other major industrial products in fifteen years'—is hardly an example of Schurmann's 'carefully worked-out blueprint of action based on a matching of goals with capabilities'.

Moreover, the approach to planning that was now proposed was what later would be called 'active' or 'long-line' planning. Both centre and provinces would draw up two sets of targets. Of the centre's two, the less ambitious had to be fulfilled, while the more ambitious formed the basis of the localities' *minimum* targets. In this way, plan targets diverged progressively from the reliable probability of achievement as they moved down from centre to locality. The objective (reminiscent of some influential ideas of Albert O. Hirschman) was to focus attention on the bottlenecks and weak points in production so as to mobilize efforts to overcome these. Years later, the veteran economist Chen Yun would comment scathingly that the most prominent result of 'long-line' balance planning was imbalance (*BR*, 23 March 1981:28).

A feature of early designs for the Great Leap that presaged its chief characteristics was an extraordinarily high investment rate. Mao proposed marginal accumulation rates of 40–60 per cent for the rural collectives in general, and 70–100 per cent for those reaching 'wealthy middle peasant' levels of income (point 16).[4] Although these rates refer to distribution of the *increases* in income (not of total income), that distinction is rather easily overlooked, especially when (as happened) increases are being statistically exaggerated. In the event, China's national rate of accumulation soared to almost 44 per cent in 1959.[5]

Excessive rates of accumulation give rise to sectoral imbalances and tensions that seem to require centralized leadership to remedy. In the case of the Great Leap, the causes of tension and imbalance were several in addition to overaccumulation, but the result was the rescinding of the decentralization measures of 1957–8, so that by 1961 the economic planning system was at least as centralized as before 1957. At the lowest level of administration, however, decentralization occurred, as the new, large communes gave up their powers to much smaller production teams and some individual farming and marketing was again permitted. These measures were necessary to counter the worst economic crisis faced by the People's Republic, as the disruption of the Great Leap and three successive bad harvests created a full-fledged famine.

This chapter discusses the main events of the turbulent period, 1958–61, focusing on the economic structural characteristics of the Great Leap Forward, and on its evaluation as an economic development strategy for China.

2 The nature of the Great Leap Forward

The principal characteristics of the Leap are grouped for discussion into the categories of technology, management and planning, and incentives and ideology. Its most important institutional innovation—the rural people's commune—is considered separately in Section 3.

2.1 Technology

The Great Leap Forward deliberately promoted technological dualism—or, as it was known in China, 'walking on two legs'. Both relatively capital-intensive, large-scale, modern production units, and relatively labour-intensive, small-scale, and technologically backward ones were to develop simultaneously, thus enabling China to make productive use of all available resources, however crude, scattered, or unskilled. The modern, large-scale 'leg' consisted of two parts: the pre-existing, formerly capitalist industries located mostly in and around Shanghai, and the new and generally much larger enterprises being built with Soviet aid. The latter in particular were a major contributor to the Great Leap in industrial output, since they were coming on-stream in increasing numbers in the late 1950s. During the first half of the 1950s, a total of

166 Soviet-aided industrial and transport projects (after consolidation from a larger number) were agreed upon between the USSR and China (Prybyla 1970:217). Of these, only 68 had been completed by the end of 1957, but an additional 45 were finished in 1958 alone, and 41 more by the end of 1960. A big impetus to modern sector output was thus provided by Soviet-aid projects coming into production just at the time the Great Leap was beginning.

These projects were less successful in providing employment, however. Highly capital-intensive, they created relatively few jobs for the expenditures involved. For example, capital per worker in the machinery and ferrous metallurgy plants was several times the national average (Rawski 1979b:52–3). Moreover, their scale and level of mechanization required large amounts of high-quality raw materials. Even when operating at full capacity, therefore, they were not able to make use of materials that were scattered in low concentrations throughout the country (a shortcoming aggravated by the underdeveloped state of China's transport system), or that were of irregular or poor quality. Nor could their output be transported from centralized production points to remote markets without exorbitant cost mark-ups. These observations provided the theoretical basis for the establishment of the 'native leg'[6] of small-scale, simple factories and workshops to supplement the modern sector.

The rationale for small, local industries did not originate in the Great Leap Forward. It had been spelled out as early as 1951, and received considerable attention in the First Five Year Plan itself.[7] However, because of the preoccupation of the political and economic leadership with the establishment of a Soviet-type, centralized system of planning and management, and with the correction of sectoral and regional imbalances that seemed to call for centralized control of the resource allocation mechanisms, little attention was actually paid to local industrialization during the First Plan period. In contrast, it was one of the pillars of the Great Leap strategy.

The small industry policy of the Leap was based partly upon the previously worked out economic rationale. On the one hand, local industries were to mobilize resources unavailable to or unwanted by the large-scale, modern sector of industry, thus expanding overall industrial production at low opportunity cost. On the other, they were to gear their production to the needs of agriculture, thereby freeing the modern sector to concentrate on its own expansion. In particular, the thousands of small shops and factories set up by the new rural communes were to bear the main burden of gradually modernizing agriculture (Riskin 1971:258–9). In other respects, however—the enormous regional dispersion of production, the stress on local self-sufficiency, the downgrading of bureaucratic control and technical expertise in favour of mass initiative—the small industries of the Great Leap departed sharply from earlier strategy. In these respects, they epitomized the social mobilizational and anti-bureaucratic aspects of Mao's 'vision', and were intended to provide China's localities with both means and motivation for extraordinary efforts on behalf of industrialization and agricultural modernization.

The Great Leap's promotion of technological dualism can also be understood as an attempt to turn China's vast quantities of underemployed labour into capital, along the lines of Ragnar Nurkse's (1953) influential ideas of the 1950s. Labour was to be used intensively not only in industrial production, but also in capital construction and agriculture. One hundred million peasants were said to be engaged in building water conservancy works during the winter of 1957–8 (Dutt 1967:23). Farm labour inputs were stepped up dramatically in an attempt to raise yields by more intensive cultivation, deeper ploughing, and especially closer planting. According to one estimate, the total number of annual labour-days in agriculture increased by about 14 per cent in 1958 and by another 23 per cent in 1959.[8]

Although the idea of mobilizing underemployed labour for production and construction has much prima facie plausibility, its successful implementation depends upon some obvious conditions. One is that labour can be transferred from agriculture to industry and construction without hurting farm production. In view of Buck's findings (see Chapter 2) from the 1930s that surplus labour in most rural localities was *seasonal*, and alternated with periodic labour scarcity, the use of such labour at low opportunity cost required that workers not be removed permanently from agriculture, and that their non-agricultural employment be limited to slack seasons. Another condition is that extremely labour-intensive techniques be capable of producing output of adequate quality. This is a very general, but obviously crucial, requirement. It means, for example, that earthwork dams put up by labour brigades must be able to withstand heavy rains, and that their construction must be preceded by a technical evaluation of their effect on the water table and soil fertility; or that iron from small-scale blast furnaces must be usable, and that its value must exceed that of its material inputs. Such obvious conditions are mentioned because, as it turned out, they were commonly ignored during the Leap. A third prerequisite is only somewhat less obvious: the intensive use of labour must raise income more than consumption. To take a simple example, if heavier labour input raises grain output per person by 25 kilograms per year and grain consumption by 50 kilograms, the prospects for continued growth will be dim.

2.2 Planning and management

Chapter 5's discussion of the 1957–8 decentralization measures concluded that they permitted the central government to retain control over the national allocation of resources, but that the power of the provinces to carry out labour and materials planning and to control the daily activities of enterprises within their jurisdictions was substantially increased. We have seen also, however, that core elements of the GLF approach were basically antithetical to rational planning. Targets continued to be put forward, but in the course of 1958 they became symbols of political enthusiasm, and lost touch with reality. The State Statistical Bureau, which made rapid progress through 1957 in establishing a reliable reporting network throughout the country, was captured by local party and government authorities intent on using statistics to spur their key construction projects and emulation drives. It quickly lost the capability to produce accurate statistics—and thus to keep the planners in touch with reality

(Li 1962). So decentralization, mass mobilization, and 'politics in command' together put an end to planning in the course of 1958.

Decentralization from the top was mirrored by centralization from below in the form of the rural people's communes, which were amalgams of the much smaller collectives of 1957. This subject is discussed in Section 3 below.

The management system in industrial enterprises also underwent rapid transformation in 1958. The goals of this change were consistent with the ideological emphasis of the Leap on combating bureaucratism, blunting the distinction between mental and manual labour, and encouraging mass participation in management. From late 1957 until the end of 1958, various experiments were carried out and then diffused throughout Chinese industry. In sum, these came to be known as the 'two participations, one reform and triple combination', or '2–1–3' system of management. 'Two participations' refers to the participation of workers in management and of cadres in labour; 'one reform' refers to the reform of irrational rules and regulations; 'triple combination' refers to technical work teams, consisting of workers, technicians, and administrative cadres, that personified the 'combination of leadership with the masses, labor with technique, and technical theory with production practice' (Andors 1977:83).

Under this system, much of the specialized management activities of functional departments of enterprises were taken over by small production groups of ordinary workers who elected their own heads. Varying combinations of such jobs as financial and statistical work, quota planning, quality control, technical control, inspection, discipline, repair and maintenance, wages and incentives, and welfare work were thus decentralized. The size of the administrative and technical staff was sharply reduced, and even those personnel kept on in specialized positions were to engage regularly in ordinary labour. This practice was intended not only to combat social stratification and bring management into contact with the problems of the shop-floor, but also to provide the expertise and skill needed by the small work groups in carrying out their new management tasks. More broadly, in response to the requirements of mass participation in technical and administrative work, factories throughout the country set up spare-time schools to train workers, and ordinary schools and universities revised their curricula to emphasize practical applications to production.

These developments contributed to the erosion of planning. Centralized administrative planning requires the continuous flow of detailed information about enterprise performance and capabilities. 'The central dilemma was that quotas and targets calculated by the mid-level departments, which served as crucial inputs into central planning, as instruments of control, and as the basis for incentives within the plants, were now all but obliterated' (Andors 1977:78). With government planning departments and banks unable to get information through ordinary channels about enterprise activity, the task of co-ordination and control shifted by default on to the shoulders of party committees. But their ability to carry out these new responsibilities was compromised by their lack of competence and preparation, as well as by prior commitment to a Great Leap ideology that had little room for the sobering influence of objective constraints.[9]

2.3 Incentives

The incentive system of the Great Leap Forward was dominated by the notion of 'politics in command'. With China in mind, Jack Gray defines political economy as 'the study of the economic implications of all relevant social relationships, and the implications of economics in turn *for* all these social relationships' (Gray 1973:115). It is in this sense that we should understand the Maoist idea of politics commanding economics: economic policies must not only expand production, but also contribute to the realization of more fully socialist relations of production. To Mao, this meant weakening the bureaucracy, the sense of privilege that went with intellectual status, the widening gulf between the material and cultural levels of urban dwellers and country people. Such progress in the realm of 'production relations' would in turn tap reservoirs of popular creativity and lead to faster economic growth: 'a great spiritual force becomes a great material force', in Mao's terms.

The approach of the Leap to technology and management was consistent with the concept of 'politics in command', as was the formation of the people's communes. The critical link between political direction and economic organization, however, is the incentive system, which directly affects the distribution of income underlying social relations, as well as the individual's perception of how just the system is. The Great Leap's attacks on functional inequalities in organization and management were reflected in incentive policies that encouraged collective solidarity and mass responsibility by greatly reducing individual income differentiation.

In the countryside, these same principles were dramatically manifested in the 'supply system', which harked back to the distributional methods used by the communist guerrillas of Yanan (Yenan) days. A portion of income was distributed to commune members in kind and free of charge, and was thus independent of their work efforts. Usually this took the form of free food, served at the public dining halls that were rapidly set up in 1958. But the list of goods and services supplied varied widely among communes, and in some places the members were guaranteed clothing, housing, education, maternity care, and even wedding and funeral services, haircuts, baths, and entertainment (Dutt 1967:42). The Central Committee was quick to warn against the general spread of these 'first shoots of the communist principle of "to each according to his needs"' and to direct that distribution 'according to work' remain the dominant system ('Wuhan Resolution', in Selden 1979:408–9). In some communes, however, including the model Weixing (Sputnik) Commune, as much as 80 per cent of members' income was freely supplied.

For that part of income distributed 'according to work', monthly wages were widely substituted for the work-points used by the collectives (Chapter 5, Sec. 2). The work-point system was basically a piece rate system that attempted to replicate, for a collective setting, the material interest of the private farmer in hard and effective work. It required careful differentiation of individual efforts and rewards, and this ran counter to the collectivist spirit of the Great Leap. Regular monthly wages seemed more industrial, large-scale, and 'public' in character, hence more socialist. The draft regulations of the model Weixing Commune called for maintaining a piece-work system until the commune 'acquires stability of income and adequate funds and ... the members are able voluntarily to consolidate labour discipline' (excerpted in Selden 1979:400)—a cautiousness also present in central directives on the communes. In fact, however, the wage system spread quickly and widely, stimulated by the 'communist wind' of 1958 as well as by the general exaggeration of farm production statistics, which briefly created the impression that scarcity had been banished for good. Wage grades were still to depend in part on work (intensity, complexity, skill), but this link was attenuated by such additional criteria as the worker's ideological awareness and attitude towards labour.

In the atmosphere of mobilization of an entire nation to wage war against nature, the system of free supply plus wages provided a compatibly egalitarian distribution method. Material incentives were at first still present, in the sense of limitless potential for quickly developing one's community or village. Articles on distribution drew analogies with wartime conditions, pointing out that victory over Japan, in the civil war, or in the Long March had not depended on work-points and material incentives: why then should economic construction, which brings its own material rewards in time? (Dutt 1967:43–4). The military analogy was carried into the organization of farmwork, and peasants marched in ranks to the fields each morning, accompanied by gongs, drums, and banners, and led by their cadres. 'Commandism' was to figure greatly in the collapse of rural incentives after the heady, early months of the Leap.

A similar attack on individual material incentives was launched in urban industries, where piece rates and personal bonuses were widely eliminated but the eight-grade wage system remained. Emphasis on individual differentiation was now seen as incompatible with the changes in factory organization discussed above, which stressed the breaking down of functional distinctions between managers and workers, the assumption of managerial and administrative tasks by shop-floor work groups, and the participation of cadres in labour. Bonuses for managerial personnel were generally eliminated, and for workers their basis was shifted from the individual to the work group. The role of nonmaterial external incentives, such as emulation campaigns, the designation of model workers and work teams, and the publicizing of accomplishments and faults by means of *dazibao* (wall posters), was greatly extended (Hoffmann 1967:97–100; Andors 1977:86).

Although external incentives (whether material or honorary) continued to play a role in the Great Leap Forward, the ideology of the Leap favoured greater reliance upon internal incentives—specifically, those related to job enlargement and worker participation in management. Workers who were part of 'triple combination' technical teams or acquired managerial responsibilities, and who were attending spare-time factory schools to upgrade their skills, were expected to identify more closely with their enterprise and to internalize its interests as their own. The collapse of central planning in 1958 probably enhanced this incentive for a while by leaving enterprises and localities with considerable autonomous authority, in which their workers shared. By the same token, the later re-imposition of central administrative planning conflicted with the participatory incentives of the Leap, since it required above all the reliable execution of orders from above. This is merely one instance of the Achilles' heel in the very conception of the Great Leap Forward: it lacked a macroeconomic organizational vision to bring overall coherence to its microeconomic innovations.

3 The communes

The rural people's communes initially were the institutional counterpart of the GLF's labour-intensive technological policy. They quickly transcended being mere instruments of convenience, however, to become vehicles for a general reorganization of rural life in preparation for a quick transition to communism. Emerging spontaneously as amalgamations of collectives trying to mobilize enough labour for the unprecedented mass irrigation campaign of winter 1957–8, they were quickly seized on and popularized by the Party. By August 1958, when central party guidelines for their formation were first promulgated in the Beidaihe (Peitaiho) Resolution, the communes already encompassed 30 per cent of rural households (see Table 5.1 above). By December, virtually all 740,000 rural collectives containing over 120 million households had been reorganized into some 26,000 rural people's communes, averaging roughly 5,000 households each. This size corresponded on the average to several townships (*xiang*). The townships, which constituted the lowest level of state administration, were absorbed by the communes, thus grafting an element of government authority to the basic collective status of the commune. Communes exceeded in size and cut across the boundaries of the traditional geographic units of local economic exchange, the 'standard marketing areas', which in 1957 roughly corresponded to the townships. In the words of a foremost student of marketing and social structure in rural China, 'the many and grave difficulties encountered by the communes during 1958–61 stemmed in significant part from the grotesquely large mold into which they had in most cases been forced, and in particular from the failure to align the new unit with the natural socioeconomic systems shaped by rural trade' (Skinner 1965, III:394).

There are several reasons for this bias towards gigantism: the identification of large scale with a more advanced position on the road to communism, and consequent pressure on local cadres to achieve the largest feasible size of commune; the desire in the radical political atmosphere of 1958–9 to escape the forces of local particularism embedded in traditional geographic units; and the relative familiarity of officials guiding the initial commune development with conditions of the North China Plain, where better developed transport and communications permitted larger units than elsewhere in China (Skinner 1965, III:384–93). By 1961 efforts were under way to reduce the size of the communes, and by 1963 their number had grown to 74,000, implying that the average commune was then only one-third the original size and corresponded fairly well to the standard marketing area. By the late 1970s the number had again been reduced, to 50,000, possibly in reflection of gradual rural development, and membership per commune averaged 15,000 (although with much variation).

From the beginning, the commune contained three tiers of organization: the commune level at the top; an intermediate level called the production brigade, which generally corresponded to the old collective and to the natural village; and the production team, which was coterminous with the old co-operative and the neighbourhood. The teams averaged thirty to forty households each, the brigades perhaps 160. It will be recalled that, after the 'high tide' of collectivization in 1955–6, the basic accounting unit in agriculture was the collective, which was thus responsible for the distribution of income among its members. Work, however, was organized and carried out by the production team or by even smaller units. This meant that the collective was able to redistribute income from richer to poorer production teams, and that this could and did hurt production incentives. In 1958, however, it was the commune that was initially made the unit of account. Income distribution and redistribution was thus carried out over a much larger population than before, which made the incentive problem worse. The status of accounting unit was later shifted downward, first to the brigade and finally, in 1962, to the team, where with some exceptions it stayed for almost two decades.

The commune was closely associated with Mao's object of eliminating the distinctions between city and countryside, worker and peasant, mental and manual labour, and with his view that attacking these distinctions would in turn release great productive energies. The commune was the institution within which industry, commerce, education, and culture would be brought to the countryside. In the words of the Beidaihe Resolution,

The establishment of people's communes with all-round management of agriculture, forestry, animal husbandry, side occupations, and fishery, where industry (the worker), agriculture (the peasant), exchange (the trader), culture and education (the student), and military affairs (the militiaman) merge into one, is the fundamental policy to guide the peasant to accelerate socialist construction, complete the building of socialism ahead of time, and carry out the gradual transition to communism. [Selden 1979:402]

By establishing community dining rooms, nurseries, crèches, etc., and thus socializing household work, the commune also freed women to participate in labour outside the home. On the one hand, the entry of millions of rural women into the labour force was a primary source of the huge increase in labour during the Great Leap Forward. On the other hand, this event, together with the organizational changes behind it, put the issue of women's equality much higher on the social agenda, and was regarded by leaders of the women's movement as creating conditions for the '"thorough emancipation of women" and the realization of genuine equality with men' (Croll 1980:260). In many areas, women for the first time did field work, learned farming techniques, engaged in industrial and construction work, improved tools, and invented implements. Such activities enhanced the social status of women; and, at least according to the press, they could no longer be regarded as filling a subsidiary role (Croll 1980:263).

Communization affected the private property of the peasants as well as property that had already been collectivized. Early commune documents called for turning over to the commune plots of land reserved for private use under the previous collectives (see Chapter 5, Sec. 2), as well as private house sites, livestock, and large farm tools. Means of consumption, such as houses, clothing, bedding, and bank deposits, were to remain private property, along with small farm tools, small domestic animals, and poultry. Private tree holdings were ambiguously dealt with: the widely publicized draft regulations of the Weixing People's Commune called for collectivizing them, whereas both the Beidaihe and Wuhan Resolutions allowed members to keep them. In the 'communist wind' of 1958, fine distinctions between what was and was not to be collectivized were widely ignored, and in some cases virtually all private property was confiscated.

Communes were set up in Chinese cities, as well, the model city in this respect being Zhengzhou (Chengchow), in Henan Province. Urban communes were a much more tentative and short-lived phenomenon, however, and only briefly in 1958 did they feature an effort to restructure urban society in a fundamental way. Thereafter, 'the emphasis of the urban commune turned from remoulding urban society to mere extension of social welfare services' (Salaff 1967:108), and they disappeared entirely in the early 1960s.

4 Highlights of the Great Leap Forward

The wave of activity that became the Great Leap Forward originated in the mass water conservancy campaign of winter 1957–8, and the subsequent merger of collectives into what would become communes in order to organize labour and other resources on a larger scale. At the beginning of 1958 the call went out to catch up with Britain in the production of steel and other major industrial products within fifteen years. At that point, China was producing about 5 million tons of steel annually and Britain, 40 million tons. Shortly thereafter, the National People's Congress called for a 'Great Leap Forward' in investment and production, over the following three years. Thereafter, factories and localities began vying with each other in raising their output targets, with many planning to fulfil their Second Five Year Plan targets (1962) in one or two years. Taking their cue from the 'Sixty Points on Working Methods' (see Sec. 1 above), localities set out to make the value of their industrial production overtake that of agriculture within three years, and small-scale, local industries grew up everywhere.

Small-scale industry, and especially the 'backyard iron and steel factories', were of course a hallmark of the Leap. Designs drawn up by central ministries in 1957–8 for local, small-scale industries, and plans for central guidance in their establishment, were swept aside in the rush to set up factories, and local initiative took over. Of necessity, the emphasis shifted to very small-scale units. The backyard iron-casting furnaces, with annual production capacity of only a few hundred tons of iron, are the best-known case. But the fact that no fewer than 7.5 million new factories and workships were set up in the first nine months of 1958, including 6 million under the auspices of the communes and their sub-units (Selden 1979:80), testifies to the smallness of scale of most such enterprises. Many, in fact, were simply formed by renaming handicraft workshops—and changing their product lines, with often disastrous results.

The main task of these small industries was to serve agriculture by producing its inputs, gradually modernizing them along the way, and processing its output. In addition, local industry was expected to supply the rural population with common consumer goods, and to serve urban industry by processing its raw materials, packaging its output, providing construction materials, and so forth. Available statistics for the end of 1959 indicate that establishments processing agricultural products were by far the most numerous among commune-run industries, followed by units manufacturing and repairing farm implements, making construction materials, and producing lumber, fuel, and chemicals. (By this time, the 'backyard iron and steel' movement had subsided.) Judging by these figures, the great majority of commune industries were oriented towards the needs of agriculture; on the other hand, only about half of the output value of these industries originated in units serving agriculture. Evidently, the larger enterprises were those that were geared to urban markets (Riskin 1971:260).

The iron and steel movement may have been the culmination of a logic of rural industrial development that began with the perception of severe shortages of farm inputs during the winter of 1957, leading at first to the attempt to produce these in newly established rural industries during the first months of 1958. Lacking the necessary material, the communes turned their attention to iron and steel from the summer of 1958 (Kojima Reiitsu; cited in Selden 1979:81). By the end of the year there were several hundred thousand small blast furnaces dotting the countryside, and some 60 million people were at one time engaged in smelting iron and mining and transporting ore (Dutt 1967:38). Unfortunately, much of this activity occurred at the peak of the harvest season, and seriously interfered with the labour supply. The farm labour force dropped from 192 million in 1957 to 151 million in 1958, a decline of 41 million, and regained its former level only in 1960 (Yang and Li 1980:196). The 1958 grain harvest was of record size, but exaggerated reports from everywhere magnified the centre's estimate of its size out of all proportion. Initial estimates put it at 375 million metric tons, which was more than double the 1957 figure. The resulting false impression of the end of food scarcity, the occupation of millions of peasants with small industries, and the ongoing creation of communes all contributed to the neglect of harvesting work, so that in fact the autumn crop was not entirely brought in (Walker 1968:443–4).

By spring 1959 food shortages had made themselves felt, the leadership had begun to grasp the realities of the economic situation, and measures began to be undertaken to correct the worst excesses of the Leap. Local cadres were urged to curtail 'free supply', return to commune members their confiscated houses, blankets, bank deposits, etc., make sure that members got enough rest during farmland capital construction campaigns, allow members to cook at home, and improve the management of the dining halls, nurseries, homes for the aged, and other collective services. The communes were to turn over more management and administrative authority to the brigades and teams. In the autumn, rural fairs were again permitted to open.

In a meeting of the Politburo in February and March 1959, Mao himself sharply attacked the levelling and overcentralizing tendencies of the Leap, and warned that there was serious unrest and resentment in the countryside.[10] He also complained of the excessive commandeering of agricultural labour for non-agricultural pursuits, and called for 'taking the entire nation as a single chess board' rather than striving for self-sufficiency in each commune without reference to the overall division of labour. Four months later, at the Lushan Conference of the Central Committee, an attack on GLF policies was led by the veteran general and defense minister, Peng Dehuai (Peng Teh-huai), who characterized them as 'petty bourgeois fanaticism', and said that Mao must share the blame. Mao's defense included a wide-ranging self-criticism, in which he acknowledged the virtual disappearance of planning during the Leap:[11]

By doing away with planning, I mean that they dispensed with overall balances, and simply made no estimates of how much coal, iron, and transport would be needed. Coal and iron cannot walk by themselves; they need vehicles to transport them. This I did not foresee . . . I am a complete outsider when it comes to economic construction, and I understand nothing about industrial planning . . . But comrades, in 1958 and 1959 the main responsibility was mine and you should take me to task.

In this same speech, Mao referred to the mass smelting of steel as 'a great catastrophe'. Peng Dehuai had stated that over 13,000 of these projects were below standards. By 1959 most were being closed down and the more successful ones were amalgamated into several production centres. By April 1960 there were some 1,300 small iron-smelting enterprises remaining, and the Planning Minister announced that about 200 of these would be developed into small or medium-size iron and steel complexes.

In August, Premier Zhou Enlai (Chou En-lai) announced a downward revision of the 1958 grain harvest estimate to 250 million metric tons. This figure, which was still an exaggeration (recent Chinese statistics put the figure at 200), amounted to a cut of 125 million metric tons, or one-third, from the original estimate. It was this kind of exaggeration that Peng Dehuai had ridiculed as 'unbelievable miracles' which had 'surely done tremendous harm to the prestige of the party' (Selden 1979:478–9).

Towards the end of 1959 the commune underwent its first major decentralization, when the brigade was made the basic unit of accounting, taxation, and income distribution.

These changes were taking place in an atmosphere of growing agricultural crisis, easily the worst faced in the brief history of the People's Republic. Official statistics put the harvests for the three years 1959–61 at 170, 143.5, and 147.5 million metric tons respectively (*ZTN* 1983:158). The 1960 figure is only 72 per cent of that of 1958 (200 million metric tons). In a poor agrarian country, one

Table 6.1. *Annual per capita grain supply and daily food energy, 1957–1964*

	Annual ave. per capita consumption of grain (kg)		(3) Daily availability of food energy (kcal)
	(1) National	(2) (Rural)	
1957	203	(204)	2167.0
1958	198	(201)	2169.6
1959	187	(183)	1820.2
1960	164	(156)	1534.8
1961	159	(154)	1650.5
1962	165	(161)	1761.2
1963	165	(160)	1863.7
1964	182	(178)	2026.1

Sources and notes: Column (2): *ZMWTZ* (1984:27). Data are in 'trade grain' and are labelled 'pingjun meiren shenghuo xiaofei liang' (average per capita amount of consumption). Column (3): Ashton *et al.* (1984:622). The two columns were estimated independently and are not necessarily mutually consistent.

year of bad harvest may exhaust available stocks of food: two or three in a row can create famine conditions.

The deterioration in national food supplies is shown in Table 6.1. Grain consumption per capita fell by 22 per cent between 1957 and 1961, the year of deepest crisis. (It did not in fact regain the 1957 level until 1979.) The estimate of caloric consumption shown in Table 6.1 suggests that China in 1960 and 1961 was supplying food energy amounts that were very low even in comparison with other recently famine-afflicted countries (Ashton *et al.* 1984:622–3). Even these figures, which are national averages, disguise the depth of the crisis in the regions most affected. Millions of deaths occurred in a major famine whose dimensions were not at the time suspected by the outside world. Section 5 below looks further into its causes and extent.

As these conditions developed, the innovations of the Leap were rolled back one by one. After 1960 the government directed that 90 per cent of rural labour was to remain in agricultural production, which meant that the majority of non-agricultural projects undertaken by the communes and their sub-units had to be dismantled. Private plots were returned to the peasants from the summer of 1960, and during the following year the government encouraged the private rearing of pigs, collective pig production having proved unsuccessful. In May 1961 the 'Sixty Articles on the Communes' were distributed throughout the countryside. As revised and later ratified at the Tenth Plenum in September 1962, this document was a kind of bill of rights for production teams and individual peasants. It made the production team the basic accounting unit for at least thirty years, and protected the team's right to refuse to provide labour to the commune and brigades. It also provided for the right of members to cultivate private plots of 5–7 per cent of cultivated land, the products of which would be neither taxed nor subject to compulsory procurement. Finally, it ratified the system of contracting various farm tasks, such as stock breeding, fisheries, and care of draught animals and farm tools, to small work groups or individuals. This item amounted to a recognition of the erosion of collective morale under the emergency conditions and political disorientation of the early 1960s, when the practice of contracting even basic farmwork to the individual household was apparently widespread in some areas.[12]

The Tenth Plenum, in addition to adopting the 'Sixty Articles' formally, also officially reordered the priorities in Chinese economic planning to place agriculture first, light industry second, and heavy industry last. This marked a major departure from the legacy of Soviet planning, and one that the Chinese had not been willing to make previously. On the other hand, the *meaning* of 'agriculture first' was left far from clear, permitting the assumption to grow in the West that agriculture was to receive the largest share of state investment. In fact, no official Chinese statement even hinted at such a definition of 'agricultural priority', nor has such a policy been carried out at any time. The Tenth Plenum resolution is much vaguer, interpreting the policy to mean that 'the unified plan for the national economy must take the expansion of agriculture as its starting point', and that 'we must begin our socialist construction with the expansion of agriculture (Union Research Institute 1971:194–5).

The notion of 'agricultural priority' thus was an analytical one (albeit not adequately defined): it identified the prior growth of agriculture as a condition of general economic growth, and stipulated that agricultural growth be treated as the first priority of the development plan. However, although this policy remained nominally in effect in subsequent years, and a shift in resources favouring agriculture and agriculture-related sectors of industry did take place in the early 1960s, the commitment of the state to this sector never grew strong enough to keep it from being the weak link in the national economy.

In mid-1960 there remained about 60,000 industrial enterprises run by the counties (*xian*) and perhaps 200,000 run by the communes (excluding the many more at brigade level). Industrial employment in the communes and brigades still accounted for 7 per cent of the rural labour force. The Party and government now moved to close down rural industries *en masse* and return their workers to the agricultural front (Riskin 1978:78–82). The 'Seventy Articles of Industrial Policy', issued in December 1961, called for halting all capital construction projects not specifically included in the national plan; closing all industrial units making losses; returning local state-owned factories that had been formed from handicraft co-operatives during the Great Leap to co-operative status; and ceasing the recruitment of rural labour for industry (Union Research Institute 1971:689–91).

Rural incentives were at the same time reverting to the *status quo ante*. The free-supply-cum-wage system was phased out and replaced by work-points based on quantity and quality of labour. The contract system, referred to above, was quite consistent with the practice of 'three guarantees and one reward' (see Chapter 5, Sec. 2) favoured in pre-commune collectives. Grain distribution to households was now debited to their working members' labour-day accumulations.

The decline of the public dining hall and of other social services established by the communes in their formative period heralded something of a retreat in the movement for women's equality. The merging of public and domestic labour represented by public dining halls, crêches, nurseries, sewing groups, and the like had promised to remove the stigma of triviality from 'women's work' and facilitate the fuller participation of women at all levels of social activity. But it proved very difficult to run such facilities well. The substitution of formal, paid labour for unpaid household labour appeared to raise costs even when it did not; the incentives of close personal relations often could not be matched by those of public institutions; variety of food and freedom of choice of menu were sacrificed; and real material costs tended to be higher—especially in north China, where the *kang*, on which food was cooked at home, doubled as the family's warm winter bed, and thus had to be heated even when cooking was done elsewhere.[13] The collapse of such services sent women back into the home and kitchen. The 'Sixty Articles', notably mute on the subject of social services except as relief for the aged and disabled, urged that the 'household chores' of women (and not of men) be taken into consideration when assigning them basic labour-day quotas.

As the economy slid from the forward momentum of the Leap to the precipitous decline of the 'three hard years', its regress was speeded by a blow from abroad. In the summer of 1960, the Soviet Union recalled all of its 1,400 scientists, engineers, and technicians working in China. According to a prominent Soviet scientist in China at the time, who later emigrated to Canada,

The abruptness of the withdrawal meant that construction stopped at the sites of scores of new plants and factories while work at many existing ones was thrown into confusion. Spare parts were no longer available for plants built according to Russian design, and mines and electric power stations developed with Russian help were closed down. Planning on new undertakings was abandoned because the Russians simultaneously cancelled contracts for the delivery of plans and equipment. [quoted in Meisner 1977:249]

It would have been impossible for Khrushchev to have chosen a moment when China was more vulnerable: a major famine in progress, the economy in organizational disarray, Chinese technical and administrative leadership scattered and demoralized, and the moves to resurrect planning and central control just beginning. Yet, although apparently ordered without warning, the Soviet withdrawal was the culmination of a quarrel between the two countries that had been escalating for some years. Mao had criticized the de-

Stalinization policy emanating from the Soviet Twentieth Party Congress in 1956 for overemphasizing Stalin's negative features. Moreover, the USSR had acted to revise its history without consultation or warning, and with no regard for the international implications of so doing. Mao also regarded Soviet domestic economic policy trends as revisionist and Khrushchev's version of peaceful coexistence as a capitulation to imperialism. More immediately, it was just after leading a Chinese military delegation to the Soviet Union in spring 1959 that Defense Minister Peng Dehuai initiated his attack on the Great Leap Forward. At virtually the same moment, the Russians reneged on a nuclear weapons technology sharing agreement that had been reached with China in 1957, and one month later, in July, Khrushchev began a series of public criticisms of the Great Leap and communes. That Peng Dehuai, a popular veteran revolutionary, should appear to be co-operating with a Soviet assault on Mao and his policies undoubtedly helps to explain the sharpness of Mao's counterattack at the Lushan Plenum in August. The quarrel continued to escalate through the second half of 1959 and the spring of 1960, with a Khrushchev–Eisenhower summit, the Chinese publication of *Long Live Lenin-ism* (a wide-ranging critique of Soviet foreign policy), and the eruption of open conflict of the Romanian Party Congress in June 1960. It was shortly after returning from Bucharest that Khrushchev recalled the Soviet experts (Meisner 1977:248–9).

From the Soviet point of view, the Leap had put great strains on their aid programme by generating sudden increases in machinery and equipment deliveries and unanticipated and capricious shifts in orders and specifications (Prybyla 1970:316). Table 6.2 does show large increases in Soviet exports to China in 1958 (17 per cent above the 1957 figure of $545 million, not shown) and in 1959, when they grew by no less than 50 per cent. The value of complete plant deliveries in 1959 was almost four times that of 1957, although this increase must have resulted in large part from the completion of previously planned projects of long gestation.

The Soviet Union also charged that the Great Leap Forward resulted in frequent and dangerous violations of technical standards by China and the consequent misuse of the equipment being furnished (Prybyla 1970:380); and that Soviet specialists were systematically mistreated in China—a charge denied by one of the Soviet scientists (Meisner 1977:249). Whatever the truth of these allegations, there is little doubt that the Soviet solution of withdrawing its experts entirely was due to the fundamental political and ideological conflict between the two powers rather than to specific conditions in China at the time.

After 1959, Soviet exports to China declined until 1964, with complete plant exports dropping to a few million dollars by 1962. During this period Chinese exports to the Soviet Union continuously exceeded imports from the Russians, as China repaid the credits extended in the first half of the 1950s (see Table 4.10 above). In 1961 the Soviet Union agreed to stretch repayment of $320 million in short-term Chinese loans over a five-year period, and China retired the debt in 1965.

Table 6.2. *Composition of Soviet exports to China, 1958–1965 (Millions of US dollars)*

	1958 Value	1958 %	1959 Value	1960 Value	1961 Value	1962 Value	1963 Value	1964 Value	1964 %	1965 Value
Total exports	634	100	955	817	367	233	187	135	100	192
Machinery, equipment	318	50	598	504	108	27	42	58	43	77
Industr. raw materials	173	27	176	189	167	127	107	58	43	72
Consumer goods	9	2	7	4	67	31	14	7	5	1
Other merchandise	17	3	12	13	6	3	2	6	4	17
Unspecified	116	18	161	107	19	45	21	8	6	25

Source: Price (1967).

5   Evaluation

The Great Leap Forward was a multi-dimensional social phenomenon. No brief evaluation can do justice to its deep and lasting impact on Chinese society. Here I confine myself principally to the direct economic consequences in drawing up a rough balance sheet for the Leap.

From a strictly short-run, quantitative perspective, the mobilized energies of the population did drive industrial output up sharply. Comparing the official statistics with three Western estimates of Chinese industrial production, Choh-ming Li (1964:14) commented that 'all the four estimates agree that there was a "great leap forward" in industrial growth from 1957 through 1959 or 1960 . . .' Table 6.3 displays in rows (1)–(4) the estimates referred to by Li, together with two more recent ones. It is apparent that, although the recent estimates sharply discount 1960 industrial performance, all agree that industrial growth in 1958 and 1959 exceeded the official estimate (18 per cent—see Table 4.2) for the First Five Year Plan.

The problem lies in interpreting these figures. During the Great Leap, quality and variety were neglected in the rush to produce greater quantities. Industrial enterprises were not constrained by the need to sell their output to users; whatever they produced counted, whether or not anyone wanted or could use it. With planning in disarray and market forces inoperative (with some exceptions—see below), much output was of too low quality to be used, or, as in the case of crude steel, was not produced in the varieties needed by users. Such output, symbolized by steel ingots rusting beside railroad tracks or farm tools breaking at first use, represents a waste of resources, yet the industrial growth statistics just cited are based on accepting it as useful output and valuing it at official prices.

It has sometimes been argued that the Great Leap Forward cost China 'almost a decade' of economic growth. Figure 6.1 (which is based on Table 6.4)

Table 6.3. *Alternative estimates of industrial growth rates, 1958–1960*

Source of estimate	Industr. net or gross output value (price base)	% increase in:		
		1958	1959	1960
(1) Liu and Yeh	Net (1952)	19.6	27.0	—
(2) Y. L. Wu *et al.*	Net (1952	19.5	32.3	15.7
(3) K. Chao	Net (1952)	30.3	31.5	—
(4) Official	Gross (1957)	66.3	39.2	29.0
(5) Rawski	Gross (1952)	45.0	22.1	4.0
(6) Field	Net (mixed)	42.1	21.5	5.1

Sources: Rows (1)–(4) are from Li (1964:14). This source identifies the official figures as being in 'net' terms, which is an apparent error. Row (5) is from Rawski (1980b:191). Row (6) is from an index of industiral production developed by R. M. Field and cited in Ashbrook (1978:231).

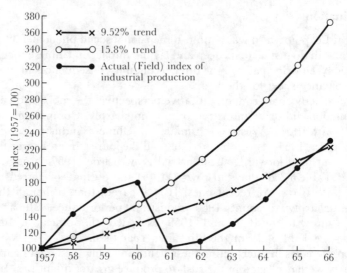

Fig. 6.1. Time paths of actual industrial production and two hypothetical trends, 1957–1966. (*Source*: Table 6.4.)

plots an index of industrial production from 1957 to 1966 and two hypothetical time trends for the same period: the first is the 15.8 per cent rate of growth shown by the same (Field) index for the FFYP period; the second is a 9.52 per cent growth path tracing the average industrial growth rate during the period 1957–77, according to official Chinese statistics (*ZTN* 1983:216). If the 'lost decade' hypothesis is taken to mean that China needed many years to recover its past peak levels of industrial output, and if we discount nominal Great Leap production levels and instead take 1957 output as the past peak in question, then the hypothesis is obviously wrong. A glance at the figure shows that actual industrial production never fell below the 1957 level, even at the depth of the post-Leap depression in 1961. On the other hand, if we treat Great Leap statistics as valid,[14] then the previous peak year becomes 1960, and it is not regained until 1965. Although five years do not a decade make, the 'lost decade' hypothesis can in this case be regarded as at least half valid. However, this conclusion requires not questioning the 1960 output figures.

A more meaningful issue might be the length of time it took China to regain its industrial growth trend line. The output lost during the time that actual production lay below the historical trend line would be a crude measure of the cost in forgone consumption and investment of the Great Leap Forward.[15] Unfortunately, there is no compelling choice of historical trend that recommends itself for this test. One possibility is to use the 15.8 per cent rate of industrial growth of the FFYP period. In this case, we see from Figure 6.1 that actual industrial production falls below the trend in 1961 and remains below it ever after (indeed, to this day). In 1965 industrial output was still slightly below

Table 6.4. *Indexes of actual industrial production and of two hypothetical time trends of industrial production, 1957–1966 (1957 = 100)*

	1958	1959	1960	1961	1962	1963	1964	1965	1966
(1) Actual industr. production	142	173	181	104	111	134	161	199	232
(2) 15.8% trend assumed	116	134	155	180	208	241	279	323	374
(3) 9.52% trend assumed	110	120	131	144	158	173	189	206	227
(4) Foodgrain output	102.5	87.2	73.6	75.6	82.0	87.2	96.1	99.7	109.7

Sources: Row (1) is taken from USCJEC (1978:231). *Row (2)* is calculated by applying the average rate of growth of the Field index (the industrial production index in USCJEC 1978:231) for the years 1953–7 (i.e., 15.8 per cent) to the years 1958–66. *Row (3)* applies to 1958–66 the average rate of growth of industrial production for the years 1957–77 implicit in index numbers for the two end years given in ZTN (1983:216). *Row (4)* is from ZTN (1984:370). For explanation see text.

the trend value for 1962. However, it is widely believed that the industrial growth rate of the FFYP period could not have been sustained very much longer, since (1) it benefited from once-and-for-all elements of recovery in the early and mid-1950s; (2) Soviet loans, which contributed to it, had ended; and (3) the slow growth of agriculture, and even more so of agricultural procurement, would have slowed industrial growth in any case.

A second possibility would be to take as the underlying historical trend the average industrial growth rate after 1957, when the special considerations operating during the First Plan period were no longer present. The 9.52 per cent trend line for the period 1957–77 (according to official statistics) is thus also shown in the figure. Actual industrial production falls below it in 1961 and exceeds it again only in 1966 (another 'lost half-decade'). The sum of annual shortfalls in the index of industrial production during the five years 1961–5 comes to 161, which is slightly larger than the trend line figure for 1962. This comparison ignores the *excess* of actual production above the trend line from 1958 to 1960 on the assumption that it was largely nominal and did not reflect real gains in consumption and investment. The real cost of the Great Leap Forward to China's industrialization effort is then equivalent to an amount of industrial output forgone which is equal to the total industrial production predicted by the trend line for 1962, and greater than the actual (nominal) output of 1958. While not perhaps a 'lost decade', this is still a substantial loss, bearing in mind that the measure is crude and imperfect.[16]

The most serious losses, however, were in agriculture, where they led to a major famine that in terms of loss of life may have been the worst on human record, but about which information is still quite scanty. To begin with, the increase in foodgrain output was smaller and shorter-lived than that in industrial production. It rose only 2.6 per cent in 1958, then fell for the following two years to reach a 1960 nadir some 29 per cent below the 1958 peak (Table 6.4 row (4)). The average per capita level of grain consumption in the countryside fell from 204 kg in 1957 to only 154 kg in 1961, and estimated national per capita daily caloric intake in 1960 was only 1,535 kilocalories (Table 6.1).

Chinese reports at the time mention the existence of 'oedema', 'dropsy', 'serious famine', and 'starvation' (Walker 1977:559), but not the magnitude of loss of life. More recent foreign analysis, based upon newly released mortality and fertility statistics for the years in question (see Table 6.5) as well as on the population age distribution emerging from the 1964 and 1982 censuses, suggests a truly appalling magnitude (Aird 1980:1982; Ashton *et al.* 1984; Coale 1981; 1984; Sun Yefang 1981). A simple application of the increases in official mortality rates to the population of the famine years (1959–61) yields excess deaths numbering over 15 million. A more sophisticated reconstruction estimates excess mortality above the 'normal' level at almost twice this figure (Ashton *et al.* 1984:619).[17] There remain many unanswered questions about the sources and quality of the statistics, which describe a period in which the statistical system itself was in disarray. At this point no exact estimate of famine mortality can be accepted with confidence. Nevertheless, all available information is consistent with a picture of demographic catastrophe.

Table 6.5. *Demographic crisis and state procurement of foodgrains, 1955–1965*

	Crude birth rate	Crude death rate	Natural increase rate	Grain output	State procurement		% of output procured	
					Total	Net	Total	Net
1955	32.60	12.28	20.32	183.9	50.7	36.2	27.6	19.7
1956	31.90	11.40	20.50	192.7	45.4	28.7	23.6	14.9
1957	34.03	10.80	23.23	195.0	48.0	33.9	24.6	17.4
1958	29.22	11.98	17.24	200.0	58.8	41.7	29.4	20.9
1959	24.78	14.59	10.19	170.0	67.4	47.6	39.7	28.0
1960	20.86	25.43	−4.57	143.5	51.1	30.9	35.6	21.5
1961	18.02	14.24	3.78	147.5	40.5	25.8	27.4	17.5
1962	37.01	10.02	26.99	160.0	38.1	25.7	23.8	16.1
1963	43.37	10.04	33.33	170.0	44.0	28.9	25.9	17.0
1964	39.14	11.50	27.64	187.5	47.4	31.8	25.3	17.0
1965	37.88	9.50	28.38	194.5	48.7	33.6	25.0	17.3

Source: ZTN (1984:83, 370). 'Net' procurement refers to gross procurement minus resales to deficit areas in the countryside.

Both natural conditions and human error contributed to the situation, although their relative shares of the blame cannot be assessed.[18] Natural disasters were widespread during the three-year period, and especially in 1960 (Freeberne 1962), but state policy undoubtedly contributed to the shortages, doing both short- and long-run damage to agriculture, as well as complicating and delaying relief measures. The construction of dams and reservoirs without prior assessment of their impact on the water table led to salinization and alkalinization of the soil. Such damage is not easily reversed and helps to explain why the grain output of the three North China Plain provinces of Henan, Hebei, and Shandong did not regain its previous peak level until the late 1960s (Walker 1977:558). Innovations such as deep ploughing and close planting, promoted by the centre beyond the bounds of rationality, also reduced output, as did the excessive drain of labour out of agriculture and into small-scale industry and transport. The military organization of farm production and the confiscation of peasants' personal property, especially in the earlier part of the Leap, the elimination in many places of private plots, the overcentralized and redistributive character of the early communes, and the adoption of the free supply system all harmed peasant incentives.

Great Leap policies not only helped create the crisis but also caused costly delay in ameliorating it. The politically motivated exaggeration of harvest size and the destruction of objective reporting systems kept the leadership in the dark about real supply conditions: 'Leaders believed in 1959–60 that they had 100 MMT more grain than they actually did' (Bernstein 1984a:13). Some local cadres, their political reputations dependent upon meeting impossibly high output commitments, failed to seek relief or even sealed off their localities to keep news of real conditions from getting out.

Excessive procurement of grain was a prime contributor to shortages in the countryside (Bernstein 1984a). Under the mistaken belief that harvests had miraculously broken all records, the government in 1958, 1959, and 1960 procured, respectively, 22, 40, and 6 per cent more grain than in 1957 (Table 6.5). In 1957 gross procurement had come to 24.6 per cent of the harvest; by 1959 it had gone up to 39.7 per cent, and in the year of highest mortality, 1960, it was 35.6 per cent. Even after resales to deficit rural areas, it remained a full 10 percentage points higher in 1959, and 4 points higher in 1960, than in 1957. Rural areas were the chief sufferers: as Table 6.1 shows, the relative advantage enjoyed by rural people in per capita foodgrain supplies during 1957 and 1958 was reversed during the crisis: in fact, rural per capita supplies remained lower than urban thenceforth until the 1980s (ZMWTZ 1984:27). Substantial grain imports, designed to supply the coastal cities and relieve pressure on the countryside, finally began in 1961, two years late.

Party and government decisions worsened the crisis in more general ways, as well. Thus, Mao was in the process of moderating the policies of the Great Leap in 1959 when the challenge from Peng Dehuai came at the Lushan Conference. The purge of Peng brought a return to the excessive policies he had criticized and no doubt thus deepened and prolonged the famine. Moreover, as Mao himself later acknowledged, preoccupation from late 1959 with the growing polemic with the Soviet Union slowed the leadership's perception of and response to the domestic crisis (Bernstein 1984:31; MacFarquhar 1983:parts 3 and 4).

In retrospect, the main institutional legacy of the Great Leap Forward was the modified rural commune with its mission of bringing industry, education, health, and culture to the countryside. The three-tiered commune turned out to be a flexible instrument for organizing farmland capital construction, facilitating technical change, introducing some social welfare protection to rural people, and instituting rural industrialization. Many of the small and medium-size industries that sprang up in the countryside after 1962 originated in the backyard factories of the Leap (Riskin 1978a:84).

The commune organization persisted for two decades before succumbing to the reforms of the Deng Xiaoping era. The primary indictment of it when it was finally dismantled was that it was the vehicle through which the state intervened directly and improperly in the affairs of agriculture, thus depriving farmers of the incentive and authority needed to develop their local economies (see Chapter 12). However, an argument could be made that the accomplishments of these semi-collective, semi-governmental institutions in developing a rural productive infrastructure made possible the unprecedented spurt of agricultural growth that attended their dissolution; and, further, that such infrastructural development could have been realized only by relatively large and collective institutions.

Could the more constructive components of the Great Leap Forward approach have been instituted more rationally, with communes formed carefully and with prior experimentation, industries built on a solid technical foundation, mass labour construction projects undertaken only after geological investigation, etc.? In short, could the underlying rational idea of stimulating local initiative and capitalizing on China's abundant labour have been implemented without the wholesale political assault on the urban-based bureaucracy and technical intelligentsia which gave rise to the irrational use of ideology to override objective constraints? To have proceeded in this way would have required either proposing an alternative to the central command planning regime as the basis for macroeconomic organization or accepting the general parameters of that regime. Mao was unwilling to accept them, yet in the end had no alternative to propose. The social upheaval embodied in discrediting the bureaucracy was quite central to the Leap, and so, unfortunately, was its ultimate irrationality.

Our evaluation of the Leap has already, of necessity, begun considering its negative aspects. These fall into several distinct categories, of which one, already alluded to, is the use of 'politics in command' to override objective constraints. A reasonable interpretation of this slogan, consistent with Maoist principle, is that the evaluation of policies must take account of their impact on social and political relations. However, during the Leap it came to mean instead that almost any desirable goal could, with the correct attitude, be quickly accomplished, regardless of objective conditions. Exemplifying this tendency was the excessive transfer of labour out of agriculture in 1958 and 1959, the belief (which experienced peasants well knew to be untrue) that yields would rise in direct proportion to the depth of ploughing and closeness of planting, and the destruction of the statistical system as it came to serve the inspirational needs of local cadres. For a brief period, as Howe and Walker (1977:200–1) show, Mao himself accepted and disseminated the grossly exaggerated statistics that resulted, and thus 'led the Chinese people to believe that miracles had happened in agricultural production'.

A second category of error in the Great Leap approach was the glorification of output quantity *per se*, without regard for quality or variety. The doubling of the steel target to 10.8 million metric tons in 1958 and its further increase to 18 million metric tons in 1959 illustrate this problem. 'Although the means of production provided by industry for agriculture doubled in this period, they could hardly make up for the decrease in the labour force on account of poor quality, unsuitability, or general ineffectivenss' (Yang and Li 1980:196).

The incentive problems of the Leap form a third category. These problems range from the initial confiscation of personal property, and the military organization of labour and commandism of cadres, to the elimination of private plots and overcentralization of commune organization. They include also the problems associated with commune social services, especially community dining halls, many of which were run in a coercive fashion.

A particularly interesting group of problems stems from the survival into the Great Leap Forward of policies and attitudes associated with past approaches and strictly at odds with the GLF strategy. One such atavism was the tendency to look to redistribution for needed resources—a 'primitive accumulation bias'[19] (Riskin 1971). Redistributive policies, such as land reform, nationalization, collectivization, taxation, and price manipulation, had been effectively used between 1949 and 1957 to generate resources for raising both investment and the consumption level of the poorest. By the late 1950s, however, with a national investment rate already exceeding 20 per cent of national product and with no significant cushion of luxury consumption surviving eight years of institutional change and income equalization, the potential for further redistribution was meager. Yet GLF policy sought to establish small industries with the resources taken from previously existing local factories and handicraft co-operatives (Riskin 1971:263). Thus, workshops making household utensils, farm tools, and arts and crafts products were transformed into 'factories' producing iron and steel and other heavy industrial goods. By May 1959, of the more than 5 million handicraft workers who had been organized in co-operatives in 1956, 35 per cent were employed in commune factories, 38 per cent in other local industries, and 14 per cent in larger, amalgamated co-operative factories. Only 13 per cent were still in their original, small co-operatives (Donnithorne 1967:224). The result was a severe shortage of essential small commodities and a consequent emergency campaign to restore both handicraft workers and their tools and materials to their original tasks (Riskin 1971:265).

The 'primitive accumulation bias' probably had several roots. The most obvious one is previous experience, for radical institutional reform and income redistribution had indeed contributed significantly to both national investment and the consumption of poorer Chinese in the early and mid-1950s. Another is Mao's oft-expressed emphasis on 'digging out potential'. Mao's view of economic development was not the standard Western economics paradigm centred on optimal allocation of fixed supplies of resources. He was interested in *enlarging* the stock of resources, both human and material, by arousing the initiative of working people. During the Great Leap, such an approach worked briefly not only to step up the intensity of production labour but also to find waste and scrap materials, ores from newly opened mines, and wild plants of various kinds in the drive to increase production. But the Leap far exceeded in scale even the considerable supplies of labour and such irregular materials as were found, and quickly turned to cannibalizing resources already earmarked for essential products.

These two bases of reliance on 'primitive accumulation' in the search for resources were probably strengthened by the tendency of peasant societies to conceive of the economy in zero-sum terms. That is, in an economy that in living memory grows very little if at all, it is quite natural to see one person's gain as another's loss. Concern about the distribution of a fixed sum, rather than with expansion through reinvestment of produced surpluses, is the rule.[20]

A second atavistic element that conflicted with GLF policies was the identification of economic progress with the development of heavy industry.[21] It might seem strange to suggest a conflict between this attitude and the Leap, which after all had as a fundamental objective the overtaking of Britain in steel production. But the Leap's 'walking on two legs' strategy was intended to free the modern industrial sector to concentrate its productive capacity on self-expansion, while the production and consumption needs of the farm population were met by the 'native' sector. As Eckstein put it,

The modern sector would become virtually an *input–input* economy . . . in the sense that every attempt would be made to minimize the leakages from the modern sector to the traditional sector, while the intermediate and final goods produced by the modern sector would be plowed back into the further expansion of that sector . . .

In contrast, the traditional sector would be pushed into involuntary autarky, with small-scale industries providing for all the consumption, production, and investment needs of this sector. [Eckstein 1977:57]

Thus, as we have already seen, the major responsibility for upgrading agricultural technology, as well as for supplying rural consumer goods, belonged to the small industries in the traditional sector. Many commune factories did indeed try to fulfil this responsibility. At the end of 1959 there were 123,000 establishments under commune auspices that were engaged in processing farm output, 20,000 making and repairing farm implements, and 11,600 making simple chemical fertilizer. But over half the output value of commune industries came from production that was not agriculture-related (Riskin 1971:260), while the quality of that which was often precluded effective use on the farms. Moreover, the heavy industry orientation of the modern sector during the Leap spilled over into the countryside to influence the choice of output mix of the rural industries. This is because of still a third 'atavism' that compromised Leap strategy, namely, the survival of the profit motive.

The Party and state certainly did not want commune industries to choose their product lines in order to maximize profits, because the arbitrary structure of state-determined prices would have dictated choices at odds with state policy. In particular, because of the low prices of agricultural goods relative to industrial ones, the peasants in general could not compete with urban industries for the products of commune factories. By directing commune industries to serve agriculture, therefore, the state was really urging them to ignore market signals. Yet, paradoxically, the breakdown of central physical and financial controls at the height of the Leap left communes with considerable freedom to follow market signals in setting up industries, and many sought to increase their incomes by contracting to supply urban construction companies with building materials or by doing processing work for urban factories (Riskin 1971:260–1).

The 'heavy industry bias' of the Leap overall can be seen from the data collected in Table 6.6. Since heavy industry consists predominantly of producer goods industries, its importance in the economy tends to be reflected in the rate of accumulation in national income. A strong emphasis on heavy industry will correspond to a high accumulation rate (i.e., a high proportion of income set aside from current consumption for purchasing new capital). As is apparent from row (1) of Table 6.6, the national accumulation rate (see note 5 of this chapter for a definition) rose from about 25 per cent in 1957 to over 33 per cent in 1958, and then—as accumulation stayed high while agricultural income dropped—to a peak of almost 44 per cent in 1959. This was the highest rate of accumulation in the history of the PRC. The policy of pushing accumulation to

Table 6.6. *Indicators of heavy industry bias in the Great Leap Forward*

		1953–7	1957	1958	1959	1960	1958–62
(1)	Accumulation rate (%)[a]	24.2	24.9	33.8	43.8	39.6	30.8[b]
(2)	Incremental capital-output ratio[a]	2.9	—	—	—	—	100
	Average consumption[a] (current yuan):						
(3)	Peasants	—	79	—	65	68	—
(4)	Workers	—	205	195	—	—	—
	% of total investment in capital construction going to:[b]						
(5)	Agriculture	7.8	—	10.5	10.5	13.0	—
(6)	Heavy industry	46.5	—	57.0	56.7	55.3	—
(7)	Light industry	5.9	—	7.3	5.2	4.0	—
(8)	All 3 sectors	60.2	—	74.8	72.4	72.3	—
	Labour force (millions):[b]						
(9)	Agricultural	—	192	151	} c. 192		—
(10)	Employed in state industr. enterprises	—	7.48	23.16		21.44	—
(11)	Heavy ind.	—	4.50	17.50	14.18	15.72	—
(12)	Light ind.	—	2.98	5.66		5.72	—
(13)	Total employment in heavy ind.	—	5.57	35.50			—
(14)	Non-agr. population	—	106.18	122.10	—	—	—
(15)	Urban population	—	99.49	107.21	—	—	—

N.B. For definition of 'accumulation rate', see note 5, this chapter. The figures for incremental capital–output ratio are calculated from their reciprocals, given in the source as 'national income increased by every one-hundred yuan accumulation (yuan)'. The method of calculation is not given. The negligibly low figure for 1958–62 obviously reflects the sharp drop in national income during that period and is not therefore an accurate reflection of the long-run productivity of Great Leap investment. No attempt is made here to compare the Chinese data presented in the table on labour force, employment, and population with various attempts to estimate such information outside of China, or to fill in gaps in the table with such estimated data.

Sources: [a]Dong (1980). [b]Yang and Li (1980:190, 192, 196).

such levels was to be harshly criticized in later years. The rate declined slightly in 1960 but stayed very high, at around 40 per cent. The lower average of 30.8 per cent for the Second Five Year Plan period as a whole (1958–62) reflects the inevitable fall in accumulation during its last two years of economic crisis when most investment activity as well as other production not immediately associated with providing food was curtailed. The rate was 10.4 per cent in 1962 (Dong 1980:12).

The lack of equipment and raw materials to support such a high investment rate kept many factories operating with much excess capacity and impeded the progress of many projects. The result was a sharp rise in the incremental capital–output ratio. During the First Plan period this had averaged around 2.9, but for the Second Plan period as whole its measured value rose to 100, according to one source (row (2) of Table 6.6). The latter figure must be regarded as rhetorical since it reflects the collapse of income in 1960–1; from the beginning of recovery in 1962, larger income flows may have been produced by GLF investments. But there is no doubt that much GLF investment activity was wasted in the pure sense of producing zero or negative income flows (e.g., irrigation works that impaired soil fertility).

The impact of increasing accumulation on the sectoral allocation of capital construction investment can be seen in rows (5)–(8) of the table. The principal trend shown by these figures is a sharp rise in the share of total capital construction investment going to heavy industry, but *not* at the expense of agriculture and light industry. Indeed, agriculture's share rose substantially during the Leap from its FFYP level. Thus, the increased shares of heavy industry (primarily) and agriculture (secondarily) pushed up the combined share of all three sectors from 60 per cent during the First Plan period to 72–75 per cent during the Leap. This of course meant a deep cut—amounting to over 30 per cent—in the share of capital construction investment going to all other sectors of the economy, such as commerce, culture, education, public health, and government administration.

The heavy industry bias of the Leap, and its attendant disruptions, lowered per capita consumption. Row (3) shows average peasant consumption decreasing from Y79 per annum in 1957 to Y65 in 1959. It may have risen somewhat in 1958 because of the good crop of that year and much wasteful consumption that accompanied the introduction of the free supply system. But such an increase, if there was one, could not be sustained when harvests failed in 1959 and 1960. Of course, some of the decline in consumption was unavoidable, given exceptionally poor weather. Worker consumption (row (4)) declined by 5 per cent between 1957 and 1958, but no figures are available for the next two years, when it must have continued to fall.

Finally, the heavy industry bias can be observed affecting labour force structure. Row (9) shows the agricultural labour force declining by some 41 million persons between 1957 and 1958, a 21 per cent drop. Although employment in state industrial enterprises tripled from 7.48 million in 1957 to 23.16 million in 1958 (row (10)), the *absolute* increase (15.68 million) amounts to less than 40 per cent of the decline in agricultural labour. Some of the remaining

25 million people leaving agriculture in 1958 moved into other non-agricultural activities in the state sector, but the bulk of them became employed in commune industries. Total heavy industrial employment rose by almost 30 million (row (13)), while that in state enterprises increased by 13 million (row (11)), implying that the iron and steel and other heavy industrial undertakings of the communes absorbed almost 17 million workers.

Data on non-agricultural and urban population for 1957 and 1958 are shown in rows (14) and (15), but they are interesting chiefly for illustrating the numerous puzzles and lacunae that are thrown up by Chinese data for which definitions and methods of collection are not revealed. Thus, the increase in non-agricultural population (15.9 million) is dwarfed by the decline in the agricultural labour force (41 million), implying that the difference—some 25 million people—moved into non-agricultural work without becoming part of the non-agricultural population. Similarly, the growth in urban population in 1958 (7.7 million) appears small when put beside the increase in state industrial employees (15.7 million), implying that half of the enormous increase in the latter consisted of urban residents who were previously unemployed or were not members of the labour force.

Although row (9) shows the agricultural labour force returning by 1960 to its 1957 dimensions, the widespread migration from countryside to cities continued into 1960. Several contemporary sources refer to a total increase of 20 million in the city population during the period 1958–60 (Hou 1968:343; Aird 1967:389). In the midst of the food crisis, the overblown urban population aggravated the problem of supplying the cities, and urgent measures were taken in the early 1960s to send people back to their villages (see Chapter 7).

From a long-run perspective, one of the most unfortunate legacies of the Great Leap Forward was its impact on the planning system. The virtual collapse of central planning, as recorded by Mao's bald statement, 'By doing away with planning, I mean that they dispensed with overall balances' (see above),[22] proved to be the first declining phase of a recurrent cycle. Cyril Lin explains the emergence of this cyclical pattern as follows:

The Great Leap in particular negated efforts to improve the planning system. The accelerated pace of decentralization beyond original intentions and beyond the 'absorptive capacity' of inexperienced local authorities . . . . and the renewed worship of the gross output deity all exacerbated the problems of plan coherence, imbalances, and disproportions. Since then the cycle of centralization–decentralization would be repeated again and again: centralization imposed order and greater balance but resulted in a rigid, lifeless economy; decentralization stimulated economic activities but resulted in chaos and disproportions. [Cyril Lin 1981]

Clearly, this pattern bears a strong similarity to the experience of Eastern Europe, where such scholars as Josef Goldmann (1965) have attributed cyclical fluctuations in growth to fundamental characteristics of the central planning system. In China, the Great Leap represented a decisive break with this system long before its full capabilities had been mastered. The alternative of administrative decentralization failed not only because of the excesses of the moment, but also, as Cyril Lin (1981) points out, because it carries some of the worst features of the bureaucratic model to the local level, perversely strengthening them. Thus, arbitrariness and subjectivity in decision-making, the lack of institutionalized pressures to economize in the use of scarce resources, and the absence of effective means to make production responsive to demand were all preserved intact in the administratively decentralized bureaucratic planning system. Yet, with the exception of a few perceptive efforts by economists such as Sun Yefang and Chen Yun in the 1950s, these problems and methods of addressing them had not been investigated in China, and any alternative to command planning was ideologically suspect. Mao's own profoundly anti-bureaucratic innovations were thus inevitably erosive of planning *per se*, since bureaucratic planning was the only kind seriously considered. The contradiction between Maoist ideology and centralized, bureaucratic planning remained with China until well after Mao's death, preventing the effective use of the latter while ruling out, on ideological grounds, the development of alternatives.

Notes

1. This statement is contained in his talk of 10 March 1958 to the Chengdu Conference (in Schram 1974:101).
2. The 'Sixty Points on Working Methods' was a draft resolution of the central committee. In his preface to it, dated 31 January 1958, Mao states that some of the points are notes of proposals by others (of whom he singles out Liu Shaoqi for mention); others are 'inspired' by discussions at various conferences, while 'only a few are put forward by me'. For the text, see Chen (1970:57–76).
3. The importance of the anti-rightist campaign as a political prerequisite of the Leap is a principal theme of early GLF literature.
4. 'Marginal accumulation rate' refers to the proportion of the increase in net income that is put into an accumulation fund for investment purposes rather than being distributed to members.
5. Yang and Li (1980). The national 'rate of accumulation' is the ratio of 'accumulation' to 'national income'. 'Accumulation' is basically 'that part of national income used to increase fixed capital assets (productive, and non-productive), working capital, and material reserves' (Chen 1967:11). 'National income', in the Marxian definition used in China, omits most services. Thus, accumulation is fairly similar to the Western concept of 'net investment', but 'national income' is smaller than the corresponding Western concept. Hence, the national 'rate of accumulation' will be larger than the net investment rate. See Field (1980) for a discussion of the relation between 'accumulation' and 'capital formation'.
6. In the Chinese terminology of the time, the two legs were referred to, respectively, as 'tu fa' (local or indigenous methods) and 'yang fa' (foreign methods).
7. See Riskin (1971:247–50), on which this section relies.
8. See Schran (1969:74). A 'labour-day' is a standard unit of work measurement and is larger than the actual average work-day. For example, one work-day of a male, able-bodied full-time worker in 1958 was equivalent to 0.88 labour-days, while that of a female full labour force member was equivalent to 0.77 labour-days (Schran 1969:31).

9. For a good discussion of enterprise management at the onset of the Great Leap Forward, see Andors (1977:68–89), on which the above three paragraphs rely heavily.

10. Mao's speeches to this conference, which took place at Zhengzhou (Chengchow), are translated in *Chinese Law and Government*, Winter 1976–7, with a useful introduction by Pierre Perrolle and Philip E. Ginsburg.

11. The text of Mao's speech to the Lushan meeting is in Schran (1974), where the quoted passage appears on p. 142. Excerpts of Peng Dehuai's criticism of the Leap appear in Selden (1979:474–80). Principal documents of the conflict between Mao and Peng can be found in *The Case of Peng Teh-huai, 1959–1968* (1968).

12. See Chen and Ridley (1969). For the text of the 'Sixty Articles on Communes', see Union Research Institute (1971:695).

13. See Croll (1980:282–6) for a good discussion of the difficulties encountered by commune social services.

14. 'Valid' here refers to the assumption that nominal output value reflects a general equilibrium in which all markets clear. The issue of whether the nominal statistics are *accurate* is of course a prior question.

15. This formulation is imperfect because it neglects the effect of forgone investment on the trend line itself. See also the following note.

16. Some of the more obvious problems of this analysis are as follows. (1) It assumes that all of the shortfall in industrial production during 1961–5 was due to GLF policies, and none to the weather and to the withdrawal of Soviet experts in 1960. (2) It measures cost only in terms of *industrial* output, ignoring agriculture and other sectors. (3) It ignores the negative effects of the shortfalls on the trend line itself, not only via reductions in investment and thus in future production capacity, but also because of the political and social legacy of factionalism, demoralization, etc., left by the Great Leap. (4) It neglects possible positive effects of the Great Leap on the trend line, discussed in the text below. (5) The trend line itself is the product of many historically unique circumstances—e.g., the Great Leap, the Cultural Revolution, the opening of China to Western trade and investment in the 1970s, etc.—and thus may not truly reflect long-run underlying forces.

17. This estimate, of 29.5 million premature deaths, also has problems associated with it. Its high estimate of above-normal deaths results in part from an unrealistically low estimate of 'normal' deaths obtained by applying normal infant mortality rates to the abnormally small number of births during the crisis. Furthermore, the ratio of child to adult mortality fluctuates in ways that are hard to explain. Unreported deaths are also assumed to fluctuate sharply—from 28 to 47 per cent of actual deaths during the famine years.

18. Liu Shaoqi (Liu Shao-ch'i) is said to have assigned 70 per cent of the blame to human mistakes and 30 per cent to natural calamities (Chao 1970:30–1).

19. For an explanation of the term 'primitive accumulation', as applied by Marx to early capitalist development and by the Soviet economist, Preobrazhenski, to the problem of socialist development in the USSR, see Erlich (1960:42–4).

20. This attitude is portrayed clearly in William Hinton's (1966) classic account of land reform in a north China village.

21. The term 'heavy industry' is ambiguous. Although it is roughly co-terminous with producer goods (and 'light industry' with consumer goods), some industries considered 'heavy'—e.g., coal and electricity—produce for consumers, and some 'light' industries—e.g., paper and small farm tools—sell to producers. See Chen (1967:28). In the discussion of the text, 'heavy industry' is understood as excluding producer goods in agriculture.

22. Cf. Howe and Walker (1977:198), who write of the GLF that 'At its most extreme, the [decentralization of economic and financial planning] created a situation where the economy was subject to central control only to the extent that it responded to direct appeals by Mao and others.'

CHAPTER 7

COUNTER-CURRENTS: ECONOMIC RECOVERY, 1962-1965

1 Introduction

The strategy and tactics of guerrilla warfare were to a degree the model for Mao's social mobilizational approach to development. Mao alluded frequently to the experience of the Yanan days, and, while aware that economic development would require new technological and organizational skills, he often held up the Yanan practices of old—and the values underlying them—as models with which to make unfavourable comparisons of the present. Action by relatively small groups under the discipline of ideology, decentralization, egalitarian distribution, abolition of formal military ranks, concentration of inferior forces to achieve tactical superiority, the waging of 'battles of annihilation', and the mass line are all modes of operation developed during the Yanan period which found expression in post-Liberation development policy.

The analogy between guerrilla war and economic development has inherent limitations even in a period of advance, as the Great Leap Forward made clear. However, it seems to lose its force altogether in retreat. Whereas military retreat is an essential part of guerrilla tactics before a superior enemy, economic retreat, especially in a planned economy with limited exposure to the world market, is likely to be a consequence of policy mistakes.[1] In the immediate aftermath of the Leap, however, Mao and others posited a 'law' of economic growth, according to which development is inevitably 'wave-like' or 'saddle-shaped'. Mao argued that it proceeds like a marching army, covering great distances swiftly and then requiring rest and recuperation; that balance is always temporary and transient, imbalance permanent.

There is truth in these homilies as general propositions about the elusiveness of perfection, but as a rationalization of the deep depression into which China fell after the Great Leap, they fail badly. The 'three hard years' were brought on in large part by the very nature of the Leap, and were not inevitable or desirable. Moreover, mobilizational economics came into discredit; Mao himself retreated to the sidelines of leadership; and direction of the economy was taken over by people committed to the maintenance of 'short-line' balance, constrained by the capacity of the weak links in the economy. Economic retreat thus brought with it a repudiation of the guerrilla analogy and a switch to a quite different strategy of economic development.

The recovery that began in 1962 proceeded quite rapidly. 'Recovery' is something of a misnomer, in fact, for industry made substantial progress in establishing new lines of production, improving quality, and increasing varieties; and it also turned out rapidly growing supplies of fertilizer, electric pumps, and other types of farm equipment and inputs. The economy in the mid-1960s was thus in many respects more advanced than at the time of the Great Leap. This was the more remarkable in view of the repatriation of Soviet experts in 1960 and the enlargement of Chinese trade surpluses as China strove to eliminate its debts to the Soviet Union. China also began in 1961 to import foodgrain from the West in annual quantities of 5–6 million tons. Yet per capita foodgrain consumption did not regain the level of 1957–8, and indeed continued to fall short of this level until the end of the 1970s.

The tumultuous events of the late 1950s and early 1960s were reflected in debates within the Party and in intellectual circles over the proper course for China to take. In the extraordinary atmosphere created by the 'three hard years', economists like Sun Yefang put forward proposals to enlarge the role of the market and make profitability the ultimate test of enterprise performance. Others suggested reorganizing industries into vertically integrated 'trusts', run professionally and largely free of political interference. With both the Soviet model and the Maoist alternative in retreat from the impact of events, the field was briefly open to alternatives. Those put forward, however, did not square with the principal social objectives of Mao Zedong—such as reducing the gaps between city and countryside and between mental and manual workers. The slogan, 'politics in command', came in a sense to represent a negative economic posture; its force was in its veto of the market-oriented and professionalistic ideas of the early 1960s, rather than in any well articulated alternative view of how to organize the economy. Partial alternative micro-models (Anshan Constitution, Dazhai, Daqing) were to emerge in the course of the 1960s, but no Maoist political economist came forward to weave these into a coherent, new theory of economic development and social change.

2 Development strategy

The guiding slogan of the recovery period was 'readjustment, consolidation, filling out, and raising standards'. This accurately covered the main points of economic strategy: the readjustment of the growth rate as well as of intersectoral relations so as to restore balance (e.g., between agriculture and industry, raw materials industries and processing industries, etc.); the consolidation of achievable output levels, supply systems, and organizational methods; the strengthening of weak links; and the shift of attention from increasing gross output to improving quality and expanding variety to meet user demand. This strategy emerged officially from the Ninth Plenum of the Eighth Central Committee in January 1961, as did its corollary of 'taking agriculture as the foundation, industry as the leading factor' of the national economy. The latter policy was sharpened in 1962 by placing agriculture at the top of the sectoral priority list: agriculture, light industry, heavy industry (see Chapter 6, Sec. 4). These two slogans amounted to the same thing: recognition of the constraining role of agriculture in China's development. Thus, Zhou Enlai (1965:10) explained: 'The scale of industrial development should correspond to the volume of marketable grain and the industrial raw materials made available by agriculture.' Mao referred to this approach as a 'revolution' in planning methods because of the tenacity with which the Soviet approach of giving priority to heavy industry had lingered on in China:

In the last few years we have been groping our way and found some other method. Our policy is to take agriculture as the foundation and industry as the leading factor. Pursuant to this policy, when we map out a plan we first see what quantity of foodgrains can be produced, then estimate how much fertilizer, pesticide, machinery, iron and steel, and so on are needed. [Mao 1974:353]

In anticipating future harvest conditions, Mao said, planners should proceed on the assumption that 'in 5 years there will be 1 year of good harvest, 2 years of ordinary harvest, and 2 years of poor harvest' (1974:353), so as to provide a realistic basis for planning the supply of food and raw materials to industry and the feasible rate of expansion of industrial production.

This, then, was the sense in which agriculture was to be taken as the foundation. Industry, in turn, was the 'leading factor' in that it was to provide the technological means of modernizing the economy, including agriculture, thus expanding the 'foundation'. But at any given time, its capacity to do so is constrained by the existing 'volume of marketable agricultural output'.

Both the severity of the crisis and the logic of its therapy required deep cuts in capital construction. Not only did resources have to be shifted to agriculture, but many workers in non-essential activities were moved to relatively well-off rural areas closer to the food supply, and those remaining behind were urged to conserve energy and reduce consumption requirements. Investment activities had developed over the Great Leap in a haphazard way; in the absence of central co-ordination and planning, many local projects were duplicative or lacking in necessary support and ancillary facilities. Even had agricultural conditions been normal and capital construction well planned, however, the *scale* of investment had become excessive, with a national accumulation rate of 44 per cent in 1959 and 40 per cent in 1960 (see Table 6.4), thus putting great pressure on consumption. As Mao explained in 1961,

We must contract industry, heavy industry, particularly on the basic construction front, and we must extend the agriculture and light industry fronts. This year we will not inaugurate new basic construction; some parts of old construction we will continue to do, while other parts we will leave where they are. Judging from the present, socialist construction cannot be too fast; we have to stress wavelike advance. Comrade [Chen] Po-ta has raised the question whether socialism has a periodic law. Just like an army on the march, it must have long and short rests; in between battles it must rest and regroup, must combine hard work and relaxation. [Mao 1974:244]

It is apparent that Mao's commitment to reducing the pace of development was temporary; the 'wave' and 'army' images implied the intention to push ahead again when conditions improved. But the economic leaders of the early 1960s, veteran economists such as Chen Yun, rejected this view and sought to substitute balanced and proportionate development for rushes and retreats. At the time, however, the two sets of views converged in the face of necessity. The slowdown in the pace of heavy industrial construction began in the second half of 1961 (Liang 1980), and as large numbers of investment projects were cut back or discontinued, the national rate of accumulation fell to 10.4 per cent in 1962. With the passage of the most acute phase of crisis, it rose again, but to the relatively modest level of 22.7 per cent for the period 1963–4 (Dong 1980).

Besides capital construction, the major victim of retrenchment in the period 1961–2 was the rural industrial sector that had mushroomed during the Great Leap. Much of the labour, equipment, and materials for the 60,000 small industrial enterprises under *xian* (county) auspices and the 200,000 run by the communes in mid-1960 had come from pre-existing handicraft co-operatives and from agriculture, causing disruption in the supply of basic consumer goods and exacerbating the agricultural crisis. Many of these enterprises produced at a loss, which automatically subjected them to closure under the terms of the 'Seventy Articles of Industrial Policy' issued in December 1961 (see Chapter 6, Sec. 4). Even those covering their costs were accused of obtaining materials 'through improper channels' so as to 'impair the State's interests and thwart the completion of planned projects and the smooth progress of production' (*Nanfang Ribao*, 15 May 1962; in Riskin 1978a:81). Most of them were closed in 1961–2, an episode that led to bitter recrimination during the Cultural Revolution when the concept of 'short-line balance', used to justify the closure, was derided as 'dragging the advanced backward' rather than 'urging the backward to become advanced' (Riskin 1978a:78). The real motive of closure was said to be an aversion on the part of the leadership to local control and mass initiative. This is probably true, for without effective planning local control had led to chaos. However, beginning in 1963, there was a resurgence of local industrial activity, particularly at the *xian* level. Many of the local enterprises involved had originated during the Leap, but the emphasis among them now was on rationalization of technology and mechanization.

The cancellation of capital construction projects, the closing of thousands of factories, and the curtailment of operations in many others left millions of urban workers without work. In ordinary times, the state handled employment problems created by sectoral readjustments by keeping laid-off workers on the payroll while seeking new jobs for them or retraining them. But these were not ordinary times. During the Great Leap Forward, as we have seen, various non-agricultural sectors had indiscriminately recruited new workers, most of them from the country. The total number of 'workers and employees' doubled from 24.5 million at the end of 1957 to 50 million at the height of the Great Leap.[2] The rural labour force declined by 23 million (Xue 1981:186), and because many of those remaining were occupied in irrigation and other capital construction projects, rural labour engaged in *grain* production declined by 40 million.[3] The influx of new workers into urban areas meant a huge and sudden increase in urban population, to a reported 130 million people (probably in 1960) from the 1957 figure of between 90 and 100 million.[4]

Thus, not only was there a shortage of rural labour for agricultural production, but the cities and towns were much harder to supply with adequate food in their swollen condition. Accordingly, large numbers of cadres and workers, especially those who had been recruited from the villages during the Great Leap, were now sent to the countryside. Some 20 million workers are said to have been thus sent down in 1961–2 (Xue 1981:186), and the urban population thereby reduced from 130 to 110 million (Strong 1964:211).[5] Periodic campaigns had been waged previously (particularly in 1955 and 1957) to return to their villages those who had migrated to the cities in search of employment or to escape natural disasters, and to send down also cadres reorganized out of administrative jobs and middle-school graduates without urban employment prospects (Aird 1967:382–8). However, none of these approached in magnitude the rustication efforts of 1961–2; indeed, at most they had reduced the growth rate of urban population, while the post-GLF campaign seems to have substantially reduced its absolute size.

The policy of 'agricultural priority' meant more than cutbacks in heavy industry, capital construction, and development plans to match the available farm surplus; it also implied an increase in investment in agriculture and in those industrial sectors supporting agriculture. We have seen that the Great Leap Forward had already produced higher shares of investment going to agriculture—from 7.8 per cent of total capital construction investment during the FFYP to 10.5 per cent in 1958 and 1959, to 13 per cent in 1960 (Table 6.4 above)—although problems of quality and general disruption cancelled much of the effectiveness of this increase. In addition, the share of total investment in heavy industry going to farm machinery, chemical fertilizer, and pesticide had doubled, from 2.9 per cent in the FFYP period to 5.7 per cent for the years 1958–62 (Yang and Li 1980:200).

During the readjustment years, 1963–5, these trends were stepped up considerably. Agriculture's share of capital construction investment grew by over one-half to 18.8 per cent (Liang 1980), while the share of the above three agricultural support industries in heavy industrial investment grew to 9.7 per cent (Yang and Li 1980:200). The tangible result of all this was a rapidly increasing flow of machinery, equipment, and current inputs from factory to farm, as can be seen in Table 7.1. By 1965, supplies of farm inputs of industrial origin were many times their 1957 levels in every category shown. However, they were still very small on a per-hectare (or a per-worker) basis; by 1964 only 10 per cent of total farmland was cultivated by tractors (Chao 1970:115). The big increase in annual production of tractors came before 1961, and output throughout the first half of the 1960s actually fell considerably short of the 1960 peak (Chao 1970:107). Not only was the technocratic leadership of the recovery period sceptical about promoting mechanization as a solution to the agricultural problem, but the organization of farm machine production and distribution had developed into a contentious issue (see Sec. 5 below).

Industrial policy during the recovery period focused investment in a small number of sectors regarded as being of high priority for economic or strategic reasons. The need to expand agricultural output quickly explains the choice of one such sector that grew extremely rapidly over the period: namely, chemicals, and especially chemical fertilizer, as shown in Table 7.2. By 1965 China was producing more than nine times as much chemical fertilizer (in terms of nutrients) as it had in 1957, and more than two and one-half times the level of 1962. When combined with imports, domestic output was supplying 13 per cent

Table 7.1. *Modernization of farm technology, 1957–1965*

	(1)	(2)	(3)	(4)	(5)	(6)	(7)
		Millions of tons		Inventory data (millions of horsepower)		Total for both categories	
	Rural power consumption (bn. kWh)	Small-scale cement output	Chemical fertilizer output[a]	Irrigation and drainage equipment	Tractors	Millions of horsepower	Horsepower per cultivated hectare
1957	0.1 (100)	—	0.8 (100)	0.6 (100)	0.4 (100)	1.0 (100)	0.01 (100)
1962	1.6	1.6 (100)	2.8	6.1	1.5	7.6	0.08
1963	2.1	2.3	3.9	6.9	1.7	8.6	0.09
1964	2.5	2.2	5.8	7.6	1.8	9.4	0.09
1965	3.7 (3700)	5.4 (338)	7.6 (950)	9.1 (1517)	2.2[b] (367)	11.3 (1130)	0.11 (1100)

N.B. Figures in parentheses are index numbers.

[a] Based on gross weight, not nutrient weight.

[b] Linear interpolation between figures for consecutive years.

Source: Rawski (1979b:80); *Zhongguo Nongye Guanghui Chengjiu* (1984:18, 26).

Table 7.2. *Production and supply of chemical fertilizer,*
1957–1965 (thousands of metric tons of plant nutrient)

	1957	1962	1965
Nitrogen	366	684	1420
Production	136	444	830
Imports	230	240	590
Phosphorus	51	103	671
Production	22	103	626
Imports	29	—	44
Potassium	10	—	4
Production	—	—	—
Imports	10	—	4
Total chemical nutrient supply	427	787	2095
% of total nutrients	3.5	6.2	12.9

Sources: Production, import and total supply estimates are from
Erisman (1975:333). Percentage of total nutrients estimates are
based on Wiens's (1980:92) estimates of organic nutrient
supplies.

of total plant nutrients in 1965, double the share of chemically derived nutrients
just three years earlier. However, chemical fertilizer application per hectare of
cultivated land was only about 20 kg in 1965, a level similar to that of the Soviet
Union and five times that of India, but only one-fifteenth that of Japan (Chao
1970:158). On the other hand, China's intensive application of organic
fertilizer—which still dwarfed chemical fertilizer use in 1965—brought the total
nutrient supply per hectare to over 150 kg (Wiens 1980:92), considerably more
than was used in the United States at the same time.

Other kinds of agricultural chemicals were also included in the buildup of the
chemical industry during the recovery period, notably insecticides and other
pesticides. Chemicals also promised to provide synthetic substitutes for
scarce raw materials of agricultural origin, and synthetic fibres were thus
vigorously promoted during this period. They, of course, depended upon
development of the petrochemical sector, which in turn was fed by a rapidly
growing oil industry.

Prior to 1960 most of China's oil came from the Soviet Union, but these
imports declined sharply after 1961. Good fortune attended China's drive for
energy independence, however, for it was in 1960 that the Daqing (Ta-ch'ing)
oilfield was discovered in the north-eastern province of Heilongjiang.
Developed between 1960 and 1963, this largest of China's oil-producing areas
came to supply over half of the total national production of crude oil. In part

because of Daqing, China's annual output of crude rose rapidly, from 1.5 million metric tons in 1957 to 10.8 million in 1965, an average growth rate of about 28 per cent per year. As a result, the share of oil in China's primary energy production rose from under 2 per cent in 1957 to almost 7 per cent in 1965, and the country's dependence on imports for oil was basically eliminated as the ratio of imports to total petroleum supply fell from 55 per cent in 1957 to about 3 per cent in 1965 (Williams 1975:228–41). This success story was a product not only of luck, but also of 'the remarkable response of domestic equipment suppliers', who were able to turn out the drilling, extracting, refining, and transporting equipment required to produce the high growth rate of oil output (Rawski 1980a:61).

Defense, and especially the nuclear industry, appear to have also received high priority during the 1961–5 period, as China adjusted to the deterioration of its relationship with the Soviet Union. Although data in this area are largely conjectural, one estimate (Rawski 1980b:159) puts the 1965 value of military weapons procurement at almost five times the 1957 level (see also Jammes 1975:462). China exploded its first atomic device in 1964, a second in May 1965, and in October 1966 fired a guided missile with a nuclear warhead. Clearly, a considerable fraction of the country's scientific and technological resources must have been thrown into the nuclear project during the first half of the decade.

China's foreign trade underwent a profound change during the recovery period. Foreign trade policy was captive to the dictates of necessity, which exerted three distinct but interrelated forces upon it: (1) the general post-GLF crisis, which reduced both export and import capacity and led to a sharp decline in overall trade; (2) the break with the Soviet Union, which caused a rapid shift in direction of trade from Soviet bloc countries to the West and Japan; and (3) the immediate food crisis, which led China to begin importing foodgrain in substantial quantities for the first time since 1949. These three vectors interacted to reduce dramatically China's imports of producer goods. First, the curtailment of investment diminished the demand for such imports. Second, the decline in output of exportable agricultural products, together with the new and large claim on foreign exchange represented by foodgrain imports, lowered the country's capacity to pay for them. Third, the Soviet bloc had been the chief source of producer goods imports, whereas the industrialized capitalist countries to which China now turned embargoed the export to China of most such goods under the COCOM system (see Chapter 3, Sec. 2).

The resulting trends are evident in Table 7.3. Between 1959 and 1962 China's total exports declined by over 30 per cent, total imports by 44 per cent. Note that the bulk of both declines occurred in trade with socialist countries, these exports and imports falling by 42 and 64 per cent, respectively. Thus, as China repaid its debt to the Soviet Union (see Chapter 6, Sec. 4), it built up a large commodity export surplus with the Soviet bloc, while its trade with the capitalist world remained almost in balance. The shift away from socialist bloc countries proved to be a long-term trend: the share of these countries in China's total trade fell from almost 70 per cent in 1959 to 53 per cent in 1962 and to 35

Table 7.3. *Commodity composition of China's foreign trade with capitalist and socialist countries, 1959, 1962, and 1964 (millions of US dollars)*

	1959			1962			1964		
	Total	Capitalist countries	Socialist countries	Total	Capitalist countries	Socialist countries	Total	Capitalist countries	Socialist countries
Exports	2205	615	1595	1525	605	920	1770	1040	730
Agricult. prods.	1100	390	720	425	285	140	650	515	135
(Foods)	(820)	(300)	(520)	(250)	(175)	(80)	(375)	(275)	(100)
Industr. mats.	360	70	290	300	125	175	320	150	170
Textiles	620	120	500	535	155	375	440	200	240
Other mfg. goods	115	35	85	265	40	225	350	175	175
Imports	2060	695	1365	1150	660	490	1475	1080	395
Agricult. prods.	10	10	—	575	455	20	820	735	85
(Foods)	(—)	(—)	(—)	(460)	(345)	(110)	(600)	(525)	(75)
Chem fertilizer	70	70	—	40	40	n.a.	60	60	n.a.
Industr. mats.	740	500	240	305	125	180	325	195	130
Mach'y, equip.	980	70	910	120	20	105	200	70	130
Other	260	45	215	110	25	85	70	20	50

Source: Price (1967:586).

per cent in 1964; by the end of the decade it stood at only 20 per cent (Batsavage and Davie 1978:710).

Exports of agricultural products fell by over 60 per cent between 1959 and 1962, while agricultural imports rose from a negligible $10 million to almost $0.6 billion in the same period as China moved into the world grain market to purchase 5.6 million metric tons of wheat in 1961 and similar amounts subsequently. By 1965 imports of agricultural products (chiefly wheat, cotton, sugar, and jute) and of chemical fertilizer together accounted for 47 per cent of total imports, as compared with only 4 per cent in 1959 (Price 1967:585). Exports of agricultural goods began to recover in 1963, and by 1965, by selling high-value foods such as rice, vegetables, and meat, China was able to make food exports roughly pay for food imports, which were of much higher bulk and calorie content. However, the share of industrial materials and machinery and equipment in total imports was only slightly above one-third in 1964, down from over four-fifths in 1959.

The depression in China's foreign trade proved to be of surprisingly long duration. Even in nominal terms, total trade turnover did not regain its 1959 peak until 1970, and in real terms not until 1972 or 1973. In proportion to GNP, it did not recover even the moderate (10 per cent) levels of the late 1950s until the late 1970s, if then.[6] One reason is that no dramatic breakthrough in Sino-Western economic relations could occur until the United States changed its policy in the early 1970s, although these relations did improve gradually. Nor did Chinese relations with the Soviet Union heal. And, of the foreign exchange available, a considerable portion continued to be claimed by food-grain imports.

Thus, China was not able to use foreign trade aggressively in development strategy for a decade and a half following the Great Leap. There were both internal and external reasons for this, but, whatever the reasons, its effect on economic development was undoubtedly significant. On the one hand, it stimulated China to achieve self-sufficiency or near self-sufficiency in many products before it would otherwise have done so, and thus to make strides in upgrading its own technology. On the other hand, it unquestionably made industrialization more difficult and costly by requiring China to reinvent the wheel on many technological fronts. In 1978 Hu Qiaomu, President of the Chinese Academy of Social Sciences, told a meeting of the State Council that after 1958 the average growth rate of labour productivity in industry, construction, transport, and communications had fallen to only one-third of the 8.7 per cent registered during the First Plan period (Hu 1978:22). While there are several factors behind such a slowdown in productivity growth, the diminished role of foreign trade must have been a significant one.

Partial insulation from the world economy had other, more subtle, effects which are difficult to evaluate. It may be the case, for example, that the relative egalitarianism that characterized income distribution and resource allocation policies during much of the post-1958 period required relative freedom from world market forces to survive. Yet the apparent inability of China's leadership over this period to combine such allocative and distributive objectives with an efficient management system and a strong 'will to economize' may also have been due to some extent to the weakness of the disciplinary force exercised by the world market. These are issues that will arise again in later chapters.

3 Planning and industrial management

Early in the recovery period, the government moved to reassert strong central control over the economy. In so doing, it cancelled the 1957–8 decentralization reforms. Those reforms had in fact never been given a chance to work, their carefully contrived mesh of central and local planning spheres having been immediately tangled by the general disintegration of planning in 1958. But the resulting anarchy, as well as the deep slump into which the economy moved, demanded a renewal of central control. Authority over resource allocation with regard to industry, commerce, finance, and labour, which had been handed down to localities in 1958, was now recentralized. By 1963 the 87 per cent of centrally controlled enterprises that had been transferred downward in 1957–8, and the three-quarters of centrally allocated goods and materials whose control had been given to local authorities at that time, were returned to the jurisdiction of the centre (He 1980:38–9); *BR* 4 February 1980:22). According to some Chinese economists, the degree of centralization was now even greater than it had been before the reforms, especially as regards financial planning (Cyril Lin 1981:25).

Mao's obvious share of responsibility for the economic crisis—indeed, his several confessions of economic incompetence (e.g., 'For a time I was in favor of producing 30 million tons of steel next year . . . I was worried only about the question of whether there was a need *and had not considered the question of whether it was possible*'—Mao 1974, I:210; emphasis added)—had badly damaged his prestige. He was subject to much criticism during the crisis years (Howe and Walker 1977:210–11), and he later complained of having been ignored by the party leadership, and especially by its General Secretary: 'Deng Xiaoping never sought me out; from 1959 until the present [1966], on no issue at all did Deng ask [to see] me' (Mao 1969:655).

Mao's performance had indeed been inconsistent. He had first given the weight of his authority to impossible targets, then backed down and urged realism; realism in spring of 1959 to Mao meant that local cadres should 'ignore' unreasonable targets handed down from above 'and simply concentrate on practical possibilities' (Mao 1974, I:174). Yet in the same year, as we have seen, he criticized the State Planning Commission and the central ministries for 'doing away with planning altogether' and failing to make overall balances with respect to crucial materials (Schram 1974:142). The ageing leader continued to try to come to terms with the Great Leap Forward, understand where it had gone wrong, and admit in part his own culpability. In April 1959, he confessed that 'We are still woefully inexperienced in running agricultural and industrial enterprises. Year by year we accumulate experience, and in another 10 years we will, step by step, come to understand objective necessity. We will then become free to a certain degree' (Mao 1974, I:172). But, in the meanwhile, Mao's favoured approach of social mobilization and administrative decentralization had been discredited; for lack of a better alternative, the professionals who were back at the helm opted for a return to tight central control.

The Second Five Year Plan period formally ended in 1962, although it had been rendered a dead letter in its first year by the GLF. The state of the economy in the aftermath of the Leap ruled out commencement of a third five year plan on schedule in 1963. Instead, planning was put on an annual basis during the period of 'readjustment, consolidation, filling out, and raising standards' until 1966, when the short-lived Third Plan was formally inaugurated.

The return to rigid centralization in the early 1960s meant that very soon the economy was facing the same problems as before the 1957-8 reforms. At this time a very far-reaching discussion took place among economists, in which the possibility of enterprise autonomy and a major role for the market was cautiously explored. Section 4 below is devoted to this discussion, which lasted into 1964 and was confined to the realm of theory: 'no attempt at practical implementation could be, or was, made at that time (Cyril Lin 1981:27).

Nevertheless, as soon as the economy was on the way to recovery, the Party felt able to loosen up somewhat, and a second decentralization reform took place in 1964. Very little is known about this episode, other than that, 'generally speaking, the changes were not very significant' (*BR*, 4 February 1980:22). Like the first reform, this one was concerned with administrative decentralization. It augmented the authority of localities over investment in nineteen non-industrial sectors of the economy, including commerce, banking, communications, and water conservancy; also, local authorities were permitted to distribute the output of small enterprises (not otherwise described) and were given 'some power to handle the allocation of funds and materials' (p. 22). Like the earlier reform (as well as the third and final one that was to occur in Mao's lifetime, that of 1970), the 1964 reform preserved intact the basic characteristic of Chinese enterprises: their integral incorporation in the government administrative system.

Recentralization of the planning system required regularization of enterprise management; it was no good issuing directives unless enterprises were prepared to carry them out as well as to provide full and accurate information to the centre. Management policy, like other aspects of industrial policy, was guided during the recovery period by the 'Seventy Articles on Industrial Policy,[7] (see Chapter 6, Sec. 4). While bitterly attacked during the Cultural Revolution as a revisionist document, the 'seventy Articles', which were largely the responsibility of Vice-Premier Bo Yibo, amalgamated some of the innovations of the GLF approach to industrial management together with some sharp retreats from that strategy. Thus, the document directed all factories and mines to institute the 'triple combination' system of technical work teams consisting of administrative cadres, technicians, and workers (Chapter 6, Sec. 2.2), a GLF institution designed to break down the barriers between mental and manual labour and to democratize the relations between leaders and rank-and-file.

Similarly, the Party was called upon to 'arouse' factory administrators to take part in manual labour.

Retreats from GLF practices were the dominant feature of the 'Seventy Articles', however. One section of the document dealt with the re-establishment of regular systems—of specialized personnel (e.g., statisticians, inspectors, materials handlers, etc.), shift rotation, record-keeping, safety, warehousing, fiscal management, and so on. With the return of system and order, workers and specialists of all grades gravitated back to their posts to shoulder responsibility for their respective fragments of the production process. Although cadres were urged to spend time on the shop-floor, the re-establishment of specialized functional departments meant the decline of direct worker participation in enterprise management of the sort that had been tried in the GLF. As for leadership, the 'Seventy Articles' emphatically assigned this to the factory director, supervised by the party committee. The leadership role of workers was now to be confined to a system of workers' congresses attended by elected representatives of the work-force, as was the case before the Leap. On paper, these congresses had the right not only to listen to, discuss, and approve leadership reports on enterprise affairs, but also to remove the factory director and his staff. In practice, however, the workers' congresses appear not to have provided much scope for worker participation in management; convened infrequently by the trade union branch and including staff personnel as well as production workers, the congresses usually confined their discussion to plan targets and welfare questions. According to Andors (1977:124), 'The agenda was made by the leadership, and the trade union had to be urged to take the congresses seriously and not turn them into an expanded meeting of cadres.'

If the 'Seventy Articles' was designed in part to get workers back to their posts and away from the specialized administrative tasks they had been encouraged to share in the Great Leap Forward, this directive also evinced concern for their health and safety. It is an ironic paradox of late Maoist policy, as it actually materialized, that the social and political *status* of peasants and workers was sometimes pursued at the expense of their tangible material welfare. The shock campaigns of the Leap had frequently been carried out without proper regard for workers' need of rest and recreation, or for their safety. The 'Seventy Articles' now strictly limited working hours to eight per day, stipulated that there be four days off each month, forbade shock campaigns in industrial units, resurrected sick leave provisions that had been granted in 1956, and gave women workers forty-five days' paid leave for childbirth.

The elaboration of functionally divided roles within the enterprise, the shoring up of its hierarchy, and the restoration of its essentially passive role within a refurbished central command planning system all had implications for incentives. So too did the erosion of ideological fervour that accompanied the collapse of the Leap and the onset of economic crisis. In no uncertain terms, the 'Seventy Articles' called for the re-establishment of an articulated system of individual material incentives, preferably one of piece rates—collective piece rates where an individual-based system was technically unfeasible—and time wages plus bonus (limited to 30 per cent of the basic wage) where no piece-work system was possible.

Recovery policy for industry and agriculture was quite different in its treatment of the market. In agriculture, administrative control was relaxed and market forces were encouraged to operate in order to restore farm incentives. But the 'Seventy Articles' made clear the leadership's aversion to giving freer play to the market in industry, forbidding state factories to market their own products or to enter into bilateral agreements to supply other factories. In the state sector, marketing was to remain a monopoly of the state commercial organs. This posture came under challenge in the theoretical literature of the period as an impediment to efficiency, a basis for bureaucratism, and a damper on any inclination of enterprises to care about user demand.

The 'Seventy Articles of Industrial Policy' charted the intended path for enterprise organization and management during the recovery period, but actual practice often blended GLF and post-GLF policies in various mixtures depending upon conditions in particular units. In a sample of fifty-three industrial enterprises studied by Andors, there was strong continuity with GLF practices with respect to the institution of 'triple combination' teams, some continuity for cadre participation in labour (both of the foregoing being favoured in the 'Seventy Articles'), but much more tenuous perseverance of GLF forms for direct participation of workers in management (Andors 1977:107–23). Continuity was generally greater in heavy industrial units than in light industry, which had deeper roots in the pre-1949 era. The greatest retreat from GLF practices occurred in management functions related to the enterprise's links to the recentralized planning system, such as quota management, accounting, and production management; functions primarily *internal* to the enterprise, such as tool and safety management, exhibited much stronger continuity of GLF institutions (Andors 1977:107–23).

Even incentive systems preserved GLF features, for piece rates did not become general practice, bonuses remained modest, and the wage spread continued to be relatively small. In general, then, this period saw some fall-back from the innovations of the Leap, and then a holding pattern containing elements of various management systems, while at the theoretical and ideological level a debate of growing sharpness took place.

As it reached the level of policy, the debate centred on the issue of whether enterprises should be comprehensive or specialized. But this apparently abstruse question was the tip of an iceberg of basic political difference, much of which remained hidden.

Consider Mao's approach of administrative decentralization and social mobilization. We have already seen how difficult it is to reconcile such a formula with central planning. In 1960 Mao put his imprimatur on a document inspired by workers of the Anshan Iron and Steel Company, China's largest steel-making complex. The Anshan Constitution, as it was called, consisted of the following five principles (Selden 1979:591–2): (1) keep putting politics in command; (2) strengthen party leadership; (3) rely on mass movements; (4)

institute the 2–1–3 system of management; (5) vigorously promote technical revolution. These principles were seen as expressing an approach to industrial enterprise management that was directly contrary to that of the Soviet Union's Magnitogorsk Iron and Steel Works, which, in Mao's view, used restrictive rules and regulations to subordinate workers to management. But the Anshan Constitution is quite silent on Anshan's important place in the national economy, on its responsibility to users of iron and steel, and on the fulfilment of various quotas and norms, whereas its first and (especially) third points referred to practices that during the Leap had proved antithetical to strengthening the external ties that integrate an enterprise with the economy around it.

This approach to enterprise management, therefore, evidently left open the question of macroeconomic—and even intrasectoral—co-ordination, that is, the question of planning itself. The tendency of the 'left' position in the first half of the 1960s was to minimize this gap by reducing the amount and complexity of co-ordination required—hence, their advocacy of 'large and comprehensive' or 'small and comprehensive' enterprises. Each enterprise would be located at the appropriate administrative level, under the leadership of the relevant party and government organ, and thus would be responsive to the needs of its locality or region. Inter-enterprise links that would compromise 'self-reliance' and remove decision-making authority from the enterprise and its political host unit would be reduced in number and importance by making each enterprise 'comprehensive'—that is, capable of 'diversified undertakings and multiple utilization', and able to produce its own materials and intermediate goods. This of course would also give the factory greater flexibility in adapting to unforeseen contingencies and changes in conditions, and is quite in keeping with common practice in central planning systems that in other respects diverge sharply from the Maoist ideal.

In sum, an industrial system in which (1) a maximum amount of activity is subsumed within individual production units; (2) inter-enterprise relations are simplified as much as possible; and (3) productive units are geared to local needs and subject to local political leadership had the best conditions, in its proponents' view, for propagating 'revolution' within the enterprise. That is, the innovations designed to break down management–worker dichotomies, reduced administrative hierarchy, create worker-technicians, and involve workers directly in management would be least hampered under such a system by external constraints and the requirements of distant co-ordinative bureaucracies.

Several model enterprises were advanced to exemplify the left's view of proper, revolutionary enterprise management. The fact that these tended to be large enterprises of national significance confirms that the local orientation of the approach was not to be confined to small, local enterprises. The two most prominent models were the Daqing Oilfields and the Anshan Iron and Steel Company.

Part of the Daqing legend was the heroic story of its construction in the dark days of the early 1960s. But once established, it was touted mainly for two

characteristics: its integration of leadership and work-force, and its combination of industry with agriculture, town with countryside. On the first point,
Daqing developed a detailed system for cadre participation in labour and
for a democratic, 'face-to-face' leadership system. 'Democracy in politics,
production, and economics' was promoted by means of a bill of rights for
workers that included the right to criticize cadres, elect basic-level cadres,
refuse improper orders, decline to work without safety measures or work
regulations, and participate in the economic accounting of the enterprise and in
the management of its dining halls. With regard to the second point, Daqing
eschewed the construction of a concentrated urban area with tall and modern
buildings, cut off from the surrounding countryside. Instead, it established a
number of small towns and several dozen residential points with 100–400
households each. Every five or six residential points made up a 'livelihood base'
and contained such facilities as a mechanized farming station, agricultural
extension station, primary school, book store, and health clinic. Dependants
of oilfield workers engaged in agricultural work, service trades, auxiliary
industrial tasks, road repair and maintenance, and management of the
residential points. They were paid on a work-point system similar to that of the
rural communes (Xu 1979:582–91).

Daqing was thus advertised mainly for its democratic and unbureaucratic
management system and for its integration with the conditions of the locality in
which it was situated. It is likely that Daqing's management system also
included detailed regulations guiding its interaction with higher-level planning
authorities. However, this aspect of Daqing, important as it was to the country
as a whole (Daqing came to produce half of China's oil at one time), was not
part of the 'Learn from Daqing' model.

Anshan was displayed for its handling of financial matters in a 'face-to-face'
style similar to that of Daqing. Rather than sit in their offices and process
written reports from the production front, cadres in finance and accounting, as
well as those from the power, mechanical, and planning departments, made
regular rounds of the production units, where they would discuss data supplied
by the workers and, from these, calculate prices, cost cœfficients, future supply
requirements, and the like (Andors 1977:148). Here, as in the Daqing case,
there was a critical *social* lesson to be drawn: that the orientation of plant
leadership and technical personnel was *downward* towards the rank-and-file and
the locality, rather than upward towards a national technocratic élite and
planning bureaucracy.

4 The renaissance of economic thought

Inherent in the 'left' position was the conviction that the main problems faced
by China lay in the realm of 'relations of production', and that the proper
function of political economy as a field was to investigate problems in this
realm. This point of view underlay one side of a debate that occurred in the
1959–63 period in the pages of academic journals and the press over the nature

of economic studies. It stressed the importance of forging new organizational and administrative forms compatible with socialist ideals, and the need to orient the field of political economy towards addressing this problem. Regarding the 'forces of production'—that is, the constellation of available means of production, including labour, and the inherited set of technologies—this school did not have a great deal to say, beyond arguing that advances in the relations of production would liberate productive forces and result in higher growth, reduced costs, etc. Thus, it implicitly assumed that issues concerning the forces of production—achievement of an optimal allocation of resources, efficiency, technical change, etc.—were valid subjects of discourse only when linked with changes in production relations; to discuss such subjects in their own right was to be guilty of 'economism': the reification of technique and the advocacy of economic measures without regard for their political and social implications.

The opposing school held that, not only were such subjects as efficiency and optimal resource allocation necessary targets of investigation in and of themselves, but to deny this was to turn Marxism on its head by trivializing the productive forces and asserting the permanent primacy of the relations of production (Cyril Lin 1981:27–38). In the opinion of this school, the virtual elimination of private ownership of the means of production in the mid-1950s had already created advanced (perhaps *too* advanced) forms of production relations in China, and now the basic contradiction facing the country was the backward economy. The Great Leap Forward had shown the folly of trying to adopt practices of advanced communism while remaining economically underdeveloped; it followed that the quickest—indeed, the only—way to make further progress on this road was to concentrate on achieving rapid economic development.

A number of reforms were accordingly advocated during this period that anticipated the reform proposals put forward from 1979 on. In accordance with the emphasis on efficiency, the idea of diversified, comprehensive enterprises was rejected in favour of specialized units and division of labour. At the level of the individual worker, specialization and division of labour meant a strictly enforced individual responsibility system with emphasis on individual material incentives to shore it up. Stressing specialization and division of labour, of course, would greatly increase the need for co-ordination, which might take the form either of strengthened bureaucratic command planning or of a greater market role. Reform ideas included both. On the one hand, the division of the country into seven economic planning and co-ordination regions was proposed, an idea that was consistent with administrative decentralization. On the other hand, several measures were advocated that would have somewhat increased the importance of market forces in the economy. These included giving enterprises relatively slack plans and the autonomy to market above-plan output and purchase inputs for above-plan capacity on their own; the re-establishment of a profit-retention arrangement (originally tried in late 1956), which would give enterprises more incentive to increase profits; and the promotion of direct, contractual relations between enterprises to reduce administrative distribution and enhance the demand orientation of production (Cyril Lin 1981:26).

Among the reform proposals that received increasing attention during the first half of the 1960s was the establishment of semi-autonomous corporations, or 'trusts', to organize production and distribution on a cost-efficient basis in individual sectors of the economy. This proposal was favoured by a dominant section of China's leadership, including Liu Shaoqi, then the Head of State. The concept of the 'trust' seems to be an amalgam of Soviet experiences with independent industrial management systems and Western corporate management methods (Stavis 1978:187–8). The basic objective was to create powerful, professional units of management that would pursue technical and economic efficiency free of daily interference by the Party and government. These would (1) have monopoly power in their respective industries (no capitalist 'anarchy' here); (2) be free to obtain raw materials and market their products; (3) strive to increase profits; (4) be self-supporting; (5) be free of local political interference; (6) promote specialization and standardization; (7) use material incentives to motivate workers and managers. It was not proposed that they be able to set prices freely or raise investment capital on their own, although the return to the idea in 1978–80 did feature both propositions (see Chapters 11, 14).

Also, while there was an implicit role for the market in the authority of trusts to obtain their own materials and sell their own products, the questions raised by monopoly power in their respective markets appear not to have been thoroughly explored. Above all, their objective seems to have been, then as more recently, to phase out the state bureaucratic economy (called 'feudal' by Liu Shaoqi), under which economic units were run by political authorities as an integral part of government administration and had no independent, material interest in demand-oriented, cost-efficient, and dynamic performance. To Mao, however, who watched these developments with growing dismay, the trust system represented corporatist bureaucratization without the benefit of political principle, the economistic glorification of profit and material incentive, and the suppression by monopolistic, profit-oriented, 'bourgeois' officials of local authority to initiate independent development activities. The clash between these views was to come to a head in the Cultural Revolution.

The remarkable debates among economists during the 1961–4 period went far beyond the specific reform proposals listed above.[8] Among the most important subjects covered was the role of commodity production and the law of value under socialism. In point of fact, this discussion had already taken place earlier, in the years 1956–8, when the inadequacies of the Stalinist approach to central planning had been recognized and had given rise to a wide-ranging search for alternatives. But the earlier debate was drowned by the anti-rightist movement and the Great Leap Forward. With the latter now discredited, the discussion burst out again with renewed vigour.

'Commodity production' refers, of course, to the production of goods and services for exchange rather than for direct use. The 'law of value' refers to the tendency, under competitive market conditions, for goods to exchange with each other at rates proportional to their relative socially necessary labour times. The two concepts are linked, in that the production of commodities for exchange presupposes exchange values satisfactory to all parties, and the workings of competition in a market commodity economy will tend to make such values gravitate towards proportionality with socially necessary labour times, given certain assumptions. It was also widely held that a commodity economy *requires* regulation by the law of value (i.e., requires regulation by a market through which the law of value determines exchange relations), but that a *non*-commodity economy—such as one with only a state sector, producing and distributing goods strictly according to plan—is free of such requirement. However, the principal participant in the 1956–8 debate, Sun Yefang, denied the latter contention, arguing instead that the law of value states a basic principle of optimal resource allocation that must be respected whether in a commodity economy or a totally planned one. For example, given that two goods have equal utility, resources should be devoted to producing the one requiring the smaller amount of socially necessary labour time as long as a condition of scarcity exists, whether the economy is completely planned or regulated in whole or in part by a market. Indeed, another discussant (Wang Yanan) argued that only under socialism could the law of value fully operate.

The importance of these apparently esoteric exercises in Marxist theory is not hard to see. The finding that socialism still provides considerable scope for commodity production and exchange constitutes a theoretical basis for relaxing centralized command planning—up to then established by Soviet theory and practice as the only orthodox form of economic organization—without betraying socialism. The proposition that the law of value must regulate resource allocation even in a planned economy is tantamount to a repudiation of arbitrary and intuitive planning. And, since central planners nowhere (and certainly not in China) have the capacity to allocate physically tens of thousands of individual goods and services in conformity with the law of value, this proposition also implies the need to replace command planning with the use of the market.

The 1961–4 discussion more or less covered the same ground as the earlier one, except that in the interim had come a contribution from Mao himself (Cyril Lin 1981:28). Mao's 1959 reading notes on Stalin's 1952 work, *Economic Problems of Socialism in the USSR*, contained a critique of Stalin's treatment of commodities under socialism. Stalin (1972) had ascribed the survival of commodity production and circulation in the Soviet Union to the co-existence of two forms of ownership, state and collective, and the consequent necessity of obtaining goods produced in the collective sector (mainly agriculture) via exchange. He also asserted that the sphere of commodity production was confined to consumer goods. Mao was critical of both points, arguing that commodity production depends on the level of development of the productive forces, as well as on the existence of different ownership forms, so that 'even under completely socialized public ownership, commodity exchange will still have to be operative in some areas' (Mao 1977c:140); and that some means of production as well as consumer goods must take commodity form, namely, those that exchange for agricultural products (Mao 1977c:145–6). Mao followed Stalin, however, in arguing that in China the law of value gives up its regulative function to planning (1977c:147).

Sun Yefang had gone well beyond the theoretical exploration of these questions to map out a series of reform proposals that would fundamentally alter the nature of China's planning and management system. The essence of his proposal was the replacement of administrative command planning with market socialism, in which autonomous enterprises would strive to maximize profits under a regime of parametric planning, with the state influencing enterprise behaviour via economic levers such as prices, taxes, and credit policies.

There are at least two levels of dispute in the arguments over economic system. One concerns the nature of the social formations associated with alternative systems of planning and management. Central administrative planning, for example, has been associated with the survival of 'feudalist' behaviour patterns, the strengthening of bureaucratism and élitism, and the growth of a privileged class; while the market has been seen as giving rise inevitably to capitalist production relations. The other level concerns basic economic theory: how to define and measure economic success and influence economic actors to take socially desired actions. In 1956–8 both strands had been pursued, with economists like Sun Yefang exploring the second, and other intellectuals engaging in broad-gauged attacks on party power that eventually led to the anti-rightist campaign. In the 1978–81 period, following Mao's death and the arrest of the ruling group around him, indictments of past economic practices focused on the arbitrary and 'feudalist' nature of the Soviet planning system in Chinese soil. But in the early 1960s with no clear resolution in sight for basic disagreements among the leadership and intellectual dissidence still largely silenced by the earlier rectification, no such sweeping indictment was possible. Rather, economists investigated the basic theoretical questions that were raised by the law of value discussions and Sun Yefang's work.

Whatever system of planning was to be established, it would have to incorporate criteria for determining economic effectiveness and mechanisms for obtaining it. While the Soviet planning system instituted in China had been effective for channelling resources into high-priority uses and in accomplishing big structural changes, it was unable to choose among alternatives the best of which was not intuitively obvious. This is because it lacked the notion of opportunity cost which underlies benefit–cost analysis (Cyril Lin 1981:29). Moreover, the use of gross value of output (GVO) as the principal target of the enterprise and the chief basis for rewarding personnel led to distortions that are well known from Soviet and East European experience (such as the inflation of gross output by extravagant use of intermediate goods, the neglect of quality and demand-oriented variety, etc.). Sun Yefang (among others) explored this problem in 1957 and advocated replacing the GVO target with enterprise profits, which, he argued, provide a comprehensive summary of an enterprise's performance. Later, in a simile made famous by Cultural Revolution attacks on it, Sun likened the profit indicator to the ring through an ox's nose, by which the whole ox could easily be led.

The early 1960s discussions threw up a number of suggestions for indicators of enterprise 'effectiveness' (*xiaoguo*), combining such measures as labour productivity, costs, profits in relation to average costs, and concepts similar to the incremental capital–output ratio (ICOR). It is evident that the validity of such value-based indicators depends crucially on the rationality of the prices on which they are based. Chinese prices, which had originally been set largely on the basis of the inherited price structure (except for a very low farm–industry price ratio), had been allowed to change only very slowly in response to rapidly changing relative costs. By the 1960s the price structure was anomalous, in the sense that the relative profitability of sectors and industries reflected the arbitrary prices of their inputs and outputs to a much greater degree than it did the efficiency of their performance.

To measure economic effectiveness accurately by means of value indicators, therefore, meant that the price system itself had to be reformed and a theoretically valid basis for setting prices worked out. The discussion accordingly examined this issue in some depth, starting from the Marxian proposition that value (to which price should tend to conform) consists of constant capital (c), variable capital (v) and surplus value (m). Whereas it was possible to calculate c and v (per unit of output), the crucial problem was how to determine m. Various solutions were put forward, of which the most significant was the 'production price' approach associated with Yang Jianbai and He Jianzhang. This approach would calculate surplus value or profit on the basis of the total capital employed by an enterprise; the profit element in the price of a good would be equal to the product of the average rate of profit on capital in the economy as whole and the average amount of capital per unit of output in the industry in question.[9] Thus, given prices calculated in this way, and ignoring external economies and diseconomies, an enterprise making greater-than-average profit on its invested capital must be more efficient than the average enterprise, and smaller-than-average profits would denote less-than-average efficiency.

Such a method of price formation, its advocates argued, would correctly reflect the interdependence of sectors in the economy as a whole and accurately separate the contribution of each individual unit from the effects of this interdependence on each unit's conditions. It would provide the basis of a planning system capable of allocating scarce resources rationally, resulting in the smallest expenditure of (living and embodied) labour to produce a given output. Of course, the notion of an average social rate of profit on capital against which individual profitability is to be evaluated is equivalent to the use of an interest rate on capital. This led to the charge that the 'theory of production prices' violated the labour theory of value, and from late 1964 on its proponents were subjected to merciless attacks as reactionaries seeking to restore capitalism.

This proposal, however, in addition to embodying an opportunity cost standard for resource allocation decisions, also addressed another fundamental problem that had revealed itself over the preceding decade: the absence of an economic mechanism to stimulate the will to economize in the use of scarce capital. With fixed and working capital allocated to enterprises through the state budget, cost-free and non-repayable, and with virtually all profits as well as the major part of inadequately small depreciation allowances reverting automatically to the state, the enterprise had no immediate material interest in applying rational economic criteria to the use of capital. The 'theory of production prices', together with proposals for enterprise autonomy and parametric planning, would have led quickly from a theoretical charge on capital (i.e., shadow price) guiding planners' choices to a real charge imposed on enterprises' use of capital. Once the enterprise was able to keep and use part of its profits, but had to pay (and could receive) a price for capital, it would develop an interest in the economic use of the latter.

Although the debate over the law of value and reform of the economic system took place largely in the academic journals, and the Tenth Plenum in September 1962 made it clear that radical changes of the sort discussed would not take place, there was not a total divorce between theory and practice. Profitability became a more important indicator of enterprise performance in the early 1960s; and, no doubt in response to the problems raised by this, the government took a critical look at the irrational price structure. In August 1962, for example, an article described the practice of levying differential taxes on enterprises to compensate for the arbitrariness of state-set prices and to enable the state to distinguish well run from poorly run industries and enterprises (USCIA 1963:16). But most of the reform proposals had to wait during another decade and a half of turmoil before getting a sympathetic hearing from a relatively united leadership.

5 Agricultural organization and technical change

Recovery in agriculture began in 1962. Total foodgrain output by the following year may have re-attained the 1957 level, and by 1964 the record level of 1958. The burden of recovery was shouldered largely by the eastern and south-eastern coastal provinces, and to some extent by the north-western provinces and Liaoning in the north-east. In contrast, the North China Plain, plagued by waterlogging and salinization, was unable to recover its 1957 output level until the late 1960s and the major producing province of Sichuan also remained depressed. Where growth occurred, it was due to the spread of improved rice varieties and of hybrid corn, to increased supplies of chemical fertilizers, and to the growth of an effective extension network (Wiens 1980:88–95). Beginning in 1964, the state carried out a policy of creating 'high and stable yield areas' (HSYA), according to which investment resources for agriculture were channelled to regions that could be made relatively impervious to the weather. The object was to make possible a good national harvest even in years of bad weather, and to ensure an adequate procurable surplus in such years.

During the 1961–3 period, the commune system underwent rapid change (Chapter 6, Sec. 4). The 26,000 original communes were split into 74,000 smaller ones, and the basic level of accounting passed downward first to the brigade and then to the team. By 1963 the average commune consisted of 9.5 brigades, 66.5 teams, and 1,622 households. The average brigade had 7 teams and 171 households, the average team, 24 households. Of course there was much regional variation around these averages (Chen and Ridley 1969:5–6).

The form of commune organization arrived at during the early 1960s remained basically stable thereafter. In what follows, the general features of commune organization during the 1960s and 1970s are described, but the special conditions that held in the early 1960s are also pointed out.

5.1   The production team

By 1962, the most important of the three tiers of commune structure was the production team. As the 'basic accounting unit', the team 'carries on independent accounting, is responsible for its own profits and losses, organizes production, and distributes income' (Chen and Ridley 1969:127). According to the Revised Draft Regulations on the Work of the Rural People's Commune ('Sixty Articles'—see Chapter 6, Sec. 4), the teams owned their own land, were entitled to dispose of their own labour forces, and had 'the right freely to manage production and distribute gains'. Strictly interpreted, these rights should have given the team the authority to decide what crops to cultivate, subject to negotiation with the state over mandatory procurement quotas for crops under 'unified and planned purchase' (Chapter 4, Sec. 4) arrangements. Such is, indeed, the way the system was described later as having been intended to work. However, it appears that, in the course of the 1960s and 1970s, the authority of production teams to make such decisions was widely infringed upon by higher levels.

The team was administered by officials elected annually by a production team congress made up of all able-bodied workers. Such officials included, among others, a team leader, deputy leader, accountant, militia platoon leader, custodian to look after team implements, animals, and granary, and a treasurer (Burki 1969:11). In the early 1960s almost all rural income was produced by the team; later, however, the development of commune and brigade enterprises elevated the income shares of those two levels, especially in relatively well-off suburban areas. Most team income came from crops, but some was earned by raising livestock and fish and from a variety of sideline activities, such as beekeeping, fodder-cutting, and native crafts.

The team's income was distributed as follows: The first obligation was the agricultural tax, which in the early 1960s came to between 5 and 15 per cent of gross output. Then, if it was a 'grain surplus team' whose normal output exceeded requirements for consumption, fodder, and seed, the state could purchase up to 90 per cent of the difference at fixed, quota prices. Practice varied regarding the quota: in the early 1980s, for example, the state used above-quota prices and even higher 'negotiated' prices to induce teams to grow and sell grain beyond their quotas.

From gross income after tax, the team set aside a portion to pay production expenses (about 30 per cent). A smaller deduction was made for an accumulation or reserve fund—perhaps 3 per cent of total income in the early 1960s, rising to 10 per cent by the mid-1970s (Strong 1964:196; Crook 1975:399). This fund financed construction and purchases of machinery and equipment. The smallest deduction, limited by the 'Sixty Articles' to 2 per cent of total income, was for the welfare fund, which helped ill and disabled persons and old people lacking family care, as well as covering some medical and educational expenses (Crook 1975:400). The remainder of team income, approximately 60 per cent of the total, was then available for distribution to individual members according to their respective earnings of work-points.

Although the team was the basic unit of work organization, the 'Sixty Articles', drafted during the crisis of the 'three hard years', permitted the establishment of 'responsibility systems' under which the team contracted tasks out to small groups or to individuals. Sideline activities such as stock-breeding, forestry, and fish-raising, together with management of draught animals, farm tools, irrigation works, and other public property, were mentioned as being subject to such a system. In the event, however, even basic farming was decollectivized in some areas of China, with fields being divided up and contracted out to individual families to cultivate. This practice, which was revived in the late 1970s (see Chapter 12), is known as 'contracting production at the household level' (*bao chan dao hu*). In Lianjiang County of Fujian (Fukien) Province, 26.5 per cent of the teams practised this system to some degree in the autumn of 1962; a little more than 2 per cent of the county's cultivated area was involved in it (Chen and Ridley 1969:99).

Land contracted to the household was still collectively owned, but at least in some cases its output was not counted in calculating the state tax and purchases quotas or to offset the basic grain ration due its cultivator (Chen and Ridley 1969:99). This made it resemble closely the 'private plots' (or, more literally, 'self-retained land' (*ziliu di*), since the produce but not the land could be bought and sold). These plots had been widely infringed upon during the GLF; the 'Sixty Articles' sought to protect the peasants' right to them, stating that they were 'generally' to occupy 5–7 per cent of the team's total cultivated land. In parts of China, however, private plots took a considerably larger fraction. This was true of Lianjiang, where they accounted for 11.3 per cent of the county's cultivated land, and in some of whose teams their share was 15 per cent or higher. In addition, peasants were allowed to cultivate privately land that they had reclaimed; a Lianjiang document of 1962 complained that some peasants were devoting 'all their efforts to the individual reclamation of barren land', which totalled 19.6 per cent of cultivated area in the county. Thus, adding together private plots, reclaimed land, and 'household contract' land, the total of privately cultivated land (called 'small freedoms land') came to about one-third of cultivated area, reaching more than one-half in some teams (Chen and Ridley 1969:18, 100).

The erosion of collectivism in the countryside during the early 1960s is testimony to the demoralization of many local cadres, who were blamed for the excesses of the Great Leap Forward, and to a disillusionment with collective agriculture on the part of many peasants when the Leap collapsed into deep depression. The influence of the spread of private farming on the subsequent recovery of agriculture, however, was mostly indirect. Private plots in Lianjiang County produced less than 6 per cent of grain output (some of which would have been produced had the plots been collectively cultivated); reclaimed land contributed somewhat more to output, but for the country as a whole it could not have made a major difference to total output over a short period of time. However, 'small freedoms' land was undoubtedly a source of reassurance to the farm population in the absence of reliable collective institutions and effective leadership, and thus it had a strong incentive function. A large proportion of nongrain products, such as vegetables, fruit, poultry, eggs, and pork, was grown on private land, which therefore played an important nutritional role in the Chinese diet; and, since these products were priced higher than staple foodgrains, their private production contributed disproportionately to the money incomes of many peasants. For example, private plots constituted 7.6 per cent of cultivated land in ten communes visited by S. J. Burki in 1965, but the average share of family income earned from these plots was 19.3 per cent (Burki 1969:40). To some extent, this disparity was also due to better care given to the private plots.

5.2   The production brigade

The production brigade, averaging 7 teams and 171 households in 1963, was the intermediate level of authority in the commune, often corresponding to the natural village.[10] It supervised the teams and was the lowest level of administration with a regular party branch. The brigade distributed important inputs to the teams, including power, irrigation water, and the use of larger machines, and ran social services such as health clinics and primary schools. Brigades also had militia units, which were often thrown into construction projects.

The brigade had its own enterprises. However, the 'Sixty Articles' directed that most of these be distributed to the teams, so that in the early 1960s the brigades, having lost both their basic accounting unit status and the bulk of their enterprises, played a very limited role. The impression of a Pakistani rural development expert who visited several communes in 1965 was that the evolution of the commune system had 'tended to play down the importance of production brigades', and that 'very few production brigades have independent sources of income' (Burki 1969:8, 12). This situation was to change noticeably after the mid-1960s, when the brigade-level economy, responsibilities, and power vis-á-vis the team expanded considerably.

Most brigade and all team cadres earned work-points by farming. In addition, their administrative activities were subsidized by their units at a level sufficient to make their incomes at least equivalent to that of an average peasant.[11] Top commune cadres, on the other hand, received a state salary that in 1965 was reported to be about Y60 (Burki 1969:150)—equivalent to the average salary of a state industrial worker and several times the average peasant income.

5.3 The commune

The commune level suffered considerable deflation between 1959 and 1962 because of its loss of basic accounting unit status, the closure of most of its enterprises, and the prohibition imposed on commandeering team labour and money. Nevertheless, it recovered its economic functions rapidly with the general economic upturn after 1962.

The commune continued to be a hybrid organization, 'combining government and co-operative into one' ('Sixty Articles'). The economic activities of the commune were regarded as collective, but the commune administration was the basic level of government administration in the rural areas, and it included such state-managed institutions as a People's Bank branch, grain management and tax collection offices, and a supply and marketing co-operative or a branch of one.[12] Communes also established hospitals and clinics, which supervised the work of brigade clinics and paramedics ('barefoot doctors'), and ran secondary and special schools. In 1964 only 22 per cent of rural primary schools were run by communes and brigades, and the establishment of hospital and clinic facilities at or below the commune level was still in a rudimentary stage (Donnithorne 1967:63–4). It was the Cultural Revolution, and Mao's attack on the urban orientation of health and education facilities, that provoked the spread of these institutions within the communes.

Large-scale water conservancy construction and irrigation projects were also organized at the commune level. In the early 1960s, however, the communes were admonished not to requisition team labour on a non-voluntary basis for such projects, and to organize the labour contributions of the teams in accordance with the distribution of benefits from the project. Under the principle of 'exchange of equal values', teams deriving little or no benefit would have to be paid for their labour. Finally, the communes were responsible for public security, and had militia regiments or battalions under the supervision of the county military authorities.

The services enumerated above consituted one aspect of commune leadership over the activities of subordinate units. In additon, the commune was supposed to provide political, ideological, and technical leadership to brigades and teams. As one report puts it,

The commune helps the brigades and teams to work out their production plans, and supervises and checks up on their implementation. It also lends a hand in improving their administrative and financial work and distribution of income, and spreads advanced experience and methods among them in order to increase production. [Wu 1975:9]

The ambiguous nature of the commune as both state and collective unit made it relatively easy for this kind of leadership to become rule by fiat, in disregard of the formal autonomy of teams. The communes were the quintessential expressions of the Maoist desire to link politics and economics by integrating economic activity into the local government structure. Under the post-Mao regime, which favoured the separation of political and economic adminis-tration, their dissolution was not long in coming (see Chapter 12).

The commune-level economy provided almost all commune income, except for a small share of the brigade and team reserve and welfare funds. (In the early 1960s, however, this source was put off limits to the commune 'for several years to come' by the 'Sixty Articles'.) Some small industries, such as food process-ing, brick-making, and farm tool manufacture and repair, survived the retrenchment of commune industrial undertakings in 1961–2, and more were established as the recovery proceeded. The commune also owned large-scale agricultural machinery, such as tractors, threshers, and trucks, which were rented for a fee by the sub-units. When communes were first established in 1958, a large number of machines were turned over to them by the state Machine Tractor Stations (MTS); however, because the communes were not prepared to maintain and run them and much waste ensued, this policy was reversed in 1961. The issue of who should own farm machinery became a highly contentious one in the leadership conflicts that led up to the Cultural Revolution, and both state and commune ownership continued to exist side by side throughout the early 1960s (see below). A final source of commune income was the specialized brigade, often run directly by communes, which engaged in such activities as construction, vegetable growing, and beekeeping.

The Commune Management Committee of ten to fifteen members was elected biennially by the Commune Congress from a slate of candidates approved at the county level. The Congress (membership of perhaps 100–150) was in turn elected for a two-year term by the production brigade congresses. Members of the Management Committee headed various functional depart-ments, such as general administration, education, culture and health, militia, industry, agriculture, women's affairs, etc.

5.4 Agricultural mechanization

The commune and brigade were often referred to in the early 1960s as 'empty shells', because their administrative forms remained while most of their substantive functions were passed down to the teams. This was probably more true of the brigade than of the commune, which continued to exercise state administrative functions and run some enterprises, and whose Party Committee was a pre-eminent institution of local authority. But the commune did lose power, and in both a downward and an upward direction; while farming activities were 'sent down' to the teams and even to individual households, the government and party leadership moved to centralize control of the development and dissemination of agricultural technology:[13]

Some of China's top leadership in the early 1960s, including Liu Shao-ch'i [Liu Shaoqi], Teng Hsiao-p'ing [Deng Xiaoping], and P'eng Chen [Peng Zhen], believed that technological reform required efficiency; that efficiency in turn required centralized administration, specialization of functions in factories and bureaucracies, and material incentives for workers and administrators; and that profits were the crucial measure of efficiency. [Stavis 1978:200]

This development was part of what came to be called the 'agricultural mechanization controversy'. The question of farm technology was central to Mao's conception of socialist development in China. It not only determines in large part the size of surpluses available to support industrialization, but also affects the relations between town and country, worker and peasant. Mao recognized that narrowing these gaps would ultimately require arming the farm population with modern technology; that higher farm incomes would require higher labour productivity; and that this meant mechanization. He had in 1955 already advocated transforming small-scale farming based on animal power into large-scale, mechanized agriculture within roughly fifteen years (Mao 1955:196–7).

Yet immediate, rapid tractorization was out of the question. It was recognized in the mid-1950s that China did not yet have either the steel for legions of tractors or the oil for running them, and that the small size of fields in much of agricultural China (especially terraced fields, which could not easily be enlarged) and the complex patterns of inter-cropping discouraged mechanization. There was also the good economics logic of Bo Yibo, who feared the depressive effect of mechanization on the demand for labour in China's overpopulated countryside (Riskin 1971:268–9). In short, the immediate problem of lagging agricultural production called for raising yields on the existing cultivated area, a solution that required more current inputs (fertilizer, water, pesticides) and more labour, but not machines. Thus, despite Mao's convictions about the ultimate need for mechanization, the Twelve Year Plan for Agriculture, which he formulated in 1956, called only for the improvement of traditional farm implements (with emphasis on the ill-fated double-wheel double-share plough).

In the autumn of 1957, however, Huang Qing, head of the State Technological Commission, published a report arguing that mechanization could play a role in raising yields without displacing labour. The key was to tailor mechanization to peak season tasks for which there were widespread *shortages* of labour. The problem of seasonal labour shortage was in fact growing as multiple cropping increased, for to fit an extra crop into the growing season required extremely intensive work in harvesting, field preparation, and planting during the switch-over period from one crop to the next. Even if some labour redundancy resulted, however, it could be absorbed by the development of industrial and sideline activities. This thought was consistent with Mao's view, as reflected in *Socialist Upsurge in China's Countryside* (1956), that rural industry, commerce, communications, science, culture, education, and public health, growing up concomitantly with mechanization, would provide sufficient employment for displaced labour. This was, after all, the trend of the future; for it would not forever require three-quarters of China's population to feed the whole.

During the Great Leap Forward the issue of mechanization was resurrected. The key event was the Chengdu Conference of March 1958, which produced a report entitled 'Views on the Question of Agricultural Mechanization'. This document outlined a strategy of mechanization that accorded with Mao's desire to have the peasants themselves control the mechanization process. Mechanization, semi-mechanization, and tool improvement were all to be pursued, with emphasis on small farm machines. The communes were to be the principal agents of change, buying machines with their own funds, building repair and manufacturing shops, training operators, and undertaking maintenance. The manufacture of farm machinery was also to be primarily local; the central government would help with technical advice, and perhaps with more tangible aid in particularly poor areas (Stavis 1978:110–12).

The view that production and operation of farm machinery should be an integral part of the activities of agricultural collectives had both political and economic roots. Politically, Mao perceived a contradiction between the state's interest in expanding the procurement of farm goods, on the one hand, and the peasants' interests on the other. To allow state institutions to monopolize control of agricultural machinery would make it easy for the state to pursue an extractive policy, using its monopoly of technology to charge exorbitant fees and 'drain the pond to catch the fish'. In drawing these conclusions, Mao had the benefit of Kang Sheng's study of the Soviet machine tractor station (MTS) and its offspring in China. In 1956, Kang had said:

Run in their present form, it is definite that tractor stations will develop greater and greater contradictions and will be detached from the masses. If we cannot operate them well, they would become in a disguised form revenue-collection organs, or organs practicing blackmail. The Soviet tractor stations are blackmailers. [Stavis 1978:96]

The *economic* basis of Mao's conclusions followed from this political analysis. A series of problems had emerged in the running of the MTSs in China, most of which appeared to stem from their administrative nature. As in the case of other state enterprise employees, the MTS personnel were evaluated according to their fulfilment of targets set from above—not according to the value of their services to their customers, the agricultural co-operatives. And, as in other state enterprises, this led to distortions, especially the overemphasis of the norm judged most important in the evaluation and reward system (usually, output quantity), at the expense of those deemed secondary (such as quality and cost). Thus, timing of service, depth of ploughing, maintenance of machinery, etc., were often arranged to suit the convenience of the station in meeting its targets.

Shortly after the Chengdu Conference, the State Council directed that farm machinery be placed under the management of the collectives (soon to become communes).[14] A large number of tractors were then purchased by communes from MTSs.

The short-term policy of the Great Leap towards agricultural technology stressed tool reform. The Leap's many labour-intensive campaigns—water conservancy construction, rural industry, deep ploughing and close planting, etc.—had quickly changed the perception of the rural labour situation from one of surplus to one of shortage, and tool improvement to increase farm labour productivity was regarded as the feasible short-run solution. However, the campaign for tool improvement depended on the backyard iron and steel movement for raw materials, and thus was plagued with quality problems. Moreover, the central authorities, failing to draw appropriate lessons from the episode of the double-wheel double-share plough, repeated the error by prematurely popularizing other intermediate technologies (in particular, a cable-drawn plough in 1958–9 and a rice transplanter in 1960) which ultimately proved unsuccessful.

In an April 1959 letter, Mao penned a line that would become famous: 'The fundamental way out for agriculture lies in mechanization.' Estimating that mechanization would require ten years, he urged all provinces, districts, and counties to establish farm tools research stations and to concentrate scientific and technical personnel and skilled workers to accomplish it (Mao 1974, I:171). This call developed into a Ten Year Plan for Agricultural Mechanization, which was publicly announced in August, at the same time that a new Ministry of Agricultural Machinery was established. The Plan was to proceed in three stages, with mechanization of big city suburbs and the major commercial growing areas by 1963; over half of the rural areas by 1966; and virtually the entire countryside by 1969.

Three things undermined the Ten Year Plan. First, the economic crisis growing out of the Leap quickly deflated expansive aims, including mechanization, and, as rural industry and other non-agricultural activities collapsed, also eliminated the previous shortage of labour. Second, the communes were unprepared to manage farm machinery well, and maintenance and safety problems were endemic. (During the Cultural Revolution, it was charged that the MTSs and their leadership in the Agriculture Ministry had sabotaged local control of farm machinery by failing to provide training, instruction, and support to the communes. Third, the decentralization of the communes, with the production team ultimately becoming the basic accounting unit, ruled out management of large farm machines by commune, brigade, or team, none of which now had sufficient resources to acquire and run them.

In 1961 and 1962, therefore, control of most tractors was returned to the state, which once again administered the machine tractor stations, now renamed 'agricultural machinery stations' (AMSs). Thus collapsed the last remaining pillar of Mao's farm mechanization strategy. Tool reform had been discredited by the premature popularization of unsuccessful innovations; local production by the excesses of the commune industrialization campaign; and now local control by the problems of commune management.

The Tenth Plenum of September 1962 demoted farm mechanization from a high-priority, ten-year campaign to merely one element in a comprehensive programme of technical change. Moreover, it was to take second place for the time being to the expansion of agricultural chemicals. As Table 7.4 indicates, the production and dissemination of tractors continued, but by 1964 they were

Table 7.4. *Tractorization in China, 1954–1964*

	Tractors[a] produced	Tractors[a] in use	Tractor–cultivated area	
			Area ('000 *mu*)	% of total cult. area
1954	0	5 061	1 225	negl.
1957	0	24 629	46 000	2.7
1959	5 598	59 000	81 000	5.0
1964	21 900	123 000	162 000	10.0

[a]Standard 15 hp units.

Source: Chao (1970:107, 114–15).

in use on only 10 per cent of total farmland, well behind the pace called for by the Ten Year Plan of 1959, which had envisioned mechanization of half the total area by 1966.[15]

The approach to farm technology after 1962 was one of centralization on all fronts. The state sought to improve efficiency and quality in farm machine production by establishing specialized, state-operated plants to make parts and accessories, importing prototype machines, and fostering high-quality research and development. Pioneer trusts were established in several industries, including agricultural machinery. The goal was a single China Agricultural Machine Company, which would control the production and repair of farm machinery, as well as the operations of agricultural machinery stations throughout China (Stavis 1978:193–4). This plan was still being promoted at the onset of the Cultural Revolution in 1966, against considerable opposition from forces, led by Mao himself, that favoured local control and self-reliance in agricultural mechanization.

The post-Tenth Plenum strategy of centralization applied also to the regional aspect of agricultural development. The burden of feeding the population in the worst stricken areas during 1959–61 had brought home to the leadership the desirability of creating modernized 'grain basket' areas, relatively impervious to the weather, from which surpluses could reliably be drawn to feed the cities and deficit rural regions. The policy of creating 'high and stable yield' areas by concentrating state investment and modern inputs in regions with favourable conditions had a net effect of shifting state investment priority 'away from the wheat and coarse grain areas of the North China Plain to the predominantly rice-growing areas of south and central China' (Erisman 1972:132; 1975:330). Such a shift was perhaps inevitable, in view of the accumulation of intractable problems facing the ambitious North China water control projects of the Great Leap Forward. In particular, both the unanticipated waterlogging and soil alkalinization that had resulted from the increased use of surface water on the North China Plain, and the failure of the large San Men Gorge dam (completed in October 1960) to solve the problem of silting, which impeded irrigation and contributed to flooding in the lower reaches of the Yellow River, led to 'forced postponement of the surface water schemes for the North China Plain' (Wiens 1978:690–1) in the early 1960s.[16] Correcting these problems would take time and rapid output gains would have to be sought elsewhere.

6   Conclusion: ideology v. policy

While the pastiche of *sauve qui peut* economic policies in the countryside and tightened central control in industry worked to lift the economy out of crisis, it was satisfactory to no one in the Chinese leadership. Mao approved the 'Sixty Articles', which protected liberalization trends in agriculture up to a point, and there is no evidence that he resisted such policies as the decentralization of the communes, tolerance of rural markets, and protection of private plots. The crisis of production, organization, and ideology during the 'three hard years' made such moves virtually mandatory, and all segments of the leadership accepted them (Chang 1968).

But what Mao accepted was a temporary expedient, not a basic principle of rural economic organization. Once the immediate crisis had eased, he was prepared to begin rectifying the political damage that individual enterprise had given rise to. Nor, as his many comments of the period on the Soviet economic system indicated, was he enamoured of the return to rigid central planning. Yet with the economic strategy of mass social mobilization and adminis-trative decentralization in disrepute after the GLF, Mao's only ground for counterattack was that of ideology; in economics, he had policies to propose (e.g., agricultural priority) but not new forms of organization and admin-istration.

Economists and others[17] who favoured reforms in the direction of 'market socialism' were equally dissatisfied with the status quo. They advocated an extended scope for individual enterprise and market-oriented activity in the countryside, and a dismantling of the command economy in favour of autonomous enterprises controlled indirectly by parametric planning. The Tenth Plenum of September 1962 made it clear that such radical extensions of economic liberalism were not to be permitted.

The group that favoured professionalization of economic management and its separation from local political control, a position that may have been shared by market advocates and is associated with the names of Liu Shaoqi and (then State Economic Commission chairman) Bo Yibo, was also frustrated. The attempt to establish 'trusts' along sectoral lines was implemented only experimentally, and was still largely stymied by Maoist opposition when the Cultural Revolution (temporarily) put a halt to it.

Thus, in the early 1960s the process of institutional development marked time while ideological confusion prevailed. The traumatic events of the turn of the decade had given rise to strong pressures among the leadership for stability, routinization, professionalism, and economic liberalization; for a shift in attention from revolutionizing the relations of production to developing the forces of production. Mao not only rejected these values, but regarded them as objects of 'class struggle', the more so as the growing polemic with the Soviet

Union led him to identify similar values as the root of 'modern revisionism' there.

While production in both industry and agriculture surged forward into the mid-1960s, therefore, disputes of growing sharpness occurred in the realm of ideology and politics. The framework for this controversy was the Socialist Education Movement and its 'Four Clean-ups' (*si qing*) campaign.[18] Launched in late 1962 in response to Mao's call at the Tenth Plenum, 'Never forget class struggle', the Socialist Education Movement was intended to rectify the problems that had appeared in the countryside as the wave of the Great Leap receded. These included not only widespread disillusionment with collective farming, growth of private economic activity, and rebirth of 'feudal' customs (e.g., payment of bride prices and observance of religious festivals), but also an equally serious demoralization among cadres and much outright corruption. Perhaps most serious of all, in Mao's eyes, was a predisposition among the leadership to turn a blind eye towards the ideological ramifications of practices that seemed to increase production in the short run.

It was in large part the effective resistance of much of the party and government leadership to Mao's call for the renewal of 'class struggle' that finally led Mao to the actions that launched the Cultural Revolution. For more than two years after its inception in late 1962, the Socialist Education Movement skirted Mao's original objectives for it, first being treated merely as another campaign to promote production and then in mid-1964 turning into a harsh purge, led by Liu Shaoqi, of local cadres for corruption. Mao attempted to salvage his original aims in early 1965 with a Central Committee directive that came to be known as the 'Twenty-Three Points'. Here he defined the nature of the movement as the contradiction 'between socialism and capitalism', and identified its chief objective to be a rectification of 'those people in positions of authority within the Party who take the capitalist road' (the first known use of this phrase, which was to figure so prominently in the Cultural Revolution). 'Capitalist roaders' were said to constitute only 'a very small minority', but one existing at all levels of the Party, even the highest. The document attacked secretive and cœrcive work methods, advocated broad united front tactics, and insisted on the need for supervision of cadres from below, by the poor and lower–middle peasants.

Schurmann (1968:544) points out that, if the rural situation in 1964 approached the condition of corruption and ideological retrogression attributed to it by Liu Shaoqi, then Mao's position would have sacrificed much of the Party's control in the villages, by permitting power to remain with traditionalist and impure peasant associations. Why should Mao, unlike Liu, be willing to take (indeed, insist upon taking) such a chance? In Schurmann's view,

There may be only one answer to the question why Mao advocated an approach which only reduced the scope of political control over the villages: he truly believed that the collectivist forces of the peasantry, aroused by education and indoctrination, and not by political coercion through the Party, would win out over individualist and kulak trends and make the commune ideal a reality. Mao was willing to loosen controls in the belief that the impulses from below would work out correctly. Liu, the orthodox Communist, believed that any loosening of controls would lead to chaos and disaster. [Schurmann 1968:544]

The 'Twenty-Three Points' failed to put the Socialist Education Movement on proper Maoist tracks. The Party proved quick to abandon Liu's punitive assaults on its middle and lower ranks, but resistant to the idea of substituting Mao's policy of mass-supervised class struggle. Increasing attention was devoted in the national press to the importance of boosting production and raising living standards, and peasant individual sideline activities were defended against 'ultra-leftist' criticism. Mao, now convinced that 'revisionism' controlled the party centre, began looking to the People's Liberation Army (PLA) under Lin Biao, and rallying supporters at the regional and provincial levels, to prepare the assult on 'capitalist roaders' at the centre that was to become the Cultural Revolution.

In the flat prose of official party resolutions, the review of party history promulgated by the Sixth Plenum of the Eleventh Central Committee in June 1981 had this to say of the Socialist Education Movement:

[I]n the course of the movement, problems differing in nature were all treated as forms of class struggle or its reflections inside the Party. As a result, quite a number of the cadres at the grass-roots level were unjustly dealt with in the latter half of 1964, and early in 1965 the erroneous thesis was advanced that the main target of the movement should be those Party persons in power taking the capitalist road. [BR, 6 July 1981:20]

Thus does official history flatten the myriad complexities and cross-currents of the recovery period into a simple case of 'left' errors increasingly encroaching on 'the correct principle of economic readjustment [carried out] since the winter of 1960' (BR, 6 July 1981:19–20). In fact, it was during this period that China came face-to-face with the contradictions attendant upon the effort to amend Soviet central planning practices according to Maoist principles under conditions of underdevelopment. The apparent futility of that effort in the view of much of the party and state bureaucracy left them pulling in directions opposite to Mao's—towards a greater role for the market, or a return to centralized controls. Yet the full implications of none of these paths were fully explored by either Mao or his opponents. Instead, apparent implications began to crystallize into hard ideological positions as Mao prepared his final campaign to topple his adversaries and return China to fundamental socialist principles as he understood these. Ironically, therefore, the same unexplored terrain was to confront Chinese economic and social policy a decade later, when the Chairman had finally left the scene.

Notes

1. In a small country, dependent on the world market, economic retrenchment before external pressures might be somewhat more analogous to military retreat.
2. The latter date is ambiguous. *Ten Great Years* (1960) shows the number reaching 45.3 million in 1958. Xue Muqiao has it growing from 24.5 million to 50 million between 1958 and 1960 (Xue 1981:186), 'while the rural labor force dropped by 23 million';

but this contradicts Yang and Li (1980), who state that the agricultural labour force returned to its 1957 size by 1960 (see Chapter 6, Table 6.4 and text).

3. Zeng (1980). The figure of 40 million given in this source for the reduction in labour engaged in *grain* production matches that of Yang and Li (1980) for the drop in *agricultural* labour force between 1957 and 1958 (see Chapter 6, Table 6.4 and text).

4. These population figures are fraught with uncertainties and inconsistencies. See Aird (1967) for a discussion, and also (at p. 381) for the source of the higher urban population statistic for 1957. The lower one is found in Rawski (1979b:25). The figure of 130 million for an unspecific year prior to 1964 was given by Bo Yibo (Po I-po), then director of the State Economic Commission, to Anna Louise Strong and is reported in Strong (1964:211). I put the year in question as 1960, because Bo reported a decrease in urban population from 130 million to 110 million, and Xue (1981:186) refers to a decline of 20 million in the urban *labour force* 'between 1961 and 1962'. Note the implication that all urban residents sent to the countryside were labour force members.

5. See note 4. The coincidence of the figure of 20 million workers sent down to the countryside, with the *net* reduction in urban population of 20 million, cited by Bo Yibo, also implies the dubious proposition that there was neither in-migration to the cities nor a positive urban natural increase rate during the period in question.

6. The ratio in question depends on how China's GNP (or NNP) is calculated, and, in particular, how it is converted into US dollars. For recent years, the CIA's method of conversion implicitly assigns the yuan far greater value than its official exchange rate with the dollar, now used by the Chinese government to express China's total output in dollar terms.

7. A summary of the text of the 'Seventy Articles' can be found in Union Research Institute (1971:689–93).

8. This section relies heavily on Cyril Lin (1981), which is the best available discussion of the history of economic thought in China since 1949.

9. The formula for price, p, would thus be: $p = c + v + rK'$, where r is the average rate of profit on capital in the economy, and K' is the average total capital employed per unit of output of the industry concerned (see Lin 1981:33, n. 60).

10. The following discussion of brigade and commune-level administration relies principally on Bastid (1973), Burki (1969), and Crook (1975).

11. In the early 1960s it was common for administrative cadres to claim 4 per cent or more of the total annual work-points of a brigade or team as their subsidy. In 1963, as part of the Socialist Education Movement, this figure was reduced to a maximum of 2 per cent, a move designed to hit at cadre bureaucratism and divorce from the masses by forcing cadres to spend more time in the fields (see Baum 1975:32).

12. The supply and marketing co-operatives which were formally collective units but in practice under strict state supervision, underwent considerable organizational experimentation during and after the GLF, being first merged with the communes, then separated out again (Donnithorne 1967:301–6). Eventually they settled into a pattern in which each served either one or a few communes (Crook 1975:382).

13. This discussion of agricultural mechanization relies chiefly on Stavis (1978), especially Chapters 4–8.

14. The Soviet Union similarly turned over agricultural machinery to the collective farms in 1958 and dismantled its MTS system.

15. Table 7.4 also suggests the probable effect of the Sino-Soviet rift in 1960 on Mao's mechanization plans. Up until 1958, China had produced no tractors of its own, and even in 1960 the great majority of tractors in use were imported from the Soviet

Union and were dependent upon the import of Soviet spare parts, which declined substantially in 1961 (Stavis 1978:145). Similarly, declining imports of high-quality steel and petroleum products were probably in part responsible for a drop in tractor production (not shown) in 1961–3 (Chao 1970:106–7).

16. Other factors involved in the change in strategy were (1) a shortage of high-grade cement and steel needed for the North China projects; (2) the Soviet withdrawal of aid that had been counted on for completing these projects; and (3) the great flooding in the region during 1959–61, which shifted attention from irrigation and power generation to flood control (Wiens 1978:689).

17. While it is not clear who if anyone in China's top leadership was favourably disposed towards the 'liberalization' position in its entirety (including the advocacy of market socialism), there is some evidence that Deng Xiaoping and Peng Zhen leaned in that direction, at least as far as agriculture was concerned (see Baum 1975:142–3, 165). The blossoming of similar but even more extensive reform proposals under Deng's leadership in the late 1970s and early 1980s lends credibility to this view.

18. For detailed accounts of this complex campaign, see Baum and Tiewes (1968), and Baum (1975), on which this account relies heavily. Texts of the major documents discussed can be found in Baum and Tiewes (1968).

CHAPTER 8

ECONOMIC CONFLICT AND CULTURAL REVOLUTION, 1966–1976

1 Introduction

For over two years, starting in mid-1966, China reverberated with convulsive and often violent social conflict. It is not clear that China suffered at this time from deeper social cleavages than most societies. What it did possess was a guiding ideology that favoured continuous development of egalitarian relations of production, a supreme leader committed to that ideology, and a brief developmental history that in many respects contradicted it. Development policy had favoured the cities over the countryside, workers over peasants, older workers and technicians with regular state positions over younger workers in contract or temporary jobs. Perhaps most seriously, administrative state planning had combined political and economic power in the hands of a bureaucracy increasingly aloof from the masses.

Mao's ideas about countering these trends through administrative decentralization and mass mobilization had been discredited by the economic chaos and crisis they had produced in 1958–61. The Party had then shown much resourcefulness in resisting mass mobilization during the Socialist Education Movement. By 1966 Mao was prepared to open up social cleavages as a means of attacking the party bureaucracy, but by doing so, he opened a Pandora's Box. Hong Yong Lee puts it aptly:

> The Cultural Revolution can . . . be best described as Mao's attempt to resolve the basic contradictions between the egalitarian view of Marxism and the élitist tendencies of Leninist organizational principles. By drawing the Chinese masses into the political process, Mao wanted to reverse the trend toward restratification caused by the bureaucratization of the Party, and he also wanted to build a mass consensus on the future direction of the society.
>
> Yet, to Mao's apparent disappointment, when he removed or weakened the control exercised by the Party organization . . ., all the latent tensions and contradictions in the society surfaced. [Lee 1978:3]

The history of the Cultural Revolution has been told elsewhere.[1] No detailed account of this complex period is attempted here. Rather, this chapter presents an analysis of the main conflicts that touched upon economic principle and strategy. These are discussed as they occurred chronologically, and the next two chapters then take up, for more detailed examination, the principal themes of late Maoism that emerged from the 'decade of turmoil'.

As for the economic achievements of that decade, an overall assessment is still very difficult. Some general indicators are presented in Table 8.1. These suggest several conclusions. First, population growth proceeded very rapidly over the decade, at an annual average rate of 2.4 per cent, contrary to the

Table 8.1. *Indicators of economic growth, 1965–1975*

	1965	1975	Av. annual growth rate (%)
Population (millions)	725.4	919.7	2.4
GNP (index, 1965 = 100)	100	191	6.5
GNP per capita (index, 1965 = 100)	100	151	4.1
Gross value of industrial output (index, 1965 = 100)	100	269	10.4
Gross value of agricultural output (index, 1965 = 100)	100	148	4.0
Consumption per capita (current yuan)	125	158	2.4
(index, constant prices, 1965 = 100)	100	124	2.2
of agric. population (current yuan)	100	124	2.2
(index, constant prices, 1965 = 100)	100	123	2.1
of non-agric. population (current yuan)	237	324	3.2
(index, constant prices, 1965 = 100)	100	133	2.9
Grain output (m. metric tons)	194	284	3.7
Grain output per capita (kg)	267	309	1.1

N.B. All indexes are calculated from data in constant prices. Growth rates for GNP, GNP per capita, grain output, and grain output per capita are estimated by least squares regression; other growth rates are calulated from endpoints.

Sources: ZJN (1981): population (p. VI-3), GVIO (p. VI-14), GVAO (p. VI-10), consumption per capita, by agricultural and non-agricultural population (p. VI-25). Ashbrook (1982:104): GNP. ZNN (1981:36): grain output. The index for GNP per capita and the figures for grain output per capita are calculated using officially published population data (which include the two population figures in this table).

contemporary judgements of some observers who thought the natural increase rate had been brought well below this level. Evidently, party and government disorganization during the first half of the decade extended to the birth control programme. Starting in the early 1970s, birth rates began falling again, but not by enough to avoid the high average decadal rate shown. Second, the nominal rates of growth for GNP (6.5 per cent) and industrial and agricultural production (10.4 and 4 per cent respectively) were quite high. Third, even consumption per capita, for both urban and rural inhabitants, grew at respectable rates of over 2 per cent annually. Fourth, grain production registered a healthy growth rate of 3.7 per cent per annum, but because of rapid population growth, this translated into a modest rate of 1.1 per cent on a per capita basis.

Aside from the population growth rate, which carried an implicit warning, there is nothing in these figures to suggest that the economy was 'approaching the brink of disaster'. On the contrary, they present an optimistic picture of vigorous growth and gradual improvements in living standards, an impression that was widely shared by outside observers during most of the period in question. Unfortunately, however, the numbers do not speak for themselves. High growth rates masked unknown degrees of statistical exaggeration as well as growing sectoral imbalances. As central planning disintegrated before the Cultural Revolution onslaught and remained crippled during the factional politics of the mid-1970s, much useless production occurred in response to arbitrary targets. In interpreting the growth rates of agricultural output and of grain production, it must be remembered that in 1965 both were still recovering to trend from the crisis of the early 1960s. Total grain output was still at the 1957 level, and grain output per capita was 11 per cent below its 1957 value. Similarly, the growth of consumption per capita must be judged against the fact that foodgrain consumption per capita at the *end* of the period was no higher than in 1956.

Thus, in most respects the performance of the national economy during the decade of the Cultural Revolution was less impressive than the bare numbers suggest. The economy's problems were structural and systemic, and it would take the literature of the economic reform period that began in 1979 to expose their full extent.

2   The Cultural Revolution decade

The Cultural Revolution proper lasted some three and one-half years, from late 1965 to early 1969, although its acute phase was considerably shorter. It can be divided into a number of more or less distinct phases. The first was the narrowly 'cultural' phase, in which a series of plays, novels, and essays written in the early 1960s and implicitly critical of party policy and of Mao were subjected to attack, their authors condemned, and their backers in the party leadership purged.

Next, from late spring 1966, the Cultural Revolution moved on to university campuses and into the streets and was dominated by the activities of the 'Red Guards', university and middle-school students who attacked 'capitalist roaders' in party, government, and school administrations, as well as manifestations of the 'four olds'—old ideas, old culture, old customs, and old habits. It was at this point that the movement became fractious and sometimes violent, as in each locality it split into two or more contending factions.

The third phase, which occurred in late 1966 and early 1967, saw workers seize power in a number of cities and in numerous factories. The most dramatic episode was the 'January Revolution' in Shanghai, in which the party and government leadership of China's largest city was expelled and a Shanghai People's Commune established on the model of the Paris Commune.[2] However, the loss of party and state control inherent in the direct democracy of the 'commune' model was too much for Mao, who opted instead for the establishment of revolutionary committees consisting of a triple alliance of mass organization representatives, cadres, and People's Liberation Army (PLA) soldiers.

Thus began the fourth stage, in which the PLA was called on to put a stop to the disruptive and often violent struggles between rival mass organizations and to prevent them from developing—as they threatened to do in mid-1967—into all-out civil war. Throughout much of the year, the army found itself embroiled in the struggle, attacked politically by some of the Cultural Revolution leadership, and even physically by rebel organizations carrying weapons seized from army arsenals.

Finally, in early September, Mao issued a directive in the name of all of the top party, state, and military organs, calling on the PLA to restore order and ordering the masses to submit. Having brought down his chief targets in the leadership, especially Liu Shaoqi (Head of State) and Deng Xiaoping (Party General Secretary), the Cultural Revolution now turned against the 'ultra-left' and purged a number of leaders associated with the radical factions and with the assault on 'capitalist roaders' in the army.

Throughout the first half of 1968, the effort to create unity among the factional organizations was compromised by continuing disputes among the leadership as well as by widespread disillusionment, vengefulness, and resentment among the rebel groups. Local violence continued to flare, and serious fighting between armed student groups occurred on Beijing campuses until Mao sent workers and soldiers into the universities to end the chaos. In the summer and autumn of 1968 some 1.75 million urban secondary school graduates and college students were sent to the countryside, commencing a post-Cultural Revolution flow that was to reach a cumulative total of 12 million rusticated youth by 1975 (Bernstein 1977:32).

The goals of this programme were several: immediately, to disperse feuding young people in the cities; more importantly, to relieve pressure on an urban economy unable to provide jobs for graduating middle-school students; to get urban educated youths to give up aspirations to privileged social status and accept the standard of living of the rural majority, and to supply their education and skills to the task of rural development. However well this programme seemed to fit objective conditions in China, it was without doubt one of the most unpopular of Mao's social policies.

'Rustication' in 1968 was not confined to students; thousands of cadres were also sent down to 'May Seventh Cadre Schools', where, through physical labour and political study, they were expected to shed bureaucratic and élitist attitudes. Ironically, even during this period of combating separation from the masses, cadres remained separated, neither living nor working with the country folk.

As the Cultural Revolution wound down in 1968, the army controlled the process of political normalization, dominating the three-in-one provincial revolutionary committees that were gradually established throughout the country. The political atmosphere of this period featured an ever more extravagant and shrill idolization of Mao, a condition later blamed on Lin Biao. In October, at the Twelfth Plenum of the Eighth Central Committee, Liu Shaoqi was formally expelled from the Party 'once and for all' and stripped of all posts 'both inside and outside the Party' (PR, 1 November 1968, Supplement: vi). The Ninth Congress of the Party, held in April 1969, declared victory for the Cultural Revolution and amended the party constitution to declare Lin Biao as Mao's successor. The end of the Cultural Revolution can formally be dated to this Congress.

The end of the Cultural Revolution proper did not, however, restore peace and stability. No sooner did one set of disputes appear to get settled than new ones erupted. The next struggle centred on Lin Biao, who apparently resisted efforts, endorsed by Mao, to rebuild the damaged Party by rehabilitating large numbers of cadres attacked during the preceding several years.

The conflict leading up to the Ninth Congress had had a devastating effect on the Communist Party: 69 per cent of the surviving members of the Eighth Central Committee were purged (i.e., were not re-elected to the Ninth Central Committee) (Klein and Hager 1971:44); 25 of 29 provincial first secretaries lost their positions (Chu-yuan Cheng 1982:43), as did 13 of the 18 members of the Central Cultural Revolution Group that had been charged with supervising the movement (Nathan 1973:54).

The urgency to Mao of restoring a degree of political normalcy may in part be explained by international developments, particularly the deteriorating relationship with the USSR. The Ninth Party Congress took place only eight months after the Soviet intervention in Czechoslovakia, which had given rise to the Brezhnev Doctrine proclaiming a Soviet right of intervention in the affairs of other socialist countries. The Soviet Union had massive military forces deployed along its border with China, and a series of sharp border clashes had occurred just before the Congress. From the Chinese viewpoint, it seemed possible that the political justification and the military means were being prepared for an attack on China. On the other hand, events in south-east Asia were making it increasingly clear that the United States was bogged down there in a war it could not win, and that the threat of escalation to China had largely passed.

Given this perception of events, Mao and part of the leadership around him sought to re-establish party and government stability at home while shifting China's foreign policy strategy towards building bridges to the West, ultimately the United States, and redefining the principal enemy and most dangerous superpower as the Soviet Union. It appears that both of these policies were resisted by Lin Biao, but without success. In early July 1971, Sino–US rapprochement began in earnest with Secretary of State Kissinger's secret visit to Beijing, and two months later Lin Biao disappeared from view, the victim, it was later claimed, of a plane crash in Outer Mongolia while fleeing to the Soviet Union after an abortive attempt on Mao's life. A wide-ranging purge of the political and military establishment followed, and Lin was denounced as leader of the ultra-leftist group responsible for the excesses of the Cultural Revolution. The reclassification of Lin Biao, whose long revolutionary career had culminated in his designation as Mao's successor and 'close comrade-in-arms', is generally credited as being for many Chinese the final blow to the increasingly fragile credibility of the top leadership. Widespread cynicism now greeted the omnipresent ideology behind which coursed byzantine factional intrigues that repeatedly turned former heroes into instant villains and vice versa.

The rebuilding of the Party and the rehabilitation of formerly denounced officials picked up pace in the early 1970s. Among the latter was Deng

Xiaoping, formerly general secretary of the Party and the second 'capitalist roader' after Liu Shaoqi. At the secretly convened Tenth Party Congress in August 1973, Deng was re-elected to the Politburo along with four ill-fated Cultural Revolution leaders supported by Mao: Jiang Qing, Wang Hongwen, Zhang Chunqiao, and Yao Wenyuan, later to be branded the 'Gang of Four'.[3] Lin Biao was now officially relabelled from 'ultra-leftist' to 'rightist'. In short, the Tenth Congress simultaneously advanced Maoist leadership figures and rhetoric as well as Deng Xiaoping and the forces of moderation, in a recipe for continued struggle and stalemate (Starr 1976:459).

The contest was at first waged within a rather obscure campaign to criticize Lin Biao and Confucius that held sway in 1973 and 1974. In spring of the latter year, Zhou Enlai entered the hospital with the cancer that was to take his life, and Deng Xiaoping took over the daily responsibilities of running China's government. In early January 1975 the Second Plenum of the Tenth Central Committee met, followed immediately by the Fourth National People's Congress, neither meeting attended by Mao. The overriding theme of the Congress was the need for unity, and it was at this gathering that Zhou Enlai put forward his famous call for 'four modernizations' in two stages: first, to build 'an independent and relatively comprehensive industrial and economic system' by 1980; second, to 'accomplish the comprehensive modernization of agriculture, industry, national defense, and science and technology before the end of the century so that our national economy will be advancing in the front ranks of the world' (PR, 24 January 1975). At Mao's specific behest, a new national constitution, adopted by the Congress, gave workers the right to strike.

After the Fourth National People's Congress, Mao issued a series of new comments that emphasized the similarity between capitalism on the one hand, and China's continued adherence to a system of commodity production, the use of money, and a system of differentiated wages, on the other. Such institutions, he suggested, inculcated bourgeois values in peasants, workers, and even party members. Therefore, it was necessary to use the 'dictatorship of the proletariat' to restrict such inherited practices.

Coming so soon after the Fourth National People's Congress, which had stressed political unity and economic development rather than further combat over the relations of production, Mao's remarks had the character of a rebuke. They gave rise to a new campaign to 'study the dictatorship of the proletariat' and to 'restrict bourgeois rights'—that is, rights, such as that of payment according to labour, that survive and are even strengthened by the achievement of public ownership of the means of production, but that treat people unequally with respect to their needs.

The most notable features of the new campaign were two articles, by Yao Wenyuan and Zhang Chunqiao, respectively, that put forward a rough but suggestive theoretical case for the rise of a new bourgeois class in socialist China. Because these were the most explicit warnings, from a Maoist perspective, against both the Soviet system and the events that were about to occur in China, it is worth pausing to examine them somewhat closer. They originally appeared in successive issues of Hong Qi (nos. 3 and 4) in 1975.

Yao's article, 'On the Social Basis of the Lin Piao Anti-Party Clique' (Yao 1975), is the cruder of the two. Yao points out that the restriction of 'bourgeois rights' amounts to a gradual reduction of the gaps between workers and peasants, town and country, and manual and mental labour; and he argues that the opposite course of 'consolidation, extension, and strengthening of bourgeois rights and that part of inequality it entails' would inevitably lead to 'polarization':

i.e., a small number of people will in the course of distribution acquire increasing amounts of commodities and money through certain legal channels and numerous illegal ones; capitalist ideas of amassing fortunes and craving for personal fame and gain, stimulated by such 'material incentives,' will spread unchecked; such phenomena as turning public property into private property, speculation, graft and corruption, theft and bribery will arise; the capitalist principle of the exchange of commodities will make its way into political life and even into Party life, undermine the socialist planned economy, and give rise to such acts of capitalist exploitation as the conversion of commodities and money into capital and labor power into a commodity . . . As a result, a small number of new bourgeois elements and upstarts . . . will emerge from among Party members, workers, well-to-do peasants, and personnel in state organs.

The growth in economic strength of such elements will lead to increasing political power and a *de facto* control of the means of production. In the end, 'a handful of new bourgeois elements monopolizing the means of production will at the same time monopolize the power of distributing consumer goods and other products.'

This apocalyptic vision is fleshed out in somewhat subtler terms by Zhang's following article, 'On Exercising All-round Dictatorship Over the Bourgeoisie' (Zhang 1975). Zhang admits that the system of ownership is the decisive factor in the relations of production, and that in this respect China had made great progress in establishing public ownership. But he adds some caveats. First is the distinction between form and reality: according to Mao, in 'a fairly large majority of factories . . . leadership was not in the hands of genuine Marxists and the masses of workers' before the Cultural Revolution. Thus, such enterprises, publicly owned though they were in form, were in reality controlled by opponents of socialism. Second, because of China's weak economic base,

bourgeois right . . . is still prevalent to a serious extent in the relations between men and holds a dominant position in distribution. In the various spheres of the superstructure, some aspects are in fact still controlled by the bourgeoisie which is predominant there . . . [Zhang 1975]

Thus, differentials in pay, status, and authority, as well as ideological, educational, legal, and other 'superstructural' phenomena, continued to reflect anti-socialist forms and attitudes and to engender their survival and extension:

[It] is incorrect to attach no importance to whether the issue of the system of ownership has been resolved in form or in reality, to the reaction exerted on the system of ownership by the two other aspects of the relations of production—the relations between men and the form of distribution—and to the reaction exerted on the economic base by the superstructure; *these two aspects and the superstructure may play a decisive role under given conditions.* [Zhang 1975; emphasis added]

In short, 'the correctness or incorrectness of the ideological and political line, and the control of leadership in the hands of one class or another, decide which class *owns* a factory *in reality*' (emphasis added).

The picture painted by Zhang thus avoids Yao Wenyuan's purple evocations of 'graft, corruption, theft, and bribery', of a coming 'bloody suppression of the people'. Zhang's message is different: a market orientation with regard to income distribution, social relations influenced by pre-socialist patterns of authority and status, and bourgeois attitudes dominating the 'superstructure' together can transform nominally public ownership into *actual* ownership by the bourgeoisie. By continuously breeding bourgeois attitudes (e.g., communists who 'have reached the point of regarding everything as a commodity, including themselves', and who 'join the Communist Party and do some work for the proletariat merely for the sake of upgrading themselves as commodities and asking the proletariat for higher prices'), these transitional forms constantly threaten to turn socialism into an empty shell within which capitalist society regenerates.

Both Yao Wenyuan and Zhang Chunqiao treat socialism as a process necessarily in motion. The retrogressive forces—commodity production, market relations, income differentials, social inequalities—are too persistent to allow stasis; they must be whittled away gradually, or they will grow larger. Yao and Zhang do not demonstrate in any detail how the restoration of capitalism as it is generally understood can occur. Rather, it is bureaucratic étatism that they fear, whose privileged élite—'new bourgeois elements . . . among party members, workers, well-to-do peasants and personnel in state organs'—take over *de facto* control of the allocation of resources and the distribution of income. Yao Wenyuan makes clear that it is the Soviet example that personifies this threat, not old-fashioned capitalism: 'Such is the process of restoration that has already taken place in the Soviet Union.'

Yet a remarkable aspect of their discussion is the sterility of its response to the threat. The crux of the problem, as they see it, is the juxtaposition of market forces (bourgeois rights) and party and state bureaucracy, the former corrupting the latter. But market forces also constitute a check on the power of the bureaucracy. To 'restrict bourgeois rights' is to weaken this check, and widen the potential scope for bureaucratic autocracy. Recognition of this leads to placing the structure of political and economic authority on the agenda. Although Mao dealt with this issue by advocating administrative decentralization, the mass line, and periodic campaigns against bureaucratism, Yao and Zhang approach it almost solely on the ideological level. It is thus not surprising that, in many respects, the rigid and arbitrary exercise of administrative power was to grow worse during the Cultural Revolution.

The elevation of Deng Xiaoping in early January 1975 at the Second Plenum of the Tenth Central Committee and the subsequent Fourth National People's Congress had made him a vice-chairman of the Party, a member of the Standing Committee of the Politburo, and the first Vice-Premier of the State Council—which left him third in the political hierarchy and the pre-eminent candidate to succeed the ailing Zhou Enlai and possibly Mao himself. While Yao Wenyuan and Zhang Chunqiao were publishing their warnings of capitalist transition, Deng was presiding over the preparation of a number of documents that mapped a coming sea-change in China's political economy.[4]

These documents undertook a wide-ranging attack on the politics of the 'left' over the preceding decade. Its adherents are accused of having a mania for creating factions, splits, and cliques; of denigrating economics by holding that correct politics automatically solves economic problems; of persecuting anyone who paid attention to economic, technical, or financial questions; of creating a widespread condition of management chaos, labour indiscipline, and general demoralization in the economy; of mistreating scientists, technicians, and researchers and thus interfering with scientific progress; of ignoring 'objective economic laws'.

It is pure nonsense to say that a certain place or work unit is carrying out revolution very well when production is fouled up. The view that once revolution is grasped, production will increase naturally and without spending any effort is believed only by those who indulge in fairy tales. [Chi 1977:227]

In industry, the (Maoist) policy of encouraging local development was accused of embodying 'serious capitalist tendencies':

A small number of enterprises . . . are sabotaging the national plan and undertaking illegal free production and free exchange . . . Class enemies . . . sabotage revolution and production, pull down good cadres, attack model workers and model collectives. Bad people are in power, while good people suffer. In these localities and enterprises, management is in chaos, production has suffered prolonged stagnation, some of the enterprises have actually changed in nature. [Chi 1977:241–2]

In short, those following such a line had imposed severe damage on the nation's economy, politics, and general morale.

To rectify this situation, a basic change in approach was necessary. To begin with, all organizations and individuals must be subject to the central leadership of the party committees. Enterprises must rebuild strong systems of management and production control, devote full attention to economic and financial norms, and develop tight and strictly implemented responsibility systems for workers and managers. More advanced technology must be imported, and to pay for it, natural resources such as coal and oil should be exported. The use of long-term foreign credits (previously ruled out) should be considered for the purpose of rapidly building up China's export capacity. In the realm of incentives, the brunt of Deng's message was aimed at 'egalitariansim'.

From each according to his means, to each according to his contribution; those who do not work will have nothing to eat. These are [the?][5] basic principles of socialism . . . An egalitarian distribution that does not distinguish between differences in the intensities of work, standards of ability, and magnitude of contribution is not conducive to the mobilization of the masses for building socialism. [Chi 1977:265]

Deng also called for reinstituting a system of regular promotions. Most workers and staff members had been frozen in place for at least a decade.

Thus, while Zhang Chunqiao and Yao Wenyuan, by claiming that existing organs of party and state were still permeated by 'representatives of the bourgeoisie', were laying the basis for renewed attacks on these institutions, Deng Xiaoping was taking exactly the opposite position. Condemning the results of such attacks over the past decade, he called for a return to system, order, discipline, production, and party leadership.

The maturing of this climactic conflict within the leadership coincided with the rapid expansion of Chinese contact with the outside world, as the leadership around Zhou and Deng moved to restore foreign trade and provide access for China to advanced technology from abroad. Throughout the decade of the 1960s, China's foreign trade, depressed by political and economic disruptions, stagnated below the peak level of 1959. At the turn of the 1970s China began a diplomatic offensive that led to a rapid expansion of its links with other countries. In October 1971, Beijing replaced Taiwan as representative of China in the United Nations. President Nixon visited China in February 1972, and signed the 'Shanghai communiqué' acknowledging the existence of only one China of which Taiwan was a part. Full diplomatic relations with Japan were established in September of that year.

Political and diplomatic ties were accompanied by a rapid growth in trade. In current dollars, China's total trade rose from $4.3 billion in 1970 to $10.3 billion in 1973, an increase of 140 per cent. Although this figure is exaggerated by the devaluation of the dollar and by inflation in the West during the period in question, even in constant dollars trade with non-communist countries grew by 80 per cent (Batsavage and Davie 1978:711). Beginning in 1972, China began contracting for plant and equipment imports from advanced industrial countries, with emphasis on chemical fertilizer and artificial fiber production facilities. A notable feature of this programme was the purchase of thirteen large urea plants from European, Japanese, and US companies. The peak year for contracting whole plant acquisition was 1973, when an estimated $1.3 billion in contracts was signed (Batsavage and Davie 1978:738–9).

These developments led to a balance of payments problem that may have become a weapon in the 1975 campaign against Deng Xiaoping. In 1974 China found itself caught by the same forces that were afflicting the economies of other Third World countries tied to the world market. Strong inflationary pressures in the West raised the prices of China's imports while world-wide recession was restricting the market for its exports. The result was a record $1.2 billion hard currency deficit in China's trade with non-communist countries. China responded in late 1974 by cancelling or postponing imports already contracted for, curtailing new imports, drastically decreasing orders for new plants (to $364 million in 1975), and striving to increase exports. 'Oil saved the day for Chinese exports as sales of crude oil and petroleum products jumped to $910 million' in 1975 (Batsavage and Davie 1978:713). As a result of these measures, the trade deficit with non-communist countries was cut in half, to $585 million, in 1975.

Throughout the first part of 1975, Deng Xiaoping vigorously pursued an anti-'left' line, promoting his 'revisionist' policy documents; preventing attempts to 'restrict bourgeois rights' by compressing wage differentials further; sending the army into the city of Hangzhou (Zhejiang Province), which was beset by violent factional strife, and arresting the most prominent 'leftist' there; attacking the leaders later to be known as the 'Gang of Four' in Politburo meetings; and purging 'leftists' in scientific and educational work who were held responsible for a drastic decline in standards (Gardner 1982:Chapter 3). Yet, contrary to general expectation, Deng disappeared from view shortly after Zhou Enlai's death in January 1976, and it was Hua Guofeng who assumed the acting premiership. There followed a large-scale campaign against Deng and the views he had advocated in his three famous policy documents.

In retrospect, it seems clear that Mao had reacted badly to these documents, which in basic ways 'reversed the verdict' of the Cultural Revolution and urged a return to previous patterns of organization and behaviour. In one of his last published statements, Mao said of Deng: 'This person does not grasp class struggle; he has never referred to this key link. Still his theme of white cat, black cat,[6] making no distinction between imperialism and Marxism' (Gardner 1982:Chapter 3).

In fact, as Selden (1979:140–2) points out, Deng's three documents contained ample verbiage of Cultural Revolution stripe about class struggle, proletarian dictatorship, and combating revisionism. But the target had changed; in Deng's hands, the enemy was not 'capitalist roaders' in Party and government, but rather those people who 'still use metaphysics' and 'talk only about politics but not economics; only about revolution but not production':

In short, the documents explicitly pinpoint the main danger rising from 'ultra-left' forces whose program of class struggle undermines national goals of modernization and development. The spearhead of criticism pointed directly at the Cultural Revolution Group. [Selden 1979:140–2]

The campaign against Deng intensified after the 'Tiananmen Incident', a demonstration that took place in April 1976 to honour the memory of Zhou Enlai and which was called a counter-revolutionary incident. Within days of this demonstration, the Politburo met and stripped Deng of his party posts as an 'unrepentant capitalist roader'.

3 The industrial policy debate

Deng's 'Certain Questions on Accelerating the Development of Industry' (the 'Twenty Points') accurately presaged the policies that would be implemented after his second resurrection in mid-1977. The attacks mounted against him in the spring and summer of 1976 represented the last expression of his opponents' viewpoints regarding China's economic organization and development and presumably would reflect their reaction, had they been able to express it, to the policies later implemented. It has become clear (and is explicitly acknowledged by the post-Mao leadership) that the views of the Gang of Four (or 'Shanghai group') on these questions closely coincided with Mao's own views at the end of his life.

The critics took issue with the 'Twenty Points' on a number of grounds,[7] of which the following are most important.

3.1 China's international economic policy

The 'Twenty Points' advocated selective import of advanced technology within a general framework of independence and self-reliance; it urged the use of oil and coal exports to pay for this, and also suggested abandoning China's refusal to consider long-term loans (Chi 1977:264). Interestingly, the critique did not directly address the last point, but did condemn the others. While recognizing the need to import 'some' advanced technology from abroad, it accused the 'Twenty Points' of overemphasizing the role of such imports, underemphasizing the importance of self-reliance, uncritically lauding the superiority of foreign technology, and seeking to export things needed by China in exchange for imports of things China could produce itself.

It is worth noting that all of these tendencies did in fact emerge in the 'foreign leap forward' of 1977–9, whether or not they were present in the 'Twenty Points'. Therefore, the critics were prescient in recognizing an incipient propensity to go overboard in treating foreign technology as the answer to China's problems. However, in view of the stagnant and underutilized role of foreign trade during the previous decade and a half, there was in 1975 much room for encouraging a more outward-looking posture, as called for by the 'Twenty Points', before a genuine issue could be made of the abandonment of self-reliance.

The Shanghai group came down particularly hard on the proposal to enter into long-term contracts with foreign suppliers, under which the latter would provide up-to-date technology for developing China's fossil fuel resources in return for eventual payment in coal and oil. This was taken to be a betrayal of national sovereignty and dignity which threatened to turn China into a dumping ground for imperialist products, a 'raw material base, a repair and assembly workshop and an investment ground' for exploitation by foreign capitalism ('Criticism of Selected Passages' 1976:4).

3.2 Enterprise management

The 'Twenty Points' attacked 'opposition to enterprise management and rules of operation' as anarchic; urged the establishment of 'strong and independent' systems of management to supervise daily production work; argued that the enterprise party committee should refrain from interfering with routine management affairs and concentrate its energies on 'major issues'; discussed strengthening various systems within enterprise management, such as those for performance evaluation, quality control, and accounting; and identified the production responsibility system as the core of the system of operational rules within the enterprise. ('Each job and each station must have a responsible person. Each cadre, worker, and technician must be assigned a specific job responsibility'—[Chi 1977:251].)

The Shanghai group's general view of this position was that, by ignoring the class character of management systems, it implicitly supported the establishment of restrictive practices and hierarchical structures such as characterize capitalist enterprises. Specifically, the attack on 'anarchy' was taken (correctly) to be an attack on the 'many forms of participation by workers in management' worked out during the Cultural Revolution; on the 'impressive changes . . . [in] the relations between people' within enterprises; and on the revolutionary committees themselves (unmentioned in the relevant section of the 'Twenty Points'). Deng's advocacy of independent management systems, together with his injunction that party committees limit their attention to major issues, was taken to be an attempt to free management from political control, to 'separate Party from government, to practice the revisionist "one chief system," to usurp the leadership of enterprises, and to turn socialist enterprises into capitalist ones' ('Criticism of Selected Passages' 1976:4–5). In fact, except for the apocalyptic last phrase, this is an accurate rendition of the reformers' platform, as was to become clear after 1976 when such proposals became more explicit and were in part enacted.

As for responsibility systems and operational rules, the critics recognized the need for these but held that the 'Twenty Points' took an overly restrictive and rigid attitude towards them, with a view to imposing 'control, checks, and coercion' on workers. They argued that such an approach exceeded the requirements of a rational division of labour (which the critics supported) and harked back to 'past narrow confines of division of work which stifled the initiative of the workers'. Examples were given in which workers had been prevented by rigid responsibility systems from helping out when problems arose outside their particular jurisdictions, with consequent harm to production. The critics instead advocated the Maoist idea of being a specialist in one job and a generalist in many. The 'Twenty Points' image of a proper responsibility system, in short, was taken to be an attempt to remove the workers from concern with politics, management, and their broader role in society and to make them subservient extensions of their machines ('Criticism of Selected Passages' 1976:6).

3.3 Incentives and welfare of workers

The emphasis of the 'Twenty Points' in this sphere is on opposing egalitarianism. It suggests that current 'material and moral conditions' did not permit excessive restriction of bourgeois rights, that egalitarianism would be 'impossible in the future' as well as now, and that income payments must differ according to variations in work intensity, ability, and magnitude of contribution. As for establishing a system of promotion, the criteria advocated are 'attitude towards work, technical and administrative skills, contribution in work and labor'. Part of the labour force should receive a wage increase every year or two. The discussion carefully includes an injunction to accompany these material measures with education of workers regarding 'the purposes of building a strong socialist country and supporting the world revolution, as well as the establishment of a communist work attitude', etc.

The critics attacked this treatment for 'essentially denying the existence of bourgeois rights in the field of distribution', which is patently inaccurate. It is true however that the 'Twenty Points' tried to have it both ways on this issue, advocating both restriction (specifying only the need to raise wages of low-wage workers so as to 'gradually reduce disparities') and expansion (i.e., reducing egalitarianism in distribution). The critics also accurately perceived that to make wages depend only upon work intensity, ability, and contribution was to embrace material incentives in practice. Here both sides were guilty of obfuscation, since the Shanghai group also endorsed payment according to work while trying to distinguish it from 'material incentives'. However, the critics undoubtedly favoured giving less weight to wage differentials and more to political education than did the reformers.

The criteria for promotion put forward by the 'Twenty Points' were attacked as a 'carrot-and-stick' system for co-opting workers and creating a labour aristocracy. Similarly, the proposal to institute regular pay increases for some workers led the critics to ask which ones would be so favoured. Their answer: those who towed the line, concerned themselves only with techniques and production, and did not 'criticize revisionism and the bourgeoisie'. Their implication was clearly that pay and promotions should be based on political as well as production criteria.

The fact that no significant wage increases had occurred since 1957 indicates how far such theoretical positions could stray from reality—in this case, with serious effects on worker morale. Workers were likely to have been impatient with an ideological defense of relatively egalitarian increases in living standards when in fact no such improvements had been forthcoming for many years. On this score, Deng Xiaoping seized the initiative and devoted one (no. 14) of the 'Twenty Points' to 'Concern for the Livelihood of the Workers'. Under this rubric, he attacked 'indifference to the problems of the livelihood of the masses' and advocated a wide range of measures, including increased construction of housing and urban public utilities; improvement in canteen facilities, day-care centres, health and medical clinics, and other social welfare projects; improvements in the supply of subsidiary foods to urban and industrial centres; effective procedures to end the practice of assigning married couples to widely separated job locations for lengthy periods of time; and allowing children to inherit the jobs of their retired or deceased parents. These were all proposals likely to win enthusiastic endorsement from urban workers and their families. (Interestingly, the last-mentioned proposal, strikingly 'feudal' in concept to have been put forward by a group that was later to condemn the persistence of 'feudal' attitudes in China, was not criticized by the Shanghai group.) The critics saw the political attractiveness of this point; they were careful not to quote Deng's detailed list of proposals, limiting their rebuttal to an indignant denial of 'indifference' to the problems in the livelihood of the masses'.

3.4 *Decentralization of industrial enterprises*

A major decentralization of economic authority occurred between 1970 and 1973, about which details became available only many years later. Almost all enterprises previously controlled by central ministries (except military industries) were transferred to local authorities, including the giant steel complex at Anshan and the Daqing oil fields. Localities were given main responsibility for capital construction, materials distribution, and financial revenues and expenditures within their jurisdictions. By 1972 the number of products subject to unified distribution by the central authorities had fallen to 31 per cent of the 1966 figure of several hundred. The depreciation funds of transferred enterprises were now put at the disposal of the enterprises themselves and of their local government supervisors. 'Horizontal' control of material allocation was strengthened; for twelve key goods (including rolled steel, cement, timber, and coal) a system was tried out in which the provinces took responsibility for supplying all enterprises within their borders, including centrally operated ones (except for defense-related enterprises, railroads, enterprises producing exports, and some unspecified 'special undertakings'), while the central government contracted with each province the amount of provincial exports or imports for a fixed period of time.

In the accompanying financial reform, the unified collection of local revenue and control of local expenditure by the central authorities was relaxed. Provincial obligations to the centre for transferring revenue and incurring expenditures were fixed in advance and the provinces were given the right to retain additional revenues and any savings realized on their expenses for their own use (He 1980:37; Wang 1982:75–6).

The degree of actual autonomy entailed by these reforms is difficult to ascertain, especially since the actual process of plan formation remained a central prerogative. As one authority puts it, 'although the localities were asked to draw up plans each year and their opinions were solicited with respect to the national draft plan, very few of these were accepted' (He 1980:37). However, in retrospect, the reforms were given both credit for stimulating much local activity during these years and some blame (most of which, however, was assigned to the 'ultra-left' line of the day) for creating serious inter-regional and sectoral imbalances (Wang Haibo 1982).

Point 5 of the 'Twenty Points' urges that this decentralization be continued. However, it strongly criticizes localities for failing to manage enterprises effectively, ignoring the national interest and central plans, changing the product line of decentralized enterprises, failing to fulfil output and supply quotas, wasting materials and funds, increasing staff size, raising the wage bill, and changing product prices at will. For these reasons, the document calls for strengthening central control over decentralized units. Large-scale enterprises 'that affect the overall national economy' were already subject to dual control; central ministries supervised allocation of their output and essential inputs, as well as their product mix, policy, and planning. However, the document went farther than this: it suggested that *all* decentralized enterprises were subject to central supervision with respect to all decisions affecting the following areas:

(1) the direction and policy of the national economy; (2) major production targets in industry and agriculture; (3) investment in basic construction and major projects; (4) allocation of essential materials; (5) purchasing and distribution of essential

products; (6) national fiscal budget and the supply of money; (7) increases of staff and workers and wages; (8) pricing of essential industrial and agricultural products.

Both sides accepted Mao's injunction in 'On the Ten Major Relationships' to 'enlarge the powers of the local authorities to some extent, give them greater independence and let them do more, all on the premise that the unified leadership of the central authorities is to be strengthened'. Deng clearly thought that the emphasis now had to be placed on the last phrase—strengthening central authority—whereas the Shanghai group saw Deng's position as an attempt to reimpose rigid central control. Both sides were perceiving events accurately; for, as a reformer later would argue, administrative control of enterprises led either to rigidity when it took a centralized form or to anarchic development in its decentralized variant. The third option, quasi-autonomous enterprises controlled by the market, which was favoured by a reform group that gained influence in 1978, was not yet openly part of the debate.

3.5   Redness v. expertise

The 'Twenty Points' endorsed the need to develop both political consciousness and technical skills in workers. However, the document made clear Deng's view that the second requirement had been given less than its proper weight in recent years. It criticized the misallocation of scientific and technical personnel to jobs in which their skills were wasted, and suggested that redness and expertise had been improperly treated as being in conflict. The critics rejected this charge, and took Deng to task for ignoring various institutions that had developed during the Cultural Revolution to promote skills—workers' theoretical contingents, 21 July workers' universities, mass scientific research activities, 'three-in-one' technical innovation groups (i.e., groups composed of workers, technicians, and administrative cadres), and so on. They accused Deng of stirring up a 'vocational typhoon', promoting expertise for its own sake.

Here again, the critics were better at perceiving the *direction* of Deng's policies than they were at accurately depicting the carefully drafted 'Twenty Points' themselves. A more frank expression of Deng's position on redness and expertise was delivered at a national science conference held in March 1978:

Scientists and technicians should concentrate their energy on scientific and technical work. When we say that at least five-sixths of their work time should be left free for their scientific and technical work, this is meant to be the minimum demand. It is still better if even more time is available for this purpose. If some persons work seven days and seven evenings on end to meet the needs of science or production, that shows their lofty spirit of selfless devotion to the cause of socialism ... We cannot demand that scientists and technicians, or at any rate the overwhelming majority of them, study a lot of political and theoretical books, participate in numerous social activities, and attend many meetings not related to their work ... How can you label as 'white' a man who studies hard to improve his knowledge and skills? ... The cause of socialism calls for a division of labor. On condition that they keep to the socialist political stand, comrades of different trades and professions are not divorced from politics when they do their best at their posts ... [PR, 24 March 1978:14–15]

Thus did Deng embrace the view that the proper division of labour leaves the Party in charge of politics and all others in charge of their work-posts—a distinctly un-Maoist view.

In sum, while both sides accepted the major slogans epitomizing economic policy—self-reliance, consistent with some foreign trade; the need for enterprise management and rules of operation; distribution according to work; restriction of bourgeois rights; decentralization of industry under unified central leadership; both redness and expertise—the differences in interpretation of these phrases evident in the documents of the debate make clear the very great conflicts that existed between Deng Xiaoping's forces and those of the Shanghai group, which to some extent spoke for Mao's views. Indeed, because these differences were partially obscured by the need on all sides to fit arguments into the slogans expressing Maoist principles, their full extent became apparent to most observers only after the change in regime, when the implementation of new policies began.

Notes

1. See, *inter alia*, Lee (1978); Ahn (1976); Karol (1974); Milton and Milton (1976); Selden (1979:107–33); Meisner (1977:Chapter 18).
2. For accounts of this event, see Hunter (1971); Meisner (1977:317–24, 354); and Walder (1978).
3. Strictly speaking, Wang Hongwen was newly elected, the others re-elected. Altogether, eight new members were added to the Politburo, including Hua Guofeng. Wang Hongwen was put on the Standing Committee, and stood third in the party hierarchy behind Mao and Zhou Enlai (see Starr 1976).
4. These documents include: 'On the General Program for All Work of the Whole Party and the Whole Country'; 'Certain Questions on Accelerating the Development of Industry' (referred to as the 'Twenty Points'); and 'Outline Report of Work in the Academy of Sciences'. A text of the first, a partial draft of the second (containing eighteen points), and excerpts of the third are available in Chi (1977).
5. The definite article is used in Chi Hsin's translation, but in Chinese the meaning is ambiguous. Since most students of Marx would agree that distribution according to work is *a* but not *the* principle of socialism, the definite article probably does not belong in the passage. Zhao Ziyang would later claim that socialism basically consisted of social ownership of the means of production plus payment according to work—thus adding another 'basic principle'.
6. The phrase 'black cat white cat' refers to a statement for which Deng Xiaoping had been fiercely attacked during the Cultural Revolution, and which came to stand for unprincipled pragmatism: 'It doesn't matter whether a cat is black or white, as long as it catches the mouse.'
7. The discussion of the Shanghai group's critique of the 'Twenty Points' is based largely on 'Criticism of Selected Passages of "Certain Questions on Accelerating the Development of Industry" ' (1976). *Study and Criticism* (*Xeuxi yu Pipan*) in which this article appeared, was the Shanghai-based organ of the 'left' faction. Quotations from the critics are all taken from this source unless otherwise identified. Quotations from the 'Twenty Points' themselves are from Chi (1977).

CHAPTER 9

LATE MAOISM, I: SELF-RELIANCE

1 Introduction

Through most of the turbulent decade chronicled in the last chapter, certain basic principles rhetorically dominated economic policy. These principles represent a culmination of Mao's thinking as regards the direction in which a socialist China should aim. That Mao himself was a critical factor in the raising and implementation of such principles can hardly be doubted, not only because of his own role in generating the Cultural Revolution to begin with, but also because of the speed with which the principles themselves were cast aside or amended after his death.

Beginning in the mid-1950s, as we have seen, and extending through the Great Leap Forward, the Socialist Education Movement, and, finally, the Cultural Revolution, Mao took aim at the concentration of political and economic authority at the centre; the growth of an urban privileged élite of officials and technocrats; and the spread of bureaucratism, reinforced by long cultural tradition. The combination of this tradition with Leninist principles of party organization gave rise to a powerful bureaucratizing momentum, against which Mao countered with unprecedented mass campaigns. The results of these conflicts were not what he desired or anticipated, and in some respects they led paradoxically to a reinforcement of the very tendencies they were meant to thwart.

It is now time to examine the principles that Mao advanced in contradistinction to the tendencies described above, principles that played such a dominant role both in rhetoric and, in part, in practice during the 'Cultural Revolution decade' of 1966–76. I have grouped them into two broad categories: self-reliance (to be considered in this chapter) and egalitarianism (Chapter 10). These categories are not independent of each other. In some respects they are contradictory; in others, the policies grouped under 'self-reliance' can be regarded as means for achieving greater economic and social equality. For example, rural industrialization, an important aspect of self-reliance in practice, was meant to reduce urban–rural differences in income, even as it led to larger income disparities between localities.

What Maoist policies had in common was their grounding in the conviction that the relations of production provide the lever for advancing both socialist society and economic development. Both his critique of Soviet experience and his observation of events in China convinced Mao that inertial forces threatening to halt progress towards a more equitable society could abort the revolution and lead to 'capitalist restoration'. Responding by means of persistent pressure on the 'three great differences' (between city and countryside, worker and peasant, and mental and manual labour), he promoted a strategy of retrenching functional bureaucracies, decentralizing economic power, and mobilizing the population under central ideological guidance. The principal policies of the 1966–76 decade are understandable in these terms.

Unlike most observers in the West and many in China as well, Mao did not regard the promotion of his values as antithetical to rapid economic development. Rather, he viewed the first as a stimulus to the second inasmuch as it led to a more thorough mobilization of the population. Mao saw human initiative as the key to success in all great endeavours, and the conditions arousing greatest initiative were those that promised greatest success.

Much human initiative was indeed aroused during the decade, and was invested in the building of rural industries, the terracing and irrigation of farmland, the establishment of co-operative medical insurance programmes, and the like. However, a great deal of the energy was devoted to sometimes savage conflict and factional politics, which generated an atmosphere of fear that corroded genuine popular initiative. Similarly, the record of achievement of left principles was mixed: interpersonal income gaps were reduced; health and education resources were redistributed to the underprivileged countryside; for a brief time workers did participate in managing their enterprises, and for a longer time cadres participated in ordinary labour; the shield of automatic authority wielded by officials was pierced, and ordinary people could put up wall posters (*dazibao*) criticizing local cadres or national leaders. On the other hand, China emerged from ten years of struggle in conditions that had strayed far from these principles. In particular, by the mid-1970s the power of the state and its leading officials was, if anything, greater than ever, for it was now relatively unchecked either by law (always a weak reed in China), by custom (a discredited part of the reactionary past), or by mass movements (either suppressed or carefully controlled by one faction or another). In addition, living standards, whose gradual but continuous rise was supposed to confirm in practice the superiority of left principles, had mostly stagnated both in cities and in the countryside, and in some areas had fallen; while, conversely, rates of capital accumulation apparently knew no bounds. Workers, made cynical by dormant wages and a decade of radical rhetoric far removed from reality, emerged more money-conscious than ever. The politicization of virtually all policy issues—one's characterization as a friend or enemy of socialism could depend on one's view about such trivial questions as whether to buy or make a piece of equipment—led to a ubiquitous fear of making decisions, with the result that buck-passing, delay, and reluctance to take responsibility—in a word, classic bureaucratic behaviour—became the norm. Goods that had no use were produced and piled up in warehouses, while goods that were acutely needed were produced not at all or in inadequate quantities. Economic sectors advanced or not under their own momentum, in accordance with their access to resources and with little relation to their links with other sectors. The quality of central planning deteriorated under the ideological assault of the anti-bureaucratic agenda and the political assault on many of the planners themselves. Allocative decisions became arbitrary, unpredictable, and subjective, forcing individual enterprises and localities to take defensive measures that were irrational from the larger, social perspective.

Many of these problems seem to have sprung not so much from inherent flaws in individual Maoist precepts themselves (although these were widely blamed by Mao's successors), as from their insufficiency collectively to address some of the main requirements of an organized economy. A lacuna in Mao's thought, it seems to me, lies in the realm of economic organization and planning. Mao's impulse was to simplify and de-professionalize administrative macro-planning. Unless China was to be a nation of small self-sufficient communities, however (an ideal that was never part of Mao's Utopia), the simplification of administrative planning would have to be matched by a strengthening of market institutions to take over the myriad allocative decisions given up by the centre. But to strengthen the market seemed to run counter to the requirements of socialist transformation. Indeed, most of the policies discussed in this chapter and the next can be interpreted as conscious rejections of the allocative and distributional trends that a relatively unfettered market would have produced, given Chinese relative factor endowments and political institutions.[1] The 1975 campaign to 'limit bourgeois rights', for example, can be given such an interpretation.

With neither market nor central planners to co-ordinate the economy, Mao sought to minimize the need for co-ordination by means of 'self-reliance'. Some notable success stories were produced at the county level and below, where vigorous and innovative local leaders seized the opportunity to carry out projects that raised local productivity and income. In such cases, Mao's conviction was borne out that the true paradigm of development is the effective release of human energies rather than the efficient allocation of fixed resources.

In general, however, appropriate institutions and political conditions proved difficult to identify and establish, and self-reliance raised as many problems as it solved. At what level should it be achieved? How much self-sufficiency did it imply? How should it be combined with 'socialist co-operation' between enterprises and localities to capture economies of comparative advantage and specialization? How could it avoid local investment in conflict with national priorities, the duplication of existing facilities with excess capacity, or competition with more efficient, large-scale plants for raw materials? Perhaps most fundamentally, self-reliance did nothing to correct the inherent weaknesses of administrative planning—especially its weakness in motivating efficient and innovative performance. Only at the lowest levels—perhaps that of the production team—might the link between self-reliant production and community income be direct enough to provide such motivation. At higher levels it was apt to be a case of arbitrary decisions made not by central bureaucrats but by local and provincial ones, possessing even less planning skill.

The rigidity of administrative planning was thus compounded by various geographic and sectoral imbalances that local and regional self-reliance introduced. The resulting disarray, to which the mass movements and disruptions of the Cultural Revolution and subsequent years contributed, called for the corrective of renewed centralization of planning. At such times the national leadership, including Mao, always opted for stronger *administrative* centralization. In this way, a 'recurring cycle' was generated, 'In which "centralization leads to rigidity, rigidity leads to complaints, complaints lead to decentralization, decentralization leads to disorder, and disorder leads back to centralization" ' (Jiang 1980:55).

In the 1970s, however, centralization seems to have lost its restorative capacity. The quality of central planning, never high in China, declined perceptibly and was marked by numerous elementary errors. While the full explanation for this peculiar technical regress in planning is complex, the main factor must have been the mutual incompatibility of central administrative planning and Maoist ideology. The former requires complete and detailed reporting of data to the centre; a stratified chain of command to ensure local compliance with central decisions; and a large corps of technicians at the centre. It assigns most important decisions to the centre and gives an essentially passive and subservient role to the direct producers and the localities. Cultural Revolution ideology, on the other hand, called for a drastically reduced and simplified planning apparatus, for decision-making power vested in localities, and for participative reforms in management that eliminated or reduced special staff departments for collecting, processing, and transmitting data upward. The locality and enterprise were to be dynamic, innovative, socially experimental bodies. Mao referred to the factory as a 'university'.

These values, repeatedly promoted by Mao until his death, survived the Cultural Revolution proper, and ruled out effective central planning. At the same time, the periodic intervention by the centre to impose order in conditions of disarray prevented the genuine implementation of the ideology and subverted its intent. The heavy hand of party, army, or bureaucracy came in fact to run the enterprise revolutionary committees and dictate sowing plans to the nominally independent production teams. With radical principles undermined by *ad hoc* manipulation from above but still strong enough to deter a true central planning regime, China seemed by the mid-1970s to have arrived at the worst of both worlds.

2   The principle of self-reliance

Self-reliance was a *sine qua non* of Cultural Revolution economic policy; to the question of how to allocate resources without recourse to a market, it posed the negative answer: let each locality, region, or enterprise rely in so far as possible on its own resources. This was the theory, if not always the practice.

The term 'self-reliance' has been much misunderstood in its Chinese usage. It is an abbreviation of a more literal translation of the Chinese term, *zili gengsheng*—'regeneration through one's own efforts'. The term has been used differently by different political forces in China (Oksenberg and Goldstein 1974). It does not necessarily connote autarky, nor is it synonymous with 'self-sufficiency'. At root, it suggests that the main resources for development should be found within the unit concerned. External relations are not ruled out, but are limited to a subsidiary role. Oksenberg and Goldstein have emphasized the principle's implication as Mao used it that

self-respect and dignity can only be earned, not received as a gift, whether by an individual, a community or a nation . . . [T]zuli keng-sheng [zili gengsheng] is a slogan that is appropriate to liberation from perceived oppression. It has much in common with the desire of some blacks in American ghettoes to control local schools . . . [Oksenberg and Goldstein 1974:6]

Self-reliance as an economic development posture includes the following principal characteristics: (1) full utilization of domestic resources, including labour and skills; (2) rejection of indiscriminate imitation of foreign methods in favour of accumulating indigenous experience suited to Chinese conditions; (3) reliance upon *domestic* saving to finance capital accumulation; (4) establishment of a comprehensive industrial system in China.[2] This definition applies to all levels of society; thus, individual provinces and even counties have at times been urged to establish 'independent and comprehensive industrial systems', as well as to rely on their own resources, capital, and experiences (Riskin 1978a).

As a broad policy stance, self-reliance was a product of the Yanan period, and the phrase itself came into common use during the late 1930s. It lay dormant from Liberation through most of the 1950s, to re-emerge at the beginning of the Great Leap Forward. The phrase has been prominent at times when the Party was inward-looking rather than (as in the 1950s and after 1976) oriented towards foreign trade and aid; was preoccupied with the countryside rather than with the urban coastline; was relatively *less* concerned with united front politics and more dependent on the social forces closely linked with the revolution; and thus was concentrating on its ties with the poorer elements of the peasantry (Oksenberg 1970).

As a principle of local initiative and non-dependence, self-reliance has broad applicability: the self-reliant individual or community will not be easy prey to autocratic authority. It is as *a principle of resource allocation* that the term is ambiguous and problematic. Of the four characteristics of self-reliance listed above, the last—establishment of a comprehensive industrial system—pertains to resource allocation, and here the analogy between the nation as a whole and individual localities within it breaks down.

On the national level, self-reliance can be understood as a strategy of import substitution designed to provide a comprehensive industrial base. In this aspect it has two broad rationales. The first is military-strategic: the ability to defend home territory and to project power abroad is enhanced by possession of a comprehensive industrial capacity. The second has to do with learning and motivation: however large a region's static comparative advantage in agriculture may be, its prospects for harnessing science and technology and achieving long-term economic development depend on mastering 'the tricks of manufacture'. From this perspective, as Rawski points out, the rationale for self-reliance lies in the widely shared conviction that excessive division of labor masks hidden technical potentials. The obvious short-term costs of trade restriction may be smaller than the long-run gains obtainable from exploiting these unsuspected capabilities. The resulting strategy is one of planned and partial truncation of commodity exchange designed to force regions, communes, and enterprises to muster latent skills in planning and administration and to foster the growth of problem-solving capabilities that come only from sustained grappling with technical difficulties. [Rawski 1980a:150]

The first (military-strategic) rationale applies to the nation as a whole, while the second refers, in addition, to 'regions, communes, and enterprises'. Although China's fear of attack has at times contributed to the impulse to promote local self-sufficiency, when the threat has faded, this policy has had to fall back on the 'learning' rationale. Examined more closely, however, this rationale really amounts to an argument for localities or enterprises to engage in *some* activities with relatively advanced and demanding technologies—not for extensive vertical integration or 'comprehensive and independent' local economies. Recent Chinese discussions have concluded that attempts to implement the latter policies resulted in great inefficiency from duplication and sacrificed economies of specialization and scale.

Why then did Mao push 'comprehensive and independent' economies for regions, localities, and even enterprises (Riskin 1978a)? As suggested above, the resource-allocative dimension of self-reliance was the Maoist answer to the problem of allocation *sans* market or large planning apparatus. Its purpose was to simplify co-ordinative requirements in the economy by localizing allocation decisions and minimizing external links, so that residual planning functions could be carried out by a smaller, less articulated, and more politically controllable bureaucracy. If self-reliance at the national level was a way of opting out of dependence on the world market, at the sub-national level it was a *substitute* for both a domestic market and administrative planning. With bureaucracies reduced in role and size and the economic relations among localities and enterprises simplified, changes in management, incentives, distribution, and other aspects of 'production relations' could proceed within each production unit or local area with few external constraints.

This interpretation of Mao's objective in promoting independent and comprehensive development at various sub-national levels is given weight by Mao's explicit comments in relation to the Soviet textbook, *Political Economy*. Rejecting the text's advocacy of division of labour among socialist countries, Mao comments:

This is not a good idea. We do not suggest this even with respect to our own provinces. We advocate all-round development and do not think that each province need not produce goods which other provinces could supply. We want the various provinces to develop a variety of production to the fullest extent . . . The correct method is each doing the utmost for itself as a means toward self-reliance for new growth, working independently to the greatest possible extent, making a principle of not relying on others . . . [Mao 1977c:102–3]

In explaining what at first glance seems a perversely irrational view, Mao points out that China's maintenance of political unity over the centuries exacted a price in the form of bureaucratism, 'under the stifling control of which local regions could not develop independently; and with everyone temporizing, economic development was very slow'. It was thus China's long bureaucratic tradition, which had not vanished with the Communist victory, that provided the main rationale for Mao's views on decentralized self-reliance.[3]

3 National self-reliance

A rough gauge of the degree of national self-reliance is the ratio of foreign trade turnover (imports plus exports) to GNP. For the period 1952–74, this has been estimated at around 6 per cent (Eckstein 1977:234), similar to that of the Soviet Union and well below the ratios of the industrialized capitalist countries. However, this average masks significant changes over time. Trade dependency rose somewhat in the 1950s, when China benefited from close economic ties with the USSR. In contrast, during the 1960s, after the break with the Soviets, trade stagnated while GNP grew substantially. China turned outward again in the first half of the 1970s; during 1970–5 the real value of trade with non-centrally planned economies increased by an estimated 78 per cent, more than twice the 36 per cent growth in GNP over the same period (see Table 9.1 and NFAC 1977:9).[4] Virtually all of this growth took place in 1970–3; 1974–5 was a period of retrenchment (Table 9.1 and Chapter 8).

Thus, China became less trade-dependent during the first half of the Cultural Revolution decade and more trade-dependent during its second half. But trade dependency ratios are not negative indicators of self-reliance. It can be argued that the policies of both halves were consistent with self-reliance. During the 1965–9 period, international conditions made any significant Sino-Western rapprochement unlikely, even had China been inclined to pursue it. Instead, to the extent that the Cultural Revolution permitted any coherent economic policy, China continued to enlarge its capacity to produce things it had previously had to import from the Soviet bloc. Industrial output grew by an average rate of 9–10 per cent per year despite the Cultural Revolution (USCIA 1979; Field, McGlynn, and Abnett 1978; Rawski 1973). On the other hand, during the 1970–3 period, in which trade grew much faster than GNP, imports contributed to self-reliance by strengthening weak points and overcoming bottlenecks in the domestic economy. Moreover, in the crucial area of machinery, the ratio of imports to production-plus-imports appears to have remained more or less constant between 1965 and 1975 at between 7 and 15 per cent, well below the figure for 1957. Imports were concentrated in a few industries, notably fertilizer, petroleum refining, petrochemicals, ferrous metallurgy, and electric power, where their chief role was 'breaking bottlenecks and introducing particular types of capacity needed to obtain essential product characteristics—a far cry from the overall dominance of Soviet equipment in industrial investment plans of the 1950s' (Rawski 1980a:101).

Thus, even during the period of rapidly growing trade, China's trade policy aimed to improve domestic productive capabilities and diminish ultimate

Table 9.1 *China's foreign trade, 1965–1975 (millions of current US dollars)*

	Total trade			With communist countries			With non-communist countries			With non-communist countries (1970 dollars)	
	Total	X	M	Total	X	M	Total	X	M	Total	Index (1970 = 100)
1965	3 880	2 035	1 845	1 165	650	515	2 715	1 385	1 330		
1966	4 245	2 210	2 035	1 090	585	505	3 155	1 625	1 530		
1967	3 915	1 960	1 955	830	485	345	3 085	1 475	1 610		
1968	3 785	1 960	1 825	840	500	340	2 945	1 460	1 485		
1969	3 895	2 060	1 835	785	490	295	3 110	1 570	1 540		
1970	4 340	2 095	2 245	860	480	380	3 480	1 615	1 865	3 322	100
1971	4 810	2 500	2 310	1 085	585	500	3 725	1 915	1 810	3 678	111
1972	6 000	3 150	2 850	1 275	740	535	4 725	2 410	2 315	4 401	132
1973	10 300	5 075	5 225	1 710	1 000	710	8 590	4 075	4 515	5 993	180
1974	14 080	6 660	7 420	2 435	1 430	1 010	11 645	5 230	6 415	5 644	170
1975	14 575	7 180	7 395	2 390	1 380	1 010	12 185	5 800	6 385	5 915	178

N.B. For current dollar figures, exports are f.o.b., imports c.i.f. The constant dollar series is based on f.o.b. estimates for both imports and exports.

Source: Batsavage and Davie (1978:736–7).

dependence on foreign trade. There seemed to be agreement among the leadership in avoiding both autarky at one extreme and an 'open-door trade policy' at the other (NFAC 1977:20). This posture, and with it the official interpretation of 'self-reliance', was of course to change dramatically after 1976, when a reform-minded leadership criticized its predecessor's unwillingness to make greater use of foreign economic relations. In retrospect, the dis-organization of the 1960s, in combination with the unfavourable inter-national environment and the xenophobic tendencies of some Chinese leaders (see Oksenberg and Goldstein 1974), imposed on China a greater degree of economic isolation than was either desirable for growth or necessary for self-reliance.

4 Regional self-reliance

Self-reliance at the regional and local levels is a much more ambiguous subject. The degree of autonomy seems to have varied by level of administration; formal policy (e.g., the autonomy of production teams) was often ignored in practice; and the situation changed significantly over time. Moreover, the general policy of self-reliance seems to have had several different dimensions, whose relative weights were subject to change. All of this makes it difficult to summarize just what self-reliance meant and how it was implemented as a general development policy.

We have already discussed how self-reliance was expected to stimulate the acquisition of new knowledge and skills. Correlated with this were some subsidiary attributes. Self-reliance was meant to stimulate the *initiative* of localities in undertaking development projects by providing economic incentives (in the form of retained profits) and political disincentives (in the form of criticism of local passivity). It was also seen as a complement to the strict controls on rural–urban migration, reducing the incentive to migrate by providing new forms of employment and higher incomes in the countryside. It was seen as a way of lowering the considerable income gap between workers and peasants by developing industry locally, distributing its products widely, and keeping entry-level wages close to average peasant incomes. Finally, local self-reliant industrialization was defended during the Cultural Revolution explicitly as a safeguard against excessive concentration of bureaucratic power at the centre.[5]

Self-reliance seems to have been least operative at the provincial level. Lardy (1978a) has established that, from the 1950s to the early 1970s, the central authorities, operating through China's national consolidated budget, which incorporates all sub-national budgets, acted to redistribute resources from richer to poorer provinces in order to reduce the large initial interregional differences in level of development. Judged by provincial gross industrial output per head, these gaps in fact continued to widen steadily throughout the entire period since 1949 (see Chapter 10), but at least in *relative* terms they narrowed—that is, the less industrialized provinces on the whole had higher

Table 9.2. *Central–provincial revenue-sharing, by province, selected years, 1956–1980*

Province	(1)[a] % of total provincial revenue retained by province				(2) % of indust'l & commerc'l tax revenue retained by province, 1980	(3) % retained by province of revenue other than ind'l & commerc'l taxes, 1980	(4) Annual transfer from central govt. to province (Y m), 1980
	(a) 1956	(b) 1957	(c) 1959	(d) Post-1960			
North-east							
Jilin	—	—	—	—	—	—	300
Heilongjiang	67.4	51.7[b]	49.5[f]	—	—	—	886
Liaoning	—	—	36.1	18.0 (1972)	0	48.7	—
North							
Beijing	—	—	48.8	36.5 (1980)	—	—	—
Tianjin	—	—	30.8	31.2 (1980)	—	—	—
Hebei	94.9	78.3	71.2	—	0	88.0	—
Shanxi	88.1	89.2	107.9	—	57.9	100.0	—
Inner Mongolia	0	88.5	100+	100+ (1972)	—	—	1063
East							
Shanghai	—	—	19.8	10.0 (1972) 11.2 (1980)	—	—	—
Jiangsu	36.6	50.8	54.4	—	—	100.0	—
Zhejiang	38.9	45.0	69.0[f]	61.0 (1980)	13.0	100.0	—
Anhui	89.5	82.4	130.7	—	58.1	—	—
Jiangxi	66.0	70.1	100+	—	—	—	138
Shandong	40.8	48.4	55.2[b]	—	10.0	100.0	—

Central South							
Henan	59.8	64.9	78.0[b]	—	75.9	100.0	—
Hubei	64.5	58.9[b]	95.8[f]	—	44.7	100.0	—
Hunan	59.0	60.6	80.4	—	42.0	100.0	—
Guangdong	40.4	43.7	56.7[b]	—	—	—	−1000[c]
Guangxi	81.5	108.6	100+	100+ (1972)	—	—	270
South-west							
Sichuan	37.5	49.2[b]	66.8	—	72.0	100.0	—
Guizhou	69.7	77.3	118.2	—	—	—	478
Yunnan	81.3	100[b]	118.0	115.0 (1974)	—	—	300
Tibet	170–180[d]	—	183.5	150+ (1960–73)	—	—	438
North-west							
Shaanxi	76.5	76.6[b]	100+	—	88.1	100.0	—
Gansu	111.0[e]	111.0[e]	100+	—	53.2	100.0	—
Qinghai	161.5	162.8	157.7[b]	—	—	—	365
Ningxia	—	—	100+	152 (1958–74)	—	—	273
Xinjiang	105.2	107.2	125.9	135 (1955–72)	—	—	827

[a] Percentages above 100 indicate net subsidy from centre to province.
[b] Budgeted. Final account not available.
[c] Negative number indicates transfer from province to central government.
[d] Figure refers to 1952–5; 1956 and 1957 not available.
[e] Figure for Gansu refers to 1953–7.
[f] Planned rate for first quarter of 1959.

Source: Lardy (1978a:76, 131, 133, 162); World Bank (1983, 1:349–50).

proportional growth rates of industrial production than the more industrialized provinces (Lardy 1978a:Chapter 4).

The chief method by which the centre achieved this redistribution was the establishment of differential revenue-sharing rates with the individual provinces. The provinces collected two-thirds of all revenues in 1965 and carried out less than 40 per cent of all expenditures; in the 1970s they collected over 80 per cent of total revenue and carried out from 40 to 50 per cent of expenditures (World Bank 1983, I:348, 355). Of the large share of revenue collected by the provinces, a disproportionate amount was raised by the richer ones. The centre extracted a large percentage of this and a smaller proportion of revenue raised by middle-income provinces and transferred some of these funds as subsidies to the poorest regions, as can be seen in Table 9.2. Column (1) shows percentages of provincial revenue retained by the provinces for various years in the late 1950s and post-1960. Whereas Shanghai kept only 20 per cent of its revenue in 1959 and 10 per cent in 1972, and heavily industrialized Liaoning kept only 18 per cent in 1972, the poorest provinces such as Xinjiang, Qinghai, Tibet, Gansu, Yunnan, Guizhou, Guangxi, and Anhui were permitted to retain all their revenues and received central subsidies as well. This policy continued into the 1980s, as indicated by Finance Minister Wang Bingqian in his report to the Fifth National People's Congress

For the five minority nationality autonomous regions, Xinjiang, Ningxia, Inner Mongolia, Tibet, and Guangxi, and the three provinces, Yunnan, Guizhou, and Qinghai, the preferential treatment they have enjoyed will remain unchanged and the subsidies provided by the central authorities will be increased progressively at a rate of 10 per cent a year. [BR, 29 September 1980:19–20]

The absolute size of these transfers for several provinces in 1980 can be seen in the last column of Table 9.2. Tibet's 1980 subsidy amounted to Y239 per capita (World Bank 1983, I:51). Provincial revenues are divided according to whether they derived from industrial and commercial (turnover) taxes or from other sources. Middle-income provinces kept all of the latter revenue, which included profits of their enterprises and the agricultural tax, and an assigned proportion of industrial and commercial tax revenue (columns (2) and (3)). Liaoning, in contrast, gave up all of its industrial and commercial tax revenue and about half of its other revenue. Industrial and commercial taxes provided about 45 per cent of total revenue nationally in the late 1970s (World Bank 1983:51).

At the highest sub-national administrative level, then, the centre has with occasional exceptions chosen strong central control of resource allocation and relatively egalitarian redistribution over the competing objectives of regional self-reliance and provincial initiative. This choice was modified in the brief experiments with decentralization (1958 and 1970), when provinces were given greater access to their own revenues and somewhat more discretionary control over their expenditures. 'At most times, however, the central government has maintained control over both the total and the composition of provincial revenue and expenditure . . .' (World Bank 1983, I:50).

5 Local self-reliance and rural industrialization

The situation was quite different below the province level. Note that in the following directive from Mao, which provided one of the chief inspirations for local self-reliance during the Cultural Revolution, provinces were to come last: 'Various localities should endeavour to build up independent industrial systems. Where conditions permit, co-ordination zones, and then provinces, should establish relatively independent but varied industrial systems' (Riskin 1978a:94). This exhortation was prominently featured in the press during 1969–70, when rural industrialization was occurring at a very rapid rate. In 1971 it stopped appearing as a quotation of Mao's and underwent a metamorphosis seemingly intended to remove 'independence' from the goal of local industrialization (Riskin 1978a:94–5).

The other text widely cited in connection with rural industrialization was Mao's famous letter to Lin Biao of 7 May 1966, which spelled out perhaps more clearly than anywhere else Mao's critical views on specialization. The letter suggested that peasants, 'where conditions permit', 'should collectively run small plants'. It was however a cautious document, which carefully pointed out that 'the main task of the peasants is agriculture (including forestry, animal husbandry, side occupations, and fishery).' Mao, like Marx, saw technology as ultimately making possible a society free of alienation by permitting its members to develop the full range of their talents. He treated this objective as a goal towards which initial steps could be taken immediately, and rural industrialization was such a step.

Chapter 7, Section 2 treats the closure in 1961–2 of thousands of rural small-scale factories established during the Great Leap Forward, and their resurrection beginning in 1963. This growth proceeded apace in the mid-1960s, with emphasis on the rationalization of technology; the rural industries of this period were larger in size and more mechanized than their tiny progenitors of 1958. The real take-off, however, occurred in the period 1968–71, when, stimulated by Cultural Revolution policies and values, rural *xian* set up and expanded small and medium-scale factories in large numbers. When essential materials and markets were available locally, the *xian* were given great freedom in establishing enterprises; as one county production chief put it, 'at that time no limits were put on such development' (Riskin 1978a:89).

The 'five small industries' (cement, chemical fertilizer, machinery, power, and iron and steel) formed the basis of the comprehensive local industrial systems of the Cultural Revolution years. The production capacity of small nitrogenous fertilizer plants grew five times between 1965 and 1969, and their share of national fertilizer output increased from 12 per cent in 1965 to 60 per cent in 1971. In 1965 there were only about 200 small cement plants, but by 1973 the number had grown to 2,800, which produced about half of China's cement. Iron and steel had been a prime target of the post-GLF closures, and small blast furnaces began again to appear in numbers only at the end of the 1960s. Yet by 1971 local small and medium-size facilities were responsible for one-fifth of national production of pig iron, and the spread of small and medium-scale oxygen top-blown converters caused local steel production to grow in many provinces, as well (Riskin 1979:56–59).

The rural small-scale power industry also grew very rapidly in the late 1960s and early 1970s. Most small power plants were hydroelectric units of only 50–100 kW capacity. They were made possible by the proliferation of small-scale water conservancy projects, and in turn provided power for irrigation machinery and industry (Clarke 1978:409, 418). By early 1972 such small hydropower stations numbered about 35,000 and provided 16 per cent of the total installed hydroelectric generating capacity (which itself constituted perhaps one-third of total power generating capacity) (Riskin 1979:56). Most farm machinery and equipment (except for the heaviest) was also produced in local small and medium-scale plants.

Local industrial systems, centred at this time on the county as the organizing and co-ordinating level, but including smaller commune and brigade facilities, were thus made up of industries with tight forward and backward linkage with each other and with agriculture. A model county in this respect was Zunhua (Hebei Province), which popularized a benign cycle of development. Funds accumulated in its profitable light industrial establishments subsidized iron and steel production, which in turn fed the farm machinery plant, whose products raised local commune income and generated demand for the light industries, thus closing the circle. The integration of industries into the production, consumption, and employment patterns of the locality made this county a model of self-reliance in the positive sense of the term (Riskin 1978a).

If rural industrialization was a key component of local self-reliance, it must be seen in perspective. The term 'rural industry' encompasses everything from very simple handicrafts to fairly large and technologically sophisticated industries, a good part of which is located in the suburbs of big cities and in county towns, some quite large. The output of rural industries of all kinds may have amounted to between 10 and 15 per cent of national gross industrial output value and employed about 15 million workers, or fewer than 5 per cent of the rural labour force in 1975 (Rawski 1979b:65). Employment at this time was expanding rapidly in commune and brigade industries, whose work-force by 1981 exceeded 30 million, or about 9 per cent of the total commune labour force (*BR*, 20 July 1981:7; Xue 1981:63). But in 1975 the macroeconomic significance of rural industry remained small, despite its substantial contribution to particular industries such as cement and chemical fertilizer.

Its importance to the peasant population increased quickly through the 1970s, however. The high growth phase for country-run industry began in the late 1960s and tapered off around 1972. Thereafter, it was industry run by communes and brigades that experienced rapid growth. By 1978 there were over 1 million such enterprises, producing over 20 per cent of the combined output of communes, brigades, and teams (*PR*, 27 January 1978:30). This ratio ran considerably higher in more developed regions. In 1979 more than two-fifths of the combined output of the three levels in several coastal provinces and the suburbs of Beijing, Tianjin, and Shanghai came from commune and brigade industries. These favoured regions were responsible for more than half the national output of such industries (World Bank 1983, I:50).

Commune and brigade enterprises were thus starting to wield muscle in rural economic affairs by the mid-1970s. It is less clear on whose behalf they operated. Besides providing a growing number of jobs for underemployed peasants, rural collective enterprises often subsidized the teams from which employees were drawn by paying part of their wages to their teams. Enterprise profits might be invested in farm machinery or in water conservancy construction, or used to expand collectively run health, education, cultural, and welfare services (Riskin 1978b:688). Policy dictated that enterprise profits go to subsidize more backward teams and poorer families within teams (e.g., Xue 1981:64); but there are also indications that cadres and party members sometimes allocated choice jobs and investments to benefit themselves (Riskin 1978b:686–87), and allegations were later made that very little of the fruits of commune and brigade activities found their way to individual households (Lin Tian 1981). In the absence of comprehensive data on the allocation of collective enterprise employment and the use of enterprise reserves, no firm conclusion can be drawn about the effect of these enterprises on rural living standards or on intra-commune income distribution.

If rural industries played an important role in the political economy of self-reliance, they also served several economic needs more narrowly defined. Employment creation was one. However, as we have seen, only a relatively modest number of jobs were directly created by rural industries. Their chief effect in this regard was on employment in agriculture. Between 1957 and 1975 agriculture absorbed a net increase of almost 100 million workers (a 40 per cent increase in the farm work-force) on a virtually constant cultivated acreage; yet output per work-year grew by an estimated 10 per cent (Rawski 1979b:71, 120). Especially towards the latter half of this period, rural industries contributed greatly to the capacity of China's farms to use new workers without encountering more severe diminishing returns. Their growing output of electric power, irrigation pumps, cement, chemical fertilizer, farm tools, pesticides, and the like, made possible a more intensive use of labour in planting high-yield seeds with shorter growing seasons, and in multiple cropping, irrigating, fertilizing, and cultivating. The fact that agriculture's absorption of labour was excessive in this period and that many peasants left farming when given the opportunity after 1978 (see Chapter 12) does not negate this contribution of rural industry.

On the whole, then, rural industry complemented farm labour rather than displacing it. However, while peasants worked considerably more on average in 1975 than they did in the late 1950s, their standard of living did not rise commensurately, while their output per work-day actually fell 15–36 per cent (Rawski 1979b:118–19). In part, this was due to the high prices they were forced to pay for new farm inputs (see Chapter 10). The resulting trend of ever-increasing labour, slowly increasing output, falling output per unit of work, and stagnant income constituted a holding pattern. Clearly, this did not satisfy peasant aspirations and could not continue indefinitely. Without rural industrialization, however, output growth would probably have been slower still, the decline in labour productivity faster, and rural underemployment greater.

In addition to creating more employment in agriculture, rural industries had other economic functions. One was to exploit differences in relative factor costs between city and village. In the latter, labour was relatively abundant and cheap and modern means of production was scarce and expensive. It thus made sense to develop industries using intermediate technologies that were relatively labour-intensive. One of the reasons for such an imperfect factor market was the limited transport network in much of the hinterland, which made it excessively costly to transport locally available raw materials to centralized, urban factories and the products of the latter back to the villages. A delegation of US rural industry specialists found in 1975 that in one county the price of coal rose 50 per cent when it was moved 25 miles. Under such circumstances, the savings in transport costs of producing a bulky item such as cement locally could easily exceed the added cost of using small-scale or backward technology. In the case of nitrogenous fertilizer, small rural factories produced ammonium bicarbonate, an inferior, volatile product that deteriorates quickly; with China's capacity to produce better-grade fertilizer still limited, however, localities could supplement their plant nutrients by making ammonium bicarbonate close to the field and using it soon after production.

In general, then, the basic economic rationale for the spread of rural industry using intermediate technologies was its ability to supplement the output of the modern, urban industries by using scattered or low-quality resources not demanded by (or not accessible to) the latter.[6] In addition to this economic justification and the broader features that made rural industrialization politically attractive to part of the national leadership, this approach had the further attraction of lightening the central government's burdens just when it was beset by problems that impeded effective administration in any case.

However, local industry was never expected to be completely self-sufficient. While initiative and most resources were to be local, there were often key pieces of equipment whose acquisition required a budget grant or a bank loan. This was true of crushers and ball mills in local cement factories (American Rural Industry Delegation 1977:94), rolling equipment and electrical machinery in small steel mills, and much of the equipment in the county chemical fertilizer plants (American Rural Industry Delegation 1977:97–8). As the US rural industry experts remarked,

The degree of 'self-reliance' was high, but not absurd. Especially at the county level, it was very common for factories to equip themselves with nearly all the basic machine tools; they quite literally made their own lathes, milling machines, rotary presses, and so on. But if a sophisticated inclined rotary gear cutter on a high-tolerance finish grinder was required, a way was found to bring one in from outside the factory . . . [American Rural Industry Delegation 1977:72]

Old or obsolete equipment was often handed down from large factories to local plants rather than being scrapped, and there was a constant two-way flow of workers and technicians between modern and rural enterprises to teach and learn industrial skills. In these various ways, self-reliance was made compatible with co-operation between units, and even with aid from advanced to backward enterprises and from higher administrative levels to lower.

A true cost-benefit analysis of China's rural industrialization programme would have to consider also its drawbacks, which were given little attention during its high-growth phase but were increasingly criticized from the late 1970s. These include not only such purely economic phenomena as high costs arising from small-scale and primitive technology, but also some problems rooted in China's system of state economic administration. The establishment of industries benefited localities in a number of ways. Even when profits reverted to higher levels under the consolidated budget, they could be used as the basis of claims for budget allocations in the next period, as could the mere existence of production facilities, with their ongoing requirement of working capital. Industrial output helped the local economy and provided jobs, at least for the administrative bureaucracy. After the *de facto* decentralization of the Cultural Revolution years and the formal one of 1970, central control over regional investment activity weakened and many localities established enterprises in furtherance of their particular interests, without regard for macroeconomic rationality. From the national viewpoint, this was clearly a misallocation of investment (Xue 1981:223). A well-known example is the motor vehicle and tractor industry, in which several hundred separate plants (several thousand, if ancillary facilities are counted) were established. As Xue Muqiao explained,

We obviously do not need this many, but these plants belong to different ministries, provinces, and counties. In view of the profits these plants can give, no unit wants to disown them . . . There are almost 1,000 municipalities and counties wishing to produce refrigerators, electric fans, washing machines, recorders and many other products this year. If all rush to set up factories at the same time, many will be forced to stop or delay their construction when half done. [Xue 1980a:615]

Although this complaint refers specifically to the situation in 1980, after a 1979 financial reform that permitted localities to retain and invest a larger share of revenues (Wang 1980:13), in fact the problem dates back at least to the reform of 1970. This gave local governments the authority to 'handle' 'a certain proportion of local financial revenues', and to 'handle' 30 per cent of total national capital construction investment autonomously and another 30 per cent in 'consultation' with the relevant central ministries. The crucial terms 'handle' and 'consultation' are in quotes precisely because of their ambiguity—it is not clear what they meant in practice regarding the division of authority between centre and localities (*BR*, 4 February 1980:22). But we do know that counties at that time were permitted to establish industries without higher-level authorization, that many of the motor vehicle plants complained about later were established before 1976, and that similar complaints were made about the farm machine industry before the decentralizing reforms of the late 1970s. Not only did such a proliferation of local investment projects, constrained neither by central plan nor by financial controls, lead to wasteful duplication of effort, shortages of raw materials, and surpluses of unwanted products; it also pushed up the investment rate and contributed to the chronic tendency towards over-accumulation and neglect of living standards. Ironically, the problem of excessively high investment rates, generally considered endemic to centrally planned economies, was if anything exacerbated by administrative decentralization.

6   Self-reliance in the factory

So far, we have considered self-reliance as a domestic policy in its application to intermediate localities (municipalities, counties, communes), where its chief characteristic was local industrialization. But it was also understood to apply to basic-level production units—factories in industry and production teams (or, rarely, brigades) in agriculture. In factories, self-reliance gave rise to the 'comprehensive' production unit that made for itself a large part of the materials and intermediate goods needed to turn out its main production line. Now it is possible for division of labour to be carried out in a large, integrated enterprise which is broken down into specialized production units. To some degree, larger Chinese enterprises functioned this way, and it is unclear the degree to which efficiencies of specialization were sacrificed in such enterprises. However, 'completeness' often meant that enterprises maintained general machine shops that turned out the odd pieces of equipment needed for expansion or technical renovation. Such 'completeness' was purchased at the expense of some inefficiency. With respect to small plants that made entire products (e.g., farm machinery factories), the case for greater specialization and division of labour among them depends of course on the extent of the market. It is arguable that, when counties were first setting up factories, neither demand nor supply conditions permitted extensive specialization among the factories, but that, as industry developed and factories spread throughout the countryside, greater division of labour among them became desirable. Whatever economic conditions in the abstract may have dictated, however, institutional and administrative considerations intervened.

In Western Marxist circles, there has been some debate over the historical origins of specialized production. Marglin (1974), for example, has suggested that the fragmentation of work into simple, repetitive tasks owed more to the capitalist's desire to supervise the labour process and decide its tempo than to any inherent superiority in technical efficiency—in other words, that it was a profit-maximizing rather than a productivity or utility-maximizing development. Many people followed with great interest China's apparent refusal to replicate this historical process of capitalist development, in the belief that self-reliance within the enterprise would make possible a less alienating work process in which workers were not confined to monotonous and repetitive tasks but shared in the creative aspect of production, including planning and decision-making, without sacrificing economic efficiency.

This kind of consideration does not seem to have played much of a role in China, however. It is true that Mao's writings favoured the idea of the generalist—for example the peasant who was part worker, part intellectual, and part soldier—as an aspect of the drive to reduce the 'three great differences'. This idea undoubtedly played an important role in providing the ideological background for rural industrialization from the late 1950s to the mid-1970s as well as for various experiments in participatory management carried out over the same period. But with respect to the work process itself, foreign observers of Chinese factories have noticed little or no deviation (other than that dictated by relative backwardness of technology) from Western practice, and little interest on the part of managers and other interlocutors in the issue of work alienation, which is commonly dismissed as a problem of a more advanced stage of development.

As for the question of whether factories should be comprehensive or specialized, the influence of Maoist ideology has been important but indirect. The predilection for 'small but complete' and 'large and complete' factories during Mao's last two decades seems to have derived, on the one hand, from the structural requirement of Maoist ideology that the bureaucratic apparatus of central planning be minimized, which, in the absence of a market to substitute for the co-ordinating functions of the bureaucracy, meant minimizing the external links of enterprises. Comprehensive enterprises, then, were not so much desirable in and of themselves, but rather were the *only* possible way to organize production with no market and only skeletal planning. On the other hand, central administrative planning, never repudiated in principle by Mao and always resurrected to rescue the economy from the effects of extreme mobilizational departures from it, could not function effectively in a climate of hostility to its organizational prerequisites and (at times) the victimization of its practitioners. The main planning institutions—the State Planning Commission, State Economic Commission, Capital Construction Commission, State Statistical Bureau, and State Price Bureau—'were merged and reduced to a skeleton staff'. Goods still had to be allocated administratively, but neither the resources nor the will existed to do so in an economically competent way. '[A]llocation decisions became more and more arbitrary and subjective as central management became increasingly ineffective' (World Bank 1983, I:46). Enterprises reacted defensively and rationally (from their viewpoint) to insulate themselves from capricious and undependable suppliers by seeking self-sufficiency.

In the late 1970s and early 1980s, Chinese economists identified these defects and the disrepute into which they brought planning itself. Ma Hong, then director of the Institute of Industrial Economics of the Chinese Academy of Social Science, wrote:

There were some mistakes and faults in planning for some time in the past . . . Thus, a plan could not be drawn up scientifically and ended in failure *in most cases*. *Some people doubted and even negated the system of planned economy* when they saw some defects and mistakes in planning . . . The authoritativeness of planning depends on the scientific nature of planning. [Ma 1982:K3; emphasis added]

Three other well-known economists (Liu Guoguang, Wu Jinglian, and Zhao Renwei) observed that '"small and complete" and "large and complete" widely spreads over China's industry', with the result that enterprises came to constitute entire 'communities':

Of course, the emergence of such a scene was not entirely due to the internal causes of an enterprise; imbalance among production, supply and marketing, failure . . . to fulfill contractual obligations (such as failing in supplying materials . . .) and many other causes also forced an enterprise to go for completeness. [Liu, Wu and Zhao 1979:12–13]

Thus, in the course of the 1960s and 1970s, self-reliance of industrial enterprises appears to have been transformed from its original conception as a bold, anti-bureaucratic stance emphasizing resourcefulness and problem-solving at the factory level to a defensive posture of survival and growth in an undependable macroeconomic environment.

7   Self-reliance in agriculture and the Dazhai brigade

In agriculture, the grass-roots model of self-reliance was the famous Dazhai production brigade, a small village in eastern Shanxi Province. When catapulted into national prominence in the mid-1960s, Dazhai had only 83 households farming 57 hectares of rocky and hilly land. It was a poverty-stricken area with unfavourable climatic conditions. By dint of extraordinary efforts, the village overcame repeated natural disasters to extend its fields, build rock-walled terraces, and construct a 4-mile-long irrigation canal. Initially refusing state aid, Dazhai gradually raised yields of grain to reach more than 7 tons per hectare in the early 1970s, a yield quite extraordinary for its terrain. As a result, annual per capita income in the village rose from Y23 in 1953 to Y180 in 1973. It is to be noted that rising income and consumption were certainly part of Mao's agricultural model, whatever may have happened nationally.

Dazhai was proclaimed *the* national model of agricultural development by Mao in 1964, and late in that year Zhou Enlai defined for the first session of the Third National People's Congress the significance of Dazhai in terms of three basic principles, one of which was 'its spirit of self-reliance and hard struggle' (*BR*, 20 April 1981:25).[7] Dazhai meant much more than self-reliance: in particular, it stood for the persistent expansion of the role of the collective in production, distribution, and consumption; constant restriction of the private sector; and relatively egalitarian distribution among individuals and units (Tsou *et al.* 1982:270). Self-reliance in Dazhai did not have any profound theoretical rationale—it wås 'a proud battle cry' (*BR*, 20 April 1981:24), affirming the strength and determination of the collective in its refusal to be a burden on the state. At no time was it made an absolute principle that aid should never be sought. The nearest thing to a general principle seems to have been sacrifice for the greater community, that is, getting along without state aid in order to contribute to the state through the agricultural tax and grain sales.

The fact that incomes rose substantially in Dazhai indicates that the spirit of self-sacrifice was tempered by a certain realism. The cynic might also remark that selflessness is an easier posture to adopt when one is a much-hyped national model. However, the question of the basis for Dazhai's self-reliance may be moot, since it was later claimed that Dazhai received Y840,000 of materials and cash from the state between 1967 and 1977, as well as labour contributions from other brigades, communes, and PLA units in building its water conservancy projects. 'As more and more aid was poured in, there was less and less of the spirit of self-reliance', according to the indictment, which thus inadvertantly accepts the original Dazhai definition of self-reliance (*BR*, 20 April 1981:25). No locality in China, however, whatever its original merit, could be truly self-reliant once caught up in the national political wars as the exemplar of one faction's views.

The other important aspect of self-reliance in agriculture was the policy of 'taking grain as the key link', which was interpreted over the Cultural Revolution decade as meaning local and regional self-sufficiency in grain. It is impossible to know just how this policy, favoured by Mao, was intended to work; there evidently was considerable variation in its application over time and between regions (Lardy 1982c:36). Stavis (1974) suggests that it was in part meant to reduce income inequalities between rich suburban communes and poor ones in the hinterland by restricting production of high-priced and profitable commodities by the former and encouraging it somewhat among the latter. Thus, in a commune near the city of Loyang, 'commune officials realized that it was more profitable to plant apples than grain, but felt constrained (by themselves and *by the government supply and purchasing plans*) to be self-sufficient in grain' (Stavis 1974:254; emphasis added).

In the event, the policy of enforcing local grain self-sufficiency may have had the opposite effect, actually increasing some interregional income differentials. This is because areas with conditions favourable for production of economic crops such as cotton or sugarcane appear to have suffered sharp declines in per capita income when forced to shift land to inefficient production of grain. Lardy (1982c) finds that a substantial number of the 211 counties identified by the Ministry of Agriculture as chronically poor in 1977–9 (i.e., as having collective distributed incomes below Y50 per capita in all three of these years) had been prosperous counties before the grain-first policy was enforced. The pattern of rural inequality produced by this policy was superimposed on the traditional configuration in which rural poverty was concentrated in remote subsistence areas.

The example given by Stavis above illustrates the state's ability to enforce the policy of regional grain self-sufficiency. By suppressing rural markets, and refusing to purchase diverse, high-value commodities or to supply grain to regions specializing in them, the state could effectively compel localities to grow grain. This indeed was widely done during the Cultural Revolution decade; in addition, 'the power of state cadres to impose specific cropping patterns on production teams was vastly increased' during this period (Lardy 1982c:35), in violation of the nominal autonomy of the farm collective.

While suppressing incomes in commercial crop areas, these policies discouraged their increase in grain-growing regions. Incentives were hurt by the dictation of cropping acreages and output targets by higher-level cadres, foreclosure of opportunities to trade grain for other desired commodities, and serious underpricing of grain relative to its inputs. This is one reason why rural incomes in general stagnated during the era of local self-reliance in foodgrain.

Notes

1. This statement can be challenged on the grounds that Mao and the left were reacting to conditions produced at least as much by bureaucratic centralism as by market forces. In some crucial respects, though—e.g., the favouring of city over countryside, or of the children of officials and workers over those of peasants—the two kinds of forces overlapped and were mutually reinforcing.
2. See Chiang (1965), cited in Oksenberg (1970).
3. Mao does not carry the point to the extreme of rejecting all co-operation among provinces. He points out that, as other provinces industrialize, Shanghai continues to be the supplier of advanced-technology items, continuously upgrading its own technological capacity. He also acknowledges the irrationality of attempting totally comprehensive development in such sparsely populated provinces as Qinghai or Ningxia (Mao 1977c:103–4).
4. China's trade with non-centrally planned economies in current dollars constituted over four-fifths of total Chinese trade during the period in question, but rose slightly from 1970 to 1975 (calculated from Table 9.1). This suggests that a constant dollar series for *total* trade would grow somewhat more slowly than that for trade with market economies.
5. The above paragraph relies heavily on Riskin (1979:71–3).
6. For a discussion of the various functions of rural industry and intermediate technology in China, see Riskin (1979).
7. The other two principles were 'putting politics in command' and 'the Communist style of loving the state and loving the collective units' (Tsou *et al.* 1982:272). In a critical review of Dazhai, which appeared in *Beijing Review* after its repudiation, the wording of the first principle was changed to 'putting stress on ideological and political work' (*BR*, 20 April 1981:25).

CHAPTER 10

LATE MAOISM, II: EGALITARIANISM

1 Introduction

If self-reliance was Mao's anti-bureaucratic principle of social organization, the positive social goal of his 'uninterrupted revolution' that began in the 1960s was gradually to eliminate the 'three great differences'. I use the term 'egalitarianism' with some trepidation to characterize this aspect of Cultural Revolution ideology, for Mao was not unambiguously a leveller. He criticized a passage in the Soviet textbook on political economy that called for the 'overall level of economic and cultural development of the various socialist countries [to] gradually draw parallel'. How can they be evened up, Mao asked, when they had different populations, resource bases, and historical conditions?

> The economic development of the various socialist countries is not in balance, nor is that of the provinces within a country, or the counties within a province. Take public health in Kuangtung [Guangdong] province. Fo Shan city and Chihlo commune have done a good job. Consequently Fo Shan is not in balance with the whole province. Chihlo is not in balance with Shaokuan. To oppose imbalances is wrong. [Mao 1977c:104]

Yet in 'The Ten Major Relationships', Mao called for locating 'the greater part of the new industry . . . in the interior so that industry may gradually become evenly distributed . . .'

A more accurate term for the basic principle at issue might be 'selflessness', of which egalitarianism is a corollary. The link between the two is made by Schram:

> In particular, Mao was persuaded that the Chinese people were inspired by the selflessness and willing acceptance of austerity which for him constituted the spiritual heritage of Yan'an. Hence the call for moral and political rather than material incentives, and the vision of a society made up of men and women whose psychology and motivation would be integrally socialist, even though the material basis of socialism was still relatively weak. Hence also the educational policies, designed to strengthen the desired egalitarian attitudes. [Schram 1981:427]

Whatever the primary basis might have been in Mao's thought, there is no doubt that the effect was the advocacy and implementation of certain policies of a highly egalitarian character, policies that after Mao's death came to be ridiculed by his successors as 'everyone eating from the same big pot'.

I argued in the introduction to Chapter 9 that such policies embodied a rejection of the influence of the market, as well as of the unequal distribution of political power, on the allocation of resources, the distribution of income, work incentives, and general social values. However, even with a weakened market, self-reliance stands in problematical relation to the egalitarian mission, tending to encourage progress in some aspects of it while discouraging it in others. *Within* administrative levels practising self-reliance (e.g., counties, communes, factories), some noticeable gains did take place (rural industrialization, reduced differential between worker and peasant income and between administrative salaries and ordinary wages, cadre participation in manual labour, worker participation in management, etc.). But *between* levels and units, self-reliance *per se* naturally tended to breed increasing differences. Urban residents could not be expected voluntarily to give up their advantages in income and access to education and medical care, nor full-status state employees their guaranteed wages and social security, nor cadres and technicians their various benefits, in order more quickly to raise real incomes of rural inhabitants, peasants, and less skilled workers.

Redistribution thus required political intervention from outside and above the self-reliant unit, often in conflict with the interests of the unit itself as well as with those of the intervening authorities, who were beneficiaries of the existing system. Not only was this a recipe for conflict, but, paradoxically, it also provided the rationale for strengthening the authority of the state. The weakening of whatever checks and balances had been provided by law, tradition, and a professional bureaucracy concentrated more power at the political apex where privilege was endemic.

The term 'egalitarianism' is ambiguous with respect to what is to be (re)distributed: wealth? income? utility? status? opportunity? capability? (Sen 1982a). Here the focus is on income and consumption, and it should be kept in mind that these are but part of the story. In contemporary China, small differences in dress or in material privilege can imply large differences in social status. This can be seen in both a positive and a negative light, since it indicates both the pressures that have been exerted to reduce inequalities in material consumption and the persistence of social stratification. Thus, while the salary of a local official may not be much higher than an average farmer's income, in the harsh words of William Hinton (1982:114), 'Anything created by a peasant who lives in the administrative sphere of a higher official, if it will enhance the latter's career, can be moved, removed, manipulated, or expropriated by that official just as if he were the lord of a feudal fief.'

Similarly, the lack of job mobility in industry and the dependence of the worker upon the good will of shop cadres for a variety of essential benefits create a sharp imbalance in power within the enterprise (Walder 1982); yet the salaries, consumption patterns, and housing of cadres have closely resembled those of workers.

High officials in China have had access to a variety of privileges—some quite illegal—that lift their real incomes above their formal salaries (Leys 1977). Some are enjoyable in their own right, such as access to special shops with imported goods or limousine travel; others, such as the particular colour of curtains on the official limousine, are important chiefly in symbolizing rank and authority. At the end of the 1966–76 decade, the more blatant of such privileges were probably confined to a small number of the highest officials. While symbolizing the continued tradition of Mandarin rule even in Mao's China, such privileges, even if measurable, would have little effect on the overall income distribution, and certainly would not negatively alter China's distribution in comparison with that of other countries (Parish 1981) whose élites at least match China's in the art of understating income.

There are several relevant ways of looking at income distribution; these amount to different ways of dividing the income pie. In the following discussion, five such 'cuts' are examined: interregional, interlocal, urban–rural, interpersonal, and (in the conclusion of the chapter) inter-class.

2   Interregional distribution

Natural economic regions coincide imperfectly with provinces or groups of provinces (Skinner 1976). The justification for concentrating here on interprovincial distribution is that relevant data exist and that national budget expenditures are allocated along provincial lines, which makes the province a distribution-relevant unit even if it did not begin as one.

Regional differentiation in China has both geographic and historical roots, some of which were discussed in earlier chapters. Lardy (1980) finds that in the 1950s interregional inequality in China 'appears to be quite high by international standards', even in comparison with countries, such as Italy and Yugoslavia, in which such inequality is a widely recognized problem. This conclusion must be qualified in two important ways. First, differences in per capita *output* (Lardy's measure) do not translate directly into *income* differentials in China, as they tend much more to do in market economies, because of state control of personal incomes in virtually all non-agricultural sectors; therefore, differences in regional per capita output in China overstate the corresponding differences in personal incomes, and this overstatement is carried into the comparison with other countries.

Second, any international comparison of regional differentiation assumes that regions are demarcated according to the same criteria, for it is obviously possible to change the measure of inequality in any country by simply redrawing regional boundaries.[1] Since this assumption is clearly not true, we are left with an ambiguity as to the meaning of (say) a similar measure of inequality for the dissimilarly defined regions of different countries. Whatever the problems of precise measurement, however, we may agree that substantial differences in economic development between Chinese provinces did exist in the 1950s.

These differences were due in large part to the regionally uneven spread of industry and commerce. Although agriculture still contributed the largest share of national income in the 1950s, the provincial distribution of agricultural production per head was much more even than that of industrial production; Lardy's (1980:161) estimated coefficient of variation for industry was more than four times as high as that for agriculture. Industrialization thus introduced new and potent sources of inequality into China, and the national leadership during Mao's tenure was committed to reducing these inequalities by encouraging industrial development in the interior, underdeveloped provinces while holding

Table 10.1. *Provincial distribution of per capita industrial output, 1957, 1965, 1974, and 1979 (percentage of national average[a])*

Province	1957	1965[b]	1974[c]	1979
North-east				
Heilongjiang	222	195	127	141
Jilin	161	148	109	120
Liaoning	385	334	300	257
North				
Beijing	481	385	617	513
Tianjin	1112	572	663	498
Hebei	55	86	122	84
Shanxi	92	n.a.	72	91
Inner Mongolia	60	251	187	63
East				
Shanghai	1517	1165	1404	1106
Shandong	62	58	77	87
Jiangsu	84	93	113	138
Zhejiang	76	72	58	85
Anhui	36	40	36	51
Jiangxi	54	n.a.	49	51
Fujian	69	56	48	59
Central-South				
Henan	30	41	43	50
Hubei	74	64	58	86
Hunan	40	41	44	63
Guangxi	33	32	37	57
Guangdong	84	94	85	79
North-west				
Gansu	51	87	100	92
Shaanxi	56	73	64	80
Ningxia	10	24	35	80
Qinghai	45	73	99	78
Xinjiang	82	86	46	54
South-west				
Sichuan	55	53	41	54
Yunnan	48	38	32	40
Guizhou	33	48	34	36
Tibet	7	13	14	11[d]
Range[e]	152:1	49:1	44:1	31:1
Coefficient of variation	1.87	1.50	1.72	1.49

[a]Underlying data for gross value of industrial output are in 1957 prices for the years 1957, 1965, and 1974, and in 1970 prices for the year 1970.

it back (via redistribution of investment resources) in the coastal, advanced ones.

We know from the work of Lardy (1975, 1978a, 1980) that relative convergence of provincial industrialization occurred from the start of the First Five Year Plan, with less industrialized provinces growing at higher proportional rates than more industrialized ones. The situation between the end of that Plan and 1979 is summarized in Table 10.1. It can be seen that, in general, the provinces (including centrally administered municipalities: Beijing, Tianjin, and Shanghai) that produced the highest per capita industrial outputs in 1957 had declining percentages of the national average up to 1979. This is true of Shanghai, Tianjin, Liaoning, Heilongjiang, and Jilin. The only exception is Beijing, which has been the beneficiary of a substantial industrialization programme. On the other hand, a large number of least industrialized provinces, such as Henan, Hunan, Guangxi, Anhui, Shaanxi, Ningxia, and Qinghai, have enjoyed big increases in relation to the national average. The major regional exception has been the south-west, which has not made significant progress in catching up with the rest of China. However, there are other exceptions as well, notably Xinjiang, Jiangxi, and Fujian.

The overall trend is summarized in the changing range and coefficient of variation of the provincial distribution. The range, measuring the ratio between the GVIO per capita of the highest province (invariably Shanghai) and the lowest (Henan, then Ningxia, Yunnan, and Guizhou—Tibet is excluded because of the greater-than-usual uncertainty about its data), fell from 152 in 1957 to 31 in 1979.[2] The coefficient of variation dropped over the same period by 20 per cent, which means that the differences between provinces as measured by the standard deviation grew more slowly than the average industrial output per province.[3]

Provincial differences in industrial output per capita do not cause equivalent differences in personal incomes. This of course affects welfare implications. Wages of all employees in the state sector are set nationally and (until recently) have not varied with labour productivity. Indeed, even in collective handicraft and street industries, where wages were nominally free to vary with collective net income, the state exercised close control and kept them well below state wages. Thus, although the more industrialized provinces had a higher

---

[b]Population figures used to compute the 1965 series are for 1964: see sources.

[c]Population figures used to compute the 1974 series are figures reported variously in 1975–7: see sources.

[d]Estimated by projecting forward from the 1977 GVIO at 7.1 per cent per year, the average growth rate for 1975–7. In 1957 prices.

[e]Excluding Tibet because of Tibet's special status and because of uncertainty about its statistics. If Tibet were included, of course, the range would be still wider, as can be seen in Table 10.3.

Sources: Population: 1952–74, Aird (1978a:3, 24); 1979, World Bank (1983, I:322). GVIO: 1957, Field, Lardy, and Emerson (1976:11); 1965 and 1974, Field, McGlynn, and Abnett (1978: Table c-1, p. 282); 1979, estimated from data given in World Bank (1983, I:322, 383).

proportion of well paid industrial workers in their labour force, these workers' wages were similar to those in less industrialized provinces where labour productivity was lower. Similarly, the benefit that enterprises and regions derive from industrialization has been limited, as enterprise profits and local budget revenues generated thereby have been subject to extensive central reallocation. In Table 9.2 we saw that rich provinces retained only a small share of their revenues, while poor ones might actually receive a subsidy in addition to all of their own revenues. Finally, the centre has controlled much of physical output as well as financial revenues; thus, the products even of industries nominally under provincial or local control may in fact be allocated by central ministries.

Industrialization thus could raise the average level of per capita income in only a limited number of ways: by increasing the number of highly paid industrial workers; by increasing the production of goods subject to local allocation (since a large number of product types not regarded as of national significance are left to local control); and by stimulating the development of commune and brigade industry, most of whose revenue 'accrues directly or indirectly to commune members' (World Bank 1983, I:85). The sheer weight of the industrialization already achieved in the most advanced areas is advantageous to their residents; the 20 per cent of its revenue that Shanghai was permitted to keep in 1959 financed much higher social expenditures per capita than did the 131 per cent of revenue kept by heavily subsidized Anhui (Table 9.2; Lardy 1978a:199), because the base was so much larger in Shanghai. Similarly, locally allocated non-strategic industries and commune and brigade industries were more developed in the industrially advanced regions than in the remote hinterland. Industrialization has its own momentum; state policies have limited but not eliminated the advantages accruing to residents of the more advanced regions.

Agricultural productivity exerts a more direct influence on living standards, for the link between output and income is much tighter in the collective farm sector. The minor burden of a small agricultural tax has been added to by continuous underpricing of farm commodities (Sec. 4.2 below). The regressiveness of the tax is counteracted by the progressive impact of underpricing, which is felt most keenly in more developed areas that market much of their output. Before the recent 'decollectivization' of agriculture (see Chapter 12), the bulk of income that escaped these two means of extraction by the state was kept by the team and distributed to its members in proportion to their accumulated work-points. Moreover, income produced on private plots, which has accounted for a substantial share of peasant income, accrued directly to the individual. Thus there has been a strong connection between a farmer's output and his or her income. This link constitutes the source of the widest and most prevalent inequalities in China today—those between rich, surburban localities and remote, poor ones. I refer to these as 'interlocal' inequality and discuss it in Section 3 below.

Much of this inequality averages out at the provincial level, however, leaving a very modest dispersion of per capita gross value of agricultural output

(GVAO) among the provinces. Table 10.2 shows this dispersion in 1957 and 1979. (When considering GVAO per capita it is more reasonable to treat the directly administered municipalities as part of their adjacent provinces, and this has been done in the table.) The modesty of inter-provincial differences can be seen from the fact that the ratio between provinces with the highest and lowest GVAO per capita was only about 2.2 in both years. The coefficient of variation was 0.22 in 1957 and 0.19 in 1979. In contrast, the coefficient of variation for industry calculated the same way (i.e., with municipalities merged with their respective provinces) was 0.81 in 1979—four times as high.

Nevertheless, some regional problems are apparent in Table 9.4, notably the lagging behind of the western provinces. Virtually every province in the north-west and south-west regions (with the possible exception of Tibet, about which 1957 data are lacking) suffered a declining agricultural output per capita in relation to the national average between 1957 and 1979. In all other regions, provincial performance was mixed. Remembering that the south-western region had also lagged behind the country as a whole in industrial growth (Table 10.1), we may conclude that China has not altogether escaped a continuing 'north–south' problem, despite a good overall record of provincial convergence in both industry and agriculture.

This problem is more general: no national division of labour between industry and agriculture has emerged to permit industrially backward areas to spring ahead in agriculture. Rather, those provinces that have done well in the one have also, on the whole, done well in the other. The World Bank (1983, I:83) calculates a correlation coefficient of 0.8 between industrial output per head and agricultural output per rural inhabitant. Thus, Shanghai and its suburbs are most prosperous both industrially and agriculturally, while remote Yunnan or Guizhou are backward in both respects.

While agricultural output per head varies much less than industrial output, its effect on personal incomes is more direct. The last column of Table 10.2 displays provincial distributed collective income per commune member in 1979, as a percentage of the national average. Comparing these figures with the data on GVAO per capita in the second column, we can see a definite relationship: the most backward provinces with respect to agricultural output also have the lowest distributed income per commune member, while the most productive provinces have the highest incomes. If GVAO is divided by each province's *rural* population, the results are strongly correlated ($R = 0.9$) with distributed collective income per member (World Bank 1983, I:85). The ratio between the distributed income of the highest (Jilin, if Tibet is excluded) and lowest (Guizhou) provinces in the distribution is 2.5, representing the difference between annual distributed income of Y116 and Y46. If Shanghai were considered separately, the highest distributed income would be its Y214.4, and the range would be 4.7. These are considerable differences, and while it must be borne in mind that there were other important sources of peasant income besides that which was distributed collectively (see Sec. 2 below), it is probably true that provinces with higher collective incomes also had better opportunities for earning incomes from other sources as well.

Table 10.2. *Agricultural output per capita, 1957 and 1979, and distributed collective income per commune member, 1979, by province (percentage of national average)*

	GVAO per capita		Distributed collective income per commune member, 1979
	1957	1979	
North-east			
Heilongjiang	166	115	137.9
Jilin	117	104	139.2
Liaoning	81	99	132.1
North			
Beijing			(150.8)
Tianjin	101	109	110.8 (145.1)
Hebei			(83.2)
Shanxi	98	98	102.9
Inner Mongolia	143	94	92.1
East			
Shanghai	78 lowest	142 highest	131.5 (257.1)
Jiangsu			(119.0)
Shandong	82	105	95.0
Zhejiang	103	133	125.2
Anhui	97	87	84.3
Jiangxi	111	101	107.1
Fujian	85	94	81.4
Central-South			
Henan	95	88	76.0
Hubei	122	125	127.3
Hunan	103	111	110.7
Guangxi	97	85	89.6
Guangdong	102	88	106.0
North-west			
Gansu	119	71	67.9
Shaanxi	135	87	95.4
Ningxia	—	79	82.4
Qinghai	119	92	117.0
Xinjiang	171 highest	104	122.8
South-west			
Sichuan	90	83	83.0
Yunnan	103	75	77.5
Guizhou	102	64 lowest	55.6 lowest
Tibet	—	139	152.9

The various measures of inter-provincial inequality that we have been considering for industry and agriculture are summarized in Table 10.3. All of the *relative* measures of inequality (the ratio between highest and lowest and the coefficient of variation) can be seen either to be declining over the period in question or at least to remain constant. The *absolute* difference in yuan between high and low provinces, also shown in the table, can be seen to widen considerably between 1957 and 1979. This is especially true for industry, where the gap grew from Y1,644 in 1957 to over Y5,000 in 1979. Even in the B series, which excludes the directly administered municipalities as well as backward Tibet, the absolute range of GVIO per capita grows from Y386 to Y1,047, an increase of more than two and one-half times.[4] This is of course a simple arithmetic result of the much lower base from which the poorest provinces began, such that, in comparison with the richest provinces, higher relative growth rates represented smaller absolute increases in yuan. It is another indication of the momentum of industrialization already achieved, and it means that, despite gradually converging growth rates, the absolute gap between rich and poor provinces widened considerably from the 1950s to the late 1970s.

A lesser degree of widening seems to have occurred in agriculture, where the difference in yuan between high and low provinces increased by Y40, or about 46 per cent. But agricultural procurement prices rose by one-third between 1957 and 1970 (recalling that the 1979 GVAO figures are in 1970 prices), and rural free market prices probably by considerably more (World Bank 1983, Annex B, Table 3.1). It is thus possible that most or all of the growth in the absolute range in agriculture is accounted for by price increases (see note 4).

The absolute range of distributed collective incomes per commune member is well below that of GVAO per capita for purely arithmetic reasons;[5] but the *relative* range (ratio of highest to lowest) is of the same order of magnitude, and the coefficients of variation in 1979 are identical and small at 0.19. Almost all provinces had collective distributed incomes per capita in the range between 75 and 130 per cent of the national average; the exceptions were the three north-eastern provinces and Shanghai–Jiangsu on the high side, Guizhou and Gansu on the low. Thus, agricultural inequality at the inter-provincial level was significant chiefly in the extremes of range, as a reinforcement of industrial

---

Notes and Sources
Gross value of agricultural output per capita as a percentage of the national average, 1957: from Lardy (1978a, Table 3.4:104), except for Qinghai, which is calculated on the basis of Wiens (1980:322). Based on provincial GVAO in 1952 yuan, with some exceptions (see source). Beijing and Tianjin are treated as part of Hebei Province and Shanghai as part of Jiangsu Province, on the basis of provincial GVAO data in Lardy (1978a, Table A.2:198) and provincial population data in Aird (1978:3a, 24).

GVAO per capita as percentage of national average, 1979: calculated by using data on GVAO by province from World Bank (1983: Annex A, Table 6.11), and on provincial populations from World Bank (1983: Annex A, Table 1.2). Beijing and Tianjin are treated as part of Hebei Province, and Shanghai as part of Jiangsu Province. Data are in 1970 yuan.

Distributed collective income per capita as a percentage of the national average is in current yuan, and is taken from World Bank (1983, I:84).

Table 10.3. *Summary measures of inter-provincial inequality, 1957 and 1979*

	Range between highest and lowest					
	Ratio		Absolute difference (Y)		Nat. ave. (Y)	Coef. of variation
	A	B	A	B		
GVIO per capita						
1957	206	13	1644	386	109	1.87
1965	93	14	2213	595	192	1.50
1974	100	9	5237	1010	377	1.72
1979	67	7	5161	1047	473	1.51
1979[a]	18[a]	—	1314[a,b]	—	473	0.81[a]
GVAO per capita[a]						
1957	2.2		87		93	0.22
1979	2.2		128		163	0.19
Distributed collective income per commune member, 1979						
Incl. Tibet[c]	2.8		81		83	—
Excl. Tibet	2.5		70		—	0.19

N.B. Series A treats Beijing, Tianjin, and Shanghai as separate provinces; Series B excludes them as well as Tibet. 1979 figures are based on 1970 prices, except distributed income, which is in current prices. Figures for other years are in 1957 prices, except 1957 GVAO per capita, which is in 1952 prices.

[a] Beijing and Tianjin included in Hebei Province, Shanghai in Jiangsu Province.
[b] If Tibet is excluded, the difference is Y1224.
[c] Tibet had the highest distributed collective income per capita in 1979.

Sources: Tables 10.1 and 10.2 and World Bank (1983, Annex B, Table 6:11).

inequality, and as a reflection of the continuing poverty characterizing some provinces.

3   Rural interlocal and interpersonal inequality

In 1979 the richest production brigade in China (in terms of 'per capita income', not otherwise defined) was the Baxiao brigade in the suburbs of Shanghai. Its members received an average of Y1,055 (*China Official Annual Report* 1981:749). On the other hand, in the same year 3.7 per cent of all households in China had net per capita incomes below Y60 (see Table 10.4). Assuming that the poorest brigade in the country had an average total per capita income of Y40,[6] the ratio of richest to poorest would be 26 to 1, and the absolute difference over Y1,000. (The average total net income of Chinese peasants in 1979 was put at Y160.2—see *ZTN* 1983:499.) The only point of

Table 10.4. *Distribution of rural income by production team, 1976–1981*

(A) Distribution of yearly collective income paid out by basic accounting unit[a]

Income class (Y per cap.)	Percentage of units (teams)[a] in each class			
	1976	1979	1980	1981
More than 300	negl.	0.23[b]	n.a.	n.a.
More than 150	negl.	7.6	8.69	15.72
100–149		17.6	17.35	21.57
80–99	57.2	15.6	15.09	15.96
60–79		31.7	19.56	16.98
50–59			11.90	9.83
40–49	18.6	11.4	11.67	8.41
Below 40	24.2	16.1	15.74	11.53
Average income	Y62.8	Y83.4	Y85.9	Y101.3

(B) Distribution of net income from all sources

Income class (Y per cap.)	Percentage of households in each class			
	1979	1980	1981	1982
More than 500	0.3	0.9	1.9	4.6
400–500	1.1	2.2	4.0	7.4
300–400	4.2	7.7	13.5	20.2
200–300	20.7	26.0	36.2	39.3
100–200	54.0	53.2	39.5	25.6
Below 100	19.6	10.1	4.9	2.9
Gini coefficient	0.26	0.24	0.23	0.23

[a] In most cases, the 'basic accounting unit' is the production team; in a few, it is the production brigade.

[b] The source for this figure, *Beijing Review*, 19 January 1981, gives it as 2.3 per cent, and it is cited thus by Vermeer (1982). But the same source, as well as *China Official Annual Report* (1981:749), makes it evident that the percentage in question should be 0.23 per cent and refers to brigades, not teams. I use it here on the assumption that it also applies to teams above Y300. This is but one of several apparent errors in this source, most notably an implausibly low percentage of teams in the 'below Y40' category (8.2 per cent). For this reason, I use here an alternative distribution for 1979 given by the State Statistical Bureau to the World Bank.

Sources: *BR*, 19 January 1981; 21 June 1982); Li and Zhang (1982); SSB (1981); World Bank (1983, I:331; 1985, I:17).

presenting such a synthetic national figure is to dramatize the continued existence of great inter-village inequality in the late 1970s. However, it should be kept in mind that this figure does not take into account state welfare subsidies to the poorest localities.

The contrast between the high–low ratio of 2.5 for the inter-provincial distribution of collective per capita income and that of more than 20 for brigades nationally suggests the amount of averaging-out of inequality that takes place at the level of the province. National statistics on rural income distribution for the late 1970s and early 1980s are displayed in Table 10.4. For comparison purposes, the table shows both national data on the distribution by 'basic accounting unit' (production teams in most cases) of collectively paid out income, and World Bank estimates, based on sample survey data, of the distribution of total rural personal income. Net personal income includes income from private plots, family sideline production, off-farm employment, and other sources as well as income distributed by basic accounting units. It is significantly higher than this last category alone.

Collective distributed income (panel A), was in 1976 compressed in the middle and lower ranges. Negligibly few teams had incomes above Y150; the majority were clustered in the Y50–150 class; more than 40 per cent were below Y50; and almost a quarter were below Y40. By 1979 over 7 per cent of teams had moved into the range above Y150 while over 15 per cent had escaped from below Y50 into the middle reaches of the distribution, which now contained almost two-thirds of all teams. The range of the distribution had widened, but concentration in the middle income classes had also increased. This pattern remained stable in the following two years, as teams moving upward out of the middle reaches were replaced by new arrivals from below. A similar pattern is evident in the data for personal income (panel B).

Keith Griffin and Ashwani Saith (1981:18–20) obtained data like those in panel A for the individual provinces of Guangdong and Hebei in 1978, and they resemble the national data for 1979 fairly closely. From them, Griffin and Saith prepared the decile ranking of Hebei's teams and counties that is reproduced in Table 10.5. It shows a distribution that is apparently marked by a low degree of inequality. The bottom 40 per cent of teams get 25 per cent of distributed income, while the top 10 per cent account for 18 per cent of income. It is difficult to make international comparisons using these data, however, because (1) other countries do not have equivalent units (production teams); (2) interpersonal differences within teams are averaged in the inter-team distribution; and (3) income other than that distributed by basic accounting units is left out of the Chinese data. On the basis of adjustments to correct for these deficiencies (as well as for undervaluation of income in kind), the World Bank (1983, I:92, 276–8, 313; 1985:17) estimated the rural *personal* income distribution for 1979 and subsequent years and compared it with that of several other developing countries. The Bank's estimate for 1979 has a Gini cœfficient of 0.26 (see Table 10.4, panel B), which 'means that rural income inequality in China is significantly less than in other South Asian countries (with Gini coefficients of 0.30–0.35)' (World Bank 1985:17).

Table 10.5. *Distributed collective income by deciles: counties and teams, Hebei Province, 1978*

Decile	% of county income	% of team income
1	5.5	5.0
2	7.0	6.0
3	8.0	6.3
4	9.0	7.7
5	9.2	9.0
6	9.3	9.2
7	11.0	10.8
8	12.0	12.0
9	12.5	16.0
10	16.5	18.0

Source: Griffin and Saith (1981:21).

We must be clear about what is being compared: the Bank estimate for China treats rural incomes after taxes but before subsidies (relief payments to impoverished teams and households).[7] It is not stated whether such payments are included in the other cases, but even if they are not their general omission biases the comparison against China, which almost certainly has had a more extensive and reliable system of relief to the destitute than most other low-income countries. Even the official revelations of widespread poverty in many parts of China in the mid-1970s referred to the reliance of these areas upon 'resold grain for their food supply, loans for production and subsidies for day-to-day living' (Wu 1980:L23), all of which formed a safety net considerably stronger than elsewhere at an equivalent level of development. The most notable competitor to China in this regard was Sri Lanka, with its extensive programme of food distribution. China's average life expectancy of 67 years in 1980 (World Bank 1985:16—the official Chinese estimate was 68 years and the 1982 census yields one of 69) and Sri Lanka's of 66 years were both far above those of virtually every other low-income country, with the possible exception of Vietnam (World Bank 1982). On balance, then, despite the difficulty of making accurate comparisons, China's record of rural personal income distribution looks very good in international perspective.

There is no doubt that land reform and collectivization in China removed the substantial element of inequality associated with property ownership. Charles Roll found that the share of the poorest fifth of rural households in total income rose from 6 per cent to over 11 per cent between the 1930s and early 1950s, a clear result of land reform.[8] As a result of land reform and collectivization, the sketchy data available suggest much greater evenness of *intra*-local income distribution in China than in India (Selden 1983:13).[9] Moreover, in mid-1970s China, perhaps as much as half of the difference in household income within a production team was explained by life-cycle variations in the dependency ratio (Vermeer 1982:31), suggesting an even greater equality of distribution of lifetime income. But Roll also points out that most of the inequality in per capita income from crops is a result of locational factors. It is this inequality that has persisted, and which some government policies may indeed have worsened. We may conclude that China's rural income distribution in the 1970s was substantially more equal than that of other Asian low-income countries; that class-based inequality was effectively reduced by China's socialist policies; and that government relief activities probably improved China's relative performance with respect to disposable income and the meeting of basic needs.

The wide rural inequalities that remained at the end of Mao's life were based upon differential access to fertile land, water, urban markets, and industrial inputs.[10] Such differences explain why some peasants in Shanghai's suburbs received up to forty times the income of some peasants in the hills of backward Guizhou Province. Given that the guiding ideology long called for greater social and economic equality, the continued existence of such large differentials requires explanation.

First, it is possible that the stress given to self-reliance throughout the period under examination effectively blocked the scale of redistribution of resources that would have been required to make major inroads on interlocal inequality. The lack of local budget data for the late 1960s and 1970s prevents us from testing this explanation quantitatively, but much qualitative evidence, such as the repeated criticisms of localities that sought help from above and praise of those that did not, supports it. On the other hand, scattered data on provincial revenue-sharing rates for the years in question seem to contradict this explanation by making it appear that substantial inter-provincial redistribution continued (Table 9.2 above). It is possible but unprovable that the goals of national balance in economic growth and the prevention of 'independent kingdoms' among the advanced provinces outweighed that of self-reliance at the provincial level, while self-reliance dominated at lower levels.

A second possible explanation is that interlocal inequalities were not highly visible to the peasants and therefore generated little political pressure for redress. Relatively little inequality *within* villages, the containment of urban–rural differentials by means of low urban wages and the role of rich suburban agricultural belts in blurring remaining urban–rural differences, together with strict limits on travel, all worked to prevent a perception of great inequality in the countryside (Vermeer 1982:33).

Third, the declining effectiveness of central planning, discussed above, probably militated most severely against the economic prospects of the poorest regions of China, since these areas were least endowed with technical, managerial, and administrative skills. More developed regions no doubt were better able to fend for themselves and to defend themselves against irrationality at the higher levels.

Moreover, the social equality that Mao and his followers were committed to fostering was primarily a class- or status-based concept rather than an income-based one. Symbolized by the elimination in 1965 of ranks and insignias in the military, and by the well-known similarity in dress of Chinese of all walks of life, this orientation was meant to weaken the status distinctions between the bureaucratic and technocratic élites and the masses and to foster better morale, organizational cohesion, and involvement by the masses in the objectives of their units (see Whyte 1973:153). From this viewpoint, the considerable income differential between peasants in, say, Ningxia and Shanghai was simply irrelevant. No discrete social barrier based in the division of labour or the organizational hierarchy separated them. Rather, they were differentiated principally by income, a gap that could be overcome in good time by mobilizing the enthusiasm of the backward and extending appropriate aid. Politically, the problem was not acute.

Inequality between localities was undoubtedly preserved and even enhanced by restrictions on migration from poorer to richer villages. Checks on such migration had existed before 1949, when they took the form of exclusionary practices by lineage groups and of rents beyond the reach of would-be immigrants. Kinship aggression against settlers from outside a village continues to exist in parts of China, such as Guangdong (Parish and Whyte 1978:59), a case of symbiotic agreement between state policy and traditional practice.

4 Urban–rural inequality

4.1 Income and consumption

Two of the 'three great differences' to which Mao and his followers pledged their opposition—those between 'city and countryside' and between 'workers and peasants'—were concerned with what is conventionally called 'urban–rural gap'. In China before 1949, as in other low income countries, urban per capita income substantially exceeded rural, although there is considerable uncertainty about the size of this gap.[11] In any case, the notion of a gap is an artifice: there were and are sizeable differences within both urban and rural income distributions, examined separately. Members of vegetable-growing communes on the fringes of big cities, for example, earned incomes greater than those of many urban workers. Moreover, because regional and local variations in income now are much greater for rural people than for city dwellers (see above), the size of the difference between average urban and rural incomes will be much greater where agriculture is backward than where it is advanced.

Yet the perception of a general urban–rural gap has been quite marked in China, and it gave rise to numerous complaints during the Hundred Flowers Movement of 1956 (Nolan 1979:447). Development policy has most of the time had a distinct urban bias, apparent not only in the preponderance of investment targeted by the state for urban sectors of the economy, but also in the many subsidies and welfare benefits guaranteed by the state to workers and staff (e.g., subsidies for housing, transport, utilities, food, medical services, child care, and pensions), as well as in the superior access of urban residents to education, medical care, and employment (Rawski 1982a:17). As Rhoads Murphey writes,

Material living standards, wages, and education are all on a higher level in virtually all Chinese cities than in rural areas—highest of all in the largest—and it is in the cities that the most desirable jobs will continue to be found, not only in terms of pay rates but in terms of the attendant attractions of power, responsibility, creativity, leadership, or simply élite status. [Murphey 1980:115]

Murphey regards this gap as inevitable in a modernizing society, and the Maoist vision of its ultimate elimination, however nobly based, as romantic illusion. That vision inspired policies, however, that seriously attempted to prevent the gap from widening. Among them were some quite drastic measures, such as the rustication of educated youth, the virtual freeze on urban wages after 1956, and Mao's Cultural Revolution assault on the Ministry of Health for ignoring the rural population. Local industrialization, widespread rural electrification, the subsidization of rural schools, and the establishment of co-operative health care systems for commune members are other examples of policies aimed at eliminating some of the most glaring disadvantages of living in the countryside.

Yet, while the state was willing to commit political and ideological resources to this objective, it was much more reluctant to shift investment funds. As we have seen, there was an increase in the proportion of capital construction investment going to agriculture and agriculture-support industries during and after the Great Leap (Chapter 6). However, as Table 10.6 makes evident, this increase was not sustained once the immediate agricultural crisis was over. The proportion of national investment going to agriculture and related sectors fell from a high of 21 per cent in 1962 to 14.6 per cent in 1965 and to 10 per cent in 1975. Moreover, the share of agriculture proper dropped even more sharply, from 7.4 per cent (1962) to less than 1 per cent (1975), while that of water conservancy was halved. All this occurred while 'agricultural priority' was still formally at the core of development strategy.

Agriculture's share in total national investment is of course not the only indicator of the state's attitude towards the welfare of the rural population and the urban–rural gap. Many forms of improvement of farm production would not show up in this statistic. Only one of the four measures given in Table 10.7 (percentage of cultivated area plowed by tractor) corresponds to investment in agriculture; the other three are current inputs for which the corresponding investment largely takes place in other sectors of the economy. These inputs can be seen to have grown quite rapidly between 1957 and the mid-1970s. While their respective growth rates were influenced by many factors, it is apparent that the Cultural Revolution Decade does not stand out as a period of special attention to their growth. If anything, growth rates seem to have been somewhat lower during this decade than they had been before it (and, in the case of chemical fertilizer use, than it was during the three years following it).

From the perspective of state support for agricultural production, then, available data do not provide an unambiguous picture of 'agricultural priority' as strong material support by the state to agriculture. The scepticism of this conclusion is strengthened by a look at available measures of urban and rural income and consumption, as well as by an examination of the terms of trade between agriculture and industry—the subject of Section 4.2.

Table 10.6. *Investment in agriculture-related sectors, 1952–1979*

	Total investment		Of which:[a]			
			Agriculture		Water conservancy	
	m. yuan	%[b]	m. yuan	%[b]	m. yuan	%[b]
1952	583	13.3	1.67	3.8	4.11	9.4
1957	1187	8.6	4.26	3.1	7.30	5.3
1962	1439	21.3	5.02	7.4	8.27	12.2
1965	2497	14.6	7.38	4.3	15.15	8.9
1975	3840	9.8	8.55	0.7	25.66	6.6
1979	5792	11.6	6.14	1.2	34.96	7.0

[a]Other components include forestry, aquatic products, and meteorology.
[b]Percentage of total national investment.

Source: ZNN (1982:45).

Table 10.7. *Growth of modern inputs to agriculture, 1957–1979*

	% cultivated area ploughed by tractor	Chem. fertilizer		Electricity used in rural areas (bn. kWh)	Pesticide output ('000 tons)
		Total use (m. tons)	per *mu* (kg)		
1957	2.4	1.794	1.0	0.14	65
1960	6.8	3.164	2.0	0.69	162
1962	8.1	3.105	2.0	1.61	88
1965	15.0	8.812	5.7	3.71	193
1970	18.0	15.351	10.5	9.57	321
1974	26.4	25.553	17.0	13.99	371
1975	33.3	26.579	17.8	18.31	422
1976	35.1	28.850	19.4	20.48	391
1979	42.4	52.476	35.2	28.27	537

Period	Average annual growth rates (% per annum)				
1957–65	25.7	22.0	24.3	50.6	14.6
1962–5	22.8	41.6	41.8	32.1	29.9
1965–70	6.3	11.7	13.0	20.9	10.8
1965–75	8.3	11.7	12.1	17.3	8.1
1976–9	6.5	22.1	22.0	11.3	11.2

N.B. Growth rates are calculated using endpoints of relevant periods.

Source: ZNN (1982:43); *SYOC* (1983:197, 247).

Some official estimates of per capita consumption of the agricultural and non-agricultural populations are shown in Table 10.8. The current price figures indicate that the former grew by about 2.5 per cent per year between 1957 and 1975 and the latter by 2.6 per cent. In terms of constant prices, however, a different story emerges. Using the indexes, which were calculated from data in 'comparable' prices, average annual growth rates of 1.1 per cent for agriculture and 2.0 per cent for non-agriculture are derived. A large part of the nominal increase in peasant consumption evidently stems from the increase in prices of a stagnating per capita food supply. The last column indicates that the relative advantage of the non-agricultural population increased by some 27 per cent between 1952 and 1975, and by over 17 per cent between 1957 and 1975. During the Cultural Revolution decade it increased by 7.6 per cent. Whatever period one looks at, the advantage of not being a farmer seems to have grown.

According to the table, by 1975 the non-agricultural population enjoyed a level of per capita consumption about 2.6 times that of the agricultural population. Some more specific information concerning this comparison is given in Table 10.9, which shows the urban–rural ratio of consumption or ownership for six specific goods. Urban residents enjoyed a per capita advantage in 1980 ranging from 60 per cent in the case of foodgrains to 400 per cent in the case of bicycles. The superiority of city dwellers in private consumption was matched by their generally superior access to education and health care, and, if they are state employees (or their dependents), to medical insurance, paid maternity leave, and pensions. Housing is the one item in which the farm population may have had an advantage—at least with respect to space, although not with respect to water and sanitation facilities (World Bank 1983:87).

A similar gap appears between estimates of urban and rural personal incomes. Numerous interpretive and data problems afflict this comparison and give rise to different estimates based on different assumptions. Rawski (1982a) puts the urban–rural per capita income ratio in 1978 at a minimum of 3.4 to 1, not including urban subsidies in urban incomes, and at 5.9 to 1 including these subsidies. The World Bank (1983: Annex A:275) finds the ratio in 1979 to be much lower, at 2.2 to 1. There are a number of reasons for this difference;[12] the principal ones, aside from the issue of urban subsidies, result in a much higher estimate by the Bank of rural per capita income (Y171 v. Rawski's Y89).[13] Because the Bank's estimate excludes subsidies, both urban and rural, and because the former are undoubtedly much larger, I would regard the Bank's 2.2 to 1 as a lower bound of the urban–rural income gap and would guess that the true figure was between 2.5 and 3.

Urban income grew faster than rural income until the late 1970s, just as consumption of the non-agricultural population outpaced that of the agricultural. The World Bank estimates annual urban per capita real income growth between 1957 and 1979 at 2.9 per cent, and rural growth at 1.6 per cent (World Bank 1983: Annex A:276). (These are higher than the rates mentioned above for per capita consumption.) The chief reason is that the latter rates stop short of the late 1970s, when a substantial increase in both income and

Table 10.8. *Consumption per capita of agricultural and non-agricultural populations, 1952–1979*

	Per cap. consumption (current Y)			Index (1952 = 100) from data in 'comparable prices'			Index of non-ag. ÷ index of ag. (1952 = 1.00)
	Nat. ave.	Ag. pop.	Non-ag. pop.	Nat. ave.	Ag. pop.	Non-ag. pop.	
1952	76	62	148	100	100	100	1.00
1957	102	79	205	122.9	117.1	126.3	1.079
1965	125	100	237	126.4	116.0	136.5	1.177
1975	158	124	324	156.9	143.1	181.1	1.266
1979	197	152	406	184.9	165.2	214.5	1.298

Source: ZJN (1981:VI-25).

Table 10.9. *Estimated ratio of urban–rural consumption and ownership per capita of seven goods, 1980 and 1981 (rural = 1)*

Consumption/ownership	1980	1981
Foodgrain[a]	1.6	—
Meat[a]	2.4	—
Sewing machines[b]	3.5	3.4
Watches[b]	7.7	7.2
Radios[b]	3.7	2.9
Bicycles[b]	5.0	4.7
TV sets[b]	11.7	9.3

Sources
[a]World Bank (1983, I:87);
[b]*SYOC 1981* (1982:450).

consumption occurred. Thus, the urban–rural income gap widened considerably between the late 1950s and the mid-1970s, despite a rigid cap on urban wages and salaries. This was due in part to a faster rise in the price index in rural areas and in part to a big increase in the labour participation rate in the cities—from 30 per cent in 1957 to 55 per cent in 1980 (*ZJN* 1981:VI–25). More people employed per family meant higher per capita incomes, even with stagnating wages.

Looking backwards, a 1979 urban–rural differential of 2.5 to 1, together with these particular growth rates, implies that in 1957 urban per capita income was about 90 per cent above the rural level. Such an average ratio is not inconsistent with the data for 1957 presented by Nolan (1979) (although Nolan emphasizes the difficulties and the ambiguity involved in making any such overall estimate). Thus, in the case of personal income, as in that of consumption, it appears that the policies of 'late Maoism' did not or could not prevent a widening gap between country people and urban dwellers.

4.2 The terms of trade between industry and agriculture

The structure of relative prices may strongly influence the urban–rural gap. This is true in particular of the terms of trade between farm products and industrial goods. It is acknowledged in China that there has existed since the founding of the People's Republic a 'scissors gap', that is, an undervaluation of agricultural prices relative to industrial prices similar to the gap maintained for many years in the Soviet Union.[14] As was true there, the 'scissors gap' has functioned as a kind of tax by which the state withdrew resources from agriculture to support its industrialization drive. Over the quarter-century from 1949 to the mid-1970s, this gap *appears* to have been narrowed by a series of price increases for agricultural goods which occurred while industrial prices remained steady or increased less rapidly. Yet in the late 1970s there were

Table 10.10. *Official estimates of terms of trade between agriculture and industry, 1930–1936 to 1979*

	Agricult. prices (1)	Indust. prices (2)	Terms of trade (1) ÷ (2) (3)	Terms of trade (1936 = 100) (4)
Ave. 1930–6	49.6	37.6	131.9	100.0
1944	—	—	50.1	38.0
1948	—	—	79.1	60.0
1951	119.6	110.2	108.5	82.3
1952	121.6	109.7	110.8	84.0
1957	146.2	112.1	130.4	99.0
1962	193.4	126.6	152.8	115.8
1965	185.1	118.4	156.3	118.5
1975	208.7	109.6	190.4	144.4
1978	207.3	109.8	188.8	143.1
1979	265.5	109.9	241.6	183.2

Sources: Figures for 1930–6, 1944, and 1948 are from *ZNJQ* (1980:100–1). Figures for other years are from *ZJN* (1981:VI-23) and Chen (1982:73). 'Agricultural prices' are more fully described in the first source as 'purchase prices of agricultural and subsidiary products', and 'industrial prices' as 'retail prices of industrial goods in the countryside.'

renewed complaints in the Chinese press that the gap remained wide, and some argued that it had actually widened. Evidently the subject is sufficiently complicated that Chinese economists themselves find it difficult to identify the size of the 'scissors gap' clearly and to agree on its movements over time.

The published data on the relations between the purchase prices of agricultural products on the one hand and rural retail prices of industrial goods on the other are set out in Table 10.10. The picture shown by this table is as follows. From a value of 60 (1930–6 = 100) on the eve of Liberation, the terms-of-trade index for agriculture rose gradually during the First Five Year Plan period to approach the prewar peak by 1957. Thereafter improvements continued, especially during the 'ten years of chaos' of 1965–75, during which the index rose by 22 per cent to a level 44 per cent higher than the prewar base period.

The problem with this picture is that in the late 1970s, after most of the improvement in agriculture's terms of trade as shown in the table had already occurred, many Chinese economists and reporters complained that relative farm prices were still far too low, creating difficulties for the peasants and depressing their standard of living. It is hard to understand how this could have been the case if each yuan of agricultural earnings really purchased 43 per cent more industrial goods than in the early 1930s and 90 per cent more than in 1950. Some Chinese economists tried to explain this contradiction between the official index and the plight of farmers unable to make ends meet by distinguishing between prices and values. They argued that, even though the 'scissors gap' of *prices* (i.e., the commodity terms of trade between agriculture and industry) had shifted strongly in agriculture's favour, that of *values* had moved in the opposite direction. The value of a commodity, in Marxian theory, depends on the amount of socially necessary labour embodied in it. Productivity change in industry had reduced the value of industrial goods relative to that of agricultural goods. Between 1957 and 1978 labour productivity in industry had risen by 75 per cent, as compared with only 15 per cent in agriculture (Chen 1982:74). Since agriculture's relative lag in productivity exceeded its relative gain in price, one unit of labour expended in agriculture was exchanging for less labour expended in industry in 1978 than in 1957. Farm prices would have had to rise by about 5 per cent more than they did in order to maintain the 1957 ratio of exchange of 'values' (Chen 1982:74).[15]

Yet it is not clear what practical significance this way of posing the problem has with respect to either motivation or equity. Peasants may respond to absolute changes in their real incomes or to changes relative to the incomes of others (such as workers). But it is unlikely that they are moved by a pure abstraction, that is, by the relative amounts of labour embodied in goods exchanged, especially since that ratio varies quite widely from the relative real incomes of workers and peasants. (Net output value per worker in industry in 1978 was 6.7 times that in agriculture (Yang and Li 1980:208), a difference substantially larger than the ratio of real incomes in the two sectors.)

A better explanation for the apparent contradiction between the official index and the hardships experienced by peasants may be that the index itself is flawed, especially in not reflecting changes in the true cost of industrial goods bought by peasants. This is implied by Yang and Li, who assert (1980:207) that the agricultural price index shown in Table 10.10 is composed of the prices of rice, wheat, cotton, pigs, and eggs, while the industrial index consists of the prices of kerosene, salt, sugar, cotton cloth, and matches. The latter index thus includes only traditional industrial goods consumed by peasants, 'while the highly priced producers' goods are not included here'. Relative prices of farm machinery, chemical fertilizer, and pesticides are singled out as being 'excessively high' in China in comparison with international market prices. For example, a kilogram of rice exchanged in China for less than half the amount of fertilizer it could command in the international market, and it took five or six times as much rice to purchase a tractor of given horsepower in China as in Japan (Yang and Li 1980:207).

Some comparisons for the mid-1970s of the purchasing power of rice over industrial consumer goods in China (Guangzhou) and Hong Kong are shown in Table 10.11. From the table it can be seen that in Hong Kong, where world market prices reign relatively unfettered, a given quantity of rice exchanged in the mid-1970s for several times as many units of industrial consumer goods as in Guangzhou (Canton), just a short distance away. One scholar has concluded that the price of rice in China was less than one-fourth its value on the world market (Liu 1980:8).

Thus, prices of both consumer and producer goods sold in the countryside in the mid-1970s remained very high relative to farm prices. In the case of

Table 10.11. *Comparison of terms of trade between rice and selected industrial goods in Guangzhou (Canton) and Hong Kong, mid-1970s*

| Industrial item | No. of kg of husked, polished rice required to buy one unit in | | Ratio: Guangzhou/ Hong Kong |
	Guangzhou	Hong Kong	
Portable radio (Guangzhou)	14	6	2.3
Thermos bottle (Guangzhou)	15.5	3.5	4.4
Sewing machine (Shanghai)	616.5	124	5.0
Bicycle (Shanghai)	582	110.5	5.3
Camera (Shanghai)	462.5	59	7.8
Alarm clock (Shanghai)	75.5	7.5	10.1

N.B. Cities in parentheses indicate place of manufacture. Data refer to identical brands sold in Guangzhou and Hong Kong.

Source: Liu (1980:5–6).

producer goods, high prices imposed severe burdens on farmers who had to adopt modern inputs in order to overcome diminishing returns to scarce land. One large-scale national survey determined that between 1962 and 1976 the average output value per *mu* of six grain crops had increased by Y16.61, but that this had been more than offset by additional production costs of Y20.33 and by Y0.39 of additional tax, so that net income per *mu* had actually fallen. As the economists Yang and Li concluded, 'there appeared not only "poor production teams with high yields" but also "poor counties with rich harvests". Isn't this the result of unreasonable pricing?' (Yang and Li 1980:207–8).[16]

Tables 10.12 and 10.13 present national data on the relations between gross income, net income, and final distribution of collective income to commune members between 1975 and 1978. As can be seen in Table 10.12, production expenses rise as a proportion of gross income from one-quarter in 1957 to one-third in 1977 (col.(5)), and net income drops from almost three-quarters of gross income in 1957 to less than two-thirds in 1977 (col.(7)). Distribution to members, cushioned somewhat by the decline in the tax burden (col. (9)), nevertheless falls from 57.5 to 51.4 per cent of gross income over this period (col. (18)). The problem of production expenses seems to become more acute in the latter part of the period; they increased only 34 per cent faster than gross income between 1957 and 1974, but 143 per cent faster between 1974 and 1977.

The impact on per capita net income and distribution can be seen in Table 10.13. Both fell between 1974 and 1977 even though gross income rose. A survey conducted in Heilongjiang Province illustrates the process at work here. Urea (a high-quality nitrogenous fertilizer), with a yield response ratio of 4 kg of corn to 1 kg of fertilizer, was priced such that 1 kg exchanged for only 3.5 kg of corn. Moreover, the 4 to 1 yield response probably depended on other additions to input cost, such as pesticide, water, etc. Little or no increase in net income resulted, yet the state urea factory made a profit of no less than 133 per cent,

Table 10.12. *Distribution of gross income of basic accounting units in the rural communes, 1957, 1974, 1977, and 1978 (millions of yuan, current prices)*

	(1) Gross income	(2) Total expenses	(3) % of (1)	(4) Prod'n expenses	(5) % of (1)	(6) Net income	(7) % of (1)	(8) Agric. tax	(9) % of (1)	(10) % of (6)
1957	36 752	9 728	26.5	9 235	25.1	27 024	73.5	3 617	9.8	13.4
1974	90 935	29 299	32.2	27 414	30.1	61 675	67.8	3 748	4.1	6.1
1977	97 593	34 729	35.6	31 978	32.8	62 980	64.5	3 710	3.8	5.9
1978	110 690	38 040	34.4	n.a.		72 650[e]	65.6	3 710	3.4	5.1

	(11) Accum. fund	(12) % of (1)	(13) % of (6)	(14) Welfare fund	(15) % of (1)	(16) % of (6)	(17) Distr. to members	(18) % of (1)	(19) % of (6)
1957	1 802	5.0	6.7	457	1.2	1.7	21 148	57.5	78.3
1974	7 019[a]	7.7	11.4	2 164[b]	2.4	3.5	48 744[c]	53.6	79.0
1977	6 617[a]	6.8	10.5	2 469[b]	2.5	3.9	50 184	51.4	79.7
1978	6 240	5.6	8.6	n.a.[d]			58 749	53.1	80.9

[a] Includes 'grain reserve fund'.
[b] Includes 'other collective reserves'.
[c] Includes cash distribution as follows: 1974: −Y12,326 (25.3 per cent of total distribution); 1977: −Y12,460 (24.8 per cent of total distribution).
[d] Not available. All public reserves other than the accumulation fund are given as totalling Y4,031 million.
[e] Calculated by subtracting total expenses from gross income. Following this procedure yields slight discrepancies for 1974 and 1977, for which net income is given by the source.

Source: ZNJQ (1980:120–4).

Table 10.13. *Selected aspects of the distribution of net income of basic accounting units, per capita: all China, 1957, 1974, and 1977 (current yuan)*

	Commune population	Income		Accum. Fund	Welfare Fund	Distrib. to members
		Gross	Net			
1957	527,242	69.7	51.3	3.4	0.9	40.1 (40.5)
1974	763,890	119.0	80.7	9.2	2.8	63.8 (65.8)
1977	796,880	122.5	79.0	8.3	3.1	63.0 (64.98)

Notes and sources: Commune population from ZNN (1982:25–6). The 1957 figures refer to agricultural production co-operatives rather than communes. The total co-operative population in that year is calculated by multiplying the number of co-operative households (given in the source) by the 1958 figure for average commune household size. Other columns calculated from commune population and data in Table 10.12. Numbers in parentheses are independent estimates of per capita distribution from ZNN (1982:45).

excluding profits made in distributing the product (Yang and Li 1980:208).

It appears, then, that the official indexes of agricultural purchase prices and prices of industrial goods sold in the countryside give a distorted view of the terms of trade between agriculture and industry. First, the index's industrial goods seem to be confined largely to traditional consumer items. Second, while prices of modern farm inputs such as chemical fertilizer, pesticides, and diesel oil did fall between the 1950s and 1970s,[17] they were hardly at all in use at the beginning of the period; whereas at the end, when badly needed to increase yields, their relative prices were still far higher than elsewhere in the world. Third, modern consumer goods (such as those listed in Table 10.11), which apparently did not figure in the index, also exchanged with farm goods at relative prices far above world market levels, adding another disincentive for farmers to modernize.

It is difficult, however, to judge the *degree* of responsibility of the price structure for lagging farm output and incomes. The rise in the share of production costs in gross output was due not only to that price gap but also to a series of arbitrary and misconceived state policies towards agriculture, such as an overemphasis on grain production, discouragement of diversification, overpromotion of multiple-cropping, and a generally 'commandist' approach to planning that relied on the dictation of quantity targets to production teams. These policies must have had a significant, if unmeasurable, negative impact on factor productivity. For this reason, some Chinese economists deny that the 'scissors gap' presented a serious constraint to agricultural progress and argue instead that ultra-leftist policy errors explain most of the plight of the peasantry. Xu and Chen (1981), for instance, call attention to areas in which the enforcement of uneconomic double-cropping had driven up production costs faster than output and gross income; when this mistake was rectified in 1978 the pattern was reversed: yields increased and production costs fell, raising peasant incomes even before the farm price increases of 1979.

Given the large disparity between relative prices in China and the rest of the world, however, and the many examples that have been featured in the Chinese press of the unprofitability to the peasants of using modern inputs, it is hard to avoid the conclusion that the 'scissors gap' played a significant role up to the later 1970s. The rise in farm prices that occurred in 1979 narrowed the difference between Chinese and world prices only somewhat, yet it seems to have greatly improved peasant incomes and incentives. Until then, however, relative prices were used to 'catch the fish by draining the pond' at the very time Mao was using this phrase to symbolize Soviet mistakes avoided by China.

5 Personal distribution

An estimate made by the World Bank of the personal income distribution of the rural population was presented in Section 3. Data are also available for urban incomes, and the World Bank has combined the two to get a personal income distribution for the population as a whole.

Some dimensions of the urban income distribution in 1981, based on a national sample of almost 9,000 households, are shown in Table 10.14. It is evident that urban income inequality was very low by any standard. Moreover, a large share of that inequality is explained by variation in the dependency ratio: the average income of the top class is 3.9 times that of the bottom class, whereas the percentage employed per household is 2.9 times as great. Variation in dependency ratio is to a great extent a life-cycle phenomenon, which of course affects our welfare evaluation of the inequality explained by it.

The extraordinarily low urban income inequality in China by international standards is illustrated in Table 10.15. No other low-income country comes close to China's record. However, it should be recalled that an important reason for China's success was its prohibition of rural–urban migration. China's poorest people are rural, and they have been administratively restricted from entering the cities, whereas rural–urban migration proceeds freely in most other

Table 10.14. *Distribution of urban income, 1981*

Income class (yuan per cap. per mo.)	% of sample pop.	Ave. income per mo.	% of total income	% employed per household
60 and over	4.9	Y72.93	8.7	84.06
50–59.9	10.4	58.68	14.7	75.41
35–49.9	40.1	44.72	43.2	60.75
25–34.9	35.1	33.25	28.1	46.78
20–24.9	6.8	24.95	4.1	37.55
Under 20	2.7	18.89	1.2	29.11
Total/ave.	100.0	Y41.70	100.0	56.37

Source: Calculated from data in *SYOC 1981* (1982:438).

Table 10.15. *China's urban income distribution in international perspective*

	Income shares of recipient groups			Gini coefficient
	Poorest 40%	Richest 20%	Richest 10%	
China, 1981	28.8	29.5	16.5	0.16
Bangladesh, 1966/7	17.1	47.2	31.5	0.40
India, 1975/6	16.9	48.8	34.1	0.42
Pakistan, 1970/1	19.1	44.4	39.7	0.36
Sri Lanka, 1969/70	16.3	47.5	31.7	0.41
Indonesia, 1976	16.0	49.4	34.5	0.43
Malaysia, 1970	11.2	56.5	40.3	0.52
Philippines, 1971	13.7	54.1	35.3	0.47
Thailand, 1975/6	17.5	46.6	32.2	0.40

N.B. The distribution is of household per capita income among persons for China, India, Sri Lanka, Malaysia, and Thailand; for the other countries, it is of household income among households.

Sources: China, Table 10.14; other countries, World Bank (1983, I:89).

low-income countries, where it contributes to a host of well-known problems while increasing urban inequality.

Restrictions on migration have probably caused China's urban–rural gap to be greater than it would otherwise have been, although those who migrate to cities are usually not among the poorest of the rural poor (who lack the assets to move). In Section 3 we treated the World Bank's estimate of the overall urban–rural income gap, 2.2 to 1, as a lower bound and estimated that the 'true' figure was closer to 2.5 or 3. This would be comparable to, or even higher than, the gap in India, Bangladesh, Sri Lanka, and several other developing countries (see World Bank 1983, I:86).

Largely because of the continuing sharp urban–rural dichotomy in China, its overall personal income distribution was not markedly more equal than those of some other low-income countries, such as Pakistan, Sri Lanka, and Bangladesh, although it was more equal than those of India and the countries in the somewhat higher income group beginning with Indonesia (see Table 10.16). China's distributional profile was notable for the low share of income going to the richest 10 per cent of the population. Like other countries that have greatly restricted the private ownership of property, China thereby eliminated the very rich and limited the share of the rich. At the same time, its poorest 40 per cent apparently did not fare especially well in comparison with those countries at a comparably low level of per capita income. As has already been pointed out, however, the distribution of conventional measured income is a misleading indicator of the distribution of entitlements to basic necessities, security, education, and health care. The availability of grants and loans to needy individuals and collectives, and the low subsidized prices of food, schooling,

Table 10.16. *China's overall income distribution in international perspective*

	Income shares of recipient groups			Gini coefficient
	Poorest 40%	Richest 20%	Richest 10%	
China, 1979	18.4	39.3	22.5	0.33
Bangladesh, 1973/4	18.2	42.2	27.4	0.34[a]
India, 1975/6	18.5	46.5	31.4	0.38
Pakistan, 1970/1	20.6	41.5	26.8	0.33
Sri Lanka, 1969/70	20.8	41.8	27.4	0.33
Indonesia, 1976	14.4	49.4	34.0	0.44
Malaysia, 1973	12.5	55.1	39.8	0.50
Philippines, 1971	14.2	54.0	38.5	0.47
Thailand, 1975/6	15.8	49.3	33.4	0.42
Yugoslavia, 1978	18.7	38.7	22.9	0.32[b]

N.B. The distribution is of household per capita income among persons for China, India, Sri Lanka, Malaysia, and Thailand; for the other countries, it is of household income among households.

[a] 1966/7.
[b] 1973.

Sources: World Bank (1983, I:64; 1982:158–9).

child care, and medical care, ensure that, despite their low share of income, 'the poorest people in China are far better off than their counterparts in most other developing countries' (World Bank 1983, I:94–5).

6 Conclusion

The complexity of the foregoing discussion of income distribution in China makes it clear that no simple conclusion about the degree of equality achieved can be drawn. Perhaps the least complicated and most significant general conclusion is that which ended the last section: that China's poor emerged from the Maoist era significantly better off than the poor of most other developing countries. But poverty remained: in 1981 some 10 per cent of China's rural households had total net per capita incomes of less than Y100 (roughly $50) per year.

The leadership has been more interested in reducing some kinds of inequalities than others. They have not always succeeded even for those targeted; as we have seen, the urban–rural differential probably grew from the late 1950s to the late 1970s. Policies tending to widen it, such as the maintenance of a low percentage of state investment allocated to agriculture, the prohibition of rural–urban migration, and the continued underpricing of farm products, had greater impact than those tending to reduce it, such as the administrative allocation of more medical and educational personnel and facilities to the countryside during the Cultural Revolution. Policies adopted since the later 1970s have caused farm incomes to grow much more rapidly (see Chapter 11), perhaps fast enough to narrow the urban–rural gap.[18]

What has here been called 'interlocal' differentials, which explain a large fraction of rural inequality in China today, have not provoked much concern from the leadership. While fiscal policy has been used vigorously and with some success to limit the widening of differences between provinces (Sec. 1), for smaller localities such as counties and villages the watchword seems to have been self-reliance. It is possible that the decade-long enforcement of local self-sufficiency in grain was in part motivated by the desire to limit interlocal differentials, as Stavis conjectures (Chapter 9); but, if so, this was a punitive way to go about it, hurting both economic crop areas and grain areas alike. More recent policies (see Chapter 12) have explicitly encouraged growing disparities, but on the Rawlsian 'difference principle' (Rawls 1971) that so doing will actually improve the position of the less advantaged (see, e.g., 'Let some Localities and Peasants Prosper First', *BR*, 19 January 1981).

Egalitarianism as a goal of the Maoist leadership was most seriously applied to relationships that had—or potentially had—a class or status character. Although from the 1950s China has kept a complex and variegated system of wage ranking scales—scales for more than sixty occupations are listed in one source (see Korzec and Whyte 1981:250–1)—visitors' reports have usually indicated a markedly small difference between the wages of top administrative and technical personnel and those of ordinary workers (Riskin 1975c). One scholar who visited thirty-eight industrial enterprises in 1966 found that 'at most enterprises the ratio between the director's salary and the average enterprise pay figure was less than 2 to 1, and the highest was only 3 to 1' (Richman 1969:799). In a sample of ten industrial enterprises visited during the period 1971–4, the maximum wage of managerial, engineering, or technical personnel averaged 2.7 times the average worker wage (Riskin 1975c:218).

These are certainly small differentials by international standards. Since most of the enterprises sampled are large, such average differences are comparable to a chief executive officer of a US corporation earning $54,000 per year when the average wage is $20,000 and the top wage $33,750. While the samples might be biased, the general impression they generate is quite consistent with the egalitarian urban distribution of income described in Section 5. Indeed, intra-enterprise egalitarianism has been roundly condemned by the post-Mao leadership, which has often complained about the difficulty of eradicating it.

Equally condemned has been the same goal of equality pursued during the 'late Maoist' period *within* the basic organizational units in the country-side—the production teams. Here, income differences between house-holds were small and were largely explained by variations in the number of able-bodied workers (Blecher 1976; Vermeer 1982). While intra-community differentials were a smaller contributor than spatial differentials to overall rural income inequality, they were directly discernible and had more serious implications. The major events in their reduction were land reform and collectivization, which first diminished and then eliminated inequality of landownership, perhaps the main source of intra-village income inequality in the past.

Once this had been accomplished, however, further progress in the direction of equality proved difficult to sustain, despite Maoist commitment to that goal. For instance, the decision of the early 1960s to make the production team the basic unit of account opened the way for large disparities between teams in a single village. But the attempt of the Cultural Revolution period (sustained fitfully in subsequent years) in many areas to shift from task rates to time rates or the Dazhai system of distribution, and to increase the proportion of 'basic grain' (distributed on a per capita basis rather than according to work-points earned), probably did significantly equalize income and consumption within teams. Certainly this is suggested by post-1976 complaints that equality was carried to the point of hurting work incentives. Parish and Whyte (1978:Chapter 5) suggest that ecological and other circumstances, such as land scarcity, size of team, and degree of affluence, have a marked effect on the appropriateness of egalitarian distribution methods, which have been accepted in teams with propitious conditions and resisted elsewhere. If so, such qualifying conditions were often overlooked by those at the top pushing egalitarianism, just as they were later ignored in the anti-egalitarian climate of the early 1980s.

The results for the urban population of the Maoist leadership's sensitivity to class- and status-related inequalities are examined more closely by Whyte and Parish (Parish 1981). Several interesting results emerge. First, there was in the 1970s a quite remarkable degree of equality among occupations in the possession of consumer durables (watches, radios, bicycles, sewing machines, cameras, etc.) and of scarce urban housing: 'statistics on consumption among those just below the top élite suggest that administrative position does not add measurably to consumption level.' Second, despite a convergence towards equal access to education by persons of all class backgrounds, in the early 1960s the children of cadres and those of former capitalists and professionals were getting more education than those of workers and peasants and were monopolizing positions in the élite boarding schools. They were also getting the best jobs, while children of workers and peasants got inferior jobs or no jobs at all. Third, the Cultural Revolution response to this situation was to emphasize class background and political commitment and de-emphasize academic achievement as the basis for school promotion, admission to college, and access to industrial employment. The data show a rapid convergence after 1966 both in level of education and in access to urban jobs:

As intended by the radicals, capitalist and other bad-class children suffered the sharpest reversals, losing their favored occupational spots to others. The children of staff and other intellectuals got jobs no better than those given the children of former peasants. In an unanticipated development, but one later singled out for comment in the press, cadre children gained in occupational terms the position of advantage they had already gained in education. With this minor exception concerning cadre children, however, the radical policies were having their intended effect of narrowing and inverting the class order. [Parish 1981:49]

Parish concludes that, after 1966, 'the fit between parental·status and children's status was reduced to near zero or to only a fraction of its former levels', and that 'Government policy to break the reproduction of status groups . . . was indeed effective' (Parish 1981:43–50).

Thus, it appears that, where radical values were most committed to the egalitarian goal, that goal was pursued quite relentlessly and effectively during the Cultural Revolution decade. Many problems have been noted with the *means* of pursuit: educational standards were badly weakened; college education practically ceased; the average wage declined; the number of new industrial jobs fell behind the supply of urban middle-school graduates entering the labour market; the reversal of status ranks was carried out in part by means of a virulent anti-intellectualism and by the attainment of new levels of arbitrariness in the exercise of political power. The violent, chaotic, and authoritarian elements of the Cultural Revolution decade cannot easily be separated from its underlying values in judging results. Yet it is at least possible that the economic problems traced to that era were more the results of these irrational and destructive elements than of the greater social equality that was sought and, to a significant degree, achieved.

Notes

1. For instance, merging the three centrally administered municipalities with their adjacent provinces (Beijing and Tianjin with Hebei and Shanghai with Jiangsu) reduces the unweighted coefficient of variation of provincial per capita industrial output in 1979 from 1.5 to 0.8 (see Table 10.1). This is because these cities are outliers in the distribution, having much higher industrial output per capita than any province. Treated as separate province-level units, they thus add greatly to the dispersion of the distribution.

2. The absolute size of the range is of course exaggerated by the treatment of three large cities as separate provinces. We are here focusing on the *change* in this measure, however, for which purpose this treatment enables us to observe Shanghai's declining but still great industrial role, and the growing one of Beijing.

3. The coefficient of variation appears to fall sharply between 1957 and 1965, then to increase up to 1974, finally returning to its 1965 level by 1979. If accurate, this would indicate, paradoxically, that during the Cultural Revolution decade, when radical redistributive policies were most in vogue, the gap between rich and poor provinces reversed its historical trend and widened. However, serious defects in the population estimates for the two intermediate years, and especially for 1965 (Aird 1978a:31), in addition to some changes in provincial boundaries during the period in question, make it impossible to accept this result at face value. The behaviour of interregional differences during the Cultural Revolution decade must be treated as a topic for research.

4. The 1979 figures are in 1970 fixed prices and the 1957 figures in 1957 prices. Industrial prices declined significantly between 1957 and 1970. The 1979 gap between high and low province, expressed in 1970 yuan, will therefore be smaller than if expressed in 1957 yuan. Thus, the increase in the gap is *under*estimated in the table. The opposite is true for the gap in agricultural output per capita: since

agricultural prices rose considerably between 1957 and 1970, the table *over*states the increase in the absolute range.

5. Only 40–50 per cent of GVAO ends up as distributed collective income, the rest being accounted for by production costs, taxes, and accumulation and welfare funds, as well as income from private sideline activities. If this percentage is the same for the highest and the lowest GVAO per capita provinces, the absolute range of collective distributed income per capita would be only 40–50 per cent of that of GVAO per capita.

6. In fact, there were even poorer brigades in terms of measured income. But bearing in mind that Y40 roughly equalled $20, the probability is zero that anything smaller is consistent with survival.

7. The Main Report (World Bank 1983:91) suggests that 'social relief' is taken into account in the estimate along with other types of non-collective distributed income, but it appears from the description of methodology in the Appendix (pp. 274–8, paras. A47–9, A51–61) that relief payments are not included. It should be pointed out that the limited reliability of rural statistics for most developing countries, and uncertainties about what kinds of income are included and excluded, about possible underreporting, and about the probable underestimation of income in kind, make such international comparisons subject to a wide range of possible error—as is acknowledged in the World Bank report (Annex A:279).

8. Charles Roll, 'Incentives and Motivation in China', paper presented at the annual meeting of the American Economic Association, 28 December 1975, and cited in Selden (1983).

9. Griffin and Saith (1981) argue that the small degree of intra-commune inequality is due in part to structural characteristics of the rural economy, quite irrespective of state policy. Using a growth model estimated on the basis of data from two communes visited, they argue that economic development within the commune is accompanied by a shift from agricultural to industrial activities and from lower (team) to higher (brigade and commune) levels of control of production. Since industrial activities require much larger amounts of fixed and working capital than does agriculture, net income per unit of expenditure on fixed and working capital falls, and, as a result, net income per worker rises at a diminishing rate. This permits poorer teams eventually to close the gap on richer ones.

It would indeed be significant if such equalizing tendencies existed in rural China independently of state policy, but I doubt that such is the case. There is nothing inherent in the nature of industrial and agricultural technology generally that would lead to this result; elsewhere in the world the opposite often occurs, industrialization leading to widening differences in productivity and net income per capita. If such a tendency exists in the Chinese countryside, then it must be due to conditions peculiar to that locale. As is now well known, provincial and local authorities frequently set arbitrary limits on the size of income differences within their jurisdictions during the mid-1970s; this took the form of setting a cap on incomes per capita or on the gap between that of the richest and poorest units within the area. 'Usually a discriminative set of state purchase and sales prices was used to achieve a redistributive effect' (Vermeer 1982:24). Even where such a policy was not explicitly invoked, the knowledge that wide differentials were frowned upon might have led better-off collectives to disguise or simply misreport their true incomes. Unusual pricing policies in China, where the ratio of farm input prices to prices of farm output was much higher than elsewhere, and where small rural industries frequently ran at a loss, must also be taken into account. These policies might well have influenced the estimates of the parameters in Griffin and Saith's model, creating the illusion of a structural tendency towards equalization where this tendency actually stemmed from the residue of Maoist egalitarian policy and from arbitrary pricing policies.

10. This conclusion contradicts a Chinese explanation that 'the differences between the poor and the rich in China . . . is essentially a manifestation of the difference in people's physical ability and labour skills' (*BR*, 21 June 1982:4).

11. For example Roll (1974:117) estimates that average per capita consumption in urban areas surpassed that of rural areas by only 14–23 per cent, whereas Rawski (1982a:24) believes the gap was closer to 2:1.

12. These reasons include the rise in peasant incomes between 1978 and 1979 and the inclusion by the World Bank of components of rural income not included by Rawski, such as income from manure sales, commune wages, and 'other'. The World Bank estimate ignores urban subsidies; both estimates ignore rural subsidies, which, although smaller than urban, must be taken account of if subsidies are to be included. There is also the hoary issue of urban costs masquerading as income: does the cost of commuting to work in the cities represent a net benefit in comparison with farmers who do not need to commute?

13. Only about 40 per cent of this difference is due to the rise in peasant income between 1978 (Rawski's year) and 1979 (the World Bank's), the rest being explained by differences in method.

14. See, e.g., Xu and Chen (1981:131): 'Agricultural tax is one of the channels through which peasants provide accumulation funds. But as the amount of agricultural tax is limited, a portion of necessary accumulation funds is provided . . . by means of the redistribution function of prices in the process of exchanging agricultural products for industrial products.' Also, see Yang and Li (1980:207): 'The "scissors" disparity . . . has narrowed in the case of some industrial and agricultural products, [but] state purchasing prices for agricultural products have generally been kept too low since the founding of the People's Republic.'

15. This argument is correct only if the 'organic composition of capital' is the same in both sectors. This assumption is not valid, however. In 1978 fixed capital per worker in state-owned industrial enterprises was Y9,400, as compared with Y240 in agriculture, a ratio of almost 40 to 1. If collective industry were included the ratio would fall somewhat but would remain quite high (see Xu and Chen 1981:132). Thus it is not clear that the value terms of trade correctly expressed to include *all* labour ('living' and 'dead') embodied in commodities, moved against agriculture. The value terms of trade are analogous to the double-factoral terms of trade in Western trade theory.

16. In their report on this survey, Yang and Li state that production costs include 'manpower'. Since, under the work-point system, the value of farm labour is determined as a residual after costs and taxes are accounted for, it is unclear how it was included in production costs and what 'net income' then consisted of.

17. According to *Peking Review* (9 August 1976, p. 26), the following prices per kilogram were paid in one county of Hunan Province:

	Chem. fertilizer	Pesticides	Diesel oil
1957	0.42	1.35	0.264
1965	0.38	1.15	0.164
1974	0.29	1.04	0.164

18. Official statistics indicate that from 1978 to 1984 per capita consumption of the agricultural population in 'comparable prices' rose by 71 per cent, while that of the non-agricultural population increased by only 27 per cent. While the relative difference thus narrowed, the absolute gap (in current yuan) widened from Y251 in 1978 to Y319 in 1984 (see *ZTZ* 1985:97).

CHAPTER 11

REASSESSMENT, 1977–1979

1 Introduction

The arrest and purge of the 'Gang of Four' brought immediate and growing change to all aspects of Chinese life. In economic policy, the stalemate resulting from the decade-long conflict gave way initially to a renewed emphasis on fast growth. But as the tide of change deepened, sweeping leaders associated with the Cultural Revolution from power and bringing back conservative and reform-oriented figures, this initial emphasis was abandoned in favour of re-examination of the basic economic principles and practices of Maoism.

Quite soon a new set of policies emerged which reversed those principles and practices in several spheres: economic structure, growth rates, incentives, the role of the market, and Sino-foreign economic links. By the turn of the 1980s, China's economy was operating in ways that would have seemed impossible five years earlier. Farm production was partly de-collectivized and the role of the market greatly expanded; light industry was growing twice as fast as heavy; local governments and enterprises were carrying out more than half of total capital construction investment; foreign private direct investment was flowing into big cities and special economic zones; small private businesses were proliferating; consumerism was being fanned by Western-style advertising campaigns; and both open inflation and budget deficits had reappeared after long absences.

On paper, the economic record of the 'late Maoist' era looks good enough to call into question the need for such fundamental changes in strategy. Industry had grown by over 10 per cent per year, agriculture by 4 per cent, grain output by 3.7 per cent, GNP by 6.5 per cent (see Table 8.1). These figures put China at the top among the low-income countries in growth performance. Yet, they also masked increasingly serious structural problems. When the new post-Mao government issued a critique of this period, it charged that the economy had in fact been pushed to 'the brink of disaster'.

We have already discussed at several points (especially the Introduction to Chapter 9) inherent problems in the Maoist strategy, in particular its embodiment of a fundamental contradiction between command planning and policies of an anti-bureaucratic, social mobilization orientation. Not only did this mismatch both weaken central planning and truncate reform, it also required central direction of policy by ideological means, which ultimately gave rise to a prudent fear of decision-making at all levels. Of course, the fact that the Maoist approach was opposed by much of the bureaucracy and intelligentsia is also significant. It is difficult to separate the effects on the economy of flaws in the 'left' approach from those of the political stalemate that obstructed economic planning during much of the 1960s and 1970s. Some of these flaws inevitably produced opposition, while opposition in turn had its own economic consequences.

In Section 2 we deal with the initial economics of the new post-Mao regime, which was vigorously expansionary on both the domestic and international fronts. Section 3 then introduces the critique developed by the reformist leadership from late 1978, which led to a slowdown in growth and a new emphasis on structural reform and sectoral readjustment. This section discusses the symptoms ('poor economic results') now being deplored, while the following two sections analyse causes. The diagnosis is rather complex and falls into two interrelated categories. First, the various imbalances and disproportionalities that characterized the economy of the late 1970s are discussed in Section 4; then, the reformist indictment of the central administrative planning and management system itself is presented in Section 5. The latter is the deeper level of explanation of China's economic problems, directly helping to explain the emergence and persistence of imbalances as well as problems of low productivity growth and poor incentives. Much of the rest of the explanation—such as the compounding effects of the Maoist reaction to these same systemic problems—derives from it *indirectly*.

2   The Ten Year Plan

After the arrest of the left leadership in October 1976, a considerable time was devoted to preparing and executing the political change of direction and rehabilitating demoted and imprisoned cadres. This was a time of much confusion: new and old ideas were in open combat, and uncertainty prevailed about the ultimate extent and duration of the changes occurring.

The first major national economic conference to take place after the purge was the Second National Conference on Learning from Dazhai in Agriculture, held in Beijing in late December 1976. At it, Party Chairman and Premier Hua Guofeng castigated the ousted leaders for a variety of sins, including in-attention to economics. But both the policies advocated by Hua and his style and rhetoric were largely vintage Cultural Revolution. 'Learning from Dazhai' was itself a policy and a slogan soon to disappear; but here also were references to the importance of cadre participation in manual labour, the 'Anshan Constitution', the central role of mass movements, and the ongoing class struggle against capitalist-roaders in the Party. Yet these were joined with references to Zhou Enlai's Four Modernizations speech to the Fourth National Party Congress in 1975, the need to develop the productive forces, and the importance of codifying rational rules and regulations and improving economic management (Hua 1977). It was left to Chen Yonggui (Chen Yung-kuei), however, to express positions most thoroughly in tune with the past.[1] He warned against the extension of private plots, the fixing of farm quotas for individual households, and the dividing up of land among households, which he said had occurred in some places, and he reiterated the left goal of 'gradual transition' from team to commune ownership (Chen 1977).

The hybrid ideological atmosphere is evident in the first major economic programme to emerge in the post-Mao period: the Ten Year Plan announced by Hua Guofeng at the First Session of the Fifth National Party Congress in February 1978 (Hua 1978). This plan reflected a sense of urgency about growth and of optimism about its achievement. Attacking the policies of the past, which it alleged had caused enormous economic losses, it now proposed a series of ambitious targets to make up for lost time. The Plan resurrected Zhou Enlai's call for 'Four Modernizations' (of agriculture, industry, national defense, and science and technology) to enable China to reach the 'front ranks' of the world at the end of the century. By then, China was to have achieved parity or superiority with respect to the advanced industrial countries in output of major industrial products, basically automated their production, and mechanized 85 per cent of major farm tasks.

The year 1985 was to be the intermediate point, and for that year specific targets were assigned to various sectors and industries. Steel output was to reach 60 million tons (1977 output was 23.7 million), foodgrain 400 million metric tons (1978 output: 304.7); between 1978 and 1985 agricultural gross output value was to grow by an average of 4–5 per cent per year, industrial output by over 10 per cent. These targets were all met.

The capital construction plans were extravagant:

the state plans to build or complete 120 large-scale projects, including ten iron and steel complexes, nine nonferrous metal complexes, eight coal mines, ten oil and gas fields, 30 power stations, six new trunk railways, and five key harbours. The completion of these projects ... will provide China with 14 fairly strong and farily rationally located industrial bases. [Hua 1978:22–3]

To implement these projects, the government planned to invest during the eight years 1978–85 an amount equal to the total capital construction investment for the previous twenty-eight years.

Accompanying this massive investment plan was an equally ambitious scale of planned capital and technology imports. China's new leaders intended to resurrect the earlier economic opening to the West which had been partially aborted in 1975. It will be recalled that China's trade (in current dollars) tripled between 1971 and 1975, and that the share of non-communist countries in that trade rose to almost 85 per cent (Chapter 8). But accelerating inflation in the West raised the cost of China's machinery, equipment, and food imports, while world-wide capitalist recession kept Chinese exports down. The result was an unexpectedly large balance of payments deficit in 1974, which may have added fuel to the left attack against Deng Xiaoping the following year. For both economic and political reasons, then, imports were sharply cut back in 1975.

Hua Guofeng's Ten Year Plan marked a return to the strategy of importing capital and technology. Japanese economists in touch with Chinese planners at the time estimated that over $70 billion of imported plant, equipment, and technology imports would be required by the Plan's various projects (JETRO, 26, 1980:18–19). With apparently little thought about the overall costs of these projects or about how they were to be paid for, various government organs began placing orders: 'By the end of 1978, TECHIMPORT, the foreign trade corporation responsible for plant and technology purchases, had negotiated for or expressed interest in about $40 billion worth of complete industrial plants' (Davie and Carver 1982:24).

In 1978, according to one Chinese source, twenty-two large-scale projects were 'introduced from abroad all at once', which not only exceeded China's ability to pay, but also saddled the country with an obligation to commit an even greater sum to the provision of ancillary equipment and parts. Moreover, projects were chosen with little regard to relative urgency of need (Commentator 1981:K8). In the midst of what was later to be pejoratively dubbed the 'foreign leap forward', China was rewarded with formal US recognition (December 1978). During only ten days of the same month China signed contracts amounting to almost $3 billion for whole plant imports, bringing the total for the year to more than $7 billion. This occurred at the same time as the Third Plenum of the Eleventh Central Committee—which was to lead to a decisive shift in economic strategy away from such import extravagance—and has accordingly been interpreted as an attempt by various officials to obtain commitments to their projects before the anticipated fall of the axe (Davie and Carver 1982:26).

The Ten Year Plan, which was widely regarded outside China as over-ambitious, was later to be attacked within the country for its continued adherence to the 'ultra-left' idea of frenetic forward leaps. Hua Guofeng's government work report, in which the Plan was introduced, was in fact a curious mixture of pre- and post-Mao ideology. On the one hand, it featured many of the positions that had become well known during the Cultural Revolution decade. For instance, it gave equal billing to 'grasping revolution' and 'promoting production', and treated the class struggle as a prerequisite to successful economic growth and scientific progress. It put much emphasis on the development of commune and brigade enterprises and on increasing their share of total commune income; it even adopted a noticeably calm tone on the key symbolic issue of competition for materials between rural and national industries. It called for provincial self-sufficiency in light industrial goods and for speeding the development of basic industries. The continued treatment of steel as the emblem of modernity was made clear by its repetition of the slogan, 'take steel as the key link'. It took a very favourable attitude towards local small and medium industries. Regarding incentives and income distribution, it judiciously came out against both a 'wide wage spread' and 'equalitarianism'. In agriculture, Dazhai remained the model to emulate; in industry, Daqing. All of these attitudes were quite consistent with the approach of the recent past.

This continuity, however, emerged in the context of a vigorous repudiation of that past. Hua Guofeng claimed, without elaboration, that the 'interference and sabotage' of the Gang of Four had cost China Y100 billion in gross industrial output value, Y40 billion in national budget revenue, and 28 million tons of steel. Strangely, he blamed followers of the 'Gang' for permitting the parcelling out of land to individual peasant households—a policy soon to be associated with the reformist leadership of Deng Xiaoping. He forbade the requisitioning of money, grain, and labour from production teams and individual peasants by higher cadres, recommended a price policy based on the exchange of equal values, and took a supportive position with respect to rural markets, private plots, and household sideline production. His strong support for upholding the 'law of value'—especially in setting price relations between industrial and farm commodities and between materials and fuels on the one hand and finished manufactured goods on the other—implied a recognition of the role of material incentives in motivating farmers, workers, and managers.

The Dengist position on the division of labour (see Chapter 8) received support in Hua's unambiguous call for strict systems of personal responsibility, from the State Council down to the grass roots. Mao's model of the generalist worker—good at many things, expert at one—was nowhere hinted at. Fixed production quotas, payment according to work performed, piece rates, and bonuses were all given support. Revolutionary committees—the leadership organs of the Cultural Revolution decade—were now to be dismantled in factories, production brigades, schools, and all other non-governmental organizations, to be replaced by directors, leaders, presidents, and managers. (The revolutionary committees of government administrative organs were soon also abolished.) Finally, Hua called for a big increase in foreign trade, to be accomplished by expanding agricultural, mineral, and industrial exports, especially from a number of new export bases to be developed.

Thus, Hua Guofeng's Government Work Report of February 1978 was an ideological hybrid in which the change of direction was marked but incomplete. Among the various vestiges of 'left' ideology within it, the one that attracted immediate attention was the dynamic, 'leap forward' posture, which committed China to continued high—and even increased—levels of capital formation.

The most influential critic of this approach was undoubtedly the veteran leader of economic work, Chen Yun, who in the course of 1978 resumed a prominent role in policy formation and strongly opposed the Ten Year Plan (Lardy and Lieberthal 1982). Chen, a long-time advocate of moderate and balanced growth, was probably the single person most responsible for the prompt shift from the Ten Year Plan to the Readjustment inaugurated at the Third Plenum of the Eleventh Central Committee in December. Behind this shift was a far-ranging critique of China's economic performance and policies since 1949, and it is to this commentary that we now turn.

3 The fruits of growth

Despite heroic investment rates and rapid measured growth during the previous two decades, the Chinese economy of the immediate post-Mao period was providing living standards that were not qualitatively higher than those of the mid-1950s. In the crucial category of grain consumption, 'average per capita foodgrain availability in 1977 was only similar to the 1955 level' (Hu 1978). Average grain consumption of the rural population for 1978–80 was several percentage points below that of 1955–7, while in urban areas it had probably increased somewhat (Walker 1982). Approximately 100 million peasants were

Table 11.1. *Total marketings and state procurement of foodgrain, selected years (millions of metric tons)*

	1952	1957	1975	1977
(1) Total marketings[a]	39.03	45.97	52.62	47.67
(2) as % of output[b]	28.7	28.4	22.3	20.3
(3) State procurement (tax + purchases)	n.a.	39.8	(52.6)[c]	47.4[d]
(4) as % of output	n.a.	24.6	22.3	20.2
(5) Net procurement (= (3) − resales to agriculture)[e]	23.40	28.11	36.48	31.17
(6) as % of output	17.2	17.4	15.4	13.3
(7) Resales to agriculture[f]	n.a.	11.7	16.1	16.3
(8) as % of output	n.a.	7.2	6.8	6.9

[a]Measured in 'trade grain', which includes some grains husked (rice and millet, according to Eckstein (1977:117) and Lardy (1983a: Table 2.1); also wheat, according to Walker (1982:577)) and others unhusked.
[b]Output figures have been reduced by 17 per cent to convert to trade grain: see Lardy (1983a: Table 2.1).
[c]Estimated as being identical to total marketings in 1975.
[d]Differs from Lardy's (1983a: Table 2.1) 47.2 m. metric tons by the inclusion of 'negotiated purchases' by the state.
[e]Figures given by source are converted from unprocessed to trade grain at ratio of 0.83.
[f]Lardy (1983a: Table 2.1) distinguishes between 'resales to rural areas' and 'resales to peasants'. The source's term, 'dui nongye hui xiao' (resales to agriculture), is equivalent to the latter term.
Sources: Row (1), Lardy (1983a: Table 2.1) and *SYOC, 1981* (1982:345); row (3), *ZNJQ* (1980:29–30); row (5), *ZNJQ* (1980:39); row (7), *ZNJQ* (1980:39) (also equal to row (3) minus row (5)).

said to have yearly per capita grain 'rations' of less than 150 kg (Jiang *et al.* 1980:53); such rations (which probably understate actual consumption)[2] would supply a daily intake of only 1,500 calories (Lardy 1982a:161, n. 9). Want of food on such a scale is not known to have existed in the 1950s. If in fact it was a new phenomenon, food distribution must have become more unequal between that decade and the 1970s, since average per capita food availability (output plus imports) did not decrease. Indeed, the state's capacity to redistribute grain may well have failed to keep pace with increasing rural differentiation. The total marketing ratio (proportion of total grain output marketed) declined from almost 30 per cent in the 1950s to only 20 per cent in the late 1970s (Table 11.1, row (2)). Although the state increased its share of the marketed portion to almost 100 per cent by the latter period, its share of total output fell from a quarter to a fifth (row (4)). Of the modest estimated increase in total state procurement between 1957 and 1975, about two-thirds (8.4 million tons) went to feed the cities while one-third (4.4 million tons) was resold to deficit rural areas. The increase in rural resales was slightly below the increase in the rural population; as a result, average resales per head of rural population declined.

Perhaps more important than total resales of grain are inter-provincial transfers. There is considerable variation in per capita grain output among the provinces. A successful effort to redistribute grain to alleviate the hunger of anything approaching 100 million people would have required a substantial transfer from grain surplus provinces. Yet inter-provincial cereal transfers appear to have declined from 7.85 million metric tons in 1953 (5.5 per cent of national output) to 4.7 million in 1965 (2.8 per cent of output) to only 2.05 million in 1978 (less than 1 per cent of output), of which all but about 325,000 metric tons were destined for export abroad (Lardy 1982b).

While rural food consumption fell and localized poverty remained widespread, it is evident that the state was less able to intervene on behalf of poor localities in the 1970s than it had been in the 1950s. Even in better-off areas, the Chinese diet remained spartan. Nationally, 80–90 per cent of total calories were derived from grains; per capita meat consumption was only 8.4 kg per year (making China ninety-eighth in the world) and that of fruit, 7 kg (Lardy 1982a:153).

Within the state sector, the general freeze of wages after 1957 and the entry of new workers into the lowest rungs of the wage ladder thereafter caused the average wage in real terms to fall 17 per cent between that year and 1977 (SYOC 1982:411–12;435–6). Only a large increase in the labour force participation rate—from 30 per cent of the urban population in 1957 to 55 per cent in 1980 (ZJN 1981:VI–25)—enabled the average per capita income of wage and salary earners to increase by 62 per cent in real terms between 1957 and 1980 (ZJN 1981:VI–25; SYOC 1982:411–12). Neglect of 'non-productive' investment over a long period (see Sec. 4 below) allowed already cramped housing space of 4.3 square metres per urban inhabitant in 1952 to decline to 3.6 square metres in 1977 (Walder 1984:24).

Of course, over the same period China scored many economic and technological triumphs: a large machine-building industry was created, earth satellites were manufactured and launched, nuclear weapons made and exploded, large ships and giant hydraulic presses turned out, insulin synthesized. Where resources were concentrated and energies exerted, great gains were made. But generally speaking, the massive buildup of productive forces that had been occurring over three decades had not yielded sufficient 'economic results' in the form of improvements in living standards, technological modernization, and productive efficiency. Between 1952 and 1980 industrial fixed assets increased 27 times, gross value of industrial and agricultural product 9.1 times, but net domestic material product only 5.2 times (Zhao 1982a:18). Although there were objective reasons for this—for example, enforced isolation from Western technology, a hostile international environment, excessive population growth and density—it was also seen to stem from longstanding mistakes in approach to economic organization and structure:

The set-up of production, the product mix, the technological makeup, the line-up of enterprises, the organizational structure, the geographical distribution of industries and

Table 11.2. *Output per worker and per yuan of capital, state-operated industrial enterprises, 1952–1978 (1952 = 100)*

	(1) GVIO	(2) No. of workers and employees (year end)	(3) Fixed and working capital	(4) Output per worker ((1)/(2))	(5) Output per unit of capital ((1)/(3))
1952	100.0	100.0	100.0	100.0	100.0
1957	233.3	146.7	225.6	159.0	103.4
1965	510.6	242.7	705.2	210.4	67.9
1978	1649.2	596.1	2222.0	276.7	74.2
Rates of growth (% per year)					
1952–57	18.5	8.0	17.7	9.7	0.7
1957–65	10.3	6.5	15.3	3.6	−5.1
1965–78	9.4	7.2	9.2	2.1	0.7
1952–78	11.4	7.1	12.7	4.0	−1.1

Sources and notes: *GVIO*: 1952, 1957, 1965 from Field (1982:317); 1978, by intrapolation from Field's (1982) estimate for 1979 on the assumption that state industrial output grew at the same rate as total GVIO (given in *SYOC* 1982:210) between 1978 and 1979. *Number of workers and employees*: *ZJN* (1981:VI-7) and *BR* (11 February 1980, p. 15). *Fixed and working capital*: *SYOC* (1982:8).

other economic undertakings, all these features of our country's economy as a whole are far from rational, and there are many defects in our system of economic management. [Zhao 1982a:18]

The problem of lagging productivity is indicated by Table 11.2, which shows change in gross value of industrial output (GVIO) per industrial worker and per yuan of fixed and working capital[3] from 1952 to 1978, and by Table 11.3, which presents a rough and impressionistic estimate of the change in output per unit of combined inputs ('total factor productivity'). While labour productivity can be seen to have almost tripled between 1952 and 1978, output per yuan of capital, after rising slightly during the First Plan Period, then fell to only three-quarters of its starting point. The decline in the output–capital ratio was in fact larger than shown here: the index of fixed plus working capital is based on current prices, which were falling throughout the period. If capital had been valued in fixed prices (like GVIO), the index would have grown still faster and output per unit of capital fallen farther.

The rough estimates in Table 11.3 of output per unit of aggregate inputs demonstrate that, however the separate factors are weighted in aggregating them, GVIO does not grow very much faster than the resulting aggregate input index. The higher growth rate of productivity, achieved when labour is given the greater weight of 0.6, is only 1.1 per cent per year over the entire period 1952–78, and almost zero for 1957–78. When labour is given a smaller weight of 0.4, the long-term productivity growth rate falls to 0.2 per cent and the rate

Table 11.3. *Growth of industrial output and inputs, 1952–1978*

	Total factor input index assuming labour share of:			Index of output per unit of combined inputs at assumed labour share of:	
	0.6	0.4	GVIO index	0.6	0.4
1952	100.0	100.0	100.0	100.0	100.0
1957	178.3	194.0	233.3	130.8	120.1
1965	427.7	520.2	510.6	119.4	98.2
1978	1246.5	1571.6	1649.2	132.3	104.9
Rates of growth (% per annum)					
1952–78				1.1	0.2
1957–78				0.1	−0.1

Source: Table 11.2.

since 1957 is slightly *negative*. (See Chapter 14 for a comparison with results since 1978.)

Without putting too much stock in the exact figures, then, it seems safe to conclude that most of China's industrial growth has come from increases in productive factors, especially fixed capital (about 70 per cent of the capital measure used here), that very little of it was due to more efficient use of inputs, and that even the growth of labour productivity was achieved principally by increases in the amounts of physical capital per worker (the capital–labour index grew from 100 in 1952 to 373 in 1978). Part of the explanation lies in the structural shift towards more capital-intensive heavy industries—a shift that has in more recent years been criticized as excessive and that has been reversed somewhat (see below).

This is the crux of the problem of 'imbalance' requiring 'readjustment'. Another part of the explanation for the limited growth of efficiency, however, is structural and systemic, meaning that it stems from deficiencies in the system of economic organization, planning, and management that are rather deep-rooted, and that require 'reform' (Sec. 4 below). The tensions and attractions between 'readjustment' and 'reform' were a principal theme of China's search for a new economic strategy after the Third Plenum of the Eleventh Central Committee in December 1978.

Finally, a somewhat unexpected but very serious problem of the post-Mao economy was high urban unemployment. For years China had claimed to have no unemployment problem, but in 1978 discussions of the subject reappeared in the press, and estimates for 1979 of the number of urban unemployed ranged upward from 10 million, or about 9.5 per cent of the estimated urban non-agricultural labour force of 104 million (Emerson 1983:2). Because of inconsistencies in the way unemployment is defined in various localities,

Emerson believes it is 'often substantially overstated in urban areas, perhaps by as much as 50 per cent' (1983:5), although there are some definitional biases that lead towards underestimation, as well. Thus, a consistent and accurate estimate of urban unemployment is not yet available.

Had large-scale urban unemployment existed unknown to the world for so many years, only to be revealed in the late 1970s, or was it a new phenomenon, the product of the changed conditions after 1976? Both explanations contribute to the story. Before 1976, open unemployment was largely avoided, although in part by some heavy-handed procedures. Some 20 million urban residents were sent to the countryside in the aftermath of the Great Leap Forward. Most of these had probably arrived in the cities only recently during the expansionary phase of the Leap. But the 17 million urban educated youth who were 'rusticated' from 1966 to 1976 were town dwellers, most of whom left relatives and friends behind. During this period job placement was handled entirely by state labour bureaux, which were responsible for placing school-leavers of various levels, demobilized soldiers, returned youth from the countryside, and released convicts. The burden on the disorganized state apparatus was excessive, and consequently many job-seekers spent long periods of time 'waiting for employment', either living with their parents or, if this was not possible, working at temporary jobs arranged by neighbourhood committees.

The job placement principle of the Cultural Revolution decade was 'take on all and provide jobs for all'. Although in practice the state's attempt to guarantee full employment fell somewhat short, its recognition of responsibility for this goal was significant and met an expectation historically associated with socalism. However, the means by which this responsibility was carried out cost heavily in efficiency and motivation, it was later claimed. The initiative of both the suppliers and users of labour was sacrificed as enterprises were formally prohibited (although in fact they often violated this structure) from recruiting workers, and individuals from seeking jobs. For reasons to be discussed more fully below, state commitment to placing everyone resulted in general overstaffing (a form of 'disguised unemployment'). The state bureaux, with more than they could handle merely in placing people, often failed to match qualifications with needs, let alone to take into consideration the personal aspirations of job-seekers. (Indeed, during much of the period in question, to harbour such personal desires was evidence of reactionary failure to 'fight self'.) Many workers thus found themselves in jobs that did not use their skills, while at higher professional levels husbands and wives were commonly assigned to positions in widely separated localities. Not the smallest cost in this sytem was borne by those young people who were unemployed for years, 'wasting the best years of their lives and withering their will to forge ahead' (Feng and Zhao 1982:131).[4]

State commitment to full employment does not necessarily imply state monopoly of the allocation of labour. Indeed, China was unusual in this respect among the centrally planned economies. Nevertheless, in the 1980s, as China moved away from full state control of job placement, it also retreated from the full employment commitment (see Chapter 14).

The emergence of large-scale open urban unemployment was occasioned by the progressive breakdown, beginning in 1974, of the movement to send urban educated youth to the countryside. In that year, a number of regulations were adopted to exempt certain categories of young people from being sent down, and, more significantly, to permit those who had already been in the countryside for two years to return if jobs or school acceptances awaited them, if they were ill, or if they had aged or infirm parents. Thus began a flow back to the cities that apparently became a flood after 1978, when most of the 17 million rusticated youth returned home. There they joined more than 10 million former peasants who had found ways to remain in the cities after having been recruited for urban work during the 1966–76 period (Feng and Zhao 1982:126–7, 132). Although it is likely that many of the former peasants had been assigned to jobs that would not otherwise have gone to urban secondary school graduates, there was undoubtedly some overlap, and thus competition, between the two groups for scarce urban jobs. In addition, from 1977 to 1980, between 3 and 5 million new junior and senior middle-school graduates required job assignments each year (net of those recruited into the army, accepted by higher educational institutions, or returned to the countryside). Finally, a backlog of unknown size remained of young people who had somehow avoided rustication and were still 'waiting for employment' in the late 1970s. It was a combination of these various factors, together with the slowdown in economi> growth that accompanied the factional strife of the mid-1970s, that turned a suppressed problem into an open crisis.

There remains the question of why the problem existed in suppressed form in the first place. Undoubtedly, the fundamental underlying factor is the size of China's population relative to that of its non-agricultural labour force, and the continuing gap between urban and rural incomes (see Chapter 10, Sec. 4). This gap implies the persistence at existing relative wages of an oversupply of labour for urban jobs, its size depending on the effectiveness of administrative forms of suppression (such as prohibition of rural–urban migration).

Other factors contributed to heightening the problem. Heavy industry, the favoured sector in China's development strategy, is capital-intensive: according to Chinese studies, Y1 million of fixed assets creates over 800 jobs in the 'nonmaterial production' sector (commerce, services, public utilities, scientific, cultural, educational, and health activities), 257 jobs in light industry, but only 94 jobs in heavy industry (Feng and Zhao 1982:129). Yet, the great bulk of capital investment during the three decades before 1979 went to heavy industry (see Sec. 4 below). Similarly, the decision to do without true production co-operatives had a negative impact on employment. Such co-operatives (or collectives) had tended to locate in labour-intensive sectors neglected by the state-run industries. After 1966 many collective enterprises were 'upgraded' to 'big collectives' (in the belief that these represented a more advanced form of socialism), which subjected them to virtually the same degree of state control as if they had been state enterprises proper. Total urban collective employment rose only by 5.5 million workers between 1966 and 1976, and it fell as a proportion of total non-agricultural employment from 24.3 to 20.9 per cent over the same period (*SYOC* 1982:107). Even the mushrooming rural industries run by communes and brigades contributed fewer than 20 million jobs in 1980 (Walder 1984).

High urban unemployment, stagnating levels of food consumption, deteriorating urban housing conditions, falling real wages, widespread rural poverty, and sluggish productivity growth—all despite rapid economic growth as conventionally measured—must be seen in the context of the debilitating conflict that sapped China's ability to make and carry through economic strategies of any kind for fifteen years. The incompatibility of Mao's political ideology with administrative planning meant muddling through in any case during the years of political conflict and stalemate. But Chinese economists have also traced these results to a number of underlying causes, only some of which can be blamed on 'left' politics or the chaos of the Cultural Revolution years. These causes are grouped in the two categories alluded to earlier: structural imbalances and systemic flaws. The first is seen as a short- to medium-term problem, the second as long-term. Systemic problems—flaws in the planning, management, and incentive systems—give rise to imbalances and dispro-portions; but, at the same time, overcoming such imbalances has been regarded as a precondition for reforming the system. This position raises two logical questions: (1) Can the imbalances be righted while the conditions that create them remain? (2) If the imbalances are redressed, will this 'prove' the lack of need for fundamental reform to the satisfaction of those with vested interests in the current system? As of the mid-1980s, there remained tension between the two goals of strengthened planning and market-oriented reform.

4 Causes: (a) imbalances and disproportions

The principal imbalances are nicely summarized in a *Renmin Ribao* commentary (9 April 1981), which in the style of the times ascribes them all to ' "left" mistakes':

> 'Left' mistakes manifest themselves mainly in high targets, high accumulation, low efficiency, and low consumption; emphasis on capital construction to the neglect of agriculture and light industry; emphasis on production to the neglect of people's livelihood; emphasis on production to the neglect of circulation; and so on. [*Renmin Ribao*, 9 April 1981]

Most of these imbalances are clearly interrelated. Underdevelopment of agriculture is due in part to overemphasis on heavy industry, which in turn helps to explain the inadequate rise in consumer goods production and standard of living.

The slow pace of agricultural growth has been a problem since the mid-1950s. We have already discussed the results in terms of food consumption, especially of the rural population. In addition, good harvests have recurrently stimulated rates of industrial expansion that were unsustainable, leading to subsequent retrenchment and the creation of an unstable pattern of growth. This happened in the late 1950s and early 1960s, when some 40 million peasants were recruited into the non-agricultural economy and then disgorged again. Similarly, a bumper harvest in 1970 induced heavy recruitment into industry in that and the following year, but this was followed by 'a slash in heavy industrial production and a general shrinkage of the scale of capital construction' (Yang and Li 1980:195).

Agriculture's differentially slow growth produced a structural anomaly. While the gross value of agricultural output fell from two-thirds of the combined value of industrial and agricultural output in 1952 to one-quarter in 1979 (Table 11.4), its share of the labour force changed little: about 75 per cent of China's labour force was still employed in agriculture in 1979, down from about 84 per cent in 1952. Over that period, the absolute size of the agricultural labour force increased by 126 million persons.

The impression of rapid decline in agriculture's share of output is exaggerated somewhat by the use of gross values, which inflates industry's relative growth. The structure of net material product shows less dramatic but still substantial change: the share of agriculture falls from about 60 to about 40 per cent, while that of industry proper rises from 20 to 46 per cent.

These structural changes imply a growing divergence between the labour productivity rates in industry and agriculture. A peasant in 1978 produced Y364 of net output value (in 1978 prices), a figure that was only 5 per cent higher than in 1952 (Table 11.5). In contrast, an industrial worker in 1978 produced Y2,809 of net output value, 4 times the figure for 1952 and 7.7 times the 1978 level in agriculture. Such large differences in labour productivity tend to give rise to gaps in personal income.

In fact, although the personal income gap between city and countryside was found to be less than half the size of this productivity ratio (Chapter 10), it was also found to have grown since the 1950s despite quite radical policies to reduce it. To improve income distribution in the face of growing sectoral differences in labour productivity is evidently quite difficult.

China's size dictates that food consumption must basically depend upon domestic production. In 1979 per capita production of foodgrain was 73 per cent of the world average, edible oil 16 per cent, sugar 9 per cent, and meat 41 per cent (Zhou Shulian 1982b:48). While food might have been distributed more evenly in China than in most other low-income countries and the direst poverty found elsewhere avoided, China's generally low level of food consumption remained the biggest and most obvious symptom of economic imbalance.

The neglect of consumption was not confined to food, but was manifested more generally in a long-term tendency towards overinvestment. The rate of investment is expressed in China as the 'accumulation rate', roughly, spending on the acquisition of fixed and working capital as a proportion of net domestic material product. We have seen how this rate was pushed up to no less than 43.8 per cent at the height of the Great Leap Forward (Table 6.4). Chinese economists have argued, however, that there has been a chronic propensity to overaccumulate ever since the First Plan period, with the sole exception of the post-Leap readjustment period (1963–5), when, because of the great

Table 11.4. *Changes in sectoral composition of output and labour force, 1952–1979*

	1952		1957		1965		1975		1979	
	m.	%	m.	%	m.	%	m.	%	m.	%
Labour force	207.3	100.0	237.7	100.0	286.7	100.0	381.7	100.0	405.8	100.0
Agricult.	173.2	83.6	193.1	81.2	234.0	81.6	294.6	77.2	299.3	73.8
Non-agricult.	34.1	16.4	44.6	18.8	52.7	18.4	87.1	22.8	106.5	26.2
	bn.Y	%	bn.Y	%	bn.Y	%	bn.Y	%	bn.Y	%
GVIAO (1970 Y)	103.0	100.0	146.9	100.0	206.8	100.0	450.4	100.0	617.5	100.0
GVAO	65.7	63.8	86.4	58.8	87.1	42.1	128.5	28.5	158.4	25.7
GVIO	37.3	36.2	60.5	41.2	119.7	57.9	321.9	71.5	459.1	74.3
Net material product (current prices)	58.9	100.0	90.8	100.0	138.7	100.0	250.5	100.0	335.0	100.0
Agriculture	34.0	57.7	42.5	46.8	64.1	46.2		39.0	131.8	39.3
Industry	11.5	19.5	25.7	28.3	50.5	36.4		45.0	153.6	45.9
Construction	2.1	3.6	4.5	5.0	5.3	3.8		4.0	13.0	3.9
Transport	2.5	4.3	3.9	4.3	5.8	4.2		4.0	12.1	3.6
Commerce	8.8	14.9	14.2	15.6	13.0	9.4		8.0	24.5	7.3

Sources and notes

Labour force: Emerson (1982:240). The agricultural labour force figure for 1975 is estimated by multiplying the rural commune labour force by 0.984, which is the average for 1970 and 1979 of the proportion of commune labour engaged in agriculture (Emerson 1982:240).

Gross value of industrial and agricultural output (GVIAO): for 1952, the 1957 definition of GVIAO in 1957 prices was first derived from data given in Wiens (1980:70–1). The 1957 GVAO in 1957 prices is also given there. GVAO for 1965 (in 1957 prices) and for 1970 and 1979 (in 1970 prices) are from World Bank (1983, I:327). Implicit price deflators used to put data in 1970 prices are from World Bank (1983, I:282).

Gross value of industrial output (GVIO): ZJN (1981:VI-4). For implicit price deflators see above.

Net material product ('National income' by China's definition): SYOC (1982:20) -contains both absolute figures and percentage shares for all years except 1975. The 1975 shares are from World Bank (1983, I:325).

Table 11.5. *Labour productivity in industry and agriculture, 1952 and 1978*

	1952	1978
Value added per worker (1978 yuan)		
Agriculture	345.8	364.3
Industry	696.4	2809.2
Ratio, industry: agriculture	2:1	7.7:1

Notes and sources: The figures for 1978 are given in Yang and Li (1980:186), which also contains 1978 total net value outputs for the two sectors in 1978 yuan and percentage increases for each, as compared with 1952, in constant prices. From these and 1952 labour force figures given in Emerson (1982:240), the sectoral values added per worker for that year were derived. (The 1952 industrial labour force figure given by Emerson, 2,464,000, should read 12,464,000.)

dislocations caused by the Leap, and under the guidance of a more moderate leadership, the accumulation rate fell to 'only' 22.7 per cent. But during the second half of the 1960s it moved back up to an average of 26.3 per cent, then to 33 per cent in the first half of the 1970s, and finally to another peak of 36.5 per cent in 1978 (Dong 1980:26).

The accumulation rate represents the proportion of material product withheld from consumption and devoted to enlarging productive capacity. The higher the rate of accumulation, the less is available for consumption. Up to a point, restricting consumption to speed up growth is an effective way of increasing future consumption. But beyond that point, it can harm morale and work motivation, push up the incremental capital–output ratio and the gestation period of investment projects, and retard growth. Such is said to have happened during much of the period since the First Plan.

However, some of the problems associated in the Chinese literature with over-accumulation really pertain to large and sudden increases in this rate. For example, the diversion of raw materials and labour to capital construction has periodically left existing factories with excess capacity for lack of materials or power, and agriculture short of labour. Capital construction projects, moreover, often lacked the machinery, materials, and skills required by their expanded plans, and thus took much longer than necessary to complete. Sometimes, as in the case of North China water conservancy projects during the Leap, planning and design for the projects were inadequate, and they ended up doing more harm than good. These are problems of the way in which accumulation was carried out and the rate at which it was sometimes increased, rather than of the high accumulation proportion *per se*. The fundamental criticism of the latter is that it prevented a satisfactory growth of consumption.

Closely connected with over-accumulation is the excessive emphasis on the development of heavy industry. There is no satisfactory definition of 'heavy' and 'light' industry; they correspond only imperfectly to producer and consumer goods sectors, respectively, but it is in this sense that the terms will be used here. Heavy industry, thought of as producer goods production, supplies most of what accumulation purchases. Thus, the two move up and down in tandem.

Yet the Chinese authorities, inheriting from Stalin an implicit sense that—in Bergson's apt phrase—bread was an intermediate good in the production of steel, continued for two decades to drive upward heavy industry's share of total fixed investment in industry: from about 85 per cent during the First Plan period to 89 per cent during 1958–62, to 92 per cent during the post-Leap readjustment and Cultural Revolution years 1963–70; only then was there a retreat to 90 per cent for the first half of the 1970s and to 87 per cent for the second half (*ZTN* 1983:328).

The reasons for this single-minded pursuit of heavy industrialization are easier to suggest than to document. There was the Soviet example of the 1930s, and the sense that national security required a quick accretion of heavy industrial capacity for the military. The conviction that the preservation of national independence depended upon fast economic growth was undoubtedly widely shared by China's leaders. Given the nature of China's system of planning and management, the only obvious way to accomplish this was by means of ever greater investment in producer goods industries; for the alternative—continuous innovation and productivity improvement in existing industry—could not be achieved from the centre.

Finally, the priority given heavy industry, once begun, tended to perpetuate itself via bureaucratic inertia; factions in the bureaucracy associated with heavy industry (e.g., the 'Petroleum Group'—Lee 1983) waxed powerful and were able to protect and enhance their shares of the budget, and of essential raw materials. Less and less rolled steel was allocated to light industry (21 per cent during the FFYP years, only 11.3 per cent during 1971–5), less and less electricity (28 per cent in 1952, 12.9 per cent in 1979) (Zhou Shulian 1982b:49).

Imbalances within heavy industry have been especially serious. Processing capacity has grown much faster than raw and semi-finished materials supplies. At the beginning of the 1980s the processing capacity of China's machine tools exceeded the supply of rolled steel by 'three or four times' (Zhou Shulian 1982b:50). In late 1980 Y50 billion of machinery and equipment was stockpiled in warehouses (an amount greater than that year's total capital construction investment), as were more than 20 million tons of steel (almost a full year's output) which had been produced in unneeded varieties (Riskin 1982:34). Yet there were severe shortages of iron ore, nonferrous metals, construction materials, transport equipment, and energy—all items within the sphere of heavy industry.

The last item on the above list, energy, warrants its own place in the panoply of imbalances. China is the world's fourth largest producer and third largest consumer of primary energy (Smil 1978). Aside from the traditional, solar-based energy sources (plant matter), which continued to predominate in the total energy picture, coal has been the chief modern source for industrialization. This continues to be true despite the rapid growth of oil production from the early 1960s to the mid-1970s, which led to much substitution of oil for coal. Although energy production has grown rapidly—by some 9.6 per cent per year between 1953 and 1978—its growth has been exceeded by that of industrial output (11.2 per cent per year for the same period, by Chinese estimates), with the result that severe shortages of energy were being encountered by the late 1970s. In 1977 the electric power industry generated about 136 billion kWh (6–7 per cent of the US level), 30–40 billion kWh short of current demand (Clarke 1978; Zhou Shulian 1982b:51). As late as 1983, no less than one-fifth of industrial capacity was idle for lack of electric power (Wang and Gu 1983:14). China's 8 million tons of diesel oil annually available to agriculture was sufficient for only fifty-odd days of use by the existing stock of farm machinery, and the nation's farm population was said generally to lack cooking fuel for three months of the year. Available energy was used inefficiently: by China's own admission, in the early 1980s it was consuming twice as much energy per unit of GNP as the average for developing countries (Wang and Gu 1983:14) and four times as much as Japan (Zhou 1982b:52). Clearly, the prospecting, development, production, and conservation of energy had been underemphasized in the process of China's industrialization.

Transport was another sector singled out as a serious bottleneck (e.g., Jiang *et al.* 1980:55), despite rapid development. By the late 1970s the overburdened railroads, carrying half of China's modern sector freight turnover, were at saturation point or beyond in the busiest eastern corridors. Thousands of kilometres of navigable inland water routes had been lost to irrigation, and to hydroelectric and flood control projects. Harbour capacity was limited by the poor transport routes leading to and from the ports. And the road system was still primitive, largely unpaved, and incapable of bearing more than a small share of the total freight burden (Peterson 1982).

In their pursuit of a growing producer goods sector, Chinese planners increasingly shortchanged activities defined as 'nonproductive'. In the classical and Marxian tradition, 'nonproductive' sectors are those that provide services whose values are not directly included in the costs of material products (as, say, freight transport is). Housing, education, medical care, cultural, sports and recreational services, military services, and administration (except within enterprises) are the principal 'nonproductive' services. Investment in this sector (e.g., construction of residential housing, hospitals, schools, and office buildings) constituted over one-third of total capital construction investment in the early days of the People's Republic (1950–2), but fell to between 12 and 15 per cent during 1958–62 and remained at that level (except for a slight rise during the Readjustment of 1963–5) through 1976.

The largest item in this category is housing. The annual average state investment in housing construction fell steadily from Y1 billion in the First Plan period (1953–7) to Y970 million in 1958–62 (the nominal Second Five Year Plan period), to Y930 million in 1963–5, to Y740 million during the Cultural Revolution years of 1966–70. It then rose to Y1.9 billion in 1971–5 (an example of 'premature readjustment'), to Y6.25 billion in 1976–81 (*SYOC* 1982:313), and to Y13.5 billion in 1984 (*ZTZ* 1985:71).

Just as nonproductive investment suffered neglect, so did trade. It might be thought that this activity, concerning the circulation and distribution—as distinguished from the production—of goods, would be included in the 'nonproductive' sector. However, perhaps because in Soviet practice national income (net domestic material product) was calculated at retail prices and thus included commercial costs, trade is considered a 'productive' sector (Nove 1961:253–4). None the less, it has not been a much esteemed sector in the making of planners' priorities.[5]

Commercial activities had been a special province of the petty bourgeoisie. The full public administration of small-scale wholesaling and retailing activities was beyond the capacity of the central planners, who therefore proceeded somewhat more cautiously towards trade than towards industry in the socialist 'high tide' of 1956. Yet, as the 'tails of capitalism', small tradespeople were particularly vulnerable to attack during the more 'radical' periods that followed. Policy towards such persons and their activities fluctuated between harshness and leniency in the years 1957–80 (Solinger 1984), but the end result was a decline in the adequacy of commerce. Table 11.4 shows that the share of commerce in net material product was halved from about 16 per cent in 1957 to 8 per cent in 1975 and fell further to 7.3 per cent in 1979. While the net material product (in current prices) increased by 270 per cent over that period, the absolute value added by commerce increased by only 73 per cent. By 1978 the average worker in retail trade was serving almost twice as many people as in 1957. In many areas there was a sharp drop in the number of shops and restaurants. For example, Liaoning Province, which underwent enormous industrial development, had only one-fifth the number of stores and service shops in 1978 that it had in 1957, and only one-tenth the number of restaurants. In Fuxin, a city of over 500,000 inhabitants, there were but 316 shops in 1978, compared with over 1,000 in 1958, when the city's population was only 140,000. In all of rural China, the number of co-operative shops and restaurants totalled 580 at the end of 1979, down from 40,000 in 1957, 'so that many communes had no shops or restaurants' (Zhou Shulian 1982b:53–4).

This was of course of greatest moment for the population as consumers. Wholesale markets supplying industry had long since been replaced with government material supply bureaux. The effect of the decline in retail trade and service industries was to replicate for the individual household the situation of the industrial enterprise: procurement was elevated to a prime activity and family members became small-scale *tolkachi*, who often had to travel considerable distances to obtain needed goods.

The neglect of trade and services was paralleled by the decline of private self-employment since these activities, together with handicrafts, had been the mainstay of the individual economy. Small trading establishments numbered 2.8 million in 1955 and employed 3.3 million people, while another 6 million were engaged in private handicraft production (Table 11.6). By the end of the socialist 'high tide' in 1956 the combined total of individual workers in these two occupations had dwindled to little more than 1 million; by the end of the Great Leap Forward it had shrunk further, to less than 500,000. After making a recovery during the moderate 'Readjustment' years (1962–5), private trade and

Table 11.6. *Individual workers, 1949–1978 (thousands)*

	Total in cities and towns	Urban and rural	
		Trade, peddling	Handicrafts
1949	7240	n.a.	n.a.
1952	8830	n.a.	n.a.
1955	6400	3300	6044
1956	160	490	544
1957	1040	700	640
1961	1650	130	300
1962	2160	130+	1000
1964	2270	568	n.a.
1965	1710	n.a.	n.a.
1976	190		
1978	150		

Sources: Total in cities and towns: *ZTN* (1984:107); Urban and rural trade, peddling, and handicrafts: Fang (1982:173–4).

N.B. 'Individual workers' refers to owners of small private businesses in commerce, handicrafts, and services and their employees.

handicraft activities were again decimated by the Cultural Revolution and their employment numbered only 190,000 in 1976 before their comeback in the post-Mao era (Tables 14.1 and 14.3). Generally the same story emerges from the figures for total number of individual workers in cities and towns (first column of Table 11.6), which fell from a high of almost 9 million in 1952 to 1 million in 1957, then recovered in the post-Leap years only to shrink again to 150,000 in 1978.

The practical elimination of small family businesses effectively removed from the market a variety of small but important goods and services. The state was not able (or, in some cases, willing) to provide the flexible, diversified, mobile, and dispersed services that had been the province of the individual worker. The collective economy might have done so had it consisted of autonomous, income-maximizing enterprises; but the actual collectives were tightly regulated and supervised by the state, and they lacked both the incentive and the means to replace the small private entrepreneur. The result was a decline in the quantity and quality of consumer goods and services that greatly inconvenienced the average Chinese:

Residents in many large and medium-size cities find it difficult to get clothing made, have their hair cut or styled, eat out in restaurants, buy nonstaple foodstuffs, buy furniture, or get repairs done. But the state and collective enterprises are unable to solve these problems for the time being. [Fang 1982:179]

5   Causes: (b) The economic system and reform

Despite the common reflex of blaming imbalances on the 'left' line, Chinese political leaders and economists began increasingly to acknowledge in the late 1970s that the system of planning and management itself was due for re-examination. They argued that this system, even before the debilitating attacks on it from Mao and the left had begun, had properties that inherently gave rise to imbalance and otherwise limited the growth of efficiency, productivity, innovativeness, and responsiveness to consumer needs and wants. In many respects their criticisms paralleled Mao's, but their proposed remedies differed quite drastically.

The Chinese analysis of the intrinsic problems of central administrative planning regimes is familiar to students of the Soviet and East European economies. In the Chinese case, however, the situation is complicated by the lingering effects of the previous Maoist assault on that same regime, which both aggravated its weaknesses and permitted the impression that a return to the *status quo ante* might substitute for systemic reform.

To the reform-minded, however, the fundamental problem was the over-centralized, administrative nature of the economic management system. The most striking criticism of this system was a political–economic one: that it encouraged dictatorial concentration of authority at the top:

[U]nder a system of centralized authority, decision-making power on [sic] economic development is virtually completely concentrated in party and government leadership organs, and within leadership organs, decision-making power is concentrated in the hands of individual leaders. The will of a minority of leaders occupies a commanding position, while the aspirations and desires of the laboring masses find no opportunity for expression. [Wu and Zhou 1980:L35]

While this is bad enough in itself, it also has a number of unfortunate consequences, including the encouragement of personal cliques, subjective decision-making ('blind guidance'), and the tendency to perpetuate mistaken policies to which the prestige of high leaders has been committed. Perhaps the outstanding example of the last is Mao's turnabout after the Lushan Conference in 1959: in response to Marshall Peng Dehaui's attack on the Great Leap Forward, Mao halted his retreat from its more extreme policies. The scale of subsequent disaster was probably thereby made greater than it would otherwise have been (see Chapter 6, Sec. 5).[6]

However, while reserving ultimate power for a few top leaders, such a system necessarily dispersed much authority because of the sheer impossibility of centralizing the myriad decisions required in a complex economy. 'Centralization by the central government actually means decentralized control by its different economic departments', as Xue (1981:205) put it. Most decisions are therefore made by the commissions under the State Council, the various economic ministries below these, the bureaus responsible for particular trades under the ministries, the finance, trade, materials supplies, and labour departments, and their local governmental counterparts. Each of these administrative systems has its particular interests, and there are no mechanisms forcing it to take account of the needs of the localities with which it deals or of the other systems with which it interacts. The administrative lines of authority are thus arbitrary and cut across 'natural' economic lines of co-ordination, specialization, and division of labour. 'An administrative control which separates the inherent connections between economic operations—this is the basic defect in our economic management system' (Xue 1981:205).

In the view of China's senior and most original economic theorist, Sun Yefang (1908–83), the central administrative planning system derived intellectually from the 'natural economy' school that dominated Soviet political economic thought. Its adherents regarded the production relations in the socialist planned economy as analogous to the technical division of labour in a single workshop, which is managed by administrative means. The category of 'circulation', by which exchanges are carried out between the hundreds of thousands of separate enterprises in an economy, was thus reduced in this view to the physical rationing of materials by a central authority. Sun pointed out the obvious: that, unlike in a workshop, where 'one glance' reveals the precise tasks being performed, 'the social division of labour dispersed over the whole of society is bound to be obscure' (Sun 1979:206). The social division of labour is realized through the sphere of circulation; Sun regarded the essence of the problem of managing a socialist planned economy to lie in the circulation process (Sun 1979:214), which, he claimed, the influence of the 'natural economy' school had caused to be ignored. The problem of constructing a system of resource allocation that was efficient—and in which the separate enterprises recognized and pursued the goal of efficiency—had therefore hardly been studied.

Of the various aspects of efficiency, one—production of the optimum output mix—is generally taken in Western economic theory to mean the output mix chosen by the market in perfect competition with an ideal distribution of income. But on a less demanding level of theory, the central command planning system is accused by Chinese economists of being particularly bad at gearing production to the needs and wants of consumers and producers; 'Since the mechanism of the marketplace could not operate normally, the needs of society and of its members could not be promptly reflected . . . The divorcing of production from demand became a common phenomenon' (Wu and Zhou 1980:L34).

The 'divorcing of production from demand' is but another name for the chronic tendency towards imbalance between industries and sectors. China's economists do not agree on the extent of culpability for such imbalance of the system itself, as distinct from incompetent use of it. One, for instance, points out that

Some countries have established largely the same economic setup as China, but they have never been bothered by economic disproportions to such a serious extent. This shows that the present proportions in China are an abnormal phenomenon which is not a necessary concomitant of her economic setup, and that they can be remedied even without a change in the latter. [Zhang Zhuoyuan 1982:19–20]

However, an opposing opinion holds that

the management system's repudiation of the regulatory function of the marketplace had
to lead inevitably to a proportional imbalance among the various sectors of the national
economy . . . Because such a system manages the economy through the administrative
system and administrative divisions, each sector and each region becomes a system
formed in and of itself, which *must inevitably* destroy the inner coherence and proportional
relationships of the national economy. [Wu and Zhou 1980:L34; emphasis added]

The latter position amounts to an assertion that central command planning
inevitably gets co-opted by the bureaucratic requirements of its executive
agencies to the detriment of macroeconomic rationality.

As for another basic aspect of 'efficiency'—producing at least cost—the
administrative planning system deprived the direct producers of both the
incentive and the means to seek and implement least-cost solutions. The state
granted virtually all fixed assets and most working capital to state enterprises
free of charge, providing no material incentive for the enterprise to economize in
the use of capital. On the contrary, faced with the unpredictability of obligatory
production quotas and of state supplies of necessary materials, the enterprise
had every reason to build up excessive inventories of fixed and working capital,
which was free, from its point of view.

On the other hand, should the enterprise nevertheless seek to improve its
equipment, institute technical innovations, or remedy material supply
deficiencies, it had few options to exercise its own initiative. It had to apply to
the state for permission to carry out any such project and for funds to finance it.
Such applications 'are often turned down by the authorities or passed on to
different levels for approval over a long time' (Xue 1981:214)—sometimes as
long as six months (Zhou Shulian 1982b:104). Not only net investment was
thus monopolized by the state; even replacement investment was at first so
handled. Depreciation allowances (except for a small amount earmarked for
'major repairs') reverted to the state as revenue, and replacement investment
had to be separately authorized and financed by a new budget grant. Moreover,
the depreciation allowance was unusually small; China has worked with a fixed
capital lifetime of around twenty-five years, implying a depreciation rate of 4
per cent. This would have discouraged technical advances embodied in new
generations of equipment, had enterprises been able to retain and employ the
fund for capital renewal. As for the small 'major repairs' fund kept by the
enterprise, policy discouraged its use to install more advanced technology
(Xue 1981:214).

The state enterprise thus found itself in the following position. Its gross
output targets, as well as seven other norms (output mix, quality, materials
consumption, fuel and power consumption, labour productivity, costs, and
profit), were handed down from above, as were virtually all funds required to
fulfil them. Its investments were determined and financed by the state, and its
output was appropriated by state material supply or commercial organs. Profits
(if any) reverted automatically to the state, while losses were just as
automatically subsidized. The enterprise personnel thus had little reason to be

concerned about the efficiency of their operations or the attractiveness of their product to users; nor had they incentive to innovate. But there was a strong impulse to hoard materials and to integrate vertically (e.g., by establishing general machine shops) to hedge against the vagaries of a capricious supply system.

By the 1970s the system had become somewhat less rigid than the above account, which is based on standard and caricatured indictments of the 1979–81 period, models it. We have seen (Chapter 8) that, as part of the decentralization reforms of 1970–3, local enterprises and (especially) their state supervisory organs were allowed to retain enterprise depreciation funds for their own use. As a result, another category of investment—for 'replacement and improvement' (*gengxin gaizao*), and originally intended to ensure the adequate replacement and modernization of worn out equipment when depreciation funds were not locally controlled—now became redundant. However, this category was not eliminated but instead became a financing source used by local authorities to build new facilities and expand existing ones (Naughton 1983:3–5). Naughton estimates that, in the 1971–5 period, depreciation reserves and 'replacement and improvement' financing (other than that provided by the central budget) together amounted to an average of about Y16 billion per year, or more than one-third of total fixed investment and almost half of the formal state capital construction category (Naughton 1983:3–5).[7]

Thus, local authorities had gained considerable control over fixed investment during the late Mao years. It is true that depreciation funds were partially recentralized in 1978, but they were rapidly returned to local control thereafter (Naughton 1983:7–8). However, it appears that, as in the case of the 1957–8 reforms, the main beneficiaries were local government organs rather than the enterprises themselves.

Criticism of the central administrative management system, particularly with respect to the suppression of enterprise initiative, has often been linked to complaints about the labour allocation and wage systems. That is, the absence of enterprise incentives is held to explain egalitarian modes of distribution within enterprises ('everyone eating from the same big pot'), on the grounds that material incentives to stimulate more efficient work are pointless if the parent enterprise derives no benefit therefrom (e.g., Ma 1983:94). The need to differentiate wage incomes has been repeated as catechism, and against much evident resistance from workers and managers, without much serious consideration of the international literature about work motivation. More to the point, the state's monopoly of labour allocation, a respect in which the Chinese system has been more rigid than those of the Soviet Union and Eastern Europe, where labour markets function, has also come under challenge. The chief objective appears to be to permit the hiring and firing of workers by enterprises, although the objective of achieving a better fit between vacancies and qualifications is also mentioned.

The basic message in the criticism of the economic system is the need to separate the political–administrative functions of government from the economic functions of enterprises. In the simile of one prominent reformer (Jiang 1980:59), the enterprises should be like living cells in an organism, each with its own metabolism, growing and reproducing itself yet linked in a complex division of labour with all the others; instead of like bricks in a wall, lifelessly put in place by the builder. Enterprises should in this view be given considerable independent authority over ordinary production, marketing, and distribution, while government agencies confine themselves to forming and implementing macroeconomic policies. Market mechanisms should govern a considerable share of the allocation of goods and services; and the price and income distribution systems should be reformed to permit a close relation between the performance of enterprises and of their workers and staff on the one hand, and of their incomes on the other. The nature of the specific reforms that were proposed and that began to be implemented after 1979 is examined in Chapter 14.

While the relationship between state and enterprise was most at issue, that between administrative levels of the state was also called into question. We recall that this issue had arisen several times before, notably in 1957–8 (decentralization and expanded local powers), 1961 (recentralization and diminished local powers), 1964, and 1970 (decentralizations). From 1971 to 1973, the previous system of unified central control over budgetary revenue and expenditure was relaxed to allow provincial governments to keep a portion of their revenues. Provincial obligations to the centre for handing over revenue and incurring expenditures were fixed, and the provinces could retain for their own use additional revenues and any savings on their expenses. They were also allowed to take charge of capital construction within their territories. However, after the ferment that followed Mao's death and the purge of the left leadership, it was decided that another recentralization was needed to 'conquer the half-planned half-anarchic situation' then thought to prevail (He 1980:37). In 1978 alone almost 1,000 enterprises reverted to central control and were again directly supplied by central organs.

Thus, by 1979 China had already experienced 'two sendings down and two takings up', as enterprises were shuttled back and forth between central and local authorities. This had mostly to do with the division of responsibility between administrative levels. 'According to my understanding, we never relaxed our control over the autonomy of enterprises, communes, and brigades . . . between 1958 and 1976 (Xue 1982b:95). The result, according to the critics, was simply an alternation between stultifying centralization and economic anarchy, as '[centralized] control caused lifelessness, decentralization caused chaos, chaos led to recentralization, which again produced lifelessness.'[8]

The average province is a very large unit with many thousands of enterprises, making direct provincial operation of enterprises clumsy and inefficient. In addition, local control, like that of the centre, cut across rational economic links, but from a different direction. Instead of limiting exchange relations to the vertical dimensions of an industrial ministry, it confined them to geographic boundaries. For example, when China moved once again after 1978 to expand provincial financial and management powers, Jiangsu was made a pilot province (Xue 1982b:99). The First Ministry of Machine Industry wanted Jiangsu, which was relatively industrialized, to become an automotive supplier to other provinces. Jiangsu had built this industry on a scale just sufficient for its own needs, so expansion required new investment. Under the new rules of the decentralized system (*Kuaikuai wei zhu guanli*, or 'management mainly along horizontal lines'), new investment financing from the Ministry required compensation in the form of a cutback in the share of provincial revenue kept by Jiangsu. This entailed complex negotiations. Also being horizontally allocated were raw materials, and since 'investment money is of no use without the materials', supply arrangements had to be worked out separately.

Evidently, local control hampered the development of exchange relations between localities. Jiangsu and other advanced areas saw further growth slowed by the lack of access to markets and resources across their borders, while backward areas used this protection to establish technologically inferior enterprises of their own. Just as vertical management had fostered comprehensive and self-sufficient enterprises within administrative sectors, so horizontal management encouraged these characteristics within localities. In their different ways, each approach obstructed the development of special-ization on a national scale (He 1980:38).[9]

When Xue Muqiao visited Jiangsu in 1979, he found the provincial authorities satisfied with their newly expanded powers, but officials of cities and towns such as Wuxi, Changzhou, and Suzhou less pleased; they had simply witnessed the replacement of one master (the centre) by another (the province). As for individual enterprises, 'They said it did not matter whether the Center or localities were in control. All they knew was that enterprises were not allowed to exercise their own control. The key should be enterprise management power' (Xue 1982b:99).

In the view of the reformers, both administrative decentralization and enterprise subordination worked to produce the chronic overinvestment that was now so widely deplored. On the one hand, the localities were eager to set up profitable industries in order to establish their own revenue bases and expand their bureaucratic domains. On the other, dependent enterprises whose investment financing came free from the Treasury always wanted more and were under little pressure to use it efficiently. This rule seemed to operate whether they were subordinate to central or to local authorities.

The intrinsic problems of a central administrative planning regime were aggravated in China by the lingering effects of the Maoist assault on it. This gave rise to the view, convenient to some, that a return to command planning without Maoism was a viable substitute for systemic reform. We recall that during the Great Leap Forward, according to Mao, the drawing up of material balances had for a while simply ceased. The different sectors of the economy steamed ahead on their own without regard to their markets and suppliers. A similar thing happened during at least parts of the 1966–76 period: 'Those who were in charge of planning and production or construction no longer devoted themselves to the study of comprehensive balancing', which predictably led to 'chaos in the economy' (Liu 1979:L4).

'Comprehensive balancing' is the heart of central command planning. How could a planned economy hope to do without it? There was no conscious intent to abandon planning *per se*; rather, the prevailing conditions made it impossible. First, a large part of the staff that prepared, implemented, and supported planning was attacked and purged. The work of the State Statistical Bureau (SSB) virtually ground to a halt, according to Sun Yefang (who was a former deputy director): 'The statistics work of the whole country was literally suspended for almost 3 years [1966–9]' (Sun 1981). During the 1966–76 period statistical offices were disbanded, personnel were transferred, and 'large quantities of materials were burned.' Even in 1981, the SSB boasted a grand total of only 193 statistical workers at the national level (Sun 1981:5). Accurate information is the first prerequisite of physical planning; it is difficult to obtain under the best of circumstances because of the sheer quantity of relevant data, constant change in demand and supply conditions, and the motivation that many have to misreport information. Without a statistical system, planning is out of the question.

Second, the atmosphere of populist enthusiasm generated by Maoist ideology clashed with the requirements of central planning: detailed delineation of responsibilities for collecting, processing, and transmitting information and directives and checking results. Such functions, even when not formally abandoned, became low-priority tasks, often ignored in the heat of the moment.

Third, as a means of dealing with the passivity ordinarily imposed by central planning on all but the top decision-makers, Mao and the left advocated 'active' (or 'positive' or 'long-term') balance as opposed to 'passive' ('negative' or 'short-term') balance (see Introduction to Chapter 6). 'Active' balancing meant planning according to the capacity of the more advanced sectors and units, whereas 'passive' balancing was based on that of the weaker links. The point of the former was to use gaps in the plan to put pressure on the weaker units to mobilize their forces and catch up. Behind this idea lay Mao's dictum that balance is always 'relative and temporary' while imbalance is 'absolute and constant'. In the mood of the 'left' periods, this idea was easily misunderstood to mean that imbalance was desirable and correcting it unnecessary.

Together, these various objective and subjective factors explain why at certain times planning was virtually abandoned and the economy left without a co-ordinating mechanism. In looking back at these experiences and the conditions they were reacting to, it seems that local initiative could be obtained only at the cost of economic anarchy, while cohesion and order exacted the price of rigid passivity below the top. What China's particular contribution to the experience of centrally planned economies consisted of was an unusual tolerance of macroeconomic disorder in the pursuit of certain populist values ('revolutionizing the relations of production'). Ironically, that very disorder provided an irresistible argument for the reimposition of centralized control, but ineffectively (without the prerequisite means), and in direct contradiction to the prevailing ideology. The gap between ideology and reality allowed the actual use of power to be extremely arbitrary, and of course it also effectively helped to discredit the ideology.

Notes

1. Chen Yonggui, former leader of the Dazhai brigade, was in 1976 a member of the Politburo and a Vice-Premier. He was later dropped from the leadership.
2. The term 'rations' (*kouliang*) is used in the source. 'Rations are usually lower than total grain consumption' (see Walker 1982:578–82). The calorie figure in the text thus probably understates actual consumption in the affected regions.
3. For definitions and discussion of these terms, see Ishikawa (1965:Chapter 3). The English-language Chinese source (*SYOC* 1982:8) uses the term 'circulating funds'. The Chinese original—*liudong zijin* (see *ZJN* 1981:VI–18)—is translated 'working funds' by Ishikawa, who states that it 'denotes working capital . . . from the enterprises's point of view' (Ishikawa 1965:105–6). It thus includes stocks of raw materials, goods in process, fuels, etc. I have used a measure of capital that includes year-end value of fixed capital net of depreciation plus 'quota working capital', rather than an alternative series containing year-end gross value of fixed capital at original prices as used by Field (1982), both to take some account of depreciation and to include in the capital measure working capital, which seems to have constituted a growing percentage of total industrial capital. In practice, the sum of these two components is very close to that of gross fixed capital at original prices, so the choice of measure makes little difference to the results.
4. Much of this discussion of unemployment is based on Feng and Zhao (1982).
5. Wiles (1962:65–6) remarks that, contrary to expectation, the Marxian definition of 'productive' is not necessarily 'emotive' in bringing excluded activities into disrepute; '[E]ducation and medicine . . . have been highly regarded [in the Soviet Union] and rapidly expanded.'
6. See MacFarquhar (1983) for a detailed examination of this episode.
7. The capital construction category included investment financed from depreciation funds but not 'replacement and improvement' investment (see Naughton 1983).
8. '*Yi tong jiou si, yi fang jiou luan, yi luan you tong, yi tong you si*' (He 1980:37). Cf. Jiang Yiwei's slightly different version of this aphorism, cited in Chapter 9, Section 1.
9. There is of course a classic and reputable argument for protecting nascent industries in economically backward areas (Bagchi 1983:17). Protected local industries in China had important external benefits unmentioned by their critics. Moreover, as I have argued elsewhere (Riskin 1969, 1971, 1979), from the viewpoint of the localities there was rarely a choice between establishing an industry and buying its product from an efficient plant located elsewhere. The usual choice was to have the industry or do without the product altogether.

CHAPTER 12

RURAL REFORM, 1979–1984: DISMANTLING THE COMMUNE

1 Introduction: the Third Plenum

Virtually all Chinese discussions of economic policy in the early 1980s cited the Third Plenum of the Eleventh Central Committee in December 1978 as the critical turning point. At this meeting Chen Yun was elevated to membership in the Politburo and made a vice-chairman of the Central Committee and first secretary of a newly created Central Commission for Inspecting Discipline; also, the reputation of the late Marshall Peng Dehuai (among others), ill-fated critic of the Great Leap Forward, was restored. These political acts sent a clear economic message: sobriety, balance, and proportion were back in favour.

The Third Plenum officially closed the campaign to discredit the ousted leadership, declared that the era of turbulent class struggles was over, and turned the focus of party work to economic development ('Communiqué of the Third Plenary Session' 1978). But its tone in dealing with economic matters was a far cry from that of Hua Guofeng's Ten Year Plan speech at the beginning of the year (see Chapter 11, Sec. 2). Reflecting the influence of Chen Yun, the Plenum's final communiqué barely mentioned the ambitious modernization programme only recently adopted. Its sections on economic policy took a different line entirely.

Passing quickly over the economic plans for 1979 and 1980, which were said to need revisions,[1] the communiqué got directly to the point: the economy was beset by major imbalances and by 'some disorder in production, construction, circulation, and distribution'; moreover, there were longstanding problems of livelihood affecting both urban and rural populations. The objective for the next few years therefore was to solve these problems, achieve 'comprehensive balance', and thus 'lay a solid foundation for rapid development' ('Communiqué' 1978). To anyone who had followed the policy conflicts and shifts of previous years, these formulations, particularly the strategic position of the key words, 'comprehensive balance' (Chen Yun's trademark) and the stress given to merely *laying a foundation* for fast growth, signalled a turn towards consolidation and restraint.

In moving away from rapid growth, the Third Plenum concentrated on elements of what would be called reform rather than readjustment.[2] The chief planks in its economic programme were: (1) attacking the over-concentration of authority in economic management; (2) reforming the commune system in agriculture and improving farm incentives; and (3) raising living standards. The first objective was seen partly in terms of another decentralization to both local governments and enterprises. More interestingly, however, and reminiscent of the 'trusts' debated in the early 1960s (Chapter 7), the communiqué called for the transfer of economic management functions from party and government organs to 'such enterprises as specialized companies or complexes'. Here again was the idea of professionalizing economic management and removing it from direct party or government control, but as yet without an expanded role for the market.

It is with respect to agriculture that the real shock came. First, the Third Plenum decided to distribute nationally, 'for discussion and trial use', two draft documents: 'Decisions of the Central Committee of the Communist Party of China on Some Questions Concerning the Acceleration of Agricultural Development' ('Zhonggong Zhongyang . . .' 1981), and a revised and updated version of the 'Regulations on the Work in the Rural People's Communes' (1979)—the famous 'Sixty Articles' of the early 1960s. The quiet act of distributing two draft documents turned out to be the first step in the metamorphosis of the commune system and the partial decollectivization of agricultural production, developments which will be discussed in the balance of this chapter.

Second, the Plenum decided to raise farm prices sharply. Grain quota purchase prices were increased by 20 per cent, beginning with the summer harvest of 1979, with an additional 50 per cent premium for above-quota sales. Purchase prices of cotton, oil-bearing crops, sugar, and other farm and side-line products were also raised. The average price increase for all agricultural purchases was about 22 per cent (Cheng 1983:19). Smaller price hikes followed in subsequent years, and the proportion of state purchases at above-quota and negotiated prices also rose from negligible levels in 1977 to reach 60 per cent in 1981 (Travers 1984:242). The resulting average purchase price increases in the years 1980–4 for farm and subsidiary goods were as follows (*ZTN* 1984:425; SSB 1985:VI):

1980	7.1%
1981	5.9%
1982	2.2%
1983	4.4%
1984	4.0%

Third, the Plenum forbade infringement by higher authorities on the rights of commune sub-units, especially the production team. Although all use of team resources (including labour), at least since the original 'Sixty Articles' of the post-Leap period, was supposed to be agreeable to the team and based upon mutual benefit and the 'exchange of equal values', in reality these principles had been widely violated. Higher-level cadres often commandeered team labour, funds, and materials and regularly dictated planting and production targets on behalf of the state. Such practices were now (again) prohibited. Later editorials on the Third Plenum decisions stated the 'imperative' that relations between collective units and between the state and collectives be those of commodity exchange, and that teams have 'the right to grow what they think fit', to make their own decisions concerning production methods and income distribution, and 'to ignore arbitrary orders from leading organs or leaders' ('China to Speed Up Agricultural Development' 1979). These Third Plenum decisions signalled the party leadership's thinking about the problem of agriculture; they ratified, directed, and in some cases trailed behind events that were rapidly changing the face of Chinese agriculture.

During 1978–80 the limit on the size of private plots was raised, the policy of enforced self-sufficiency in grain gave way to one of encouraging a diversification of production and the development of family side-lines, and rural free markets proliferated in which side-line and private plot output could be bought and sold. During the 'Cultural Revolution decade' private plots had averaged 5–7 per cent of cultivated land and had been under pressure in some areas. With the future premier, Zhao Ziyang, leading the way with 'experiments' in Sichuan Province, this limit was progressively raised until decollectivization began to erode the distinction between collective land and private plots. Limits on what could be produced on these plots were also relaxed (Khan and Lee 1983:14–15).

With the easing of the pressure to produce grain and the encouragement of specialization and division of labour, many of the rural counties that had been impoverished by the former policy now recovered rapidly. Previously unable to exploit their comparative advantage in such commercial products as sugar and cotton, they used their new freedom to bring about large increases in per capita income (Chapter 10; Lardy 1983a: Chapters 2, 5). Nationally, while gross agricultural output was growing by very high rates (see below), side-line production and animal husbandry grew even faster, rising respectively from 14.6 and 13.2 per cent of GVAO in 1978 to 19.4 and 15.0 per cent in 1984 (see Table 12.2). Not only were rural free markets expanding to absorb part of this output, but from early 1979 peasants were also able to sell their goods at private markets in towns and cities (Khan and Lee 1983:15).

Of the many changes occurring in the countryside, however, the two most fundamental were the virtual decollectivization of work organization and the end of the commune as a composite unit combining political and economic authority.

2   The decollectivization of agriculture

'Household responsibility systems' (HRSs), which became nearly universal in the countryside by the end of 1982, were not in fact sanctioned by the Third Plenum.[3] Article 31 of the original '60 Articles' of 1962 ('Nongcun Renmin Gongshe . . .' 1962) permitted the contracting of output between the production team and the individual household. Not so the new version distributed by the Plenum ('Regulations . . .' 1979:105): 'It is forbidden to fix output quotas or to distribute the land according to the individual households.' But the new 'Sixty Articles' did permit quotas to be set for small work groups within the team. Under this system of 'contracting output to the group' (baochan daozu), work-points, inputs, and output would be agreed to by the group and the production team, and there might be a bonus for overfulfilment. Planning, the control of tools and draught animals, irrigation, farmland capital construction, and the distribution of income remained in the hands of the production team, except that the division of work-points among members of a small group was now left to the group.

The small group responsibility system was thus a relatively gentle break with the past. It maintained the major landmarks of collectivism while establishing a closer link between work and reward, in keeping with the slogan (much emphasized by the reformers), 'from each according to his ability, to each according to his work'. Its difference with Cultural Revolution ideology lay principally in its rebuff to the equation of socialist advance with large-scale collective units.

But the small group was merely a way-station on the quick trip back to the household. Experiments with contracting output to the individual household (*baochan daohu*) had already begun in Anhui Province at the time of the Third Plenum, and by the end of 1979 16 per cent of Anhui's teams were practising it (Watson 1983:712). By the time the Fourth Plenum formally approved the new 'Sixty Articles' in September 1979, they no longer contained the prohibition on household quotas (Zweig 1982:69).

In late September 1980 the Central Committee issued Document 75, 'Announcement Regarding Several Issues Concerned with the Further Strengthening and Perfection of the Production Responsibility System in Agriculture' ('Zhonggong Zhongyang Banfa . . .' 1981). Acknowledging that there was an 'extensive debate' going on among cadres and masses over whether contracting to the household was permissible, Document 75 for the first time embraced it as central government policy[4] in two kinds of circumstances: (1) in poor and backward areas, where the population had 'lost faith in the collective', and (2) where household contracting had already been carried out and found satisfactory. In general, however, where collective agriculture was firmly established and production had increased, household responsibility should not be implemented ('Zhonggong Zhongyang Banfa . . .' 1981:7/52). However, the document provided a quite transparent invitation to circumvent this stricture; for, if the second clause sanctioned prior violations of it, why should future ones not also be forgiven? Also, the document permitted a spectrum of less radical systems of household responsibility (e.g., for short-term specialized tasks), which could easily be used to disguise adoption of the genuine article.

Under the indicated constraints. Document 75 permitted both contracting output to the household (*baochan daohu*) and the more radical system of contracting everything to the household (*baogan daohu* or *da baogan*). The first allowed the household the use of a particular piece of land; a given amount of its output would go to the team in exchange for an agreed number of work-points. The household might be allowed to keep for its own disposition any surplus output, or it might receive a bonus for overfulfilment; it would also be penalized for a deficit. Either the household or the team could be responsible for providing current inputs (seed, fertilizer, insecticide, etc.) Plans for planting, irrigation, and the use of draught animals and machinery remained under team control.

Also, the value of the work-point remained dependent upon total team output.

Thus, there was now a contradiction between the collective arrangement of distribution and the privatization of production: the income of each family remained dependent upon the efforts of others, but the individualized labour process did not foster the group morale that might make such interdependence work on behalf of diligence (the 'Dazhai spirit'). On the other hand, by linking the number of work-points awarded unambiguously to output, *baochan daohu* did avoid the opposite tendency of solidary organization: to minimize social friction by giving every member (more or less) the same income. Which of these characteristics had been dominant in the years of collective agriculture? Had closely linked fates produced an impetus towards collective advance and discipline of slackers (Riskin 1975b), or a weakening of work incentives and a palsy of creative effort? There must have been great variation in the effectiveness of collective organization, but it appears that the latter problem was widespread. To realize the positive potential of collective solidarity demands collective autonomy and a supportive environment. With the state dictating cropping plans and putting arbitrary caps on team income, with unfavourable terms of trade between inputs and outputs, and with the denial of opportunities for specialization and exchange, collective agriculture in many places turned passive and uninspired.

Baogan daohu resolved the tension between private production and interdependent distribution by privatizing distribution. In this system, draught animals, tools, and equipment are divided among households. The team retains planning authority in setting sales quotas and tax obligations for the households. However, this authority entails the power to allocate profitable activities among households. Emerging from an era in which efficient allocation of agricultural resources had been deliberately suppressed in the name of grain self-sufficiency, China was now rife with opportunities for making big profits quickly by producing items in short supply. The authority to allocate such opportunities meant a considerable retention of local cadre power in the villages.

After meeting its sales and tax obligations and paying a contribution to the team to maintain some collective services, the household is free to dispose of its output as it wishes. It may sell to the state at above-quota prices and, beyond that, at still higher 'negotiated' prices; or it may sell in the free market. Work-points are eliminated.

Baogan daohu resembles tenant farming with the collective and state as landlord. Because the 'rent' (agricultural tax plus contribution to collective plus the tax implicit in low-priced quota sales) is fixed, while access to the higher prices from above-quota, negotiated, and free market sales is achieved only with higher output, increased productivity brings the household a more than proportional increase in income. 'In this sense, the principle of distribution goes beyond the officially endorsed one of "to each according to his work" ' (Khan and Lee 1983:33, 36). Land was originally to be distributed on an equal per capita basis, or according to available labour power, number of adult family members, or adult equivalents (children as fractions of adults), or in a manner based on these factors in combination. Because quality as well as quantity must be fairly distributed, fields were again broken up into parcels in many areas.

In early 1983 the Central Committee issued the first of two watershed directives labelled 'Document No. 1' (the second was issued at the beginning of 1984—see below), which further ratified the development of the HRS as the dominant mode of rural organization. Document No. 1, 1983 (CPCCC 1983) explicitly promoted HRS ('We should actively support the masses' demand for adopting this practice wherever they are'—p. K3). It permitted individual farm households to hire labour, buy and own motor vehicles and farm machinery, freely market their surpluses of goods subject to state quota, and transport goods long distances and across administrative boundaries to market.

Document No. 1, 1984 ('Zhonggong Zhongyang . . .' 1984; CPCCC 1984)[5] added several important provisions to the now explicit party endorsement of household contract farming. In order to prevent predatory use of land and encourage its improvement, it lengthened the duration of contract to 'more than 15 years' (p. 133) for ordinary crops, and longer for those with long gestation periods. It encouraged the concentration of land in the hands of more efficient producers by permitting lease-like arrangements between households; and it promoted the free flow of peasant investment into various kinds of private and co-operative enterprises (p. 133).

Both documents favoured the trend towards specialization among peasant households, which began to

contract mountain forests, orchards, tea plantations, mulberry fields, beaches, fishponds, herds of livestock or various kinds of workshops from the collective; or they engage independently in such undertakings as raising chicken[s], ducks, rabbits, pigs, or cows as well as weaving, processing, transportation, repair, services, and commerce. [Lin 1983:118]

Such specialized activities offer opportunities to earn higher incomes than contract farming, and the state hopes that many households will find it advantageous to give up their contracted land and devote themselves fully to the more lucrative activity (see Sec. 4.4). In addition to peasants who contract their specialized activities with the collective and use collectively owned equipment, increasing numbers have been striking out on their own as private entrepreneurs ('self-managing' households), often adding their private activities to their contract farming.[6] Such diversification is seen as a means of relieving population pressure on the land as well as raising rural incomes. At the end of 1984, about one-quarter of the rural labour force was said to be working in industry, construction, transport, commerce, catering, and services (*BR*, 24 December 1984:10), and specialized households of all kinds were estimated to account for 14 per cent of all rural households nationally and almost 33 per cent of households in developed coastal provinces such as Jiangsu (Delfs 1984b:68).

The HRS quickly became the overwhelmingly dominant form of organization in agriculture. In October 1981, 97.8 per cent of basic accounting units in China were on some form of responsibility system, 45 per cent were on a household system, and 38 per cent were contracting everything to the household. The more limited *baochan daohu* system seems to have peaked at 17 per cent in the spring or summer of 1981, thereafter declining in favour of *da baogan*. By mid-1982 the HRS had been adopted by 74 per cent of basic accounting units (by now a term of questionable accuracy, since the basic income-earning and -distributing unit had become the household rather than the team)[7] and this figure had grown to 93 per cent by May (Watson 1983:719; *BR*, September 1983) and 98 per cent by November of 1983 (*BR*, 28 November 1983:19).

3 Agricultural performance after 1979

The rural reforms can be broken down into several distinct aspects: (1) substantial purchasing price increases for farm products; (2) increased independence of decision-making authority for the collective; (3) the replacement of a policy of forced local self-sufficiency in grain with one of encouraging diversification and specialization; and (4) rapid decollectivization of the labour and income distribution systems. These changes were accompanied by a dramatic improvement in production performance, the broad dimensions of which are shown in Table 12.1. Agricultural gross output value (GVAO) grew by no less than 9 per cent per year between 1978 and 1984, an unprecedented accomplishment in China for so sustained a period. There is an element of exaggeration in this picture, however: farmers, permitted greater authority over crop acreage, shifted resources from relatively low-priced grain to relatively high-priced economic crops, and from farming generally to more lucrative side-lines; this change in the composition of GVAO in favour of higher priced goods pushes up the overall index. Nevertheless, even taking this bias into account, the growth record after 1978 was remarkable.

Table 12.1 reveals the shift out of crop growing ('agriculture', in the table). The growth rate of 'agriculture', although a very respectable 6.7 per cent, is lower than that of all other components of GVAO; side-line production and animal husbandry did particularly well, with average annual growth rates of 18.6 and 9.4 per cent, respectively. Within the category of 'side-lines', industries formerly run by brigades and teams (now called 'rural enterprises' or 'township enterprises') grew fastest of all, by 21.1 per cent.

The structure of rural production has become more diversified (see Table 12.2 since the 'grain-first' policies of the past were relaxed. In particular, by the early 1980s the share of side-lines (including rural industries) had grown to almost one-fifth of GVAO, while that of crops had fallen to under three-fifths from over four-fifths in the 1950s.

Both rapid growth and diversification in agriculture finally began to improve the quantity and quality of the average diet. Table 12.3 shows per capita foodgrain output growing by 3.8 per cent per year between 1978 and 1983, after remaining almost constant for two decades. This growth rate is far exceeded by those of edible oils (14 per cent), whose production per capita had actually fallen between the 1950s and 1978, and of meat (9 per cent). For the first time in many years, then, China's spartan diet began to improve, with significant additions of

Table 12.1. *Increase in gross agricultural output value and its principal components, 1978–1984 (1978 = 100)*

	GVAO (bns. 1980 yuan)	GVAO	Agriculture	Forestry	husbandry	Side lines		Fishery
						Total	Brigade & team ind.	
1978	197.03	100.0	100.0	100.0	100.0	100.0	100.0	100.0
1979	213.98	108.6	107.2	101.4	114.6	112.4	116.4	96.6
1980	222.30	112.8	106.6	113.7	122.6	133.5	141.2	103.9
1981	236.92	120.2	112.9	118.4	129.8	148.5	158.4	108.5
1982	263.23	133.6	124.3	128.5	147.0	167.4	173.5	121.8
1983	288.18	146.3	134.6	141.6	152.7	200.2	211.3	132.2
1984	329.97	167.5	146.6	164.0	170.6	273.9	307.4	150.0
Average annual rate of growth (%)	9.0	9.0	6.7	8.7	9.4	18.6	21.1	7.1

Source: ZTZ (1983:451); ZTN (1984:133); SSB (1985:I–II).

Table 12.2. *Composition of GVAO, 1952–1984 (percentage share of each branch in GVAO)*

	Agriculture	Forestry	Animal husbandry	Fishery	Side-lines Total	Brigade & team industry
1952	83.1	0.7	11.5	0.3	4.4	
1957	80.6	1.7	12.9	0.5	4.3	
1965	75.8	2.0	14.0	1.7	6.5	
1978	67.8	3.0	13.2	1.4	14.6	11.7
1979	66.9	2.8	14.0	1.2	15.1	12.5
1980	63.7	4.2	15.3	1.7	15.1	11.2
1981	63.2	4.2	15.2	1.7	15.7	11.7
1982	62.8	4.1	15.5	1.7	16.0	11.5
1983	62.1	4.1	14.7	1.7	17.4	12.9
1984	59.3	4.2	15.0	2.1	19.4	15.7

N.B. This table reflects the changing fixed prices in which GVAO has been calculated. 1952–7 figures are based on 1957 prices, 1978–9 figures on 1970 prices, and 1980–3 figures on 1980 prices. Thus, the change in structure does not exactly match Table 12.1's sectoral growth rates, which are based on 'comparable prices'.

Sources: ZJN (1984:III-19); SSB (1985:I–II).

protein and fats. Moreover, cotton production also ended its stagnation with an average annual increase of 17.5 per cent between 1978 and 1984.

Growth rates of these magnitudes imply a serious prior misallocation of resources. Indeed, the many press accounts of peasants becoming instantly wealthy by raising a few hundred chickens or ducks—enterprises that take readily available skills and little capital—reinforce the impression of prior distortion in the mix of farm output. So does the fact that grain production continued to grow at a healthy rate even as diversification continued. A survey in Gansu Province revealed that specialized households with 100–200 chickens recouped their investments in one year and made net incomes of Y1,000–2,000 the second year. 'Raising chickens has become one of the avenues leading to wealth' (Zhou and Du 1984:51). Such opportunities cannot be expected to last very long as peasants rush in to exploit them.

With growing output came higher incomes. Average per capita net real income of a sample household survey of the rural population more than doubled between 1978 and 1984 (ZTN 1984:453; SSB 1985:VIII).[8] The official estimate of real rural per capita consumption shows an increase of 51 per cent between 1978 and 1983 (ZTZ 1984:454). Since consumption is estimated using the personal consumption component of 'national income', however, it omits some fast-growing categories of consumption.[9] The official estimates of real income growth, based on the rural sample surveys, are derived by valuing farm income (including income in kind or production for own use) at current

Table 12.3. *Per capita output of major agricultural products, 1952–1984 (kilograms divided by mean annual population)*

	Grain	Cotton	Edible oil	Pork, beef mutton	Aquatic products
1952	288	2.3	7.4	6.0	2.9
1957	306	2.6	6.6	6.3	4.9
1965	272	2.9	5.1	7.7	4.2
1978	319	2.3	5.5	9.0	4.9
1979	343	2.3	6.6	11.0	4.5
1980	327	2.8	7.8	12.3	4.6
1981	327	3.0	10.3	12.7	4.7
1982	351	3.6	11.7	13.4	5.1
1983	380	4.6	10.4	13.7	5.3
1984	397	5.9	11.6	14.9	5.9
Rates of growth per Annum (%)					
1952–57	1.2	2.5	−2.3	1.0	11.1
1957–78	0.2	−0.6	−0.9	1.7	0
1978–84	3.8	17.5	14.0	9.0	3.3

N.B. Relative growth rates are calculated between endpoint years for 1952–7 and 1957–78. For 1978–84 they are calculated as the average of the five annual percentage increases.

Sources: ZJN (1984:III-21); 1984 figures calculated from outputs in SSB (1985:II) and mean population.

prices—average farm purchase prices rose by 47.7 per cent between 1978 and 1983—and then deflating by a general retail price index, which increased by only 16.7 per cent (*ZTN* 1984:426).[10] This disparity implies that a given physical quantity of self-consumed products was given a higher monetary value each year after 1978. The biggest such effect occurred in 1979, when the average purchase price rose by 22 per cent while the 'cost of living' index increased by only 1.9 per cent. The growth of the self-consumed portion of income was greatly exaggerated in that year.[11] More generally, it is evident that price increases explain a significant portion—on the order of one-fifth—of the increase in rural per capita real income.[12]

Although income inequality has widened in several of its dimensions as a result of the agricultural reforms (see Sec. 4.5), in one respect—namely, the urban–rural gap—it may have narrowed. The sample surveys of households in cities and villages indicate that, while average per capita 'disposable income' of urban workers and employees grew by 42.7 per cent between 1978 and 1983, net per capita income of peasants was rising by 98.4 per cent (*ZTN* 1984:453).[13] Workers and staff are not the only urban residents, but there are unfortunately no data on the net income of the urban population as a whole. As a proxy for consumption, however, we can examine per capita retail sales of consumer goods in urban and rural areas. In carrying out this exercise, Travers

(1984:246) made the startling discovery that almost all of the considerable increase in per capita consumer good sales between 1978 and 1981 had taken place in the villages. Table 12.4, which presents such sales from 1978 to 1984,[14] seems to show the same results for the longer period. Sales in urban areas fall from 48 per cent of total sales in 1978 to 41 per cent in 1984, while rural sales correspondingly rise from 52 to 59 per cent. Since this trend is accompanied by an extraordinarily fast growth in urban population (by 91 per cent over the six-year period), urban sales per capita actually fall, while rural per capita sales increase by 1.3 times. The rapid urbanization seems to have been due to the fast accretion of new towns (*zhen*), especially after the standard for defining a town was relaxed in 1984 (*ZTZ* 1985:18). It is unclear at present whether the retail sales statistics accord with the same definitions of 'urban' and 'rural' as the population statistics, so Table 12.4, which seems to show that country folk have carried away *all* of the per capita increase in purchased consumer goods, should be treated with great caution. Also, this comparison understates both urban and rural purchasing power by omitting increases in housing and other services and possibly free market purchases (Travers 1984:247).[15]

Up to the mid-1970s, agricultural growth had been squeezed reluctantly out of the land with massive increases of inputs, including labour. Rawski (1979b:119–21) has estimated that agricultural labour productivity, measured in terms of gross output value per worker-year, rose by all of 10 per cent between 1957 and 1975; and, because of a large increase in intensity of work measured in terms of the number of days worked per year, the output per worker-day actually declined by 15–36 per cent. His rough estimate of 'total factor productivity' (gross output per unit of combined factor inputs) falls by an average annual rate of between 1.7 and 2.4 per cent. Tang (1980:25) finds 'total factor productivity' falling by an average of 0.6 per cent per year over the longer period 1952–77. In theory, if inputs and outputs are all included and correctly measured, only 'technical regress' can explain a decline in 'total factor productivity'—not a credible explanation in the Chinese case. Using a somewhat different method, Chow (1984: Chapter 3) finds that GVAO actually grew a little faster than inputs through 1980.[16]

This kind of 'growth accounting' is fraught with ambiguities, for example concerning the choice of appropriate weights for aggregating the various inputs. Even apparently straightforward data lend themselves to conflicting interpretations. For example, tractors are treated as an agricultural input, yet in China they are, more often than not, used for transport rather than for farming. The most important input remains labour, which is found by Chow (1984) to have contributed about 29 per cent of the growth of GVAO between 1952 and 1980. But labour is not a homogeneous input of unvarying quality and intensity. Its effectiveness, and thus measured 'total factor productivity', is influenced by institutional arrangements, including work organization, relative prices, the availability of market exchange opportunities, tax rates, and other aspects of the income distribution that affect work motivation. It is precisely these consequential conditions that were evolving rapidly after 1978. The large apparent increases in farm labour inputs after 1957 now appear to have been

Table 12.4. *Retail sales, per capita, in urban and rural areas, 1978–1984*

	1978	1979	1980	1981	1982	1983	1984
Retail sales of consumer goods (bn. Y)							
Total	155.8	180.0	214.0	235.0	257.0	284.9	337.6
In urban areas	74.8	81.5	95.0	102.6	109.0	117.9	137.7
In rural areas	81.0	98.4	119.0	132.4	148.0	167.0	199.9
Urban population (m)	172.45	184.95	191.40	201.71	211.54	241.26	330.06
Rural population (m)	790.14	790.47	795.65	799.01	803.87	783.69	704.69
Price index (1978 = 1.00)	1.00	1.02	1.10	1.12	1.15	1.17	1.20
Per capita retail sales of consumer goods (Y 1978)							
National average	161.0	180.8	197.1	209.7	220.1	237.6	271.9
In urban areas	433.7	432.0	451.2	454.1	448.1	417.7	347.7
In rural areas	102.5	122.0	136.0	148.0	160.1	132.0	236.4

Source: ZTZ (1985:18,82,95). The price index used is that of 'General Index of Cost of Living Prices of Staff and Workers'.

partly illusory—that is, disguised unemployment—because large quantities of labour left food production after the 1979 reforms while foodgrain output was increasing (Table 12.3).[17] Nothing illustrates better the dangers of growth accounting when institutions and motivational conditions are in flux.

Land estimates are subject to their own uncertainties. Satellite photographs and aerial spot-checks by the government have revealed a substantial concealment of cultivated acreage (Egawa 1981:13).[18] Sun Yefang stated in 1981 that such under-reporting had existed 'ever since the policy of emphasizing increased per-acre yield of grain was implemented' and, further, that grain output increases were especially subject to similar under-reporting as a hedge against subsequent declines (Egawa 1981:13). It is thus evident that estimates of sown area, its rate of change, and its relation to grain output are all subject to a wide margin of error.

Nevertheless, it is of interest to see how the apparent relations between inputs and output changed after 1978 in order to get some idea of the effects of institutional changes on the nominal 'productivity' of aggregate inputs. Table 12.5 reveals startling change in this measure after 1978 compared with the previous two decades. Agricultural gross value output (in constant prices) grew by an average of 7.9 per cent per year between 1978 and 1983, which implies an annual increase in labour productivity of 5.8 per cent, or more than 32 per cent for the five-year period. The table shows that, of the inputs listed, only farm machinery and chemical fertilizer grew faster than GVAO. Weights similar to those used by Rawski (1979b:119–21) to construct his aggregate input index for 1957–75 produce an annual growth rate of GVAO per unit of aggregate input of 5.7 per cent for the years 1979–83. Even if the weights are changed to increase the relative importance of fast-growing modern inputs and reduce that of slow-growing traditional ones, the factor productivity growth rate comes down only to 4.8 per cent, still far above its historical level.[19]

In addition, the commercialization rate finally began rising after stagnating since the 1960s (see Chapter 11). The marketed portion of grain output, having declined to only 20 per cent in 1977 (13.3 per cent net of state resales to the countryside), increased to 30.9 per cent (net 22 per cent) in 1983 (*ZTN* 1984:370).[20] The ratio of commodity sales to total agricultural production exceeded 53 per cent in 1984 (SSB 1985:I).

Unfortunately, it is not possible here to decompose the several changes that together produced these remarkable results and assign relative weights to them. It is very likely that part of the spurt in output was due to incentives catching up with the technological and infrastructural improvements of the collective era which were not fully exploited then.[21] More efficient allocation of land and other resources following the abandonment of the 'grain-first' policy also played a major role (Stone 1985:114–17). One significant factor is purely nominal: the change in composition of GVAO as farmers shifted resources from foodgrain to higher-priced products (Tables 12.1 and 12.2). Stone (1985:118) argues that 'by far the most impressive source of growth' has been the doubling in quantity and rise in quality of chemical fertilizers between 1978 and 1984. Generally favourable weather also played a role. Furthermore, it is possible, in view of our

Table 12.5. *Average annual growth rates of farm output and inputs, 1979–1983*

	% per year
Outputs	
Gross value of agricultural output	
(yuan, constant prices)	7.9
Foodgrain (tons)	5.0
Inputs	
Labour (agricultural labour force)	2.0
Land (sown area)	−0.8
Farm machinery (horsepower)	9.0
Draught animals (year-end stock)	4.1
Chemical fertilizer	13.6
Organic fertilizer (see notes)	1.0
Estimated total nutrients (see notes)	6.0
Labour productivity	5.8
Aggregate input	2.0–2.9
GVAO per aggregate input	4.8–5.7

Sources and notes
Gross value of agricultural output: ZTN (1984:132).
Foodgrain: ZTZ (1985:32).
Labour: ZTN (1984:109).
Land (sown area): ZTN (1984:137).
Farm machinery (hp): ZTN (1984:169).
Draught animals: ZTN (1984:159).
Chemical fertilizer: ZTN (1984:175).
Organic fertilizer: assumed to grow at same rate as stock of large animals and pigs: ZTN (1984:159–60).
Estimated total nutrients: estimated as weighted average of growth rates of chemical fertilizer (weight = 0.4) and organic fertilizer (weight = 0.6).
Labour productivity: index of annual growth of GVAO (107.9) divided by index of annual labour force growth (102.0).
GVAO per aggregate input: index of annual growth of GVAO divided by index of annual growth of combined inputs. The range shown results from the use of alternative weights in deriving the aggregate input index. The higher is the weight given to fast-growing, modern inputs, the higher the aggregate input growth and the lower that of GVAO per aggregate input. See text and note 19 to this chapter.

earlier discussion of under-reporting of cultivated land and output, that some of the increase in reported production is purely statistical, that is, represents output that had already existed but had been concealed before the HRS became widespread.

It is interesting, moreover, that the beginning of the spurt in agricultural growth preceded both the price changes and the more radical decollectivization measures. Total agricultural output surged forward by 8.9 per cent in 1978 and 8.6 per cent in 1979 (ZRGGTJ 1979:7; *SYOC 1981* 1982:136). Yet the new prices took effect only with the summer harvest of 1979, and in early 1980 only about 1 per cent of farm households had adopted any form of HRS (Watson 1983:719). While year-to-year fluctuations in agriculture owe much to the weather, and therefore cannot be taken too seriously, this record at least suggests that the acceleration of agricultural growth may have been a response as much to the general relaxation of state pressure on the peasants as to specific policies to enhance incentives, and it raises questions about the attempts by some Chinese economists to argue that the HRS alone explains the improvement.[22]

Indeed, it raises the broader question why the Party decided to bring back individual farming rather than permit and encourage autonomy for the existing collectives. As one scholar puts this question,

If China's Cultural Revolution dampened individual material incentives by promoting egalitarian distribution, generating fears of personal enrichment, and reducing the economic autonomy of rural collectives as well as that of their member households, then why not reverse the trend within the framework of the classical commune system—that is, by improving the work-metering quality of work-point distribution systems, removing the stigma from household enrichment, allowing greater income differentials, raising producer prices where appropriate, and increasing the decision-making autonomy of the collective units? [Putterman 1984:3]

Such a policy would have captured many of the same benefits for production while avoiding problems that privatism has given rise to.

But the Party chose to bypass this course. Against considerable resistance from rural cadres and peasants in successful collectives, the leadership made acceptance of the HRS a question of 'line' that could not be legitimately opposed. Cadres were pressed to break up even strong and viable production teams, making the HRS nearly universal, in the familiar pattern of *yi dao qie* ('a single cut of the knife') (Zweig 1982:75–7; Hinton 1983:2–3; Bernstein 1984a: Part 3). Past collectivization was now seen as a fatally flawed process, both intrinsically encouraging state interference in collective decisions and weakening the link between individual performance and income.

However, new forms of co-operation based upon voluntary association are being encouraged in the countryside. Households may pool savings to buy expensive equipment or pay for plant protection or seed selection services; they may contribute labour or cash to the establishment of a small enterprise, such as a kiln, a construction team, or a flour mill, taking their returns in wages and dividends. Counties or collectives may also be the organizing force; one county in Henan Province established a 2000-member co-operative to mine bauxite and manufacture glazed tiles, exporting its $3.5 million annual output (*CD*, 9 January 1983, also 7 January 1983). Growing rural incomes and the inability of the individual household to provide many of the services previously supplied by the team (or not supplied at all) have raised the demand for goods and services both for production and consumption. On the other hand, the rural population, with more savings, a big surplus of labour revealed by the HRS, more bank credit available, and the right to buy and sell on the market, has been in an increasingly strong position to meet many of these needs itself (Watson 1983:722–4).

The new co-operative combinations and associations are still mostly small in scale, but they are touted for pointing the direction of future co-operation in the countryside. That direction is not entirely clear, however. It remains to be seen, for example, whether the two forms of investment—money and labour—characterizing the new associations will socially differentiate their members as some accumulate shares while others become *de facto* wage-earners. Also unclear is whether the Party, which has encouraged such combinations precisely because of their self-starting character, will continue to favour them if they gain strength and become an economic and political force outside the planning system.

The Party has fostered such a separation of political and economic authority by depriving the communes of their political and administrative powers. The new Constitution adopted in December 1982 mandated the resurrection of the old township (*xiang*) governments to take over these functions; by the end of 1984 this change had been implemented everywhere except Tibet (*BR*, 7 January 1985). The communes as such have virtually disappeared. Commune enterprises have been absorbed into newly formed joint companies with shares owned by the former brigades and teams. Brigade enterprises are now village-level companies owned by the former teams, and/or by households. Such enterprises are now commonly leased out to their managers to run on an independent basis.

In the past, brigades looked after capital construction that transcended team boundaries and communes looked after capital construction that transcended brigade boundaries. This was matched by the authority of the higher levels to mobilize labour from the lower units, the workers receiving work-points from their teams. This system in effect imposed a proportional tax on all team members' collective income. With the dismantling of the commune, it was abolished (Khan and Lee 1983:46).

Officially, these changes were made because (1) the higher levels routinely abused the former system by appropriating labour and funds belonging to lower levels; (2) commune management imposed artificial administrative boundaries on economic exchange and co-operation, preventing a rational divison of labour; and (3) the combination of political with economic authority weakened both at the local level (Khan and Lee 1983:40–5; Shue 1984). But the question raised above concerning the new co-operative associations is also relevant here: will the Party refrain from intervening directly in the affairs of the new 'companies' and 'corporations' and use only economic methods to influence them?

4 Problems of decollectivization

Although the household contract system has been given much of the credit for the success of agriculture since the late 1970s, it is not surprising that such a large and sudden transformation also gave rise to many new problems. This section discusses the most important of these.

4.1   Conflict between plan and market

Although contracting farmers were encouraged to maximize net incomes or profits, these depended upon the structure of prices of outputs and inputs, which did not accurately reflect planners' preferences with respect to the output mix. For example, the area sown to foodgrain fell by 7 million hectares between 1979 and 1982, a decline of about 6 per cent, in defiance of planners' wishes. (However, see the discussion in Section 2 of suspected under-reporting of cultivated land.) Cash crop acreage grew by over 4 million hectares (Table 12.6; also *CD*, 31 December 1983). In 1982 the area sown to winter grain fell by 600,000 ha, while that sown to tobacco was increasing well beyond its planned expansion (*RMRB*, 27 May 1982). Suburban farmers abandoned vegetable farming to engage in more lucrative commercial activities, and a shortage of vegetables developed (Zhang Jingfu 1982:21). In many places, farmers treated contracted land as their own and built houses and put graves on it. Arable land was 'recklessly' taken for other uses, including factories for urban and rural enterprises. In early 1985, arable land was said to be decreasing by an annual rate of 0.5–1 per cent (*CD*, 13 March 1985:3; Hinton 1983:27). All this led to the reassertion of administrative controls on the use of the land and on crop acreage.

The erection of houses and graves on farmland was prohibited (CCPCC 1982:23), and a new national law to protect arable land was prepared in 1985 (*CD*, 13 March 1985); but administrative regulation of cropped area is a touchier matter. A decline in grain output in 1980, chiefly for reasons of

Table 12.6. *Sown acreage of agricultural crops, 1952–1984 (millions of hectares)*

	Total: all crops	Foodgrains		Economic crops	
		Area	% of total	Area	% of total
1952	141.3	124.0	87.8	12.5	8.8
1957	157.2	133.6	85.0	14.5	9.2
1965	143.3	119.6	83.5	12.2	8.5
1978	150.1	120.6	80.3	14.4	9.6
1979	148.5	119.3	80.3	14.8	10.0
1980	146.4	117.2	80.1	15.9	10.9
1981	145.2	115.0	79.2	17.6	12.1
1982	144.7	113.4	78.4	18.8	13.0
1983	144.0	114.0	79.2	17.8	12.3
1984	144.2	112.9	78.3	19.3	13.4

Sources: ZTN (1984:137); ZTZ (1985:30).

weather, temporarily alarmed the leadership, which began urging 'stabilization' of the grain sown area as well as exploring economic means of accomplishing this, such as raising the proportion of higher-priced above-quota and negotiated purchases in grain basket areas. But the reduction in sown acreage had been to some degree an inevitable product of the relaxation of the 'grain first' policy and concomitant encouragement of diversification. Grain output resumed its upward trend in 1981 despite further reductions in acreage.

Nevertheless, the leadership resurrected the syllogism that, because planning was 'dominant' and the market 'supplementary', decisions about sown acreages for specific crops must proceed according to plan (administrative order) rather than in response to market signal (Zhang Jingfu 1982:20). Peasants were thus responsible not only for meeting their purchase quota and tax, but also for planting according to directive the particular crop that would remain theirs to sell or consume. The output mix of major farm products was in large degree still determined administratively, with plan and market in some conflict. The reason seems to lie as much in obstacles to the adoption of a more flexible pricing policy as in ideological resistance to a freer market; indeed, the two have been mutually reinforcing (see Chapter 14).

At the beginning of 1985, Zhao Ziyang, calling price reform 'what we have hoped for but dared not carry out', announced that the Party had decided to phase out mandatory quotas in agriculture and rely increasingly on the market. Prices of all agricultural goods except grain and cotton were to be set free to accord with supply and demand. The state would contract to buy smaller quantities than before of grain and cotton, leaving the peasant free to market above-quota output. The state was motivated chiefly by a desire to reduce the large subsidies it was providing through its purchases of great amounts of grain at above-quota and negotiated prices considerably higher than the urban retail prices at which it was sold.[23] The leadership seemed convinced that five years of fast agricultural growth and successive bumper harvests had created a buyers' market in which freer prices would not rise sharply. Agriculture was thus chosen to pioneer general price reform intended eventually for industry as well (Zhao 1985a; *BR*, 8 April 1985:8; Du 1985:16).

4.2   *Conflict between agricultural reforms and the centrally administered economy*

The compatibility of market signals and planners' preferences is only one aspect of this conflict. Another, closely related, concerns the links between the newly market-oriented agriculture and the rest of the economy. Farm households deal with this other economy when they purchase inputs or sell output.

If the state economy with which the peasants deal is not responsive to their needs, these intersectoral links can dampen the effectiveness of market incentives. For instance, shortages of chemical fertilizer and of construction materials for building new houses have been encountered; state commercial departments sometimes refuse to purchase goods exceeding their plans from the peasants (Jing 1983:21); and storage facilities have been wholly inadequate: 'It is amazing that in some places, large amounts of fruit, milk, fish, shrimp, and grain have gone bad. The problem of people finding it difficult to buy and sell is still fairly common' (Wan 1985:20).

Even when these problems are overcome, farmers who cannot find attractive consumer goods to buy with new cash earnings will begin to doubt the value of hard work and effective management. The seven-fold rise in rural savings deposits from Y5.6 billion in 1978 to Y47 billion in 1984 (*ZTN* 1984:482; Zhang 1985:K3) suggests that the farm population may have encountered some difficulty in spending its new earnings.[24] *People's Daily* remarked in May 1983 that it had 'continuously received letters from commune members in rural areas, reflecting various unhealthy tendencies in the supply of goods and materials for agricultural use'. These included speculation, price-gouging, kickbacks, and product adulteration by state and collective commercial and industrial units taking advantage of their monopoly position and the shortage of farm inputs (Commentator 1983:K7). Some of these phenomena are well-known in market economies and others are typical of constrained markets. The point is not that *laissez-faire* is best, but that the mutual interdependence of market-oriented and bureaucratically administered sectors introduces special problems that are apt to increase as the former sector grows and becomes more dependent on the latter.

4.3   Increase in the rural birth rate

Since at least the early 1970s, China's leadership has promoted a vigorous population control policy. With some 1.04 billion people in 1984, an annual net increment of 13 million, a youthful age structure, and scarce arable land, China's urgent need for a decline in population growth is evident. The seriousness of the issue increased in the late 1970s as Chinese demographers worked out the consequences of various population growth rates for future population size. In 1980, when it had been grasped that an average of two children per family would produce a population exceeding 1.5 billion by the middle of the next century, the Party and state 'firmly adopted the one-child limit' (Banister 1984a:721–2). The government's ambitious goal since 1980 has been to stabilize the population size at 1.2 billion by the end of this century and then gradually reduce it to around 700 million over the next century (Liu 1981:20; Song 1981:31). However, after a rapid fall during the 1970s, the crude birth and natural increase rates began to edge upward again in 1980, the former rising from 17.9 per 1,000 population in 1979 to 21.1 in 1982 (Table 12.7). This was no doubt partly due to the changing age structure of the population, as the baby boom cohorts born in the 1950s and 1960s began to swell the proportion in the prime reproductive ages (Tian 1984:197–8; Banister 1984b:243–7; 'Age Distribution of China's Population' 1984). This put upward pressure on the crude birth rate, offsetting the decline in age-specific fertility.

The HRS is also a cause, however. First, it puts a premium on family labour power, the primary source of household income in a still very labour-intensive rural economy. Especially as diversification of household activity became profitable (see below), the economic utility of children in farming, side-line, or

Table 12.7. *Crude birth, crude death, and natural increase rates, 1970-1984 (percentages)*

	Cr. birth rate	Cr. death rate	Rate of nat. inc.
1970	33.6	7.6	26.0
1971	30.7	7.3	23.4
1972	29.9	7.7	22.3
1973	28.1	7.1	20.9
1974	25.0	7.4	17.6
1975	23.1	7.4	15.8
1976	20.0	7.3	12.7
1977	19.0	6.9	12.1
1978	18.3	6.3	12.0
1979	17.9	6.2	11.7
1980	18.2	6.3	11.9
1981	20.9	6.4	14.5
1982	21.1	6.6	14.5
1983	18.6	7.1	11.5
1984	17.5	6.7	10.8

Sources: 1970-9, Liu (1981:4-6); 1980-3, *ZTN* (1984:83); 1984, SSB (1985:VIII).

off-farm activities rose. For this reason, school attendance dropped after the introduction of the HRS (Hinton 1983:26-7; Bernstein 1984a:59). Moreover, having children, who will eventually be workers, is a means of ensuring access to land, which is distributed according to family size or available labour power.

Perhaps even more important, the HRS has reinforced the sense of the family's responsibility for its members in their old age. As one demographic researcher confessed, 'For various reasons, the "five guarantee" or "honour old age" homes are at present still not well run' (Cheng 1982:56). With the dividing of land, co-operative brigade-medical clinics in many areas were discontinued, frequently being leased to paramedics ('barefoot doctors') who then charged fees for their use (Latham 1983:59-60). The welfare fund, which supported the care of indigent elderly, was in many areas maintained in name only (*RMRB*, 22 May 1982, 24 July 1982). The decline in collective support of social services implies that families have had to turn increasingly to their private incomes to finance education and health care (Travers 1984:252).

Some of this may have been a temporary manifestation of the confusion attending the initial stages of decollectivization. That this is so is suggested by the very sharp increase in rural welfare activity in 1984, when the number of indigent people aided by rural collectives jumped 50 per cent and the number of elderly people in homes for the aged increased by 43 per cent (SSB 1985:VIII). Nevertheless, the HRS has clearly heightened the tension between individual and collective interests and made it more difficult to redistribute income to the indigent (Latham 1983:70).

Social, economic, and cultural elements have all favoured high rural birth rates; only the stringent government population policy, with its quota of one child per family enforced by a mixture of education, material incentives, and coercion (Weisskopf 1985), has countered these factors (Cheng 1982:56). Official government statements have blamed the survival of 'feudal attitudes'—wanting many children and especially sons—for peasant resistance to smaller families. But such attitudes are eminently rational in post-reform conditions. Daughters marry out of their family and village and become responsible for their *husbands'* parents; it is imperative to have sons to ensure one's wellbeing in old age. In a 1981 survey carried out in Hubei Province, 51 per cent of the 808 respondents gave as their (primary?) reason for wanting children the assurance of their security in old age; continuing the family line was cited by 25 per cent, obtaining more family labour by 21 per cent, and enjoyment of children by the few remaining per cent (Cheng 1982:56). Rather than commit significant resources to provide social welfare substitutes for family self-reliance, the Party at first moved in the opposite direction, throwing families back on their own resources.

The official reaction to the rising birth rate was to increase pressure of all kinds on would-be violators of local birth quotas (Bernstein 1984a:57). Economic incentives laid out in 1979–80 to encourage the one-child family proved ineffective, yet they constituted a drain on limited state and collective budgets (Wong 1984:230; Bernstein 1984a:56–7; Banister 1984a:723–5). The state therefore stepped up the disincentives to include such dire punishments for having a second or higher-order child as dismissal from one's job and confiscation of contract land (Wong 1984:224; Banister 1984a:726), measures that blur the distinction between incentive and cœrcion and inevitably affect the innocent children involved (Wong 1984:230).

The conflict between official population control policy and the plethora of objective and subjective factors supporting peasants' desire for large families and several sons has inevitably provoked aberrations, including a resurgence of female infanticide, the abandonment of female infants, and the divorce and abuse (including killing) of wives who bear daughters. The 1982 national census revealed a male–female sex ratio of 1.085 (the normal ratio is 1.06). In three provinces that collected age-specific sex ratios, the proportion of females was abnormally low for ages 0–2 (Aird 1983:618–19). The intransigence symbolized by such behaviour in turn triggered widespread local cœrcion, including forced sterilization and forced abortion well into the third trimester of pregnancy (Weisskopf 1985; Wong 1984:230). While the combination of crippling disincentives, administrative harassment, and compulsion brought the crude birth rate down again in 1983 and 1984 (see Table 12.7), the Party's need to resort to such measures in its population policy raised questions about the likelihood of its long-run success. In 1985, however, preparation for a 'relaxation' in the one-child policy was announced (*BR*, 24 June 1985).

4.4   Surplus labour in agriculture

The establishment of the HRS quickly revealed that a large percentage of the farm labour force could leave agriculture without reducing output. Indeed, a smaller farm labour force was accompanied by rapid *increases* in output (see Sec. 3). The rural labour surplus is said to have amounted to between one-third and one-half of the total labour force in many areas (Lin 1983:112).

The juxtaposition of fewer workers with rising output under relatively constant technology does not imply that labour's marginal product had been zero (or even negative). Rather, it suggests that much of the huge increase in work-hours per worker-year between 1957 and 1975 had been illusory, that is, had been offset by slack, badly planned, and/or poorly motivated work. When given the incentive and opportunity, many farmers reorganized to do better work in less time. Such massive disguised unemployment in agriculture before the late 1970s implies that the stagnant labour productivity and declining 'total factor productivity' found by Western economists were also partly illusory. These findings were based on the assumption that the reported increases in annual labour inputs between 1957 and 1975 were real increases of standard quality and intensity, an assumption that must now be doubted. Ironically, 'factor productivity' did not fare so poorly: the reason agricultural output lagged is that inputs did not grow faster, and incentives were poor (see Sec. 3 above and note 17).

At first blush, the surplus labour revealed by the HRS seems in conflict with its positive impact on the birth rate: why would farmers want more children if labour were already redundant? But this is to confuse the farming of basic crops with the general range of opportunities now open to the rural population. The changes in party policy favouring rural diversification and encouraging individual initiative created many profitable opportunities outside of food production, and even outside of farming in general. Peasants were now able to compare the returns from different occupations and choose accordingly. In many cases, commercial activities, transport, crafts, or itinerant labour offered far higher profit than farming. Families with several working members in particular would find it attractive to keep only part of their labour on the land. 'In some areas, particularly near towns or factories, unacceptably large numbers of peasants wanted to engage in commercial activities rather than work in the fields' (Latham 1983:108–9).

Rural non-agricultural undertakings have continued to develop as sources of income and employment in the countryside. They include enterprises owned by townships and villages (successors to, respectively, the communes and brigades) and by individual households or groups of households. These produced a gross output value of Y170 billion in 1984, over half as great as the GVAO net of rural industrial output,[25] and employed 52.06 million workers, equal to about 16 per cent of the agricultural labour force.[26] Of all enterprises, 71 per cent were industrial (of which machinery, building materials, and textiles were the most common), 13 per cent were in construction, and the rest were distributed among transport (4 per cent), agriculture (4 per cent), and service trades (8 per cent) (Du 1985:17). Perhaps a third of all rural industrial output is currently produced in the Changjiang (Yangtze) Delta provinces of Jiangsu and Zhejiang (Delfs 1985e).

Rural enterprises operate to a large extent outside the system of central planning and allocation, getting their materials on the market and selling their output 'through a variety of channels, including direct contacts with suppliers and customers, private traders, and an emerging rural–collective trading network' (Delfs 1985e:93). To officials who do not fear them as a threat to socialism and economic planning, they represent the path of the future for much of the rural population. By the year 2000, the proportion of the rural labour force engaged in agriculture is 'expected' to decline from 80–85 per cent (1984) to only 30 per cent, the difference being absorbed by rural industry and commerce, mining, forestry, animal husbandry, fishing, and services (Delfs 1984b:67; Wang Dacheng 1985:4). Such massive structural change, whose implications for population distribution, agricultural productivity, and the growth of industrial output are immense, has no precedent in the pattern established by the first thirty years of economic growth and is unlikely to be fully realized. Yet it does indicate the direction in which the reformers wish to see the countryside evolve to eliminate surplus farm labour and raise rural incomes.

4.5   Polarization

While narrowing the gap between city and countryside, the rural reforms have given rise to growing inequality within the countryside itself. Before 1979 the most significant differentials were those between localities with different ecological conditions or proximity to urban markets, whereas income within villages was distributed quite evenly (Chapter 10). Since 1979, large gaps have opened within localities, too, as the incomes of individual households have come to conform more closely to their particular characteristics (labour power, skills, education, political influence,[27] etc.) without the equalizing intermediation of a common work-point and central distribution. Arguing that egalitarianism had been carried too far earlier, the Party has deliberately encouraged differentiation through a policy of 'helping some peasants to prosper first'. For example, peasants with special or superior skills are provided with funds, technical assistance, and materials to develop special lines of production, from carpentry to running clinics, nurseries, or schools (Jing 1983). Their incomes are expected to rise much faster than average.

The national sample surveys of rural households show a sharp decline in the number and percentage of poverty-stricken households and a rapid rise in well-off ones. Households with annual per capita net incomes below Y150 constituted 5.1 per cent of all rural households in 1984, down from a third of all households in 1978. Those with incomes Y500 or above reached almost 12 per cent in 1983 and over 15 per cent in 1984, whereas in 1978 only 2.4 per cent of rural households had net per capita incomes above Y300 (ZTN 1984:473; LLi 1985:20). Although these figures contain much statistical exaggeration,[28] the impression conveyed of general improvement is no doubt accurate. Much of the increase in inequality is due to the rising incomes of the successful.

In the prefecture that pioneered the HRS, Chuxian in Anhui Province, rapid general growth of incomes was accompanied by increased differentiation. By 1981, 1.2 per cent of families had moved up to an income of Y500 per capita while another 5 per cent earned less than Y60 each—a gap said to be significantly higher than before; moreover, Chuxian was regarded as representative of the relatively underdeveloped one-third of China's countryside in this respect (*BR*, 21 June 1982). In Jiangsu's Suqian County in 1982, about 3,400 households out of the 200,000 total earned more than Y1,000; at the same time, 5 per cent of households got less than Y100 per capita (Jing 1983). Again largely because some farmers were increasing their incomes faster than others, the income gap was growing. Using the rural household surveys (which are of questionable representativeness), Li Chengrui (1985:21–2) finds that the Gini coefficient for rural distribution rose from 0.237 in 1978 to 0.264, which indicates a small increase in inequality, although its degree remains low by international standards.

With private ownership of property, from tractors to shares in enterprises, the opportunity arises to accumulate wealth. In March 1983, William Hinton found a peasant in Fengyang County, Anhui, who owned two tractors, each of which could earn Y1,000 per month, paying for its own price in six months. Another had become a trader, distributing reed mats woven locally to purchasers in the north-east. He made Y20,000 in a single year, paid three-fourths of it in income tax, and still ended up with fourteen times the county average income. Hinton comments:

He could plow this money back into his own business, put it in the bank to draw interest, or buy shares in some of the new industries under construction. Whatever he did with it, the income derived from the investment . . . must eventually accumulate as a substantial capital holding . . . Surely the commercial freedom that now pervades the market threatens to throw up some merchant princes. [Hinton 1983:26, 24]

In the early 1980s, the Chinese leadership was touting such successes much as it earlier had acclaimed Dazhai. It is denied that polarization can give rise to exploitation or a resurrection of classes based on property ownership. China's leaders have decided that in Chinese agriculture private ownership of land is the only possible basis of class exploitation; as long as land remains collective or state property, such danger is averted. That capital can now be privately accumulated and inherited is not discussed as a potential threat.[29] Yet, as Kenneth Lieberthal points out,

[T]he logic of current policy is that a new rural élite stratum will emerge that will enjoy leverage across many aspects of rural life. The new policy permits peasant families that have prospered . . . to use their surplus capital to acquire more extensive land holdings, to set up transport companies, to invest in local enterprises, and so forth. Such wide-ranging economic activity will inevitably produce pressures for enhanced social and political power. [Lieberthal 1985:109–10][30]

The degree to which party policy has favoured this emerging rural élite is suggested by the eulogy accorded it by a principal reformer, Vice-Premier Wan Li (1984:19), who said its members were transmitters of 'the fine traditions of the Chinese peasants' and 'representatives of advanced productive forces in the countryside'.

Although the press has featured stories of poor peasants who bone up on new technology, borrow money to buy some chicks, and become rich in a year, a 1984 survey of 21,000 prosperous households in a county of Shanxi Province indicates a different picture. There, 43 per cent of prosperous households consisted of brigade and team cadres or former cadres, another 42 per cent of returned educated youth and demobilized soldiers. People skilled in industry or trade made up another 9 per cent, leaving only a residual 5 percentage points for 'peasants skilled in business and management' (Lu 1984c:26–7).

Those left behind by events include residents of remote and hilly regions with poor land and no access to major markets, and also those without the family labour, skills, or political connections necessary to take advantage of the new conditions. Guizhou, a hilly, poor province that was one of the first to adopt the HRS, is nevertheless a site of such areas (Wren 1984). Beggars, some of them peasant migrants, again openly ply the railroad stations and thoroughfares of towns and cities.[31] The Minister of Civil Affairs estimated in January 1985 that about 8 per cent of the rural population, or 70 million people, were in poverty and required aid. Some delegates to the March 1985 National People's Congress, however, criticized the leadership's depiction of rural conditions as 'exaggerated in that the real grass roots situation is far from rosy' (Lee 1985b:13).

Policies to help the rural poor include the reduction or remittance of taxes, the provision of low-interest loans, priority in purchasing their output and in supplying improved seed and other farm inputs, subsidies to buy such inputs, and the provision of technical education and advice (FBIS, 7 January 1985:K17).[32] Cadres in some areas have taken it upon themselves to help indigent families work out plans to overcome their problems (Hinton 1983:22; BR, 19 January 1981; BR, 21 June 1982; Jing 1983:20–1). In 1980 the national government established a special fund to help impoverished localities (BR, 19 January 1981), but this fund was not mentioned in subsequent budgets. Annual spending from the state budget for rural relief averaged Y0.8 billion between 1979 and 1982 (ZTN 1984:424). In short, party policy has been to smooth the way for peasants in favourable circumstances to forge ahead while providing some help for those left farthest behind.

4.6   Destruction of collective property

In the confusion that accompanied the initial division of collective land among households, collective assets were often destroyed or damaged. Trees were felled and forests cleared for building materials and fuel (CPCCC 1983:K11; Latham 1983:49), compounding a long-term problem of deforestation and erosion. Collectively owned equipment and facilities were frequently distributed along with the land (*RMRB*, 22 May and 24 July 1982). Water control works generally remained under collective management, but there seems to have been a halt in significant construction activity to extend them (Latham 1983:46).

Among the most serious manifestations of this tendency was predatory use of the land by its new occupiers, who, afraid it would be taken away again, treated it as a short-run asset and failed to replace soil nutrients or to invest in improvements. In early 1984 the Party moved to correct this problem by extending the duration of contracts to fifteen years or more (see Sec. 2).

4.7 Leadership

Wan Li, one of the leading reformers, stated in late 1982 that a majority of leading cadres 'are not convinced of the responsibility system, hesitate to act, or even resist it' (FBIS, 4 January 1983:K5; quoted in Bernstein 1984b:30). Ideological misgivings and self-interest were both, no doubt, involved in different degrees.[33] Many local cadres were losers in the adoption of the HRS. They lost command authority and direct control over the work process and the distribution of income. Many could no longer be supported from collective income and had to return to farming, while others chose to do so out of disgruntlement over the course of events and/or the impulse to take personal advantage of the new conditions. However, these conditions in fact required new and complex leadership qualities. The formulation and enforcement of household and group contracts called for rather sophisticated financial skills. Many new sources of conflict arose among households, and between these, the collective, and the state, which required mediation and dispute resolution abilities that were in short supply.

4.8 Insecurity

Linked to the polarization problem is that of peasant insecurity, affecting especially the less aggressive and less well endowed farmers who have been less able to take advantage of the new conditions. Under the HRS, individual households became responsible for purchasing a range of inputs and services that previously were the responsibility of the collective. These include fertilizers, improved seeds, insecticides, tractor ploughing services, and supplementary labour in the heavy seasons, as well as tools and equipment. The decisions themselves, as well as the individual financial burden entailed, have been a source of anxiety to many peasants. Moreover, they were now dealing directly with banks for needed loans, rather than with their teams as before, and thus 'were exposed increasingly to impersonal, distant, and not necessarily responsive financial bureaucrats' (Latham 1983:116). As banks themselves began to stress profitability in their loan operations, they naturally tended to avoid lending to poor peasants (1983:117-18).

Of the several problems discussed above, some were the inevitable products of the rapidity and scope of the changes that occurred after 1979. Others, such as polarization and intersectoral tensions, are harbingers of long-term dangers present at first in only embryonic form. On the whole, the problems in the early 1980s looked pale next to the new dynamism of the rural economy. But whether that dynamism had become a permanent feature of China's agriculture was still uncertain.

Much of it, as we have seen, was due to once-for-all changes in policies affecting farm incentives, and to the consequent catching up of production to its potential. For the potential itself to continue growing quickly, however, a strong flow of investment will be needed to bring capital and technical improvements to the farms. In this respect the record, as summarized by Stone, has been equivocal:

As of 1979 the proportion of the state capital construction budget devoted to agriculture during the Cultural Revolution decade (around 10 per cent) was heavily criticized as being too low . . . The proportion was raised from 10.7 per cent in 1978 to 14 per cent in 1979 and was scheduled to increase to 18 per cent during 1980–82 . . . But owing to budgetary problems in 1980–81, the total state construction budget declined by 21 per cent in 1981 and the proportion allocated to agriculture, forestry, water conservancy, and meteorology fell to 6.6 per cent, and then to 6.1 per cent of a recovered 1982 construction budget. [Stone 1985:119–20]

Budgeted state aid to agriculture in 1984 was only 6 per cent of total state expenditures (Delfs 1984c:68). Although decollectivization has stimulated peasant purchases of small farm machinery and equipment, much of the increase in peasant incomes has gone into consumption, including such traditional activities as weddings and religious celebrations, and into housing. Long-term investment of all kinds, by the collectives as well as the state, declined substantially (Walker 1984:800), as a result of which the irrigated area actually fell between 1978 and 1983 (*ZTN* 1984:175).

Foreign scholars, such as Nicholas Lardy (1984), Bruce Stone (1985), and Kenneth Walker (1984), see the failure to sustain higher levels of investment in agriculture as threatening the long-term maintenance of higher growth rates. Chinese researchers agree that continued progress after 1987 will depend in part on more and better material inputs to agriculture. The development of the rural economy (including non-agricultural activities) during the last fifteen years of the twentieth century is expected to require investments totalling Y1,000–Y1,500 billion, but current plans call for the state to provide only a minor share of this, perhaps one-fifth (Du 1985:22; Delfs 1984b:68). The great bulk of it must come from the savings of rural enterprises, households, and collectives, either invested directly or intermediated by the banking system. The main purveyor of credit is the Agricultural Bank of China (ABC), re-established in 1979 to specialize in the mobilization of savings from and provision of credit to the rural economy. The ABC's accumulated loans in the five years after its reopening totalled Y180 billion, about five times the amounts of state budgeted expenditures in agriculture (Delfs 1984c:69). However, three-quarters of its portfolio in 1983 consisted of loans to rural industry and commerce and to other banks (Delfs 1984c:70); its potential as a major source of funds for agriculture proper was still unrealized.

Small-scale family farming has its advocates in the economic development literature, and it has been capable of bringing about impressive growth of output and yields under the right conditions. K. N. Raj (1983) argues that in China these conditions were created by the farmland consolidation and capital construction programmes of the collective era, a point made also by Stone (1985:121). In Indian agriculture, by way of contrast, Raj argues that inequality of holdings, fragmentation, and irrational land use have impeded the improvement of yields under a family farming regime. It is these conditions, so evident in J. L. Buck's description of Chinese agrarian conditions in the 1930s, that were eliminated by collectivization and large-scale labour-intensive construction in agriculture.[34]

With the land consolidated, irrigated, terraced, and then divided equitably, can small-scale family farming in China be a dynamic and socially stable arrangement? The answer depends on whether the infrastructure can be further developed, the flow of technological improvements maintained, and income polarization avoided under the new conditions—and also on whether market-oriented farmers can get the inputs and consumer goods they want from the more rigid state economy. In the not-much-longer run, a vital issue will be the impact of peasant individualism on the growth rate of China's massive population.

Notes

1. The Third Plenum approved these plans 'in principle' and directed the State Council to submit them 'after revisions' to the National People's Congress session due early the following year. Somewhat ambiguously, the communiqué declares that 'these arrangements are both forward-looking and feasible.' In view of the immediately following shift in attention to the problem of economic imbalance, this treatment was a polite but unmistakable signal that ambitious annual plans based on the Ten Year Plan were to be scaled down.
2. The elevation of agriculture to the position of highest priority was consistent with readjustment policy. But, as the text indicates, the means stressed by the Third Plenum were those of institutional reform.
3. This discussion of the production responsibility system in agriculture relies especially on the following sources: Domes (1982); Latham (1983); Watson (1983); Wu (1980); Zweig (1982).
4. The Anhui Provincial Party Committee had affirmed household contracting as a legitimate form of responsibility system some nine months earlier (Watson 1983:712).
5. Citations are to the *China Quarterly* translation.
6. The distinction between 'contracting' and 'self-managing' specialists tends to break down, however, as contractors accumulate their own capital and self-managers find various ways to use collective resources (Zhou and Du 1984).
7. '[T]he principal characteristic that makes a collective unit a basic accounting unit is that all workpoints earned in it have the same value. Once contracting with individual households is practised no collective unit . . . can claim to satisfy this criterion. Indeed, under the most widespread type of contracting the calculation of workpoints is no longer necessary. Thus, in current usage the term "basic

accounting unit" appears to have come to mean something quite different from what it meant in the past' (Khan and Lee 1983:13).

8. Travers (1984:243–5) argues that the rural income gains shown by the household sample surveys are biased upward. His own estimate of net rural per capita real income for the years 1978–81 shows it growing by a total of 37.9 per cent, compared with the sample survey estimate (when deflated) of 49 per cent. The survey methods are broadly described in Hong (1984:48), which reveals that sample households are chosen in advance, and must then keep careful accounts which are discussed by the cadres and masses. This alone would tend to produce biased results by activating the 'Hawthorne effect', in which subjects do better than usual merely because they are being studied.

9. China still follows Soviet practice in excluding the output of 'non-material production sectors' from 'national income'. These include service trades, education, scientific research, and cultural and health services. The disparity between the growth rates of real consumption and real income may be due in part to a slower growth in material consumption than in the consumption component of the excluded services over the years in question. It is also likely that the estimates of real income growth, which are based on rural sample household surveys, are biased upward, as Travers (1982, 1984) contends.

10. The implicit deflator used in *ZTN* (1984:453) is almost identical to the index of 'cost of living' (*shenghuo feiyong*) of workers and staff, and slightly higher than the national retail price index. Lardy (1984:861) discusses the reasons why this index may understate the true rate of inflation and points out that there is no official cost of living index published for rural residents. He also points out that the procedure for valuing distribution of income-in-kind in the rural sample surveys is not specifically disclosed. It is possible, contrary to my assumption, that this income is valued in constant prices, but, if so, one would suppose that this would be mentioned in the notes to the relevant tables, and it is not. See *ZTN* (1984:453, 471).

11. In subsequent years, not only did the gap between the two price indexes grow smaller, but the non-marketed proportion of agricultural output also diminished. A smaller upward bias in measured income each year after 1979 implies a downward bias in its growth rate for those years.

12. Rural per capita real income grew twice as fast as the 47 per cent increase in GVAO per rural inhabitant between 1978 and 1983. Part of this difference is due to greater efficiency, that is, to an increase in the ratio of net income to gross output. But part of it is due to the fact that farm purchase prices rose faster than general retail prices. If all farm income were received from either sales or self-consumed output valued at current purchase prices, the total proportional increase in net income could be analysed as follows:

$$\frac{\text{Total increase}}{\text{in net income}} = \frac{\text{growth of net income}}{\text{in base year prices}} \times \frac{\text{purchase price increase}}{\text{'cost of living' index}}$$

or

$$1.984 = 1.565 \times \frac{1.477}{1.165} = 1.565 \times 1.268.$$

The 26.8 per cent net price increase above the 'cost of living' index would constitute 27 per cent of the overall net income increase of 98.4 per cent. However, some rural income comes from wages, overseas remittances, relief payments, and other sources to which purchase prices do not apply; hence my rough estimate that price rises explain only 20 per cent of the total. (All figures are taken from *ZTN* 1984.)

13. These figures must not be taken too literally. The rural surveys are probably biased upward (see n. 8). Moreover, 'disposable income' of workers excludes expenses for supporting relatives, gifts to relatives, and certain other supplementary household expenses, while no such deductions are made from peasant net income. The considerable increase in recent years in urban housing at subsidized rents is also omitted. Finally, a wide range of other subsidies available to urban workers are not counted. On the whole, the comparison probably understates the size of the remaining urban–rural gap while correctly indicating its narrowing.

14. The figures in Table 12.4 differ somewhat from Travers's. The urban population numbers are larger than those implied by Travers's table, and the rural populations correspondingly smaller. A different price index is used to deflate the sales data and no attempt is made to add free market sales to the official totals. There may be other differences as well. The trend results are the same, however.

15. Lardy (1984:862–3) cautions that 'one cannot necessarily infer that policy since 1978 has reversed the longstanding trend of increasing differentials in urban and rural living standards', since various subsidies and fringe benefits aiding the urban population, but not the rural, have grown very rapidly in recent years, and 'the relative prices faced by urban and rural consumers diverge more widely than ever before.'

16. Chow shows that Tang's method (also used by Rawski) employs a weighted arithmetic mean input index, which yields a high estimate of input growth and a correspondingly low one of the growth of total factor productivity. For his own calculation, Chow constructs a geometric mean input index.

17. It is also possible that much collectively organized labour was thrown into relatively unproductive construction activities, or otherwise misallocated, which if true would rescue the productivity calculations to some degree. However, the logic of such growth accounting exercises assumes the efficiency of resource allocation.

18. During a research visit to Beijing in 1980 I was told the same thing by members of the Chinese Academy of Social Science.

19. The weights used by Rawski, and chosen originally by Anthony Tang (1971), are as follows: labour, 0.55; land, 0.25; current inputs (total nutrients), 0.11; draught animals, 0.081; aggregate horsepower of farm machinery, 0.009. The new weights referred to in the text are: labour, 0.45; land, 0.18; draught animals, 0.1; farm machinery, 0.05; current inputs, 0.22. The increase in the weights of relatively fast-growing inputs is consistent with empirical evidence from other countries that substitution elasticities tend to be above one in agriculture (Yotopolous and Nugent 1976:151–63).

It should be pointed out that my method of estimating input growth rates differs from Rawski's. In particular, I make no attempt to estimate changes in intensity of work per year over the 1978–82 period, but take the reported growth in the agricultural labour force to be the growth of labour inputs. Any increase in work intensity will therefore cause the growth rate of the productivity index to be biased upward, whereas a decline in work intensity will cause it to be biased downward. Also, in estimating total nutrients I have changed the relative weights of chemical and organic fertilizer to reflect the change in composition of total nutrients between the 1960s and the 1980s. Finally, in the absence of an up-to-date study of organic fertilizer collection, I have used an extremely simple method (as indicated in the notes to Table 12.5) of estimating its growth.

20. Lin (1983:113) claims that marketed farm and side-line output per head of the agricultural population rose between 1978 and 1981 by 67.8 per cent. But this figure is inflated by the substantial (average 38.5 per cent) price increases of agricultural products over this perod.

21. As Stone (1985:121) puts it, 'recent growth has had some of the character of cashing in on autonomous rural progress and unrealized gains from the groundwork laid during the 1970s . . .'

22. Thus, Lin (1983:112) points out that agricultural labour productivity rose by 2.7 per cent per year between 1979 and 1981, which equals the entire increase between 1952 and 1978. 'In other words, the rate of increase in labour productivity in a single year after the output-related contract system was adopted is equivalent to that of the past 26 years. The statistical method used for these two periods is the same and there is no problem in the comparability of the derived data.' Lin neglects to mention that other things were changing as well, that the rate of labour productivity increase would have been even higher had 1978 been made the starting point, and that therefore the data do not demonstrate that the contract system alone was responsible for the improvement.

23. The rise in farm procurement prices had created a glut of some products in 1984, notably grain and cotton, while others were still in short supply. Zhao's plan permits a greater share of grain to be sold on the free market. The state, rather than guaranteeing to purchase all grain, would fix its total purchases at 75–80 million metric tons, 30 per cent at low quota prices, 70 per cent at higher above-quota prices. Zhao claimed this would leave only 5 million metric tons of additional surplus above self-consumption for the free market (Zhao 1985a:K3). In 1983 the state purchased 120 million metric tons, 31 per cent of total output (ZTN 1984:370) and 40 million metric tons above the new maximum planned purchase figure. Such a quantity thrown on the market without state price support would probably bring grain prices down markedly. As part of the plan, however, the state would intervene to buy additional grain at the quota price if the free market price falls below this. The net result in the case of a large harvest would seem to be to reduce the price at which the state is obliged to purchase the surplus. See also Oi (1986).

24. This problem may be more pronounced in the cities, where per capita savings had risen from Y74 to Y370 between 1978 and 1984 (Zhang 1985:K3).

25. GVAO net of village industrial output in 1984 was Y306.2 billion. However, it should be kept in mind that the ratio of net to gross value is much higher in agriculture than in industry. Therefore, in terms of net value the relative importance of rural non-agricultural activities would look much less impressive.

26. Of this number, 32 million were employed by township enterprises (BR, 7 January 1985:7), the rest by village and co-operative and private enterprises.

27. For a discussion of the development of patron–client relations in the countryside, as well as of cadre pressure on successful peasant entrepreneurs, see Bernstein (1984b: Part V).

28. Aside from questions about the representativeness of the yearly samples, it should be kept in mind that a significant part of the increase in incomes (measured here in current prices) was due to the higher prices attached to self-consumed output (see Sec. 3 above). There is also some question about the comparability of pre- and post-1981 figures (see Hong 1984:48). Finally, the 1984 figures given in the text are my interpretation of a misprinted table in Li (1985:20).

29. Hinton (1983:24) observes that the leadership position would have amused the classical political economists (Marx included), who pointed out that 'Private

ownership of the land hinders rather than advances this ability [to profit from wage labour], forcing entrepreneurs to share their profits with a non-productive class of landowners.'

30. Lieberthal points out that reported and potential activities of prosperous peasants, from local philanthropy to buying higher education for their children, are reminiscent of the role of the 'enlightened gentry' before 1949 (1985:109–10).

31. For the story of one such peasant, see the *Washington Post* (3 February 1985): 'Some Chinese Fail to Benefit From Reforms'. This man's wife died in childbirth, leaving him with an infant for whom he could not provide on the one acre of land contracted to him in his North Hebei village. He had gone with the baby to Beijing to beg, then illegally stowed away on a train to warmer Guangzhou in an attempt to keep the infant alive over the winter. This man mourned the time of Mao, when the villagers looked after those in trouble. Picked up by the Guangzhou authorities, he was released again to resume his begging.

32. Curiously, the Minister 'pledged' that 'his ministry would continue to raise money to support the poorer peasants', making it sound much like a private charitable organization rather than one funded by the state budget. Unable to offer sufficient hard cash, he instead proferred his conviction that assistance would be gradually increased as the economy improved (FBIS, 7 January 1985:K17).

33. See Bernstein (1984b: Part III) for a discussion of the various dimensions of cadre opposition to the HRS.

34. Raj suggests that the efforts that have gone into water conservancy projects, mostly in the north, have permitted that region to contribute 44 per cent of the increment in foodgrain production between 1955–7 and 1978–80, when the already high yields in the south made increasing output there ever more difficult.

CHAPTER 13

THE OPEN DOOR: INTERNATIONAL ECONOMIC POLICY

1 Introduction

The 'open door' symbolizes China's sharp turn towards participation in the world market to speed up economic growth and technological modernization. Only developments in agriculture rival in magnitude the post-Mao changes in foreign economic policy, which are the more startling because during most of the previous two decades this area played a peripheral role at best. China lived implicitly by the old rule, developed as a rationalization of necessity bred by Soviet isolation in Stalin's day, that foreign trade is 'merely a means of balancing surpluses and shortages', that is, a way of 'filling gaps in domestic supply' (Wang Linsheng 1983:57; Yuan and Wang 1983:26). The more universal was domestic production, the fewer the gaps, the smaller the role of foreign trade, and the happier the leadership.

This view suited China's objective conditions during the decades of isolation from the world market by the US-led embargo: 'For many years, China could not have expanded her foreign trade freely even if she had wanted to' (Chao 1982:20). The melting of the embargo since the early 1970s, however, together with the general improvement in China's international position, gave rise to a change in its view of foreign economic relations. Premier Zhao Ziyang in 1981 called on his people to 'abandon once for all the idea of self-sufficiency' (Zhao 1982a:47). Chinese economists began to study the law of comparative advantage and to urge participation in the international division of labour. Zhao himself seemed to embrace these ideas when he explained:

By linking our country with the world market, expanding foreign trade, importing advanced technology, utilizing foreign capital, and entering into different forms of international economic and technological co-operation, we can use our strong points to make up for our weak points through international exchange on the basis of equality and mutual benefit. [Zhao 1982a:47]

Not only has trade soared after a decade of virtual stagnation, but, more significantly, foreign capital has been solicited, tourism promoted, and a remarkable series of institutional changes made to create an environment attractive to foreign investors. Trade Minister Li Qiang announced in 1979 the breaching of the last two remaining 'forbidden zones': acceptance of government-to-government loans, and private direct foreign investment: 'By and large we now accept all the common practices known to world trade' (Brown 1983:27). This is all a far cry from the days when China insisted on paying its way in cash, rejected foreign investment as inherently imperialistic, and practised a form of 'self-reliance' that had only marginal room for trade and almost none for tourism.

Like several other socialist countries, China has found it easier to develop links with the world market than to reform the home economy. Indeed, the thought must have occurred to some leaders that trade and foreign capital, by making possible the importation of new technology and innovative management methods, might let them side-step the hard choices of reform. The reformers, however, clearly see the 'open door' policy as complementing their domestic goals by exposing China to instruction in—and competition with—the more efficient ways of the developed capitalist world.

2 Trends in foreign trade

Recent trends in China's merchandise trade, together with some earlier figures for comparison, are shown in Table 13.1. They reveal the rapid expansion of trade after its virtual stagnation during the 1960s. Two-way trade almost quadrupled in value between 1976 and 1984, and, although some of this

Table 13.1. *Merchandise trade, selected years, 1950–1984 (billions of current US dollars)*

	Exports	Imports	Balance	Merchandise trade Total	Per capita (Y)
1950	0.55	0.58	−0.03	1.13	2.06
1952	0.82	1.12	−0.30	1.94	4.03
1957	1.60	1.51	0.09	3.11	4.81
1959	2.26	2.12	0.14	4.38	6.52
1965	2.23	2.02	0.21	4.25	5.85
1970	2.26	2.33	−0.07	4.59	5.53
1972	3.44	2.86	0.58	6.30	7.23
1974	6.95	7.62	−0.67	14.57	16.03
1975	7.26	7.49	−0.23	14.75	15.96
1976	6.86	6.58	0.28	13.44	14.34
1978	9.75	10.89	−1.14	20.64	21.44
1980	18.27	19.55	−1.28	37.82	38.31
1981	20.89	19.48	1.41	40.37	40.34
1982	21.82	17.48	4.34	39.30	38.70
1983	22.20	18.53	3.67	40.73	39.74
1984	25.02	26.75	−1.73	51.77	50.05

N.B. Exports are f.o.b., imports c.i.f. Since an increasing amount of China's trade has used Chinese ships, this somewhat exaggerates import costs. For a different trade series, giving imports f.o.b., see USCIA (1985: Table 1).

Sources: 1950–83, *ZTN* (1984:395); 1984, SSB (1985:vi), converted into US dollars at 1984 average exchange rate of Y2.32 = \$1 (*International Financial Statistics*, 6 June 1985:152). Per capita figures derived using population figures from *ZTN* (1984:81).

Table 13.2. *Merchandise trade as a percentage of aggregate product, 1933–1984*

	1933	1957	1977–8	1980	1984
China	8	11	9.2	13.3	16.8
India			13.0		
Indonesia			41.3		
Bangladesh			24.1		
Turkey			14.3		
Brazil			15.5		
Mexico			14.0		
Japan			21.2		
USA			15.0		
USSR			10.8		
All developed countries 1978			31.5		
Low-income developing countries 1978			23.5		
Middle-income developing countries, 1978			37.7		

Sources: 1933, 1957, Falkenheim and Rawski (1983: Table 3); 1977–8 (China and other countries and groups of countries) and 1980, World Bank (1983, II:412); 1984, author's estimate based upon growth rates of 'national income' and trade between 1980 and 1984. 'National income' and trade figures from *ZTZ* (1985:7, 90) and *ZTN* (1984:29, 395).

increase is ascribable to world-wide inflation, much of it is real. By 1984 total trade came to $50 per capita, as compared with well under $10 just a decade earlier.

This record, in itself, is not remarkable. China's subjection to international boycott and its own policy of 'self-reliance' had kept total trade very small before the late 1970s. Much or all of the surge since then can be interpreted as a return to something like a normal trade ratio for a country of China's size and level of national income. This can be seen in Table 13.2, which shows trade ratios for China in selected years and those of several other countries and groups of countries in 1977–8 for comparison. China's trade ratio rose from very low levels in the 1930s and early 1950s to over 10 per cent in the late 1950s, from which point it dropped through the next decade as aggregate output rose while total trade fell below its 1959 peak. By 1977–8 it had recovered somewhat as a result of the surge of trade in the early 1970s, and from there it rose to almost 17 per cent in 1984. This was of the same order of magnitude as other large countries (including the USA), higher than India, and significantly higher than the USSR.

The fast growth of trade has increased China's weight in the international market, especially in those particular markets in which its trade is concentrated. China's exports constituted only 1.4 per cent of world imports in 1983 (compared with 8.8 per cent for Japan), and its imports were 1.3 per cent of world exports (against 6.7 per cent for Japan), but China had become a significant purchaser of grain, chemical fertilizer, metals, machinery, and equipment as well as 'one of the world's biggest developing-country markets'

(Delfs 1985a:94). And in the first half of 1985 China was Japan's second-largest trading partner (Smith 1985).

If the ratio of total trade to GNP was not remarkable, that of imports was, and so was the trade balance. China's imports–GNP ratio in 1977–8, at 4.7 per cent, was below that of all of the other countries in the table. The World Bank (1983, II:139) calls this 'especially striking' in comparison with many other developing countries that have large import surpluses financed by substantial capital inflows.

This point is underlined by the trade balance figures in Table 13.1, which reveal that surpluses on trade account have been larger and more numerous than deficits. China also runs a regular surplus in its 'invisibles' account (shipping, insurance, services, overseas remittances). Thus, by the end of 1983, foreign exchange reserves totalled $15,690 million, equivalent to more than three-quarters of that year's imports. In addition, China held 12.67 million ounces of gold, worth around $4 billion (FBIS, 10 July 1984:K14). Unlike most developing countries, China has been a net exporter of capital, lending more money than it borrows and earning net positive interest on capital account (JETRO, November–December 1983:16). With a very low debt service ratio (under 12 per cent in 1982), China has clearly been careful to avoid financial dependency.

An exception to this conservatism occurred in 1978–80, when the short-lived Ten Year Plan gave rise to a 'great leap outward'. Japanese consultants to the State Planning Commission estimated the overall investment programme contemplated by the Plan to require $70–80 billion in plant and technology imports (JETRO, June 1980:18–19).

In addition, China began decentralizing the management of foreign trade in 1978. Under the new conditions of greatly increased trade, the old system, in which all decisions had to go through sectoral Foreign Trade Corporations under the Foreign Trade Ministry, proved hopelessly inefficient. Authority to engage in foreign transactions was therefore given to various other ministries and to local governments. From there, in an attempt to bring domestic customers and suppliers into direct contact with their foreign counterparts, it devolved further, so that 'there are dozens of corporations, enterprises, and factories authorized to conclude business with foreigners, and a bewildering array of government agencies involved in approving, supervising, and coordinating foreign economic relations' (Clark 1984:8).[1]

As various units went on a buying spree, the centre lost control of import and export decisions. Import *volume* (corrected for price changes) rose by an estimated 51 per cent in 1978 and 21 per cent in 1979 (Falkenheim and Rawski 1983:Table 2). China signed contracts in 1978 alone for twenty-two large-scale plants and related equipment worth $7.8 billion. Much waste occurred as imports were improperly selected or lacked the necessary support facilities—especially transport and power—in China. Beginning in 1978, there were three successive trade deficits, leaving China 'dangerously low on foreign exchange; reserves had fallen to less than $2 billion by the beginning of 1979' (Davie and Carver 1982:26).[2]

This situation prompted some thought about how the Ten Year Plan projects were to be financed, as well as about what principles of selection and planning ought to be followed in foreign trade, and was one of the main factors precipitating the sharp downward 'readjustment' in capital construction plans that began in 1979. In February of that year, China temporarily suspended $2.6 billion of contracts with Japanese firms, subject to further exploration of financing conditions, and declared a moratorium on major new contracts. It was at this time that the Bank of China was split off from the People's Bank and a Foreign Investment Control Commission established, both moves intended to establish firmer central control over access to foreign exchange (Davie and Carver 1982:28). China also decided to de-emphasize its policy of importing whole plants and to concentrate more selectively on technology and equipment that could not easily be produced at home (World Bank 1983, II:420). Imports were cut heavily (remaining well below the 1980 peak in the three subsequent years) while exports were stimulated, and substantial surpluses were run in 1981-3. In September 1984, foreign exchange reserves stood at almost $14 billion.

At this point, a new set of 'reforms' in the monetary and foreign trade systems set off another crisis. More local units were empowered to use foreign exchange; banks began issuing great amounts of credit, much of it unsecured, open-ended, and at low interest rates (Ross 1985:47; Lee 1985b:72); and the Bank of China began automatically approving letters of credit on previously restricted imports (Smith 1985:47). The result in late 1984 and early 1985 was 'an "orgy" of importing by local authorities', especially of Japanese consumer goods, for the purpose of 'raising funds quickly for local development programs' (Smith 1985:47). In the six months from September 1984 to March 1985 foreign exchange reserves fell over $5 billion (Smith 1985:46; Burns 1985). The government then re-imposed various central controls on the use of foreign currency. (See Section 3 for further discussion of this episode.)

Tables 13.3 and 13.4 show changes in the composition of China's imports and exports, respectively, from 1970 to 1984. The structure of imports has clearly shifted, although not as profoundly as in the 1960s, when grain, crude materials, and semi-manufactures advanced at the expense of machinery and equipment. These items have remained dominant components of total imports. However, a succession of good harvests since 1979 have called into question China's willingness to continue purchasing large quantities of grain and other farm staples; the share of grain in fact fell from 15 per cent of imports in 1982 to 6 per cent in 1983, and that of primary products as a whole dropped from almost 40 per cent to only 19 per cent (ZTN 1984:382; SSB 1985:VI). Also, the beginnings of the surge in imports of consumer durables—televisions, tape and video recorders, watches, cameras, etc.—can be detected in the breakdown by end use and in the series for 'miscellaneous manufactured goods'. In the Chinese division of imports between 'means of production' and 'means of subsistence', the latter rose from 6–8 per cent of the total in the 1950s to 44 per cent in the early 1960s (largely because of the beginning of large-scale grain imports) and then fell back to below 20 per cent at the turn of the 1970s. By the early 1980s, however, it had recovered to almost 30 per cent (SYOC 1983:421).

Table 13.3. *Imports, by type of commodity, 1970–1984 (f.o.b., millions of current dollars)*

	1970	1975	1979	1980	1981	1982	1983	1984
By SITC no. and category								
All commodities	2 051	6 818	14 364	19 180	17 949	16 633	18 399	25 101
Shares of total (%)								
0 Food and live animals	16	12	13	15	17	20	12	9
1 Beverages & tobacco	6	2	0	0	0	1	1	1
2 Crude materials (excl. fuels)	12	11	13	17	18	15	12	10
3 Mineral fuels, lubricants, etc.	2	2	1	1	1	1	1	1
4 Animal & vegitable oils & fats	0	1	1	1	1	1	1	0
5 Chemicals	15	12	10	11	11	13	12	12
6 Semi-manufactured goods	34	32	32	24	22	25	30	29
7 Machinery and transport equipment	20	29	27	28	26	20	24	31
8 Misc. manufactured goods	1	1	2	2	3	4	5	6
9 Other	0	0	1	1	1	1	1	1
By end use								
Total	2 045	6 825	14 285	19 350				
Shares of total (%)								
Foodstuffs	18	12	13	14				
of which:								
Grain	12	8	10	12				
Consumer durables	negl.	negl.	2	3				
Industrial supplies	65	58	59	58				
Capital goods	17	30	26	25				
of which:								
Machinery	9	17	16	n.a.				
Transport equipment	7	12	9	n.a.				

N.B. The totals for the two different classification systems differ slightly because they come from different CIA estimates. The estimates for the SITC classes were made more recently than those for the end-use groups.

Sources: SITC (Standard International Trade Classification) categories: 1970–81, USCIA (1984b:53); 1983–4, USCIA (1985:10–11); by end use: Davie and Carver (1982:43–4).

Table 13.4. *Exports, by type of commodity, 1970–1984 (f.o.b., millions of current US dollars)*

	1970	1975	1979	1980	1981 CIA	1981 Off.	1982 CIA	1982 Off.	1983	1984
By SITC no. and category										
All commodities	2 163.1	7 120.6	13 458.5	18 875.0	21 495.7		22 900.3		23 519.8	27 439.8
					CIA	Off.	CIA	Off.		
Shares of total (%)										
0 Food & live animals	31	29	20	17	16	13	14	13	14	12
1 Beverages and tobacco	1	1	1	1	1	0	1	0	1	1
2 Crude materials (excl. fuels)	18	12	12	10	10	9	8	7	9	9
3 Mineral fuels, lubricants, etc.	3	14	18	23	22	24	23	24	20	21
4 Animal & vegetable oils & fats	1	1	1	0	0	0	0	0	0	
5 Chemicals	5	5	6	6	6	6	6	5	5	5
6 Semi-manufactured goods	27	23	26	23	24	21	21	19	21	22
7 Machinery and transport equipment	3	4	3	3	4	5	3	6	3	4
8 Misc. manufactured goods	11	11	15	16	17	17	18	17	19	21
9 Other	0	0	0	0	0	4	6	8	7	5

N.B. The official shares are based on yuan statistics, and thus differ from the dollar-based CIA shares because of pricing and exchange rate factors.

Sources: 1970–80, USCIA (1984b:1); 1981–4, totals and 'CIA' columns, USCIA (1984a:8–9; 1985:8–9); 'Official' columns, *SYOC* (1983:405).

Marked shifts are also apparent in export performance (Table 13.4). Both food and crude materials (excluding fuels) fell sharply, while oil and miscellaneous manufactures (which include textiles) steadily advanced. Manufactured goods (including semi-manufactures) now make up about half of all exports. Although China's natural conditions and population density make inevitable a long-run decline in the relative importance of agricultural exports, this trend was no doubt given a strong push by past farm policies, just as it is being retarded by the remarkable upturn in agricultural growth rates since 1978 (see Chapter 12). Exports of textiles and light manufactures, in which China's comparative advantage now lies, are impeded by protectionist policies in industrialized countries, where economic stagnation and high unemployment in the 1970s and 1980s have created strong coalitions favouring restrictions on imports. A well-known case in point is the US quota for Chinese textiles. China has expanded rapidly into one relatively open market—weapons—exporting $1.5 billion worth in 1983 (USCIA 1985:9).

The phenomenal growth of oil production through the 1960s and 1970s, which brought oil exports from nil in 1961 to 13.4 million tons in 1979, was one of the more important factors behind the ambitious expectations of the Ten Year Plan (See Chapter 11). At the very time this plan was being formulated, however, oil production was peaking (output declined in 1980 for the first time in thirteen years), as existing wells (especially Daqing) were depleted while new offshore explorations were just getting under way. Chinese factories had shortsightedly shifted from burning abundant coal to using the apparently cheap and plentiful oil, and had paid little attention to conservation or efficiency of use (the sorts of mistakes planning is supposed to avoid). Now that the growth of oil production had virtually ceased, export commitments and growing domestic requirements together claimed more than the available supplies. Although both production and exports resumed growth in 1984,[3] they are unlikely to be able to maintain high growth rates in the near future.

The sharp change in direction of trade that occurred with the Sino-Soviet split two decades ago persists into the 1980s, as is seen in Table 13.5. The great bulk of China's trade is with developed capitalist and Third World countries (including Hong Kong); only about 5 per cent of exports and 9 per cent of imports involved other centrally planned economies, and the Soviet Union played a distinctly minor role even in this group. In 1983, however, Sino-Soviet trade began reviving towards more normal levels and it virtually doubled the following year (see also Kawai 1985:9). In 1985 the two countries signed a five-year, $14 billion trade agreement.

China's largest trading partners have been Japan, Hong Kong, and the United States, in that order. With some fluctuation over the four years shown, it is apparent that China has been more than covering small deficits in its trade with developed capitalist countries by means of large surpluses with developing areas, with Hong Kong alone responsible for almost half of the latter.

The importance of the colony to China is only suggested by these data, for it is also related to Hong Kong's role as a financial centre, a source of investment, and a window on new international technical and commercial developments. In

Table 13.5. Direction of trade, 1981–1984 (f.o.b., billions US dollars)

	1981			1982			1983			1984		
	X	M	Balance	X	M	Balance	X	M	Balance	X	M	Balance
World	21.5	17.9	3.6	23.4	16.7	6.7	24.0	18.4	5.6	27.4	25.1	52.5
Less developed countries	10.2	3.9	6.3	12.0	4.2	7.8	12.7	5.0	7.7	14.0	7.6	21.6
Hong Kong	5.2	2.0	3.2	5.4	2.0	3.4	5.8	2.5	3.3	7.1	5.0	12.1
Developed capitalist countries	10.0	12.7	-2.7	10.2	10.8	-0.6	9.9	11.7	-1.8	11.9	15.4	27.3
USA	1.9	3.6	-1.7	2.3	2.9	-0.6	2.3	2.2	0.1	3.1	3.0	6.1
Japan	5.0	5.1	-0.1	5.1	3.5	1.6	4.8	4.9	-0.1	5.7	7.2	12.9
Western Europe	2.6	2.5	0.1	2.3	2.4	-0.1	2.4	2.9	-0.5	2.5	3.4	5.9
USSR	0.1	0.1		0.1	0.2	-0.1	0.3	0.3		0.6	0.6	1.2
Eastern Europe	0.7	0.7		0.7	0.9	-0.2	0.6	0.9	-0.3	0.6	1.0	1.6
Asian communist countries and Cuba	0.4	0.5	-0.1	0.4	0.6	-0.2	0.4	0.5	-0.1	0.3	0.5	0.8

Source: USCIA (1984a: Tables 2–3; 1985: Tables 2–3).

1984 Britain and China agreed to a formula for Hong Kong to revert to Chinese control at the end of Britain's lease in 1997. The agreement incorporates a Chinese promise to maintain for fifty years the colony's current social system, including the present judicial system, freedom of travel, and a convertible currency. China's delicate task has been to recover a goose still able to lay golden eggs. While there is no doubt of its ability to accomplish the first part of the task, Hong Kong business and the global corporate world to which it is tied retain the power to deny the second.

3 Foreign investment

3.1 General trends

While expanded reliance on trade is an important part of China's new economic strategy, it is its decision to encourage foreign private capital investment, in joint ventures and even wholly foreign owned enterprises, that constitutes the sharpest break with the past. China has devised a parade of new institutions, political and legal, designed to turn the frown directed at foreign capital during the Mao years into a welcoming smile. 'Special economic zones' (SEZs), the most successful being Shenzhen on the northern border of Hong Kong, have been set up in coastal areas of Guangdong and Fujian Provinces with favourable tax, profit repatriation, and other provisions for foreign investors; and similar benefits have been extended to important coastal cities. China has encouraged the formation of joint equity ventures with foreign partners, especially for larger industrial projects involving sophisticated technologies in key sectors (Brehm 1983:16).[4] For other kinds of projects it has promoted various types of arrangements with foreign business, such as joint operations, co-operative production, compensation trade, countertrade, and export processing agreements.[5] At this writing, some forty laws and decrees have been enacted specifically concerning foreign investment matters, including joint ventures, taxes, SEZs, foreign exchange control, join exploration for offshore oil, and patent protection (Gu Ming 1984:16), and over one hundred others relevant to foreign economic matters (Graham 1983). Eighteen multinational oil companies have been contracted with to explore the South China and Yellow Seas for oil and several are actively drilling as China's joint venture partners.

    In the same vein, China participates in various international economic bodies, such as the International Monetary Fund (IMF), the World Bank, and the Food and Agriculture Organization. United Nations aid was used in preparing and carrying out the national population census of 1982; and loans have been taken from the World Bank for various agricultural and infrastructural projects (Ross 1985:48) and from Japan for large-scale energy and transport development programmes. Not least significant is the sending abroad of thousands of Chinese students and hundreds of delegations of specialists, and the reception of many similar delegations from abroad. In 1984, moreover, 12.85 million tourists—including 11.72 million overseas Chinese and residents of Hong Kong and Macao—visited China, spending almost $1.13 billion in foreign exchange (SSB 1985:VII).

The welcoming posture extends to the terms offered potential investors. These improved considerably in 1983 and 1984 in a deliberate attempt to step up the still cautious pace of foreign capital inflow. The industrial and commercial (turnover) tax was lowered for joint ventures and made subject to adjustment in the event of losses—an act that amounts to softening the budget constraint on joint ventures. The latter were also relieved of all income tax liability for the first two profitable years, and half in the third year. The machinery and equipment imports of foreign firms and joint ventures were exempted from import tariffs and industrial and commercial taxes, and virtually all imports by joint ventures producing to export were excused from these taxes. Although a chief aim was to stimulate exports and earn foreign exchange, the domestic market was made available for part of the output, and in fact, as of spring 1985, only one-third of SEZ production was being exported (Delfs 1985b). The income tax rate in SEZs and 'open' cities was limited to 15 per cent (as compared with 18.5 per cent in Hong Kong); SEZs and 'open' cities were given powers, normally kept at a higher level, to approve investments, and entry and exit procedures in them for foreigners were simplified (Kawai 1984; Gu Ming 1984; Williams and Brilliant 1984). The legal environment also improved considerably (see below). Other aspects of China's embrace are more problematic, as we shall see.

The resulting scale of investment has been significant, if not up to the leaders' hopes. Through 1983, Chinese organs, from the centre to individual enterprises, had 'actually utilized' US $14.6 billion of intergovernmental loans, bank loans, and direct investment; 1,780 foreign companies had invested in China (Chiang 1983:26); 190 Sino-foreign joint ventures had been formed; 1,123 joint operations and 31 joint prospecting and resource exploitation projects had been carried out (FBIS, 26 July 1984:K13–14). In 1984 another $2.66 billion was absorbed, including $1.32 billion in loans and $1.34 million of direct investment (SSB 1985:VII); and 741 additional Chinese–foreign joint ventures were approved (Zhao 1985a:VI). By 1984 many of the world's best known corporations were engaged in operations in China, from Volkswagen, American Motors, IBM, and Mitsui to Beatrice Foods, Gillette, and Coca Cola.

China has also begun engaging in undertakings abroad, earning foreign exchange from the export of labour and services and learning relevant technologies by investing in foreign enterprises. From 1979 to 1983 construction and other labour-oriented projects were carried out in fifty-seven countries and regions, involving $2.2 billion of contracted value. Another $1.68 billion of contracts were agreed to in 1984, and $0.55 billion were fulfilled in that year (SSB 1985:VII). Over forty contracting corporations in China send out labour for construction and other services in a wide range of activities, from building harbours, railways, and hotels to agriculture and fishing (Cao 1983:27). Most such activities so far have been in Third World Countries, especially oil-exporting Middle Eastern countries with foreign exchange to spend. In mid-1984, over 30,000 Chinese workers and technicians were working abroad.

China has also invested in joint ventures of various kinds with foreign partners in some sixteen countries as of mid-1984 (FBIS, 26 July 1984:K14).

3.2   Labour

There are two distinct kinds of contradictions between China's socialist economy and the norms of international business. One, involving bureaucratic power and prerogatives, is the difficulty of pursuing market requirements in a rigid administrative planning regime; this will be explored further below. The other concerns the clash of values in a country that had outlawed private business of any size years before.

Consider, for example, the use of labour in foreign enterprises and joint ventures. No issue is more sensitive to socialism's self-image than the treatment of the proletariat; for instance, it was fear of unemployment, more than any other factor that limited the scope of Hungary's market reforms (Granick 1975), and this sensitivity would be expected to be even greater where foreign capital was involved. Thus, a bone of contention between foreign corporations and their Chinese hosts, and between foreign and Chinese partners in joint ventures, has been the cost of labour and the right to recruit and dismiss workers. Joint ventures have found it difficult to recruit workers freely despite provisions to that effect in the SEZ regulations; they commonly must obtain them from labour service companies (Falkenheim and Rawski 1983:32). Similarly, dismissal has been rare, although it is sanctioned under certain circumstances. The Regulations on Rewards and Punishments for Enterprise Staff and Workers, adopted in 1982, and the interim provisions governing labour relations in the SEZs of Guangdong Province, adopted in 1981, both permit dismissal for disciplinary reasons after approval at a higher level (and, in the former case, also by the enterprise workers' congress or trade union). Relevant regulations also permit dismissal, with severance pay, when technological or production changes make workers redundant (Horsley 1984:23–5). Experience indicates, however, that the Chinese are very reluctant to permit dismissals except in extreme circumstances.

State industrial workers, as we have seen, are a relatively privileged group, with higher pay, job security, and a gamut of social welfare benefits. In other words, their price, like other prices, does not reflect the market equilibrium 'shadow price' of labour. It is precisely the *cost* of their treatment that has confined it to full-status state employees and reduced the latter's representation in total non-agricultural employment in recent years (Chapter 14). Thus, the concept of 'labour cost' is ambiguous: it could refer either to the low 'shadow price' that would clear a theoretical free labour market in China's abundant labour circumstances, or to the higher real cost of contract or temporary workers, or to the much higher cost in wages, benefits, and subsidies of a full-status state worker. The government, while advertising China's low labour costs to the business world, has on the whole charged this last amount for labour.

Table 13.6. *Standard wage schedule, Shenzhen SEZ, 1983 (yuan)*

Grade	Basic wage	Industr. zone increment	'Frontier' allowance	Price suppl.	Total
Apprentice	32	32	15	5	84
1	40	44	15	5	104
2	47	51.7	15	5	118.7
3	55	60.5	15	5	130.5
4	64	70.4	15	5	154.4
5	75	82.5	15	5	177.5
6	87	87	15	5	194
7	102	102	15	5	224
8	120	120	5	5	260

Source: Kobayashi (1984:10).

The average annual wage of state workers and staff in 1982 was Y832, or around Y70 per month. The basic time or piece rate component was about 72 per cent of the total, or Y50 per month. Bonuses constituted about 11 per cent, overtime pay 1.5 per cent, and supplementary payments of various kinds, 1.5 per cent. Also included were enterprise subsidies (14 per cent), such as the Y5 instituted in 1979 to compensate for price increases of nonstaple foods, as well as subsidies covering home leave for workers living apart from their spouses or (if single) parents, maternity leave, child care, sick leave, and medical expenses of workers and their dependants, housing rent, coal for heating, commuting expenses, baths, haircuts, etc. (Horsley 1984:20; *SYOC* 1983:485, 491). At the average exchange rate of 1982, the total figure would come to around US$440, or $37 per month.

In contrast, joint ventures in 1983 paid monthly wages of Y110 ($55)–Y250 ($125)—in other words, from one and one-half to almost three and one-half times this average (Horsley 1984:19; *AWSJ*, 18 April 1983:8). A standard schedule of wages for workers in the Shenzhen SEZ is shown in Table 13.6. One Shenzhen enterprise (the Hua Yi Aluminium Factory) paid the following wages in 1983 (Kobayaski 1984:10):[6]

Office workers	Y100–145
Operatives	Y130–180
Assistant engineers	Y160–220
Department managers and engineers	Y200–260
General manager	Y240
Chief engineer	Y300

The wage was generally paid not directly to the worker but to a labour service company (in the case of Japanese enterprises in Shekou, to the China Merchants Steam Navigation Co.), which deducted a varying proportion (20 per cent in the above case) to cover labour insurance and welfare fund contributions and returned the rest to the worker or the enterprise (Kobayashi 1984:10)[7]

Part of the differential in wages paid to workers in foreign-connected enterprises is justified by the Chinese on the grounds that workers in foreign enterprises or joint ventures are expected to be more qualified and productive than the average state worker. But much of its represents the 'social wage'—costs borne by the state and enterprise in subsidizing workers (in addition to enterprise subsidies) in one way or another.

For instance, state enterprises paid a total of Y15.4 billion (an amount equal to 21.7 per cent of the total wage bill) into labour insurance and welfare funds in 1982 (SYOC 1983:491). These funds finance pensions, injury, disability and other relief payments, death benefits, recreational, educational and day care facilities, and clinics (Horsley 1984:20–1). In addition, however, China's price structure contains within it large subsidies, covered by the state budget, for the urban population. The government announced that these price subsidies cost Y20 billion in 1980 (FBIS, 4 February 1981:L11),[8] an amount equal to about one-third of the total wage bill of all state-owned units in that year. Most important in this category was the state subsidy of foodgrain and vegetable oil, which were purchased by the state at prices well above their selling prices. One estimate puts this subsidy alone, which grew rapidly with increasing grain procurement prices, at about Y330 per worker in 1983 (or about 40 per cent of the total wage given above) and the total value of all subsidies and fringe benefits available to each state worker in 1982 at almost Y900 (Lardy 1983b:23). Added to the average 1982 money wage (net of enterprise subsidies) of Y716, this brings the annual total social wage, including all subsidies, to the neighbourhood of Y1,616 ($808), or Y135 ($67) per month, two and one-quarter times the money wage. This is well within the range (Y110–Y250) of wages mentioned above as paid by joint ventures, and suggests that the Chinese government wants to make foreign firms and joint ventures pay at least the full social cost of a state employee.

It is true that these subsidies, which dwarf those available to the much larger rural population, have exacerbated the urban–rural income gap, prevented greater reliance on the market, imposed the additional cost of a huge and 'unprecedented' rationing system, and complicated the containment of rural–urban migration (Lardy 1983b:23). It is also true that China's leaders have begun acting to reduce the subsidies (Chapter 14). Yet the fact remains that workers were among the chief economic winners in the Chinese revolution. This outcome is embodied in their high social wage, although new policies towards urban workers threaten to erode their privileged position (see Chapter 14, Section 3).

3.3 Administrative planning and the open door

For many foreign businesses, the open door has revealed a maze of bureaucratic obstacles that have to be negotiated at every turn. As in the case of the agricultural reforms, a constraint on the development of new forms of foreign trade and investment has been their inevitable links with the domestic economy, which lacks the flexibility and incentives to respond quickly to the needs of a dynamic new sector.

Attempting to spell out the relationship between joint ventures and the planned economy, the 1983 joint venture regulations in fact give the former considerable autonomy, including 'the right to do business independently' under Chinese law and the provisions of their contracts, and to develop their own capital construction, production, and operating plans. Joint ventures are subject to the guidance and supervision of administrative authorities, but may not be issued directives (Cohen and Horsley 1983:45; 'Regulations for the Implementation . . .' 1983). At the same time, however, they (together with wholly foreign-owned firms) are dependent upon the administrative supply network and commercial departments for their materials and supplies. Many of the manufactured exports (clothing, consumer goods, textiles, machinery) that now fall within China's comparative advantage are subject to rapidly changing world market conditions, yet they must rely for inputs on other enterprises whose plans are set many months in advance (Falkenheim and Rawski 1983:28). Firms within the SEZs have complained of an inability to get needed materials on short notice (Lee 1984:17). Moreover, they are subject to the same bottlenecks and shortages that have afflicted industry generally, sometimes finding themselves without power or cement, for instance (Falkenheim and Rawski 1983:30). On the other hand, there is fear that the priority access promised joint ventures to some domestic supplies, such as construction materials and utilities,[9] will worsen shortages in the domestic economy (Lee 1984:19).

There are two possible avenues for addressing this kind of problem. One is to isolate the foreign-oriented sectors from the domestic economy, permitting them to develop in their own way, outside the planning framework and oriented to the world market. There are some signs of this approach in China; indeed, the very concept of 'special economic zone' is of a differentiated area subject to its own rules. Although the intention is to make the SEZs a gateway for the entry of advanced techniques to the core economy, such zones in other developing countries have been notorious for lacking spread effects. Often consisting of 'screwdriver industries' that import equipment, components, and materials for assembly and re-export, they gain little for the domestic economy beyond the non-repatriated value added. Falkenheim and Rawski discovered several instances in the Shenzhen SEZ in which equipment such as earth-moving machinery and material such as sugar and steel sections were imported rather than being obtained from within China, because of unresponsive domestic supply or inflexible pricing (1983:36). In fact, a key piece of Shenzhen's infrastructure is an 85 km border around the zone, consisting of a patrol road, six port inspection stations, thirteen rural inspection stations, and thirty barracks. Ostensibly to curb smuggling inland of duty-free imports, this internal border actually has somewhat broader purposes (Kobayashi 1985b:16):

After completion of the boundary, the SEZ will be able to carry out what it terms 'special policies', which it has not defined as yet, but which are likely to be somewhat incompatible with the economic system prevailing in the rest of China. These policies are expected to be more flexible, providing overseas investors with a more attractive, more stable environment in which to invest their capital. [Williams and Brilliant 1984:13]

This latter-day version of the old foreign enclave is costly in foreign exchange, as we have seen, since it relies heavily upon imports. More importantly, it locks within the enclave precisely those modern skills, methods, and technologies whose spread throughout the economy is the host country's prime objective, and it thus gives rise to the classic problem of dualism.[10]

In opening more and more of its territory to foreign-oriented activity, however, China seems intent on avoiding such a result. The bulk of foreign investments, especially the larger projects, have in any case located outside the SEZs, which have tended to attract mostly overseas Chinese investment in relatively small undertakings.[11] Unresponsiveness of the planned economy to the needs of foreign traders has been attacked by setting plans slack and permitting enterprises to market their above-quota output freely. Moreover, although the fourteen opened coastal cities[12] include the original 'treaty ports' of old, today they contain a considerable fraction of China's industry; opening them to foreign investment would seem incompatible with isolating the domestic economy. It is China's express intention to concentrate foreign capital in coastal cities, which 'are better grounded industrially, scientifically and technologically, and . . . have richer experience in economic and technological exchanges with foreign countries' (Zhao 1984:ix). These are to assimilate the new techniques and methods and gradually pass them on to the rest of the country. While trickle-down may occur eventually, the short-run effect will undoubtedly be to increase regional inequality.

Thus, the second possible response to friction between the foreign-oriented sector and the domestic economy is reform of the latter to activate market forces, relax administrative controls, and make enterprises responsive to demand and sensitive to cost (see Chapter 14). The State Council, in fact, announced its intention to use foreign investment activities in the coastal cities as an opening wedge to bring about general reform:

Reform and opening to the outside world must not be separated, [the State Council official] said. These cities would . . . carry out a series of reforms to make the system of management conform to the open policy. Some of the successful methods practiced in the special economic zones may also be tried out in the port cities. [FBIS, 13 July 1984:K13–14]

What this portends is still far from clear. The quoted official did not elaborate, but turned instead to the need for competent cadres and well trained personnel, which invokes the ever-present ambiguity in discussions of 'reform' as to whether it means relaxation of the command economy or better commanders. Moreover, after ambitious statements from the leadership about the intended opening of the entire east coast to foreign investment (e.g., *BR*, 25 March

1985:31), it was announced in July 1985 that, at least temporarily, only the four largest of the fourteen 'open cities' (Shanghai, Guangzhou, Tianjin, Dalian) would pursue this goal seriously (Burns 1985; *FEER*, 25 July 1985:13).

The legal and administrative machinery has evolved rapidly to try to meet the requirements of foreign investors but within a planning framework. Allusion has already been made to the myriad new laws and regulations that have emerged to shape the legal framework of rights and obligations with respect to protection of property, taxation, profit repatriation, access to foreign exchange, dispute settlement, labour management, and a host of similar issues. This is an ongoing process, often responsive to the expressed concerns of foreign firms reluctant to commit resources in an environment with less specific legal protection than they are used to. As the Deputy Secretary-General of the State Council, Gu Ming (1984:16), acknowledged in July 1984, 'Some foreign investors still take a wait-and-see attitude. Others . . . wonder about the risks'. Many have remained aloof because of China's continued vagueness about protecting proprietary information. Lack of a patent law, for instance, was a significant obstacle to technology transfer until one was finally adopted in March 1984; but, in common with practice in many low-income countries, the new law provides little or no protection in a number of areas, such as chemicals, pharmaceuticals, foods, medicines, and scientific discoveries (*CBR*, March–April 1984:5). Finally, basic concern about the longevity of the current policies, aggravated by frequent swings in policy that reflect internal disagreements within the leadership, inhibit would-be large investors.

It is generally felt that the foreign investment attracted as of the mid-1980s accordingly failed to fulfil the reform leadership's expectations: 'officials have spoken of billions of dollars. But probably less than a billion dollars has trickled in in the first five or six years' (Burns 1985). The total through 1984, in fact, came to $840 million, with an additional $3.2 billion of potential inflow represented by contracts signed through April 1985. While these are not trifling sums, even the latter one probably does not exceed by much, if at all, the infrastructural investment (roads, harbours, housing, etc.) already expended in the SEZs alone (Delfs 1985b:70; Burns 1985).

Improvement in the business environment in 1983 was due in part to the promulgation of detailed regulations for implementation of the joint venture law,[13] and in part to favourable adjustment of laws and regulations governing import tariffs, corporate income taxes on joint ventures, foreign exchange controls, and mediation of contract disputes (Kawai 1984:21). A trademark law took effect in March 1983, the long-awaited patent law in 1984, and a law on economic contracts involving foreign interests in 1985 (Cohen 1985); at this writing the process of developing a legal framework supportive of foreign economic relations proceeds apace (Kawai 1984; Gu Ming 1984:16–17).

While China has been adept at producing laws and regulations to meet foreign (and, to some degree, domestic) demand, similar efforts to adjust the administrative framework have proved less successful. At the interface between free-wheeling international capitalism and central command planning, administrative reform has reflected all the contradictions inherent in this uneasy match.

Decentralization of the administrative apparatus governing foreign economic policy was at the cutting edge of this reform. Most of the business previously handled at the centre by foreign trade corporations (FTCs) under the Ministry of Foreign Trade was taken over by branch offices newly established in provincial capitals throughout the country. New FTCs were set up under other ministries (e.g., China National Machinery and Equipment Import-Export Corporation, or EQUIMPEX, under the Ministry of Machine Building Industry, and China National Offshore Oil Corporation, under the Ministry of Petroleum Industry); while still others were created in Beijing, Shanghai, Tianjin, Guangdong, Guangxi, Fujian, Liaoning, and Hebei under the shared leadership of the localities and the Ministry of Trade. Some of the new sectoral corporations, established to cut across administrative lines and permit more rational planning and resource use (see Chapter 14), have been given powers to engage in foreign trade and receive foreign investment in their particular sectors. Provinces and cities have received similar authority. Shanghai and Tianjin in 1985 were authorized to approve investment projects up to $30 million. The limit for Beijing and Liaoning was $10 million, and for other provinces and municipalities $5 million (Imai 1985b:3). Some enterprises were given authority to engage directly in trade deals with foreign businesses (Clarke 1984:8–9; Chao 1982:212–13).

This diffusion of authority led to a change in the exchange rate mechanism. Under the old system, all foreign trade was in the hands of FTCs under the Ministry of Trade. The corporations exported and imported goods at world prices and bought and sold them in China at domestic prices. World market prices were not permitted to affect the very different domestic prices. In general, world prices of China's manufactured exports, converted to *renminbi* at the official exchange rate, tended to be below the domestic prices at which they were procured by the FTCs, causing the latter to make losses in their export operations. On the other hand, FTCs made profits on their import operations because world prices of many imported goods, at the official exchange rate, were also below the level at which such goods sold in China. The only 'bottom line' that mattered, however, was that of the trading system as a whole, for the profits and losses of individual FTCs were aggregated at the level of the Ministry of Trade (now Ministry of Foreign Economic Relations and Trade, or MOFERT), whose net profit or loss became part of the national budget. Whether individual FTCs made profits or losses was merely an accounting question. With decentralization, however, the profitability of foreign trade to particular units empowered to engage in it began to affect their behaviour—in particular, to encourage imports and discourage exports. This situation may well have contributed to the balance of trade deficits of 1978–9 (see Section 2 above).

At the beginning of 1981, therefore, the yuan was given a new 'internal settlement rate' of Y2.8 to $1.0 (the old rate was Y1.5 = $1.0 for foreign-trade-related transactions. This is the rate at which foreign exchange needed for imports was to be obtained and at which that earned by exports was converted back into yuan. The effect was to make exports more profitable and imports less so.[14] However, depreciation of the yuan against a strong dollar gradually narrowed the difference between the 'domestic settlement rate' and the official exchange rate until it disappeared in 1984.[15]

In any case, depreciation of the yuan did not result in any greater conformity of Chinese *relative* prices to those of the world market. To bring these into greater harmony would of course require fundamental price reform (see Chapter 14). The effective isolation of producers and consumers in China from international prices has cut them off from world market signals, to which they, moreover, have had no incentive to respond. Some efforts have been made to remedy this; for example, in 1983 it was decided that joint ventures would pay international market prices (in yuan) for such Chinese goods as oil, coal, and lumber, but only when these goods were to be embodied in exports (Kawai 1984:21). Moreover, the logic of fast-moving events in Shenzhen—a new currency, the elimination of customs duties for trade with Hong Kong, simplification of entry and exit procedures for foreigners, and the construction of the border separating the SEZ from the rest of China—suggests that many prices there are being allowed to fluctuate freely, in which case they would tend to align themselves with those of Hong Kong (*CBR*, July–August 1984:5; Kobayashi 1985b).[16]

The price problem has many ramifications. Lack of price flexibility means that domestic producers of exports have no incentive to make improvements that enhance their products' marketability because they cannot recover the costs. The Shanghai No. 1 Sewing Machine Plant, for example, loses profits from its exports because of the extra costs of the instruction manuals and special packing required. The result is a system of negotiated subsidies, as in purely domestic arrangements (see Chapter 14), which both are time-consuming to arrive at and disguise the true pattern of China's comparative advantage (Falkenheim and Rawski 1983:39). As one Chinese economist put it,[17]

Under the current system of economic management, prices, taxes, revenue, and profit rates have long distorted the 'true' value of our exports. By the same token, current foreign exchange rates are so distorted that it is difficult to compare accurately foreign and domestic prices. In short, we have not yet made a penetrating study of foreign trade theory, the significance of macroeconomic effects, and the terms of trade. In the absence of such theory, the Foreign Trade Ministry itself can hardly resolve these problems practically. [Wang Linsheng 1983:62]

Price rigidity is part of the more general problem of incentives—the lack of reward for improvement and innovation, of penalty for its absence (Chapters 11, 14). This problem, for example, explains a discovery that astonished two China experts: almost none of China's textile and clothing exports is made with domestic machinery, because, despite half a century of production experience, Chinese sewing machines still leak oil (Falkenheim and Rawski 1983:44).

At the same time as foreign trade and investment powers were being decentralized, various new national planning and co-ordinating bodies were established, such as China International Trust and Investment Corporation (CITIC), giving rise to much confusion over the division of responsibilities between the individual actors and the national bodies. Particular uncertainty has attached to the question of jurisdiction over particular product lines. Clarke (1984:9) cites cases in which 'bloody and protracted bureaucratic battles' over turf took place between various administrative bodies.

Initially to overcome this problem, the government created the Ministry of Foreign Economic Relations and Trade (MOFERT) in March 1982 by merging the Ministry of Foreign Trade with the Foreign Investment Control Commission and the Import–Export Commission. MOFERT, which was to be superordinate in both trade and foreign investment matters, including joint ventures (Cohen and Horsley 1983:45), engaged in a number of actions to achieve greater control of the market: establishing a licensing system for both imports and exports, imposing export duties to curb exports of goods in short supply at home and tap local export profits, and establishing port commissioners' offices in Shanghai, Tianjin, Guangzhou, and Dalian to co-ordinate trade activity in these major coastal urban regions (Clarke 1984:10). In March 1984, the ministry announced a policy of further tightening central control over trade by increasing the number of commodities subject to export licences, fixing commodity prices, establishing quotas, and enforcing monopoly trading privileges for the national foreign trade corporations over important commodities such as oil, grain, cotton, sugar, steel, and timber (Delfs 1984a:84).

This approach lasted only six months; it was then replaced by a diametrically opposite policy, approved by the State Council in September 1984, aimed at *reducing* the monopoly powers exercised by the national FTCs and separating MOFERT, as a government agency responsible for overall policy-making, from actual participation in foreign trade transactions. Henceforth, trading would be done mainly by a variety of specialized companies, which would compete for the free patronage of the ultimate buyers and sellers. Actual profits and losses of foreign transactions would accrue largely to the importers and exporters, instead of being absorbed by the FTCs (Delfs 1984a:84). By the end of 1984 there were already 944 foreign trade corporations, both national and local (Kobayashi 1985a:1). And the Bank of China supported the new approach by permitting '"thousands" of domestic enterprises to borrow foreign exchange to import equipment and repay in renminbi' (Lee 1985a:50).

This victory of the liberalizers was no doubt aided by by the fact that foreign exchange reserves had reached the record level of $17 billion in mid-1984, which was felt to be excessive; the government had been desirous of expanding imports in 1984, but had failed to prevent a continuing trade surplus from further expanding reserves in the first half (Imai 1985b:2–3). High growth rates at the end of the year, a runaway 23.1 per cent industrial growth rate during the first half of 1985, and a rapidly expanding money supply all then contributed to raising imports (*CD*, 31 July 1985; Delfs 1985c; Ross 1985; Lee 1985b:72).

The result, which paralleled that of the first decentralization of 1978–80, was a precipitous fall in China's foreign exchange reserves (see Section 2 above) and the consequent imposition once again of central controls. Access to foreign exchange was curtailed; the issue of letters of credit to provinces and cities for imports of most types of durable consumer goods was suspended; new taxes were imposed, sharply raising import prices; and many impending foreign deals were cancelled or deferred (Smith 1985:46; Lee 1985b:72).

Closely linked to the turmoil occasioned by relaxing central control over foreign trade has been the problem of corruption. The 'open door' has let in a variety of unsavoury Western values and given play to the operation of some domestic ones. 'Wherever the discipline inspection commissions cast their eye, they find misuse of powers by party and government organizations and their officials' (Kobayashi 1985a:1). '[K]ickbacks and other finagling . . . smuggling rings and corruption among officials in a position to profit from contacts with outsiders', the use of official funds by a senior Yunnan party official to import pornographic videotapes—even an attempt to smuggle opium from the Shenzhen SEZ into Hong Kong—have become common fare in the Chinese press (Burns 1985). A particularly egregious example, exposed in summer 1985, occurred on Hainan Island, an open district. There, the head of the local government and vice-secretary of the regional party committee led his colleagues in using their access to foreign exchange to import (tax-free) an astonishing 2.86 million colour television sets, 252,000 video cassette recorders, 122,000 motorcyles, and 10,000 cars and minibuses, most of which were resold throughout the country at double or triple the original prices. A large part of the population of Hainan Island seems to have been involved in this activity (CD, 1 August 1985; BR, 12 August 1985).[18] Similar entrepreneurship was displayed in 1984 by military units in Fuzhou (Delfs 1985a:59).

Such cases exemplify some of the difficulties facing economic reform. The widespread participation of the local Hainan community suggests that many people thought themselves within the new bounds of propriety established by rhetoric about 'getting rich' and relying on the market. It was, after all, the market, in combination with Hainan's privileged access to foreign exchange and duty-free imports, that created a golden opportunity to wheel and deal. And the Hainan authorities had in fact been permitted to (1) use foreign exchange at their own discretion, and (2) resell imported goods as a means of raising funds for regional development (Kobayashi 1985a:1). Where personal gain is legitimized but administrative fiat still basically runs the show, the distinction between private gain and public responsibility is easily blurred. In the case of a Chongqing steamship company that planned to build a tourist hotel to earn foreign exchange for importing tug boats (Delfs 1985a:59), the motive may have been less objectionable, but the activity itself is no more conducive to social efficiency.

As of mid 1986, considerable uncertainty remained about the ultimate scale and impact of China's turn to foreign capital. The volume of capital absorbed had risen unevenly and substantially, but less than the leadership had hoped (see above). The country has moved with dispatch to improve conditions for foreign investors and to establish an effective legal machinery, but at this writing the fundamental problems of the planning and administrative system have not been solved, and the state accordingly has had to swing back and forth between loosening and tightening administrative controls, adding to the already rampant confusion in the minds of both Chinese and foreigners about the division of rights and responsibilities within the bureaucracy. On the other hand, China has managed to avoid financial dependency and maintain a robust international financial position.

The reform leadership of Deng Xiaoping, Party General Secretary Hu Yaobang, and Prime Minister Zhao seems firmly committed to expanding foreign economic relations (Barnett 1984). It also appears determined to use foreign capital not only to supplement Chinese savings (indeed, China on balance has exported capital, as we have seen) but to introduce technology, manufacture goods that China is as yet unable to produce, raise export earnings, educate managers and technicians, and change attitudes. Contradictions between the needs of foreign capital and China's conventional practices can be used to change conventions—a very Maoist notion. The ways of the advanced industrial capitalist economies are seen as 'modern', and the Four Modernizations therefore must imitate them. What better way to do so than to have them on Chinese soil, where they can be observed at first hand?

The ultimate fate of this bold experiment, however, is linked to that of domestic economic reform, for reasons discussed above. If the progress of reform is minimal, the tendency will probably grow to isolate foreign activity in self-sufficient enclaves, where it will have little impact. In a thoroughly reformed environment, the large party–state bureaucracy, which is ill-equipped to administer a market–socialist economy, would lose much of its present functions, status, and authority. Many of its members and others who hold older Marxist values at variance with the views of Deng, Hu, and Zhao may use the failings of reform as well as the resurgence of corrupt practices to attack the 'open door' policy itself. The 'anti-spiritual pollution' campaign that was waged inconclusively in 1983, targeting not only crime, corruption, and pornography but also Western liberal humanist ideas and relationships with foreigners, reflected the objections of that group. But foreign investment has a way of creating its own interest groups among the élites with which it deals in host countries—one reason it is widely distrusted in the Third World. Such groups may come to imitate the ways and appreciate the viewpoints of the global corporations to whose fortunes their own careers become tied, and, given enough time, may become a counterweight to the domestic bureaucracy.

Until the leadership identifies the core socialist values and institutions that it hopes to protect from what Mao called the 'sugar-coated bullets of the bourgeoisie', however, it is difficult to know how far it intends to go both in introducing reform and utilizing the world market. There is an implicit assumption, reminiscent of the 'ti-yong' dichotomy of China's nineteenth century modernizers ('Western learning for use, Chinese learning as the essence'), that the foreign presence can be used to learn modern techniques without changing China's socialist essence. Thus, the SEZs

should boldly introduce advanced technology and methods of management from abroad and make use of foreign capital. Our aim is to promote China's socialist modernization; we should adhere to the characteristics of the socialist system in our work in the special zones, and the workers, staff, and other inhabitants should be imbued with socialist morality. [Zhao 1982a:49–50]

But unlike in the nineteenth century, when there was at stake a cultural identity that every Chinese knew and understood, what constitutes socialism today is no longer self-evident. In much of the world, political divisions consciously express the deep tensions between traditional socialist values—such as security, solidarity, equality, co-operation—and the values required and rewarded by the market: individualism, tolerance of risk and uncertainty, inequality, and the treatment of all things, talents, and people as potential commodities. Zhao Ziyang's words, ignoring such tensions, help little to chart the prospects for China's love affair with the world market.

Notes

1. Clarke (1984) provides a short guide to the status and problems of decentralization of foreign trade authority as of early 1984, as well as to the more important agencies involved.

2. However, these were alleviated considerably by surpluses in transport, services, and transfers, so that the current account balances were much better than those for trade alone. In fact, according to the same source (Davie and Carver 1982:47), the current account balances were actually positive in all three years: $0.9 billion in 1978, $0.2 billion in 1979, and $1.2 billion in 1980.

3. Crude oil production rose by 8 per cent to 114.5 million tons in 1984. Exports of crude (in quantity terms) rose unexpectedly sharply—by 45 per cent to 22 million tons—while exports of refined petroleum products increased by 11 per cent to 5.7 million tons (*FEER*, 11 July 1985:54; *ZTN* 1984:408). The dollar value of exports of both together rose 15.5 per cent (USCIA 1985:8).

4. *Joint ventures* are jointly owned enterprises, in which the foreign owner's share generally must be *at least* 25 per cent, but is not limited at the upper end, and has tended to be around 50 per cent. Sectors in which joint ventures are encouraged include: energy, building materials, metallurgy, machine building, offshore oil exploration equipment, electronics and computers, communications equipment, textiles, foodstuffs, medical apparatus, packaging, agriculture, animal husbandry, aquaculture, tourism, and service trades. See 'Regulations for the Implementation . . . (1983:Article 2).

5. Brief definitions of these forms are in order. In *joint operations*, also called 'contractual joint venture' or 'co-production venture', the foreign party provides capital in the form of equipment to an enterprise managed by the Chinese side, and receives a negotiated share of the profit; the capital is repaid after no more than ten years, usually in half that time. *Compensation trade* is an arrangement under which the foreign side supplies equipment, technology, or training and is paid in resulting products. *Countertrade* involves an explicit or implicit agreement that the party selling to China will purchase an equivalent value of Chinese products. *Co-operative production* resembles both joint ventures and compensation trade: the foreign party licenses a product or technology to the Chinese side and plays a major initial role in supplying the equipment and technology, helping set up the factory, and training the management and work-force; often payment is made in the form of the factory's product, as in compensation trade. Under *export processing* arrangements, the foreign firm supplies the materials or components for processing or assembly according to

its specifications by the Chinese side for a fee, and then takes the product back. For fuller discussions of these forms, see World Bank (1983, II:433–42) and various issues of *China Business Review*.

6. This source states that the general wage level in Shenzhen is less than half that in Hong Kong, while labour productivity and production costs are 75–80 per cent and 60–70 per cent, respectively, of Hong Kong's level.

7. A later wage reform in the Shekou industrial district of Shenzhen changed the wage formula to increase the proportion of total compensation tied to performance. In the first quarter of 1984, the average monthly wage there was Y193.8, of which 40.8 per cent was base wage (including 'frontier' allowance and food subsidy), 37.2 per cent performance-based increment (bonus?), and 22 per cent 'floating wage' (connected to enterprise profitability). See Kobayashi (1985:16).

8. Of this total, Y12 billion went for subsidies to basic consumer goods such as grain, cotton, edible oils, meat, eggs, vegetables, and coal; Y5 billion financed increased prices paid for above-quota purchases of agricultural goods; Y3 billion covered prices of industrial inputs to agriculture. The total does not include other state subsidies, such as for rental housing and transport (Wang 1980:16).

9. The 1983 regulations provide for preferential access by joint ventures to materials needed in their construction, but not for those required in production. See 'Regulations for the Implementations for. . .' (1983: Articles 54–9); Cohen and Horsley (1983:45).

10. This critique of the role of 'special economic zones' has been made in China. For instance, an economist with the People's Bank of China, writing in *Guangzhou Yanjiu*, mentions the inevitably modest scale and technical level of investment going to the SEZs as well as the limit to spread effects imposed by the barriers separating the zones from the rest of the economy. He urges the attraction of foreign investment directly into advanced northern industries as well as making available for domestic market to foreign investors (see Delfs 1985b:70).

11. See the list of joint equity ventures within and outside of the SEZs, as of September 1983, in *CBR* (September–October 1983:21–5).

12. They are Dalian (Dairen), Qinghuangdao, Tianjin (Tientsin), Yantai, Qingdao (Tsingtao), Lianyungang, Nantong, Shanghai, Ningbo (Ningpo), Wenzhou, Fuzhou (Foochow), Guangzhou (Canton), Zhanjiang, and Beihai. These cities have authority to approve foreign investment projects and to offer tax incentives to foreign investors (either joint ventures or entirely foreign-owned firms). Their profits tax is set at 15 per cent, as in the SEZs. Imports of machinery and equipment by joint ventures, co-production projects, and wholly owned foreign firms are exempt from import duties and the industrial and commercial tax, and their exports are exempt from export taxes. They are allowed some access to the domestic market.

13. Two authorities on Chinese law, Jerome Alan Cohen and Jamie P. Horsley, conclude after examining these regulations closely that, 'although questions inevitably exist, the Regulations provide much useful guidance and represent yet another major step forward in China's long march to create a legal environment attractive to foreign business' (Cohen and Horsley 1983:48).

14. However, the domestic cost of many industrial exports continued to exceed the yuan equivalent of their world market prices even at the new exchange rate, necessitating continued subsidies to exporters. At the same time, because domestic retail prices of basic foodgrain are kept very low, raising the price of foreign exchange has resulted in the need for an estimated Y400 per ton subsidy for imported wheat (Falkenheim and Rawski 1983:40–1).

15. This eliminated the rationale for criticism, including legal complaints, from some US businesses, which attacked the dual exchange rate system as a form of export subsidy (Imai 1985b:2).

16. This result is in fact argued to be desirable in Chinese journals, which advocate for the SEZ a state capitalist economy with prices closely reflecting those of the world market and with an international capital market (Kobayashi 1985b:14–16).

17. I have made some minor grammatical corrections to the translation.

18. According to a Party Central Committee report released on 30 July 1985, 872 companies, 88 departments under the regional government, several bank branches, and even schools and kindergartens participated; *see BR* (12 August 1985:9–10).

CHAPTER 14

REFORM

1 Introduction

Having successfully changed the face of agriculture and foreign economic relations, China's leaders turned next to the most formidable task: basic revision of the planning and management system of industrial production and circulation. The success of the agricultural reforms emboldened the Party to concentrate its attack on the urban economy. Major changes in planning, enterprise management, and ownership; in the handling of employment, wage, and labour issues; and in pricing, banking, and trade were introduced in quick succession. Signs of change were everywhere: in the proliferation of private enterprises and markets, the reappearance of advertising on the streets and in the media, the phenomenon of suddenly rising money incomes and prices, the growing gaps in personal income symbolized by the arrival of luxury consumer goods, such as colour television sets, never before available, the emergence of wealthy peasants who owned tractors, farm machines and consumer durables, and the spread of corruption, made easier by growing 'enterprise autonomy'. What is in question is the nature of the end product to which the many efforts at reform have added up.

Such efforts had in fact been under way since 1979, when, intrigued by the promise of improved efficiency and impressed by the weaknesses of the existing system of planning and management, the leadership began putting forward a stream of piecemeal reform measures. A key theme was to make greater use of the market and reduce reliance on administrative planning. State enterprises were allowed to keep a share of profits, and their managements were permitted to exercise more autonomous authority over production and supply decisions. The collective sector was expanded, and for the first time since the mid-1950s small private undertakings were promoted in commerce, service trades, and handicrafts. Joint stock companies were formed with private purchases of stock by individuals and enterprises and domestic joint ventures floated to circumvent administrative barriers and develop complementary links between units in different regions or under separate vertical chains of command. Enterprises adopted material incentive schemes, imposed strict systems of work-place discipline, and promoted personnel with higher levels of education and technical training. But these measures tended to conflict with one another and with the unreformed aspects of the economy, creating as many problems as they solved. Despite all the motion, there was little movement.

An economy in greater-than-normal disequilibrium marked by an irrational price structure, big surpluses, and simultaneous shortages is not fertile ground on which to set free market forces. Moreover, *non*-market-oriented changes in policy, especially a new and sweeping administrative decentralization of control over investment, jeopardized the central government's budget revenues; this in turn has made the centre hesitate to relinquish real control to the enterprises. Finally, a large, entrenched bureaucracy has been resistant to reforms that would eliminate its *raison d'être*.

The 'Decision of the Central Committee on Reform of the Economic Structure', adopted on 20 October 1984, recognized the ineffectiveness of many of the partial reforms already tried; it made the very same indictment of the economic system, discussed in detail in Chapter 11, as had been raised five years earlier. Now, however, the Party voiced determination to carry out an urban economic 'revolution' (Deng Xiaoping's term) equal to the one put through in the countryside. Government was to be divested of its economic management role, enterprises given decision-making autonomy, the scope of mandatory planning sharply reduced, that of the market correspondingly increased, and price reform finally undertaken.

Halfway through the 1980s, the economic scene was marked by cross-currents of confusion. The old sources of economic dynamism were no longer available, but the new foundations—foreign trade and investment, technology, 'scientific management', individual incentives, the market—were not yet working in tandem. Moreover, they brought with them values and attitudes at odds with older conceptions of socialism and with the interests of the party bureaucracy, which responded with a brief and inconclusive campaign against 'spiritual pollution'. The party leadership seemed intoxicated with the promises of the market, determined to proceed with reform, yet unable to anticipate and prevent its negative consequences.

In Section 2 we consider the progress of reform in the industrial management system since 1979. Section 3 considers changes in the way labour issues have been handled and examines the problem of unemployment and the proliferation of private and collective undertakings designed in part to alleviate it. Commerce and the ongoing efforts to multiply the channels for goods circulation are the subject of the fourth section. Finally, we assess in some detail the overall impact of reforms generally on central control of investment and planning (Section 5) and on industrial productivity (Section 6).

2 Industrial reform

The main approaches to reform of the industrial management system can be listed as follows.

First, there was the expansion of enterprise autonomy. A prime motive of the reformers was to free industry from the embrace of the state administration. Initially, expanded autonomy meant a right to a share of enterprise profits, but it was later to include as well greater authority over plans, supply of materials and equipment, sale of output, and other aspects of operations (Liao 1981:24; Zhao 1984:IV). The progress of the effort to increase enterprise autonomy has been marked by repeated tactical shifts and considerable backing and filling.

Second, the role of the market in guiding output and motivating producers was to be expanded, in accordance with the theoretical conclusions drawn by Sun Yefang and others regarding the importance of commodity production in the socialist economy (see Chapter 11).

Third, considerable authority over budgetary revenues and expenditures was handed down to provinces and localities with a view to linking their expenditures to their revenues and thus arousing their initiative.

Fourth, enterprises were to use a variety of means to break down horizontal and vertical administrative barriers to specialization and division of labour. Specialized companies arose, while joint ventures and compensation trade deals flourished as means of linking together different localities, state and collective enterprises, and rural commune and brigade (now 'township') industries.

Fifth, the practice of budgeting all fixed and circulating capital free of charge was to be replaced by the use of repayable bank loans bearing interest. This move was aimed at the waste in capital construction investment and the stockpiling of excessive inventories, both of which were exacerbated by the fact that capital was provided without charge to the enterprise (Liao 1981; Ma 1983:102–12).

Sixth, enterprise management has been urged to stress material incentive schemes, to develop strict systems of work-place discipline, and to promote personnel with higher levels of education and technical training. Seventh, the system of incentives and property rights concerning the development and diffusion of knowledge is being reformed. Patent and trademark legislation has been developed and paid consulting by individuals or enterprises legitimized.

Finally, after much trepidation and delay, the October 1984 'Decision on Economic Reform' (see above) put price reform at the top of the agenda.

Although, in the course of these reforms, a considerable amount of authority went to the individual enterprise, in fact the reform in large part turned into another—and an unprecedentedly thorough—*administrative* decentralization.[1] Its roots go back to 1967–71, when, during and just after the Cultural Revolution proper, the central government stopped collecting enterprise depreciation funds as budget revenue. These funds added greatly to the financial resources available to local governments. Together with the decentralization of 1970, in which most enterprises under central ministries were passed down to provincial and local authorities (Chapter 11), they contributed to the local initiatives in investment that characterized the 1966–76 decade. By 1972, moreover, central authorities were directly allocating less than 40 per cent of the materials they had handled in 1966 (Wang 1982:75). The post-Mao regime, seeking to control excessive dispersion of economic authority, moved in 1978 to collect for itself one-half of enterprise depreciation funds.[2] It also made plans to regain direct control of thousands of locally operated enterprises. The period 1978–9 was thus one of *re*-centralization analogous to that which had occurred in the early post-Great Leap Forward period.

Simultaneously, however, pressures were developing in both intellectual and leadership circles for a separation of government from economic management and a strengthening of the autonomy of enterprises (Chapter 11, Section 5). Experiments with expanded enterprise autonomy began in October 1978 in

Sichuan Province, whose First Party Secretary was then Zhao Ziyang, and then in Yunnan and Anhui (*Economic Readjustment* . . . 1982:93). The State Council in July 1979 issued five documents on reform dealing with the expansion of enterprise autonomy in selected experimental enterprises. Reforms to be tried out included enterprise retention of profit, free marketing of above-plan output, and exaction of a charge for the use of fixed capital and of interest on circulating capital. The number of enterprises retaining a share of profits rose to 4,000 in 1979 and to 6,600 by mid-1980. Although only 16 per cent of the 42,000 enterprises included in the state budget, these were generally the largest and most profitable ones, accounting for 60 per cent of output value and 70 per cent of profits (Wang 1982:83). Of them, 191 experimented with a more advanced form of autonomous management under which the enterprise paid prescribed taxes to the state and kept after-tax profits (and were responsible for losses). With the exception of the few enterprises on this system, known as *zifu yinkui* (self-responsibility for profits and losses), the experimental units all practised a form of profit retention.

Generally, these enterprises were asked to fulfil eight state-set norms concerning output: quantity; quality; variety; consumption of materials, fuel, and power; labour productivity; cost; use of working capital; and profit. Successful fulfilment entitled the enterprise to establish an 'enterprise fund' consisting of 3–5 per cent of its planned profit and 15–25 per cent of above-plan profit. It was also entitled to keep 60 per cent of its depreciation fund and, for two years, any additional profit attributable to self-financed technological innovation. In some cases, retention was tied to surpassing the previous year's profit. Retained earnings were to be divided between capital investment, collective consumption (such as construction of worker housing), and bonuses (Wang 1982:83–4).

This phase of reform ended in December 1980, having thrown up some thorny problems. The aim of giving enterprises authority over a portion of their own profits was to provide them with an incentive to be both more innovative and more responsive to demand and cost. For such an incentive to be effective, profitability must closely reflect economic performance. In China, however, relative profitability still depends mainly on the relation of fixed prices of outputs and inputs. In some industries (oil) prices were such as to generate high profits, whereas in others (coal) they gave rise to low profits or losses. Even among high-profit industries, differences in tax rates caused arbitrary variations in after-tax profits (e.g., high for watches, low for cigarettes). Moreover, well-equipped units enjoyed relatively low costs and high profits while those that had not recently received state investment did not. If a common profit-sharing ratio were applied across the board, the result would be 'unequal fortunes' (*kule bujun*), bearing no relation to enterprise management or conduct.

Thus it was necessary to vary the profit-sharing formula by sector and even by enterprise to reflect objective conditions fairly. A 'very complicated system of profit retention' developed, with considerable variation among regions and sectors in the formulas used. Because these formulas directly affected the revenues of government departments, localities, and enterprises, their determination involved frequent disputes 'among central ministries, between central ministries and provinces, municipalities, and autonomous regions, between rich and poor provinces, between provinces and the districts, municipalities, and counties under their jurisdiction, between all the above and enterprises, and between rich and poor enterprises' (Xue 1982b:103).

In addition to the intrinsic contradictions of the profit-sharing reform, there was concern about its implications for the state budget and the price level. When it appeared in 1980 that the central government was losing control of investment priorities and the inflation rate (see below), strict price control was reinstated in early 1981 (FBIS, 5 February 1981:L6), investment expenditures were cut drastically, the newly acquired right of enterprises to finance fixed investment with bank loans was suspended, and the spread of profit retention was halted (Naughton 1984a:10–11). The cutbacks in investment and production plans were softened later in the year, having made matters worse by lowering profits and, therefore, state revenues.

During this brief austerity period, many enterprises found themselves in a bind: they could not meet their profit targets on the basis of their low output plans. They began individually negotiating 'profit contracts' (*yingkui baogan*) with the state, thus giving rise to a new kind of 'reform' (Naughton 1984a). Even the limited dependence of the earlier profit-sharing reform upon such relatively objective factors as planned profit was now replaced by purely *ad hoc* arrangements.

The 'profit contract' epitomized what Kornai (1979, 1980a, 1980b) calls the 'soft budget constraint'. Because its terms depended upon the particular conditions facing individual enterprises—all of which were victimized in one way or another by the ineffective planning system—the plea of adverse conditions was almost always a convincing defence against high targets or penalties for non-fulfilment. Chinese commentators echoed Kornai in complaining that enterprises under the 'profit contract' system were happy to assume responsibility for profits but always found an excuse for losses (e.g., Gong 1983:3).

The negotiation of profit shares threatened to make the anticipated and much needed reform of the price structure more difficult, for each price adjustment would affect retained earnings and thus be a ripe source of conflict. With negotiated shares, prices would not serve to balance supply and demand, since price reductions for abundant goods would trigger a re-negotiation of share rates, leaving the enterprise no incentive to reduce production, and vice versa for scarce goods (Xue 1982b:111). Nor did profit contracts solve the other problems associated with profit-sharing, such as the difficulty of setting the base and sharing rate under the widely varying (and constantly changing) conditions facing different sectors and enterprises, the resulting disputatious relations between enterprises and government economic departments, and the tendency for the latter to intervene frequently in the affairs of the former (Xue 1982b:111). The last point bears further comment.

The real power behind the enterprise was the economic department or local government of which it was a branch and which allocated the bulk of the retained earnings technically held by the enterprise.[3] This parent body seized on the 'profit contract' system as a source of enhanced local revenue and an excuse to establish new industries for generating income, regardless of real demand and supply conditions or national need. As Naughton (1984a:16) observes, 'the fundamental determinant of how revenues were divided remained the interactions between the various levels of the hierarchy. Bargaining over profit became one of the main activities of the industrial hierarchy, replacing bargaining over plan targets.'

Reluctance on the part of the bureaucracy to relinquish direct control of economic resources has been a potent barrier to enterprise autonomy. Xue Muqiao, having in 1980 identified cadre opposition as the first of three main reasons for the many difficulties encountered by the reform programme,[4] bluntly warned that the unwillingness of party and state organs to give up direct control 'for fear of losing their share of the profit' would put 'the chance of ever realizing the general direction of reforming economic institutions . . . in doubt' (Xue 1982b:109, 101).

By early 1982, four out of five state enterprises covered by the budget were on some form of profit-sharing system. The core of the industrial reforms, this system encountered resistance both for what it did and for what it did not do; it was vulnerable for aggravating inflation and the state deficit, while the reformers were unhappy with its deep compromise on enterprise autonomy. Xue (1982b:109, 101) had advocated 'replacing this system of profit delivery with income tax collection', and this indeed was the next step that began in late 1982 and was generalized in stunted form to all firms on 1 July 1983.

The 'tax-for profit' system was intended to substitute an objective basis of income distribution between state and enterprise for the negotiations of the profit-sharing system. Enterprises would pay a series of well defined taxes and keep net profits. Taxes would include the fees imposed for the use of fixed and circulating capital, the industrial–commercial (sales) tax, a profits tax, and, finally, an 'adjustment' tax to collect differential rents arising from arbitrary conditions, such as location, natural resource endowment, and the price structure. The key problem, of course, was in the 'adjustment tax' provision, which simply ensured that the focus of negotiation would shift from profit-sharing formula to appropriate adjustment tax rate.

The 'tax-for-profit' system was implemented in truncated form, with large and medium-sized state enterprises paying a 55 per cent profits tax and small ones a progressive income tax. The government then *claimed a share of after-tax profits*, just as before. In some enterprises this additional division took the form of the 'adjustment tax', whereas in others this tax remained disguised as a profit-sharing arrangement. Clearly, the only substantive change represented by this system was to guarantee that the state would get at least 55 per cent of enterprise profits, as was acknowledged to be one of its prime objectives (e.g., Gong 1983:4; 'A Major Breakthrough . . .' 1984:K4).

This was hardly the major reform step hailed at the time. Indeed, almost a year later, Premier Zhao Ziyang (1984:III–IV) identified the central task of reform to be 'to eliminate the practice of making no distinction between well run and badly run enterprises', thus implying that a primary objective of the 'tax-for-profit' system had not been achieved. The State Council therefore decided to push ahead and, beginning in late 1984, 'gradually [to] switch' to a pure tax collection regime, eliminating the vestiges of profit-sharing.[5] Since the state dependend upon *after*-tax profit for revenue, its renunciation of rights to this income implied the need to raise taxes. Accordingly, Premier Zhao announced a readjustment of the industrial and commercial tax and the introduction of a 'resource' tax on coal, oil, and metallurgical enterprises, a value-added tax, and some local taxes. The 'adjustment tax',[6] designed to offset irrational prices and make profits more closely reflect enterprise performance, was to be imposed on net income after the income tax (Zhao 1984;IV; *RMRB*, 12 May 1984; Fujimoto 1985). By the end of 1985, 81 per cent of enterprises in China had switched to the tax payment system (SSB 1986:29).

First among the anticipated fruits of this reform listed by Zhao was the placement of financial distribution between state and enterprise on an objective, legally defined basis. It was hoped that this would harden the enterprise's soft budget constraint, improve its incentives, and simultaneously ensure that growing profits would be equitably shared by the state treasury and the enterprise. Even before going into effect, however, the reform was watered down by reassurances that 'enterprises which have temporary difficulties' would get tax exemptions or reductions ('A Major Breakthrough . . .' 1984:K4). Moreover, since part of the new tax structure (especially that of the 'adjustment tax') has the function of skimming off excess profits left by the basic taxes (Gong 1983:4), specific tax burdens still have to be negotiated, and constantly changing conditions—especially any attempt at price reform—will require frequent renegotiation. It is not obvious how much more 'objective' this process is simply because revenue collection is called taxation rather than profit-sharing.

Evidently, many problems could be alleviated with price reform. Because prices are rigid and do not reflect cost or demand, both profit shares and tax rates must be tailored to each enterprises's specific conditions—an endlessly trying and conflict-laden task. In April 1979 a Central Committee work conference decided that 'a total readjustment of the entire pricing system' was necessary (Zhang 1984:38). Three years later, Premier Zhao Ziyang (1982a:31), calling price reform 'imperative', nevertheless said it could not be undertaken before 1986. In early 1984 he reiterated that 'the price system, irrational as it is, lacks the conditions for overall reform in a short period of time' (Zhao 1984:II). However, because it had become clear from experience that the prevailing price system was an insuperable block to general change, the Central Committee in October announced that price reform, 'the key to reform of the entire economic structure', would gradually be implemented. This wariness about price reform, however 'imperative', is as firmly based in Chinese realities as is the need for it.

There are two aspects to the problem. One concerns the possibility of the planners restructuring fixed prices to reflect relative costs, and realigning them frequently. Even with powerful computers and a modern statistical capability, this would be an overwhelming task. In China's circumstances it seems out of the question. Explaining why past attempts to adjust prices according to plan failed, Xue Muqiao remarks:

The reason was that there were up to one million prices. Cost calculation for each and every product was extremely complicated. There were endless disputes between producers and users with their divergent interests. Therefore, no single price control agency, no matter how competent, could hope to handle this complicated problem well through subjective plans. [Xue 1982b:76]

Indeed, in the case of the one substantial industrial price reform that occurred before the October 1984 decision, namely a 1983 readjustment in textile prices which raised the price of cotton and lowered that of synthetics, more than six months were needed for preparation and nearly 10,000 price department personnel were directly involved (Zhang 1984:40). This is due as much to the political sensitivity of price reform as to its inherent complexity. So delicate an issue is it that only the State Council may make the decision to carry out a price reform (Zhang 1984:38). Frequent price adjustment of all (or even of many) commodities are clearly beyond China's technical or political capabilities.

The second aspect of the problem concerns the extent and method of controlling prices. If mandatory price control on a continuing basis cannot approximate rational prices, then the only way to do so is to allow the market a much greater role in price determination. This indeed was Xue Muqiao's conclusion (1982b:65,68,75,76), and it is the path chosen by the October 1984 'Decision of the Central Committee'. It alleviates to some degree the technical problem, but not the political one.

The price structure embodies a distribution of income to government enterprises, and households which each has come to regard as its entitlement. In particular, it determines government revenue, which is derived from enterprise profits and taxes. The increase in procurement prices for agricultural goods between 1979 and 1982 cost the Treasury Y26 billion—equal to one-quarter of total budget revenue—in the latter year alone (Zhang 1984:37). State subsidies of the urban prices of grain, cooking oil, cotton, coal, meat, fish, poultry, vegetables, and other nonstaple foods were estimated to surpass Y20 billion in 1984: 'This is the main reason for the country's budget deficit' (Xue 1984:K5). Despite these massive subsidies, the urban population 'strongly objected' to increases in prices of fruits, vegetables, and other nonstaples over this period (1984:K5). This predicament, more than anything else, has brought home to the government the complexities of price reform, however implemented.

Nevertheless, the State Planning Commission in October 1984 issued a set of proposals for reducing the number of products subject to mandatory planning and allowing prices to fluctuate in response to market conditions (New York Times, 13 October 1984), and in 1985 the prices of meat, poultry, fish, eggs, and vegetables were decontrolled, boosting consumer prices in Beijing immediately by an average of 30 per cent.[7] This was to be the beginning of a five-year effort to construct a rational price system (BR, 27 May 1985:4).

The distribution of income between state and enterprise is of course only part of the overall issue of enterprise autonomy, which also requires that enterprise management have the authority to use its resources on behalf of its own objectives. The State Council issued in 1984 'Provisional Regulations on Further Extending the Decision-Making Power of the State Industrial Enterprises' (*RMRB*, 12 May 1984; Zhao 1984:IV), which sought to increase enterprise authority over production and operations planning; sales; pricing; materials purchase; management of assets, funds, and personnel; wages; and relations with other establishments.[8] Under the reforms proposed by the State Planning Commission (see previous paragraph), the number of industrial product categories subject to mandatory plans would fall from 120 to 60. Moreover, Premier Zhao announced the intention of restoring supreme authority over enterprise operations to the manager or director in an attempt to banish the party committee from day-to-day administration while preserving its paramount role in supervising general policy.[9] And mandatory purchase quotas in agriculture were to be reduced from 29 types of products to 10 (Fujimoto 1985:6).

Of the various aspects of price reform, some economists have felt that one in particular is crucial, namely, the price of investment funds. In the past, these funds have taken the form of free and non-repayable budget allocations, on which enterprises have accordingly felt little impulse to economize. Such problems as the 'overextended capital construction front', the building of extravagant projects, and the hoarding of materials and parts (Chapter 11) are all seen as stemming at least in part from the enterprise's view of fixed and working capital as free.

China's conversion to the use of repayable, interest-bearing bank loans for financing fixed investment and working capital is intended to alleviate these problems, irrespective of progress (or lack of it) in rationalizing the general price structure. On the other hand, Kornai, speaking from East European experience, argues that the soft budget constraint vitiates the effectiveness of such measures: as long as bankruptcy is a virtual impossibility and the enterprise is always confident of state aid, imposing a charge on capital is of minor disciplinary value.[10] Be that as it may, progress in instituting this reform has been slow. As of spring 1984, the most significant steps in charging for the use of fixed capital provided by the state had been taken in Shanghai, where the annual rate came to about 9.6 per cent, and was levied on net, after-tax profit (i.e., it did not reduce the enterprise's tax liability). Elsewhere, less progress had been made and the rates charged were lower (Naughton 1984a).

In conformity with the requirements of a bank credit-financed economy, and stimulated in the first instance by 'the acute shortage of construction funds' ('Yao Yilin and Tian Jiyun . . .' 1984:25), a banking reform was carried out to restore more centralized control of the money supply and to differentiate the central bank functions of the People's Bank of China (PBC) from the new investment functions of various specialized banks. The latter include the Agricultural Bank of China (which handles credit for agriculture and rural savings), the People's Construction Bank (which provides investment funds for capital construction), the Bank of China (which specializes in foreign exchange transactions and relations with foreign governments and banks), and the

Investment Bank of China (which absorbs foreign capital for investment in China and handles investment credits), several of which were initiated or rejuvenated after 1979. Other institutions with a funds-managing role were also established—the People's Insurance Company of China and the International Trust and Investment Corporation, for instance.

With the growth in bank deposits (by 18 per cent annually between 1979 and 1983) and the use of bank credit, the People's Bank increasingly found itself in the anomalous position of being both regulator of and competitor with the specialized banks. Its nominal regulatory role suffered, and this is said to be one of the factors contributing to the loss of central control of investment after 1979. Accordingly, in what appears to be only the beginning of a period of banking institutional reform, the Industrial and Commercial Bank of China was established at the beginning of 1984 to take over from the PBC the handling of industrial and commercial credit and bank deposits, leaving the latter exclusively a central bank to carry out national monetary policy, issue currency, control interest rates, control foreign exchange and gold reserves, act as the bank of the government and of the specialized banks, and supervise the monetary system as a whole ('Banking Reform . . .' 1984; 'China's 1980 Monetary Statistics' 1981). At about the same time, the banking system was finally given full control over the allocation of working capital to enterprises, a function it had been sharing with the Ministry of Finance. From the discussion that accompanied this move, it seems apparent that it too was aimed at tightening control of credit and reducing the 'excessive amount of circulating funds tied up by the enterprises' (Shen 1984:27).

If enterprises do become empowered under the reforms, they will continue to be subject to vertical and horizontal administrative barriers to their operations (see Chapter 11) unless the 'organizational setup' of the economy is also changed. In the reformers' view, the essential step is to reorganize industry according to the principles of specialization and division of labour, for which purpose they have encouraged the formation of integrated corporations, organized along industrial or sectoral lines and equipped with the power to carry out the reorganization of, and to co-ordinate the division of labour among, their constituent enterprises. Through 1982 some 2,000 such specialized corporations, embracing almost 5.5 per cent of all enterprises, had been established nationally; in Beijing, Shanghai, and Tianjin such corporations covered 31 per cent of enterprises (Ma 1983:126). In addition, enterprises were encouraged to enter into joint production arrangements, joint ventures, and other co-operative relations with one another.

As happened in 1964, when a similar reform established twelve national industrial 'trusts', the usual Chinese method of carrying out change by uniform decree from above has created problems. Corporations were set up and given monopoly control of virtually all aspects of industrial activity: labour, material supply, finance, production, marketing. The enterprises below found themselves once again stripped of authority, albeit to a nominally new boss. Some regions and departments protected their own enterprises from integration with outsiders by forming corporations of unrelated enterprises. As in the 1960s, it seems that integration has pitted vertically organized corporations against the localities. Administered integration has been at the expense of the localities. However, for a period in 1980, the Central Committee tried out a policy of relaxing administrative intervention and allowing enterprises to integrate nominally on their own initiative. This, it seems, meant that local administrations were free to establish new factories, which they did on a grand scale, aggravating the shortage of construction materials, competing with large enterprises for scarce energy and raw materials, and increasing the national investment rate when state policy sought to reduce it. The response of the State Council was to issue, in July 1980, 'Provisional Regulations on Promoting Economic Integration', which decreed greater administrative (i.e., vertical) intervention in the reorganization process (Ma 1983:128–30).

Thus, once again the issue was defined as vertical control of industry that is technocratically led (i.e., free of party or government control of day-to-day operations) v. local, horizontal control.[11] The issue of 'enterprise autonomy' has been distinctly subordinate in this discussion, as has the role of the market. The same viewpoint, favouring more competent and enlightened administration rather than the abandonment of administrative control *per se*, is apparent in another reform institution, the 'industrial association'.

A somewhat looser and more voluntary form of integration, the 'industrial association', is being promoted for essentially the same reasons as the specialized corporation: to circumvent the arbitrary administrative boundaries that have defined and restricted economic activity, and to permit rational allocation of resources according to economic criteria. The industrial association is conceived of as a kind of trade association: 'an organ of democratic management voluntarily formed by enterprises in a particular line of industry to co-ordinate the development of the industry concerned'.[12] But the degree of its independence of government administration is carefully hedged, as indicated in a description worth quoting at some length:

It could be considered a kind of integration along industrial lines, with management carried out by the board of directors democratically elected by the enterprises participating . . . An industrial association can make regulations on the rights and duties of participating enterprises. One of its characteristics is that it is not a state administrative organ, but *is rather an organization under state guidance which is part-official and part-civilian, as well as part-administrative and part-economic. It is not an administrative organ of the government, but it has certain administrative powers; it is not a combined economic organization, but it has certain economic functions*. It plays the role of a bridge not only between the state and enterprises but also between different enterprises. *It speaks on behalf of an industry before the government; it represents the government in conducting democratic consultations with enterprises*. [Ma 1983:140–1; emphasis added]

This conception of the industrial association makes it all things to all people, representing at one and the same time state, enterprise, and industry. It symbolizes the contradictions inherent in seeking to produce dynamic, self-motivated economic actors without giving up direct control over their activity.

By late 1984 the direction of economic reform had become apparent. China proposed to follow Hungary's use of a three-tiered price system: fixed prices for the most important goods, upper and lower limits to price fluctuations for an intermediate range, and freely floating prices for a host of consumer and small producer goods (Mochizuki 1985). Industries with greatest and most general forward linkage, such as steel, coal, and petroleum, would remain under tight central control and be subject to continued mandatory plans. At the other end of the spectrum, production of most ordinary consumer goods and many producer goods as well would respond relatively freely to market conditions. An intermediate range of goods would be subject to state 'guidance' but not to mandatory plans.[13] While this has a judicious ring to it, it leaves most of the important questions about industrial organization and the real distribution of authority unresolved. How binding will the rough 'guidance' plans be, how free the competition? The 'Decision on Reform of the Economic Structure' called for floating prices on the one hand, and 'absolutely' ruled out raising prices 'at will' on the other; it rather confusingly distinguished that competition among enterprises which allows 'only the best to survive', from the capitalist 'law of the jungle', which means nothing if not survival of the fittest. Its statement of purpose, that 'the enterprise should be truly made a relatively independent economic entity', in its tortured ambiguity encompasses all of the real issues still to be decided.

3   Policy towards labour

Unlike peasants, who have been given greater independence in everyday work life, workers appear to be a subject of reform rather than its object. In industrial labour relations the emphasis has been on work discipline and greater wage differentiation. The Maoist ideal of worker participation in management and cadre participation in ordinary labour has faded, to be replaced by 'scientific management' and the 'responsibility system': each person's tasks are to be carefully defined and remuneration tied as specifically as possible to their fulfilment. A much touted model is the Shoudu (Capital) Iron and Steel company in the Beijing suburbs, which uses a work-point system for determining wages. The flavour of the new regime's approach to work organization is conveyed by a Shoudu worker, quoted approvingly in the press: 'Everything is so rigid now. You can't afford to do wrong; if you do, you lose some points.' Indeed, although the Party continues to hold that workers are the 'masters of their own jobs' and 'the true masters of the enterprises' in China, it now defines that condition to mean: 'Those who worked diligently were awarded [sic] and those who idled about, penalized' (Li 1983:22–3). In short, there is little to distinguish the current Chinese view of 'scientific management' from that of Frederick Taylor, circa 1910.

It is true that Chinese enterprises have returned to the formation of elected congresses of representatives of workers and staff, whose nominal role includes 'examining' and 'deciding on' major enterprise policies and protecting the rights and interests of state employees; and that such congresses are sometimes referred to as the ultimate authority in the enterprise (Jiang 1980:69–70; Zhou Ping 1982; Zhao 1984:V). Experience in the 1950s and early 1960s with workers' congresses, however, suggests that they were prone to domination by cadres and did not play an independent role in management (Andors 1977:124).[14] Moreover, attention has shifted away from congresses towards the opposite principle of strengthening the authority of the enterprise director and the new management committee, in whose list of participants workers' representatives bring up the rear (see n. 9). In such a setting, the oft-repeated slogan, 'The workers and staff are the real masters of any factory in China' (e.g., Jin 1984:4) takes on a somewhat Orwellian air. The previous rhetoric of participatory management may have been only fleetingly implemented in practice (Walder 1982), but it remained the statement of a principled objective. Now, the rhetoric had shifted from worker participation to a metaphysical assertion of worker rule, the practical manifestation of which—workers' congresses—appears to have little actual status.

Piece rates and bonuses are now the preferred methods of tying income to work. In 1984, bonuses and premiums paid for above-quota piece-work came to 16 per cent of base wages, an increase of 48 per cent over 1983 (SSB 1985: VIII). The literature reports considerable resistance to using bonuses as a differentiating device, and also a tendency to distribute them more equally than intended by the leadership,[15] which has waged a constant struggle against 'egalitarianism'. In late 1984, as in earlier years, the 'indiscriminate' issuance of bonuses and premiums to workers was a 'grave problem' (SSB 1985:VIII). Parish and Whyte discovered, in interviewing *émigré* factory workers, that their subjects had not been much bothered by relatively equal pay *per se*, but rather had objected to the various *inequities* in compensation that developed during the Cultural Revolution decade (see Chapter 10). Nevertheless, in the late 1970s and early 1980s the quest for greater inequality of compensation was the principal theme in Chinese wage policy pronouncements.

Chapter 11 discussed the re-emergence of large-scale open unemployment as a public issue in the late 1970s. Some sources put the number of urban unemployed in early 1979 at 20 million, or over 20 per cent of the urban labour force of 95 million.[16] A more recent source gives the 1979 figure as 15.38 million and states that it was reduced to 6.6 million by the end of that year (Ren and Yue 1983:21). Many of the unemployed, as we have seen, were young people who had returned from rural areas or recently graduated from middle school. In the five years 1979–83, the state claims to have found jobs for over 38 million people, including both those who had been unemployed for some time and new entrants to the labour force (*BR*, 6 June 1983:5; SSB 1984:XI). The 1984 plan called for creation of another 5.4 million urban jobs in that year ('Report on the 1984 Economic Plan' 1984:20), but in fact only 3.53 million jobs were found (SSB 1985:VII). Despite 6.65 million new jobs in 1982, there were still said to be 3.04 million unemployed at the year's end, only 'slightly fewer' than one year earlier (*BR*, 6 June 1983:5). Clearly, new entrants to the labour force from the large cohorts born after the 'three hard years' far outnumbered departures from death or retirement, making it difficult to absorb the backlog of jobless. Since somewhat fewer jobs (6.28 million) were provided in 1983 than in 1982, a similar stock of unemployed must have remained as 1984 began, and a somewhat larger one at the beginning of 1985.

In 1984 (but not in 1985), the official communiqué on plan fulfilment (SSB 1984:XI) used the term 'unemployment', rather than the euphemism, 'waiting for jobs'.[17] The state no longer guarantees employment, even in principle. The compatibility in official eyes of socialism with unemployment is highlighted by the announced intention to establish an unemployment insurance programme.[18]

Unwilling to accommodate all of the unemployed with full-status jobs in already overstaffed state establishments (which would also burden the budget with the generous fringe benefits accorded state employees), the government has encouraged them to form service and craft collectives or go into business as self-employed individuals. Stories of resourceful and frugal individuals who quickly became rich by opening restaurants or other service trades have abounded in the press. Less well advertised are those who earn a meagre living as hawkers, street corner cobblers, knife sharpeners, and the like. Some who have followed this route out of necessity consider it temporary and hope eventually to find the security of a regular state job—a hope that runs counter to the Party's intention to de-emphasize such jobs.

Considerable ideological legerdemain has been devoted to rationalizing the hiring by individual entrepreneurs of workers called 'apprentices' or 'helpers' (of whom the widely ignored legal maximum in 1984 was eight). The absence of exploitation is asserted; yet, in one widely reported example an individual employer was making twenty times the income of his 'helpers' (Sun 1984:28).[19] These individual workers do not get free medical care, retirement pensions, and the various subsidies available to state employees. The government is said to be studying a contributory plan under which they would pay premiums for insurance and retirement benefits (Sun 1984:27), but the social status of urban individual workers has remained low, despite government efforts to prop it up.

The growth of employment in urban collectives and in private sector pursuits is shown in Table 14.1. Both have evidently been growing rapidly in absolute terms and as a percentage of total employment. Indeed, virtually all of the 1984 net increase of 4.83 million in non-agricultural employment (including urban but not rural self-employed workers) occurred in collective (4.72 million) and private (1.08 million) establishments. These numbers add up to more than the total increase because state sector employment actually *declined* by over one million (ZTZ 1985:25). In 1984, just over half of urban collective employment was in industry, which was followed in importance by commerce, catering, and service trades (24 per cent), construction (10 per cent), and transport (7 per cent). Individual self-employed workers, having declined in numbers precipitously during the Cultural Revolution decade, began increasing again only in 1979; by 1984 this sector had doubled its level of twenty years earlier. Its occupational distribution had changed, however: 83 per cent of the self-employed were engaged in commerce, catering, and service trades, as against under 30 per cent in 1963 (ZTN 1984:122; ZTZ 1985:26).[20] The

Table 14.1. *Collective and private sector employment in cities and towns (millions)*

	Private sector workers in cities and towns	Employment in urban collectives
1975	0.24	17.72
1980	0.81	24.25
1981	1.13	25.68
1982	1.47	26.51
1983	2.31	27.44
1984	3.39	32.16

Sources: *SYOC* (1983:134, 137); SSB (1984:K14); ZTZ (1985:25).

objective was not only to provide jobs, but also to expand services that the state had proved unable to supply and whose shortage had been a general source of inconvenience (see Chapter 11).

The Ministry of Labour in February 1983 called for the hiring of new workers on short- or medium-term contract rather than as full-status employees entitled to all the associated protection, security, and fringe benefits. Such contracts are a means to eliminate the so-called 'iron rice bowl' of lifetime employment at fixed wages and to make credible the threat of dismissal and wage reduction as disciplinary weapons. At the same time, they are advertised as giving more freedom of choice to both workers and employers than is permitted by the state labour allocation system. In conditions of labour surplus the change may create more jobs in the state sector while reducing job security and social welfare provisions there. In mid-1986 the number of contract workers totalled 3.5 million (*BR*, 4 August 1986).

Contract workers have of course always existed in the PRC. Their angry demonstration in Beijing for equal treatment provided one of the tenser moments of the Cultural Revolution.[21] That the perception of contract work as inferior persists is suggested by the fact that the Labour Ministry's promotion circular 'pointed out that contract workers are part of the working class, and as such they enjoy the same political rights and have equal opportunities for political and vocational training as regular workers' (BR 4 April 1983:5).

In the construction industry, the increase in full-status workers from 50 per cent of all workers in the 1950s to over 80 per cent in 1984 was associated with a big increase in the proportion of administrative overhead personnel in total employment, leaving 'only a small number of people engaged in actual production work'. The contract system is to be used to 'sharply increase' the number of temporary and seasonal workers, including peasant construction crews, as a means of raising the ratio of production workers to administrative personnel (Zhao 1984:VI). Both the problem and the solution imply a trend towards a segmented labour market, with 'mental workers' occupying permanent posts and manual workers, temporary and insecure ones.

Thus, the old system, in which industrial workers *per se* formed a relatively privileged stratum with generous health, retirement, and other benefits as well as job security and high incomes, is ending. The industrial labour force itself is becoming sharply stratified. As early as 1981 permanent state employees comprised only 42 per cent of total industrial employment, the rest being made up of urban and rural temporary and collective workers without the security or benefits of full-status state employees (Walder 1984:35). Many of the latter are retiring to be replaced by their children, for the practice of job inheritance (*dingti*) is 'in force everywhere' (Falkenheim and Rawski 1983:32–3). The familiar combination of surplus labour, generous welfare benefits, and capital-intensive technology in state industry makes it impossible for the state to absorb into full-status jobs even the additions to just the urban labour force, leading Walder (1984:41) to predict that 'the rapid improvement in benefits, welfare, and standard of living that accompanied the rapid spread of state sector employment in the 1950s will give way to a stable pattern of inequality with the highest status reserved for a fixed and perhaps shrinking minority.

4 Commerce

The objective of replacing administered allocation of resources with commodity production for the market immediately called into question the adequacy of the circulation system, which had become a weak link in the economy even under mandatory planning. At thirty years of age, the PRC economy suffered from commercial hardening of the arteries, and a classic 'shortage economy' (in Kornai's phrase) had developed. Inability to move and obtain supplies and products affected production and caused what was produced to be hoarded (see Chapter 11).[22]

The goods circulation system prior to reform was made up of three parts. (1) Government procurement and supply agencies, under the leadership of the State Bureau of Supplies (set up in the early 1960s), allocated the overwhelming bulk of raw materials and producer goods. The Bureau was abolished in 1970, together with most of its provincial counterparts, to be re-established in 1975. In the interim, industrial ministries gained control over materials allocation, which exacerbated the tendency to lock materials into exclusive administrative channels (Naughton 1984b:6–7). (2) The state commercial departments distributed consumer goods via an elaborate wholesale and retail network. (3) Supply and marketing co-operatives—which despite their name were *de facto* state agencies before 1977, *de jure* after[23]—handled the marketing of farm products and the supply of consumer goods and agricultural inputs to the farmers. This system was supplemented by regular 'ordering conferences', held semi-annually, in which major users and suppliers of particular products would meet to draw up contracts (Naughton 1984b:8), and also by occasional 'materials exchange conferences' for enterprises to trade their surplus inventories, by rural fairs and periodic markets at which farmers individually or collectively sold produce and sideline products, and by collectively owned neighbourhood shops in towns and cities. These institutions provided some flexibility in an otherwise impossibly rigid central allocative regime. They were periodically suppressed as 'tails of capitalism', springing to life again between campaigns (see Solinger 1984).

The difficulties encountered by the commercial system stemmed from the decline of effective central planning generally and the concomitant spread of bureaucratism, from the inability of state agencies, even at their best, to handle the distribution of the myriad goods and services produced by the national economy, and from the prevalent ideological view that commodities and their circulation disappear under socialism and that trade is a backward, capitalistic activity. Technological backwardness and Maoist antipathy to central administrative planning had combined to keep the allocation of resources a crude and primitive process in comparison with other centrally planned economies. For instance, only some 500–700 different goods were balanced by central departments, compared with over 10,000 in the Soviet Union. The products balanced centrally thus were highly aggregated generic types (finished steel, lumber, cement), whose many varieties, qualities, and grades had to be allocated by individual ministries, provinces, and localities (Naughton 1984b:5). These units had their own agendas on behalf of which they used what power they had over resources. Neither plan nor market was able effectively to assert higher-order priorities over these parochial interests.

Although state supply and commercial work could be improved immensely, the reformers argue that in principle it could never adequately respond to changing supply and demand conditions or promote the full exchange of commodities from millions of separate factories, farms, shops, and households. Aside from the question of feasibility, it is argued, the provision of proper incentives to producers requires a functioning market. In the past, shops sold whatever they were allocated, paying no attention to profitability or to the popularity of their merchandise. There is reason to believe that this is something of an exaggeration, and that many commercial workers strove hard to match supply with demand under the general motivation of 'serving the people' (foreign visitors often remarked on the well-stocked department stores and shops they observed in major cities—see, e.g., Richman 1969); but it was probably an increasingly common attitude during the Cultural Revolution decade as the planning system broke down and cynicism spread.

Reform has therefore concentrated upon breaking the state trade monopoly and giving the market a larger role. The objective has been to 'increase the number of channels and reduce the number of links' ('links' referring to the separate steps that goods must go through on their way to the final consumer).[24]

With respect to producer goods, factories are being permitted to market their above-plan output directly, to vary prices of industrial producer goods within limits, and to purchase materials directly from other factories, bypassing the state distribution mechanism (see n. 6). In 1982, according to Ma Hong (1983:109), about 15 per cent of gross industrial output value was 'manufactured according to market demand', and this proportion reached almost 50 per cent for enterprises under the former First Ministry of Machine-Building Ministry.[25] Specialized companies in charge of specific goods, first established in the early 1960s and resuscitated in the last half-decade, are playing a bigger role in linking buyers and sellers (Koziara and Yan 1983:691–2, 699). By early 1984, 120 such super-companies—related to the 'trusts' so vilified in the Cultural Revolution (Chapter 9)—had been set up, with branches throughout the country.[26] Cities have opened trade centres (2,248 by the end of 1984) for industrial goods (1,254), farm and side-line products (753), and all-purpose trading (241) (SSB 1985:VI). These are in principal accessible to any buyer or seller, whether state, collective, or individual. In 1984 over 58,000 small state retailing establishments were leased to collective management (46,600), turned over entirely to collective ownership (5,600), or leased to private management (SSB 1985:VI). In general, the state distribution network is being strengthened, with the addition of stores, warehouses, and trade personnel (see Table 14.2).

An administrative reform has created regional economic zones organized around core cities, which have been given authority over their surrounding prefects. By the end of 1983, 121 of China's 286 designated 'cities' had taken control of 541 counties previously subordinate to prefectures, putting about one-quarter of all counties under municipal jurisdiction (CBR, May–June 1984:4). An attempt to break down restrictions on goods circulation and planning by permitting city governments to manage the entire areas of which they are the economic nuclei, this reform is in fact an attempt to rationalize planning (see 'Facts Behind the Shanghai Economic Zone' 1984).

The reformers seek to replace government administrative allocation of goods with professional economic agencies operating independently of day-to-day political control. The state should retain direct control over only a few of the most essential producer goods and materials, the rest being handled 'in the open market as commodities' (Li 1982:129). Zhao Ziyang's May 1984 Report on the Work of the Government contained the following commitment:

Apart from certain kinds of essential means of production and badly needed consumer goods, which will remain under the control of the state and be supplied according to plan, all goods produced over and above the plan or not covered by it can be traded freely at the trade centres and wholesale markets. Erection of trade barriers and, consequently, protection of the sale of inferior goods is impermissible. [Zhao 1984:VII]

The changes that have occurred in the distribution of urban consumer goods and services are perhaps more striking. Industrial consumer goods have had to negotiate two levels of the supply and marketing network plus a wholesale stage before finally reaching the retail shop (Xue 1981:121). This three-tier network (centre–province–county) is to be replaced, in accordance with a State Council directive of July 1984, by a system of urban wholesale companies (state-owned) and trade centres to facilitate direct links between producers and consumers and between different localities (Wang Dacheng 1984:4; BR, 27 August 1984:10–11). But the most striking change has been the widespread proliferation of collective and private service establishments, which has made available to townspeople many more restaurants and food stalls, service and repair trades, and small retail shops. As Table 14.2 shows, recent growth rates

Table 14.2. *Retail sales, by ownership sector, 1981–1984 (billions of current yuan)*

	Total	State units	Collective units	Private units	Peasants to non-agr. pop.
1981					
Value	235	188.1	34.2	3.7	8.9
% of total	100	80	14.5	1.6	3.8
1982					
Value	257	196.9	41.4	7.5	11.1
% of total	100	76.6	16.1	2.9	4.3
% change from previous yr	9.1	4.7	20.2	102.7	24.7
1983					
Value	284.9	205.4	47.4	18.5	13.3
% of total	100	72.1	16.6	6.5	4.7
% change from previous yr	10.9	4.3	14.5	146.7	19.8
1984					
Value	337.6	153.8[a]	133.7[a]	32.4	17.0
% of total	100	45.6[a]	39.6[a]	9.6	5.0
%change from same period prev. yr	18.5	−25.1[a]	182.1[a]	75.1	27.8

[a] Retail sales of supply and marketing cooperatives are included in the state sector through 1983 and in the collective sector in 1984.
N.B. A small amount of retail sales by 'jointly operated' units is omitted from the table. Comprising only 0.1 per cent of total sales through 1983, this sector's sales grew by 100 per cent in 1984. It includes various kinds of joint ventures including Sino-foreign.
Source: ZTZ (1985:83).

of retail sales by collective and private units have both been much higher than those of retail sales as a whole; sales by private units grew by eight times between 1981 and 1984, an indication both of the low level to which private economic activity had fallen by the mid-1970s and of the rapidity with which it has been restored. By 1984, collective and private businesses together accounted for about half of total retail sales.

The rapid expansion in the number of 'circulation channels' for consumer goods and services can also be seen in terms of employment in the relevant sectors: retail trade, catering, and service trades (Table 14.3). Total employment in the first two sectors almost tripled between 1978 and 1983, while that in service trades quadrupled. Although these rates are far in excess of the growth of total non-agricultural employment, they are themselves dwarfed by the growth of *private* employment in all three sub-sectors: from 136,000 jobs in 1978 to over 4 million in 1983 for retail trade; from 73,000 to 1 million in catering; and from 53,000 to 930,000 in service trades. Collective employment

Table 14.3. *Employment in retail trade, catering, and service trades by form of ownership, 1978–1983 (thousands of persons)*

	1978	1979	1980	1981	1982	1983
Total employment in retail, catering, and service trades	6 078	7 905	9 268	11 224	12 921	16 676
Retail trade	4 474	5 627	6 377	7 628	8 709	11 689
State	2 586	3 565	3 840	4 069	4 238	4 346
Collective	1 752	1 911	2 061	2 570	2 907	3 221
Private	136	151	473	985	1 559	4 116
Joint state–private			3	4	5	6
Catering	1 044	1 394	1 765	2 113	2 388	2 713
State	783	734	739	724	706	669
Collective	188	575	778	947	1 039	996
Private	73	85	246	441	639	1 042
Joint state–private			2	1	4	6
Service trades	560	884	1 126	1 483	1 824	2 274
State	451	426	451	483	506	502
Collective	56	395	495	646	803	838
Private	53	63	178	353	512	930
Joint state–private			2	1	3	4

Sources: *SYOC* (1983:339); *ZTN* (1984:376).

has grown almost as fast in catering and even faster in service trades. By 1983 collective and private employment together came to 63, 75, and 78 per cent respectively, of total employment in retail trade, catering, and service trades.[27] Total employment in privately owned industrial and commercial enterprises came to almost 7.5 million in that year (2.3 million in urban areas), some sixteen times the 1978 figure (*BR*, 6 August 1984:25).

Despite this progress, the outlook for collective and private enterprise remains uncertain. These businesses must deal in various ways with the state economy (e.g., in obtaining fuel, raw materials, and power). They are 'not assured of the supply of raw materials and are subject to all kinds of restrictions when they want to make purchases on their own'. Moreover, they are frequently still not treated as independent enterprises, permitted to make their own decisions about production and operations. It is therefore understandable that they are reluctant to assume sole responsibility for profits or losses (Gu Baofu 1984:K9).

'Among the channels of commodity circulation in China, the most serious bottlenecks are found in those for the purchase of farm produce and side-line and native products' (Xue 1981:122). Xue Muqiao is here suggesting that the incapacity of the centralized state commercial apparatus to handle the multiplicity of peasant side-line products was in part responsible for the decline in production of many such goods. After the 'socialist high tide' of 1955–6, the pedlars who had supplemented the formal trading system in handling their transport and sale were all transferred to other jobs. Peasant attempts at trade activity under the communes, except during the crisis years of the early 1960s, were condemned as 'capitalist road' activities. With nobody attending to this trade, production of many small commodities (e.g., castor oil, sunflower seeds) fell drastically, and peasant incomes suffered (Xue 1981:122).

Since the late 1970s, rural markets have expanded and provided outlets again for farm subsidiary products. Moreover, individual and collective commercial activity, including transport and sales over long distances, has proved a lucrative alternative to farming for many rural inhabitants. By mid-1984 more than half of the suburban commune population of Beijing, Shanghai, Tianjin, Jiangsu, Zhejiang, Guangdong, Liaoning, and elsewhere had left farming for other trades (*BR*, 9 July 1984:9), among which commerce is prominent. Nation-wide, one-quarter of the rural labour force was working in non-agricultural pursuits by the end of that year (*BR*, 24 December 1984). Among these, industry in the form of 'township enterprises', the heirs of the former 'commune and brigade industries', employed 32 million rural inhabitants nationally, or 9.3 per cent of the agricultural labour force, in 1983 and produced one-fourth of total agricultural income (*BR*, 9 July 1984). The state monopoly on grain trade was relaxed to permit individuals and collectives to buy and sell grain, and in 1985 the quotas themselves were abolished in favour of contracts between households and the state (see Chapter 12, Section 3).

In 1982 the denationalization and return to collective ownership of supply and marketing co-operatives began. Peasants were urged to buy shares at Y2–Y5 each, and by January 1984 40 million of them had bought Y250 million worth of shares.[28] This change is supposed to have given peasants 'a say' in running the co-operatives, which are to have some price-setting powers. By early 1984 over 20,000 'young staff members' had been elected to administrative positions in the more than 35,000 basic-level co-operatives. It is curious that, after two years of this particular reform, Premier Zhao Ziyang, in his Government Work Report of May 1984 (p. VII), made no reference to progress in its implementation. Rather, he spoke as if it were still to be inaugurated:

[T]he system of supply and marketing co-operatives must be reformed. The essential thing is to change them from being run by the government to being run by the people, that is, to change them into co-operative commercial enterprises that are collectively owned by the peasants. It is necessary to restore . . . mass participation, democratic management and flexible operation and boldly encourage peasants to buy shares . . . to reform the labour and personnel system . . . so that cadres can be elected . . . [etc.]

5 Financial effects

The various reforms impacted negatively on the central government in two ways: first, they produced a series of alarming budget deficits; second, they channelled an increasing proportion—finally, a major share—of investment

Table 14.4. *State revenue and expenditure, 1978–1984 (billions of current yuan)*

	Total revenue	Total expend.	Net surplus (+) or deficit (−)	Total borrowing	Net deficit (−) incl. borrowing
1978	112.11	111.10	1.01	0.15	0.86
1979	110.33	127.39	−17.06	3.64	−20.70
1980	108.52	121.27	−12.75	4.30	−17.05
1981	108.95	111.50	−2.55	7.31	−9.86
1982	112.40	115.33	−2.93	8.39	−11.32
1983	124.90	129.25	−4.35	7.94	−12.29
1984	146.50	151.50	−5.00	7.65	−12.65

Sources: *SYOC* (1983:445–6); Wang Bingqian (1984:K1–K4; 1985:I); Fujimoto (1983).

into the hands of local governments, which used it to confound the planned reduction in the national investment rate and to circumvent plan priorities.

The state budget situation is summarized in Table 14.4. Chinese practice is to include foreign and domestic loans in revenue, so the last column of the table shows net surplus or deficit with borrowing excluded from revenue in accordance with standard accounting practice. This table reveals why the situation in 1979–80 seemed threatening to a government accustomed to balancing its budget or running a surplus. Starting from approximate balance in 1978, the budget suddenly showed a deficit of almost Y21 billion, or one-sixth of total expenditures, in 1979.

On the revenue side, the chief culprit was a decline in profits turned in to the Treasury by state enterprises. There were several reasons for this. First, the 1979 increase in purchase prices of farm products caused great losses to state supply and marketing agencies. Second, rising wages meant higher costs and lower state enterprise profits. Third, the reform permitting enterprises to retain some profits resulted in a total of Y28.1 billion, which previously would have gone to the state, remaining with enterprises from 1979 to 1981 (Fujimoto 1983:4). Finally, 'readjustment', and especially the sharp cutback in capital construction in 1980, which produced a depression in heavy industry, impacted severely on the profits and taxes that that sector was able to remit to the state.

On the expenditure side, the main contributors to the deficit were the border war with Vietnam in 1979 and the additional spending required by the higher farm procurement prices, together with the additional subsidy granted urban workers to offset inflation.

The decline of direct central command of resources is seen in its broadest dimensions in Table 14.5. State revenue can here be seen to have fallen as a proportion of national income (Chinese definition) from an average of 32–34 per cent during the 1950s, 1960s, and 1970s (discounting the highly unusual Great Leap Forward period of 1958–62) to about 25 per cent in the 1980s. Moreover, the absolute amount of revenue stagnated from 1979 to 1982

Table 14.5. *Central command of resources: state revenue as proportion of 'national income' (billions of current yuan)*

	'National income'	State revenue	Revenue as proportion of 'nat. income'
1953–7 (ave)	80.7	25.8	0.32
1958–62 (ave.)	109.6	41.6	0.38
1963–5 (ave.)	118.4	40.5	0.34
1966–72 (ave.)	174.9	57.7	0.33
1973–8 (ave.)	254.2	86.3	0.34
1979	335.0	106.7	0.32
1980	368.8	104.2	0.28
1981	394.0	101.6	0.26
1982	424.7	104.0	0.24
1983	467.3	117.0	0.25
1984	548.5	138.5	0.25

N.B. 'State revenue' here *excludes* domestic and foreign borrowing (which is included in Chinese official revenue statistics), in accordance with standard international practice. 'National income' refers to China's definition of this term, which excludes most services included in the Western definition.

Source: *SYOC* (1983:22, 445, 446); *ZTN* (1984:29); SSB (1985:I); Wang Bingqian (1984:K1–K2, 1985:I).

although output and income both grew. Chief contributors to this problem have been (1) the proliferation of extra-budgetary financial resources available to localities and enterprises, (2) the low efficiency—and therefore low profitability—of state enterprises, and (3) growing state price subsidies of large grain harvests. Discussion in Chinese journals indicates a target value for the ratio of state revenue to national income of about 30 per cent in order to guarantee sufficient resources to key state construction projects (Tanaka 1984:3).

Slippage in central control of investment priorities came about as the decentralization of financial authority gave localities access to an increasing amount and variety of funds. These included (in rough order of importance) depreciation funds—already available to enterprises and their local administrators since the Cultural Revolution period (see Chapter 11)—and now loans, retained profits, extra-budgetary funds of local government and non-profit organizations, and foreign capital. Naughton (1983:8–19), who has studied the evolution of these sources, estimates that the centrally controlled proportion of total capital construction investment in state enterprises has declined, as shown in Table 14.6 (see also Xu and Chen 1984b:495–6).

Financial decentralization was, as we have seen (Section 3; Naughton 1984b), accompanied by local acquisition of command over materials. After 1979, this control was enhanced by the newly enlarged power of enterprises to market their above-plan output, especially during the severe recession of 1980,

Table 14.6. *Decline in central control of investment: fixed investment in state enterprises (billions of yuan)*

	Total	Centrally budgeted	Locally controlled	% centrally budgeted
1977	54.8	33.0	21.8	60
1978	66.9	44.4	22.5	66
1979	69.9	45.7	24.2	65
1980	74.6	38.2	36.4	51
1981	66.8	28.7	38.1	43
1982	84.6	31.0	53.6	37
1983	95.2	38.7	56.5	41
1984	118.5	45.4	73.1	38

N.B. *ZTN*(1985) gives for 1984 the centrally budgeted amount of capital construction investment, only. I have added to this 11.4 per cent of other fixed investment, which is the centrally budgeted proportion of other investment in 1982 and 1983. Note also that 'locally controlled' is here defined as not being included in the central budget.

Sources: 1977–82, Naughton (1984a: Table I); 1983, *ZTN* (1984:302); 1984, *ZTN* (1985:66, 68).

when machinery and other heavy industrial enterprises were able to sell large proportions of their output unwanted by the state (Naughton 1984b:12). But local *administrative* control of materials is far more significant, accounting, for example, for an estimated 70 per cent of cement output in 1981, compared with 27 per cent handled by the centre and 3 per cent by enterprises independently (Naughton 1984b:15). The change from 1962 to 1982 in the proportion of four principal producer goods allocated by the centre is as follows (Hama 1983:12):

	1965	*1982*
Rolled steel	95%	53%
Cement	71%	25%
Coal	75%	51%
Timber	63%	57%

Thus, decentralization of the resource allocation process since the late 1970s has been real and sustained. On the one hand, it was a deliberate part of the reform effort to disperse authority and incentive more widely; but on the other, it gave rise to an unanticipated and undesired consequence, namely, an out-of-budget local investment boom that contravened the centre's intention of reducing the investment rate and defeated its policy of concentrating resources in key construction projects.

It will be recalled that a prime objective of the 'readjustment' policy was to cut the national rate of investment and reduce the number of capital construction projects. Yet, as Table 14.6 indicates, total fixed investment has continued to grow despite state efforts to limit it, and it has regularly exceeded plans by substantial amounts.[29] Total fixed investment in state-owned enterprises in 1984 exceeded that of the previous year by 22 per cent, increasing pressure on the inadequate supplies of construction materials and causing the percentage of project and housing completions to fall (SSB 1985:V). It is apparent that the centre has had to bear the entire burden of controlling investment, while that administered locally has continued to climb. Even when the centre was able temporarily to force aggregate investment spending down in 1981, it did so by cutting its own spending by 34 per cent from the peak level of 1979, while that of the localities rose by 57 per cent in the same period. Thus, the decline in the centre's proportion of total investment stems in part from the proliferation of new funding sources available to the localities, and in part from its own attempts to balance the economy by cutting back central expenditures in the face of growing local investment.

The result was that the centre lost the ability to direct resources to key projects and sectors. Thus, although the energy and transport sectors were the two most serious bottlenecks and policy was committed to giving them high priority in construction, the State Planning Commissioner complained in June 1983 that the 'overextension of capital construction and excessively decentralized use of investment funds' had siphoned resources away from key projects in these sectors: 'Energy and transport projects, in particular, were adversely affected by a lack of funds, materials and construction workers. This was extremely harmful to the overall interests of the national economy' (Yao 1983:K4). In fact, the proportion of capital construction investment going to energy fell from 20.7 per cent over the 1976–80 period to 18.3 per cent in 1982, while that going to transport and communications fell from 12.9 per cent in 1976–80 to 10.3 per cent in 1982 (Table 14.7). The planners were also unable to raise the share of investment going to other sectors which had been promised increases, such as agriculture, education, and scientific research. (The improvement in this situation in 1983 will be dealt with below.) In 1982 the central government's inability to procure and allocate the planned amounts of rolled steel, cement, and coal caused it to have to purchase large amounts of

Table 14.7. *Priority sectors' share of capital construction investment (percentage of total investment in capital construction)*

	1971–5	1976–80	1981	1982	1983	1984
Agriculture	9.8	10.5	6.6	6.1	6.0	5.0
Energy	15.8	17.4	20.7	18.3	21.3	21.4
Transport and communications	18	12.9	9.1	10.3	13.1	14.2
Education and scientific research	n.a.	n.a.	7.1	6.3	7	n.a.

Source: *SYOC* (1983:324–5, 328–34); ZRGGTJ (1984:294); ZTZ (1985:70).

these materials from abroad and from local governments (Hama 1983:13). Governments at all levels down to the county, as well as their planning commissions, economic commissions, finance offices, and banks, were permitted to authorize investment projects (1983:13). No serious financial constraints discouraged the localities from multiplying their revenue sources by establishing factories in high-profit sectors, even in defiance of central priorities. The resulting over-investment, duplication of facilities, shortages of construction materials, and inflationary pressures also made market-oriented reform more difficult by aggravating sectoral imbalances and causing relative scarcities to depart that much farther from inflexible relative prices.

As it became clear in mid-1983 that spending was out of control, the Central Committee and State Council reimposed administrative restraints on investment to regain control of priorities. The heads of the provinces, municipalities, autonomous regions, ministries, and banks were made personally responsible for cutting back capital construction in their jurisdictions and assuring adequate supplies of resources for key projects (Song 1984:K2; Hama 1983:7–8). The centre imposed a 10 per cent levy on all non-budgetary funds, receiving in 1984 from this source some Y12 billion, an amount equal to 16 percent of all capital construction investment (Wang Bingqian 1985:I). To control investment based on locally raised funds, a rule was adopted in July 1983 requiring local governments and enterprises to provide 30 per cent down-payments from their own funds for all such projects (Hama 1983:13). The State Council also decreed that from the beginning of 1984 locally raised funds for capital construction must be deposited in the State Construction Bank in advance of their use (Song 1984:K8).

These measures were effective in the latter half of 1983 in restraining local capital construction and channelling resources to key projects. As Table 14.6 shows, the precipitous decline in the central share of investment was finally reversed, and it recovered somewhat to 41 per cent of total investment. Locally funded capital construction (including that financed by bank loans) actually declined by almost Y2 billion (Song 1974:K3; ZRGGTJ 1984:294).[30] In addition, the centre was more successful in concentrating resources in priority sectors, as is indicated by Table 14.7, which shows the proportion of capital construction investment going to energy, transport, and education and scientific research all rising significantly.

Having regained some control, the centre promptly gave it up again in mid-1984, permitting the banking system to expand its lending freely and allowing a large number of organizations access to foreign exchange (Lee 1985b). A new boom developed, which saw gross industrial output take off during the third quarter of 1984 and grow at an annual rate of over 23 per cent during the first half of 1985 (see Chapter 13, Section 3.3). Once again it was necessary to clamp down with administrative controls on lending, spending and importing in order to cool the overheated economy. Total investment in fixed assets nevertheless grew by 35 per cent in 1985 and came to 36.5 per cent of 'national income' and 31.8 per cent of gross domestic product, estimates of which China began to make public in 1985 (SSB 1986).

REFORM   367

It was vital for the centre to control the overall scale of investment as well as broad sectoral priorities, to maintain greater macroeconomic balance, control inflationary tendencies, and promote reforms oriented towards a greater reliance on the market. What recent experience indicates is that China's economic system generates strong 'investment hunger' in its various parts and that economic constraints to overinvestment and to socially irrational investment choices are as yet weak or non-existent. The centre has therefore had to renew and strengthen administrative methods to constrain and control local investment choices.

The character of the administrators themselves has in the meantime been changing as an extensive overhaul of the leadership at the provincial level and below has brought many new cadres into leading positions. 'The new leaders are in their fifties or early sixties, are better educated, and their careers exposed them to technical problems' (Oksenberg 1984:11). Four-fifths of state enterprises were reported to have younger and more competent directors at the end of 1984 (Lu 1985:17).

The deeper reform issue, namely, replacing the administered economy with an 'enterprise-based' one (in Jiang Yiwei's term—see Chapter 11), is not necessarily promoted by having more competent administrators. As China has found itself having to reassert administrative controls in a number of areas, its ability to do so successfully constitutes an argument in the arsenal of the influential faction that prefers a technocratic management of planning to wider reliance on the market. This is but one of the contradictions that haunt current reform policies.

While the planners have wrestled with controlling investment, other dimensions of planning have not progressed rapidly. This is most apparent in comparing annual plan targets with actual performance. For broad aggregates, the two have borne little relation to one another, as the comparison below for industry makes clear:

	1982	1983	1984	1985
Growth rate of GVIO (%):				
Planned	1.0	4.1	5.0	8.0
Actual	7.7	10.5	14.0	18.0

Nor were sectoral growth rates closer to target. Gross industrial output value in 1983 actually surpassed the Sixth Five Year Plan target for 1985, as did individual outputs of thirty-three major industrial products. The chairman of the State Planning Commission explained that 1984 plans had been set the previous November, too early to take the rapid growth of 1983 into account (Hama 1984:6); and the State Statistical Bureau identified the chief economic problems of 1985 as 'total demand outstripping . . . total supply', 'excessive investment', 'intemperate increase in imports', and 'substantial price hikes for some goods'—all symptoms of ineffective planning (SSB 1986:27).

Thus it is evident that Chinese industry continues to plunge ahead under its own steam rather than in conformity with carefully balanced plans, as repeatedly called for by Chen Yun and other economic leaders. The result has been a notable lack of progress in improving various indicators of efficiency, as will be discussed in Section 6. This has been duly noted in annual reviews of the economic situation, but with decreasing sense of urgency. Probably, the extraordinary performance of agriculture in the years since 1978 has lessened immediate concern about inefficiency and provided a margin of security for pro-growth forces, just as it always has in the past.

6 Industrial performance

The changes in industry have been much less thorough than those in agriculture, but it is nevertheless of interest to see whether they have given rise to a similar improvement in performance.

Gross industrial output grew somewhat more slowly between 1978 and 1982, at an average rate of 7.0 per cent, than the 11.4 per cent per year it had registered from 1952 to 1978 and the 9.4 per cent from 1965 to 1978 (Table 11.2). This was the result of a deliberate intent to curb excessive growth in keeping with the readjustment policy. A further part of this policy was the retardation of heavy industrial growth to 3.6 per cent per year, well below the 12.0 per cent growth rate of light industry.

Thus, the leadership succeeded, at least temporarily, in increasing supplies of consumer goods of various kinds to meet the growing incomes of rural and urban households, improve general living standards, and provide incentives to the working population. From 1982 to 1985, however, growth accelerated year by year so that the average annual rate of growth for the whole period 1978–85 exceeded 10 per cent (Table 14.8). Unlike in the past, light industry kept up with (indeed, exceeded) heavy. Neither enterprise management nor the price system had yet been substantially reformed, however, so that the resumption of high growth brought with it many of the same problems—wasteful use of material, inflation of gross value, duplication of product lines, etc.—as it had earlier.

While the shift in priorities favouring light industry was a product of readjustment, the results of reform must be sought in measures of efficiency, productivity, and demand orientation. To this end we examine the relations between output, labour, and fixed assets to see whether there is any sign of a departure from the productivity results of the pre-reform period as outlined in Chapter 11 (see Tables 11.2 and 11.3 and their discussion in the text). As before, we are limited by the available data to investigating state industrial enterprises, which produce between 70 and 80 per cent of total industrial output.

Table 14.9 shows that labour productivity in state industrial enterprises grew by 4.2 per cent per year between 1978 and 1984, which compares favourably with past periods (Table 11.2).[31] The value of fixed assets grew somewhat faster (at 8.6 per cent per year) than industrial output. These two observations—that employment grew more slowly than output and fixed assets more quickly—imply that the estimate of growth of output per unit combined inputs

Table 14.8. *Gross value of industrial output, total, heavy, and light industry, 1978–1985*

	1978 (1)	1979 (2)	1980 (3)	1981 (4)	1982 (5)	1983 (6)	1984 (7)	1985 (8)	Ave. ann. growth rate (9)
(1) GVIO (bn. Y, 1970 prices)	423.1	459.1	499.2	517.8	557.7	616.4	702.7	829.2	
(2) Incr. over prev. yr. (%)		8.5	8.7	4.1	6.8	10.5	14.0	18.0	
(3) Ave. ann. growth rate (%)									10.1
Index, heavy industry									
(4) 1978 = 100	100.0	107.7	109.2	104.1	114.4	128.6	146.9	173.2	
(5) Incr. over prev. yr. (%)		7.7	1.4	−4.7	9.9	12.4	14.2	17.9	
(6) Ave. ann. growth rate (%)									8.4
Index, light industry									
(7) 1978 = 100	100.0	109.6	129.8	148.1	156.5	170.1	193.7	228.8	
(8) Incr. over prev. yr. (%)		9.6	18.4	14.1	5.7	8.7	13.9	18.1	
(9) Ave. ann. growth rate (%)									12.6

Sources and notes: Row (1): ZTN (1984:194) gives GVIO for 1978–83. It appears to be in constant 1970 prices. The figures for 1984 and 1985 are derived using the percentage increases given in SSB (1985 and 1986). Rows (4) and (7): 1978–83, calculated from index in 1952 prices given in ZTN (1984:196); 1984–85, estimated from percentage increases given in SSB (1985 and 1986).

Table 14.9. *Growth of industrial output, employment, fixed assets, and productivity, state industrial enterprises, 1978—1984*

	1978 (1)	1979 (2)	1980 (3)	1981 (4)	1982 (5)	1983 (6)	1984 (7)	Ave. ann. rate of growth (8)
(1) Gross industrial output value (bn, 1980 yuan)	338 463.3	368 043.4	392 116.8	404 172.4	425 019.0	464 069.9	515 117.6	
(2) Increase over previous year (%)		8.7	6.5	3.0	5.2	9.2	11.0	7.3
(3) Employment (millions)	30.4	31.1	32.5	34.1	35.0	35.5	36.3	
(4) Incr. over previous year (%)		2.2	4.4	5.0	2.8	1.4	2.3	3.0
(5) Output/worker	11 130.0	11 838.0	12 080.0	11 863.0	12 133.0	13 049.0	14 184.0	
(6) Increase over previous year (%)		6.4	2.0	−1.8	2.3	7.5	8.7	4.2
(7) Fixed assets, state ind'l enterprises (bn. yuan, orig. prices)	319.3	346.7	373.0	403.2	439.1	477.1	522.1	
(8) Increase over previous year (%)		8.6	7.6	8.1	8.9	8.7	9.4	8.6

Sources and notes: Row (1): 1978–83, product of row (5) × row (3); 1984, derived from percentage increase given in SSB (1985:II). *Row (3):* 1978–83, *ZTN* (1984:114); 1984, row (1) divided by row (5). *Row (5):* 1978–83, *ZTN* (1984:270); 1984, derived by applying growth rate in row (6) to 1983 figure. *Row (6):* 1984, SSB (1985). *Row (7):* 1978–81, Field (1983:659); 1982, roughly estimated by multiplying the increase in fixed assets between 1980 and 1981 by 1.19. This is equal to the percentage by which investment in fixed assets of state-owned units in 1982 exceeded that in 1981 (1.266), divided by the assumed rate of inflation of construction materials (1.064). The latter, probably an underestimate, corresponds to the officially listed inflation rate for the rural market price of bamboo and timber, the only construction material price given in *SYOC* (1983:462); 1983, 1984, estimated by similar methods as for 1982. Investment data from *ZTN* (1984:301); for 1984, from SSB (1985).

Table 14.10. *Growth of output per unit inputs, state industrial enterprises, 1978—1984*

	Ave. ann. rate of growth (%)
Gross value of industrial output	7.3
Factors of production	
Employment	3.0
Fixed assets	8.6
Aggregate inputs	
Labour weight = 0.4	6.4
Labour weight = 0.5	5.8
Labour weight = 0.75	4.4
Output per unit inputs	
Labour weight = 0.4	0.8
Labour weight = 0.5	1.4
Labour weight = 0.75	2.8

Source: Table 14.9.

is very sensitive to the weights given the two inputs. The illustrative weights used in Chapter 11 (labour = 0.5 and 0.75, respectively) are applied to the data for 1978–84 in Table 14.10. With the smaller of these two weights for labour, the unexplained residual is 1.4 percentage points of growth while with the larger weight it is 2.8 points.

While it is unclear what the 'right' weights are, there appears to be some improvement in output per unit combined input in comparison with the 1965–78 period, when its higher estimate was 1.7 per cent. However, this result depends largely upon the year 1984: had the period estimated been 1978–83, the input–output relation would have been very similar to that of the earlier period.[32] Moreover, using a weight of 0.4 for labour, as suggested by an estimate of Gregory Chow,[33] the residual is 0.8 per cent for 1978–84, which is not particularly impressive. Given the crudeness of the data, it would seem that no clear case either for or against an improvement in 'factor productivity' can be made from this test.

This result is not surprising. Reform in the urban economy has only recently begun and, as we have seen, has encountered myriad setbacks and difficulties that are only starting to be addressed. Nor have the Chinese themselves yet claimed any great improvement: quite the contrary. Their own indicators of 'economic results' (*jinqji xiaoyi*)[34] include material consumption rates, quality indexes, ratios of profits to gross output value and to fixed and total capital, rate of cost reduction, period of turnover of working capital, and ratio of actual to planned completions of capital construction projects. In most of these respects, planners have remained dissatisfied with progress. For example, Ma Hong (1984:3) points out that tax revenues increased much less rapidly than state industrial production in 1983, while the ratio of profits to sales fell: 'this indicates that economic results have not made any great improvement and in some respects have even retrogressed.' Economic reports in the early 1980s continuously complained about overemphasis of gross output, neglect of efficiency goals, ignored demand, and unfinished construction (see, e.g., SSB 1984:VI). The communiqués on plan fulfilment for 1984 and 1985 were somewhat more upbeat, but the State Economic Commissioner in early 1985 reported that only 15 per cent of enterprises were beginning to use their new powers to improve management, while 20 per cent were in difficulty and the rest showed no change (*BR*, 4 March 1985:10).

Evidently, then, China's planners and economists agree that there had been no substantial improvement in efficiency of industrial performance through 1984 under the reform regime. Spectacular agricultural progress shielded the economy from the most serious ramifications of its inefficiency, keeping wage goods and materials of agricultural origin cheap and permitting consumer goods industries to advance and living standards to rise.

Notes

1. This account makes use of the analysis of Barry Naughton (1984a).
2. This was reduced to 30 per cent in May 1984. See Fujimoto (1985:4).
3. In arguing that the current reform, once the rhetoric of 'enterprise autonomy' is penetrated, has like earlier ones been an *administrative* decentralization, Naughton (1984a) points out that in 1980 (the one year for which data are available) profit-retaining enterprises actually disposed of only a small proportion of total retained profits (perhaps 20 per cent) and an even smaller proportion of all decentralized financial resources.
4. The other two barriers to progress were (1) the conflict between the reforms and the unreformed bulk of the economic system, and (2) lack of planning and co-ordination in introducing reforms.
5. The shift from profit-sharing to tax-paying was reported to have been implemented beginning in 1985. See Lu Dong (Director of the State Economic Commission) (1985:17).
6. The 'adjustment tax' is sometimes officially (and misleadingly) translated as 'business regulatory tax', in imitation of Western parlance.
7. In Beijing, the municipal government provided residents with a per capita subsidy of Y7.5 per month to partially offset the effects of the price increases (*BR*, 27 May 1985:4).
8. Issued on 10 May 1984, these regulations give businesses the right to produce for the market after fulfilling their plans; to sell these products as well as overstocked items and goods rejected by state purchasing agencies; to vary prices of marketed producer goods by up to 20 per cent on either side of the state price or to negotiate them with purchasers (this right does not extend to consumer goods or to producer goods for agriculture); to choose their suppliers of state-distributed materials; and to bypass the state distribution network and buy raw materials directly from producers. Other expanded powers involve the use of retained profits, the leasing

and sale of surplus equipment, personnel and wage matters, and the formation of joint ventures that cut across official administrative divisions. See Fujimoto (1985); *BR* (19 June 1984:10–11).

9. The dominance of the party committee is to be exercised through its secretary's position on the enterprise management committee, together with the director, trade union chairperson, technical personnel, and workers' representatives. This committee is to be the equivalent of a board of directors, making major production and operational decisions, while the director as chief executive officer is given a relatively free hand in carrying them out. See Jin (1984).

10. Speaking to the Workshop on Comparative Economic Systems at Columbia University in May 1984, Kornai observed that in Hungary there is virtually no correlation between original enterprise profit rate and that remaining after state fiscal intervention. Under these circumstances, it is doubtful that any single fiscal disciplinary instrument, such as an interest rate, can have much effect.

11. Although Ma Hong treats it as being a matter of too much administrative intervention *v.* too little, his description of events makes it apparent that these poles actually correspond to the familiar dichotomy of vertical and horizontal control. Ma Hong is former President of the Chinese Academy of Social Sciences and advisor to the State Planning Commission.

12. Its primary tasks are to draw up annual, medium-term, and long-term development plans; plan for innovation and technical change; formulate enterprise and product standards; organize intra-industry co-operation between enterprises; promote the industry's products on the international market; 'report to the government on the industry's production and management activities and put forward related demands and suggestions'; and other similar aims (Ma 1983:140–1).

13. For an economist's description of this schema, see He (1984).

14. According to Andors, the congress's agenda 'was made by the leadership, and the trade union had to be urged to take the congresses seriously and not turn them into an expanded meeting of cadres' (Andors 1977:124). A Chinese student in the United States related to me the experience of his friend, who, having won election to his factory's congress, was told at its first meeting that he must serve the party committee rather than his constituents in case of conflict. For the official view of the role of workers' congresses, see 'Provisional Regulations Concerning Congresses of Workers and Staff Members' (1982).

15. Thus, after several years of such exhortations, Zhao Ziyang (1984:IV) in mid-1984 was still urging 'smashing the "big pot" practice within the enterprises' and 'doing away with egalitarianism in income distribution'.

16. The clearest statement of this figure is in Zhou Shulian, 'Sanshinian lai woguo jingji jiegou de huigu' (A review of our country's economic structure in the past thirty years), Chapter 1 of Ma Hong and Sun Shangqing (eds), *Zhongguo Jingji Jiegou Wenti Yanjiu* (Problems of China's Economic Structure), Vol. 1, Beijing; quoted in Chow (1984:Ch. 4).

17. The term 'unemployment' had actually been used prior to 1984 in press and academic discussions. For instance, writing in *Renmin Ribao* in 1982, Feng Lanrui characterized as 'meaningless and impractical' the usual distinction drawn in China between 'waiting for jobs' and 'unemployment', namely, that the first refers to young recent graduates and the second to those who have lost their job for any reason; see Feng (1982:K2).

18. See, e.g., Yan (1985), who insists that '[b]ankruptcy is ... common to all commodity economies', and speaks casually of 'the labour market' in China.

19. This extraordinary article, however, contends that the income differential was only 2

or 3 to 1, by projecting hypothetical monthly wage increases three years into the future while assuming that the employer's income remains fixed!

20. In 1963 private urban agricultural and farm side-line activities (730,000 people) were extensive in the wake of the collapse of the Great Leap, and almost a half a million people were engaged in private industrial (handicrafts) pursuits as against only 160 million in 1982 (*SYOC* 1983:137).

21. The demonstration ended by being labelled 'counter-revolutionary'. See Milton and Milton (1976) for a dramatic eyewitness account of this episode; see also Andors (1977:Ch. 7).

22. For discussions of China's domestic trade system, see Li (1981); Koziara and Yan (1983); Xue (1981:116–25); Li (1982).

23. Ending the fiction of collective ownership, the National Federation of Supply and Marketing Co-operatives was formally absorbed by the Commerce Ministry in that year (Koziara and Yan 1983:691; FBIS, 9 January 1984:K23). Still more recently, however, the government has moved to return local rural co-operatives to genuine collective status; see below.

24. An example of the complexity of these links is given by the noted sociologist, Fei Xiaotong (1984:27). The peasants of southern Jiangsu Province, not far from Shanghai, receive manufactures from that city only at the end of a process of five distinct stages. First, the goods are shipped from Shanghai to the regional centre, Suzhou, from which the materials department distributes them to Wujiang County. The county commercial office divides them among the county's communes, whose supply and marketing co-operatives send them to the collective shops, from which they finally reach the peasants. Farm staples and side-line products move in the opposite direction via a similarly complex route. Another example concerns oranges from Guangdong Province, to which the 'links' in bringing them to Beijing add 119 per cent to their local price (*Economic Readjustment and Reform* 1982:125).

25. This ministry was merged with the Ministry of Agriculture Machinery and two other units in May 1982 to form the Ministry of Machine Building. The ambiguous nature of the claim made by Ma should be noticed. Under the former First Ministry of Machine Building's jurisdiction are automotive and consumer electrical products, both notorious problem sectors, the first hampered by a multiplicity of small, high-cost factories, the second by an over-supply of products such as electric fans. Consumer goods can be said always to have been 'manufactured according to market demand', since commercial departments were supposed to do market research before placing orders. Moreover, the former ministry's enterprises produce a considerable number of export items, which would also be included in the claim.

26. For more on the role of specialized companies, see Xue (1981:117–20). The counterparts of specialized companies on an industry-wide scale are 'industrial associations'. See Section 5 of this chapter for a discussion of these.

27. Note, in comparing Tables 14.2 and 14.3, the disparity between the share of collective and private retailers in sales value (23 per cent in 1983), on the one hand, and in employment (62 per cent), on the other. Clearly, employees in state retail trade were almost three times as 'productive' as their counterparts in collective and private units. This advantage was undoubtedly offset by opposite differentials between the sectors in the amount of assets per employee.

28. The sources are rather confusing on this point. Xinhua of 2 January 1984 (in FBIS, 9 January 1984:K23) puts the number of shareholders at 40 million but states that the SMCs 'now embrace' over 80 per cent of peasant households, which implies that being embraced does not require investing in shares. *BR* (21 May 1984), however,

gives the same total share capital (Y250 million) but states that it was purchased by 'about 70 per cent of China's peasant households'—far more than 40 million. The explanation may lie in the return of ownership of Y360 million of capital nationalized in 1977 to the original peasant investors along with credit for Y95 million in bonuses accumulated (but not paid) over the years (FBIS, 9 January 1984:K23).

29. Plans have in fact tended to be raised during the year to catch up with actual investment amounts. Thus, actual capital construction investment in 1981 exceeded the February plan by 48 per cent and the revised mid-year plan by 17 per cent. In 1982 it exceeded the April plan by 46 per cent and the revised plan by 25 per cent. In 1983 it exceeded the original plan by 17 per cent, but various additions to the plan in the course of the year brought the latter to within 2.4 percentage points of the actual result (Hama 1983:8; Song 1984:K3). These figures refer to 'capital construction' investment only, excluding 'restructuring and reform' expenditures that are included in total fixed investment in Table 14.6.

30. However, 'restructuring and reform' (gengxin gaizao) investment, most of it locally funded, rose by Y6.8 billion, which is why locally controlled fixed investment as a whole rose.

31. Because the period is short, the annual averages reported here are very sensitive to year-to-year fluctuations. Thus, labour productivity grew by only 2.2 per cent per year from 1978 to 1982—about the same as in the 1965–78 period. Large increases in 1983 (7.5 per cent) and 1984 (8.4 per cent) pull the average up to 4.2 per cent.

32. The range of residuals for 1978–83 is 0.7–1.9 percentage points.

33. Gregory Chow has estimated the labour and capital weights for state industry, using only seven observations for which official input and output data were available (1952, 1957, 1965, 1975, 1979, 1980, and 1981) and assuming, alternately, a Cobb–Douglas production function and a production function whose elasticities are not constrained to add up to one. Under the Cobb–Douglas assumption, the estimate of the elasticity of output with respect to capital is 0.6, implying a weight for labour of 0.4. The correlation coefficient r is very high (0.9948), and the standard error of the regression coefficient is 0.028. The elasticity estimates for the unconstrained equation are 0.524 (labour) and 0.535 (capital). Chow compares the observed output values for the reform years 1979–81 with the values predicted by the latter equation and finds the deviations extremely small and in one case negative. He concludes: 'there is no evidence that the outputs in the years 1979 to 1981 were higher than can be accounted for by the labour and capital inputs, using a production function estimated for the period 1952 to 1981' (Chow 1984:Ch. 4). In other words, the industrial reforms had not by 1981 stimulated productivity increases large enough to show up in the simple growth accounting permitted by Chinese statistics. However, industrial reforms were still at a very early stage in 1981, which was also a year of deliberately engineered stagnation, which would bias any productivity estimate downward.

34. For a discussion of the meaning of jingji xiaoyi, see JPRS (1983:23–4).

CHAPTER 15

CONCLUSION

In 1955, when Mao Zedong delivered his fateful speech on agricultural co-operation and ushered in what has been called here the 'late Maoist period', much of the party leadership was facing the other way. They favoured slowing the formation of co-operatives, even dissolving those whose foundations were weak, whose cadres lacked the ability to manage such an unprecedented peasant organization. In a sense, rural policy after Mao's death reverted swiftly to what those leaders had wanted a quarter-century earlier, now that the Chairman's olympian presence was finally removed from the scene. Similarly, something like the urban reforms, which resemble those attempted earlier in Eastern Europe, might well have occurred much sooner but for Mao's objections and the circumstances of the new regime's birth: Korea and the era of high Cold War.

Yet the post-Mao policies cannot be understood in isolation from their forerunners. Indeed, they were shaped and continue to be expressed in terms of an escape from what came before. Both 'late Maoism' and the regime of central command planning with which it was intertwined are sticks that drive the reformers towards the carrot of 'modernization'. As a reviewer of a recent book by several Chinese economists comments, 'The essays tell us what should not be done (in the light of past experience) but not what exactly should be done' (Cyril Lin 1984:873). Policies are justified by their departure from the egalitarianism or the indiscipline or the autarky of the bad old days. But what sort of society the reformers hope to build is less clear, except that it is to be a richer one.

If rising per capita income is the ultimate measure of economic development, then China has made signal progress since the period of reform began. We have seen (Chapter 12, Sec. 3) that peasant income and consumption have both risen sharply in the years since 1978, as has the real disposable income of urban workers and staff. From 1978 to 1984 the official measure of real annual consumption per capita for the entire population rose by 58 per cent. Per capita consumption of grain rose 29 per cent, that of edible oil 194 per cent, of pork 70 per cent; housing space per capita rose by a half in the cities and by even more in the countryside (ZTZ 1985:96). Consumer durables such as radios and television sets are becoming common in the cities and richer suburbs. Of course, incomes high enough to permit such luxuries are still few, and there has been some increase in income inequality. But the strong general upward trend in personal income and consumption has kept that issue from becoming acute, at least temporarily.

Sustaining such growth rates of income will be difficult if not impossible, since they result in large part from the simultaneous occurrence of several once-for-all changes. For instance, as Lardy (1984:863) points out, over one-sixth of the rise in per capita material consumption between 1978 and 1983 derived solely from the increase in the share of consumption in national income. But this share, 63.5 per cent in 1978, in fact peaked at 71.5 per cent in 1981, then fell slightly and is not likely to rise further in the near future (*ZTN* 1984:32). Similarly, urban per capita income grew by one-fifth between 1978 and 1982 merely because of rising labour force participation rates (Lardy 1984:859, 863); with three out of five worker family members already employed in 1983 (*ZTN* 1984:462), there is little room for further improvement on this score. Moreover, the big increases in wages and bonuses of the early reform period have already tapered off and are unlikely to be repeated in the near future.

In agriculture, as we have seen, a substantial part of the improvement in peasant incomes after 1978 came from more rational allocation of resources permitted by renewed diversification and specialization after a period in which these were discouraged. Another major contributor was the big increase in farm prices, especially in 1979. But the most profitable opportunities for diversification are disappearing as they are discovered and exploited by new rural entrepreneurs; while, on the other hand, the state slowed the rate of farm price increase in the early 1980s and made it clear that further income growth must come from advances in productivity. Moreover, the state evidently reneged on its earlier promise to give agriculture a large share of public investment: this sector (including forestry, water conservancy, and meteorology) received only 5 per cent of basic construction investment in 1984, down from 11 per cent in 1979 (*ZTZ* 1985:70). It appears, then, that the sources of farm personal income growth in the second half of the 1980s will be more modest than they were in the first half.

A less pleasant development of the new period is the open flowering of economic privilege for cadres, after decades of sub rosa existence in an unfriendly public atmosphere. As Oksenberg (1984:7) remarks, 'High officialdom is the first to enjoy the fruits of modernization. Arrogance, corruption, and abuse of office in China as elsewhere afflict a bureaucracy removed from those it governs. Balancing the need for organization against the danger of bureaucratism is one of the key problems in China today.'

The ultimate shape of China's emerging political economy, then, is still in shadow. Where the older Mao's response to the classic question of how to build socialism in a pre-capitalist agrarian society had emphasized the role of human ideas and attitudes, his successors have asserted that backward conditions breed retrogressive ideas. In their view, the requirement is rather for a massive expansion of the productive forces accomplished by means of quasi-capitalist institutions (commodities, markets, corporations, material incentives, 'scientific management', and the like) and the attitudes concomitant to them, over which the Party will rule as trustee of the workers' objective interest in the now distant goal of communism. In this posture, the post-Mao regime moves much closer to a strain of Marxism that rules out absolutely the possibility of skipping historical stages. Marx himself argued that a premature political seizure of power by the proletariat when 'the material conditions are not yet created which make necessary the abolition of the bourgeois mode of production' could be 'only a temporary victory, only an element in the service of the bourgeois revolution itself', and he insisted that 'no effort of mind or will can free [men]' from the requirement of producing the *material conditions* of a new society' before they can produce that society itself (Marx 1956, emphasis added; quoted in Meisner 1982:37).

Mao's 'effort of mind or will', it has been argued here and elsewhere, was not unconnected with the underlying realities of Chinese economy and society and reflected a shrewd appreciation of the intractable difficulties facing socialist development under those conditions. It sought in ideology, decentralization, mass campaigns, and collective incentives an alternative to the highly bureaucratized command planning regime with which the country started in the early 1950s. For all its successes, however, and for reasons some of which I tried to identify in this book, it was unable to provide the organizing principles for a non-bureaucratic socialism that could survive the great prestige of its founder and unite the Chinese people. Instead, it gave rise in the end to a violent and repressive episode in which heady idealism degenerated into warfare between dogmas and factions. Despite remarkable accomplishments by many ingenious and hardworking people, the economy as a whole drifted, cut loose by the disintegration of rational planning, and veered sharply away from meeting the needs of the population.

The Utopian goals of Mao Zedong[1] have been abandoned in the wake of these economic and political aberrations, and the current leadership has consciously turned away from his 'effort of mind or will' and towards 'producing the material conditions'. Starting from a modest conception of socialism as 'public ownership of the means of production plus payment according to labour', they leave maximum room for manœuvre. They have adopted an ethic of pragmatism which holds that whatever expands production *ipso facto* serves the socialist cause, and they have tried to harness the goal of 'modernization' to the twin engines of individual self-interest and advanced technology. Mao crippled central command planning and would not countenance the market as a substitute. Having experienced the economic cul-de-sac that resulted, the reform leadership has concluded, like its Eastern European counterparts, that socialism must make considerable use of market forces to provide incentives and signal relative scarcities. Undoubtedly, a liberation of individual energy explains much of the economic progress since the late 1970s, especially in agriculture. But the specific manner in which market and plan are to co-operate, as well as the more general question of the nature of the economy and society in the making, are both still blurred.

Of course, China is not the first country to explore the historical compromise between backwardness and classical socialism. But with vastly more people than its predecessors, a still more backward starting point, and a new world of technology to contend with, China must find its own path. Where Mao kept alive Utopian principles to light the distant goals but failed to chart the way there consistently, his successors focus on the immediate footsteps ahead but neglect the goals. In so doing, they have moved into very new territory, where there are both new and old forces they do not welcome: corruption, selfishness, superstition, bureaucratism, as well as social and philosophical ideas at odds with party dogma. As the ideological glue has dissolved, they have again had to resort to other means of exacting compliance, including coercion. As long as the energies released by the reforms continue to feed, clothe, and house people better, China can live with its contradictory path. But if, as Mao (and Marx) might have put it, these contradictions begin to impede development of the productive forces, China will once again be forced to redefine its path towards modernity, and, in the process, to clarify which aspects of the modern world it truly covets.

Notes

1. See Meisner (1982) for an enlightening treatment of Mao's Utopianism.

BIBLIOGRAPHY

Journals, reference works, and translation services cited

Beijing Review (BR)
China Business Review (CBR)
China Daily (CD)
Far Eastern Economic Review (FEER)
Foreign Broadcast Information Service—*Daily Report, People's Republic of China* (FBIS)
International Financial Statistics
Joint Publications Research Service (JPRS)
Japan External Trade Research Organization, *China Report* (JETRO)
Nanfang Ribao (Southern Daily)
Renmin Ribao (RMRB) (People's Daily)
Statistical Yearbook of China (SYOC), compiled by the State Statistical Bureau, Beijing. Hong Kong, Economic Information and Agency.
Tongji Gongzuo (Statistical Work)
Zhongguo Jingji Nianjian (ZJN) (Economic Yearbook of China), ed., Xue Muqiao et al. Beijing, Jingji Guanli Chubanshe.
Zhongguo Tongji Nianjian (ZTN) (Statistical Yearbook of China). Chinese Statistical Publishing House, Beijing.
Zhongguo Tongji Zhaiyao (ZTZ) (Statistical Abstract of China). Beijing, Chinese Statistical Publishing House (1983 edition reprinted with translations of table headings in JPRS 84111).

Books and articles cited

'A Major Breakthrough—The Aim and Significance of Carrying Out the Second-Stage Reform in Substituting Tax Payments for Profit Delivery' (1984), *RMRB*, 8 July; in FBIS, 11 July 1984:K3.
'Age Distribution of China's Population' (1984), *BR*, 3, 16 January.
Agrarian Reform Law of the People's Republic of China, and Other Relevant Documents (1959), Peking, Foreign Languages Press.
Agriculture in New China (1953), Peking, Foreign Languages Press.
Ahn, Byung-joon (1976), *Chinese Politics and the Cultural Revolution*, Seattle, University of Washington Press.
Aird, John S. (1967), 'Population Growth and Distribution in Mainland China', in US Congress, Joint Economic Committee (1967).
—— (1978a), 'Recent Provincial Population Figures', *CQ*, 73, March.
—— (1978b), 'Population Growth in the People's Republic of China', in US Congress, Joint Economic Committee (1978).
—— (1980), 'Reconstruction of an Official Data Model of the Population of China', US Department of Commerce, Bureau of the Census, May.

—— (1982), 'Population Studies and Population Policy in China', *Population and Development Review*, 8(2), June.

—— (1983), 'The Preliminary Results of China's 1982 Census', *CQ*, 96, December.

American Rural Industry Delegation (1977), *Rural Small-Scale Industry in The People's Republic of China*, Berkeley, University of California Press.

Andors, Stephen (1977), *China's Industrial Revolution*, New York, Pantheon.

Ash, Robert (1976), 'Economic Aspects of Land Reform in Kiangsu, 1949–52', in two parts, *CQ* 66:261–92 (June) and 67:519–45 (September).

Ashbrook, Arthur G., Jr. (1975), 'China: Economic Overview, 1975', in US Congress, Joint Economic Committee (1975).

—— (1978), 'China: A Shift of Economic Gears in Mid-1970s', in US Congress, Joint Economic Committee (1978).

—— (1982), 'China: Economic Modernization and Long-term Performance', in US Congress, Joint Economic Committee (1982).

Ashton, Basil, Hill, Kenneth, Piazza, Alan, and Zeitz, Robin (1984), 'Famine in China, 1958–61', *Population and Development Review*, 1 (4), December.

Bagchi, A. K. (1983), *The Political Economy of Underdevelopment*, Cambridge University Press.

Banister, Judith (1984a), 'Population Policy and Trends in China, 1978–83', *CQ*, 100, December.

—— (1984b), 'An Analysis of Recent Data on the Population of China', *Population and Development Review*, 10(2), June.

'Banking Reform Favors Centralization' (1984), Interview with Lu Peijian, President of the People's Bank of China, *BR*, 15, 9 April.

Barnett, A. Doak (1981), *China's Economy in Global Perspective*, Washington, DC, Brookings Institution.

—— (1984), 'A Peek at China's Foreign Policy Process', *New York Times*, 13 August.

'Basic Program on Chinese Agrarian Law' (1947), in Selden (1979).

Bastid, Marianne (1973), 'Levels of Decision-making', in Schram (1973).

Batsavage, Richard E., and Davie, John L. (1978), 'China's International Trade and Finance', in US Congress, Joint Economic Committee (1978).

Baum, Richard (1975), *Prelude to Revolution*, New York, Columbia University Press.

—— and Tiewes, Fred (1968), *Ssu-Ch'ing: The Socialist Education Movement of 1962–1966*, Berkeley, California, University of California, Center for Chinese Studies Research Monograph.

Berliner, Joseph (1957), *Factory and Manager in the USSR*, Cambridge, Massachusetts, Harvard University Press.

Bernstein, Thomas P. (1967), 'Leadership and Mass Mobilization in the Soviet and Chinese Collectivization Campaigns of 1929–30 and 1955–56: A Comparison', *CQ*, 31, July–September.

—— (1977), *Up to the Mountains and Down to the Villages: The Transfer of Youth from Urban to Rural China*, New Haven, Connecticut, Yale University Press.

—— (1984a), 'Stalinism, Famine, and Chinese Peasants', *Theory and Society*, 13, May.

—— (1984b), 'Reforming China's Agriculture', paper prepared for the conference, 'To Reform the Chinese Political Order', June 1984, Harwichport, Massachusetts, sponsored by the Joint Committee on Chinese Studies of the American Council of Learned Societies and the the Social Science Research Council.

Blecher, Mark (1976), 'Income Distribution in Small Rural Chinese Communities', *CQ*, 68, December.

Brehm, Carolyn, L. (1983), 'Flex Trade', *CBR*, 10 (5), September–October.

Brown, David, G. (1983), 'Sino-foreign Joint Ventures: Contemporary Developments and Historical Perspective', *Journal of Northeast Asian Studies, 1983*.

Buck, John Lossing (1937), *Land Utilization in China*. Vol. III: *Statistics*, University of Nanking.

—— (1964), *Land Utilization in China*, New York: Paragon Book Reprint Corp.

Burki, Shahid Javed (1969), *A Study of Chinese Communes, 1965*, Cambridge, Massachusetts, Harvard University, East Asian Research Center.

Burns, John F. (1985), 'China's "Open Door" to West Begins to Close', *New York Times*, 4 August.

Cao Guanlin (1983), 'Construction Contracting and Labour Co-operation Abroad', *BR*, 52, 26 December.

Case of Peng Teh-huai, 1959–1968, The (1968), Hong Kong, Union Research Institute.

Chang Kia-ngau (1958), *The Inflationary Spiral: The Experience in China, 1939–1950*, New York, Technological Press of MIT and John Wiley.

Chang, John (1969), *Industrial Development in Pre-Communist China*, Chicago, Aldine.

Chang, Parris (1968), 'Struggle Between the Two Roads in China's Countryside', *Current Scene*, 6 (3) 15 February.

Chao, Arnold (1982), 'Economic Readjustment and the Open Door Policy', in Wei and Chao (1982).

Chao I-wen (Zhao Yiwen) (1957), *Xin Zhongguo de Gongye* (New China's Industry), Beijing, Tongji chubanshe (Statistical Publishing House).

Chao, Kang (1970), *Agricultural Production in Communist China, 1949–1965*, Madison, University of Wisconsin Press.

—— (1975), 'The Growth of Modern Cotton Textile Industry and the Competition with Handicrafts', in Perkins (1975c).

Chao Kuo-chun (1960), *Agrarian Policy of the Chinese Communist Party*, Bombay, Asia Publishing House.

Chen, C. S. and Ridley, Charles P. (1969), *The Rural People's Communes in Lienchiang*, Stanford, California, The Hoover Institution.

Chen Han-seng (1936), *Landlord and Peasant in China*, New York, International Publishers; reprinted by Hyperion Press, Westport, Connecticut, 1973.

Chen, Jerome (1970), *Mao Papers, Anthology and Bibliography*, New York and Toronto, Oxford University Press.

Chen Kaiguo (1982), 'A Tentative Inquiry into the Scissors Gap in the Rate of Exchange Between Industrial and Agricultural Products', *Social Sciences in China*, 2.

Chen, Nai-ruenn (1967), *Chinese Economic Statistics*, Chicago, Aldine.

—— (1975), 'China's Foreign Trade, 1950–74', in US Congress, Joint Economic Committee (1975).

—— and Galenson, Walter (1969), *The Chinese Economy Under Communism*, Chicago, Aldine.

Chen Po-ta (1948), 'The Labor Policy and Tax Policy for Developing Industry', FBIS, 26–28 April; in Selden (1979:265–70).

Chen Yung-kuei (1977), 'Report at the Second National Conference on Learning from Tachai in Agriculture', *PR*, 2, 7 January.

Cheng, Chu-yuan (1963), *Communist China's Economy, 1949–62*, South Orange, New Jersey, Seton Hall University Press.

—— (1982), *China's Economic Development: Growth and Structural Change*, Boulder, Colorado, Westview Press.

Cheng Du (1982), 'Nongcun renkou de zaishengchan—dui yige diaocha baogaode fenxi' ('Reproduction of population in the countryside—analysis of an investigation report'), *JJYJ*, 6 June.

Cheng Zhiping (Director of State Price Bureau) (1983), interview in *BR*, 35, 29 August.

Chi Hsin (1977), *The Case of the Gang of Four*, Hong Kong, Cosmos Books.

Chiang Chen-yun (1965), 'Study Chairman Mao's "Regeneration Through Our Own Efforts" . . .', *JJYJ*, 1 January; trans, *JPRS* 30704.

Chiang, Jeanne (1983), 'What Works and What Doesn't', *CBR*, September–October.

China Official Annual Report (1981), Hong Kong, Kingsway International Publishers.

'China's 1980 Monetary Statistics', (1981), *BR*, 29, 20 July.

'China to Speed Up Agriculture Development' (1979), *BR*, 16 March.

Chow, Gregory (1984), *The Chinese Economy*, New York, Harper and Row.

Clarke, Christopher M. (1984), 'Decentralization', *CBR*, 11 (2), March–April.

Clarke, William (1978), 'China's Electric Power Industry', in US Congress, Joint Economic Committee (1978).

Coale, Ansley, J. (1981), 'Population Trends, Population Policy, and Population Studies in China', *Population and Development Review*, 7(1), March.

—— (1984), *Rapid Population Change in China, 1952–1982*, Report no. 27, Committee on Population and Demography, Washington, D.C., National Academy Press.

Cohen, Jerome A. (1985), 'The New Foreign Contract Law', in *CBR*, 12 (4), July–August.

—— and Horsley, Jamie P. (1983), 'The New JV Regulations', *CBR*, 10 (6), November—December.

Commentator (1981), 'Straighten Out Guidelines for Economic Work—On Leftist Mistakes in Economic Construction', *RMRB*, 9 April; in FBIS, 16 April 1981.

Commentator (1983), 'Stop the Unhealthy Tendencies in the Supply of Goods and Materials for Agricultural Use', *RMRB*, 23 May; in FBIS, 31 May 1983, K7.

'Communiqué of the Third Plenary Session of the 11th Central Committee of the Communist Party of China' (1978), *PR*, 52.

Communist Party of China Central Committee (CPCCC) (1982), 'Summary of the National Conference on Rural Work', *BR*, 24, 14 June.

—— (1983), 'Some Questions Concerning Current Rural Economic Policies', Document no. 1; excerpted in FBIS, 13 April 1983: K1–K13.

—— (1984), 'Certain Questions Concerning the Current Rural Economic Policy', Document no. 1, 1 January; in FBIS, 13 June 1984; also translated in *CQ*, 101, March 1985.

'Criticism of Selected Passages of "Certain Questions on Accelerating the Development of Industry" ', *Xuexi yu Pipan* (Study and Criticism), 14 April 1976, trans. in SPRCM 76–15, June 1976.

Croll, Elizabeth (1979), *Women in Rural Development*, Geneva: International Labour Organization.

—— (1980), *Feminism and Socialism in China*, New York, Schocken.

Crook, Frederic (1975), 'The Commune System in the People's Republic of China, 1963–74', in US Congress, Joint Economic Committee (1975).

Davie, John L. and Carver, Dean W. (1982), 'China's International Trade and Finance', in US Congress, Joint Economic Committee (1982).

Delfs, Robert (1984a), 'Reverse for Full Ahead', *FEER*, 11 October.

—— (1984b), 'Agricultural Yields Rise, But The Boom Cannot Last', *FEER*, 13 December.

—— (1984c), 'Financing From Within The Extended Rural Family', *FEER*, 13 December.

—— (1985a), 'Rapid Growth to a Small Role', *FEER*, 28 February.

—— (1985b), 'Reform upon Reform', *FEER*, 7 March.

—— (1985c), 'Changing the Pattern', *FEER*, 9 May.

—— (1985d), 'Revolution Run Riot', *FEER*, 11 July.

—— (1985e), 'The Delta Factor', *FEER*, 18 July.

Denny, David (1970), 'China's Agricultural Marketings and Industrial Development: 1950–59', paper prepared for SSRC Conference on 'The Economy of China', Cambridge, Massachusetts, 11–12 December 1970.

Dernberger, Robert F. (1975), 'The Role of the Foreigner in China's Economic Development, 1840–1949', in Perkins (1975c).

—— (ed.) (1980), *China's Development Experience in Comparative Perspective*, Cambridge, Massachusetts, Harvard University Press.

—— and Fasenfest, David (1978), 'China's Post-Mao Economic Future', in US Congress, Joint Economic Commitee (1978).

Dobb, Maurice (1966), *Soviet Economic Development Since 1917*, New York, International Publishers.

Domes, Jurgen (1982), 'New Policies in the Communes: Notes on Rural Societal Structures in China, 1976–1981', *Journal of Asian Studies*, 41 (2), February.

Dong Furen (1980), 'On the Relation between Accumulation and Consumption in China's Development', paper delivered at the US–China Conference on 'Alternative Strategies for Economic Development', Wingspread, Racine, Wisconsin, 21–24 November 1980.

Donnithorne, Audrey (1967), *China's Economic System*, New York, Praeger.

Du Runsheng (1985), 'Second-stage Rural Structural Reform', *BR*, 25, 24 June.

Dutt, Gargi (1967), *Rural Communes of China*, New York, Asia Publishing House.

Ecklund, George (1966), *Financing the Chinese Government Budget: Mainland China, 1950–1959*, Chicago, Aldine.

Eckstein, Alexander (1954), 'Reconstruction and Control, 1949–1952', in Rostow (1954).

—— (1961), *The National Income of Communist China*, New York, Free Press.

—— (1966), *Communist China's Economic Growth and Foreign Trade*, New York, McGraw-Hill.

—— (1968), 'The Economic Heritage', in Eckstein, Galenson, and Liu (1968).

—— (ed.) (1971), *China's Trade Prospects and US Policy*, New York, Praeger.

—— (1973), 'Economic Growth and Change in China', *CQ*, April–June; reprinted in Eckstein (1976).

—— (1976), *China's Economic Development: The Interplay of Scarcity and Ideology*, Ann Arbor, University of Michigan Press.

—— (1977), *China's Economic Revolution*, Cambridge University Press.

—— (ed.) (1980), *Quantitative Measures of China's Economic Output*, Ann Arbor, University of Michigan Press.

——, Galenson, Walter, and Liu, Ta-chung (eds) (1968), *Economic Trends in Communist China*, Chicago, Aldine.

Economic Readjustment and Reform (1982), 'China Today (3)', *BR* Special Feature Series.

Egawa, Hiyoshi (1981), 'Chinese Statistics: How Reliable?' JETRO, *China Newsletter*, no. 33.

Ellman, Michael (1979), *Socialist Planning*, Cambridge University Press.

Elvin, Mark (1970), 'Early Communist Land Reform and the Kiangsi Rural Economy: A Review Article', *Modern Asian Studies*, 4 (2).

—— (1973), *The Pattern of the Chinese Past*, Stanford University Press.

—— (1975), 'Skills and Resources in Late Traditional China', in Perkins (1975c).

Emerson, John Philip (1965), *Nonagricultural Employment in Mainland China: 1949–1957*, Washington, DC : US Census Bureau, series p. 90, no. 21.

—— (1967), 'Employment in Mainland China: Problems and Prospects', in US Congress, Joint Economic Committee (1967).

—— (1982), 'The Labor Force of China, 1957–1980', in US Congress, Joint Economic Committee (1982).

—— (1983), 'Urban School Leavers and Unemployment in China', *CQ*, 93, March.

Erisman, Alva Lewis (1972), 'China: Agricultural Development, 1949–71', in US Congress, Joint Economic Committee (1972).

—— (1975), 'China: Agriculture in the 1970s', in US Congress, Joint Economic Committee (1975).

Erlich, Alexander (1960), *The Soviet Industrialization Debate, 1924–1928*, Cambridge, Massachusetts, Harvard University Press.

Esherick, Joseph (1972), 'Harvard on China: The Apologetics of Imperialism', *Bulletin of Concerned Asian Scholars*, 4, December.

'Facts Behind the Shanghai Economic Zone' (1984), *BR*, 16, 16 April.

Falkenheim, Victor C. and Rawski, Thomas G. (1983), 'China's Economic Reform: the International Dimension', unpublished paper, June.

Fang Sheng (1982), 'The Revival of Individual Economy in Urban Areas', in Wei and Chao (1982).

Fei Xiaotong (1984), 'Smooth Commodity Flow Needs More Avenues', *BR*, 25, 18 June.

Feng Lanrui (1982), 'We Must Study the Socialist Theory of Employment', *RMRB*, 26 February; in FBIS, 4 March 1982.

—— and Zhao Lukuan (1982), 'Urban Unemployment in China', *Social Sciences in China*, 1.

Feuerwerker, Albert (1959), *China's Early Industrialization: Sheng Hsuan-huai (1844–1916) and Mandarin Enterprise*, Cambridge, Massachusetts, Harvard University Press.

—— (1968), *The Chinese Economy, 1912–1968*, Michigan Papers in Chinese Studies, no. 1. Ann Arbor, University of Michigan, Center for Chinese Studies.

—— (1969), *The Chinese Economy, ca. 1870–1911*, Michigan Papers in Chinese Studies, no. 5. Ann Arbor, University of Michigan, Center for Chinese Studies.

—— (1976), *The Foreign Establishment in China in the Early Twentieth Century*, Michigan Papers in Chinese Studies, no. 29. Ann Arbor, University of Michigan, Center for Chinese Studies.

—— (1977), *Economic Trends in the Republic of China, 1912–1949*, Michigan Papers in Chinese Studies, no. 31. Ann Arbor, University of Michigan, Center for Chinese Studies.

Field, Robert Michael (1980), 'Real Capital Formation in the People's Republic of China', in Eckstein (1980).

—— (1982), 'Growth and Structural Change in Chinese Industry: 1952–79', in US Congress, Joint Economic Committee (1982).

—— (1983), 'Slow Growth of Labour Productivity in Chinese Industry, 1952–81', *CQ*, 96, December.

—— (1984), 'Changes in Chinese Industry Since 1978', *CQ*, 100, December.

——, Lardy, Nicholas, and Emerson, John Philip (1976), *Provincial Industrial Output in the People's Republic of China: 1949–75*, Foreign Economic Report no. 12, Washington, DC., US Department of Commerce.

——, McGlynn, Kathleen M., and Abnett, William B. (1978), 'Political Conflict and Industrial Growth in China: 1965–77', in US Congress, Joint Economic Committee (1978).

First Five Year Plan for Development of the National Economy of the People's Republic of China in 1953–1957 (1956), Peking, Foreign Languages Press.

Freeberne, Michael (1962), 'Natural Calamities in China, 1949–1961', *Pacific Viewpoint*, 3, September.

Fujimoto, Akira (1983), 'China's State Finances in the Course of "Readjustment"', JETRO, *China Newsletter*, 45, July–August.

—— (1985), 'China's Economic Reforms: The New Stage', JETRO, *China Newsletter*, 54, January–February.

Gardner, John (1969), 'The *Wu-Fan* Campaign in Shanghai: A Study in the Consolidation of Urban Control', in A. D. Barnett (ed.), *Chinese Communist Politics in Action*, Seattle, Washington London, University of Washington Press.

—— (1982), *Chinese Politics and the Succession to Mao*, London, Macmillan.

Garson, John R. (1971). 'The American Trade Embargo Against China', in Eckstein (1971).

Geography of China (1972), Peking, Foreign Language Press.

Goldmann, Joseph (1965), 'Short- and Long-term Variations in the Growth Rate and the Model of Functioning of a Socialist Economy', *Czechoslovak Economic Papers*, 5.

Gong Zhi (1983), 'Guoying chiye li gai shui fuhe jingji tizhi gaoge de fangxiang' (Tax-for-profit in state enterprises suits the direction of economic structural reform), *JJGL*, 6.

Graham, Marianna (1983), 'Laws', *CBR*, 10 (5), September–October.

Granick, David (1954), *Management of the Industrial Firm in the USSR*, New York, Columbia University Press.

—— (1975), *Enterprise Guidance in Eastern Eugrope: A Comparison of Four Socialist Economies*, Princeton University Press.

Gray, Jack (1970), 'The Hightide of Socialism in the Chinese Countryside', in Jerome Chen and Nicholas Tarling (eds), *Studies in the Social History of China and Southeast Asia*, Cambridge University Press.

—— (1973), 'The Two Roads: Alternative Strategies of Social Change and Economic Growth in China', in Schram (1973).

Griffin, Keith and Saith, Ashwani (1981), *Growth and Equality in Rural China*, Singapore, International Labour Organization.

Gu Baofu (1984), 'Some Problems in Collective Enterprises . . .', *JJGL*, 5(5), May; FBIS, 20 July 1984, K7.

Gu Ming (1984), 'Investment Environment Seen as Favourable', *BR*, 29, 16 July.

Gurley, John G. (1976), *China's Economy and the Maoist Strategy*, New York, Monthly Review Press.

Hama, Katsuhiko (1983), 'Systemic Reform and Financial Problems—The "Investment Fever" Mechanism', JETRO, *China Newsletter*, 47, November–December.

—— (1984), 'New Era in Economic Reform', JETRO, *China Newsletter*, 51, July–August.

Harper, Paul (1969), 'The Party and the Unions in Communist China', *CQ*, 37, January—March.

He Jianzhang (1980), 'Wo guo quanmin suoyouzhi jingji jihua guanli tizhi cunzaide wenti he gaige fangxiang' (Current problems and the direction of reform in the planning and management system of China's state-owned economy), *JJYJ*, 5 May 1979; trans. in *Chinese Economic Studies*, 13(4), Summer 1980.

—— (1984), 'The Necessity of Socialist Planned Economy', *Hong Qi*, 3(1), February.

Hinton, William (1966), *Fanshen*, New York, Monthly Review Press.

—— (1982), 'Village in Transition', in Selden and Lippit, (1982).

—— (1983), 'A Trip to Fengyang County: Investigating China's New Family Contract System', *Monthly Review*, November.

Ho, Ping-ti (1959), *Studies on the Population of China*, Cambridge, Massachusetts, Harvard University Press.

Hoffmann, Charles (1967), *Work Incentive Practices and Policies in the People's Republic of China, 1953–1965*, Albany, State University of New York Press.

—— (1974), *The Chinese Worker*, Albany, State University of New York Press.

Hong Nongyun (1984), 'Quanguo nongmin renjun shouru shi zemmeyang jisuan-chulaide?' (How is national per capita total income of the peasants calculated?), *Hong Qi*, 15, 15 August.

Horsley, Jamie P. (1984), 'Chinese Labor', *CBR*, 11(3), May–June.

Hou, Chi-ming (1965), *Foreign Investment and Economic Development in China, 1840–1937*, Cambridge, Massachusetts, Harvard University Press.

—— (1968), 'Manpower, Employment and Unemployment', in Eckstein, Galenson, and Liu (1968).

Howe, Christopher (1971), *Employment and Economic Growth in Urban China, 1949–1957*, Cambridge University Press.

—— (1973), *Wage Patterns and Wage Policy in Modern China, 1919–1972*, Cambridge University Press.

—— and Walker, Kenneth (1977), 'The Economist', in Dick Wilson (ed.), *Mao Tse-tung in the Scales of History*, Cambridge University Press.

Hsueh Mu-ch'iao, *et al.*: see Xue Muqiao.

Hu Qiaomu (1978), 'Anzhao jingji guelü banshi, jiakuai shixian sige xiandaihua' (Observe economic laws, speed up realization of the four modernizations), *RMRB*, 6 October; trans. in *PR*, nos. 45–47, November 1978.

Hua Guofeng (1977), 'Speech at the Second National Conference on Learning from Tachai in Agriculture', Beijing, Foreign Languages Press.

—— (1978), 'Report on the Work of the Government', *BR*, 10 March.

Huang, Philip C. C. (1975), 'Analyzing the Twentieth-century Chinese Countryside: Revolutionaries versus Western Scholarship', *Modern China*, 1(2), April.

Hunter, Neale (1971), *Shanghai Journal: An Eyewitness Account of the Cultural Revolution*, Boston, Beacon Press.

Imai, Satoshi (1985a), 'Reform of China's Foreign Trade System', in JETRO, *China Newsletter*, 56, May–June.

—— (1985b), 'China's Foreign Reserves', JETRO, *China Newsletter*, 57, July–August.

Ishikawa, Shigeru (1965), *National Income and Capital Formation in Mainland China*, Tokyo, Institute of Asian Economic Affairs.

Jammes, Sydney H. (1975), 'The Chinese Defense Burden, 1965–74', in US Congress, Joint Economic Committee (1975).

JETRO (1983), 'China's Economy: Aiming at Stable Growth', JETRO, Special Report, *China Newsletter*, 47, November–December.

Jiang Junchen, Zhou Zhaoyang, and Shen Jun (1980), 'Lun shengchan he shenghuode guanxi wenti' (On the relations between production and livelihood) *JJYJ*, 9.

Jiang Yiwei (1980), 'The Theory of An Enterprise-based Economy', *Social Sciences in China*, 1(1).

Jin Qi (1984), 'Reforming Enterprise Leadership System', *BR*, 25, 18 June.

Jing Ping (1985), 'Contract Purchasing of Grain is a Major Reform', *Red Flag*, 10, 16 May; trans. JPRS, CRF-85–015, *China Report*, 26 July 1985.

Jing Wei (1983), 'Responsibility System Revives Jiangsu Countryside', *BR*, 48, 28 November.

JPRS (1983), 'JPRS Newsletter for Chinese Translators', no. 6, April.

Kallgren, Joyce (1985), 'The Concept of Decentralization in Document no. 1, 1984', *CQ*, 101, March.

Karol, K. S. (1974), *The Second Chinese Revolution*, New York, Hill and Wang.

Kawai, Hiroko (1984), 'Direct Investment in China in 1983', JETRO, *China Newsletter*, 48, January–February.

—— (1985), 'China's External Trade in 1984', JETRO, *China Newsletter*, 56, May–June.

Khan, Azizur Rahman and Lee, Eddy (1983), *Agrarian Policies and Institutions in China After Mao*, Bangkok, ILO.

Klein, Donald and Hager, Lois (1971), 'The Ninth Central Committee', *CQ*, 45, January–March.

Kobayashi, Hironao (1984), 'Shenzhen SEZ: Mirror of China's Open Door Policy', JETRO, *China Newsletter*, 49, March–April.

—— (1985a), 'Trade Controls Toughened', JETRO, *China Newsletter*, 57, July–August.

—— (1985b), 'Special Economic Zones and China's Open Economic Policy', JETRO, *China Newsletter*, 57, July–August.

Kornai, Janos (1959), *Overcentralization in Economic Administration*, Oxford University Press.

—— (1971), *Anti-equilibrium: On Economic Systems Theory and the Tasks of Research*, Amsterdam, North Holland.

—— (1972), *Rush vs. Harmonic Growth*, Amsterdam, North Holland.

—— (1979), 'Resource Constrained vs. Demand Constrained Systems', *Econometrica*, 47 (4), July.

—— (1980a), *Economics of Shortage*, vols. A and B, Amsterdam, North-Holland.

—— (1980b), 'The Dilemmas of a Socialist Economy: The Hungarian Experience', *Cambridge Journal of Economics*, 4(2), June.

Korzec, Michel and Whyte, Martin King (1981), 'Reading Notes: The Chinese Wage System', *CQ*, 86, June.

Koziara, Edward Clifford and Yan, Chiou-shuang (1983), 'The Distribution System for Producers' Goods in China', *CQ*, 96, December.

Kueh, Y. Y. (1983), 'Economic Reform in China at the "Xian" Level', *CQ*, 96, December.

—— (1985), 'The Economics of the "Second Land Reform" in China', *CQ*, 101, March.

—— and Howe, Christopher (1984), 'China's International Trade: Policy and Organization Change and their Place in the "Economic Readjustment" ', *CQ*, 100, December.

Kuznets, Simon (1966), *Modern Economic Growth: Rate, Structure and Spread*, New Haven, Connecticut, Yale University Press.

Lardy, Nicholas R. (1975), 'Economic Planning in the People's Republic of China: Central-Provincial Fiscal Relations', in US Congress, Joint Economic Committee (1975).

—— (1978a), *Economic Growth and Income Distribution in the People's Republic of China*, Cambridge University Press.

—— (1978b), *Chinese Economic Planning: Translations from Chi-hua Ching-chi*, Armonk, New York, M. E. Sharpe.

—— (1980), 'Regional Growth and Income Distribution in China', in Dernberger (1980).

—— (1982a), 'Food Consumption in the People's Republic of China', in Randolph Barker, Radha Sinha, and Beth Rose (eds), *The Chinese Agricultural Economy*, Boulder, Colorado, Westview Press.

—— (1982b), 'Prices, Markets and the Chinese Peasant', Discussion Paper no. 428, Yale Economic Growth Center, New Haven, Connecticut.

—— (1982c), 'Comparative Advantage, Internal Trade, and the Distribution of Income in Chinese Agriculture', paper prepared for the Trade and Development Workshop, Yale University, 25 January 1982.

—— (1983a), *Agriculture in China's Modern Economic Development*, Cambridge University Press.

—— (1983b), 'Subsidies', *CBR*, 10(6), November–December.

—— (1984), 'Consumption and Living Standards in China, 1978–83', *CQ*, 100, December.

—— and Lieberthal, Kenneth (1982), 'Introduction', in 'Chen Yun's Strategy for China's Development: A Non-Maoist Alternative', *Chinese Economic Studies*, 15 (3–4).

Latham, Richard J. (1983), 'The Political, Social and Economic Implications of the Household Production Responsibility System (Bao Gan Dao Hu)', chapter of doctoral dissertation.

Lee, Edmund (1983), 'Economic Reform in Post-Mao China: An Insider's View', *Bulletin of Concerned Asian Scholars*, 15(1).

—— (1984), 'China's Special Economic Zones (1979–1981)', unpublished paper.

Lee, Hong Yong (1978), *The Politics of the Chinese Cultural Revolution*, Berkeley, University of California Press.

Lee, Mary (1985a), 'The Curtain Goes Up', *FEER*, 31 January.

—— (1985b), 'Heed: Speed and Greed', *FEER*, 18 April.

—— (1985c), 'Change from the Top', *FEER*, 9 May.

Leys, Simon (1977), *Chinese Shadows*, New York, Viking Press.

Li Chengrui (1984), 'Are the 1967–76 Statistics on China's Economy Reliable?' *BR*, 12.

—— (1985), 'Economic Reform Brings Better Life', *BR*, 29, 22 July.

—— and Zhang Zhongji (1982), 'Remarkable Improvement in Living Standards', *BR* 17.

—— and Zhang Zhuoyuan (1984), 'An Outline of Economic Development (1977–1980)', in Yu Guangyuan (1984).

Li, Choh-ming (1959), *Economic Development of Communist China*, Berkeley, University of California Press.

—— (1962), *The Statistical System of Communist China*, Berkeley, University of California Press.

—— (1964), 'China's Industrial Development, 1958–73', *CQ*, 17, January–March.

Li Haibo (1983), 'Shoudu Steel—A Success Story', *BR*, 15, 11 April.

Li Kaixin (1981), 'Zhongguo de wuzi guanli' (Materials management in China), *ZJN*.

Li Zhisheng (1982), 'Commercial Reforms', in *Economic Readjustment and Reform* (1982).

Liang Wensen (1980), 'Balanced Development of Industry and Agriculture in the Economy of China', paper presented at the US–China Conference on 'Alternative Strategies for Economic Development', Wingspread, Racine, Wisconsin, 21–24 November 1980.

Liao Jili (1981), 'Zhongguo jingji tizhi gaige de xin jinzhan' (New progress in the reform of China's economic system), in Xue Muqiao (ed.), *Zhongguo Jingji Fazhan Xin Qushi* (New trends in China's economic development), Beijing, Social Science Publishers.

Lieberthal, Kenneth (1985), 'The Political Implications of Document No. 1, 1984', *CQ*, 101, March.

Lin, Cyril (1981), 'The Reinstatement of Economics in China Today', *CQ*, 85, March.

—— (1984), review of Wei and Zhao (1983), in *CQ*, 100, December.

Lin Tian (1981), 'Inquiry into the System of People's Communes', *JJGL*, 1, 15 February.

Lin Zili (1983), 'The New Situation in the Rural Economy and its Basic Direction', *Social Sciences in China*, 3.

Lippit, Victor D. (1974), *Land Reform and Economic Development in China*, White Plains, New York, International Arts and Sciences Press.

—— (1978), 'The Development of Underdevelopment in China', *Modern China*, 4(3), July.

Liu Guoguang (1979), 'Several Questions Regarding Comprehensive Balancing', *RMRB*, 13 April; FBIS, 30 April 1979.

—— (1984), 'Some Important Problems in China's Strategy for Economic Development', *Social Sciences in China*, 4.

—— and Wang Ruisun (1982), *Zhongguo de Jingji Tizhi Gaige* (Reform of China's Economic Structure), Beijing, People's Publishing House.

—— (1984), 'Restructuring of the Economy', in Yu Guangyuan (1984).

——, Wu Jinglian, and Zhao Renwei (1979), 'Relationship between Planning and Market as Seen by China in Her Socialist Economy', *Atlantic Economic Journal*, VII (4), December.

Liu, Jung-chao (1980), 'A Note on China's Pricing Policies', paper presented to Workshop of the Department of Economics, State University of New York, Binghamton, 19 March.

Liu, Ta-chung and Yeh, Kung-chia (1965), *The Economy of the Chinese Mainland: National Income and Economic Development, 1933–1959*, Princeton University Press.

Liu Tzu-chiu (1956), 'Wage Reform in China', *People's China*, 16 October.

Liu Wai (1953), *Rural Economics on the Chinese Mainland*, Hong Kong; cited in Zao (1964).

Liu Zheng (1981), 'Population Planning and Demographic Theory', in Liu *et al.* (1981).

—— *et al.* (1981), *China's Population: Problems and Prospects*, Beijing, New World Press.

Lu Dong (1985), 'Reforms Invigorate 1984 Economy', *BR*, 10.

Lu Yun (1984a), 'Gap Between Rich and Poor is Bridged' (Rural Responsibility System, III), *BR*, 46, 12 November.

—— (1984b), 'Is It A Retreat to Capitalism?' (Rural Responsibility System, I), *BR*, 45, 5 November.

—— (1984c), 'Specialized Households Emerge' (Rural Responsibility System, V), *BR*, 49, 3 December.

Ma Hong (1982), 'Strengthen Planned Economy, Improve Planning', *Zhongguo Caimao Bao*, 20 April; trans. FBIS, 12 May 1982.

—— (1983), *New Strategy for China's Economy*, Beijing: New World Press.

—— (1984), 'Jiaqiang shehuizhuyi gongye jianshe zhongda lilun wenti de yanjiu' (Strengthen research on the major theoretical issues concerning socialist industrial construction), *JJGL*, 5, 5 May.

—— and Sun Shangqing (eds), *Zhongguo Jingji Jiegou Wenti Yanjiu* (Research on Problems of China's Economic Structure), 2 vols., Beijing, People's Publishing House.

MacFarquhar, Roderick (1983), *Origins of the Cultural Revolution. 2: The Great Leap Forward 1958–1960*, New York, Columbia University Press.

Mah, Feng-hwa (1968), 'Foreign Trade', in Eckstein, Galenson, and Liu (1968).

—— (1971), *The Foreign Trade of Mainland China*, Chicago, Aldine.

Mao Zedong (Mao Tsetung) (1955), 'On the Cooperative Transformation of Agriculture', in Mao (1977a:184–207).

—— (1967), *Selected Works*, Vols. I–IV, Peking, Foreign Languages Press.

—— (1969), *Mao Zedong sixiang wansui* (*Long live Mao Zedong thought*), selected speeches and writings of Mao. (No other publication information.)

—— (1974), *Miscellany of Mao Tse-tung Thought*, Parts I and II, JPRS, 61269–2, Arlington, Virginia.

—— (1977a), *Selected Work*, Vol V, Peking, Foreign Languages Press.

—— (1977b), 'On Agricultural Cooperation', in Mao (1977a).

—— (1977c), *A Critique of Soviet Economics*, ed. and trans. Moss Roberts, New York, Monthly Review Press.

—— (1977d), 'On the Ten Great Relationships' (1956), in Schram (1974); official version in *BR*, January 1977.

Marglin, Stephen (1974), 'What Do Bosses Do? The Origin and Functions of Hierarchy in Capitalist Production', *Review of Radical Political Economics*, 6(2).

Marx, Karl (1956), 'Die moralisierende Kritik und die kritisierende Moral', in Karl Marx, *Selected Writings in Sociology and Social Philosophy*, London, Watts.

Meisner, Maurice (1977), *Mao's China: A History of The People's Republic*, New York, Free Press.

—— (1982), *Marxism, Maoism, and Utopianism: Eight Essays*, Madison, Wisconsin, University of Wisconsin Press.

Milton, David and Milton, Nancy (1976), *The Wind Will Not Subside: Years in Revolutionary China, 1964–1969*, New York, Pantheon.

Mochizuki, Kiichi (1985), 'Chinese, Soviet, and Hungarian Economic Reforms Compared', in JETRO, *China Newsletter*, 54, January–February.

Moise, Edwin (1977), 'Downward Social Mobility in Pre-revolutionary China', *Modern China*, 3 (1), January.

Moulder, Frances (1977), *Japan, China and the Modern World Economy*, Cambridge University Press.

Murphey, Rhoads (1970), *The Treaty Ports and China's Modernization: What Went Wrong?* Michigan Papers in Chinese Studies, no. 7, Ann Arbor, University of Michigan, Center for Chinese Studies.

—— (1980), *The Fading of the Maoist Vision*, New York, Methuen.

Myers, Ramon H. (1970), *The Chinese Peasant Economy: Agricultural Development in Hopei and Shantung, 1890–1949*, Cambridge, Massachusetts, Harvard University Press.

—— (1977), 'Trade in Agriculture, 1911–1949', unpublished paper; cited in Rawski (1979a).

—— (1980), *The Chinese Economy, Past and Present*, Belmont, California, Wadsworth.

Nakamura, James I. (1966), 'Meiji Land Reform, Redistribution of Income, and Saving from Agriculture', *Economic Development and Cultural Change*, 14(4), July.

Nathan, Andrew, J. (1973), 'A Factionalism Model for CCP Politics', *CQ*, 53, January–March.

National Foreign Assessment Center (1977), *China: Real Trends in Trade with Non-Communist Countries Since 1970*, Washington, DC, NFAC.

Naughton, Barry (1983), 'State Investment in Post-Mao China: The Decline of Central Control', unpublished paper.

—— (1984a), 'False Starts and Long-run Prospects: Financial Reforms in China's Industrial System', in Elizabeth Perry and Christine Wong (eds), *The Political Economy of Reform in China*, Cambridge, Massachusetts, Harvard University Press.

—— (1984b), 'Economic Reforms and Decentralization: China's Problematic Materials Allocation System', unpublished paper prepared for the Regional Seminar in Chinese Studies, University of California, Berkeley, 6 April 1984.

Nee, Victor and Peck, James (1975), *China's Uninterrupted Revolution*, New York, Pantheon.

'New Achievements in Rural Economy' (1983), *BR*, 36, 5 September.

Nolan, Peter (1979), 'Inequality of Income Between Town and Countryside in The People's Republic of China in the Mid-1950s', *World Development*, 7.

'Noncun renmin gongshe gongzuo tiaoli (xiuzheng caoan)' (Work regulations for the rural people's communes, revised draft) (1962), Taiwan, State Security Office.

Nove, Alec (1961), *The Soviet Economy*, New York, Praeger.

Nurkse, Ragnar (1953), *Problems of Capital Formation in Underdeveloped Countries*, Oxford, Basil Blackwell.

Oi, Jean C. (1986), 'Peasant Grain Marketing and State Procurement: China's Grain Contracting System', *CQ*, 106, June.

Oksenberg, Michel (1970), 'Mao's Foreign Policy of "Self-Reliance" ', paper presented to Columbia University Seminar on Modern China, 4 March 1970.

—— (1984), *President Reagan's China Trip: A Background Paper*, New York, China Council of The Asia Society.

—— and Goldstein, Steven M. (1974), 'The Chinese Political Spectrum', *Problems of Communism*, 23(2), March–April.

Orleans, Leo A. (1961), *Professional Manpower and Education in Communist China*, Washington, DC, US Government Printing Office.

Parish, William (1981), 'Egalitarianism', *Problems of Communism*, January–February.

—— and Whyte, Martin King (1978), *Village and Family in Contemporary China*, University of Chicago Press.

Perkins, Dwight H. (1966), *Market Control and Planning in Communist China*, Cambridge, Massachusetts, Harvard Universty Press.

—— (1968), 'Industrial Planning and Management', in Eckstein, Galenson and Liu (1968).

—— (1969), *Agricultural Development in China, 1368–1968*, Chicago, Aldine.

—— (1975a), 'Introduction: The Persistence of the Past', in Perkins (1975c).

—— (1975b), 'Growth and Changing Structure of China's Twentieth-Century Economy', in Perkins (1975c).

—— (ed.) (1975c), *China's Modern Economy in Historical Perspective*, Stanford University Press.

—— (1980), 'Issues in the Estimation of China's National Product', in Eckstein (1980).

Peterson, Albert S. (1982), 'China: Transportation Developments, 1971–80', in US Congress, Joint Economic Committee (1982).

Potter, Jack M. (1968), *Capitalism and the Chinese Peasant*, Berkeley, University of California Press.

Price, Robert, L. (1967), 'Communist China's Balance of Payments, 1950–65', in US Congress, Joint Economic Committee (1967).

'Provisional Regulations Concerning Congresses of Workers and Staff Members in State-owned Industrial Enterprises' (1982), in *Economic Readjustment and Reform* (1982).

Prybyla, Jan S. (1970), *The Political Economy of Communist China*, Scranton, Pennsylvania, International Textbooks.

Putterman, Louis (1984), 'Work Motivation and Monitoring in A Collective Farm', Brown University Department of Economics Working Paper no. 84–28.

Raj, K. N. (1983), 'Agricultural Growth in China and India: Role of Price and Non-price Factors', *Economic and Political Weekly*, 18 (3), 15 January.

Rawls, John (1971), *A Theory of Justice*, Cambridge, Massachusetts, Belknap Press.

Rawski, Thomas G. (1973), 'Recent Trends in the Chinese Economy', *CQ*, 53, January–March.

—— (1979a), 'China's Republican Economy: An Introduction', paper presented to the Columbia University Seminar on Modern China, 8 March.

—— (1979b), *Economic Growth and Employment in China*, New York, Oxford University Press.

—— (1980a), *China's Transition to Industrialism*, Ann Arbor, University of Michigan Press.

—— (1980b), 'China's Industrial Performance, 1949–73', in Eckstein (1980).

—— (1982a), 'The Simple Arithmetic of Chinese Income Distribution', *Keizai Kenkyu*, 22 (1).

—— (1982b), 'Economic Growth and Integration in Prewar China', Discussion Paper no. 5, University of Toronto–York University Joint Centre on Modern East Asia.

—— (1983), 'Economic Growth in Prewar China', unpublished draft chapter.

'Regulations for the Implementation of the Law of the People's Republic of China on Joint Ventures Using Chinese and Foreign Investment' (1983), *BR*, 41 (10), October.

'Regulations on the Work in the Rural People's Communes (Draft for Trial Use)' (1979), *Issues and Studies*, 15(8), 100–12; 15(9), 104–15.

Ren Tao and Yue Bing (1983), 'Population and Employment', *BR*, 13, 28 March.

'Report on the 1984 Economic Plan' (1984), *BR*, 22, 28 May.

'Resolution of the Eight National Congress of the Communist Party of China' (1956), in *Eighth National Congress of the Communist Party of China*, 3 vols., Beijing: Foreign Languages Press.

Richman, Barry M. (1969), *Industrial Society in Communist China*, New York, Random House.

Riskin, Carl (1969), 'Local Industry and the Choice of Techniques in Planning of Industrial Development in China', in *Planning for Advanced Skills and Technologies*, New York and Vienna, UNIDO.

—— (1971), 'Small Industry and the Chinese Model of Development', *CQ*, 46, April–June.

—— (1975a), 'Surplus and Stagnation in Modern China', in Perkins (1975c).

—— (1975b), 'Maoism and Motivation; Work Incentives in China', in V. Nee and J. Peck (eds), *China's Uninterrupted Revolution*, New York, Pantheon.

—— (1975c), 'Workers' Incentives in Chinese Industry', in US Congress, Joint Economic Committee (1975).

—— (1978a), 'China's Rural Industries: Self-reliant Systems or Independent Kingdoms', *CQ*, 73, March.

—— (1978b), 'Political Conflict and Rural Industrialization in China', *World Development*, 6(5), May.

—— (1979), 'Intermediate Technologies in China's Rural Industries', in E. A. G. Robinson (ed.), *Appropriate Technologies for Third World Development*, London, Macmillan.

—— (1982), 'Market, Maoism and Economic Reform in China', in M. Selden and V. Lippit (eds), *The Transition to Socialism in China*, Armonk, New York, M. E. Sharpe.

Roll, Charles R. (1974), *The Distribution of Rural Incomes in China*, Ph.D. dissertation, Harvard University.

—— and Yeh, Kung-chia (1975), 'Balance in Coastal and Inland Industrial Development', in US Congress, Joint Economic Committee (1975).

Rosenberg, William G. and Young, Marilyn (1982), *Transforming Russia and China*, New York, Oxford University Press.

Ross, Madelyn (1985), 'China Heads Toward 2000', *CBR*, 12(4), July–August.

Rostow, W. W. (1954), *The Prospects for Communist China*, New York, John Wiley.

Saith, Ashwani (1981), 'Economic Incentives for the One-child Family in Rural China', *CQ*, 17, September.

Salaff, Janet (1967), 'The Urban Communes in Communist China', *CQ*, 29, January–March.

Schram, Stuart (ed.) (1973), *Authority, Participation and Cultural Change in China*, Cambridge University Press.

—— (1974), *Chairman Mao Talks to the People*, New York, Pantheon.

—— (1981), 'To Utopia and Back: A Cycle in the History of the Chinese Communist Party', *CQ*, 87, September.

Schran, Peter (1969), *The Development of Chinese Agriculture, 1950–1959*, Urbana, University of Illinois Press.

Schurmann, Franz (1968), *Ideology and Organization in Communist China*, 2nd edn., Berkeley and Los Angeles, University of California Press.

—— and Schell, Orville, Jr. (eds) (1967), *Imperial China*, New York: Vintage.

Selden, Mark (1979), *The People's Republic of China: A Documentary History of Revolutionary Change*, New York, Monthly Review Press.

—— (1982), 'Cooperation and Socialist Transition in China's Countryside', in Selden and Lippit (1982).

—— (1983), 'Income Inequality and the State in Rural China', unpublished paper.

—— and Lippit, Victor (eds) (1982), *The Transition to Socialism in China*, Armonk, New York, M. E. Sharpe.

Sen, Amartya (1981), *Poverty and Famines: An Essay on Entitlement and Deprivation*, Oxford, Clarendon Press.

—— (1982a), *Choice, Welfare, and Measurement*, Oxford, Basil Blackwell.

—— (1982b), 'How is India Doing?' *New York Review of Books*, 29 (20), 16 December.

—— (1983), 'Development: Which Way Now?' *Economic Journal*, December.

Shen Renhang (1984), 'The Unified Management of Circulating Funds by Banks Represents a Major Reform', *Sichuan Ribao*, 23 January; JPRS, CEA–84–037, 14 May 1984.

Shen, T. H. (1951), *Agricultural Resources of China*, Ithaca, New York, Cornell University Press.

Shue, Vivienne (1981), *Peasant China in Transition*, Berkeley, University of California Press.

—— (1984), 'The Fate of the Commune', *Modern China*, 10(3), July.

Skinner, G. William (1964, 1965), 'Marketing and Social Structure in Rural China', *Journal of Asian Studies*, 24(1), November 1964, 3–44 (Part I); 24(2), February 1965, 195–228 (Part II); 24(3), May 1965, 363–400 (Part III).

—— (1976), *The City in Late Imperial China*, Stanford University Press.

Smil, Vaclav (1978), 'China's Energetics: A System Analysis', in US Congress, Joint Economic Committee (1978).

Smith, Charles (1985), 'A Crisis of Plenty', *FEER*, 1 August.

Socialist Upsurge in China's Countryside (1956), Beijing, Foreign Language Press.

Solinger, Dorothy J. (1980), 'The Socialist Transformation of the Small Merchant by Economic Regulation, 1954–1980', paper presented at Midwest Regional Seminar on China, Chicago, 27 September 1980.

—— (1984), *Chinese Business Under Socialism*, Berkeley, University of California Press.

Song Jian (1981), 'Population Development—Goals and Plans', in Liu *et al.* (1981).

Song Ping (1984), 'Report on the Draft 1984 Plan for National Economic and Social Development', FBIS, 5 June.

Stalin, Joseph (1972), *Economic Problems of Socialism in the USSR*, Peking, Foreign Languages Press (originally published in 1952).

Starr, John Bryan (1976), 'From the 10th Party Congress to the Premiership of Hua Guo-feng: The Significance of the Colour of the Cat', *CQ*, 67, September, 457–88.

State Statistical Bureau (SSB) (1958), *Major Aspects of the Chinese Economy Through 1956*, Beijing, Statistical Publishing House.

—— (1981), 'Communique on Fulfillment of China's 1980 National Economic Plan', *BR*, 19, 11 May.

—— (1982), 'Communique on Fulfillment of China's 1981 National Economic Plan', *BR*, 20, 17 May.

—— (1984), 'Communique on Fulfillment of China's 1983 National Economic Plan', *BR*, 5, 14 May.

—— (1985), 'Guanyu 1984 nian guomin jingji he shehui fazhande tongji gongbao' (Statistical communique on fulfilment of China's 1984 economic and social development plan), *RMRB*, 10 March 1985; trans. in *BR*, 12, 23 March 1985.

—— (1986), 'Communique on the Statistics of 1985 Economic and Social Development', *BR*, 12, 24 March.

Stavis, Benedict (1974), *Making Green Revolution: The Politics of Agricultural Development in China*, Rural Development Monograph no. 1. Ithaca, New York, Cornell University Rural Development Committee.

—— (1978), *The Politics of Agricultural Mechanization in China*, Ithaca, New York, Cornell University Press.

Stone, Bruce (1985), 'The Basis for Chinese Agricultural Growth in the 1980s and 1990s: A Comment on Document No. 1, 1984', *CQ*, 101, March.

Strong, Anna Louise (1964), *The Chinese People's Communes—and Six Years after*, Peking, New World Press.

Stuermer, John R. (1984), 'The Way Ahead', *CBR*, 11(1), January–February.

Sun Ping (1984), 'Individual Economy Under Socialism', *BR*, 33(13), August.

Sun Yefang (1979), *Shehuizhuyi Jingji de Ruogan Lilun Wenti* (Theoretical problems of the socialist economy), Beijing, People's Publishing House.

—— (1981), 'Jiaqiang tongji gongzuo, gaige tongji zhidu' (Strengthen statistical work, reform the statistical system), *JJGL*, 2, 15 February; trans. FBIS, 26 March 1981, L4–L9.

Tanaka, Akio (1984), 'Vitalization and Balanced Growth of the Chinese Economy', JETRO, *China Newsletter*, 49, March–April.

Tang, Anthony M. (1968), 'Policy and Performance in Agriculture', in Eckstein, Galenson, and Liu (1968).

—— (1971), 'Input–Output Relations in the Agriculture of Communist China, 1952–1965', in W. A. Douglas Jackson (ed.), *Agrarian Policies and Problems in Communist and Non-Communist Countries*, Seattle, University of Washington Press.

—— (1980), 'Food and Agriculture in China: Trends and Projections, 1952–77 and 2000', in A. Tang and B. Stone (eds), *Food Production in The People's Republic of China*, Research Report 15, International Food Policy Research Institute.

Tawney, R. H. (1939), 'Introduction', *Agrarian China: Selected Source Materials from Chinese Authors*, London, Institute for Pacific Relations.

Ten Great Years (TGY) (1960), Beijing, State Statistical Bureau.

Tian Jiyun (1985), 'Price System Due for Reform', *BR*, 4, 28 January.

Tian Xueyuan (1984), 'On Changes in the Age Composition of the Population and Policy Options for Population Planning', *Social Sciences in China*, 3, September.

Travers, Lee (1982), 'Bias in Chinese Economic Statistics: The Case of the Typical Example Investigation', *CQ*, 91, September.

—— (1984), 'Post-1978 Rural Economic Policy and Peasant Income in China', *CQ*, 98, April.

Tsou, Tang, Blecher, Marc, and Meisner, Mitch (1982), 'National Agricultural Policy: The Dazhai Model and Local Change in the Post-Mao Era', in Selden and Lippit (1982).

US Central Intelligence Agency (USCIA) (1963), *The Short-lived Liberal Phase in Economic Thinking in Communist China*, Washington, DC, CIA.

—— (1972), *People's Republic of China: International Trade Handbook*, Washington, DC, CIA.

—— (1979), *China: Major Economic Indicators*, Washington DC, CIA.

—— (1984a), *China: International Trade, Fourth Quarter, 1983*, Washington, DC, CIA.

—— (1984b), *China: International Trade, Annual Statistical Supplement*, Washington, DC, CIA.

—— (1984c), *China: International Trade, Fourth Quarter, 1984*, Washington DC, CIA.

—— (1985), *China: International Trade Annual Statistical Supplement*, Washington, DC, CIA.

US Congress, Joint Economic Committee (USCJEC) (1967), *An Economic Profile of Mainland China*, 2 vols., Washington, DC, US Government Printing Office.

—— (1972), *People's Republic of China: An Economic Assessment*, Washington, DC, US Government Printing Office.

—— (1975), *China: A Reassessment of the Economy*, Washington, DC, US Government Printing Office.

—— (1978), *Chinese Economy Post-Mao*, 2 vols., Washington, DC, US Government Printing Office.

—— (1982), *China Under the Four Modernizations*, Parts 1 and 2, Washington DC, US Government Printing Office.

—— (1986), *The Chinese Economy in the Eighties*, Washington, DC, US Government Printing Office.

Union Research Institute (1971), *Documents of the Chinese Communist Party Central Committee*, Vol. 1I, Hong Kong, Union Research Institute.

—— (1974), *Documents of the Chinese Communist Party Central Committee*, Vol. II, Hong Kong, Union Research Institute.

Vermeer, E. B. (1982), 'Income Differentials in Rural China,' *CQ*, 89, March.

Vogel, Ezra (1969), *Canton Under Communism*, Cambridge, Massachusetts, Harvard University Press.

Walder, Andrew (1978), *Chang Ch'un-ch'iao and Shanghai's January Revolution*, Ann Arbor, University of Michigan, Center for Chinese Studies, Michigan Papers in Chinese Studies, no. 32.

—— (1982), 'Some Ironies of the Maoist Legacy in Industry', in Selden and Lippit (1982).

—— (1984), 'The Remaking of the Chinese Working Class, 1949–1981', *Modern China*, 10(1), January.

—— (1985a), 'China Turns to Industry Reform', *Challenge*, March–April.

—— (1985b), 'The Informal Dimension of Enterprise Financial Reforms', in US Congress, Joint Economic Committee (1986).

Walker, Kenneth R. (1965), *Planning in Chinese Agriculture*, Chicago, Aldine.

—— (1966), 'Collectivization in Retrospect: The "Socialist Hightide" of Autumn 1955–Spring 1956', *CQ*, 26, April–June.

—— (1968), 'Organization of Agricultural Production', in Eckstein, Galenson, and Liu (1968).

—— (1977), 'Grain Self-sufficiency in North China', *CQ*, 71, September, 555–90.

—— (1982), 'Interpreting Chinese Grain Consumption Statistics', *CQ*, 92, December.

—— (1984), 'Chinese Agriculture During the Period of the Readjustment, 1978–83', *CQ*, 100, December.

Wan Li (1984), 'Developing Rural Commodity Production', *BR*, 9, 27 February.

Wang Bingqian, (1980), 'Report on Financial Work', report on the final state accounts for 1979, the draft state budget for 1980, and the financial estimates for 1981, *BR*, 11, 29 September.

—— (1983), 'Report on the Final State Accounts for 1982', FBIS, 24 June.

—— (1984), 'Report on the Final State Accounts for 1983 and the Draft State Budget for 1984', FBIS, 4 June.

—— (1985), 'Report on the Execution of the State Budget for 1984 and on the Draft State Budget for 1985', *BR*, 17, 29 April.

Wang, Dacheng (1984), 'Major Reform under Way in Commerce', *BR*, 35, 27 August.

—— (1985), 'Chinese Peasants Favour Small Towns', *BR*, 13, 1 April.

Wang Haibo (1982), 'Greater Power for the Enterprises', in Wei and Zhao (1982).

Wang Linsheng (1983), 'On the Role of Foreign Trade Under Socialism', trans. from *Guoji Maoyi* (International Trade), 2, 1982; in *Chinese Economic Studies*, 16 (3), Spring.

Wang Qingyi and Gu Jian (1983), 'How Will China Solve Energy Problem?' *BR*, 35, 29 August.

Wang Zhenzhi and Wang Yongzhi (1982), 'Epilogue: Prices in China', in Wei and Chao (1982).

Watson, Andrew (1983), 'Agriculture Looks for "Shoes that Fit": The Production Responsibility System and Its Implications', *World Development*, 11(8), August.

Wei, Lin, and Chao, Arnold (1982), *China's Economic Reforms*, Philadelphia, University of Pennsylvania Press.

Weisskopf, Michael (1985), 'Abortion Policy Tears at Fabric of China's Society', *Washington Post*, 7 January.

Whyte, Martin King (1973), 'Bureaucracy and Modernization in China: The Maoist Critique', *American Sociological Review*, 38 (2), April.

Wiens, Thomas (1978), 'The Evolution of Policies and Capabilities in China's Agricultural Technology', in USCJEC (1978).

—— (1980), 'Agricultural Statistics in the People's Republic of China', in Eckstein (1980).

Wiles, Peter (1962), *The Political Economy of Communism*, Cambridge, Massachusetts, Harvard University Press.

Williams, Bobby (1975), 'The Chinese Petroleum Industry: Growth and Prospects', in USCJEC (1975).

Williams, Tim and Brilliant, Robin (1984), 'Shenzhen Status Report', *CBR*, 11(2), March–April.

Wong Siu-lun (1984), 'Consequences of China's New Population Policy', *CQ*, 98, June.

World Bank (1982), *World Development Report 1982*, New York, Oxford University Press.

—— (1983), *China: Socialist Economic Development*, Vols. I–III, Washington, DC, World Bank.

—— (1985), *China: Long-Term Issues and Options*, Vol. I, Annexes A–E, Washington, DC, World Bank.

Wren, Christopher (1984), 'Despite Rural China's Gains, Poverty Grips Some Regions', *New York Times*, 18 December.

Wright, Mary Clabaugh (ed.) (1969), *China in Revolution: The First Phase, 1900–1913*, New Haven and London, Yale University Press.

Wu Chou (1975), *Report from Tungting*, Beijing, Foreign Languages Press.

Wu Jinglian and Zhou Shulian (1980), 'Correctly Handle the Relationship Between Readjustment and Restructuring', *RMRB*, 5 December; FBIS, 29 December 1980.

Wu Xiang (1980), 'The Open Road and the Log Bridge—A Preliminary Discussion on the Origins, Advantages and Disadvantages, Nature and Future of the Fixing of Farm Output Quotas for Each Household', *RMRB*, 5 November; FBIS, 7 November 1980.

Xu Dixin and others (1982), *China's Search for Economic Growth*, trans. Andrew Watson, Beijing, New World Press.

Xu Jinqiang (1979), 'Hold High the Great Red Banner . . .', in Selden (1979:582–91).

Xu Yi and Chen Baosen (1981), 'On the Necessity and Possibility of Stabilizing Prices', *Social Sciences in China*, 2(3), September.

—— (1984a), 'Finance', in Yu (1984).

—— (1984b), *Caizheng Xue* (Finance), Beijing, Chinese Finance and Economic Publishing House.

Xue Muqiao (Hsueh Mu-ch'iao) (1977), 'The Two-road Struggle in the Economic Field During the Transition Period', in four parts: *BR*, nos. 49–52, 2, 9, 16, and 26 December.

—— (1979), *Shehuizhuyi jingji lilun wenti* (Theoretical Problems of the Socialist Economy), Beijing, People's Publishing House.

—— (1980a), 'Guanyu jingji tizhi gaigede yixie yijian' (Some opinions on reform of the economic system), *RMRB*, 10 June; trans. FBIS, 25 June 1980.

—— (1980b), 'Jihua tiaojie yu shichang tiaojie' (Plan regulation and market regulation), *RMRB*, 13 October.

—— (1981), *China's Socialist Economy*, Beijing, Foreign Languages Press.

—— (1982a), 'Problems to be Solved in Reforming the Enterprise Management System', *JJYJ*, 1, January; trans. FBIS, 24 February 1982, K11–K17.

—— (1982b), *Current Economic Problems in China*, Boulder, Colorado, Westview Press.

—— (1984), 'How Are We To View Prices and People's Livelihood?' *Beijing Ribao*, 11 July; FBIS, 24 July 1984, K3.

——, Su Xing, and Lin Tse-li (1960), *The Socialist Transformation of the National Economy*, Peking, Foreign Languages Press.

Yan Kalin (1985), 'How to Deal with Losing Enterprises', *BR*, 10.

Yang Jianbai and Li Xuezeng (1980), 'The Relations between Agriculture, Light Industry and Heavy Industry in China', in *Social Sciences in China*, 2.

Yao Wenyuan (1975), 'On the Social Basis of the Lin Piao Anti-Party Clique', *PR*, 10.

Yao Yilin (1983), 'Report on the 1983 Plan for National Economic and Social Development', FBIS, 24 June.

'Yao Yilin and Tian Jiyun Discuss Restructuring of China's Banking System' (1984) *Jingji Ribao* (Beijing), 28 January; JPRS, CEA–84–037, 14 May 1984.

Yeh, K. C. (1964), *Capital Formation in Mainland China: 1931–36 and 1952–57*, unpublished doctoral dissertation, Columbia University.

—— (1968), 'Capital Formation', in Eckstein, Galenson, and Liu (1968).

—— (1979), 'China's National Income, 1931–36', in Hou, Chi-ming and Yu, Tzongshian (eds), *Modern Chinese Economic History*, Taipei.

—— (1984), 'Macroeconomic Changes in the Chinese Economy During the Readjustment', *CQ*, 100, December.

Yen Chung-ping *et al.* (eds) (1955), *Zhongguo jindai jingi shi tongji zilao xuanji* (Selections from statistical source materials on modern Chinese econonomic history), Beijing, Science Publishing House.

Yotopolous, Pan A. and Nugent, Jeffrey B. (1976), *Economics of Development, Empirical Investigations*, New York, Harper & Row.

Yu Guangyuan (ed.) (1984), *China's Socialist Modernization*, Beijing, Foreign Languages Press.

Yu Zuyao (1984), 'New Developments in China's Socialist Commodity Economy', *Social Sciences in China*, 4, Winter.

Yuan Wenqi and Wang Jianmin (1988), 'We Must Review and Reevaluate the Role of Foreign Trade in the Development of the National Economy', trans. from *Guoji Maoyi* (International Trade), 1; in *Chinese Economic Studies*, 16(3), Spring.

Zao, Koe-tseng (Paul) (1964), *La Réforme Agraire en Chine Communiste*, Louvain, Ancienne Lib. Desbarax.

Zeng Qixian (1980), 'The Problem of Employment in the Economic Development of China', paper delivered at US–China Conference on 'Alternative Strategies for Economic Development', Wingspread, Racine, Wisconsin, 21–24 November 1980.

Zhang Chunqiao (1975), 'On Exercising All-round Dictatorship over the Bourgeosie', *Peking Review*, 14.

Zhang Jingfu (1982), 'Upholding Planned Economy in Agriculture', *BR*, 12, 22 March.
—— (1984), 'Talk Given at National Price Work Experience Exchange Conference', in *Jiage Lilun yu Shijian* (Price Theory and Practice), JPRS, CEA-84–037, 14 May 1984, p. 37.
Zhang Yi (1985), 'Will Readjustment of Prices Lower People's Standards of Living?' *Xuexi yu Yanjiu*; trans. FBIS, 18 July 1985, K3–K4.
Zhang Zhuoyuan (1982), 'Introduction: China's Economy After the Cultural Revolution', in Wei and Chao (1982).
Zhao Ziyang (1982a), 'The Present Economic Situation and the Principles for Future Economic Construction', Report on the Work of the Government, 1981; in Zhao (1982b).
—— (1982b), *China's Economy and Development Principles*, Beijing, Foreign Languages Press.
—— (1984), 'Report on the Work of the Government', Delivered to 2nd Session, 6th National People's Congress 14 May 1984, in *BR*, 24, 11 June.
—— (1985a), 'Loosen Control Over the Prices of Farm Products to Promote the Readjustment of the Production Structure in Rural Areas', *Hong Qi*, 3; FBIS, 31 January 1985.
—— (1985b), 'The Current Economic Situation and the Reform of the Economic Structure', Report on the Work of the Government, 27 March 1985, in *BR* 16, 22 April.
'Zhao on Price and Wage Reform' (1985), *BR*, 1, 7 January.
'Zhonggong zhongyang banfa "guanyu jinyibu jiaqiang he wanshan nongye shengchan zerenzhi de jige wenti de tongzhi" ' (Directive of the Central Committee of the Chinese Communist Party on several questions concerning further strengthening and perfecting of the production responsibility system in agriculture) (1981), *Zhong Gong Nian Bao* (Yearbook on Chinese Communism), pp. 7.50–7.53. Taibei, Institute of International Relations.
'Zhonggong zhongyang guanyu jiakuai nongye fazhan ruogan wenti de jueding' (Decisions of the Central Committee of the CCP on some questions concerning the acceleration of agricultural development) (1981), in *ZJN* (1981).
'Zhonggong zhongyang guanyu xijiubasi nian nongcun gongzuo de tongzhi' (Directive of the Central Committee of the Chinese Communist Party concerning rural work in 1984) (1984), *RMRB*, 12 June.
Zhongguo Gongye de Fazhan, 1949–1984 (China's industrial development, 1949–1984) (1985), State Statistical Bureau. Beijing, Chinese Statistical Publishing House.
Zhongguo Maoyi Wujia Tongji Ziliao, 1952–1983 (ZMWTZ) (Statistical material on China's commerce and prices, 1952–1983) (1984), Office of Commerce and Price Statistics, State Statistical Bureau. Beijing, Chinese Statistical Publishing House.
Zhongguo Nongye Jiben Qingkuang (ZNJQ) (Basic Situation of China's Agriculture) (1979), Policy Research Office, Ministry of Agriculture. Beijing, Nongye Chubanshe.
Zhongguo Nongye Nianjian 1980 (ZNN) (Agricultural Yearbook of China) (1982), excerpts with tables translated in JPRS, *China Report, Agriculture*, no. 192, JPRS, 80270.
Zhongguo Nongyede Guanghui Chengjiu, 1949–1984 (Brilliant accomplishments of China's agriculture, 1949–1984) (1984), Office of Agriculture Statistics, State Statistical Bureau. Beijing, Chinese Statistical Publishing House.
Zhonghua Renmin Gongheguo Guojia Tongji Ju (ZRGGTJ) (1979), *Guanyu yijiuqiba nian guomin jingji jihua zhixing jieguo de gongbao* (Communiqué of the State Statistical Bureau of the PRC on Fulfilment of China's 1978 National Economic Plan), Beijing, Financial and Economic Publishing House.

—— (1984), 'Guanyu yijiubasan nian guomin jingji he shehui fazhan jihua zhixing jieguo de gongbao' (Communiqué on Fulfilment of the 1983 Plan for National Economic and Social Development), in *Zhonghua renmin gongheguo guowuyuan gongbao*, no. 9, 20 May 1984.

Zhou Chuan (1982), 'Jin sannian wo guo cheng xiang renmin de shenghuo zhuangkuang' ('The State of the Urban and Rural People's Livelihoods in the Last Three Years'), *JJGL*, 5.

Zhou En-lai (1965), 'Report on the Work of the Government to the First Session, Third National People's Congress', *Peking Review*, 1, 1 January.

Zhou Ping (1982), 'Workers' Congresses: A Step Towards Democratic Management', in *Economic Readjustment and Reform* (1982).

Zhou Qiren and Du Ying (1984), 'Specialized Households: A Preliminary Study', *Social Sciences in China*, 5(3), September.

Zhou Shulian (1982a), 'The Market Mechanism in a Planned Economy', in Wei and Chao (1982).

—— (1982b), 'Changing the Pattern of China's Economy', in Wei and Chao (1982).

Zweig, David (1982), 'National Elites, Rural Bureaucrats, and Peasants: Limits on Commune Reform', in *The Limits of Reform in China*, Washington, DC, Wilson Center.

INDEX

Studies of the East Asian Institute

The Ladder of Success in Imperial China, by Ping-ti Ho. New York: Columbia University Press, 1962.

The Chinese Inflation, 1937–1949, by Shun-hsin Chou. New York: Columbia University Press, 1963.

Reformer in Modern China: Chang Chien, 1853–1926, by Samuel Chu. New York: Columbia University Press, 1965.

Research in Japanese Sources: A Guide, by Herschel Webb with the assistance of Marleigh Ryan. New York: Columbia University Press, 1965.

Society and Education in Japan, by Herbert Passin. New York: Teachers College Press, 1965.

Agricultural Production and Economic Development in Japan, 1873–1922, by James I. Nakamura. Princeton: Princeton University Press, 1966.

Japan's First Modern Novel: Ukigumo of Futabatei Shimei, by Marleigh Ryan. New York: Columbia University Press, 1967.

The Korean Communist Movement, 1918–1948, by Dae-Sook Suh. Princeton: Princeton University Press, 1967.

The First Vietnam Crisis, by Melvin Gurtov. New York: Columbia University Press, 1967.

Cadres, Bureaucracy, and Political Power in Communist China, by A. Doak Barnett. New York: Columbia University Press, 1968.

The Japanese Imperial Institution in the Tokugawa Period, by Herschel Webb. New York: Columbia University Press, 1968.

Higher Education and Business Recruitment in Japan, by Koya Azumi. New York: Teachers College Press, 1969.

The Communists and Peasant Rebellions: A Study in the Rewriting of Chinese History, by James P. Harrison, Jr. New York: Atheneum, 1969.

How the Conservatives Rule Japan, by Nathaniel B. Thayer. Princeton: Princeton University Press, 1969.

Aspects of Chinese Education, edited by C. T. Hu. New York: Teachers College Press, 1970.

Documents of Korean Communism, 1918–1948, by Dae-Sook Suh. Princeton: Princeton University Press, 1970.

Japanese Education: A Bibliography of Materials in the English Language, by Herbert Passin. New York: Teachers College Press, 1970.

Economic Development and the Labor Market in Japan, by Koji Taira. New York: Columbia University Press, 1970.

The Japanese Oligarchy and the Russo-Japanese War, by Shumpei Okamoto, New York: Columbia University Press, 1970.

Imperial Restoration in Medieval Japan, by H. Paul Varley, New York: Columbia University Press, 1971.

Japan's Postwar Defense Policy, 1947–1968, by Martin E. Weinstein. New York: Columbia University Press, 1971.

Election Campaigning Japanese Style, by Gerald L Curtis. New York: Columbia University Press, 1971.

China and Russia: The 'Great Game', by O. Edmund Clubb. New York: Columbia University Press, 1971.

Money and Monetary Policy in Communist China, by Katharine Huang Hsiao. New York: Columbia University Press, 1971.

The District Magistrate in Late Imperial China, by John R. Watt. New York: Columbia University Press, 1972.

Law and Policy in China's Foreign Relations: A Study of Attitudes and Practice, by James C. Hsiung. New York: Columbia University Press, 1972.

Pearl Harbour as History: Japanese–American Relations, 1931–1941, edited by Dorothy Borg and Shumpei Okamoto, with the assistance of Dale K. A. Finlayson. New York: Columbia University Press, 1973.

Japanese Culture: A Short History, by H. Paul Varley. New York: Praeger, 1973.

Doctors in Politics: The Political Life of the Japan Medical Association, by William E. Steslicke. New York: Praeger, 1973.

The Japan Teachers Union: a Radical Interest Group in Japanese Politics, by Donald Ray Thurston. Princeton: Princeton University Press, 1973.

Japan's Foreign Policy, 1868–1941: A Research Guide, edited by James William Morley. New York: Columbia University Press, 1974.

Palace and Politics in Prewar Japan, by David Anson Titus. New York: Columbia University Press, 1974.

The Idea of China: Essays in Geographic Myth and Theory, by Andrew March. Devon, England: David and Charles, 1974.

Origins of the Cultural Revolution, by Roderick MacFarquhar. New York: Columbia University Press, 1974.

Shiba Kokan: Artist, Innovator, and Pioneer in the Westernization of Japan, by Calvin L. French. Tokyo: Weatherhill, 1974.

Insei: Abdicated Sovereigns in the Politics of Late Heian Japan, by G. Cameron Hurst, New York: Columbia University Press, 1975.

Embassy at War, by Harold Joyce Noble. Edited with an introduction by Frank Baldwin, Jr. Seattle: University of Washington Press, 1975.

Rebels and Bureaucrats: China's December 9ers, by John Israel and Donald W. Klein. Berkeley: University of California Press, 1975.

Deterrent Diplomacy, edited by James William Morley. New York: Columbia University Press, 1976.

House United, House Divided: The Chinese Family in Taiwan, by Myron L. Cohen. New York: Columbia University Press, 1976.

Escape from Predicament: Neo-Confucianism and China's Evolving Political Culture by Thomas A. Metzger. New York: Columbia University Press, 1976.

Cadres, Commanders, and Commissars: The Training of the Chinese Communist Leadership, 1920–45, by Jane L. Price. Boulder, Colo.: Westview Press, 1976.

Sun Yat-Sen: Frustrated Patriot, by C. Martin Wilbur. New York: Columbia University Press, 1977.

Japanese International Negotiating Style, by Michael Blaker. New York: Columbia University Press, 1977.

Contemporary Japanese Budget Politics, by John Creighton Campbell. Berkeley: University of California Press, 1977.

The Medieval Chinese Oligarchy, by David Johnson. Boulder, Colo.: Westview Press, 1977.

The Arms of Kiangnan: Modernization in the Chinese Ordnance Industry, 1860–1895, by Thomas L. Kennedy. Boulder, Colo.: Westview Press, 1978.

Patterns of Japanese Policymaking: Experiences from Higher Education, by T. J. Pempel. Boulder, Colo.: Westview Press, 1978.

The Chinese Connection: Roger S. Greene, Thomas W. Lamont, George E. Sokolsky, and

American–East Asian Relations, by Warren I. Cohen. New York: Columbia University Press, 1978.

Militarism in Modern China: The Career of Wu P'ei-Fu, 1916–1939, by Odoric Y. K. Wou. Folkestone, England: Dawson, 1978.

A Chinese Pioneer Family: The Lins of Wu-Feng, by Johanna Meskill. Princeton: Princeton University Press, 1979.

Perspectives on a Changing China, ediated by Joshua A. Fogel and William T. Rowe. Boulder, Colo.: Westview Press, 1979.

The Memoirs of Li Tsung-Jen, by T. K. Tong and Li Tsung-jen. Boulder, Colo.: Westview Press, 1979.

Unwelcome Muse: Chinese Literature in Shanghai and Peking, 1937–1945, by Edward Gunn. New York: Columbia University Press, 1979.

Yenan and the Great Powers: The Origins of Chinese Communist Foreign Policy, by James Reardon-Anderson. New York: Columbia University Press, 1980.

Uncertain Years: Chinese–American Relations, 1947–1950, edited by Dorothy Borg and Waldo Heinrichs. New York: Columbia University Press, 1980.

The Fateful Choice: Japan's Advance into South-East Asia, edited by James William Morley. New York: Columbia University Press, 1980.

Tanaka Giichi and Japan's China Policy, by William F. Morton. Folkestone, England: Dawson, 1980; New York: St. Martin's Press, 1980.

The Origins of the Korean War: Liberation and the Emergence of Separate Regimes, 1945–1947, by Bruce Cumings. Princeton: Princeton University Press, 1981.

Class Conflict in Chinese Socialism, by Richard Curt Kraus. New York: Columbia University Press, 1981.

Education under Mao: Class and Competition in Canton Schools, by Jonathan Unger. New York: Columbia University Press, 1982.

Private Academies of Tokugawa Japan, by Richard Rubinger. Princeton: Princeton University Press, 1982.

Japan and the San Francisco Peace Settlement, by Michael M. Yoshitsu. New York: Columbia University Press, 1982.

New Frontiers in American-East Asian Relations: Essays Presented to Dorothy Borg, edited by Warren I Cohen. New York: Columbia University Press, 1983.

The Origins of the Cultural Revolution: II, The Great Leap Forward, 1958–1960, by Roderick MacFarquhar. New York: Columbia University Press, 1983.

The China Quagmire: Japan's Expansion on the Asian Continent, 1933—1941, edited by James William Morley. New York: Columbia University Press, 1983.

Fragments of Rainbows: The Life and Poetry of Saito Mokichi, 1882–1953, by Amy Vladeck Heinrich. New York: Columbia University Press, 1983.

The US–South Korean Alliance: Evolving Patterns of Security Relations, edited by Gerald L. Curtis and Sung-joo Han. Lexington, Mass.: Lexington Books. 1983.

Discovering History in China: American Historical Writing on the Recent Chinese Past, by Paul A. Cohen. New York: Columbia University Press, 1984.

The Foreign Policy of the Republic of Korea, edited by Youngnok Koo and Sungjoo Han. New York: Columbia University Press, 1984.

State and Diplomacy in Early Modern Japan, by Ronald Toby. Princeton: Princeton University Press, 1983.

Japan and the Asian Development Bank, by Dennis Yasutomo. New York: Praeger Publishers, 1983.

Japan Erupts: The London Naval Conference and the Manchurian Incident, edited by James W. Morley. New York: Columbia University Press, 1984.

Japanese Culture: third edition, revised, by Paul Varley. Honolulu: University of Hawaii Press, 1984.

Japan's Modern Myths: Ideology in the Late Meiji Period, by Carol Gluck. Princeton: Princeton University Press, 1985.

Shamans, Housewives and Other Restless Spirits: Women in Korean Ritual Life, by Laurel Kendall. Honolulu: University of Hawaii Press, 1985.

Human Rights in Contemporary China, by R. Randle Edwards, Louis Henkin, and Andrew J. Nathan. New York: Columbia University Press, 1986.

The Pacific Basin: New Challenges for the United States, edited by James W. Morley. New York: Academy of Political Science, 1986.

The Manner of Giving: Strategic Aid and Japanese Foreign Policy, by Dennis T. Yasutomo. Lexington, Mass.: Lexington Books, 1986.